International Human Resource Management

Thank you for choosing a SAGE product!
If you have any comment, observation or feedback,
I would like to personally hear from you.

Please write to me at **contactceo@sagepub.in**

Vivek Mehra, Managing Director and CEO, SAGE India.

Bulk Sales

SAGE India offers special discounts
for bulk institutional purchases.

For queries/orders/inspection copy requests,
write to **textbooksales@sagepub.in**

Publishing

Would you like to publish a textbook with SAGE?
Please send your proposal to **publishingtextbooks@sagepub.in**

Get to know more about SAGE

Be invited to SAGE events, get on our mailing list.
Write today to **marketing@sagepub.in**

International Human Resource Management

Srinivas R. Kandula

Chief Executive Officer, Capgemini Technology Services India Limited

Los Angeles | London | New Delhi
Singapore | Washington DC | Melbourne

First published in 2018 by

SAGE Publications India Pvt Ltd
B1/I-1 Mohan Cooperative Industrial Area
Mathura Road, New Delhi 110 044, India
www.sagepub.in

SAGE Publications Inc
2455 Teller Road
Thousand Oaks, California 91320, USA

SAGE Publications Ltd
1 Oliver's Yard, 55 City Road
London EC1Y 1SP, United Kingdom

SAGE Publications Asia-Pacific Pte Ltd
3 Church Street
#10-04 Samsung Hub
Singapore 049483

Published by Vivek Mehra for SAGE Publications India Pvt Ltd, typeset in 10/12 pt Cambria by AG Infographics, Delhi.

Library of Congress Cataloging-in-Publication Data

Name: Kandula, Srinivas R. (Srinivas Rao), author.
Title: International human resource management / Srinivas R. Kandula.
Description: Thousand Oaks : SAGE Publications India Pvt Ltd, [2018] | Includes bibliographical references and indexes.
Identifiers: LCCN 2018009036 | ISBN 9789352806812 (pbk.)
Subjects: LCSH: International business enterprises—Personnel management. | Personnel management.
Classification: LCC HF5549.5.E45 K36 2018 | DDC 658.3—dc23 LC record available at https://lccn.loc.gov/2018009036

ISBN: 978-93-528-0681-2 (PB)

SAGE Team: Amit Kumar, Indrani Dutta, Vandana Gupta, Madhurima Thapa, and Ritu Chopra

Brief Contents

Detailed Contents

Preface

*I*nternational Human Resource Management (IHRM) is a classic case where theory is running far behind the practice, unlike many other disciplines where theory takes the lead by a significant distance. Today, every business is looking to expand itself beyond its home country, and this pursuit of many organizations is challenged due to people-related issues. There is a dearth of guiding information on hiring, training, compensating, developing, retiring, culture and compliance to laws as a single thread. The literature of IHRM is largely dominated by the expat phenomenon rather than enabling the understanding of full lifecycle of human resource management (HRM) and a framework to understand the dynamics and relations between parent and host countries with regard to people management. Further, even though some of the works are helpful they are more conceptual than pragmatic, at least from a practitioner's perspective. Of course, it is also an undeniable fact that though there is greater convergence among various nations relating to human resource (HR) practices and emergence of a common labour law framework like European Union directives on labour and employment, a substantive difference does exist among nations making it very complex to derive a common theme of HRM.

IHRM, like other subjects of HRM, is fast becoming interdisciplinary, with each of the players trying to understand it from a particular dimension. Culture experts have been focusing on cross-cultural areas, legal experts concentrating on bringing out labour laws and regulation brochures for each of the nations, recruitment agencies contributing to building hiring models for multinational companies, information technology experts trying to offer digital tools for cross-border HR information system and financial experts offering solutions for payroll process and taxation in different nations. Though all these attempts are valuable and help in better understanding of HR matters in the international context, the onus to put all these pieces together and make sense out of them lies on HR practitioners and business managers. This book is an attempt to bridge that gap. The book consisting of nine chapters endeavours to cover the lifecycle of HRM, focusing on 18 countries in 4 continents: procurement (international staffing), development (international training), compensation (international compensation), maintenance (labour codes, laws and regulations) and integration (international performance and international culture management). However, this book is a beginner's text to attain a fundamental base for IHRM practice rather than presenting an advanced perspective.

Despite feeble attempts to promote protectionist economic and political philosophy and trends like Brexit and Right-wing nationalism, cross-border economies and international movement of people are going to grow and strengthen, and globalization will garner more steam in coming years. More than anything else, people will be at the core of this movement and HR professionals will have a unique opportunity to enable this transformation. I sincerely hope this book can support this evolution.

About the Author

Srinivas R. Kandula is leading Capgemini Technology Services India Limited as its chief executive officer and a doctoral fellow at XLRI (Xavier School of Management), Jamshedpur. He has authored nine books in the areas of HRM, organizational behaviour, organization development and self-management, published in multiple languages. His work has also been published in over 50 papers in national and international journals. He is a preferred speaker in premier business schools and management forums across the globe. Dr Kandula is a management practitioner with over 25 years of experience, in both public sector and private sector organizations.

International Human Resource Management: An Introduction

LEARNING OBJECTIVES

The objectives of this chapter are to:

❑ present a historical evolution of International Human Resource Management (IHRM), both in theory and in practice.
❑ enable understanding of similarities and dissimilarities between single nation-centric human resource management (HRM) and IHRM.
❑ illustrate global HRM challenges.
❑ discuss the role and emergence of the global human resource (HR) manager.

With the increasing globalization of trade and business and a highly mobile workforce, the significance of International Human Resource Management (IHRM) has been growing manifold. As per the estimates of the United Nations, there are about 80 million people working in over 100,000 multinational companies whose affiliates are spread across the globe, virtually leaving not even single nation untouched. An interesting development during the last decade is that small and medium enterprises have begun to spread their operations beyond the home country and often across the continents as opposed to the trend of only big corporations enlarging their transnational operations. Fuelled by everdecreasing transportation and communication costs, transfer of technologies among nations, emergence of a global economy and convergence of research and development, the international workforce is growing rapidly. The nature of issues one needs to confront and deal with and the perspectives required to manage a globalized workforce is qualitatively different from that of a single nation-centric workforce. Though the basic tenets and theory of HRM may not vary that much, its demonstrations and the modus operandi have huge variations. These variations are threefold: first, the cultural texture of the immediate society where the corporate is operating; second, the laws and regulations of that society; and third, the emphasis given to the kind of human resources practices (HRP). It is essential for students, practitioners and academicians of HRM to focus on international dimensions of workforce as the future belongs to a globalized workforce rather than a workforce of single nation concentration.

Managing International Workforce

Perlmutter (1969) in his paper 'The Tortuous Evolution of the Multinational Corporation' suggests that international workforce is managed in three different ways in consonance with orientation of managers. These are as follows:

Ethnocentrism: In this approach, organizations extensively use expats. The influence and oversight of headquarters is overwhelming. The tendency is to extend the headquarters' policies and programmes to subsidiaries. Decision-making is centralized. Headquarters' managers wield all power and demonstrate a behaviour that only limited managerial discretion should be extended to branch/subsidiary countries in order to garner the sustainability of values and business processes. Therefore, all HR policies and programmes of headquarters are simply applied in other countries. Also, HR managers are generally drawn from headquarters as expats.

Polycentrism: Organizations adopting this approach tend to prefer local HR managers to run people programmes. Only the salient features and cardinal principles of headquarters are applied providing adequate flexibility to alter them in order to suit local prevailing conditions. Typically, regions appear to take lead in this case rather than headquarters.

Geocentrism: This is an evolved stage of managing organizations and people. The best in class practices and excellence can originate from any region or country and are evaluated and extended to remaining countries of operations. The motive here is to drive fundamentally uniform strategy and practices across the organization. Expatriates are used only to fill certain gaps in terms of skills and talent rather than as a source of oversight or as a representative of headquarters. Further, expatriates can come from any country and not necessarily from headquarters. In fact, in this scenario, locals dominate and exert equal amount of influence and authority as do headquarters. HR managers can be either locals or outsiders with sole criterion of cultural and functional fit.

IHRM: Meaning and Definition

HRM has a distinct meaning and scope in an international context. The mandate of IHRM would include building and operationalizing internationally amenable HR systems, policies, practices and processes. Several organizations fail to succeed not due to a lack of global infrastructure, capital investments, technology or other logistical apparatus but because of a lack of understanding and appreciation for a workforce in an international context and an inadequate understanding of how to motivate and manage such a workforce. IHRM, as a discipline, focuses exclusively on attracting, developing and retaining talent internationally. The scope of IHRM would include all facets of standard HRM frameworks such as recruitment, development, compensation and benefits, industrial relations (IR), culture and values, leadership development and separation management. It also covers all the industries and corporate and non-corporate organizations. The critical aspect that distinguishes IHRM is its focus on an international workforce.

IHRM is defined as 'planning, organizing, directing and controlling of hiring, nurturing, motivating, rewarding and retiring of international workforce in an equitable manner to accomplish people and business objectives'. It focuses on the approaches and methods beneficial to understand a workforce that has no national boundaries and also on ways to create such an international workforce.

Briscoe, Schuler and Claus (2009) have defined the field of IHRM as 'the study and application of all human resource management activities as they impact the process of managing human resources in enterprises in the global environment'.

IHRM provides no espousal for either replicating or extending the home country HR policies to host country or vice versa or for following country-specific HRM framework. It emphasizes pursuing a singular HR model which is fundamentally uniform across all the countries in which an organization is present with superstructure modifications as required due to country-specific regulatory framework and cultural ethos.

IHRM: Evolution

Though the history of IHRM is almost a century old, a phase when imperialism was an accepted phenomenon, the professional phase of IHRM began in the 1960s, with the research of Geert Hofstede who had discovered cultural implications of various nations and societies for the practice of IHRM. This movement was further strengthened in the 1980s with the growing acceptance of globalization and omnipresence of multinational enterprises. The initial phases of HRM heavily concentrated on understanding and analysing the management of expatriates, wherein many multinational organizations were challenged with issues like how to treat and deal with employees posted from a parent country to host country. In fact, IHRM has been treated synonymously with expat management for the larger part of foregone decades. Global organizations continued to have centralized HR structures, systems and processes till the 1970s, even though they often discussed about HRM in an international context. It was not until the 1980s, when cultures started integrating and employees were exposed to international trends, regardless of their place of their work, that organizations started building expectations of a single HR policy and practice across the company, independent of the number of countries the company might be operating in. The expectation of attaining global standards of HRP is not just limited to multinational companies but is also relevant to regional players with or without global aspirations for business growth. In the wake of the aforementioned expectation, IHRM has made two parallel journeys, both in theory and practice. One continued to explore and practice IHRM from an expat perspective: remuneration, taxation, housing, insurance and family welfare of expats. Attempts were also made to internationalize American managerial practices in the name of IHRM. The other was to build a true IHRM practice wherein companies started to attempt to design globally benchmarked HR systems, applicable to all employees working in various countries, equally and equitably. The history of IHRM has also seen conflicting arguments between unified and divergent HRM practices. Advocates of a unified practice believed that it did not make a business case to differentiate HRP from one nation to the other since national boundaries have no implication on people management or the ever-evolving cultural ethos. The believers of a divergent HR practice, on the other hand, argued that the needs of people working in every country, and their cultural underpinnings, are very different from each other, and imposing a unified culture may be fraught with the danger of disrespecting and depriving people's beliefs and preferences. This conflict has weakened the progress of IHRM quite a bit as a full-fledged discipline for quite a while since the divergent perspective of HRM was considered as going against the development of IHRM. However, the evolution in the 1990s helped resolve this issue with the realization of the fact that unification and divergence are two sides of the same coin, both enriching the scope and depth of IHRM. This led to the creation of global HR-shared services, global HR directors and eventually a global HR agenda. In acknowledgement of this trend, many reputed universities around the world have built IHRM as an important part of their curriculum and teach it as a part of their management courses. The evolution of IHRM as a distinct discipline has not been random, ad hoc or merely an expansion of the existing HRM practice, but instead as systematic growth through critical thinking and as a pragmatic necessity caused by market, technological, economic and social changes occurring in the world. However, IHRM is relatively recent and is yet to build a comprehensive base of theoretically and practically validated body of knowledge, even though several concepts and models developed as a part of HRM remain applicable and relevant for IHRM.

Emergence of IHRM

The following factors have specifically contributed in the evolution of IHRM as a distinct discipline:

- **Increasing cross-border trade and business:** Economics of the twenty-first century has seen globalization of business at a scale and size like never before. There is a realization across businesses and governments that if trade and commerce are to survive, they cannot be restricted to a nation or boundaries. Capital has been moving swiftly from those nations with a surplus to those with an opportunity. This has given a big push for exploring methods and approaches to manage HR internationally.
- **Increasing mergers and acquisitions and joint ventures:** There is a continuously growing trend in cross-border mergers and acquisitions. HR issues are expectedly the dominant focus in such contexts and require a greater understanding of employee matters, along with a need to integrate this understanding to build solutions.
- **Merging cultures:** Societies are connected to each other much more closely, and this connect has evolved into not only appreciation for each other's culture but has also led to melding them into one. The importance of cultural differences is diminishing at a rapid pace. This mosaic of cultures, paving a way for folded identity, implies there has to be a uniform method of people management, and excessive local standardizations can create inequality and eventually inefficiencies in management of people.
- **Technological advancements:** Developments in technologies such as telecommunications, media and information technology (IT), especially the Internet explosion, have brought people from various nations on the same plane and wavelength, modernizing them into a single human force. This, in turn, has led to a greater emphasis on the application of IHRM practices.
- **Internationalization of work:** Global transfer of work, particularly offshoring and nearshoring the projects, has seen work getting more and more internationalized. This has necessitated creating global teams. Employees working in one country are provided with opportunities to work with employees in another country, resulting in incorporation of IHRM practices.
- **Internationalization of management practices:** Management has become increasingly global and ideas are exchanged freely across countries. Organizations are keen to adopt and implement management practices that are proven to be successful, regardless of their geography. European organizations are keen to implement American and Japanese management methods, while the Japanese organizations are intrigued to experiment with American management concepts. This has led to a greater convergence of thoughts followed with practices.

IHRM: Challenges

The main challenges involved with the management of HR in an international context are the following.

Headquarters/host country centric: The biggest challenge comes from a perspective that HR policies, practices and processes built and applied at headquarters can be extended to other countries. Many organizations and managers tend to believe that HRP especially those which succeeded at headquarters should be applied in other countries of operations, and in some cases merely as a demonstration of authority of headquarters' managers. In situations such as these, HRM has often failed to deliver any functional results. Bringing mindset change in managers of such organizations is very challenging and also critical for IHRM.

T-shirt @ USD 55 Million

General Electric (GE) had acquired a France-based company Cie Generale de Radiologie dealing with medical systems. In the integration workshops, the French employees were made to wear T-shirts labelled in English. GE managers of the United States had also displayed English language posters in the conference hall. French employees saw these practices as aggressive, a display of American dominance and lacking sensitivity. The newly acquired French Unit which was to make about USD 30 million profits had incurred USD 25 million losses in the first year. The saga of loss-making continued for another two years until GE took serious steps to integrate and respect the employees working locally.

Lack of practitioner models: IHRM as a discipline is yet to be developed and there is dearth of a systematic body of knowledge. Largely, IHRM is comprised of anecdotal works and prescriptions. There is a need for practitioner readings and handbooks which can help HR managers drive international HRP.

Inadequate global HR managers: There is a serious dearth of well-trained global HR managers who are capable of managing and supporting an international workforce. As a result, most of the HR managers prefer to extend either headquarters or home country HR policies to the rest of the world without realizing their efficacy and implications for employees working in such countries.

Narrow understanding of IHRM: There exists a limited understanding that IHRM simply means either aligning the overt cultural nuances of a nation or implementing country-specific tax laws. In some cases, IHRM is treated as nothing but immigration management facilitating visa grants to employees.

IHRM as expatriate management: More often than not IHRM is understood as expatriate management. In such a scenario, the efforts are scoped to identifying, providing peripheral culture training and fixing compensation and benefits.

Multinational corporations centric: IHRM is understood as something only required in multinational enterprises. Though this is largely true, IHRM is also needed to address issues of a multinational workforce even when operations are confined to a particular country.

The Big Five HR Global Challenges

Mendenhall, Black, Jensen and Gregersen (2007), based on their survey and interviews conducted covering 30 firms, have identified big five HR global challenges as described below:

1. **Enhancing global business strategy:** HR managers have pivotal role in shaping the global business strategy. In order to achieve this, they need to focus on three critical aspects: first is integrating global HR issues into the company's mission, second is to encourage senior managers to be catalysts for integrating HR with global strategy development and implementation, and third is to keep global HR issues on managers' radar screens throughout the strategy building and implementation process.

2. **Aligning HR processes and programmes with overall global business strategy:** This is an essential element in the successful execution of global business strategy, but unfortunately many organizations miss this resulting in either slow or lack of progress in internationalization of business. Therefore, paying due attention during the implementation of global business strategy is of utmost importance. Instead of maintaining a headquarters approach or an exclusive localized approach to HR, it is important to sharply align HRM practices and processes with the pace of internationalization of business. Pursuing either approaches, that is, extension of the headquarter HR framework, especially with the mindset that such an HR framework is tested and validated or allowing local, national operations/business to create their own HR framework can be counterproductive for effective execution of global business strategy. Therefore, the big challenge is ensuring alignment of HR processes and programmes with overall global business strategy implementation.

3. **Assisting in leading global change initiatives:** Designing and driving organizational change management programmes is the primary responsibility of HR managers. Any change management programme has huge ramifications for the people working in such organizations. HR managers need to enable and assist the people to adapt to the change, and drafting all key managers for successful implementation of such organizational change management programme is not merely desirable but essential. Organizational change would generally lead to skill upgradation, reassigning of employees, new team structures, counselling initiatives and recast of career planning programmes apart from a special focus on leadership. HR mangers need to anchor all such programmes which directly fall within the purview of HR management.

4. **Strategically assisting in building corporate cultures:** The fourth big global HR challenge for HR managers is providing leadership to organizations in building a strong corporate culture that is capable of sustaining the internationalization, ensuring that principal corporate norms are followed across the global operations and yet providing enough flexibility to absorb local realities. HR managers need to remember that a strong culture not only contributes to an organization's aspiration to be truly global but also acts as a unifying force by aiding in strong unification of operations across the countries.

5. **Developing future leaders:** Despite having built sound organizational structures and systems, some organizations could not sustain the internationalization strategy due to weak global leadership mettle. HR managers can significantly influence the success chances through building global leadership competencies, training and mentoring programmes and through building global mindsets. This is the single most important initiative that can create a substantial difference to organizations in their efforts to internationalize their business.

Source: Mendenhall et al. (2007).

Cultural variations: The most fundamental challenge for IHRM as well as the essence of IHRM is a precise understanding of cultural underpinnings of workforce in different nations and continents. Languages, behavioural demonstrations, mannerisms, protocols, symbols, artefacts—all have different meanings and acceptances which ought to be harmonized and integrated through a robust IHRM framework and process for its effectiveness and efficiency. For example, some nations pursue control and command structures, while others prefer ideation models.

Political and economic variations: Due to historical reasons and driven by a particular ideology, every sovereign nation has its own polity and economic doctrine that have a subtle bearing on the way HR is managed in organizations located in these nations. There are different political ideologies: socialist, communist, democratic, capitalistic and dictatorial. The kind of economic policies pursued also differ due to these political affiliations. The combination of both the political ideology and the economic policy influences the organizational structures, regulatory frameworks, psychological expectations, the way the work is carried out and mobility of people. IHRM is expected to create integration between all these features in order to drive cutting-edge HRM practices.

Regulatory framework variations: Each nation draws its regulatory framework from its constitutional directives and political, economic and sociological spirit. For example, the kind of employee and work regulations preferred and enforced depends upon the nation's political and economic policies. They influence the HRM framework in a significant manner.

Workforce variations: The nature, academic and experiential background of workforce tends to have variations among the nations. For example, the chronological age of the average workforce in developing countries is much younger than that of the workforce in developed countries. These demographic factors pose a definite challenge to the practice of HR policies and processes.

Variations in appreciation of HRM: The state of HRM practice and its appreciation has significant variations in different countries. The practice of HRM is in an evolved stage in a few nations and nascent in others. This gap can be formidable to bridge, especially when trying to create a universal IHRM framework for a company.

IHRM: Objectives

Though the objectives of IHRM are no different from those of standard HRM theory and practice, IHRM has certain distinct objectives such as the following:

Creating international talent acquisition models: One of the key objectives of IHRM is to create and operationalize the methods and practices that help in hiring workforce internationally. The recruitment and selection models are to be designed to attract, evaluate, select and bring the right talent on board. Often, many organizations, even multinational ones, engage in hiring models that fall short of hiring the right talent in an international context. These models seldom include competencies such as appreciation for cross culture and comprehension of complex managerial systems as critical competencies in the selection process.

Creating international training systems: Though the core of the training curriculum remains similar or identical across nations, organizations need to create an internationally amenable training methodology, evaluation and delivery style. Very often, training efforts developed in a single nation context fail to deliver results due to inappropriate and unsuitable teaching frameworks, case studies and examples. IHRM can play a pivotal role by building learning models and methodologies that help in imparting skills and competencies to an international workforce.

Creating international compensation and benefits model: Compensation and benefits management in an international context is a critical area for many organizations. The model will need to include aspects related to compensation design, structure, tax deductions, payroll administration and local statutory compliances. While it is extremely challenging to create compensation and benefits model that can be applied to the workforce internationally due to variations in tax structures and currency valuations and cost of living, IHRM can create a systematic understanding of international compensation management models.

Creating international work culture: IHRM can contribute to a systematic understanding of cultural variations and ethos, and their implications for organizations operating globally. Communication protocols, negotiation methods, teamwork, leadership, conflict management and motivational structures tend to be different while they can also have sources of integration due to fundamental similarities. The analysis and understanding of cultural variations would help to draft internationally suitable work culture building interventions.

Creating international performance and career management systems: The purpose of performance and career management systems appears to be the same across the globe but the importance accorded to various parameters is widely different. In some cultures, more importance is given to potential and past credentials while others accentuate on task and present contextual performance. Similarly, some view it as important to include aspects such as discipline and loyalty, and others believe that dynamism and ideation are critical. Likewise, some national cultures view career as merely involving vertical movements and others see it as competency enrichment. IHRM can create models of performance and career planning that can be applied across the organization internationally.

Creating international employee relations framework: Currently, the practice of HRM is limited by the fact that there are few or no models of employee relations that students and practitioners can follow in pursuit of employee engagement and harmony in an international perspective. This is due to variations in employee regulatory frameworks added with a lack of clear understanding in managing employee relations functions in multicultural scenario. The other challenge is that organizations and managers in some nations understand employee relations as a function of employee and employer conflict management, while other understand it as pure employee commitment and fulfilment activity. The objective of IHRM in this backdrop is to build employee relations models that can be adopted in international settings.

Creating international separation management: Exit management is always considered an important HRM function from both people and business perspective. Many organizations and HR managers have fears when venturing into a new territory since exit laws in some countries are stringent making it difficult to pull out in adverse conditions. Further understanding of exit laws as well as social customs underpinning separation of employees is a complex issue. IHRM has an exclusive focus to provide a clear understanding of employee separation management in different nations.

IHRM Versus Single Nation-centric HRM

There are comparisons and contrasts between IHRM and single nation-centric HRM. The similarity as discussed earlier comes from the basic tenets of HR theories and models, and the contrast arises from the way HRP is designed and implemented. The focus here is on the contrast which includes the following:

Profile of workforce: The preliminary difference is obvious. The profile of workforce in a single nation-centric model would be identical, whereas in an international context the profile is complex and varied. This has significant implications for the design and application of HRP.

Administrative overload: The number of administrative activities to be carried in an international HR set-up is huge and requires a thorough understanding. For example, the type of transfer policy and assistance programme to be adopted since employees can virtually be transferred to any part of the world. Assisting them in their relocation, their orientation, education for their children, medical and taxation issues are other aspects to consider. The sheer range of these activities can be mind-boggling.

Macro perspective: A local or national mindset is adequate to manage workforce in a single nation-centric organization but this mindset is utterly inadequate to manage an international workforce. In fact, most of the failures of multinational organizations in the area of HRM practice have come from engaging HR managers who are trained to deal with workforce issues of just a single nation.

HR framework: Issues ranging from talent hiring, development to retention are qualitatively different when an organization is targeting the international arena. For example, the leadership is required at a global level and so the training will need to have substantial focus on international perspectives and on doing and managing business in a multinational context. Similarly, various HR policies and programmes encompassing performance management, career management, succession planning, talent panning and others are to be accorded international treatment through integration of various cultures, regulations and characteristics of the varied workforce. Hence, the HR framework developed ought to be very different from the single nation-centric HR framework.

Conventional Categorization of Employees

Host country nationals: Employees are called host country nationals if an international organization employs nationals locally in that country's operations. For example, Unilever hires and places Indians in India operations.

Parent country nationals: Employees are called parent country nationals when such employees hired or already working in the organization's country of origin or headquarters are placed in another country where either its subsidiary or branch is located.

Third country nationals: When employees of a developing country are transferred to another developing country, they are termed as third country nationals. For example, employees of Indian nationality hired and already working in India if placed to work in Malaysia are called third country nationals.

Expatriate: This refers to an employee working in a foreign country. This employee can be a host or parent country national or a third country national. However, the word expatriate is generally used when employees of a parent country are temporarily assigned to a host country. Technically speaking, the term expatriate refers to all the three nationals as above.

Inpatriate: This word was added to the technical jargon of IHRM recently. It refers to an employee who is working in host country (subsidiary or branch operations) and is transferred to parent country.

Repatriate: This refers to a parent or host company employee transferred to another country and called back either on expiry of the assignment or after a defined term.

External influence: An important differentiator between single-centric organizations and international organizations is that the external influence is too high on international organizations. Sometimes they are susceptible to formidable challenges in the form of local government regulations which can be comparatively more stringent from those faced by single nation-centric and owned organizations. This could have several implications for HRM practices. For example, some nations impose hiring restrictions or exit restrictions on international operations that may not be valid for single nation-centric organizations.

Geo perspective: Another obvious factor that distinguishes a single nation-centric organization from an international organization is the spread of geography. Managers in an international context are required to possess reasonable knowledge of the world map and where the operations are located. This in itself calls for a specific competency. In fact, the training of HR managers in IHRM needs to start from the issue of geographical knowledge in terms of location of operations and its nature and significance.

Risk factor: Risks associated with managing an international workforce outpace the single nation-centric workforce in many ways due to the susceptibility of international workforce to external influence as discussed before. Any change in regulations or change in social, political and economic issues can have significant implications for management of HR in an international context. This can be a limiting factor at times, both for strong emergence of international workforce and for effective HRM.

IHRM: Approaches

A much debated issue in the management of international business and an international workforce is which approach to choose: integration or differentiation, or a combination of both. This has ramifications for IHRM framework and the resultant HR policies and practices. Basically, there are three approaches to IHRM based on the growth stage of an international workforce and the life cycle of an organization.

Integration approach to IHRM: A stout argument advanced by many academicians and practitioners is that the basic purpose of IHRM practice is to integrate otherwise disintegrated HR policies and practices. Their point is that the differentiation has always been favourably biased towards headquarters or parent country employees as most of the HR policies are designed and applied keeping in view the parent country workforce context. According to this school of thought, the differentiation also leads to centralization of decision-making and many executive decisions made concerning reward, career and plum assignments tend to benefit parent company staff. In such an environment, employees working in subsidiaries and in host countries are liable to develop subordinate attitudes and a loss of initiative. Further integration had many virtues including optimization of resources, achievement of cost-effectiveness, increased innovation and infusion of competitive spirit within the organization involving workforce from all nationalities. The root of differentiation lies in causing advantages to one section of employees at the cost of the other section depending upon which side the authority and power is centred on. Hence, the advocates of integration-oriented IHRM put integration as the core objective of IHRM origin and existence.

Differentiation approach to IHRM: The argument in favour of differentiating IHRM is that every nation and region is unique. External factors such as polity, economic policies, labour regulation and cultural factors vary so much that no single HR framework can address and fulfil all the requirements of an international workforce. Hence, there is a dire need for localized treatment and enough differentiation in HR policies and practices. This way, providing autonomy and appropriateness in management of HR is a possibility. Managerial practice cannot go against the very nature of the differentiation that exists in different nations and people. Ignoring this reality would be insensitivity and imposing a single perspective of thinking and doing believed at one place to another place which can have negative implications for organizations and people. The differentiation is indeed good for the organization as it can create variety and dynamism which are essential for organizational spirit.

Mid path approach to IHRM: In this approach, a combination of integration and differentiation is suggested. The essence is that integration is imperative to bring oneness in an organization, and differentiation is the key to ensure easy adoptablity and absorption of cultures and people. Corporate drivers such as strategy, quality, research and development need to follow an integration approach, whereas compliance and operations can follow a differentiation approach to attain optimization and effectiveness. In the context of IHRM, it is argued that organization-wide HR strategy needs to have an integration approach, while compliance to labour regulations and employee welfare and cultural aspects should be given a differentiation approach implying that they should be influenced by local operations.

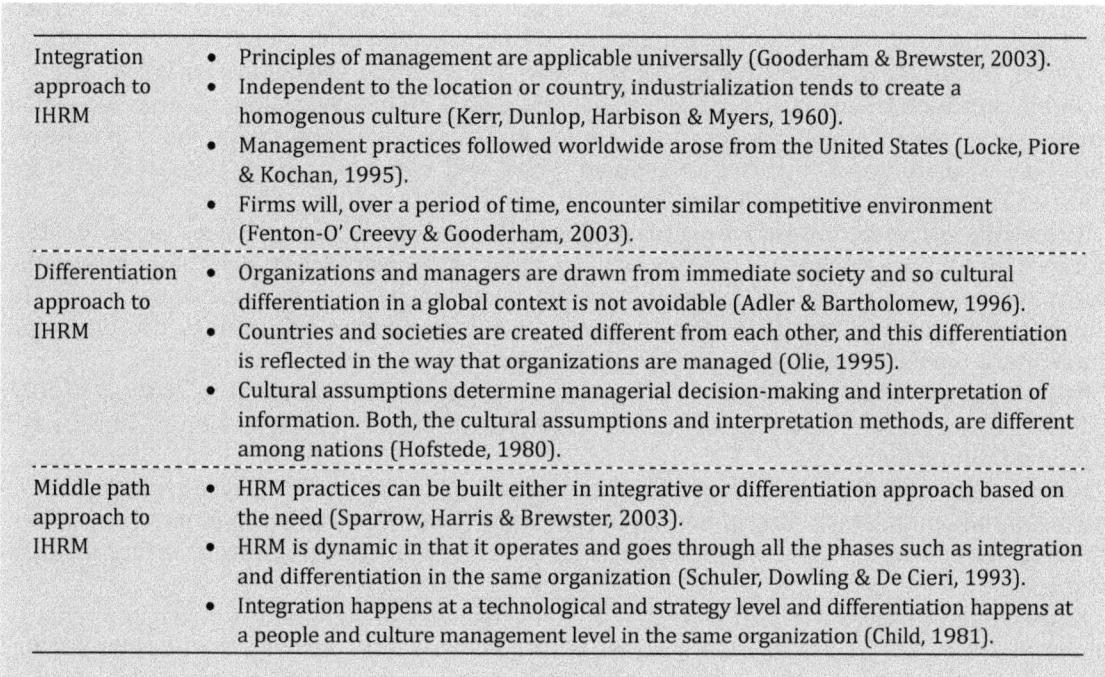

Integration approach to IHRM	• Principles of management are applicable universally (Gooderham & Brewster, 2003).
	• Independent to the location or country, industrialization tends to create a homogenous culture (Kerr, Dunlop, Harbison & Myers, 1960).
	• Management practices followed worldwide arose from the United States (Locke, Piore & Kochan, 1995).
	• Firms will, over a period of time, encounter similar competitive environment (Fenton-O' Creevy & Gooderham, 2003).
Differentiation approach to IHRM	• Organizations and managers are drawn from immediate society and so cultural differentiation in a global context is not avoidable (Adler & Bartholomew, 1996).
	• Countries and societies are created different from each other, and this differentiation is reflected in the way that organizations are managed (Olie, 1995).
	• Cultural assumptions determine managerial decision-making and interpretation of information. Both, the cultural assumptions and interpretation methods, are different among nations (Hofstede, 1980).
Middle path approach to IHRM	• HRM practices can be built either in integrative or differentiation approach based on the need (Sparrow, Harris & Brewster, 2003).
	• HRM is dynamic in that it operates and goes through all the phases such as integration and differentiation in the same organization (Schuler, Dowling & De Cieri, 1993).
	• Integration happens at a technological and strategy level and differentiation happens at a people and culture management level in the same organization (Child, 1981).

Evolving approach to IHRM: Another emerging approach can be "evolving approach." The advocates of this approach mainly come from the practicing managers community who aver that it is neither integrative not differentiation nor mid path approach but a combination of all these depending upon the growth stage of an organization and the state of its operations in a given country or region. According to this approach, HR policies and practices as well as HR strategy tend to be the same across an organization when business operations of such an organization are in an evolved stage and a differentiation approach is prevalent if the organization is in a growing stage and an integrative approach is enforced during the nascent stage. To summarize, all these approaches are present in the same organization depending upon the growth cycle stage it is currently in.

Emergence of Global HR Manager

The future belongs to HR managers who are globalized, since more and more organizations tend to go international. This is because domestic markets can no longer provide the scale and opportunities required for them to remain in business. Hence, becoming an international organization is not so much a growth aspiration as it is a fundamental necessity. In such a scenario, the demand is more for global HR managers and less for localized and single nation-centric HR professionals. On the other hand, HR managers must play a significant role in shaping an organization's business strategy into a global strategy and beyond political boundaries. This is certainly a fertile opportunity for HR professionals who had almost lagged behind in leading business strategy and being at the core of organization in the foregoing business revolution phase. People mobility and global talent play a pivotal role in the era of internationalization of business and growth of world economy. In the coming decades, competitive organizations are more concerned about performance-driven talent than nationality. So emergence of strong global HRM appears to be imminent. The profile of global HR manager will need to incorporate the following aspects.

Global mindset: HR managers in order to become global HR managers should possess a global mindset. Awareness of global businesses and trends, and more importantly of how an international workforce is shaping up in terms of demographics and competencies, is a prerequisite for someone aiming to be a global HR manager.

Knowledge of international business: Global HR managers should have a great deal of appreciation and knowledge of international markets and business. Studies have repeatedly shown the need for a robust alignment between business strategy of organizations and HR strategy. In this context, an HR manager ought to understand how HR strategy can align and contribute to internationalizing the businesses in a systematic manner.

Knowledge of labour markets: It is important for global HR managers to possess a deep understanding of labour and employment markets which include concentration of various HR skills and training hubs.

Knowledge of labour regulations: Local and national government employee regulations and unionism, and an understanding of how such regulations and IR possibly can impact businesses, especially for an international organization, is an important functional requirement for a global HR manager.

Knowledge of macro societal changes: The effectiveness of a global HR manager is greatly enhanced if the role holder has the awareness of macro societal changes that are happening, especially from a sociological perspective, since such changes can have huge implications for the type of people management policies and programmes required in an international context.

Cultural perspective: A multicultural perspective and ability to leverage them for organizational success and growth is another important competency that a global HR manager must acquire and practise. The history of organizations that have taken initiative to internalize their businesses in the last three decades is formidable evidence that these originations could not achieve their intended goals or failed owing to poor cultural alignment and management. In fact, some of the experiences point to the significance of culture management as fundamental to internationalization of businesses.

Apart from the ones listed before, the standard soft competencies such as positive regard, power of socialization, a high degree of self-awareness and the ability to manage group processes are essential for global HR managers to succeed.

IHRM: Overview of the Book

This book is organized into nine chapters focusing on the multifaceted dimensions of IHRM. The endeavour is to balance HRP and IR perspectives, departing from a traditional theoretical divide between IR and HRP, since both sides, apart from enabling a comprehensive understanding of IHRM, are equally important and enriching. This book is also designed to cover all important geographies, spanning 18 countries, and reflect the international nature of HRM. Business cases, contemporary global trends, benchmarking practices, data analysis and conflicting views are presented within each HR practice and IR practice to enrich the readers' understanding of IHRM. Chapters are sequenced on the basis of a typical lifecycle of HRM, beginning from the procurement of HR to enriching them, keeping the maintenance phase of HRP (industrial relations practices, IRP) in the middle, and ending with international culture management that glues the entire practice together.

Chapter 1: IHRM—the meaning, concept, challenges and its historical evolution and implications are vividly discussed in this chapter. The objective of the chapter is to introduce IHRM and debate approaches such as integration, differentiation and middle path models, as well as global trends in the context of rapid economic, technological and societal changes. Often there is a question in the minds of students and practitioners about the precise similarity and dissimilarity between single nation-centric HRM versus multination-centric HRM. This is amply deliberated in this maiden chapter to clear the conceptual and practical dilemma. The growing emergence of a global HR director and how it is becoming more common than in the past is illustrated in the context of business organizations. The chapter also dwells upon the kinds of friction an organization goes through when the time comes for it to internationalize the company HR policy, and how unwittingly the parent company's HR policies influence this course of progress.

Chapter 2: In this chapter, we discuss how the workforce is becoming global, the staffing trends in an international arena and the quest of organizations worldwide to access talent in a borderless fashion. How factors such as expanding cities, rise of immigration, global outsourcing, demographics, technological advancements, especially digitization, automation and analytics are driving the practice of international staffing (IS) are also discussed in this chapter. International recruitment trends, strategies being adopted by organizations and IS process maps, benchmarking practices and sophistication of international human capital inventory practices and valuations, expatriates as source of IS and immigration regulations of 18 nations impacting the global sourcing of talents are illustrated with contemporary examples and citations. Contrary trends that can potentially slow down IS such as de-globalization and protectionism and their ramifications are evaluated. Discussion on leadership hiring, trends and pitfalls in international context is accorded a special focus to enable the readers to grasp the topics in their respective contexts in order to draw parallels with their leadership staffing practices.

Chapter 3: International trends in higher education, training and development are discussed in this chapter. Training models encompassing training needs assessment (TNA), design of courses, instruction methodologies, global digital libraries, evaluation models in the international context along with best practices are given focus. Leadership competencies and development, and their significance in IHRM, are illustrated with examples of approaches adopted by global corporations. Technological trends aiding efforts of global companies to enhance the reach of training delivery and accessibility and virtual learning environment (VLE) are the key topics. Though there are great similarities in training approaches followed in both domestic and international organizations in a few contexts, efforts are made to describe the directional difference in them. The key objective of this chapter is to understand how the content, design, delivery and evaluation of learning management can be planned and managed in an international context with wider reach and impact. The chapter also dedicates additional focus on classic training models and designs which are not new but remain fundamental even in IHRM context.

Chapter 4: Macro and micro compensation trends and their ramifications to wage management of global corporations are vividly described with the support of comprehensive data and its interpretation. Trends such as productivity, inflation, wage inequality, executive compensation, increasing legislative measures to minimize the compensation arbitrariness, along with various compensation models and strategies that can assist in designing international compensation, are included in the discussion. Setting up of payroll processes in various countries to meet employees' expectations as well as to comply with legislative stipulations has been a tricky function for global HR managers, and therefore exclusive focus is accorded to this topic to provide practical tips and illustrations. Compensation practices, incentives, fringe benefits, pay taxation provisions, along with emerging trends and pay structures of 18 countries are described, making this a rare effort. The objective of this chapter is to enable global HR managers to create a compensation model tailor-made to their respective organizations while considering national and international compensation dynamics and mechanisms that have relevance to compensation management as a competitive and motivational tool apart from being an economic and HR function.

Chapter 5: The chapter captures salient labour and employment laws and labour codes of the United States and Canada. Precise understanding of various laws and their implication at the workplace is a complex exercise which is made easy and reader-friendly, enabling students and practitioners to grasp them at a glance without losing the rigour, essence and meaning of various provisions. Selective laws of the United States are covered with their interpretation, both from a federal perspective and from a state perspective. The provincial legislative measures in case of Canada have been taken care of while creating the text. Contextual case studies are illustrated to drive the implementation process of selective legal provisions which are key and fundamental in IR management. Comparative analysis of the legislative landscapes in the United States and Canada is discussed briefly to provide the underlying assumptions of such legal measures in each country, even though they fall under a single geography (North America).

Chapter 6: This is the most voluminous chapter of the book, which is dedicated to labour legislation, employment regulations and labour codes in the European countries. European Union directives on labour and employment have emerged as cardinal to the evolution of labour legislation and regulations in the member European nations. Hence, a detailed discussion is held on this topic covering all the pertinent aspects. Selective legislation measures and labour codes are presented using an application-oriented approach, covering the United Kingdom, Germany, France, the Netherlands, Switzerland, Finland, Denmark, Hungary, Poland and the Czech Republic. The objective is to provide all the important labour laws along with their interpretation in all the major European countries in one place for ease. The chapter provides a pragmatic understanding for the students and practitioners of IHRM, who today need to search in various places for relevant information and analyse it to gain a perspective on the subject.

Chapter 7: Following the logical sequence, this chapter addresses the labour laws and regulations in Asian countries, such as the People's Republic of China (PRC), Singapore, Japan and the Philippines, and all territorial labour and employment legislations of Australia. Each of these countries has evolved the labour laws in tandem with their political and economic history and developments, and as a result, one can see a stark difference in their approach to same topics, along with varying importance of the issues. The chapter tries to explain these dynamics while providing a detailed coverage of laws and their interpretation.

Chapter 8: International performance management (IPM) framework, approaches, strategies, benchmarking practices and trends are covered in this chapter, with a special focus on high performance work practices (HPWP). This is a difficult chapter from the point of view of delineating a domestic performance management approach from an international one, as readers may look to understand from a global context, what factors, apart from cultural consequences, are likely to play a role in execution of performance management practices. Hence, some of these aspects are covered with examples and practices.

Chapter 9: The concluding chapter is designed to describe and discuss the concepts, models and profiles of culture in an international context. Organizational culture in the best-run multinational organizations, together with a multicultural organizational development model is illustrated in detail. The causes of cultural breakdown in a multicultural environment and remedial measures and model to build and install a multicultural model that could address the needs of an organization operating in a global environment are the topics of study in this chapter. Communication, which is a vital part of culture management, is given a special focus in terms of coverage and discussion.

Summary

The introductory chapter dwells upon (a) significance of IHRM in the backdrop of an increasingly mobile workforce across all nations, (b) ways of managing international workforce, (c) meaning and scope of IHRM, (d) international HR challenges and objectives, (e) single nation-centric HRM versus IHRM approaches and (f) emergence of global HR manager. It is also argued that students, practitioners and academicians must focus on international dimension of workforce as the future belongs to a globalized workforce rather than a workforce of a single national concentration.

QUESTIONS FOR DISCUSSION

1. Is there a need to develop IHRM as a distinct discipline?
2. Compare and contrast the theory and practice of HRM of a single nation-centric with IHRM.
3. What competencies are required to be an effective global HR manager?
4. What are the factors accelerating the emergence of IHRM as a practice?
5. Describe the characteristics of globalized workforce.

CASE STUDY

Future Drugs and Pharmaceuticals Ltd is an Australia-based, family-owned company engaged in formulations/generics of immunity suppressant medicines with over AUD 6 billion in annual revenues, employing over 11,000 employees out of which about 10,200 employees work in the home country. The company has decided to diversify into bulk drugs manufacturing and set up operations in China and Poland with twin objectives of leveraging costs and to spread itself into Asian and European markets. The new operations would create about 4,000 jobs in the coming two years. HRM is identified as one of the most strategic areas for success of this business intervention since talent is the core. Currently, HR policies, processes and practices within the company are Australia centric which may not cater to workforce needs of countries such as China and Poland. The entire HR department is concentrated in Australia itself, with no associated staff anywhere else. Further, the company has decided that it needs an IHRM framework and practices to strengthen its endeavour to internationalize the company. However, management of the company strongly believes that they have a robust people practice in their Australian units which should not be diluted. Discuss how you will approach the issues and what steps are necessary to build an IHRM model that can meet the business and people objectives of Future Drugs and Pharmaceuticals Ltd.

Bibliography

Adler, N. J. and Bartholomew, S. (1996). Building Networks and Crossing Borders, in P. Joynt and M. Warner (eds), *Managing Across Cultures: Issues and Perspectives* (pp. 7–32). London: International Thomson Business Press.

Briscoe, D. R., Schuler, R. S. and Claus, L. (2009). *International Human Resource Management: Policies and Practices for Multinational Enterprises*. London: Routledge.

Child, J. (1981). Culture, Contingencies and Capitalism in the Cross-national Study of Organizations, in L. L. Cummings and B. M. Staw (eds), *Research in Organizational Behavior, 3*, 303–356. Greenwich, CT: JAI Press.

Fenton-O'Creevy, M. and Gooderham, P. N. (2003). International Management of Human Resources. *Scandinavian Journal of Business Research, 17*(1), 19–37.

Gooderham, P. N. and Brewster, C. (2003). Convergence, Stasis or Divergence? Personnel Management in Europe. *Scandinavian Journal of Business Research, 17*(1), 6–18.

Hofstede, G. (1980). *Culture's Consequences: International Differences in Work-related Values*. London: SAGE Publications.

Kerr, C., Dunlop, J. T., Harbison, F. and Myers, C. A. (1960). *Industrialism and Industrial Man*. Cambridge, MA: Harvard University Press.

Locke, R., Piore, M. and Kochan, T. (1995). *Employment Relations in a Changing World Economy*. London: SAGE Publications.

Mendenhall, M. E., Black, S. Jensen, R. J. and Gregersen, H. B. (2007). *Readings and Cases in International Human Resource Management*. London: Routledge.

Olie, R. (1995). The Culture Factor in Personnel and Organization Policies, in A. W. K. Harzing and J. Van Ruysseveldt (eds), *International Human Resource Management: An Integrated Approach* (pp. 124–143). London: SAGE Publications.

Perlmutter, H. V. (1969). The Tortuous Evolution of the Multinational Corporation. *Columbia Journal of World Business*, 4, 9–18.

Schuler, R. S., Dowling, P. J. and De Cieri, H. (1993). An Integrated Framework of International Human Resource Management. *The International Journal of Human Resource Management, 4*(3), 717–764.

Sparrow, P. R., Harris, H. and Brewster, C. (2003, 4–6 June). *Towards a New Model of Globalizing HRM*. Paper presented at the 7th International Human Resource Management Conference. Limerick, Ireland.

International Staffing Management

LEARNING OBJECTIVES

The objectives of this chapter are to:

☐ discuss contemporary approaches of international recruitment and their implications for business organizations.

☐ illustrate international recruitment trends and leveraging different sourcing channels for attracting top global talent.

☐ demonstrate different types of practices and process maps in international hiring, along with their interpretation.

☐ analyse the IS plan step by step.

☐ describe the immigration processes of 18 countries for greater global mobility of HR.

There are about 3 billion productive employees employed in a variety of industries, private and public institutions, across the world, of which 2.2 billion are in developing nations and the rest are in advanced industrialized nations such as the United States, Central Europe and other high-income nations. Every year, approximately 50 million people join the global workforce as per International Labour Organization (ILO, 2016) estimate. Leveraging talent across the borders has been a significant development for both the world economy and global corporate, and most importantly for the practice of HRM which has catapulted into the international scene more emphatically than ever before. Research amply proves that the ability to attract and hire good talent is the single most important determinant of an organization's strategic effectiveness. According to a KPMG survey (2016), 75 per cent of respondents were quoted saying that their workforce is becoming more global. Imbalance that existed in micro talent markets especially in managerial, technical and niche skill categories has given fillip to open up the borders for talent hunt at an international level. Talent demand at both leadership and specialist levels in emerging markets has thrown very significant challenges. Hiring for international market is fraught with unique challenges which do not otherwise exist while hiring for domestic needs. Each nation's focus on talent, methods of hiring and outlook to recruitment and onboarding is qualitatively different from other nations due to economic, social and cultural differences in addition to level of maturity in staffing management. Hence, as the forthcoming contents reveal, the initial hiring at international level has witnessed more failures than successes like any other new experiment. However, the success rate has seen a positive climb in the last five years with more and more leaders hired from one country heading the businesses in other countries proving that talent matters rather than nationality in growing the business. Talent Mobility Research Report 2015 published by Lee Hecht Harrison, a global talent mobility consulting firm covering 257 organizations representing 20 industries and deploying a reliable diagnostic survey, points out that almost 75 per cent of organizations recognize well that effective talent management is critical for success of global corporations. The report also reveals that though many organizations acknowledge the importance of a talent strategy, they are struggling to put in place a coherent and well-executed model. PricewaterhouseCoopers' (PwC) annual global CEO survey reveals that 55 per cent of respondents believe that they will look to change their approach to global mobility. Based on findings, the survey also predicts that the mobility of talent at a global scale is likely to increase at a faster pace as this can be a powerful determinant of organizational success. In this context, this chapter explores the trends, challenges, solutions and practices of IS as discussed further.

International Staffing: The Trends

There are a number of trends directly or indirectly impacting the practice of IS. Indirect trends include demographics, governance, expanding cities, digitization, automation, growing strength of knowledge economy, outsourcing, rising nationalism, de-globalization and globalization forces. Direct trends include: workforce composition and mix, and changes and growing recognition of IS as a distinct business strategy and a full-fledged function led by senior-level leadership and investments.

Globalization

Globalization has contributed to closer integration of nations than ever before. According to global consulting firm McKinsey (2016), the amount of cross-border bandwidth that is used has grown 45 times since 2005. Multinational companies are greatly influencing the pace of globalization. Two-thirds of international trade is accounted for by 500 multinational corporations. International trade has grown 12 times since the 1960s and is estimated to grow almost 6 per cent annually. FDI flows have reached almost USD 600 billion by 2010 and total borrowings on international capital markets increased from an annual average of USD 95 billion in 1980 to USD 819 billion by 1993 which is 35 per cent growth. Developments in both communications and transport have fuelled the pace of globalization further by making conduct of international business cost-effective. For example, cost of international airfares fell by almost 60 per cent between 1960 and 1990, and cost of international telephone calls fell by more than 80 per cent between 1970 and 1990. Take an example of EU: in 2015, imports accounted for 43 per cent, while exports accounted for 42 per cent, implying the level of interdependency on other nations for trade and business. As per World Trade Organization (WTO, 2016) data, world merchandise exports have grown from USD 5,168 billion to USD 19,002 billion by 2014, and world export of commercial services has escalated from USD 1,179 in 1995 to USD 4,872 by 2014. In brief, despite the financial crisis, the share of world trade in GDP, that is, average share of exports and imports of goods and commercial services as a percentage of world's GDP, is much higher today than it was 20 years ago standing at 30 per cent. The growing trend of globalization means there shall be more international practice of HRM than domestic practice, and this must start from design and deployment of robust IS practices to support and accelerate the rate of globalization.

De-globalization

While globalization has reached a state of maturity, forces of de-globalization are sweeping quite a few nations. Some experts call it 'guarded globalization'. Often quoted examples in support of de-globalization are: BREXIT, growing state capitalism (65 of 73 Chinese companies listed in the Fortune Global 500 are state owned, more than 50 per cent of Moscow's exchange value is owned by the government and most Middle East countries' wealth is owned and controlled by the respective governments, and quite a few other nations such as Brazil, North Korea, Taiwan, Cuba, Germany and France fall in this cluster where governments control large investments, trade and business) and rising protectionism both in Europe and the United States. Many political leaders, especially in Europe, have started focusing on ideologies that further the localization of economy rather than promoting free economies or fostering regional economic cooperation. Governments of a few developing nations have become cautions in opening their economy fully to global corporations with a fear of domination and are protecting their industries vociferously. Cyber espionage and political subsidies too are contributing to this trend. Global trade has seen a slowdown from its normal pace. Cross-border migration is stagnant. Apple announced that it would set up a Mac computer production unit back in the United States with an investment of over USD 100 million, while GE is contemplating moving white goods manufacturing and Otis to move elevator manufacturing from Mexico to South Carolina. However, experts believe that reversing over USD 18 trillion worth exports internationally would be an impossible task. Many economists believe that de-globalization means restructuring the global economy rather than dismantling global economic cooperation and alliances. This is more of a reconfiguration of world capital structure. Therefore, international HRM and IS practices are here to stay and of course there can be slowdown in cross-border hiring if de-globalization forces really gain the momentum.

Demographics

There is contraction and a downward trend of population growth in developed economies which will cause major shortage of workforce for these economies. Population decline is expected to continue in countries which are engines of economic growth and account for three-fourths of world economic growth. The population of the more developed countries is falling from 32 per cent of the world in 1950 to 16 per cent of the world in 2030. On the other hand, though the population continued to grow in developing economies such as China, India, Eastern Europe and South America, the demand for more productive workforce to cater to domestic talent needs and leadership talent availability and the need to meet aspirations of the younger population to work outside their own country are causing new developments. Further, the population is also ageing in all countries resulting in a less productive workforce. Today the ratio of children to older people stands at 3:1, but by 2040, this ratio can be inverted. It is argued in the Global Monitoring Report of the World Bank (2016) that global demographic trends and patterns are at a turning point, with the proportion of people aged between 15 and 64 people most likely to be in the workforce having reached a peak of 65.8 per cent by 2012 will decline in the coming years, while elderly population will rise to almost 16 per cent from the current 5 per cent of the total population. Middle class across the world, especially in emerging economies, is growing at a tremendous pace accounting for almost 3 billion by 2015 up by a billion in 10 years. Demographic change brings unique opportunities and challenges since countries face differences in demographic change resulting in imbalance. While nations have worked on removing trade barriers and increasing movement of capital across borders, the political landscape that has not changed much is continuing to cause stringency in immigration practices by restricting movement of workforce from one country to another country. Much needs to be done to meet the global staffing demands though global immigration is on the rise, as discussed next. The real test for globalization would come from nation's willingness to open borders for free talent mobility. This will have huge implications for IS.

Rise of Global Immigration

The United Nations data show that global migration is growing rapidly. About 60 million people were living outside their countries of birth in 1960 and the same is reported to be 244 million people in 2015 equal to 3.2 per cent of world population. Only a minuscule number of this migrant population have moved to another country as refugees, while majority of them had moved for better careers and livelihood. The United States, Germany and Russia occupy the first, second and third places in highest absorption of migrant employees excluding the Gulf region which in fact accounts for the highest migration. For example, the foreign born population accounts for 88 per cent of the total population in United Arab Emirates, 76 per cent in Qatar and 74 per cent in Kuwait. International migrants make up a third of the total population in cities such as Sydney, Singapore and London as per the Global Migration Data Analysis Centre. Almost one in five of the world's migrants lives in the top 20 largest cities. World Economic Forum reports that in the last 20 years the number of women among migrants has increased worldwide. In 2016, women will comprise more than half of the world's 244 million migrants. A growing proportion of these women are migrating independently as breadwinners for their families. The millennials have greater expectations of working internationally than the older population. PwC, the global consulting firm, in its analysis titled 'A Global Generational Study' states that in the past, talent has tended to flow from East to West, but by 2020, a more globally interconnected market will see global talent moving in all directions. Further, it adds that 93 per cent of working people in Africa, 81 per cent of Latin America and 74 per cent in the Middle East would like to work outside their home country at some point of time in their career, and in the last decade the number of mobile employees increased by 25 per cent and this number is likely to accelerate by 50 per cent by 2020. Migrant employees contribute significantly to the economy of destination countries by filling important jobs and skill gaps. However, it is often seen in many countries that migrant employees are not dealt with fairly in terms of wages, rights and social protection. The situation is also complicated by stringent immigration rules, role of placement agencies in collecting excessive recruitment fees and improper recruitment methods. Percentage of foreign-born and non-citizens in the total population is growing in OECD countries as shown in Table 2.1. IOM-Gallup report on public perceptions on migration worldwide reveals that contrary to what is often portrayed in the media, in every region of the world, people are more likely to be in favour of migration than against it. Despite barriers, migration is likely to grow and will grow to help nations by fulfilling the talent demands and internationals staffing practices will have a critical role in this context.

Expanding Cities

It is estimated that 70 per cent of the world's population will be living in urban cities by 2050. This figure currently stands at about 34 per cent. Top 20 cities of the world contribute to nearly 55 per cent of the world economy. Population size and economic activity in the cities have been growing

| Table 2.1 | Percentage of Foreign-born and Non-citizens in the Total Population in OECD Countries |

Country	Percentage of Foreign Born	Percentage of Non-citizens
France	10.0	5.6
The Netherlands	10.1	4.2
Greece	10.3	7.0
Ireland	10.4	5.9
Belgium	10.7	8.2
Sweden	12.0	5.3
The United States	12.3	6.6
Germany	12.5	–
Austria	12.5	8.8
Canada	19.3	5.3
New Zealand	19.5	–
Switzerland	22.4	20.5
Australia	23.0	7.4
Luxembourg	32.6	36.9
Japan	–	1.0
Korea	–	0.3
Mexico	0.5	–
Turkey	1.9	–
Poland	2.1	–
Slovak Republic	2.5	0.5
Finland	2.5	1.7
Hungary	2.9	0.9
The Czech Republic	4.5	1.2
Spain	5.3	3.8
Portugal	6.3	2.2
Denmark	6.8	5.0
Norway	7.3	4.3
The United Kingdom	8.3	–

Source: https://data.oecd.org/migration/foreign-born-population.htm (accessed on 7 March 2018).

without a pause. Developing countries such as China and India are in the forefront in creating new cities causing huge urbanization. There were just 16 cities in the world at the beginning of the twentieth century which had a population size of one million and above, and today there are 400 cities with a population size equalling or more than one million. As mentioned in the foregoing content, one out of five people who live in the cities is a migrant. IS practices have to gear up to meet the demands and provide necessary solutions not only for hiring of migrant resources but also native citizens of cities who need to be put on international platform to garner competitive advantage.

Global Outsourcing

Several factors, including fast-changing technologies, imperatives of innovation, need to address skill shortage and leadership talent challenges, need to be flexible, need to optimize costs and need to be competitive on a global scale, are forcing corporations to embrace outsourcing as a key business strategy. The outsourcing industry is not just limited to technology and business process service sectors but also includes other industries such as drugs and pharmaceuticals, automobile, infrastructure, manufacturing, banking, e-commerce and knowledge professions like legal and medical services. Total number of jobs outsourced from the United States alone accounted for about 2.4 million in the year 2015 valuing about USD 29 billion. As per an IBISWorld estimate (2017), globally the outsourcing industry amounted to USD 136 billion in 2015 from the United States alone and worldwide the outsourcing business is estimated to have generated USD 507 billion in revenue in 2014. Further, there are about 53 million freelance employees in the United States catering to outsourced work. Since 2001, the United States has been witnessing a jobless growth which is primarily attributed to outsourcing practices. Bardhan and Kroll (2003) who have done an empirical study on US outsourcing practices estimate that more than 14 million jobs in 49 service occupations representing about 11 per cent of total employment in the United States as of 2011 have attributes that could allow outsource to outside of the United States. The vulnerability of offshoring and outsourcing of many jobs in manufacturing industry is ripe. This trend is likely to grow regardless of the ever hotly debated topic of whether outsourcing would help or harm the economies and societies. IS has an important role to play in addressing the challenges posed by this outburst of outsourcing trend. Many organizations that outsource the work to third-party companies have varied quality of talent and staffing practices. Inability to service an outsourcing deal primarily arises from lack of able talent. The model and practice of staffing shall meet international standards and there is an urgent need to come up with state-of-the-art selection and induction practices. Undoubtedly, global outsourcing is a macro trend that could create an enormous impact on IS management.

Digitization and Automation

Digital marketing, digital manufacturing, automation, artificial intelligence, robotics, smart machines, cloud computing, big data, and mobile and Internet of things are widely used buzz words in the corporate world for the last five years. *SiriusDecisions* (2015) B2B marketing automation study has found that almost 63 successful marketing firms deploy marketing automation extensively. The top digital techniques that are transforming marketing include: mobile marketing, search engine optimization, communities, social media marketing, marketing automation, big data and content marketing. Technavio's (2015) market research analysis predicts that global digital manufacturing will grow steadily at a CAGR of more than 7 per cent by 2020. Digital manufacturing technology will outpace all other methods and tools. It is evident that all manufacturing companies, in order to compete, seek to deploy product life cycle management software to effectively transform their product engineering, design engineering and manufacturing. According to a PwC survey, 59 per cent of manufacturing organizations are already using some form of robotic technology to enhance their competitiveness. Big data and mobile technologies have become necessary to manage businesses. All these trends solicit advanced skills which are scarce. An organization aspiring to compete cannot confine itself to one or two micro talent markets but needs to focus on a global level. An organization's ability to be agile to demands of technological changes would be squarely dependent upon its ability to attract right skills. For example, an estimated 4.4 million IT jobs around big data are generated already. IS is a practice that is more a necessity in this situation than a tool for creating marginal value.

Direct Trends

Acknowledgement of IS not only as a distinct practice but as a strategic intervention is the most impactful direct trend. The changing mix of workforce and talent pools distribution are the other factors impacting the practice as discussed next.

Presence/Absence of International Recruitment Practice

Companies lose millions of dollars because they fail to recruit timely or rightly. Though this challenge has existed for several years, it has gotten compounded recently with the demands of changing technological and managerial landscape. The availability of talent in the immediate labour market has become the real business challenge and organizations that lack the practice of global recruitment have become serious casualties. *iCIMS* (2012) in its talent benchmark practices study covering a number of global corporations has found that many organizations do not have strategic global recruitment plans in place. The reasons for lack of focus on this practice are centred on: (a) being unable to unify HR team on a global scale, (b) manual nature of recruitment operations, (c) lack of expertise or knowledge in ensuring compliance to international laws and regulations, and (d) lack of a shared service model to manage recruitment globally from one location. Also, the study reveals that only 24 per cent of organizations have a defined global recruiting strategy. According to the International Confederation of Private Employment Services' (CIETT) economic report of 2016, the global employment and recruitment industry has seen annual growth of 9 per cent with cumulative revenue of EUR 48 billion. Staffing industry analysts predict that the global online staffing sector which earns revenues of USD 1.6 billion in 2013 will grow to USD 16 billion by 2020. The power has shifted away from employers to candidates in recruitment cycle. However, more and more organizations are realizing this and setting up international recruitment function and practice. One more challenge that haunts international recruitment practice is the absence of competent leadership. A study conducted by Chartered Management Institute (CMI) in 2011 reveals that only one in five recruitment managers are qualified, 63 per cent of them have no formal training and 56 per cent of employers said their recruitment managers are not proficient and 71 per cent of business managers have stated that effective leadership in recruitment is the real challenge. Hence, it is very important for global organizations to create a formidable international recruitment practice.

Changing Mix of Workforce in Talent Market

Changing mix of talent in terms of skills and their distribution has started impacting the trends of international recruitment. Many organizations have launched programmes to ensure right mix in terms of gender, social and cultural background in hiring the talent. This has become further challenging given the shortages of requisite talent in local talent market pushing organizations to look beyond borders. More and more organizations need experienced leaders on one hand and specialist skills on the other hand, while emerging markets face severe crunch for leaders and the developed nations are facing acute shortage of skilled people. The challenge is accentuated by the fact that there is a clear lack of alignment between the courses taught in academic institutes in many countries and the skills that industry is looking for. All these challenges can be minimized if not eliminated by opening the boundaries for talent and making it a clear global play. There is also a mix of talent, members of different generations with their own unique approaches to work: Baby boomer generation (1946–1964 born), Generation X also known as baby bust (1969–1979 born), Generation Y also known as the millennial (1980–1995) and Generation Z (born after 1996). Generational divide has its implications for the approaches to be adopted by international recruitment teams.

Changing Recruitment Trends

Data analytics, digital technologies and use of social networks like LinkedIn are playing a pivotal role in New Age recruitment management which helps international hiring considerably. Legacy concepts such as paper resumes, manual screenings and stepwise long hierarchical and personal interviews are giving way to new open-based systems of recruiting wherein passive candidates can be turned up much more easily. Traditional metrics of hiring effectiveness such as cost per hire, turnaround time and source to hire have become very basic, and organizations are now increasingly focusing on metrics such as job fitment and performance criteria. Flexibility, adaptability and diversity are the core themes running across the international recruitment practice. LinkedIn's (2016) fifth annual report which uncovers worldwide recruiting trends suggests that 39 per cent of talent leaders believe that quality of hire is the most valuable metric for performance of recruitment function but majority of them lack confidence in measuring the same. A study conducted in the United Sates by Taleo Research and Human Capital Institute in 2010 has found that only 17 per cent of the HR and business executives had access to reliable quality of hire data. Referrals as a source of hiring is gaining good traction and 32 per cent of hiring done worldwide is through referrals, beating most of the traditional sources of hiring. The other trends include increasing evidence of recruitment leaders partnering with marketing to create a talent brand of companies and focus on retention of new recruits. However, the study points out the glaring failure of global corporations to put in place a well-crafted international recruitment strategy and plan despite realization that it is core and critical for their success.

Hays 12 International Recruitment Trends to Watch

1. **Growth of flexible workforces:** More and more organizations seek project- and assignment-specific hiring in both duration and engagement points of view.
2. **Focus on STEM careers:** There will be more demand than ever before for science, technology, engineering and mathematics skills with growing focus on innovation.
3. **Digital influencers and analytics:** With the increased focus on use of digital technologies and big data and analytics, the skills associated with these occupations will grow multifold.
4. **Focus on cyber security:** Laws across the world are becoming stringent to protect data privacy and ensure foolproof data protection from theft and hacking resulting in greater demand for cyber security professionals.

5. **Digital and mobile apps:** User-friendly and simpler apps are the key properties to manage New Age customers. Organizations are seeking people with skills that can create these apps with a context.
6. **DevOps:** Experts possessing development and operations skills in software development and application deployment experience will be at the centre of international hiring in the technology industry.
7. **Customer experience:** Organizations have no choice but to put customers at the centre in a competitive world. To better serve the customers, data and understanding of data is the key. Therefore, more and more organizations seek candidates with data sense apart from their core skills.
8. **Candidates need to be adaptable:** Interviewers will focus more on the ability of candidates to adapt and be context sensitive rather than merely skill centric.
9. **HR to harness content marketing:** As recruitment market is becoming more candidate centric, it is important for HR to create more content about companies.
10. **Workforce diversity:** Gender diversity is key for all recruitment, especially leadership levels. More organizations today seek women candidates than in the past and are ready to incentivize women hiring efforts.
11. **Health care:** Recruitment in health care sector especially in developed nations is on the rise.
12. **Revolution of recruitment outsourcing:** Medium and smaller organizations prefer to outsource their recruitment since their reach is limited and these organizations are eager to access the international talent. This trend is likely to strengthen in the coming years.

Source: http://www.hays.co.uk/salary-guide/index.htm (accessed on 26 February 2018).

International Staffing: The Practice and Process Map

Though IS has been a decades-old practice, it is largely restricted to hiring few leadership and managerial levels from the nations outside parent country keeping in view the future expansion plans in the host countries or expat hiring. However, this trend has been changing with the experiences gained from outsourcing business practices. It started with cost arbitrage wherein hiring talent from host nations was dominated by cost considerations which has evolved more towards merit considerations and to effectively deal with skill shortages in present times. For example, a study finds that only 4 per cent of nurses were hired internationally for National Health Services, UK, in 2003 and this figure has grown to 43 per cent by 2014.

There are quite a few challenges when recruiting for domestic versus international as discussed in the following:

- **Who should hold positions:** Often the big questions are, which are the positions that shall be held in headquarters and which shall be in subsidiary nations? People working in headquarters would like to protect their interests and resist moving the positions to subsidiaries and even if they agree for movement, these roles tend to be inconsequential and management obviously would like to move roles to subsidiaries based on business needs.
- **Immigration rules:** The common requirement in most of the countries is that there shall be good evidence as to why local nationals should not be employed. To discourage further, countries have started stipulating high wages for employees recruited internationally and some European nations have mandated that all positions open for recruitment must first be run through trade unions/works councils before seeking candidates internationally to fill the positions.

- **Cultural and institutional variations:** Several experiences with international placements, especially expat management, prove that culture is the key factor followed by institutional variations. Macro cultural differences while recruiting for domestic needs is not an issue while it is a dominant aspect here. Cross-cultural adjustments is often quoted as the critical reason for success or failure of IS.
- **Labour legislation:** Employment and labour laws and their execution have severe differences from country to country. Therefore, terms and conditions of employment vary significantly which impact international hiring. This creates a paradoxical situation to the objectives of IS which strive for standardization at global level while labour laws continue to be region and nation specific.
- **Type of labour market:** Hiring practices are also influenced by the nature of the labour market that exists in the geography. For example, studies have found that a country like India is very good for bulk hiring of technical HR while the United States is ahead of everybody in its leadership hiring practices.

Lou Adler Group (2012) estimates that hiring the right person for the right job yields the monetary value of 100 times the annual compensation of that employee.

International Human Resource Planning

For more than a decade, companies have given little more than lip service to HR planning but all that has changed. New business imperatives have led to adoption of sophisticated tools for improved planning of HR at international level. Companies across the world are recognizing the need to plan their HR needs as carefully as they do their financial and technological needs. Korn Ferry's economic analysis of human capital in 2016 puts the value of human capital as being nearly 2.5 times (about USD 1.2 quadrillion) more valuable to economy than physical assets such as technology and real estate (valued at USD 521 trillion). The uniqueness of HR planning, albeit a fundamental function and richly described practice in HRM literature, in an international setting is underexplored. While the basic process map is akin to a standard approach to HR planning, there are stark differences in the orientation and dynamics in HR planning as a practice at an international scale. Some of these differences along with steps involved in HR planning are discussed next. HR planning is the first step that helps in integrating HRM with strategic planning and business objectives of any organization. Several benchmarking studies covering multinational enterprises have found that though applying HR planning globally is challenging, this practice has huge potential to create significant business value. Factors such as diversity, affirmative actions and equal opportunities have become as important as technological and market changes in the planning process. Despite innumerable benefits with application of HR planning covering all the nations of operations of an enterprise (enterprise-wide HR planning), it has continued to be largely very country specific and often ad hoc. However, this trend is gradually changing due to influencing factors discussed before such as skills shortages, innovation drive and cost advantages.

As discussed in foregoing content, the decision of locations of positions is critical in a multinational context. While forecasting techniques may be relevant to predict the number of job openings along with their timelines, where the job is expected to be performed from is always a subject of decision-making. One way to resolve this issue is to look at it from an efficiency perspective implying from where this job can be effectively performed in an organization. However, that may not always be possible because of various dynamics that exist in a firm. Each company chooses to set up its operations based on multiple considerations. Some companies are set up to be in close proximity with customers, some others decide based on where talent is easily accessible and some weigh on cost effectiveness measure while others where leadership is dominantly present. In international HR planning, the decision of job locations is often seen as highly contentious. There is always pull and push among various units/branches/subsidiaries to gain the jobs, particularly in leadership, middle and supervisory levels. The other challenge has been standardization of candidate's educational and experience profile that brings all candidates internationally on the same scale and measurement. Unless there is a robust method that is capable of providing reliable comparison of candidates globally, it will be difficult to plan HR requirements on a global scale. It is widely acknowledged that although all academics appear similar, they are not exactly received and treated that way and same goes with the experience profile of people in different countries. HR planners and business managers in multinational enterprises strongly believe that academic standards maintained in developing nations are not quite comparable to Ivy League schools of the United States or the United Kingdom or other developed nations. Hence, establishing equivalence is an added challenge. For example, many multinational companies launch fresher programmes that are both country specific and also international but graduates are drawn from developed nations for global hiring.

Benchmarking International Human Resource Planning Flow

Research has shown that HR planning has been widely criticized for its failure to align forecasting techniques with turbulent environmental changes of businesses. There is also extensive use of qualitative HR forecasting techniques such as succession planning, personnel inventories, supervisor estimates, non-statistical formulae such as rules of thumb, network flow models instead of use of quantitative techniques such as stochastic models, regression analysis, Delphi technique or renewal models. The situation is further complicated by lack of precision in business operating plans, inadequate commitment from business and line managers and inadequate database. However, wherever HR planning has adopted sophisticated techniques and aligned with changing business environment, it has resulted in a strengthened relationship with strategic planning and generated positive perceptions.

In contemporary multinational corporations, forecast techniques are largely automated using enterprise resource planning software. Of course, their utility is immense especially to multinational corporations given their spread and complexity of operations. Requirement of HR both from quantity and quality perspective can be projected as well as other parameters such as location, diversity and tenure are effectively dealt with. Benchmarking studies on global organizations such as Microsoft, GE, Bechtel and Mylan in the area of HR planning practice reveal that the following flow can help to gain business value out of such exercise.

Step 1: Strategic objectives and business plans: Maiden step in HR planning is to study and capture the essential data that is relevant to HR planning from a firm's strategic objectives and long-, medium- and short-term business plans. Typically, a firm's strategic and business plans should have factored markets, customers, technological and policy changes while drawing up growth strategy and tend to contain specific details such as where, when, what and how. These data pieces can serve as the basis for developing HR requirements. However, using this method, HR planning can meet business demands well in long and medium terms. It is a well-established fact that these plans are susceptible to continuous evolvement and are subject to mid-course corrections having direct implications for HR planning exercise in short term. Operational plans though are consistent with strategic plans and tend to vary in tandem with ground realities so short-term plans are helpful in HR planning but as witnessed these are quite dynamic. All these plans shall be reckoned for a real-time HR planning. As discussed before, added challenge is bringing in executive decisions for some location-neutral roles as well as new and existing roles in deciding the exact location and country of jobs. Increasingly, benchmarking studies have shown that talent availability and cost of talent acquisition and management have played a key role in this process. Often seen and recorded trend during the current decade is greater offshoring of jobs from expensive locations to low-cost locations/nations with talent market as contributing factor. For example, the biggest location for Microsoft after Redmond has been India. Many multinational enterprises had moved their strategic business enabling functions, support functions, shared services to countries such as India and the Philippines by opening captive business process centres, while others have opened up their innovation labs. Several thousands of jobs in manufacturing plants and units have been moved from developed nations in Europe and North America to countries such as China, Vietnam and Taiwan. Therefore, location has become an important element in international HR planning process because the exercise is not just limited to forecasting HR requirements for growth but also for restructuring and offshoring.

Best Practice in International Human Resource Planning: Colgate-Palmolive Company

Brian Smith, Director, Global HR Strategy has presented the process of HR planning as a part of global strategic HR strategy of Colgate-Palmolive. Believing the best sustainable competitive advantage arises from unleashing the power of people, Colgate undertook development of a global HR planning strategy aligned with global equities strategy and global manufacturing strategy. This programme known as 'building organizational excellence' is defined as the continuous alignment of Colgate people, organization structure and business processes consisting of three levels: (a) generating organizational excellence which helps select and develop people, (b) reinforcing organizational excellence which helps in focusing on and aligning Colgate people and (c) sustaining organizational excellence which helps in continuous improvement.

Source: Smith, Borski and Davis (1993).

A study conducted by Doving and Nordhaug (2010) covering a large number of companies numbering a total of 3,877 over 21 countries across the world has found that many of them have adapted HR planning practice for the purpose of analysing competence needs with varying success rates as shown in Table 2.2. While the HR planning practice is present, utilization of the practice appears to be limited although this has changed in the recent times.

Step 2: Analysis of current inventory of human capital: The vitality of HR planning comes from assessing HR needs from both quantity and quality angles afresh on annual basis instead of merely restricting it to the new expansion plans or restructuring programmes of a corporation in an ever-evolving business environment. Human capital analysis is a method through which an organization can take stock of competencies and culture. There are a number of off-the-shelf tools that are available which can be deployed to suit the requirements of any organization. For

| Table 2.2 | Investing in Human Resource Planning: An International Study |

Country	Analysis of Competence Needs	Number of Firms
Austria	91.8	147
Belgium	94.0	149
Bulgaria	89.0	82
Canada	90.4	281
Denmark	86.2	398
Estonia	93.3	75
Finland	89.1	129
Germany	89.3	196
Greece	86.0	136
Greek Cypriot	80.4	56
Iceland	76.1	46
Israel	91.1	90
The Netherlands	92.0	262
New Zealand	96.1	262
Northern Cyprus	64.7	34
Norway	58.6	29
Slovenia	61.2	129
Sweden	79.8	163
Switzerland	95.7	255
Turkey	55.0	91
The United Kingdom	98.2	896

Source: Doving and Nordhaug (2010).

example, Gartner's 'People' is a well-designed, web-based skill inventory tool that provides a quick and easy way to collect skills information from an IT organization. This model suggests organizations to follow a seven-step process: (a) understand business needs and special client requirements, (b) create skill categories and skills list, (c) reporting requirements, (d) communication templates, (e) project administration, (f) management deliverables and (g) client satisfaction. The Sibson's approach to human capital inventory analysis is presented next. Kurt Salmon (a global management consulting firm) has developed a human capital assessment methodology focused on three primary dimensions: (a) skills inventory measuring hard and softs kills associated with business value and benchmarked to industry standards, (b) tasks assessment measuring metrics on task priorities, job function alignment and task focus and (c) leadership capabilities measuring effectiveness of leadership within an organization.

Sibson's Approach to Human Capital Inventory Analysis

New York-based Sibson Consulting has established a human capital inventory approach which is scientific and reliable as described here:

Review and assess: The model advocates that a thorough review of following shall be carried out for objective understanding of current human capital inventory:

- *Structures:* Review and assess current organizational structures, roles, responsibilities and accountabilities of the existing employees.
- *Trends:* Review and assess historical and current workforce trends, patterns and costs.
- *Policies and practices:* Review and assess relevant policies, processes, practices, controls, data and measurements affecting or impacting workforce performance, organization's operations and culture.
- *Performance:* Review and assess current levels of workforce and performance (cost, quality and speed to deliver) and assess stakeholder satisfaction levels.

Identify, assess and quantify: This phase consists of the following actions:

- *Resources:* Identify and quantify current resources (human, financial, physical and technological) used to support the mission and key operations of an organization).
- *Skills/culture:* Identify and assess the competencies, skills, culture, morale and overall effectiveness of workforce.
- *Gaps:* Identify current gaps and future needs for workforce development and training.
- *Other factors:* Identify all other factors directly or indirectly impacting the performance, culture and organizational operations. Also, identify any issues that are contributing or hindering or a SWOT analysis to assess potential impact of future performance, culture and organizational operations.

Source: http://www.sibson.com/who-we-help/overview/higher-education/organizational-human-capital-strategy/ (accessed on 26 February 2018).

These tools, which are automated and can be made online (web based), can be deployed to collect data across geographies and operations of a global firm with ease and reliability. Jon Walker, global leader of HR at USD 40 billion Dow Chemical Company, says that his company is undergoing a global exercise in assessing the skills inventory to execute its broader business strategy across geographic locations and functions. Winch (2001) found that in times of major change the obsolescence rate of a firm's existing skill base increases rapidly and many firms are ill equipped to face the task. HR planning particularly taking stock of current human capital inventory analysis shall therefore be adopted as a strategic move to prepare organizations globally to compete and grow.

Step 3: Analysis of human capital inventory data: An effective human capital inventory analysis exercise would provide reliable data on what skills and attitudes are necessary in relation to realization of a firm's strategic objectives and business plans apart from giving the existing inventory statement of human capital assets a firm owns. Essentially, step 2 generates the gaps in competencies and culture globally as well as by geography, unit, function and technology/market segment. This will form the basis for building HR requirements for placement actions. Many times, global human capital inventory analysis also leads to understanding of talent surplus and shortage within an organization. IBM research has found that there is a big difference between the people who are formally supposed to have certain skills and the people who actually have them in an international context and this can be fixed only by executing a well-crafted global human capital inventory analysis and data approach. Human capital is an illusive concept for many in corporate since it is intangible and for a long time lack of sophistication in human capital inventory analysis and skill audits have contributed to this notion. Usage of HR analytics is fast becoming a mainstream management practice and increased sophistication in inventory analysis and forecasting techniques are fast removing these illusions. Contrary to popular belief, human capital or skill inventory is not necessarily always a positive capital asset but can also be a statement of liability for a firm operating at a global scale. Traditional models have advocated skills as assets regardless of their relevance to changing technologies, and costs are never subjected to comparison between countries or talent markets (if the same skills can be acquired at competitive cost in other markets comparing). This step which is the final action in international HR planning exercise leads firms to plan recruitment as well as redundancy management or retraining and redeployment.

International Recruitment and Selection

A systematic international HR planning as discussed before paves way for international recruitment and selection practice. Analytics and automation have potential to transform international recruitment function. Until recently, recruitment in multinational companies too has been organized by geography on the grounds that the data, actual administration and recruitment process is conducted locally. However, this trend is changing as reported in ERE conference held in 2014 with the extensive use of analytics: both predictive and data, virtual hiring methods and Internet-based recruitment processes as presented in Box 2.1. Organizations are certainly moving beyond Skype interviews and online shortlisting of resumes using job portals or mass mail techniques. Predictive analytical tools can help to anticipate and optimize talent acquisition, pipelines planning and response time. Organizations have the opportunity to save millions of days of recruitment effort to reach right talent at right time. Global organizations such as Google, Sears, Cisco and others are extensively applying predictive analytics to secure both quantity and the quality in hiring. Google which processes over 2 million applications a year, for example, uses analytics to secure four objectives: (a) to transform hiring process and administration to become fast, efficient and reliable, (b) to expand the candidate universe and enhance quality of candidates pipeline, (c) ensuring candidate experience is delightful through fast feedback and by making the entire conversations interactive and (d) to apply analytics for decisions in relation to shortlisting and selection. Sears uses predictive analytics to screen and grade resumes to meet their various requirements, cutting down the process time significantly while eliminating errors. It has applied analytics to automate the entire recruitment cycle including job postings, resume screening, job responses, scheduling and analysis for final selection decision and capturing candidate's experience and expectations. Some organizations went a step ahead to extend application of analytics to predict the retention and job fit level of candidates, while some others are trying to digitize behavioural competency assessments to ensure cultural fitness of candidates.

Pressures are also mounting to optimize recruitment costs and at the same time enhance a firm's ability to attract the right talent. These changes would also lead to dramatic shift in the way recruitment teams are organized and managed. Algorithm has become the emerging recruitment leader in the New Age multinational corporations. Though the legal validity of virtual hiring method is still a debatable issue, the use of virtual hiring techniques is on rise. There are experts who question how virtual hiring model can address the need to ensure cultural fit and behavioural adaption of candidates. While the argument that virtual hiring cannot replace in person-based

Box 2.1   Top 10 International Recruitment Practices

ERE conference which was held in Chicago in 2014 identified the following top 10 trends in international recruitment:

1. **Analysis of talent market data:** In order to gain deep insights into talent market and provide valuable information to the business, the analysis of talent market and talent mapping is a proactive action that helps business leaders immensely.
2. **Market intelligence:** There shall be a specialized team to gather market information about talent polls, leadership, compensation trends, demand and supply of certain skills which would contribute to precision in recruitment planning and execution.
3. **Branding:** Studies show that candidates' preferences and interests are influenced by the brand perception of a firm. Therefore, firms must make efforts to generate awareness about profile of the company in as realistic a manner as possible without exaggeration.
4. **Infusing sales culture into recruitment:** Recruitment activity and teams shall be managed the way sales processes and teams are managed in that they will be target driven, incentivized for good performance, penalized for failures, action oriented and with functional pressures applied on the team.
5. **Standardization of recruitment processes and teams:** Several organizations are not successful in optimizing efforts of recruitment due to lack of standardization of recruitment process and organization of recruitment teams based on skills or levels or recruitment sub-activity. Standardization can create value to multinational enterprises given their size and scale.
6. **Create dedicated teams:** It is beneficial and efficient to create international recruitment teams based on skills and levels of employees.
7. **Focus on passive candidate identification and relationship building:** Essentially this practice suggests building talent pipeline through cold calling, accessing niche professional networks sites and semi-social sites such as LinkedIn.
8. **Realistic preview of job openings:** Description of job opportunities and profiles must be precise and clear to attract right candidates using the web tools and job sites. Sizable efforts are wasted both by recruitment teams and candidates due to absence of clarity of job openings.
9. **Leverage social sites and engagements:** Power of social media and relevance of sites and blending that with employee referrals can give an edge in sourcing right candidates timely with lesser recruitment process costs.
10. **Virtual events:** Virtual instead of physical recruitment events are the most ideal for international hiring activity where talent is available in multiple locations.

Source: https://www.ere.net/top-10-future-recruitment-trends/ (accessed on 26 February 2018).

hiring process is valid to some extent, virtual hiring can help in initial round of interviews where the questions tend to be standard. The time organizations allocate to these initial rounds of interviews and screening are substantial costing millions of dollars. This is particularly true in case of multinational corporations. Virtual interviewing and screening can also help in greater standardization that organizations seek. Nestle Purina which has moved its campus recruitment from on campus to virtual covering 125 universities reports that 'converting our traditional recruitment practices into virtual best practices has helped our number of qualified applicants and quality of hires soar, which brings us where we are today: a robust recruiting team with a virtual recruiting model that works time after time'. According to Lindsey Nelsen and Blake

Witters (2015) of National Association of Colleges and Employers (NACE), the success of virtual hiring depends on the ability to create a level of engagement that would mirror in-person interactions and assessment programmes that duplicate in-person regular assessment processes as much as possible. They also advocate three key actions to build a robust virtual recruiting programme: (a) streamline the process for consistency and better candidate experience, (b) keep a calendar for the virtual recruiting programme and (c) be flexible and strategic to make mid-course changes. Forbes, in a study conducted in 2016, reports that virtual recruiting is already a major part of many organizations' recruitment process and these organizations deploy Google Cardboard and Samsung's Gear VR in addition to software-driven analytics and automation. UK military is reported to have been using virtual reality for recruiting using a simplified app that supports recruiting candidates with the right fitness for soldier-level vacancies. Capco, the multinational management consultancy, uses the tool from Saberr to find out whether candidates will fall in love with a job or not to establish the person's fitness for the job. Emma Codd, the talent head of Deloitte, says that recruitment is a discipline where technology is evolving in fascinating ways, from programmes such as Textio which help organizations to avoid unconscious bias when wording job advertisements. GE, using virtual technologies, has managed an international hiring programme in Saudi Arabia, employing 1,000 women and has been awarded the Award for Corporate Excellence by the US Secretary of State for this achievement.

In brief, apart from direct and indirect trends, technological and automation trends as discussed before are fast integrating the recruitment processes and teams across the globe realizing international recruitment practice. Basically, firms shall take three steps in establishing a robust international recruitment practice.

Step 1—Establishing universal recruitment processes: Global organizations with an objective to attain greater efficiencies and universal consistency shall define and execute a universally applicable recruitment process capable of meeting its HR needs projected as per the international HR planning process. The process shall describe application of automation/technology in publication of job openings, job competencies, application screenings, shortlisting process, interview process, selection criteria, reference/background check, offer management and pre-placement engagement. Process must factor various recruitment laws and regulations as applicable including equal opportunities, diversity and affirmative compliances. The differences in recruitment processes that exist in various geographies have, over a period of time, become barriers to the practice of international recruitment. The fragmented recruitment process is more evident in multinational organizations due to traditional belief that hiring has to follow local processes. The process standardization not only helps in automating it but also ensures consistency and uniformity. According to Watson Wyatt Worldwide (2014), a management consulting company which conducted a global study covering 405 companies, recruitment has the greatest impact on an organization's market value. The consulting firm has also estimated in the study that good recruitment processes and execution can increase an organization's market capitalization by over 10 per cent. Quality of recruitment and success with talent are largely dependent on the quality of recruitment processes of an organization. A good recruitment process is not only capable of attracting right talent but can also deter unsuitable candidates from applying. Several organizations in services sector mistakenly feel proud that their actual selection ratio is 1:20 or more implying that these organizations select 1 person out of 20 or more candidates applying for a position. This is a colossal waste of effort, time and money. No one applies for a job to be rejected so candidates too want to approach an organization for a job opening that suits their skills and experience. When organizations fail to communicate preview of jobs, the number grows beyond a practical sense. On the other hand, a common occurrence is right candidates either not being responded to or not being shortlisted since they are lost in the heap of innumerable applications or in the riddle of unorganized big data. Hence, automation and standardization of recruitment process is a sure way for creating an international recruitment that can garner right talent in a global organization. A benchmarking recruitment process must be in-built with right templates, formats and user-friendly directions so that recruitment staff can deliver performance without stress. Building right metrics and standards are essential to measure effectiveness of recruitment process at every level. Both conventional process adherence metrics such as turnaround time, cost per hire, ageing of openings, recruits per recruiter and various ratios such as number of applicants per select are as important as outcome metrics such as role-recruit fitness, candidate experience with hiring process, cost elimination rate, business value addition and service longevity of new recruits in an organization. Recruitment processes shall also consider immigration rules and regulations of various nations relevant to a global firm's operations and presence. Immigration rules currently applicable to selective countries are presented in Appendix 2.1.

Recruitment process outsourcing is a growing trend with some organizations though multinational organizations have scale and size to organize the function in house. Cost considerations, overhead of supervision, unfamiliarity with talent markets, need for liquid hiring as the hiring numbers are not firmed up, and hesitation to redefine existing recruitment processes and reluctance to recast the recruitment teams are found to be contributing to this trend. There are also organizations which have outsourced to a third party on the basis of build, operate and transfer mode so that they have enough flexibility to pilot and test the efficacy of creating an international recruitment practice. There are number of third-party companies with global footprint in recruitment process outsourcing business such as Accolo, Pinstripe, Randstad, Futurestep, Pontoon Solutions, ADP, TalentFusion and Kelly. However, the need for a well-designed universal recruitment process remains valid even in outsourcing scenario to ensure a systematic international recruitment practice. Organizations would not be successful in driving third parties towards competitive performance in the absence of their own recruitment process map. Outsourcing would lead to loss of market intelligence, poor perception about the company's commitment to HR and compromise on company brand.

Career Website

Career website occupies a central place in the management of IS. Effective career website management can result in a number of benefits that would include: elimination of manual interventions in staffing cycle, elimination of errors and low value adding processes, access to enlarged pool of talent, improved quality of candidates, cost savings and speed in managing the hiring cycle. An international career website ideally should have the following features.

- **Description of people centricity of company:** More than products, services, technologies and financials of the company, candidates surfing the website will look for information on HR policies, culture and career-related aspects. Therefore, highlighting information on company vision, mission, values, ethics, leadership, working environment, facilities, locations, affirmative actions, performance parameters, developmental interventions and more importantly culture of the company helps candidates to make positive decisions.

Career website must also be directly linked to the home page so that marketing branding can be leveraged.

- **Job listings:** Seldom job listings of the companies follow the principle of urgent openings first and future openings later. It tends to mix up all positions opened up or put in hierarchical or in a clustered manner. Candidate's attention can be drawn easily if calendar of hiring is published conspicuously with urgent openings as the banner. Many candidates work with timelines in their head about job changing so letting them know of the timelines is definitely helpful.

- **Social media websites:** Linking career website with social media sites such as Facebook, Twitter and WhatsApp leads to generation of more candidates uploading their resumes. This also leads to greater publicity and awareness apart from positioning the company as contemporary. Companies must encourage employees also to post the openings reflected in career page on social websites so employee referrals would gain a platform without incurring any costs.

- **Installing job search engine:** A career website is as good as the job search engine. The engine must enable candidates to search for suitable openings as quickly and correctly as possible. Search criteria must include skill, experience, location and category. Often search engines fail to respond meaningfully due to design fault so utmost care must be exercised to make it intuitive and user-friendly. A good search engine can help in reducing administrative burden for the recruiter and saves time for candidates and can make the entire experience meaningful.

- **Intelligent career website:** A career website ideally should have in-built pre-screening. Instead of candidates merely uploading their profiles, it is more efficient to have an interactive checklist wherein a candidate by answering few profile-related questions can know whether he or she is qualified for shortlist or not. In order to enable this feature, a career website shall be designed beyond a generic online resume uploading machine. In other words, it shall be a more tailor-made interactive career website application.

- **Candidates data management:** Career website shall also have a feature wherein all candidates relevant to the business of an organization can upload their resumes regardless of the status current job openings. Candidates can update them on regular basis and tag them to various standard job categories so that these profiles can be picked up automatically as and when job openings arise. This helps organizations to deploy analytics to understand talent market much more scientifically apart from establishing relationship between a future potential employee and the company.

- **Data protection:** Privacy and confidentiality are sacrosanct in managing a career website and candidate database. This has both compliance to legal provisions and implications to moral standards since many countries have well laid down laws in relation to this. Anonymity of candidates is crucial as many of them are employed with other organizations. In an organization, where multiple recruiters work and have access to the database of international career websites, data protection can be complex. Organizations shall have strict process and code of conduct defined and implemented to protect this.

- **Maintenance:** A study of career websites by the Association of Executive Recruiters points out that several of them are non-operative and not updated as fast as required. In many cases, career websites generate counterproductive results with candidates frustrated with lack of correct information and dysfunctionality of the site. This can cause severe damage to company brand and contribute to losing good candidates. So maintenance of career website is essential to accrue real benefits to companies failing in which the very objective is nullified.

Step 2—Establishing a universal recruitment team: Having well-defined universal recruitment processes is a job half done because forming, nurturing and norming an international team that is capable of executing universal process is critical for the practice of international recruitment. Organizations need to acknowledge that recruitment function is a pure business function and closely tied with organizational performance and growth. It is a transformational step for many global HR departments because recruitment teams are generally organized by geography with the assumption that localized recruitment teams can be held accountable easily for performance. Unless recruitment team is one and geography agnostic, it is challenging to attain execution of universal recruitment process. A localized recruitment team creates silos and maximizes duplication of work especially in sourcing phase apart from tendency to reinvent the wheel on recruitment techniques and processes. Teams shall be trained on the global recruitment process and also need to be organized aligning with each sub-process adopting assembly line approach. The process of forming, developing and motivating recruitment teams is akin to the process adopted for sales teams: it is target driven, measurable and results that count. An incentivized and results-based variable compensation structure for recruitment professionals is more appropriate than a base salary reward. Training of recruitment staff on use of technologies and analytics shall be integral part of development programme. There are various models for structuring recruitment teams. Some teams are structured based on skills/technologies/functions, some on levels of employees and others on the basis of business profile. However, all these teams shall be integrated in consonance with the recruitment processes. Effectiveness and quality of recruitment leadership and ethical standards can play an important role in building and managing formidable recruitment teams. Though recruitment falls within the functional ambit of HRM, organizations shall explore possibilities of deploying line managers preceded by recruitment process training and orientation along with HR professionals to create right blend of recruitment teams. Training programmes for recruitment teams shall be designed keeping in view both internal and external environmental factors of an organization such as organizational culture, values, people policies, salaries, careers, technologies, intellectual property, financials, branding and of course recruitment strategy and processes on one hand and talent market, geographical dynamics of business, competition, customers, investors and global workforce trends and immigration rules and regulations of different nations as relevant to a company's operations on the other hand. Training of interview panels and line/business managers associated with candidate selection process is an element that global organizations shall not neglect as this is a common error that is witnessed. Infusion of cultural sensitivity in hiring activity is core to the success of international hiring as this is often cited reason for not internationalizing the recruitment. Recruiters regardless of nationality can be trained to manage recruitment across the nations through language and culture sensitivity orientation. In brief, creating, developing and charging an international recruitment team is different from organizing domestic recruitment team as discussed before. Global organizations can successfully realize international hiring with the help of global recruitment processes and global recruitment team as described in steps 1 and 2.

Step 3—Establishing a universal pre-employment engagement model: Organizations loose thousands of potential employees post selection and after issuance of employment contracts mainly due to lack of an effective pre-employment engagement with potential employees. According to Aberdeen Group (2013) which had conducted a comprehensive study on onboarding in 2013 covering 230 organizations, 91 per cent of employees were retained in organizations where pre-employment engagement model is in place as compared to 30 per cent of employees at laggard organizations, 62 per cent of employees hired in the last 12 months met first performance milestones on time as compared to 17 per cent in laggard organizations and 33 per cent year-over-year improvement in hiring manager satisfaction as compared to a 3 per cent increase among laggard organizations. The study also points out that only 37 per cent of organizations have invested in a formal onboarding programme. Organizations fail to reap benefits proportionate to the recruitment efforts and carry weak return on investment (ROI) due to callousness with onboarding initiatives. Time between the offer and actual joining of a candidate is very crucial. This time can be used as boon or bane depending on an organization's commitment to the talent management. This period can be used to share information with prospective employees about company vision, mission, values, culture, leadership, HR policies (HR handbook), organization structure, clients, services and business portfolios and information relating to that person's career and role. A good deal of onboarding paper work and forms filling can be done during this phase. A common practice is organizing a get-together of all prospective employees with leadership over lunch or dinner so that candidates can get a definite sense of leadership and will be able to share rich information and have the opportunity to exchange dialogue. Few organizations are also found to hand over gift hampers or mementos to the candidates along with job offers. The most effective pre-employment engagement tool used by very few organizations is allocating mentors as part of a buddy programme to enable a candidate to have candid conversations with someone familiar with the organization. The objective of pre-employment engagement model is to also improve retention and engagement of employees. Research has provided wide evidence that about 65 per cent of employees decide to engage fully or partially, or not at all during the first month of joining. In such a scenario, pre-employment engagement can be of significant use to knock down this failure rate early on. In other words, an organization, through pre-employment engagement model, can target to decrease the number of new hires who quit the jobs within six months to one year. It is also helpful to start the relationship with new recruits on a good professional note apart from shortening the lead time for them to be productive. FedEx experience with pre-employment engagement shows that engaging an employee before actual joining can improve their performance on joining by 20 per cent and reduce their probability of departure by about 87 per cent. Pre-employment engagement is much more challenging where recruitment is globalized and is not globalized. Usually, organizations follow localized practices for pre-employment engagement of candidates or onboarding activities lacking standardization and a universal appeal. Transforming staffing as an international function would importantly involve making pre-employment engagement a global experience with global processes while deploying local leadership for personal contact wherever international leadership contact is not feasible. There are a few automated and Internet-based tools that are available and that meet the criteria of onboarding as a part of pre-employment engagement and can contribute for standardization. As discussed before, establishing a universal pre-employment engagement model is the final critical step in ensuring a scientific international recruitment practice.

Expatriates as a Source of International Staffing

This part of the chapter makes an attempt to discuss issues related to expat management incisively as it is a key source of IS. Reasons for staffing positions through expats, experiences of organizations with expat route, precautions while posting expats and their management are included in the discussion.

Expat management plays a pivotal role in IS. Many global organizations today strive to create a workforce that is global in its outlook and management through expatriate staffing since IS is no longer a strategic advantage but a competitive necessity. Black and Gregersen (1999) in their Harvard classic paper after studying management of expats at about 750 US, European and Japanese companies state that nearly 80 per cent of mid-size and large companies currently send professionals abroad and 45 per cent plan to increase the number they have on assignment. In accordance with OECD statistics, on an average about 6 per cent of the British population live abroad as expats. According to the Department of Statistics, Singapore Government, more than 2 million expats are working in Singapore by 2012. An estimated 4.6 per cent of the total working population in Hong Kong is comprised of expats. Though the definition of an expat is not universal, as per the research report published by Finaccord in 2013, the total number of expats worldwide amounted to around 50.5 million and estimated to grow at a compound annual rate of 2.4 per cent. State Department of the United States has published in 2011 that about 6.32 million Americans work and reside outside the United States and majority of them are expats. In Gulf countries, expats account for nearly 48 per cent of managerial staff. The United States, the United Kingdom and Australia lead the population of expats though other nations such as India, USSR and China are catching the trend fast. According to a 2012 survey by Brookfield Global Relocation Services, the top five new emerging locations for international assignments are China, Brazil, Australia, India and Russia.

The Expat Explorer Survey by HSBC, 2014

The survey is based on 9,000 foreign worker respondents in over 100 countries' salient findings.

- Expats in Asia earn almost three times (USD 250,000) what their counterparts in Europe earn.
- Switzerland, Singapore and China are the leading destinations for a balanced expat lifestyle.
- High growth 'EAGLE' economies such as Brazil, Turkey, India, China, Mexico and Taiwan are popular destinations for companies looking to send their employees abroad.
- Canada takes the crown as the top expat retiree spot with three times more expat retirees than the global average.
- Canada and the United States offer expats an easy set-up and great quality of life.
- A significant number of expats move to the Middle East looking for better job prospects and to boost their income.

Source: https://www.expatexplorer.hsbc.com/survey/files/pdfs/overall-reports/2014/HSBC_Expat_Explorer_2014_report.pdf (accessed on 26 February 2018).

There is a widespread concern with the application of expats as a key source of IS across the board, though it has produced quite a few good results for some organizations. A study estimates that failure rate of expats is as high as 70 per cent in China. It is difficult to draw a final verdict on the topic since the data on failure and success rate of expats is inconclusive. According to EY (2013) Global Mobility Effectiveness Survey, 46 per cent of respondent organizations were not tracking the effectiveness of expats. The popular framework that is used to assess the success of expats is applying a three-factor formula: adjustment, performance and turnover. There are other models using financial parameters to analyse efficacy of expat method. Failure of an expat is very expensive to organizations in terms of both investment and loss of growth opportunity. For example, Zeira and Banai way back in 1985 estimated that the average cost of failure of each expat manager is about USD 200,000. Black and Gregersen (1999) estimate that international assignments do not come cheap and on an average expats cost two to three times (salaries ranging from USD 300,000 to 1,000,000 per annum) what they would in an equivalent position back home. Yet another study focusing on Australian expats working in Hong Kong estimates that each expat manager costs anywhere between AUD 250,000 to 1.2 million per annum. As per NatWest IPB Expat Wealth Ranking Survey of 2007, the average annual income of a British expatriate was about GBP 100,000. In conclusion, failure of expats can cost organizations in both direct and indirect costs. Therefore, given that deployment of expats is an expensive proposition to organizations, let us examine the success and failure experiences of organizations.

Expatriate Trends Study 2013 by HSBC
Key Findings

- Gaps in communication of benefits programmes: Employer providing services but expats not very aware.
- One size does not fit all: Customization by country of assignment is necessary.
- Expats state that more needs to be done post assignment.
- Expats desire more support and understanding from HR regarding challenges abroad.
- Family status plays a big role in identifying what is important and leads to employee satisfaction.
- Preparedness is viewed as very important in health care.
- Assignment types: Long- and short-term continue to evolve.

Source: https://www.expatexplorer.hsbc.com/survey/files/pdfs/overall-reports/2013/report.pdf (accessed on 16 February 2018).

It is also important to understand why organizations are motivated to deploy expat model as a source of IS.

- **Management control of their assets and processes:** Global organizations have a tendency to trust the home country manager's ability to set up and control their assets, business and processes in ethical standards consistent with their own. There is surely an advantage in posting an expat who has a great understanding of a company's business plans, processes, products, services, values, attitudes and priorities.
- **Communication and fast decision-making:** An expat is known to all key decision-makers and influencers at headquarters. This facilitates a clear communication and faster decision-making process. Decision-making can get very contextual with many global organizations so a seasoned manager of that organization would be at ease to make relevant decisions.
- **Imparting skills and setting up processes:** An expat manager who is well trained himself on technologies, functional competencies and has mastery over the company processes can set up a subsidiary and train local employees faster and maintain consistency with the company's design and objectives.

- **Building international talent:** Global organizations see expat model as an opportunity to build international management talent. In addition to creating training opportunities for managers, this can also serve to upgrade careers.
- **Source of IS:** Selecting an internal candidate to perform a role in another country is quicker and a more reliable recruitment method than hiring from outside.
- **Shortage of managerial talent in the host country:** One of the reasons cited often for expat staffing is lack of adequate managerial talent in the host country.

Expat as Staffing Model: Successes and Failures

Pre-mature return of expats (repatriation) is understood and used extensively to demonstrate the failure of expat model to fill up international positions. An estimated 45 per cent of expats repatriate before end of their agreed tenure of assignment. However, there are others who argue that selection process of expats, cross-cultural knowledge, effectiveness of company induction programmes meant for expats, company policies, actual performance of expats, financial issues and family factors are equally important in understanding the successes and failures of expat model. For example, Tung (1987) through his research titled 'Expatriate Assignments: Enhancing Success and Minimizing Failure' has found that inability of an expat's spouse to adjust to a different physical and cultural environment, expat's personality or emotional maturity, expat's lack of motivation to work in overseas and lack of managerial competence are core reasons for expat failures. Expats generally lack a good understating of local market, culture, language, local education system, talent markers, processes and government's way of functioning. Studies have also found that large number of expats experience adjustment issues. The most commonly used framework to explain adjustment challenges of expats is U-curve framework of cross-cultural adjustments. The U-curve basically identifies four stages of cross-cultural adjustment: the first stage is called 'honeymoon' which describes the stage when the expat and family are fascinated with the home country set-up, the second stage is 'cultural shock' and describes the stage when frustration creeps in, 'adjustment' is the third stage by when an expat and family learn to adjust and fourth stage is 'mastery' at which stage an expat and family are able to live in the host country happily. The adjustment issues from culture perspective are discussed in detail in Chapter 9, titled 'International Culture Management'. Compensation and training and development-related aspects are discussed in their respective chapters of this book. Let us understand here the selection criteria of expats and their induction which are an integral part of IS and largely lead to success and failure of expats.

Selection and Induction Process of Expats

There is no standard model that organizations adopt in selecting expats. This entirely depends upon the culture and management style of an organization. Some follow a formal process and others an informal process. In a formal process, selection criteria are set in line with objectives of setting up a subsidiary or the expat role, assignment is defined, applications sought, and evaluation and selection completed. In an informal process which is also known as coffee machine decision syndrome, decision-maker chooses the candidate based on his or her personal knowledge of people and based on recommendation of senior managers in casual discussions.

Many researchers have found that there is heavy emphasis on technical competence rather than relational abilities in selection of expats and this seems to have marred the probability of success. According to Harvey and Novicevic (2001), selection process of expats focuses only on skills directly linked to technical and functional capabilities neglecting skills such as global awareness, cultural empathy, international negotiation skills and ethical understanding. It is easier to assess technical competence than social and cultural skills and so organizations are driven to depend solely on technical competence as a criterion for selecting expats. Jeffrey A. Joerres, formerly McKinsey consultant and currently an expat coach, after surveying over 200 expats in 2011 has identified five successful behavioural characteristics of expats: open-minded, adventurous, culturally sensitive, curious and flexible. An expat's language proficiency and familiarity of host country too is an important factor apart from cultural understanding. However, organizations seem to have not accorded the right level of consideration for language and culture. For instance, only 30 per cent of global organizations are found to be using expat's culture adaptability assessment tools as per the 2010 study published by National Foreign Trade Council titled 'Global Mobility Trends Survey Results'. Carlson (2005) in his research has found that companies that invested in language training for expats and their spouses have increased success rate from 34 per cent in 1999 to 42 per cent in 2005. Still, there are other factors like family that could impact selection of right expat. Often, although organizations have in the parent country the most suitable managers for an expat assignment, they end up choosing candidates who are willing to accept the assignment as refusal to accept an overseas assignment due to personal constraints is a growing phenomenon. A study conducted in 2014 by Cartus has revealed that 76 per cent of the respondents cited family constraint as the reason for refusing an international posting. According to this study, it is challenging for organizations to draft right talent for international assignments as many of them refuse due to family reasons in an ever growing dual career society. Therefore, it is important for organizations to develop a more robust and wholesome expat selection process in order for them to be successful with this model. A selection process must involve an assessment of technical competence, social and cultural adaptability, commitment to learn, language proficiency, family requirements, organization and employee-specific requirements.

Onboarding of expats (expat induction): A systematic onboarding is highly critical for the success of expats. An estimated 30 per cent of success with expat model comes from an effective onboarding management. There is no one-size-fits-all kind of induction programme since each expat's journey tends to be unique. An expat induction shall not be a one-time activity but an ongoing process till an expat adjusts to the new environment. It is ideal if an orientation programme of expat is part of the overall talent development of an international manager. It is desirable to subject an identified expat to assessment of development needs in technical, functional and social competencies from an international assignment backdrop based on which a customized orientation plan can be developed and executed. Expats are faced with multiple challenges as discussed before that include lack of knowledge of local issues, culture, language, food, adjustment challenges, home sickness, health care, tax and financial issues. A comprehensive orientation programme in addition to a standard suite of induction, visit to host country, dialogue with local employees, enlisting a prospective expat in social forums of host country business and sensitivity training will go a long way in enabling expats to adjust to and perform an assignment successfully. They must be provided with videos, books and mentoring with an expat veteran. Many expats are also concerned about their repatriation procedure which shall be dealt with as a part of onboarding orientation to remove the anxiety.

Appendix 2.1: Immigration Regulations

The United States

In order to bring employees into the United States as non-immigrants for work purpose, organizations as employers shall file a non-immigrant petition on behalf of employee with United States Citizenship and Immigration Services. This is also called the temporary worker visa process. However, there are different types of temporary worker visas as discussed here. The visa rules have mainly originated from Immigration Act of 1990 though there were a number of amendments and reform acts that followed this legislation.

L-1A Non-Immigrant Visa: This visa enables a US employer to transfer an executive or manager from one of its affiliated foreign offices to one of its offices in the United States. The employer must file a form I-129 petition for this purpose along with requisite fee on behalf of the employee. An executive in this context is referred to an employee who has decision power of wide latitude without much oversight and manager is referred to someone who has supervisory control of employees and for both categories the employee must have worked in that capacity for at least one year out of three years preceding the application date. Under this category, employees are allowed to stay for an initial period of three years with extension up to a maximum of cumulative seven years. Organizations can also follow intra company transfer of employees (L1-A visa) by filing blanket petition known as I-129S subject to certain conditions such as an organization shall have a workforce of at least 1,000 employees in the United States.

L2 Non-immigrant Visa and Form I-765: Family of employee (spouse and children under the age of 21) can accompany an employee entering the United States under a L1-A category visa by filing L2 petition and spouse of L1-A employee can apply for work authorization by filing form I-765.

L1-B Non-immigrant Visa: The L1-B non-immigrant visa enables a US employer to transfer a professional employee with specialized knowledge of the organization's interests from one of its affiliated foreign offices to one of its offices in the United States by filing a petition using Form I-129 along with requisite fee. Specialized knowledge here means either special knowledge possessed by an employee of the petitioning organization's product, service, research, techniques, management or an advanced knowledge or expertise in the organization's processes and procedures. Employees under this category can stay in the United States for up to a maximum of five years including extensions. Form I-539 for entry of family of the employee and I-765 for spouse work authorization is applicable here as well.

H-1B/H-1B1/E-3: This visa category is applicable to the people who perform or wish to perform services in a specialty occupation, services of exceptional merit and ability relating to a Department of Defense (DOD) cooperative research and development project or services as a fashion model of distinguished merit and ability. Petitioner must file form I-129 along with form ETA-9035 and Labor Condition Application (LCA) by prospective employer. Countries such as China and India are the biggest beneficiaries of this visa category. This is known as H-1B1, a variant of H-1B for workers from Singapore and Chile and E-3 for workers from Australia. Employees should have a bachelor's degree equivalent to a US bachelor's and the job to be performed shall have prerequisite of a bachelor's degree qualification and the degree qualification shall be associated with nature of work of the job. Some of the key requirements for an H1-B visa are that: (a) a person must have an employer–employee relationship with the petitioning US employer for which evidence like employment contract would be adequate, (b) an employee's job must qualify as a specialty occupation as per the *Occupational Outlook Handbook* (OCH) issued by the Department of Labor (DOL; generally a bachelor's degree relevant to the area of work of an employee would be an adequate condition), (c) an employee's job must be in a specialty occupation related to the field of study, (d) an employee must be paid at least the actual or prevailing wage of that employee's occupation, whichever is higher (to demonstrate that an employee will be paid appropriate wage, petition must be supported with a LCA for that position, certified by the Secretary of Labor) and (e) an H1-B visa number must be available at the time of filing the petition, unless the petition is exempt from the numerical limits (the H1-B visa has an annual numerical limit of 65,000 visas each fiscal year). Under this visa category, a person will be admitted to stay in the United States for a maximum period of six years including extensions after initial period of three years though some exceptions do apply. If an employer terminates employment before completion of the approved term, an employer is responsible to bear the cost of return transportation of an employee.

Other visa categories applicable to temporary non-immigrant employees: The other categories include: CW-2 meant for transitional workers, E-1(3) for treaty traders and qualified employees, E-2(3) for treaty investors and qualified employees, E-2C for long-term foreign investors, H-1C (2) for registered nurses, H-3 for trainees other than in medical or academic fields, I for media representatives, O-1 for persons with extraordinary ability in sciences, arts, education, business, athletics, motion picture or TV production and TN for temporary professionals from Mexico and Canada.

Canada

Canada issues work permits to eligible persons to work in the country. Visa categories are different for temporary workers, permanent workers and interns. These are known as 'open work permits' that allow persons to work for any employer in Canada except for an employer who has been notified as ineligible employer and 'employer-specific work permits' that allow persons to work according to the conditions of the said work permit such as name of the employer one can work for, tenure of work and the location of the work. Organizations popularly resort to intra company transfers who are eligible to apply for work permits. The eligibility criteria here include that a person: (a) must currently be employed by a multinational company and seeking entry to work in a parent, a subsidiary, a branch or an affiliate of that company, (b) is being transferred to a legitimate and continuing establishment of that company in Canada and 18–24 months can be a reasonable period to qualify the condition of continuity, (c) is being transferred to a position in an executive, senior managerial or specialized knowledge capacity and (d) has been employed in the company for at least one year. After intra-company transferees have reached their maximum work permit duration, seven years for executives and senior managers and five years for specialized knowledge workers, they must complete one year of full-time employment in the company outside Canada if they wish to reapply as an intra-company transferee.

The United Kingdom

Organizations in the United Kingdom can use the Tier 2 procedure of the UK immigration system to employ other nationals to fill jobs which cannot be filled by local workers. A multinational organization can process a visa for its employee working outside the United Kingdom in order to transfer this employee to the United Kingdom for the purpose of training or to fill a skilled position if a local person with these skills is not available to fill that position. Grant of a visa in the United Kingdom is based on points system. In order to acquire a UK visa, a person must score a minimum of 50 points for attributes which include having a sponsor and a valid certificate of sponsorship and appropriate salary, 10 points for English language skills (however, this is not applicable in case of intra company transfers) and 10 points for maintenance (financial). The certificate of sponsorship must confirm that the job is at National Qualifications Framework (NQF) level 6 as stated in the codes of practice although this does not mean a person must have been educated at that level but that the job must be at that level. The appropriate minimum salary stipulated for intra company transfer for long term is 41,500 GBP per annum and 30,000 GBP per annum in case of short-term transfer. Further, an application under intra company transfer is subjected to general grounds for refusal criteria.

There are three categories in intra company transfer route as discussed here:

1. **Graduate trainee:** This scheme enables graduate recruits of a company to transfer to the UK branch/affiliate for the purpose of training as part of a structured graduate training programme for a period of 12 months. The said training programme shall clearly define the progression of graduate trainee into a specialist or managerial role on completion of the training.
2. **Long-term staff:** A person who has been working with a company for at least 12 months and is being transferred to the UK branch to fill a skilled job which cannot be filled by a local person. A visa under this category can be given for a tenure of up to five years and nine years in case the person's earning is GBP 155,300 or more per annum.
3. **Short-term staff:** A visa under this category can be granted for stay in the United Kingdom for a maximum period of 12 months based on transfer of an employee to the UK branch to fill a skilled position which cannot be filled by a local employee. However, the UK Government has closed the short-term Staff Scheme effective April 2017 to new applications and extensions.

There is an annual limit on the number of certificates of sponsorship available under the Tier 2 route. Salary to an employee in this context can be paid in the United Kingdom or abroad and if paid abroad, exchange rate published in Canada must be followed to convert to pounds sterling.

Germany

Primarily two sets of immigration rules are applicable for people entering to obtain visas and work permits in order to work in Germany: one set of rules is for EU citizens and the other is for non-EU citizens. There are three types of work permits that are applicable to non-EU citizens:

1. *Aufenthaltserlaubnis* is a temporary permit granted to those moving to Germany for a specific purpose such as to get employed in an organization or to study or to do research and the duration of a visa validity will equal length of stay required by such an assignment.
2. The EU Blue Card is applicable to the highly educated or skilled workers such as doctors, engineers and other professional specialists. A graduate degree is a must to apply for a visa under this category. The salary that shall be offered in this category is stipulated at a

minimum of EUR 46,400 per annum. However, this can be relaxed to lower the limit to EUR 36,192 per annum in case of professions for which there is an acute skill shortage in Germany.

3. *Niederlassungserlaubnis* is an unrestricted residence permit for permanent residency in Germany. Generally, this visa is granted to professionals who have completed a reasonable period of residency such as five years and have been employed in Germany through the five years and there is sufficient evidence that the persons will continue to be employed in future. Sufficient knowledge of German language is a requirement. In some special cases such as for political reasons, this visa is also granted automatically on arrival into Germany.

In all the discussed categories, spouses and children of those who already hold a permit are granted a settlement permit.

France

There are a number of different visas in order to reside and work in France and there are many exemptions. Generally, the work permit in France is closely linked to the residential status of a person. A precondition for obtaining a work permit in France is that one should have a job in France. Basically there are two categories of immigration rules which are applicable based on country of citizenship.

1. **EU citizens:** No work permit is required for an EU citizen except for Croatian nationals who would require a work permit during their first year of work. All EU citizens can walk freely into France and work.

2. **Non-EU citizens:** Nationals from countries other than EU countries would need a work permit in order to work in France. Employers need to organize an authorization certificate before a visa and residence permit can be granted to any person. There are four types of work visas majorly applicable to non-EU citizens though there are a few other variants which are very specific such as AU Pairs, seasonal workers permit: (a) temporary work permit: this is applicable if a person is going to work in France for less than 90 days. An employer must obtain a work permit approved by the French Ministry of Labour and by using this work permit, a person can apply for a visa with the French Consulate in their respective home country. However, citizens from select countries such as Australia, Singapore, Canada, the United States, Japan, Israel, Brazil and Mexico are exempted from this process and can directly enter France for jobs of less than 90 days' duration; (b) a long-term work permit/visa: persons intending to stay more than 90 days for work need to apply for a long-term stay visa. In this case, the employer first needs to draw up a work contract and send it to the French Ministry of Labour and based on the approval of the Ministry, the same work contract can be forwarded to the French Consulate of home country of that person for issuing a visa. The length of stay permitted under this category varies depending on the type of the long-term visa which in turn depends on type of work and worker. Generally it is for a three-year term with possibility of extension if the visa is for a skilled worker; (c) EU Blue Card is for highly skilled/educated workers who possess a graduate degree and a minimum of five years of professional experience and earn a monthly salary of at least 1.5 times the French average gross annual salary which is currently pegged at

EUR 2,105 per month and (d) expatriate employee permit basically applies to secondees. If an employee has been working for at least three months in a company outside France and is seconded to one of the employer's companies based in France and earning 1.5 times the minimum wage, he or she will be eligible for this visa and will be allowed to work for three years with possible extensions.

Spouse and children of a person who has been issued a work permit/visa will be eligible to be issued residence visas and the spouse will also be allowed to work in France legally.

Switzerland

Two different sets of conditions are applicable for obtaining work permits in Switzerland: one is for the citizens of EU or EFTA and the other is for the citizens of Third-World countries as discussed next:

1. **EU citizens:** Citizens of EU/EFTA nations can enter into Switzerland freely but need to apply for work authorization.
2. **Non-EU citizens:** No person of other nationalities other than EU citizens can enter into Switzerland freely without a visa/residence permit. Non-EU citizens would require both a residence permit and work permit in order to stay and work in Switzerland. Non-EU citizen cannot enter into Switzerland without a valid visa or work permit. An employer who issues offer of appointment shall seek authorization for a work visa while the person who is in receipt of appointment must apply for a visa in respective home country. Employer shall first submit an application to the local cantonal employment service that will review the application and refer it to the Federal Office for Migration for approval of work permit. The grant of authorization to work depends upon a person's educational background and work experience and subject to the condition that no person from EU is available to fill that particular job. Generally, work permits are granted for specialist positions. There are different types of residence and work permits as explained further and these are granted depending upon the duration of stay required and in consonance with the offer of appointment.

   - **Permit L:** It is a short-term residence permit that allows a person to stay for up to one year and it is extendable by a year more but not more than that.
   - **Permit B:** Under this category, a person would be issued work permit for a year initially which can be extended on an annual basis till the employment lasts with a condition that there shall be no change in the employer and the person shall work in the same canton that issued the work permit and will not move out of that canton.
   - **Permit C:** This is more akin to Swiss citizenship and permanent residence process. This is also known as settlement permit. Persons living on work cum residence permit in Switzerland for 10 or more continuous years are eligible for grant of a settlement visa. However, this condition is not applicable and it is only five years of continuous stay for the citizens of the United States and Canada.

A common rule that is applicable for all work permit visas here is that a person applying for permit shall possess a minimum of a bachelor's degree.

The Netherlands

The Netherlands is one of the most immigration-friendly nations in the world for people with specialized skills and good educational background. The demand for highly skilled workers is high and it has a multilingual and diversified workforce. In fact, the country offers tax benefits and incentives for international employees to relocate to the Netherlands. Stay and work permits are very different here and they are governed by different set of regulations though in some cases there can be a single application for work cum residence permit. However, highly skilled workers, Blue Card holders and recently graduated students on an orientation year and self-employed persons if given residence permit need not obtain a work permit to work subject to a labour market test. A market test entails that a person needs to earn what is deemed a competitive salary and employer needs to show evidence that a citizen of the Netherlands is not available to fill the position despite efforts. A partner or spouse, or relative of a work permit holder will be eligible for grant of work cum residence permit, and partner of a permanent work permit holder does not need a separate work permit to be employed in the Netherlands. All EU national citizens except citizens of Croatia require neither a residence permit nor a work permit. Japanese citizens too do not require any work permit but will need to obtain residence permit for long stay. There are multiple work permits to legally work in the Netherlands which are applicable to non-EU migrants as discussed next:

1. **Highly skilled migrant permit:** This is also known as knowledge worker visa. In order to obtain work permit under this category, a person shall have a written employment contract lasting for duration of more than four months with a monthly salary of minimum EUR 4,240. The work permit is valid and equivalent to the period of the employment contract validity and such employment shall be with an employer who is recognized by the Dutch government.
2. **EU Blue Card:** This is also applicable to highly skilled workers. To be eligible for this card, a person shall have an employment contract of a minimum of one year with a Dutch employer and with a minimum monthly salary of 4,968 euros excluding holiday pay and should be a diploma holder of three years' duration. This card is a work cum residence permit and also allows intra EU mobility rights.
3. **Intra-company transfer permit:** If a person is employed with a Dutch employer for more than a year outside the Netherlands, he or she can seek work permit based on intra-company transfer. Employer is expected to file the papers on behalf of an employee being transferred and based on the work permit the employee can apply for a residence visa in respective home country.
4. **Permanent residence status permit:** After living in the Netherlands for more than five consecutive years on a residence permit, it is possible to obtain permanent residence status which gives the right to work for any Dutch employer or as a self-employed person without the need for a work permit.

Finland

Broadly there are three types of visas applicable to persons intending to work in Finland and these are known as 'residence permits'. The first type is no requirement for residence permit and is applicable to citizens of Nordic countries who can directly enter into Finland to live and work. The second type of permit is applicable to citizens of EU countries and Switzerland who can also enter directly into Finland to live and work but shall register with a police station if their stay is expected to be for a period of more than three months. However, this does not mean that EU citizens require a special work or residence permit but it is merely a registration. The third type of residence/work permit is applicable to non-EU citizens who need to apply for a residence permit at the Finnish embassy located within the home country of the person seeking the permit. This work permit is generally issued for duration of one year or based on the length of the employment/assignment. Employment contract issued by an employer in Finland is compulsory for issuance of residence permit. If a person has resided continuously for more than four years in Finland, he or she is eligible for a permanent residence permit.

Sweden

Sweden has the most simple and direct immigration rules. There are two types of visas. One is meant for EU citizens and the other for non-EU Citizens. EU citizens can enter into Sweden based on an employment offer issued by Swedish employer and can start work by registering with the Ministry of Labour. The other is for non-EU citizens who shall apply for work permits to be issued by Swedish Migration Agency. In both the cases, an offer of employment issued by a Swedish-based employer is compulsory. An employer needs to initiate the application for work permit in respect of non-EU citizens attaching an offer of employment that has been approved by a relevant trade union. An employer must have issued an advertisement for a job at least 10 days prior and made efforts to fill the same with Swedish and EU citizens before an offer of appointment for that job is issued to a non-EU citizen. Minimum wages to be paid in these cases shall be SEK 28,500 per month. An employee is eligible for permanent residency on completion of continuous stay of 48 months. Spouse and children accompanying a residence permit holder are eligible for the grant of residence permits. Residence permits are issued from Finland embassies of respective home countries after following the requisite process including photographs, fingerprints and collecting information around citizenship, education and contact address.

Denmark

Denmark actively encourages citizens of all nationalities with specialized skills to apply for a work visa in order to fill skill gaps that exist in the country. Denmark maintains a large listing of skill shortage occupations called the Positive List which is organized into several sections such as engineering, medicine, IT, education and academia. If a person has a job offer from a Danish employer in an occupation on the Positive List, he or she can apply for and obtain a work and residence permit under the Positive List Scheme. A person who is given work permit under the Positive List Scheme can stay in Denmark as per the length of employment specified in the employment contract. Generally work permits are granted for a period of four years initially which is extendable if the employment contract is permanent in nature. If the employment contract is not a permanent one, then a work permit cum visa is granted for the duration of employment plus six months to stay and work in Denmark. The second type of visa is known as the 'Pay Limit Scheme'. If a person has a job offer from a Danish employer that pays more than DKK 375,000 per annum, he or she is eligible for a work and residence permit in Denmark. Spouse and children under the age of 18 years are eligible for residence permit, and the spouse is additionally eligible for a work permit for the entire period of residence.

Hungary

EU citizens and non-citizens of EU but spouse of a Hungarian citizen do not need a work permit and residence visa to get employed and reside in Hungary. However, they need to obtain a registration card which enables them to stay as long as they need to stay and work. Registration card is issued based on the proof of accommodation and employment contract papers. All non-EU citizens require a work visa and permit to be able to enter and then work legally in Hungary. In order to obtain a work visa, a person shall have a valid work permit, labour agreement and proof of accommodation to stay in Hungary. The work permit application must be filed by an employer after complying with due conditions such as not being able to successfully recruit a Hungarian citizen after advertising the job at the Hungarian Labour Office by giving 15 days' time so that Hungarian citizens can apply for the position. Attaching the work permit, a person can apply for a residence visa at the Hungarian consulate in the home country. The work permit and stay visa is granted for two years initially which can be extended in consonance with the employment contract.

Poland

Poland being a member of EU allows all EU citizens to enter and work in Poland without the requirement of work permit and a visa. All other nationalities shall need work permit and a visa to stay and get employed in Poland. Broadly, five types of work permits are applicable to non-EU nationality citizens to legally work in Poland as discussed here:

1. **Type A:** This work permit is applicable to non-EU citizens working for an employer whose registered office/affiliate/residence/other form of business is located in Poland.
2. **Type B:** This is applicable to persons whose length of stay is between 6 and 12 months and who are performing roles in the management board or have established own business.
3. **Type C:** This type of visa is relevant to persons who are employed in non-Polish organizations with a branch or facility in Poland and who are intending to work there for more than 30 days.
4. **Type D:** This is applicable to non-EU nationality citizens working for a non-Polish employer and delegated to Poland for the purpose of execution of a service which is for a temporary period or in other words, a non-EU citizen entering into Poland for export business.
5. **Type E:** This visa covers all not covered in A, B, C and D, and persons intending to enter into Poland for work with for a period of three to six months and working for a non-Polish employer.

Visa and residence permits are different for Poland. A visa allows a person to work in Poland, while residence permit is for stay. The duration of a visa depends upon the contract of employment or engagement. The duration can vary from three months to five years. Usually, residence permit is given for all categories mentioned before for duration of three months to five years and maximum for one year at a time with an extension for another few years on annual basis. All residence permit holders need to mention upfront the place of residence and need to register with local city council on grant of residence permit.

The Czech Republic

Basically there are two types of work permits that are applicable to non-EU citizens known as Employee Card and Blue Card. The Employee Card is meant for unskilled workers and the Blue Card, as in many EU nations, is for skilled workers. Both these cards serve dual purpose of work cum residence permit. These cards are generally valid for two years initially but extendable repeatedly based on the validity of employment contracts or need as assessed by the immigration authorities. However, expats can apply for work permit and residence permit separately if they wish. Applications under the Blue Card category can be filed if a person is highly educated and possesses specialized skill and has received an employment contract from an employer of the Czech Republic after due process of local advertisement and efforts to fill the position internally with the Czech Republic citizens and EU citizens failed. The Employee Card is meant to cater to non-highly skilled positions but for which there is shortage of people within the country or to meet self-employment opportunities. EU citizens and their family members require neither a work permit nor a residence permit. A foreign national refers to either a non-Czech EU national citizen or a non-EU national citizen, both of whom are eligible to apply for permanent residence on completion of five years' continuous stay in the country on the basis of a long-term visa/residence permit.

The People's Republic of China

Multiple types of visas based on the need and purpose are granted to enter, work and reside in PRC. Depending on the nationality, the rules for grant of a visa vary. These are known as the F/M visa, applicable to business persons; the X visa, for pursuing studies by students; the Z visa, for employment and work; the D visa, for residing in China; the R Visa, which is applicable to highly educated and skilled persons; the J1 and J2 visas, for journalists; and the S visa, for family members of a visa holder. Residence permits are different from visas. China residence permits are classified into two types: temporary residence permit and permanent residence permit. Relevant visa categories are discussed below in detail:

1. **China work visa (Z visa):** Persons intending to work in PRC for pay shall obtain a work visa. A person applying for the Z visa, which is popularly known as the expert visa, shall have an employment offer issued by a Chinese organization which is accredited to employ foreigners. The employer has to obtain a certificate from the Foreign Employment Office of PRC that a person complies with the requirements of an expert to be employed in China. An employee must apply for a visa at the Chinese consulate in respective home country attaching government-issued employment permit and visa notification letter sent by an employer. The Z visa is valid for 30 days from the date of arrival into China during which period an employee must obtain a temporary residence permit for stay equivalent to duration of employment which can be for a minimum period of 90 days to a maximum of 5 years. Family members accompanying a Z category visa holder must apply for S1 or S2 visa submitting an invitation letter from the relative.

2. **Chinese talent visa (R visa):** This type of visa is issued to foreign high-level personnel and much-needed highly talented people who need to stay in China. This category of visa is complementary to the Z type visa and was introduced by the Chinese government to show its sincerity towards global talent and to create a friendly environment for foreigners to get employed and work in China. All highly skilled persons with specialized qualities who are in shortage in the country and wanting to work in China are eligible to obtain a visa. A person or employer shall first obtain the qualification approval from the provincial government before an application for grant of a visa is made. This is a flexible programme in terms of duration of stay and other requirements.
3. **Residence permits:** All visa holders, especially those fall under the Z and R categories, shall apply at the local public security bureau exit and entry administration office for temporary residence permit on arrival within 30 days. Sponsoring organization/employer shall obtain an appointment with the office and also a visa holder is subjected to a physical examination. Temporary residence permit is issued for a minimum of 90 days to a maximum of five years with possibility of renewals. Permanent residence permit is issued for duration of 5–10 years. There are different qualifying requirements for the issuance of this permit. Persons who qualify are generally those with major and outstanding contribution to China, having direct investment and sound taxation record, spouses of citizens or unmarried children less than 18 years old who come to live with their parents.

Singapore

Non-Singapore citizens intending to work in Singapore shall obtain a work visa commonly known as a valid pass. There are different types of work passes and permits depending upon the need and profile of person seeking permission to enter into Singapore for work. The visa types relevant to employment and business are discussed as follows. These are primarily two types: one applicable to professionals and the other for semi-skilled workforce.

1. **Employment pass:** The employment pass is applicable to professionals, executives and managers who are intending to work in Singapore. The basic condition here is that a person shall have an employment offer that pays a minimum SGD 3,600 a month and shall possess acceptable qualification which is usually a university degree or a specialized certification. Employer on behalf of a prospective employee must apply for the work permit. The duration allowed for stay in Singapore under this category is up to two years initially which can be extended by another three years.
2. **Personalised employment pass (PES):** This visa offers greater flexibility and is meant to attract high net worth individuals earning a minimum of SGD 18,000 per month as the last drawn fixed salary overseas. It is not tied to an employer. Candidates can apply directly for this visa. Stay allowed under this category is for three years and non-renewable. However, on expiry of the visa, candidates can seek Employment Pass to continue to work in Singapore. However, a person intending to start a business or any form of entrepreneurial activity or a freelancer or a proprietor/sole owner is not eligible to apply for PES.
3. **EntrePass:** This visa allows eligible foreigners to start and operate a new business in Singapore. The company which shall be registered with the Accounting ad Corporate Regulatory Authority shall have at least SGD 50,000 in paid-up capital and person applying for

a visa shall hold at least 30 per cent of the shares of the company. There is no stipulated minimum salary here and stay permitted is up to one year initially which can be extended.

4. **S pass:** This is applicable to mid-level skilled staff earning at least SGD 2,200 a month and possess relevant qualifications and work experience. This visa is given initially for two years which can be extended depending upon the need and on meeting the criteria.

5. **Semi-skilled workers:** There are four sub-categories in this visa type: (a) work permit for semi-skilled foreign workers in the construction, manufacturing, marine, process or services sector from approved source countries for stay permit up to two years with provision to renew, (b) work permit for domestic workers to work in Singapore for which approval is required for both the workers and the employer for stay up to two years with provision to renew, (c) work permit for confinement nanny and (d) work permit for foreign performers working in public entertainment outlets for stay up to six months which cannot be renewed but a fresh visa can be issued for a year after expiry of this visa.

Spouses and children of eligible employment pass or S pass holders are eligible for dependent's pass.

Japan

The visa procedures and approvals are regulated by Immigration Control and Refugee Recognition Act in Japan. The visa rules are very simple in Japan, they allow very few people the status of residence, and most people can enter Japan only through a Temporary Visitor Visa that does not allow a person to work for pay in Japan. Persons intending to stay and work in Japan must first obtain a 'Certificate of Eligibility' issued by the Ministry of Justice after having examined whether or not the activities that a foreigner wishing to enter Japan intends to carry out within the country meet the conditions of landing. A person who is successful in obtaining the said 'Certificate of Eligibility' can apply for a visa with the respective Japanese consulate in the home country of that person. Alternatively, a person who is in receipt of the 'Certificate of Eligibility' can land in Japan directly and seek a necessary visa with the immigration authorities at the port of entry. The purpose of 'Certificate of Eligibility' is stated to be to expedite and simplify the procedure of immigration and make it more efficient. A person intending to apply for the 'Certificate of Eligibility' must have an offer of appointment from an employer in Japan and obtain the 'Certificate of Authorized Employment'. An employee on self-basis or through a legal representative can apply for the 'Certificate of Authorized Employment' attaching necessary documents such as the passport, offer of appointment and proof of residence.

The Philippines

The Philippines offers a range of visas depending upon the need and purpose. The visa policy of the Philippines is regulated by the Philippine Immigration Act enforced by the Department of Foreign Affairs. Employment-related visa provisions are discussed as follows:

1. **Pre-arranged employee visa:** This is also popularly called 9G visa. Foreign nationals who are proceeding to the Philippines to engage in any lawful employment for wages fall within

this category. A person to be eligible must be occupying a technical, executive or a managerial position in a company for at least one year. An employer must submit a letter of request, Alien Employment Form, issued by the Department of Labour and Employment along with other routine documents such as copy of passport, educational qualification and residence proof certificates. A candidate can apply for a visa in the Philippines embassy of his or her home country for issuance of work visa once pre-arranged employment visa application is approved and a notification is received. The process may involve personal interview of the applicant by an immigration officer at the embassy. This visa is valid equivalent for the duration mentioned in the Alien Employment Form. An employer shall adhere to the process of searching for a Filipino national to fill the position before the said Alien Employment Form is issued.

2. **Special non-immigrant visa:** This visa, also known as 47 A-2 visa, is granted to foreign investors by the Secretary of the Department of Justice on the basis of public interest consideration. Generally, this is given to investors engaged in industries such as power generation, oil exploration and infrastructure, and to those registered with the Philippines Economic Zone Authority. Valid duration of this visa is maximum one year. This visa is also granted to executives, supervisors, specialists, consultants and personal staff at enterprises registered with special economic processing zone.

3. **Special work permit:** This is issued to professional athletes, professionals who perform emergency operations and services, artists, musicians and other performers and other professionals who could not acquire the 9G visa and entered into the Philippines through a tourist visa or a temporary visa. This visa is issued for three months initially and can be extended by another three months.

4. **Special visa for employment generation:** This is known as the SVEG visa. This is a non-immigrant visa granted to foreign nationals and their dependents who employ at least 10 Filipinos in a lawful business or enterprise. Persons who are granted this visa shall be considered as special non-immigrants with multiple entry privileges.

Dependent family members of all visa holders as discussed are eligible to apply for a dependent visa that allows them to stay as long as the original visa holder is legally permitted to reside and work.

Australia

Four types of visas are relevant in the context of our discussion. These are work-related visa which include skilled and employer-sponsored work and other short-term work, a visa programme for entrepreneurs, permanent residency applicable to people who want to migrate to Australia to live there and the partners/spouse visa to accompany a valid visa holder. These are discussed briefly here. Australian visa programme is highly transparent and objective. It is based on a system wherein in almost in all cases applicants by subjecting their application through point measurement or balance tests can assess the likelihood of a visa grant and approvals.

1. **Work visa:** There are three types of visas applicable to skilled workers: the Skilled Independent Visa, the Skilled Nominated Visa and the Skilled Regional Visa. These are popularly known as General Skilled Migration (GSM) visas. As part of the first step in this

process, a person shall submit an Expression of Interest through Skillset, an online service that manages Australia's skilled migration programme. Based on the skill (occupation) and experience, and other relevant parameters, the Skillset allocates points to an applicant. Higher the points greater the chance for a visa approval. Skillset is not mandatory for employer-sponsored visas. Rules governing the grant of visas are different for different types of visa. The other major visa category is the Temporary Work Visa which is relevant for a person intending to stay and work for a minimum of one day to a maximum of four years. This is known as the 457 Visa which shall be sponsored by an employer and the applicant must be a skilled worker and sponsoring organization shall be an approved business sponsor. Organizations that are operating in Australia for a minimum of three years with an annual turnover of over AUD 4 million can also seek recognition under sponsor accreditation scheme that provides additional qualifications for the visa sponsorships. The objective of this visa programme is to encourage skilled workers to travel to Australia to fill the skill shortages. Application for grant of a visa under this category goes through a three-step process of sponsorship, nomination and visa application. An employer is also required to reach a labour agreement with the department of labour in order to recruit a specified number of overseas workers. This recruitment of overseas workers shall be in occupations which are identified as having skill shortages in Australian market.

2. **Business innovation and investment visa programme:** This visa programme is meant for entrepreneurs who are intending to undertake an entrepreneurial venture in Australia. However, ventures related to real estate, labour hire and purchasing an existing business do not fall within the purview of this programme. To qualify, an applicant must have submitted an Expression of Interest and registered with Skillset, developed a business plan outlining the venture and its plans and shown evidence of ability to invest a minimum of AUD 200,000. A holder of this visa can progress to permanent residency after four years if they can successfully meet the parameters specified around business turnover and number of Australians employed.

3. **Permanent employer sponsorship programme:** This is also known as the 186 Visa. It is for skilled workers who want to work permanently in Australia. This visa process involves a two-step process. First, nomination by an approved Australian employer and then an application under the nominated stream. There are three sub-types here: (a) the temporary residence transition stream that allows conversion of the 457 visa into the 186 visa, (b) direct entry stream applicable to persons who have either never worked in Australia or briefly worked and not eligible for grant of a visa under 457 category and (c) the agreement stream which is applicable to persons sponsored by an employer through a negotiated formal labour agreement.

4. **Family/partners visa:** Australian visa programme to bring spouse, children, parents, partner, relatives and adoptions is very exhaustive. The partner calculator will help to determine whether someone is eligible to apply for a visa under partnership programme. An applicant under this category can seek both temporary and permanent residency. An Australian permanent resident who has been living in Australia is eligible to apply for the parents' visa and can be granted a visa in the same category of the applicant subject to meeting the 'Balance of Family Test'. A temporary visa holder or an applicant can apply for a family members' visa with the supporting documents which is usually granted on the same conditions applicable to the visa holder. Dependent children below the age of 23 years are only allowed to apply for a visa under family members' category.

Summary

Direct and indirect trends impacting the practice of IS along with changing international hiring practices are discussed in this chapter. Processes and practices of IS including international HR planning together with the best practices such as human capital inventory management and investment plans are also presented and analysed. Expats as sourcing model to strengthen the leadership and associated managerial hiring practices are also given a detailed focus. Immigration policies of nations are strong determinants of not only on the migration of international workforce but also the effectiveness of IS. Hence, immigration policies of selective nations are covered as a part of the chapter.

QUESTIONS FOR DISCUSSION

1. Discuss the challenges and remedies to deal with staffing leadership positions in international organizations.
2. Is international mobile workforce a boon or bane for staffing management?
3. What macro and micro trends are contributing to emergence of IS as a strategic HR function?
4. Describe international recruitment trends.
5. Analyse the significance of human capital inventory and planning in globalized context.
6. Describe the role of automation tools in IS management.
7. Debate pros and cons of expats as source of international hiring.
8. What are the best practices in IS management?
9. Analyse immigration trends and their impact on IS.

CASE STUDY

EG is a highly diversified multinational corporation headquartered in the United States with operations virtually across the globe spanning over 109 countries. A study conducted on the diversity and inclusion of the company has revealed that: (a) though the operations are truly multinational, the leadership is not, (b) majority of leadership positions are occupied by persons of a particular nation and (c) several countries where the company has operations are left unrepresented in the leadership structure. Reasons offered by HR executives are: (a) not enough leadership talent available in the countries where the positions are held by expats, (b) historical reasons as the company has the practice of deputing senior people from the host country to oversee the subsidiary operations, (c) comfort factor since most of the business heads reside and work from host country and they feel assured in posting someone who has been close to them, (d) trust factor as leaders tend to believe in their own people more than people of subsidiary nations, (e) unwritten company practice of posting host country managers in all important and sensitive positions and (f) lack of confidence in the capabilities of managers of subsidiary operations. The top management has realized that many leaders in the company

(Continued)

(Continued)

believe that globalization means just ensuring host country managers spread across all countries of operations rather than spreading leaders from all nations. A decision has been taken at board level to transform the company leadership structure with representation from all the nations in three years. Initial efforts have corroborated the fact that there is indeed a leadership deficit internally due to long neglect in training, grooming and mentoring of senior managers in many nations where the company has operations. The approach of resolving the issue through capability building initiatives is considered as a medium- and long-term approach and hiring leadership talent from external market as an immediate solution. Accordingly, the HR department is advised to launch leadership hiring across 27 nations in Asia and Eastern Europe. The HR department has started drawing up a plan for hiring. During the process, it has encountered many dilemmas such as: (a) whether leadership positions in a country shall be filled by talent from the same country or from the talent pool of another subsidiary country. (b) Which positions: operations, maintenance, project management, sales and business development, marketing, support functions such as finance, HR, public relations should be targeted first to launch leadership hiring or should they only identify positions currently being occupied by expats? (c) What tools and methods should be followed in leadership hiring? (d) Should there be one team across all the countries to work on leadership hiring or should it be decentralized? (e) What other challenges are likely to crop up in the progress?

Discuss what approach will you take. How can you resolve the dilemma being faced by EG HR executives.

Bibliography

Aberdeen Group. (2013). *Onboarding 2013—A New Look at New Hires*. Retrieved 29 January 2018, from http://deliberatepractice.com.au/wp-content/uploads/2013/04/Onboarding-2013.pdf

Association of Americans Resident Overseas. (2011). *AARO Annual Report 2011*. Retrieved 27 February 2018, from https://aaro.org/about-aaro/aaros-historic-achievements/96-about-aaro

Bardhan, A. and Kroll, C. (2003). *The New Wave of Outsourcing*. Research Report. Fisher Center for Real Estate & Urban Economics, University of California, Berkley.

Black, S. J. and Gregersen, H. B. (1999). The Right Way to Manage Expats. *Harvard Business Review, 77*(2), 52–57.

Brookfield Global Relocation Services. (2012). *Global Relocation Trends: 2012 Survey Report*. Retrieved 29 January 2018, from https://espritgloballearning.com/wp-content/uploads/2011/03/2012-Brookfield-Global-Relocations-Trends-Survey.pdf

Carlson, L. (2005, June). Complications Abound in Managing Expatriate Benefits. *Employee Benefit News*, 19, pp. 28–39.

Cartus. (2014). *Global Mobility Policy & Practices*. Retrieved 29 January 2018, from https://www.cartus.com/files/2214/8796/3083/Cartus-2016-Global-Mobility-Policy-and-Practices-Survey_Full_Survey_inclusive_of_all_charts.pdf?

Chartered Management Institute. (2011). Developing True Management Professionals. Retrieved 27 February 2018, from https://www.managers.org.uk/~/media/Files/Apprenticeships/CMDA_Flyer.pdf

CIETT. (2016). Annual Economic Report. Retrieved 29 January 2018, from http://www.wecglobal.org/economicreport2016/

Doving, E. and Nordhaug, O. (2010). Investing in Human Resource Planning: An International Study. *Management Review, 21*(3), 292–307.

Dumont, J.-C. and Lemaitre, G. (2015). *Counting Immigrants and Expatriates in OECD Countries: A New Perspective*. Directorate for Employment, Labour and Social Affairs: OECD.

Economic Intelligence Unit, KPMG International. (2016). *Rethinking Human Resources in a Changing World Report*. KPMG.

ERE. (2014). *ERE Recruiting Conference Proceedings*. Retrieved 27 February 2018, from www.ererecruitingconference.com

EY. (2013). *Your Talent in Motion: Global Mobility Effectiveness Survey 2013*. Retrieved 27 February 2018, from http://www.ey.com/Publication/vwLUAssets/EY-Global_Mobility_Effectiveness_Survey_2013/$FILE/EY-Global-Mobility-Survey.pdf

Finaccord. (2013). *Global Expatriates: Size, Segmentation and Forecast for the Worldwide Market.* Retrieved 27 February 2018, from http://finaccord.com/uk/report_global-expatriates_size-segmentation-and-forecast-for-the-worldwide-market.htm

GE. (2017). *Empowering Youth and Women.* Retrieved 27 February 2018, from https://www.ge.com/sa/stories/empowering-youth-and-women

Harvey, M. and Novicevic, M. M. (2001). Selecting Expatriates for Increasingly Complex Global Assignments. *Career Development International, 6*(2), 69–87.

Hays. (2016). *Top 12 Talent Trends for 2016—What Should be on Your Radar?* Retrieved 27 February 2018, from https://www.hays.com.au/press-releases/HAYS_310989

HSBC. (2013). *Expatriate Trends Survey 2013.* Retrieved 27 February 2018, from https://www.expatexplorer.hsbc.com/survey/files/pdfs/overall-reports/2013/report.pdf

———. (2014). *Expat Explorer—Moving and Living Abroad.* Retrieved 27 February 2018, from https://www.expatexplorer.hsbc.com/

IBIS. (2017). *Business Process Outsourcing Services: Market Research Report.* Retrieved 27 February 2018, from https://www.ibisworld.com/industry-trends/specialized-market-research-reports/advisory-financial-services/outsourced-office-functions/business-process-outsourcing-services.html

iCIMS. (2012). *Strategic Talent Acquisition: Are You Prepared to Hire the Best?* Retrieved 27 February 2018, from https://www.icims.com/resources/e-book/are-your-ready-for-the-future-of-talent-acquisition

International Labour Organization. (2016). *World Employment and Social Outlook Trends.* Geneva: ILO.

International Organization for Migration. (2015). *How the World Views Migration: IOM-Gallup World Poll.* Retrieved 27 February 2018, from https://www.iom.int/news/how-world-views-migration-results-new-iomgallup-report

———. (2016). *IOM's Global Migration Data Analysis.* Retrieved 27 February 2018, https://gmdac.iom.int/data-and-analysis-search

Korn Ferry. (2016). *Korn Ferry Economic Analysis: Human Capital Nearly 2.5 Times More Valuable to Economy than Physical Assets Such as Technology, Real Estate & Inventory.* Retrieved 27 February 2018, from https://www.kornferry.com/press/korn-ferry-economic-analysis-human-capital-nearly-2-5-times-more-valuable-to-global-economy-than-physical-assets-such-as-technology-real-estate-and-inventory/

Joerres, J. A. (2011). *Beyond Expats: Better Managers for Emerging Markets.* Retrieved 30 January 2018, from https://www.mckinsey.com/business-functions/organization/our-insights/beyond-expats-better-managers-for-emerging-markets

Lee Hecht Harrison. (2015). *Mobilizing Your Workforce.* 2015 Talent Mobility Research Report. Los Angeles, CA: Lee Hecht Harrison.

LinkedIn. (2016). *Global Recruiting Trends 2016.* Retrieved 27 February 2018, from https://business.linkedin.com/talent-solutions/c/14/1/product-updates-tutorials/tips-and-insights/2016-global-recruiting-trends-report

Lou Adler Group. (2012). *Sourcing Problems are Rarely the Problem of Scarcity Versus Surplus.* Retrieved 27 February 2018, from https://louadlergroup.com/sourcing-problems-are-rarely-the-problem/scarcity-vs-surplus-2/

McKinsey Global Institute. (2016). *Digital Globalization: The New Era of Global Flows.* New York: McKinsey & Company.

National Foreign Trade Council. (2010). *Global Mobility Trends Survey Results.* Retrieved 27 February 2018, from https://www.cignaglobalhealth.com/assets/docs/we-know-expats/global-mobility-trends-study-brochure.pdf

NatWest International. (2015). *NatWest IPB Quality of Life Report.* Retrieved 27 February 2018, from https://www.natwestinternational.com/nw/global/quality-of-life-study.ashx?intcam=qol_2015

Nelsen, L. and Witters, B. (2015). *National Association of Colleges and Employers Conference Proceedings.* Retrieved 27 February 2018, from https://www.naceweb.org/conferenceexpo/files/nace15-program.pdf

PwC. (2014). *The New Hire: How a New Generation of Robots is Transforming Manufacturing.* Retrieved 27 February 2018, from https://www.pwc.com/gx/en/hr-management-services/pdf/pwc-key-trends-in-human-capital-2014.pdf

———. (2015). *PwC's NextGen: A Global Generational Study.* Retrieved 27 February 2018, from https://www.pwc.com/gx/en/hr-management-services/pdf/pwc-nextgen-study-2015.pdf

———. (2016). *19th Annual Global CEO Survey: Redefining Business Success in a Changing World.* PwC. Retrieved 7 March 2018, from https://www.pwc.com/gx/en/ceo-survey/2016/landing-page/pwc-19th-annual-global-ceo-survey.pdf

Reuters Technology News. (2013). *Apple to Return Some Mac Production to U.S. in 2013.* Retrieved 30 January 2018, from https://www.reuters.com/article/us-apple-manufacturing/apple-to-return-some-mac-production-to-u-s-in-2013-idUSBRE8B50R120121207

Sibson Consulting. (2016). *Human Capital Inventory.* Retrieved 27 February 2018, from http://www.sibson.com/who-we-help/overview/higher-education/organizational-human-capital-strategy/

SiriusDecisions. (2015). *The BtoB Marketing Automation Study.* Retrieved 27 February 2018, from https://www.siriusdecisions.com/blog/marketing-automation-study

Smith, B., Borski, J. and Davis, G. (1993). Human Resource Planning. *Human Resource Management*, Spring–Summer, 81–93.

Taleo Research and Human Capital Institute. (2010). *United Talent Management: A Global View*. Retrieved 4 February 2018, from http://taleohrguys.files.wordpress.com

Technavio. (2015). *Technavio Forecast of Digital Manufacturing Analysis Report*.

The World Bank. (2016). *Global Monitoring Report. Developmental Goals in an Era of Demographic Change*. Retrieved 27 February 2018, from http://pubdocs.worldbank.org/en/503001444058224597/Global-Monitoring-Report-2015.pdf

Tung, R. L. (1987). Expatriate Assignments: Enhancing Success and Minimizing Failure. *Academy of Management Executive, 1*, 117–125.

United Nations Department of Economic and Social Affairs. (2015). *United Nations Global Migration Database*. Retrieved 7 March 2018, from https://esa.un.org/unmigration/

Visualise. (2015). *British Army VR Recruitment Experience*. Retrieved 29 January 2018, from http://visualise.com/case-study/british-army-vr-recruitment-experience

Wall Street Journal (2011). *Why Otis Elevator Returned from Mexico*. Retrieved 27 February 2018, from http://www.wsj.com/video/why-otis-elevator-returned-from-mexico/EE8347BC-ED72-44DF-85FA-032AA31BBB81.html

Watson Wyatt Worldwide. (2014). *Human Capital Index*. Retrieved 27 February 2018, from https://www.towerswatson.com/en-BM/Insights/IC-Types/Survey-Research-Results/2014/08/the-2014-global-workforce-study

Winch, G. (2001). Management on the Skills Inventory in Times of Major Change. *System Dynamics Review, 17*, no. 2, 151–159.

World Trade Organization. (2016). *World Trade Statistical Review*. Retrieved 4 February 2018, from www.wto.org/statistics

Zeira, Y. and Banai, M. (1985). Selection of Expatriates Managers in MNCs: The Host Environment Point of View. *International Studies of Management & Organization, 15,* no. 1, 33–51.

International Training Management

LEARNING OBJECTIVES

The objectives of this chapter are to:
- ☐ discuss contemporary approaches of international training and their implications for business organizations.
- ☐ illustrate international training management trends and leveraging technology for effective delivery of training across the geographies.
- ☐ discuss the methods of international training renewals.
- ☐ illustrate benchmarking training models, enabling for deeper insights into the state of training in selective global corporations.
- ☐ enable designing courses and pedagogical methods in an international context.

Training employees is indispensable for international organizations in order to remain competitive. International organizations are far more exposed to challenges than domestic businesses because they not only cater to global markets but also face competition from everywhere. Competition theories emphasize that technology, products, capital, strategy and markets can be created much faster and can be replicated relatively much more easily than an organization can create highly skilled workforce. The lead time to transform raw skilled or under skilled or differently skilled workforce to skilled is complex and often fraught with several economic, social and emotional upheavals. Further, this is an ongoing journey rather than a one-time fix. An organization can aspire to remain highly competitive and be 'first' on arrival if it can master the art and science of international training management. Brian Benton (2016), author of several AutoCAD training tools, content and videos, states that if there is no upfront cost, no rational person ever will choose an untrained pilot over a trained pilot. This reality applies everywhere but organizations often pay scant attention putting themselves into uncompetitive mode. Lack of a systematic international training system causes multiple disorders in organizations, which include the following: untrained employees tend to be inefficient, less productive and expensive as they make mistakes creating low self-esteem leading to low morale and loss of customers, declining revenues and profits ultimately putting their very survival at stake. On the other hand, organizations that make good investment and efforts to build an international training system enjoy high productivity, innovation, low employee turnover and higher employee morale.

Table 3.1	Training Budgets

Year	Total Budget Spent (Billion US Dollars)
2015	97
2014	108
2013	101
2012	103
2011	112

Source: https://www.ifla.org/FR/node/17154 (accessed on 7 March 2018).

However, training is not cheap. It is expensive as well as time-consuming. Cheng and Ho (2001) aver that training is an expensive investment, particularly when some studies establish that only 10 per cent of total investment made on training could deliver positive results. Data from several organizations and countries show that training budget is the first one targeted to save profits. For example, Association for Talent and Development (ATD; 2014) reports that overall training spend by the industry in the United States has seen a downward trend in the last few years as illustrated in Table 3.1.

While a major chunk of this budget is pertaining to government spending, it still provides a perspective that the conviction in training is inadequate in quite a few organizations. However, selective data from New Age technology organizations contradicts this view as their focus and dedication to training seems unquestionable. For example, e-learning budget spent in technology organizations from Europe and North America demonstrates a double-digit (18 per cent) budget growth for the period between 2012 and 2015. The *Training Magazine*'s survey of 2015 covering 125,778 companies concludes that for 2015 the total US training expenditures, including payroll and spending on external products and services, have seen upward trajectory growing at 14.2 per cent. However, average training spend of large companies has seen a marginal decrease. It is very complex to assess the budgetary trends of training as there is conflicting data where some surveys show that budgets are on rise and some concluding that budgets are shrinking. Training budget data for all the global corporates is hard to access and selective data tends to provide inaccurate inferences. The general trend continues to be the same with New Age companies and growing organizations focusing on training as a strategic investment, and stagnant and declining companies seeing training budgets as cost that needs to be controlled.

Research conducted across countries shows that training has strong positive correlation with profitability of companies. For example, Hansson (2007), based on the data analysis of nearly 5,800 private corporates operating in over 26 countries, has found that the single most important factor contributing to profitability is the extent to which an organization makes investments in training and development. In yet another study conducted by Akhtar, Ding and Ge (2008), covering a sample of 465 Chinese companies, it has been found that there is a significant positive relationship between training and financial performance of the sample organizations. Bassi et al., in a study of select companies in the United States, state that training had led to an 18 per cent increase in financial return to the shareholders compared to 12 per cent financial returns offered by organizations that did not invest in training. Guerrero and Barraud-Didier (2004) based on a study of about 1,530 large organizations in France point out that 4.6 per cent of the variance in financial performance is on account of training and development initiatives. A study conducted in Spain with a sample size of 380 large organizations too reports that training positively correlates with profits of a company. Using 359 firms with over 12 years of longitudinal firm level profit data, Kim and Ployhart (2014) of University of South Carolina suggest that internal training directly influences firm's profit growth through its effects on labour productivity. There are various studies which reveal a positive impact of training on productivity. Black and Lynch (1996) based on a survey of manufacturing organizations have found that 10 per cent increase in training leads to an 8.5 per cent increase in productivity. A detailed study conducted on manufacturing organizations in the United Kingdom also establishes positive contribution of training in various spheres such as quality, productivity and financial returns. A study conducted by 'Expertus' to assess the impact of customer service training on customer satisfaction has found that the satisfaction rate increases by almost 31 per cent when before and after training scores are compared. Training also has a strong positive impact on performance of employees. Arthur Jr, Day, McNelly and Edens (2003) who have conducted a meta-analysis of 165 sources of training research found that implementing training had an overall positive effect on job-related behaviours compared to no training efforts. Barber (2004) based on his study of mechanics in automobile industry in India has found that on-the-job training lead to great innovation and development of tacit skills.

However, Chatterjee (2016), professor of strategy at the University of Washington, in his research paper focused on global software services industry argues that all training initiatives will not yield financial results for companies. For instance, his research conducted in the year 2008 exploring the relationship between training and profits, using data from 347 software development projects with a staff over 5,500 employees, found that technological training such as computer language training did not boost projects profits.

A higher education trend which is the prime feeder of top talent for global corporations is positive. For example, the global population of students who move to another country to study continues to rise, reaching almost 5 million in 2014 with annual increase of 10 per cent. Most estimates expect the figure to reach 8 million by 2025. International students mobility is likely to see revolutionary changes in the future, owing to political changes in the United States and Europe, two regions traditionally attracting most international students.

International Trends in Higher Education, Training and Development

Driven by technological changes, international training function is in the middle of major changes. Until the beginning of the current decade, the biggest barrier for globalizing training of employees has been lack of infrastructure, information facilities and coaching aids. With the advent of digital technologies, these barriers are fast disappearing. International federation of Library Associations and Institutions (IFLA) based on its global study of knowledge management in 2016 predicts the following five major trends:

1. Online education will democratize and disrupt global learning.
2. Hyper connected societies will listen to and empower new voices and groups.
3. The global information environment will be transformed by new technologies.
4. The boundaries of privacy and data protection will be redefined.
5. New technologies will both expand and limit who has access to information.

Training and Development: Domestic Versus International Organizations

The profile, management and type of training programmes tend to have similarities as well as dissimilarities in domestic and international organizations due to obvious reasons such as difference in their focus, spread, reach and objectives. Typically, domestic organizations prefer training models which help in enhancing functional and technical expertise, while the emphasis on soft skills is accorded incidentally. In domestic organizations, the choice of instruction methodologies is mostly drawn keeping in view in-person training and classroom teaching, whereas international training organizations seek application of technology in training instructions so that programmes can be delivered remotely, with standardization also becoming much easier. International organizations also prefer trainings which not only enhance technical and functional skills but also build cross-cultural sensitivity, languages and leadership. This helps in managing multi-country operations, in addition to further the expansion of their operations across the globe. Experiences show that international organizations are in a better position to leverage both domestic and global techniques, tools, knowledge and practices enriching the training and development efforts. These organizations also have better access to quality international faculty and content and due to this, employees in international organizations significantly benefit in terms of both exposure and support in their learning. However, unlike domestic organizations, these organizations face their own set of challenges often related to the methodology to implement training and development programmes. As employees working in different parts of the world are not equally ready to receive the same content, the reception to these programmes would be very different too. Creating content and methodology suitable for each nation can nullify the standardization of learning and development. It is seen quite often that the learning standards of employees in the same nation or location can be very different, ranging from quick learners to slow acquirers. Tying them to the same notion can weaken the training effort, apart from demoralizing the performing group of employees. Keeping this reality in view, many international organizations have started devising training and development programmes at different levels of proficiency, offering these across groups of employees based on their existing performance standards. International organizations are seen utilizing international assignments, tenure-based deputations to other nations and special assignments involving a different country of operations from the home location of work for employee development, especially in building leadership which is cross-national. Language and cultural sensitivity training has become almost basic in many of these organizations due to the increasing use of inter-country teams working on global projects. Communication and presentation skills are equally important as technical skills, and sometimes even more important for employees in leadership positions. Some empirical studies show that few employees could not succeed in international organizations, despite having worked in domestic organizations and proven themselves very successful, due to gaps in communication and presentation styles. However, all the gaps discussed before between domestic and international organizations are disappearing quickly and are not as stark as they used to be few years ago, primarily because many domestic organizations are benchmarking themselves with global practices too.

Emerging Learning and Development Model in International Organizations

Though the basic training model comprising of TNA, design of training courses, implementation and evaluation is quite similar in all organizations (domestic or international), the methodologies and learning model in terms of few courses practised in international organizations are different and are discussed below:

Self-instruction: This is more commonly found in international organizations where employees learn at their own pace, self-instructing with the help of courseware provided by organizations. There is neither a time limit nor restrictions imposed on employees to access the course, except in few segments where the learning is involved with patented designs or where learning under supervision is a must, owing to safety and asset dilution situations. Availability of faculty or teaching assistance is provided in selective courses where required, with an aim to help solve certain complex problems and cases.

Self-evaluation: Employees are not only given an opportunity to learn on their own but are also empowered to self-evaluate in order to measure the proficiency attained with the help of web-enabled tools. Though self-evaluation is limited to few courses, it is being promoted much more than it was in the past. Self-evaluation modules are built with tests and problem-solving cases to instil credibility to such an exercise. The advantage with this model is that employees can test themselves as and when they are ready and can also subject themselves repeatedly or whenever a renewal is required.

Usage of technology/Internet applications: It is observed that international organizations have quickly adopted technologies such as Internet-based applications to enhance reach, access, standardization and cost optimization. A technology-centric instruction methodology is also seen to drive learning much faster since it is learner-friendly. Using artificial intelligence techniques has also helped create an interactive experience, and, as a result, the only criticism against using web-based tools stating that they were not interactive has been addressed. Virtual classrooms and accelerated solution environment techniques are commonly used to institutionalize learning at various work locations set up across the countries. Physical classroom instructions are slowly being replaced by Internet-enabled virtual classrooms.

International assignments: Short-term assignments spanning from one week to eight weeks are found to be a widely deployed learning technique. This usually occurs in two different ways: first is when a multi-country representative team is formed to work on a global task so that all employees, apart from building a solution to the given problem, are also exposed to work together in a multicultural and multi-language environment. Second, employees working in one country are given an assignment to work in another country for a duration spanning one week to four weeks.

Deputations: Employees are deputed to work on a specific issue or to work in collaboration with a team operating in another country for a fixed tenure so that it helps to build leadership and also to gain knowledge of operations in a different country.

Transfers and global posting: International organizations avail global postings as a valuable source of learning, especially in leadership development. This has been popularized as expatriate postings in the past, but in contemporary times, this has taken a shape of global postings. Expatriate postings were just limited to postings between the parent and host country and vice versa, whereas global postings allows for posting of employees from and to any location. This helps employees gain true global exposure.

Global leadership cadres: Several international organizations have designed in-house global leadership modules consisting of work assignments and rotations among functions/departments and locations across the globe in order to build not only global knowledge-driven leadership but also to build an appreciation for the dynamics and realities of various nations. This has worked as a major source of learning and development for international organizations and is not feasible in domestic organizations.

Cultural sensitivity and language learning: There is a great emphasis on cross-cultural and multi-language training in international organizations. This works as a foundation for creating global citizens, paving the way for learning technologies and management approaches with a global perspective. Cultural training, which used to be confined to leadership echelons in most organizations, is now being seen extended to all employees. This effort is resulting in building a learning environment wherein all employees are ready to access global level technological, functional and managerial learning as language occupies a central place in nurturing a higher order of zeal and ambition among employees of all nations. As a result, cross-cultural and language training is emerging as the foundation for global learning.

International Training Management: Basic Concepts and Models

International training management primarily consists of five stages: (a) determination of training needs, (b) design of training courses, (c) implementation of training courses, (d) assessment of training utility and (e) renewal of training system. These stages are discussed further. As training becomes more global, the dynamics of performing these stages also are undergoing significant changes. Use of technology has become fundamental for international training management, replacing purely person-based initiatives.

Stage 1: Determination of Training Needs

This is an essential part of training management since any systematic training effort must start with understanding the real training needs. However, various studies on this subject reveal that only a miniscule percentage of organizations undertake TNA in a rigorous manner. Majority of organizations move with a belief that any training connected with principal operations of organization is good, without studying the precise nature of training needs. Even organizations that implement TNA tend to carry out a generic survey rather than scientific analysis of organizational, functional and individual training needs. Ferreira and Abbad (2013) based on comprehensive review of TNA studies and review of over 51 research articles on the subject conclude that: (a) there is little agreement on how to measure training needs and (b) majority of TNA practices and models are reactive and do not include contextual factors. Further, studies reveal that few organizations are sceptic about the benefits of TNA believing TNA is meant to serve the purpose of TNA administrators more than yielding any material benefit to the organization; findings of TNA not being realistic or pragmatic in the context of immediate business goals and lack of concrete action on the findings of past studies.

However, failure to convert training investment into proportionate positive gains for organizations mainly arises from neglect of proper TNA. There are many other maladies associated with conducting training courses not based on needs study but on a generic understanding of training requirements such as overtraining, duplication of training, waste of time, loss of faith in training system, productivity loss, decline in quality of products, services, customer satisfaction and loss of innovative capability. Training assessment study in international organizations, covering employees in a number of countries, has quite a few natural advantages but is also challenging, because operations of a company may be at different stages of evolution in different countries with variances in skill proficiencies and more importantly the interference of cultural differences that may impact a global study. However, with the right preparation and a good TNA framework, these challenges can be remedied. In this context, time-tested TNA models that can be immensely handy in designing and applying a TNA framework are discussed here.

Three-tier Training Needs Assessment Model

McGehee and Thayer, way back in 1961, developed a well-acclaimed three-tier approach to conduct training needs analysis encompassing all the facets of an organization. This model is also popularly known as O-TP model of training needs analysis. The model as the title suggests consists of three approaches as discussed here:

- **Tier 1: Organizational analysis.** This is an organizational-level analysis. In order to craft and execute an organizational strategy what skills and competencies are required is analysed at this level. Elements such as vision, mission, business goals, business plans, growth plans, technology, customers and markets are integral part of the strategy of an organization. Training needs analysis at this level focuses on identifying the skills availability to attain this strategy and gap if it exists.
- **Tier 2: Task analysis.** This is task-level analysis of training needs. In order to carry out various operations and projects in an organization, whether all the skills and competencies associated with such tasks are sufficiently available or not and the precise gap that exists are studied at this level.
- **Tier 3: Person analysis.** While tiers 1 and 2 focus on creating TNA study with organization and functions as units of study, this level is dedicated to study each individual employee in the context of his or her respective job specifications and determine if any gaps exist at all.

McClelland's 11-step Training Needs Assessment Model

This is also known as open system model of TNA. This model consists of 11 steps, guiding through the needs assessment from defining TNA goals to drawing final inferences and recommendations based on which training courses can be designed and rolled out. These steps are:

Step 1: Defining goals. McClelland says that a sound TNA practice must begin with setting and understanding the assessment goals: what purpose does it intend to serve? How will it benefit organization and employees? What is the output expected out of such study? How will the results of the study be used? What is the success criterion?

Step 2: Determining unit of study. It is important to clearly identify the functions/departments/groups which will fall within the purview of the study and unit of analysis. Aspects like whether a sample will be chosen or all the employees working in the unit are to be covered and the organization of the same are addressed at this stage.

Step 3: Identifying resource persons. A leader and the team required to conduct the study and their selection is an important step. Competent people within or outside an organization who have requisite skills and competencies such as research, understanding of related domain of work/operations, data analytics and report writing skills are desirable. Engagement of right persons to conduct and oversee the needs assessment will strengthen the quality of study.

Step 4: Obtaining management sponsorship. Adequate financial support in the form of budget allocation, right level of management commitment, espousal and sponsorship is a prerequisite for a successful study. Many TNA studies fail to garner the right level of seriousness within an organization merely reducing it to a ritual leading to poor outcomes attributable to lukewarm reactions of senior management towards the study. Senior leadership must spread the message and support the process which will help significantly.

Step 5: Deploying suitable methods and tools of TNA. The TNA team along with the leader is expected to review all the needs assessment methods and tools in order to identify right ones, keeping in view the nature and goals of the study. Choosing right methodology is important to diagnose and deliver accurate needs report. Incidents of making mistakes in deploying suitable methods and tools are not uncommon. Hence, this process must be well thought out and evaluation of methods needs to be rigorous.

Global Training at Unilever

Unilever's focus on training comes from the belief that all the best practices, ideas, knowledge and skills shall be shared among all the employees of the company globally. The training approach known as 'winning with people' within the company is closely aligned with the company strategy called 'the Compass'. Unilever's training programmes are predominantly global in design and delivery focusing on two key areas. One is skill and task-centric training that is intended to equip employees to perform their roles very well. Functional skill training such as operations, product development methods and general training such as safety and compliances fall in this category. Second type of training is focused on building leadership and behavioural skills such as negotiation and people management skills. While functional and behavioural training is compulsory to all, aimed at continuous upgradation, the leadership development training is need based and tied up with succession planning and potential assessment process. The leadership development programme is titled 'Unilever Future Leaders Programme' (UFLP). Unilever also follows an approach of judiciously mixing on-the-job, off-the-job and e-learning methods. As a part of training, employees are rotated across countries and operations in a systematic manner. For example, in 2014 alone, over 4,000 employees from Southeast Asia were rotated in other countries for periods ranging from 6 months to 12 months.

Step 6: Determining timelines. To ensure steady and timely progress, a TNA study must have milestones and critical steps along with timelines. The study must be treated as a strategic activity and be accorded a status of business priority. Few organizations initiate and treat the study as something desirable but not essential for organizational success and growth. Therefore, the plan of study tends to be liberal and moves at its own pace. This style will not only nullify the purpose of study but also harm the developmental projects. Hence, the study shall be designed with watertight timelines and pursued to its spirit.

Step 7: Rolling out implementation. The TNA team is required to develop a schedule of activities and publish it within the organization well ahead of time. In order to avoid surprises, it is also better to seek feedback on the schedule from key stakeholders or run a pilot to test the plan. Once the phase of feedback/pilot study is complete, the refined schedule must be rolled out with precision and without deviations. This is the most critical step in the entire study because the accuracy of results will be as good as the execution.

Step 8: Collecting data. The implementation of TNA schedule leads to collection of rich primary and secondary data. The data must be maintained diligently and in an organized form preparing it for scientific analysis.

Step 9: Analysis of TNA data. Data collected and organized is subjected to analysis at this phase. Using suitable analytical tools, both quantitative and qualitative, is important and application of these tools must be drawn based on the type and nature of data that was gathered. Incorrect selection/application of tools can lead to wrong analysis; so, it is critical to identify the right tools. Statistical tool like Statistical Package for Social Sciences (SPSS) is relevant in this context.

Step 10: Deriving inferences. Inferences and major themes are drawn in this step based on the analytical findings of the study. These inferences are subjected to qualitative evaluation using a sample representing the unit of study to validate further, in the light of experts' views, and to test the inferences emerging against the alternative data that might exist in an organization.

Step 11: Drawing conclusions and recommendations. Validated analytical results are translated into findings. Conclusions are drawn based on the findings, and recommendations are made in consonance with conclusions and findings of the study. The objectives and goals of TNA study as identified at step 1 of the process are qualified at this step against the backdrop of recommendations.

Mager and Pipe's Performance Analysis-based TNA

Mager and Pipe (1970) had developed a performance analysis flow in 1970 which can be adapted for identifying training needs. This model offers precise or a point solution to locate training needs distinguishing from non-need. This model essentially drives performance optimization by selecting the right solution. The performance analysis model stipulates the following steps:

- Is the problem serious? If not serious, do nothing now but monitor the situation.
- If the problem is serious, identify root cause for the problem. Is this because of lack of knowledge or skill?
- Can the task-causing problem be simplified? If the answer is yes, simplify and provide extra support performance aids.
- If answer to simplification possibility is no, then find out if the task is being carried out correctly. Provide feedback to correct the way of doing if the task is not being carried out correctly.
- Find out whether there is reward for doing the task properly. Is there a punishment for not doing a task properly? If not, install proper reward–punishment process.
- Find out whether there are any environmental or situational constraints causing the problem. If yes, remove these barriers.
- If the problem is not the way the task is organized, is the problem with the skill proficiency? Can people be trained on this?
- If the answer to training is yes, training to handle the task must be organized enabling employees to acquire the skill and practise it.

US Coast Guard Model of TNA

US Coast Guard follows a three-tier training needs analysis model interconnecting individual, group and organization's performance analysis as illustrated here:

- **Tier 1: Investigative analysis.** The study at this tier includes organizational mission, strategy, goals, work, organizational and competitive environment and identifying desired workforce performance standards versus actual state of workforce performance.
- **Tier 2: Root cause analysis.** Deciding whether the gap between desired and actual performance is due to skill deficiency or due to some other problem. Here the study would

involve collecting data pertaining to skills, knowledge, controls, standards, motives, expectations, support, resources, tools and measurement criteria.

- **Tier 3: Intervention selection and design.** In this tier, based on the root cause that was identified in tier 2, appropriate interventions are considered and designed to rectify or improve the situation. The illustrative interventions are introducing or modifying the appraisal systems, career development, coaching, culture change, compensation, documentation, environment, engineering, reengineering, information systems, health/wellness, job aids, job/work design, leadership, organizational design, staffing, supervision, team building, training and education.

Burton and Merrill's Six Needs and Four-phase TNA Model

According to this model which was developed in 1977 by Burton and Merrill, there are six types of training needs and four phases to establish the actual training need causing the gap between desirable and actual performance. These are briefly discussed here:

1. **Normative need:** This occurs when employees fail to meet certain defined standards.
2. **Felt need:** This need refers to what employees perceive as their training need.
3. **Expressed need:** A felt need when not addressed timely and suitably will develop as expressed need, when an employee or group of employees with the same need tend to express in the form of a demand.
4. **Comparative need:** This training need arises when performance of two groups engaged on the same task is very different.
5. **Future need:** An organization's future business plans and goals would lead to new training needs and this is called as anticipated or future training needs.
6. **Critical incident need:** As the name suggests, this need implies to the instances where a significant breakdown or an important operation collapses due to failure to anticipate and correct it. This critical incident often leads to the identification of the skill gap expressed in a training need.

The following four-phase TNA cycle helps in identifying precise training need out of the said six needs:

- **Phase 1: List goals.** Training goals are identified based on the study of organizational performance, functional/departmental performance, existing training courses, interviewing employees, managers and customers, and observing the existing work processes versus benchmark practices.
- **Phase 2: Determine performance levels.** This phase involves study of current performance levels of employees and what efforts are being made to bridge the skill gaps.
- **Phase 3: Map the gaps.** The difference between actual performance and desired performance is mapped keeping in view the data gathered in phases 1 and 2. The data pertaining to gaps study must be measurable and precise, highlighting the performance standards required versus current in various spheres/units of organization, as well as factoring each employee as unit of analysis.
- **Phase 4: Set priorities.** Based on the goals identified in phase 1 and gaps reported in phase 3, priorities must be defined for the training needs. Factors such as implication of a training need to the business performance, magnitude of gap, the number of employees that need to be trained can be considered while arriving at the priorities.

Witkin and Altschuld's Three-phase Training Needs Assessment Model

This model which came into existence in 1995 prescribes three principal phases for an objective TNA study as illustrated next.

- **Phase 1: Pre-assessment.** This phase must drive exploration activities such as defining the purpose, gathering existing data, characterizing the population and determining the data collection methods and sources.
- **Phase 2: Assessment.** This phase is dedicated to implementing the TNA. Activities such as determining sampling strategy, piloting test data gathering instruments, gathering and analysing data and producing the study findings and conclusions are carried out in this phase.
- **Phase 3: Post-assessment.** Once assessment study on the ground is complete, efforts must be made to communicate the results/findings of the study to all important stakeholders. Focus groups may be formed to (a) debate over the issues, (b) identify solutions and (c) develop an action plan for executing solutions to fulfil the gaps arisen due to skill deficiencies. The solution may be development of specific training courses and training suitable number of employees to bridge the skill gap.

Rothwell and Kazanas's Five-phase Training Needs Assessment Model

This model which is comprehensive in its approach stipulates a precondition of answering certain questions before launching TNA study such as: What is the current situation? What is the ideal? How important is the gap? What solutions are appropriate? What collateral damage the corrective action may create? The five phases are:

- **Phase 1: Establish purpose of needs assessment.** The purpose must arise from detecting a performance problem. The objectives definition must include how and what benefits the objective achievement will offer to resolve the performance issue.
- **Phase 2: Identify the target audience and select a sample group.** This is the process of identifying the universe of the needs assessments study and finalizing the sample from within.
- **Phase 3: Select data collection methods and prepare instruments.** There are different data collection methods and instruments which can be deployed based on the purpose and nature of study. Organizations can develop tailor-made data collection instruments or use a readily available instrument. Reliability and validity of instruments assumes importance in this process.
- **Phase 4: Determine the methods of data analysis:** Tools and techniques that are required to be used to analyse data must be identified. Usually, the nature of data collected and organized and data collection methods used would lead to identifying right data analysis methods and tools. It is advisable to run pilot analysis on the methods of analysis as well as on tools before large-scale deployment.
- **Phase 5: Assess the feasibility of the needs assessment plan:** This is the most critical phase that occurs just before launch of the needs assessment study. It involves checking: whether resources are adequate to implement the study; whether the needs assessment plan and method suit the organizational context; whether there is a right team in place to conduct the study; is the time apt for launching the study.

Kaufman's Organizational Elements Model of Training Needs Assessment

Kaufman's (2013) model known as Organizational Elements Model (OEM) separates means from the ends during the TNA consisting of five systems: (a) inputs, (b) processes representing means of organizational efforts, (c) products, (d) outputs and (e) outcomes. These are briefly discussed here.

- Inputs system involves studying the resources required for an organization such as raw material, resources to achieve organizational ends and gaps identification.
- Processes system study focuses on applying methods and approaches employed in an organization as a means to achieve the organizational ends and gaps identification.
- Products system focuses on what an organization is producing at each level and what are the results and the gaps constraining desired performance.
- Outputs system study is dedicated to analyse the organizational accomplishments, aggregated products, portfolio and impact of these on customers and what gaps exist.
- Outcome system study involves identifying the outcomes for customers of an organization: whether products and services delivered by an organization are able to meet expectations of customers and whether organization's results address the needs of all stakeholders and performance gaps that exist.

The first two address the means and remaining three systems are focused on ends.

Harless Front-end Analysis Model of TNA

In 1987, Harless proposed a front-end analysis model that helps not only in identifying training needs and skill gaps but also in building competencies and improving productivity through two methods discussed below:

- **Diagnostic front-end analysis:** Diagnosis is taken up to identify the exact reason for non-performance or what is known in the model as goal deficit. Diagnosis initiative comprises of several actions: defining the general problem in terms of what business or performance goals are not being met; defining the root performance deficit by comparing a poor performance with exceptional performance; determining the root cause for the performance gap in terms of skills and knowledge issues, situational causes and determine the solution describing the probable effects on the performance after rectification/improvement and cost estimates.
- **New performance front-end analysis:** This step enables to experience the effect of new performance hypothetically when a performance gap is identified and a solution is developed to address the issue through a series of actions such as: defining the new performance areas by answering questions such as what performance standards to be achieved and what new work behaviours are expected to emerge, defining the new interventions to be developed and implemented, contributing to realizing new performances and planning the design and roll-out of each intervention.

The other front-end analysis models which can be referred in this context would include Gordon's Front-end analysis model and Gilbert's Behavioral Engineering Performance Matrix.

Rummler and Brache Process Relationship Model of TNA

According to the authors, the process relationship model is a picture of the input/output relationships between the major work processes in an organization. This model helps in training needs analysis from a perspective of looking at processes more than at people to fix the performance gap. The premise of this model is that even a good performer tends to show poor performance if the processes are not designed or applied properly or both. This situation can constrain the functional relationship between inputs and outputs. The authors have also developed many tools which can help organizations self-drive the process improvement initiatives. The methodology of this model is strong which can be applied to training needs analysis. The methodology consists of six phases as described next.

- **Phase 0: Performance planning.** Performance metrics/standards are identified at this stage.
- **Phase 1: Project definition.** The existing performance level is compared with ideal benchmarks to identify gap and build the objective.
- **Phase 2: Process analysis and design.** The processes associated with the performance area/units are analysed and improvement areas are identified. The new processes are designed and tested.
- **Phase 3: Implementation and change.** This is the most critical phase in process relationship model. The newly designed processes are rolled out.
- **Phase 4: Performance management.** The performance goals as set during the planning phase are validated against the actual results and the performance of new processes is managed.
- **Phase 5: Managing the organization as an adaptive system.** The model advocates transforming an organization as an adaptive system with a process relationship model for better business results and emphasizes that process improvement is a continuous process and therefore an organization must be adaptive to change all the time.

Stage 2: Design of Training Courses

The first question is: whether training management is different in an international organizational set-up as compared to a domestic organizational set-up. The answer is yes and no. The curriculum and contents can be same, while the methodology and case studies can be different to address international profile of employees. Further, there will be pressure on international organizations to adopt same curriculum and standards across the countries to ensure uniformity, though the practice of pushing outdated technologies to developing countries exists, albeit this is on decline progressively. International organizations have the scale, depth and reach to build and elevate training to all operations. However, the alternative argument is although the course design and curriculum shall be uniform across the countries, at same time the content must include the local factors as much as possible, since realities can be different in few disciplines.

Instructional Design Models

Once TNA is done successfully, the sequential activity is to design a training course based on the findings of such study. The design of a training system or course is mainly drawn from the nature of training need, audience and type of the course to be imparted. The instructional design method assumes significance since it has profound bearing on actual imparting of skill in order to fill the performance gaps that exist. There are various instructional design models (IDMs) contributed by experts in different disciplines and contexts which can be adapted in tandem with an organization's requirement. Few prominent models are discussed further.

ADDIE Instructional Model

ADDIE is an instructional design model which is well acknowledged and adopted by instructional designers and trainers worldwide. This model consists of five phases with each one of these producing tangle outcomes as discussed below:

- **Analysis phase:** This is the first stage in building a training system which helps in identifying and developing: instructional problems, instructional goals, learning logistics, existing knowledge and skills, and gaps. Data is collected on important aspects such as: Who is the audience? What are their expectations? What are the key characteristics and background of the audience? What is the success criteria, effectiveness measurement? What are the learning constraints likely to exist and occur? What are the delivery options? Which are the appropriate pedagogical methods for the nature of subject to be imparted? And what are timelines for project completion?

- **Design phase:** Successful execution of first phase (analysis) yields rich information that helps design a state-of-the-art training system. During this phase, curriculum and case studies are developed and pilot tested. An integrative method is adopted to create a well-connected programme rather than disjointed capsules that are commonly seen as point solution initiatives. The preliminary design is improved based on the feedback received during pilot testing. Standard steps applied here are documentation of instructional, visual and technical design strategy, determination of instructional design keeping in view the expected behavioural outcomes such as cognitive, affective and psychomotor, creation of case studies and storyboards, design of user interface and user experience, prototype creation and application of graphic design capturing the concept. Towards the end of this phase, a meaningful training system is seen in a conceptual/planning form.

- **Development phase:** In many instances, design of curriculum and instructional tools are spread into several areas ending up with myriad components. This phase is dedicated to assemble all the components to create a well-integrated and comprehensive training system or a course. Once again, the entire assembled model is tested and improved based on the feedback.

- **Execution phase:** This phase begins with training of faculty and coaches on the curriculum (train the trainer), teaching methodologies, instructional tools, method of delivery, testing procedures and outcomes expected from the training course. Selection of audience/ attendees and their registration, logistics, infrastructure and courseware, both digital and manual, are readied. The course is rolled out as per the plan that is frozen during development phase without deviation and for the length of time it was conceived.

- **Evaluation phase:** This is the most critical phase since it has the potential to reveal the efficacy of all the effort. The model prescribes two types of evaluation—one is called formative evaluation and the other summative evaluation. Formative evaluation is used to evaluate the effectiveness of the imparting of a course at each meaningful stage, more like assessment of transfer of learning or evaluating at the completion of each components delivery. Summative evaluation refers to evaluating the effectiveness of the course from users' and recipients' points of view with tangible evidence. The phase also is deployed to check whether course goals and objectives set at analysis and design phase are met.

Five Steps in International Leadership Development

Leadership training and development, an important element in international training management, is strategic to global corporations. Corporate Leadership Council which is acclaimed for its leadership development research and insights stipulates five steps in building a world-class leadership training programme as illustrated below:

1. Senior leadership commitment and direct participation of senior leadership in training
2. On-the-job experience training modules
3. A professional network initiative that facilitates contacts of leaders regardless of formal working relationship/hierarchy
4. Practice of setting stretch goals for good performers
5. Engagement of leaders with high potentials on regular basis

Dick and Carey Model

The nine-step training system approach model which was developed way back in 1978, by Walter Dick, Lou Carey and James Carey is by far the most popular and widely practised as benchmark instructional design framework in global organizations. This model particularly accords a comprehensive treatment to training system recognizing the need to integrate course objectives, course curriculum, learning methodology, instructional behaviour of coaches and learning behaviour of trainees. In a nutshell, the model focuses on creating entire training ecosystem by following a nine-step approach as described here. The model which was basically crafted to address the needs of e-learning systems can also be extended to all types of training systems because it is rational and sequential.

Step 1: Identifying goals and objectives. What a course intends to deliver to benefit organizations, or to a process or bridging a skill gap must be clear to all—trainers, trainees, course designers, training administrators and recipient managers. Trainee must be able to apply the skill in real world once the virtual training is complete.

Step 2: Analysing instructional needs. The learning needs of each participant/trainee or a group of participants should be mapped clearly for effective delivery of course. Hence, the skill gaps or existing skill proficiency of participants must be analysed and the information obtained is expected to be fed into course design and delivery plan. Often, training courses fail to accomplish the objectives due to variations of learning behaviours and neglect in factoring existing skill status of trainees forcing the training course to meet lowest denominator.

Step 3: Determining entry criteria. Entry criteria determination can happen in two parts—first, based on course objectives and instructional needs, the entry standards must be arrived at. Entry standards in turn need to be translated into assessment tools. Second part is meant towards understanding trainee behaviours and their characteristics for baking them into the instructional design. Course design, courseware and instructional methodology that are not well connected with the audience will not succeed to deliver identified goals. Weak entry criteria are one of leading factors for training ineffectiveness.

Step 4: Deciding success criteria. What is intended to achieve by imparting a skill ultimately is crucial. Sometimes training system may be successful in imparting the skill which can be applied in real-life work setting the way it was envisaged but it may fall short of creating a tangible benefit to organizations. Therefore, what a skill is intended to deliver in terms of business value must be addressed. A skill imparted is a means to achieve a business goal and therefore should not be an end in itself. Business value goals can be converted into milestones for gauging performance of a training system or a training course.

Step 5: Developing criterion-referenced learning assessments. Strengths and weaknesses of instruction design, courseware, tools and overall progress against the criteria set must be assessed at regular intervals for mid-course correction. No matter how stringently a pilot test was done before roll-out, the actual delivery of courses always spring surprises. Since this assessment is done for each component of the overall training system, it provides precision.

Step 6: Creating instructional learning strategy. Based on steps 1 to 5, an instructional strategy is developed during this step. Information obtained on variety of factors provides an opportunity to build a learning strategy that is comprehensive, purposeful and meaningful. The learning strategy as developed can be validated against existing well-established learning models as a final checkpoint.

Step 7: Selecting course material and online medium. Based on audience preferences and learning effectiveness, mode of course material and exercises should be selected. Range of course material aids includes multimedia-based instructional kits, online tutorials, personal coaching episodes and interactive lessons. This is an important component of the training system because it is the course material that creates sustainable learning. Course material both in terms of content and form must be created not only keeping in view preferences of trainees but also to act as the best carrier of skill imparting.

Step 8: Applying formative evaluation. This evaluation can be applied before deploying the training courses on a large scale covering wide audience. In the first phase, a course must be conducted with all its features on a focus group and feedback must be sought at different levels including creation of actual value. In line with the feedback, actions can be undertaken to carry out the final corrections to make the course free from any flaws.

Step 9: Applying summative evaluation. This is the final evaluation which occurs on completion of roll-out of training system or a particular course on a large scale. This is the test of efficacy. Whether training system is able to create business value and whether it is able to meet the training objectives and goals set at the beginning of the exercise are determined at this step. Even though the summative assessment happens towards end, this can still be carried out at various levels such as transfer of learning to workplace, trainees' reactions and feedback, trainees' performance in tests and examinations, and feedback from managers of trainees, coaches, course designers and implementers. Data that is generated from all these sources is consolidated and validated against each other in order to draw summative evaluation report.

Training Course Design at Motorola

Motorola has adapted a five-step approach to build high-quality training courses which are also centred on the company quality initiatives. These are:

1. **Statistical quality control:** The concept of Six Sigma originated from Motorola though it was popularized by GE. Motorola not only applied this methodology in training design but also made sure that each and every training course designed at Motorola University invariably covered training on seven quality tools.
2. **Basic industrial problem-solving:** All courses are designed keeping in view the problem-solving approach/methodology that are in existence in the basic industrial problem-solving system.

3. **Case study presentations:** Every course design should consist of presentations by trainees since it is strongly believed that making practical sense of concepts is possible through this approach. This is an integral part of course material at Motorola, where workers were asked to read through concepts and make presentations to their supervisors applying the said concepts at the shop floor.
4. **Effective meetings:** All courses consist of a chapter on how to conduct effective meetings that emphasize the role of all participants of a meeting and how meetings must be progressed to attain the core objectives.
5. **Goal-setting:** The approach of setting goals and defining objectives, measuring them and providing feedback is also a compulsory part of training course design.

ASSURE Model of Instructional Design

ASSURE is an acronym that refers to various steps involved in building an effective learning system. Even though the model appears simple, it has valuable practical insights particularly with rigour in its sequence. The steps are discussed here:

Analyse learners: As the title suggests, the first step in building a scientific training system is to understand the learners' behaviours, learning styles, aspirations, goals and capabilities. A training system however perfect it may be, if it exists in isolation and is not aligned with attributes of learners will not succeed. This step helps in bridging that gap and also to build tailor-made learning solutions.

State standards and objectives: Learners data thus collected in the first step is used to build the course's standards and objectives. The model stipulates ABCD framework to accomplish the task of setting standards and objectives. A stands for audience: for whom is the objective intended? B for behaviour: what is the performance or behaviour to be demonstrated? C for conditions: what are the conditions under which the behaviour or performance will be observed? D for degree: To what degree will the knowledge or skill be mastered?

Select strategies, technology, media and materials: Selecting right learning delivery methodology and tools is the key for effectiveness of training system. What technology or medium and materials are to be used will be totally dependent upon the learning styles data of audience. Unless there is complete agreement between audience/trainees attributes and training methodologies and curriculum, the model will fall short of meeting course objectives. Data available from analysis of various international courses and training programmes reveal that many times use of inappropriate instruction methodology and tools is the root cause for training not delivering the right value. Organizations and training managers tend to spend enormous amount of time in audience selection criteria and courseware development and less time in designing teaching techniques with the aid of technology and media. Using interactive media where not required and not using when required can deprive learning excitement.

Utilize technology, media and material: This step emphasizes the deployment sensitivities of the previous step. The model exhorts us to follow five Ps in this context:

- **Preview the technology, media and materials:** Organizing tools and material well in advance, subjecting them to dry run before they are actually rolled out is critical in ensuring good standards.
- **Prepare the technology, media and materials:** This is sequential step and meant to ensure that all the tools are up and running and there is alignment among all the tools and materials.

- **Prepare the environment:** Making sure that classroom setting and infrastructure is in order, suiting the course design and ensuring there is no noise or interfering factors in smooth delivery of course.
- **Prepare the learners:** Before commencement of actual course, trainees should be informed about the course objectives and performance criteria.
- **Provide the learning experience:** Carrying out the implementation of the course and observing every step of instruction carefully.

Require learner participation: Participation of trainees is as important as the role of coaches in delivery of a training course. Sometimes, this is possible through teaching methodologies and tools such as case studies, exercises, group discussion, solving puzzles, presentations, debates and simulations. It needs to be decided beforehand which elements of the course will be subjected to greater interaction and dialogue with the reason for it. Trainee participation during imparting the training course is vital in adult education and any attempt to make it solo or a one-sided lecture tends to breed learning boredom. However, if not planned and implemented properly, trainee participation can lead to distortion in actual learning of the skill.

Evaluate and revise: The final step in the model is evaluation of all components together as well as on stand-alone basis to establish whether they are successful in meeting the training objectives—has the trainee acquired the skills? Was the coaching effective? Has the courseware helped in acquiring skill? Was the coaching methodology appropriate? In all, if the trainees on qualifying are able to perform the task efficiently in real work life? Is there a scope to improve? Based on answers to all these questions and on testing reliability of analysis, the findings must be leveraged for revising the training system by restarting from the step 1 of the model.

Backward Design Model

Wiggins and McTighe (2011) had proposed the backward design model in 2005 in their widely acclaimed book *Understanding by Design*. The basic argument of the model is twofold; one is 'how' something is taught is more important than 'what' is taught in a training course. However, this argument has been widely criticized because course design or teaching methodology or style of coaching is merely a means and not substitute to the course itself and therefore thinking that the means (of delivery) is more important than the need (end) is misplaced. The second factor is it looks at the training system from a reverse perspective compared to typical IDMs (content first and methodology later) by highlighting that methodology dominantly decides what is and what can be imparted rather than content determining the design of methodology. Backward design model is made of three phases as illustrated below:

Phase 1: Identify desired results (big ideas and skills). what trainees should learn and acquire is expected to define the entire design. The cognitive learning map needs to be built based on the desired results, and coaches are ought to build a taxonomy that guides the trainees through learning sequence and process. The model exhorts that learning design must consider few sub-goals such as:

- *Remember:* Ability to refer to historical knowledge and evolution skill techniques as and when required.
- *Understand:* Ability to grasp context, interpret, classify, associate, summarize and construct meaning.

- *Apply:* Ability to apply knowledge thus acquired at workplace to produce/perform the task or in problem-solving real time.
- *Analyse:* Ability to organize, differentiate and attribute and see through the pattern leading to predictability.
- *Evaluate:* Ability to build opinion, judge, reason and critique.
- *Create:* Ability to build big idea, innovate and produce new knowledge to the existing body of knowledge.

Global Digital Libraries

Physical library is becoming obsolete fast worldwide as all publishers increasingly opt for e-publications. Digital libraries are growing rapidly than many have anticipated due to cost advantages, avoidance of shipping problems apart from many qualitative advantages. This is a major booster for international training practice. In all probability, the number of libraries across the globe will be less than 5 per cent of today's number in a decade. Some of the key trends are:

- In the United States, 95 per cent of all libraries have an e-book collection.
- Libraries such as 3 M Cloud Library, Baker & Taylor, Hoopla and OverDrive are gaining fast traction.
- The numbers of digital loans are growing rapidly with an estimated 12 per cent growth per annum.
- A new trend of audiobooks is gaining popularity with companies like 'Audible' releasing over 35,000 audiobooks in 2014 alone. The global audiobook industry is worth almost USD 3 billion with *The New York Times* predicting the growth of audiobooks outstripping e-books.
- Libraries worldwide are expected to forgo print books/CDs altogether to embrace digital 100 per cent.
- Obsession with the present drives people to endorse digital libraries.

Though the trend of digital libraries is real for global corporations and it can augment the efforts of internationalizing training function, some experts believe that given Internet access only to 35 per cent of world's population, pursuing digital libraries at the cost of conventional libraries can be an elitist approach nullifying the principle of equal opportunity.

This phase also must address questions such as: What must the students be fundamentally familiar with? What is important to know and what could be optional or supplementary or trendy? What should be the enduring and sustainable knowledge and skill that a trainee necessarily possesses? Answers to these questions can become a rich source for building courseware leading to producing desired results.

Phase 2: Determine appropriate criteria for evaluating trainee's progress. This phase is meant for designing an evaluation system and criteria for both: (a) ongoing evaluation to gauge real-time progress towards the desired learning outcomes and (b) final evaluation towards end of the course to measure whether trainee has acquired the skill for deploying it in real-life work. Further, the evaluation criteria can also cover two types of evaluations—one is direct assessment to test the core content and subject knowledge thus imparted and the other is testing latent skills such as diagnosis of an issue, analysing and problem-solving approach because any course is meant to build both core and application-driven skills. The criteria should be drawn from the nature of course and type of skills the course is expected to impart. Lack of reliability of evaluation criteria will render training course ineffective and invalid. The scientific evaluation criteria are ones which not only help in assessment to establish training effectiveness and proficiency of skill but also can be leveraged as milestones to gauge progress and guide trainees and coaches.

Phase 3: Plan the instructional methodology and learning experience. The final step in designing a course is planning the most appropriate instructional methodology keeping in view the nature of course in order to enhance the learning experience. This is at the core of backward design model. The model strongly argues that if the methodology is not exciting enough for trainees, the course will fail to impart the skill regardless of richness of the course design and content. In contrast, a good course methodology not only enhances experience of trainees but gives a fillip to acquire skill proficiency more than what was anticipated. The difference between a best course and mediocre course is not in its course content, which is generally accessible, but the way it is imparted making it unique and creating all the difference between well-taught institutes and the not so good. Though there are various techniques that are employed in design of methodology, the thumb rule is that all these techniques must be followed by interactive experience.

Morrison, Ross and Kemp Model

This is a non-linear instruction design model comprising of nine interrelated components. This is also popularly known as circular model that is blended with approaches from multiple disciplines. The model allows significant flexibility to course designers because they can start from any of the nine components, and the components are neither sequential nor orderly but appear random yet are powerfully interconnected and interdependent. It is also not a must that the course designer is ought to follow all the components but can chose those relevant for building the course and can approach all the components if required simultaneously. The component-wise work can also be improvised, while other components are at different stages of evolution. The nine core components are:

1. Determine the specific goals and purpose of a training course or training system. In relation to achievement of the goals set, identify the potential instructional design challenges. This would involve understanding skill/subject knowledge requirements of trainees in order to perform a task/job.
2. Understand behavioural/learning attributes of trainees and their learning styles/ preferences which will be critical information for designing the training course.
3. Define course content and analyse the proposed task components in relation to the stated goals and purposes of the training course. Design of the course content must also reckon the learners existing capabilities.
4. Define instructional objectives and desired learning outcomes. It largely depends upon the nature of skill/knowledge to be imparted and the proficiency level.
5. Ensure that content for each instructional unit is structured sequentially and logically to facilitate learning. Human mind tends to receive a subject matter/content effectively that is well organized and meaningfully arranged but tends to create a burden on the learner and causes learning distortions if the content set-up is fluid.
6. Design instructional approaches and methods enabling individual as well as group of trainees to master the subject and achieve desired learning outcomes.
7. Plan the instructional message and the appropriate mode of delivery that is apt for the learning style of trainees and teaching mode of coaches.

8. Develop evaluation instruments suitable for measuring and assessing learners' progress towards achieving course objectives. This should preferably be a continuous process rather than a step process for real-time gauging of learning progress.

9. Choose the suitable complimentary resources that will facilitate both teaching and learning activities.

Gerlach and Ely Design Model

This IDM founded by Vernom Gerlach and Donald Ely way back in 1971 is time tested and suitable to media-rich instructional methods as well as classroom situations and can cater to both advanced skill training as well as in imparting fundamental concepts. The model basically focuses on two broad elements: the first is related to training goals and second pertains to training methodologies. These two elements are achieved through the following 10 steps: (a) specification of content, (b) specification of objectives, (c) assessment of entering behaviours, (d) determination of strategy, (e) organization of groups, (f) allocation of time, (g) allocation of space, (h) selection of resources, (i) evaluation of performance and (j) analysis of feedback.

Stage 3: Implementation of Training Courses

The logical step when a training course design is complete is planning, preparing and rolling out the course to the target audience. Often, this is the most crucial stage since the manner in which implementation is carried out has significant bearing on the effectiveness of the course. Meticulous preparation and arrangements are must for a professional start. Empirical data reveals that there are enough instances where organizations have failed to translate the objectives into reality due to gaps in execution which is particularly evident in roll-out of international training courses. Some of the common pitfalls are:

1. **Audience mix:** A training course delivery is as good as the quality and suitability of audience. A training programme which was designed keeping in view a particular audience/trainee group if extended to a different group or to a mix of relevant and not relevant, then participants will result in mixed feedback. A training course is designed based on a premise of familiarity, a pre-knowledge/preparation and certain standards as well as relevance of the trainees. It is essential to define criteria for selection of audience and adhere to it.

2. **Faculty standards:** Faculty must be trained and coached on the specific topic of the course. A common mistake is choosing a faculty who is good in that particular discipline but not necessarily proficient on the specific topic. Mere knowledge of a topic/skill is not adequate to impart the skill to others but intensive understating of nuances in application of the skill is equally important.

3. **Pre-course engagement:** Studies and experiences with implementation of training courses point out that lack of pre-course engagement particularly with newly launched courses causes (a) unrealistic expectations from the course by the trainees, (b) delay in progress of the course delivery due to absence of preparation from trainees side and (c) loss of precious time in the initial phase of training course implementation by engaging in socialization and with the process of setting context. Therefore, the implementation plan must factor pre-engagement schedule to warm up the training course administrators,

trainees and faculty which will contribute to the success of a training course. A good communication involving all the players and a well-designed connect programme is highly desirable.

4. **Infrastructure arrangements:** Implementing a training course globally calls for a different level of planning and preparation. Aspects such as time zones, electronic media set-up, digital equipment, virtual classrooms as well as physical classroom facilities, course material delivery should be monitored closely while ensuring they function properly, failing in which the course delivery will get adversely impacted threatening the very objective of training course roll-out. Technical malfunction has been noticed as the most common occurrence so training administrators must pay special attention to this challenge.

5. **Ongoing feedback and mid-course actions:** While it is customary to obtain feedback from the participants and faculty towards end of a training course roll-out, this only helps in analysing the pitfalls and identifying positive elements but does not present an opportunity for mid-course corrections. Implementing a training course in classroom in a conventional way can accommodate feedback at the end, because it would be difficult to validate the feedback applicability universally, since the feedback comprises experience of a small sample. This situation is qualitatively different in rolling out a training course globally in international organizations because it has the potential to host a large number of participants running into hundreds and thousands. Therefore, applying a conventional feedback system to the new era of electronic and virtual class-centric training course can lead to heavy dilution of the implementation rigour. Hence, it is mandatory for international training course administrators to create an in-built ongoing feedback system to tap the experiences, suggestions and critique in real time. The feedback that is obtained must be analysed, validated, inferences drawn and should be actioned without loss of time so the course effectiveness can be enhanced manifold.

6. **Coordination/integration mechanisms:** Cross-functional teams such as communication, administration, IT/electronic equipment department, information service department, content creators, course administrators, faculty, trainees and managers of an organization are typical players in roll-out of a training course. The role, priorities and eagerness of different players can create coordination and integration challenges. Hence, this should be sorted out upfront and clarity of who will play what role and the extent must be defined, removing all ambiguities. There must be a designated programme director for each course roll-out who is authorized to take all decisions keeping course objectives in mind.

7. **Cultural sensitivity:** Keeping in view and factoring cultural sensitivities assumes greater importance in international roll-out of courses. The introduction of courses, medium of instruction, symbols, examples and case studies used in the course delivery must reflect local scenario as much as possible. Even if international examples and case studies are used, caution must be exercised to avoid gathering these instances from a single country or culture as it may ultimately lead to perceiving domination or imposing of a particular social fabric.

8. **Piloting:** Piloting roll-out of a course on a controlled experiment group is highly recommended in case of complex course structures and curriculum. The complexity of the courses can lead to certain level of ambiguity or difficulty in acquiring the knowledge and skills so it is beneficial to run a pilot which can provide first-hand insights into what needs modification or improvement and what needs to be eliminated or included into the course. Administrators of international training need to keep in mind that online training and

virtual classes leave no time and room to retract from something that ought to not have been there. Therefore, adoption of pilot studies is a good strategy in the circumstances as described.

9. **Big bang versus gradual:** If training is expected to cover few thousands of employees, for example, in a large international organization with operations in several nations, then they may evaluate a big bang launch versus gradual implementation of training course depending on merits of each situation. Sustainability and rigour is more important than hype for establishing credibility of a training course.

10. **End of a training course:** A training course roll-out must consider winding up on a positive note and providing summary of the course background, key learnings and how these learnings have led to acquisition of skills to bridge the performance gaps. Essentially this enables trainees to see the skills they have acquired from an application and real work setting perspective.

Stage 4: Evaluation of International Training

Measuring effectiveness of training and evaluation of ROI is an important step in establishing international training as a distinct function in organizations. There are also many advantages in evaluating a training that includes the following: (a) appropriateness of training courses, pedagogy, selection and assessment criteria can be tested and actions can be taken to improvise, (b) contribution of training to business growth in revenue, margins and to some extent market capitalization can be established, (c) contribution of training towards improvement of products, processes and operational efficiencies can be studied and inferences drawn, (d) budget allocation and investments in training can be substantiated and (e) the overall confidence in training function can be enhanced. In the absence of a timely evaluation programme, training function tends to receive sceptic reactions on its efficacy and contribution and the overall function tends to become subdued in an organizational set-up. Therefore, international organizations must make evaluation on integral part of business performance appraisal. However, evaluation process is time-consuming and a one-size-fits-all approach does not work. Each organization may have to develop its own training evaluation model and also different evaluation models for different training courses depending on the nature and length of these courses. Training evaluation models should be validated before any executive action is taken on findings/inferences drawn out of such evaluation projects. Clive Shepherd (2011) of Fast Track Consulting, UK, suggests that the following costs must be factored in order to build ROI model commonly known as the process of calculating ROI while factoring savings on account of labour, productivity and revenue due to improved innovation:

- **Design and development costs:** This item of costs must include days of time spent by internal training staff to design the course, methodology and content, costs incurred on hiring from outside and any material or tools sourced from outside market on commercial payment.
- **Promotion costs:** All direct and indirect costs incurred to publicize and create awareness of training courses (marketing design and campaign) must be factored. Often internal or external marketing teams work on this assignment so these costs need to be accounted to arrive at promotional costs.

- **Administration costs:** Costs associated with enrolling trainees, selection administration-testing and selecting of trainees and days of wages of administrative staff equivalent to time spent on admissions, actual conduct, coordination and facility management.
- **Faculty costs:** Faculty salaries, expenses and all other incidental costs associated with design, delivery and assessment of training courses and proportionate infrastructure/overhead costs to look after faculty and their assistance. Many times, there would be a visiting faculty for internal and external courses so that cost needs to be included as well.
- **Trainee costs:** Salaries of trainees undergoing the course, replacement costs and hours spent prior to commencement of training for enrolling and preparing for training and trainee turnover costs.
- **Material and tools:** Course material and tools obtained that include simulators and software costs, excluding capex costs.
- **Facilities:** These include capex costs including all infrastructure—classrooms, labs, hardware, robots, simulators and operating costs—aligned to managing facilities such as electricity, air-conditioning and transport.
- **Leadership costs:** Time spent by leaders in debating and deciding the training courses and resources spent in evaluating various proposals including the exercise of training evaluation and its costs are to be factored in the cost model.

It is also pertinent to measure monetary benefits accrued on account of training apart from the costs as discussed before:

- **Labour savings:** Training often results in improved operational efficiencies and optimization of manpower. A well-trained staff can reduce requirement of number of people engaged in a task/operation. Estimates indicate this saving of manpower can be anywhere from a minimum of 20 per cent to a maximum of 50 per cent of the existing strength. Opportunities to eliminate surplus engagement of labour shall be identified and redeployment can be taken up. This in turn will lead to significant savings of labour costs which can be attributed to training.
- **Saving of operational/production/service support costs:** A well-trained staff not only tends to be efficient but can be highly productive and find new ways of working thus contributing to enhancement of service quality, operational precision and enhancement of production rate. These positives contribute towards a substantial monetary gain for companies and if properly evaluated and measured, this can be accounted against training initiatives.
- **Innovation and reengineering:** There are case studies and empirical data supporting the argument that good training and application of post-training skills contribute to growth of innovation rate and reengineering of work methodologies. Companies such as Toyota and Canon have cited enough examples on how training has led to development of new products and continuous improvement of not only production systems but also various components of automobiles and the evolution of digitalization of its camera product range, as quoted by Canon.
- **Non-monetary benefits:** Training also leads to a number of non-monetary benefits such as improved morale of workforce, job satisfaction, low employee turnover and growth of human capital/talent. However, it is difficult to translate these befits in quantitative terms.

Kirkpatrick Learning Evaluation Model

A well-acclaimed model for evaluation of training, this is known as four levels of training evaluation model. Donald Kirkpatrick (1994) has developed four levels to establish efficacy of training course from both trainee and organizations points of view. The four levels are:

Reaction evaluation (level 1): What is the response of trainees for a training course? What are they appreciative of? What they are critical of? Did they enjoy attending the course and felt excited or not? How do coaches perceive the entire experience of imparting course to trainees? How was the engagement of trainees with the course while being delivered such as asking questions/seeking clarifications/voicing opinions/views/debating? The model says that though a delighted experience may not necessarily indicate effectiveness of a training course in meeting its objectives, a cynical reaction or disappointment of trainees would definitely signal that training was ineffective. Data collection techniques such as questionnaire-based feedback from trainees on various items of training course can be obtained towards end of the course, verbal feedback, smile sheets, comments and online assessments of reactions are also useful to understand trainees' reactions towards a training course. The data thus obtained must be analysed and inferences drawn for betterment of a training course.

Learning evaluation (level 2): Evaluation of a training course at this level is primarily focused on whether trainees have actually learned the skills and knowledge that the course intended to impart or not. Is there a positive change in skill proficiency post training participation? Do the trainees feel more confident with their skill set now? What trainees could not learn and why? Evaluation of a training course at this stage is very challenging since mere paper-based testing of skills of trainees cannot be a conclusive evidence to establish success. Therefore, a combination of evaluation tools needs to be deployed to measure success of a training course which can include interview of trainees, practical demonstrations, assignments, comparing pre- and post-training scores of trainees, comparing scores of control group versus experiment group, post-course examinations and observations by peers and instructors. The evaluation framework must follow the course objectives set at the beginning of the course or during the design phase as trying to evaluate effectiveness of a course different from original objectives can be misleading.

Transfer evaluation (level 3): This evaluation can ideally take place after about six months from the completion of a training course. Testing actual use of skills and knowledge by the participants at workplace is done at this level of evaluation. Sometimes, trainees conceptually or in a simulated setting might demonstrate the skill proficiency successfully but may not be successful in actually transferring the acquired skills to solve a problem or fix a solution in real-life work setting. Evaluation at this stage is very complex because many a times it takes few trials and attempts for trainees to apply the skill in a perfect manner and attempting to evaluate prematurely cannot provide reliable results. Therefore, time of carrying out this evaluation holds significance for obtaining valid data. Tools such as observations by neutral experts, performance appraisal, written self-reporting, written supervisor assessment, observations of peers and a 360-degree type feedback and surveys can be used to carry out the transfer of skill/learning evaluation. In brief, this tests if a positive skill behaviour change has occurred or not.

Results evaluation (level 4): This is fundamental and final form of evaluation that can establish conclusively whether objectives of implementing training course have been achieved or not. The assessment is basically done to understand what the business gains out of a training course? Has the productivity increased? Have costs of production come down? Is the quality of produce better post-training? Has the organizational performance or performance of a department/function improved? Are there fewer accidents? Is there a lesser defect occurrence? Improved customer satisfaction? Better solution building? Better profits? Data must be collected during pre- and post-training periods on exact parameters that are reliable enough to get to the truth in consultation with trainees and coaches of the training course. Data collection tools can be selected based on type of parameters of evaluation.

Facebook's Five Leadership Competencies

1. **Passion:** Zuckerberg says, 'Find that thing you are super passionate about.' The mission statement of Facebook is 'to give people the power to share and make the world more open and connected'. Facebook promotes employees to find their passion rather merely fulfilling a job requirement/expectation. When you are passionate, you see failure as a learning opportunity and if you are not, you see a failure as a stumbling block! Perseverance is considered as key to nurture the passion.
2. **Purpose:** Every great institution is fuelled by its purpose. The purpose guides all actions; it is at the root of all ideas and functions as centrifugal force. Facebook is not just a social networking site, it is a way of staying in touch with people around the world, a place to bring people together and build communities and a tool for sharing information. Leaders at Facebook are expected to keep purpose on their mind all the time.
3. **People:** Inspiring people is the kingpin of Facebook's leadership competencies. At Facebook, leaders' role in managing people is not merely setting goals and appraising and rewarding them but inspiring them, encouraging them to find their passion and motivating them to innovate hitherto not existing or challenging the status quo. In Zuckerberg's language, 'I think as a company, if you can get those two things right: having a clear direction on what you are trying to do and bringing in great people who can execute on the stuff—then you can do pretty well.'
4. **Product:** Facebook strongly believes that leaders must nurture innovation, they need to stand as examples and every innovation is meant to further the goal accomplishment of simplifying products and services. Mark Zuckerberg says that 'The Hacker way is an approach that helps in building a culture of continuous improvement.' Hackers' view that nothing is ever complete and always there is a defect and therefore there is a scope for improvement.
5. **Partnerships:** This refers to power of teams and teamwork. Facebook espouses a management value that no one person can or ever will be able to do everything in order to run a company and grow a company. It is teamwork and therefore team sport is a key competency of leadership. Great leaders recognize their weaknesses as much as their strengths and bring the right people in to form partnerships that drive success.

Stage 5: Renewal of Training System

Comprehensive review and renewal of a training system is an ultimate action in managing international training system. The findings of a training system or a training course evaluation create a path for review and renewal of action. However, the evaluation or assessment of a training course is mostly done from the angle of ROI and whether a training met its objectives or not rather than whether the training in its existing status will be able to cater to the new business and employee paradigm or not. The renewal phase helps in answering that question. The renewal action may lead to scrapping of a training system or a course altogether or making modifications and updating despite the fact that the existing course has met its objectives and is able to provide a good ROI because continuation of the same may create losses and liability due to changes. This is also linked to business focus and several other organizational changes occurring in all the functional, market and technological spheres. Hence, the review and renewal cycle is developed based on the combined source of evaluation studies and renewal studies of a training system as discussed in the following:

1. **Revisiting TNA:** The TNA reports and findings created during the first phase of the international training system must be revisited and reviewed in the light of emerging business strategy, and technological and market changes. In a rapidly changing business world, revisiting the TNA is a necessity at least once in two years or as frequently as possible, particularly for international organizations for whom change is very fast, and any change or the first impact that occurs anywhere in the world will be felt by these organizations being global entities. Hence, continuous update of TNA repository helps organizations to be agile.

2. **Actions post-TNA revisit:** If the revisit of TNA findings in the light of business strategy reveals gaps, the curriculum of the courses should be reviewed and the process of course design, implementation and evaluation phase as applicable will follow the same method as illustrated in the content before. The actions may further lead to introduction of new training courses, withdrawal of existing courses and sometimes renewal of entire training system.

3. **Revisiting training design, implementation and evaluation programmes:** It is important to re-evaluate various phases—the training course design methodology, implementation of the training courses system and the evaluation of the training system and courses at regular intervals—to tone and keep them as high performing systems as well as to ensure their currency in changing times. If this process is not followed, it may lead to methodologies being irrelevant and not matching the demands of news skills and style of learning.

Leadership Training and Development in International Organizations

The most strategic dimension of international training revolves around leadership training and development. There is ample evidence that organizations may not be equally fast in adapting international training practices of shop floor skills but they have shown great speed and agility in transforming and internationalizing leadership development. In fact, internationalization of training function can be attributed partially to leadership development initiatives since this is the area where organizations have realized benefits of moving away from localization of training particularly the design and development of training courses. Today, increasing number of global organizations have built a globally valid leadership competency framework based on which leadership development courses are designed and delivered. Companies such as Microsoft, Amazon and Google have their own leadership development centres imparting and evangelizing leadership development aligning to their company vision and culture as illustrated through an example in Box 3.1.

Box 3.1 | Amazon's 14 Leadership Competencies

Amazon is considered to have a tough and highly result-oriented culture. Consistent with this philosophy, Amazon has developed a 14 principles-centric leadership competency framework that is applicable to all employees in the organization. Employees are trained and coached on these competencies consistently. Though this framework is lauded for its comprehensiveness as well as progressiveness, it is also criticized for excessive focus what must be delivered negating how it should be done. These competencies are as follows:

1. **Customer obsession:** Observe customers and not competitors to tone up products and services. Leaders are coached to observe customers and study their expectations and work backwards to orient internal strategy.

2. **Ownership:** Leaders are not expected to say 'it is not my job' regardless of whether a task is within their ambit or not. All decisions are to be made keeping the long term in view and never short-term considerations.

3. **Invent and simplify:** Core purpose of innovation is find new ways, new products, new services that simplify anything and everything. Do not believe what we have is the best solution and do not believe that if something exists for long it is logical.

4. **Are right, a lot:** Leaders are right a lot but are encouraged to seek diverse perspectives to disconfirm their beliefs.

5. **Hire and develop the best:** Leaders raise the performance bar with every hire and promotion. Leaders develop leaders and take serious participation in coaching and mentoring others. They have an eye for exceptional talent; identify them and move them across the organization.

6. **Insist on the highest standards:** Leaders push and motivate their employees to surpass the existing standards of performance and to create superiors products, services and solutions. Leaders ensure that defects do not get set down the line and that problems are fixed so they stay fixed.

7. **Think big:** Thinking small is a self-fulfilling prophecy. Leaders create and communicate a bold direction that inspires results. They think differently and look around corners for ways to serve customers.

8. **Bias for action:** Action and execution are more important than endless debates and thinking. Speed of decision-making matters in business. Many decisions are reversible and do not require a detailed study. Calculated risk is encouraged.

9. **Frugality:** Growing fixed costs/capex is not encouraged and growing head count and enlarging budgets are not the indicators of real growth. Doing more with less is what an effective leader does. Constraints and resource limitations breed innovation, new ways of working and create resourcefulness and self-sufficiency.

10. **Learn and be curious:** Leaders never learn and always seek to improve themselves. They are curious about new possibilities and act to explore them.

11. **Earn trust:** Leaders listen attentively, speak candidly and treat others respectfully. They are vocally self-critical, even when doing so is awkward or embarrassing. Leaders benchmark themselves and their teams against the best.

12. **Dive deep:** Leaders operate at all levels, stay connected to the details, audit frequently and are sceptical when metrics and anecdotes differ, no task is beneath them.

13. **Have backbone; disagree and commit:** Leaders are required to disagree with the proposals or decisions when they hold different views but they must do it respectfully and with rational explanation even if it is uncomfortable and exhausting. Leaders have convictions and are tenacious. They do not compromise for the sake of social cohesion. Once a decision is determined, they commit wholly.

14. **Deliver results:** Leaders focus on the key inputs for their business and deliver them with the right quality and in a timely fashion. Despite setbacks, they rise to the occasion and never settle.

Technology in International Training Management

The technological developments in learning have given a big push and played as a catalyst in realizing the international training practices. Given the pace of tech changes taking place in learnings space, it is imprudent for organizations to manage training locally. For example, e-learning industry based on the actual usage of training technologies by corporate organizations has identified the following as the widely deployed tech solutions for international training management. These technologies and tech training devices can offer multiple benefits to international training practice that would include cost, access, standardization, world-class course content, instruction design and highly reliable pedagogy.

Automation and adaptive learning: The big boon for international training practice is wide adaption of digital medium and digital solutions in learning activities that include content management. Corporate universities and training centres can deploy automated solutions in order to create content and training material and also make it available across the countries and provide access to all employees at the same time. The automated tools are much more efficient, precise and cost-effective. Learners' preferences and requirements can be automatically customized to enhance the pace of learning of trainees apart from creating unparalleled optimization. Automated tools also can provide algorithmic solutions to evaluate user's knowledge and skills individually.

Microsoft Leadership Competency Framework

Microsoft has developed a tailor-made leadership competency framework in alignment with its business strategy and vision that is used to groom leaders as well as for leadership potential assessment. The framework comprises of six distinguishing competencies as descried below:

1. Executive maturity
2. One Microsoft
3. Impact and influence
4. Deep insight
5. Create business value
6. Customer commitment and foresight

Mobile learning: There is an estimated 2.2 billion mobile users in the world. There would hardly be any employee who does not possess a mobile phone and most of them with very few exceptions use smartphones. In addition to mobile telephony, it is very common among the employees of all levels in global companies to use tablets, IPad, personal computers and other mobile instruments. All these devices can be leveraged for imparting training. International organizations which are struggling to ensure reach and consistency in their training courses can effectively utilize mobile communication technology. It is also estimated that mobile training industry will grow to over USD 37 billion by 2020. Apart from access and reach, this technology also provides greater flexibility. Employees can be organized to learn the modules individually, in small groups as well as in large groups. They can also participate in training as per their work and personal schedules. This facility also provides the advantage of being connected to co-trainees globally, enhancing exposure and lifting standards.

Five Technology Trends in International Training

Professor Karl Kapp (2017) at Bloomsburg University and an expert on instructional technology predicts five major trends which will sweep the training function across the globe, as illustrated below:

Trend 1: Micro learning. Karl argues that e-learning as medium of training is no longer valid as increasingly mobile technology is available which can be used to tap training opportunities. Micro learning refers to small duration capsules of five- to eight-minute courses which trainees can watch and learn at ease. Even a long course can be organized into small meaningful capsules and delivered. This will create better learning and enhances learnability. The length can be modified to suit the trainees' pace of learning. Technologies like Google Primer can be a relevant example here.

Trend 2: Gamification. Though online gaming started as fun, it can be leveraged widely for interactive learning. Gamification as technology and methodology has huge potential to deliver some very complex and abstract education. There is ample evidence of usage of gaming technology in basic education like engineering and medicine courses already and this trend will grow. This platform suits the learning style of millennials well.

Trend 3: Social learning. This is not really new, since social learning platforms are in use for more than a decade. There are generic social network platforms and organization-specific social learning platforms hosted on the respective intranet sites. These networking sites and platforms can be used widely for training and can also serve as an interactive learning device. This medium has dual advantage—it can work as formal learning platform as well as informal learning medium.

Trend 4: Adaptive learning. Various tools like 'DreamBox' are available which can be modified to suit to training in organizations. This is essentially a personal learning medium using which pace of teaching, instruction and content can be organized to match the speed and style of trainees individually. Also depending upon the nature of content and in consonance with difficulty being experienced by the trainees as gauged by the learning analytics tool, content delivery can be altered to bring down the withdrawal intents.

Trend 5: Immersive learning. Devices such as Google Cardboard, Oculus Rift, 3-D games, online streaming and gamification can transform learning into highly immersive activity. The biggest challenge faced by organizations worldwide in training employees is to sustain their attention and participation because most of the courses and imparting of training is monotonous and uninteresting for adults. The use of interactive technologies and analytics in organizing content can make training highly participative.

Online digital training: Online streaming technologies have gained greater momentum in the current decade replacing existing technologies such as CDs and pen drives. Companies such as YouTube, Netflix and Hotspot have popularized this medium extensively and YouTube has emerged as a highly surfed Internet search engine. Technologies such as Skype, Google Hangouts are creating entirely new medium which is being effectively utilized by global companies for imparting not only refresher courses but also conventional training courses. With the advent of video-based training which can replace in-person training for all practical purposes with lot more convenience, the training standards are set to increase and all employees regardless of where they are located would get access to global standards of training. This is not only cost-effective but can save millions of instructor hours.

HTML and responsive design: HTML is available on almost all the browsers and platforms which can be stored even offline. Also, a responsive design can help make a training course modify progressively in tune with learning pace of trainees as well as features of mobile devices. These technologies can bring ease, precision and authenticity to the entire learning experience.

Googler to Googler Training Model

Employees teach one another in Google which is based on the methodology of mentoring. Instead of driving formal classroom training programmes and in order to ensure global reach, Google encourages one-to-one coaching modules across the company. Google also practises training using a two-tier approach. The first approach is where employees are given training on relevant skills (core and job-specific courses) and the second approach is providing employees with additional opportunities to develop what is learned in training. Google is also formalizing training based on data analytics to ensure employees learn what they need to know precisely rather than in generalized manner. Google also advocates the following five principles in securing a strong global training practice:

1. Keep learning material up to date.
2. Ask employees about their course preferences.
3. Identify potential mentors within management.
4. Motivate employees to coach one another.
5. Give employees projects to practise new skills.

All global companies must make sure international training management is set up using these technologies. Technologies like Google Glass can work as interactive learning device.

Virtual Learning Environment

Virtual learning environment is gaining momentum not only in traditional school systems but more importantly the way training is imparted in international organizations. Given the differences in time zones, faculty limitations and infrastructure challenges, many international organizations have localized the actual delivery of training practices. With VLE, now trainings can be organized internationally replacing local delivery. VLE, an online learning platform, has many distinct advantages. There is no need to be physically present; all the course material is available at all times; tests, tools, exercises and case studies are available; video and audios can be embedded; one is able to interact with co-learners and faculty globally while providing feedback and seeking clarifications almost real time. Fronter, Moodle, Frog, LP+ and Kaleidos are some of VLE tools available off the shelf.

Data and analytics: Digital technologies are contributing to widespread adaptation of data and analytics in all spheres of management and international training management is no exception. Huge bits of data get collected while online training is in progress as well as on its completion and assessment that include trainee's reactions, learning pace, suitability of content, methodological appropriateness, case studies and assessment, and so on which is immensely useful to further refine the courses and instruction design. Training data can be linked directly to job performance and employee motivation and morale scores to measure the alignment.

Robotic-assisted learning: It may be an old practice to use simulators to train people but the new thing is using robots to train humans with the help of AI technologies. Complex training courses need person-assisted teaching and this often creates limitations due to deficit of trainers. Imparting these complex skills has become easier and more accessible with robots.

Summary

How to deliver skill development programmes in a standard, consistent and informal manner to employees working across business units spread across many nations is a big challenge for international organizations. Medium, case studies, simulations and language can be facilitators as well as inhibitors to these organizations. Employees' expectations are clear that regardless of their location of work, they seek same training and development opportunities. The present chapter explores some of these topics and also role of technology and life cycle of HR development in international context. Time-tested training design, delivery and evaluation models together with best practices were illustrated. Integration and assimilation of work practices also provides opportunities and digital technology-driven tools support optimization efforts to leverage training and development to further the goals of internationalization of organizations.

QUESTIONS FOR DISCUSSION

1. What are the pitfalls with parent organization-centred leadership development initiatives?
2. Proving benefits of training and development programmes to organizational success is a myth or reality? Discuss with examples.
3. Discuss trends focusing on virtual training and digital libraries and how effective these models are to impart technical and functional skills.
4. Write critique on IDMs and how relevant are these to today's international organizations.
5. Discuss leadership development initiatives and leadership competency programmes in international organizations.
6. Employees working in company headquarters are at advantageous position compared to employees working in subsidiary nations in receiving advanced and latest skill development programmes! Do you agree or disagree?
7. Describe the latest trends in training and development practices in corporate organizations in the international context.
8. Discuss the role of medium in imparting of training courses and discuss approaches to overcome national barriers in training management.
9. Training budget is a function of organizational profitability! Write pros and cons along with latest status on training budgets in corporate industry.
10. Discuss common mistakes with leadership development programmes in international organizations.

CASE STUDY

Acclaim Consulting is an IT and consulting multinational engaged in IT services business, offering testing, enterprise resource planning, business intelligence, infrastructure management and process services apart from application maintenance and development programmes. Technology and markets and also client expectations are changing fast for the company, necessitating it to launch a massive retraining and reskilling programme for its 200 thousand employees working in 51 countries. Though at a macro level the company is clear that it shall train its employees on emerging technologies such as digital, cloud and automation, it is yet to build a pragmatic plan at micro level identifying what skills can be imparted to which category of employees and also design- and delivery-related plans. The company has decided to launch a comprehensive study to identify the precise developmental needs in the context of organizational strategy and objectives and tailor-make rest of the programme. Discuss how you will go about this initiative with the help of entire life cycle of international training management.

Bibliography

Akhtar, S., Ding, D. Z. and Ge, L. G. (2008). Strategic HRM Practices and Their Impact on Company Performance in Chinese Enterprises. *Human Resource Management, 47*(1), 15–32.

Arthur, W., Jr, Day, E. A., McNelly, T. L. and Edens, P. S. (2003). A Meta-analysis of the Criterion-related Validity of Assessment Center Dimensions. *Personnel Psychology, 56*(1), 125–153.

ATD (2014). *State of the Industry Report: Spending on Employee Training Remains a Priority.* Retrieved 30 January 2018, from https://www.td.org/magazines/td-magazine/2014-state-of-the-industry-report-spending-on-employee-training-remains-a-priority

Barber, J. (2004). Skill Upgrading Within Informal Training: Lessons from the Indian Auto Mechanic. *International Journal of Training and Development, 8*, no. 2, 94–172.

Benton, B. (2016). *How I use AutoCAD.* Retrieved 7 March 2018, from https://knowledge.autodesk.com/support/autocad/learn-explore/caas/video/youtube/watch-v--bvJVijo9kg.html

Black, S. E. and Lynch, L. M. (1996, May). Human Capital Investments and Productivity. *American Economic Review, 86*, no. 2, 263–267.

Burton, J. K. and Merill, P. F. (1977). Needs Assessment: Goals, Needs and Priorities, in L. J. Briggs (ed.), *Instructional Design* (pp. 21–45). Englewood Cliffs, NJ: Educational Technology Publications.

Chatterjee, J. (2016). *Can Employee Training Lead to Higher Profits?* Retrieved 7 March 2018, from https://www.linkedin.com/pulse/does-employee-training-lead-higher-profits-joydeep-chatterjee

Cheng, W. L. and Ho, D. C. K. (2001). A Review of Transfer of Training Studies in the Past Decade. *Personnel Review, 30*, no. 1, 201–213.

Ciraso-Cali, A., Pineda-Herrero, P., Quesada-Pallares, C. and Janer-Hidalgo, A. (2014). *Training for Innovation in Spain.* Retrieved 27 February 2018, from www.elmmagazine.eu/articles/training-for-innovation-in-spain

Corporate Leadership Council. (2005). *Six Mistakes That Drive Away Your Rising Stars.* Retrieved 27 February 2018, from wango.org/NGONews/February11/CLC.pdf

Dell, J., Fox, J. and Malcom, R. (1998). Training Situation Analysis (US Coast Guard): Conducting a Needs Analysis for Teams and New Systems. *Performance Improvement, 7*, no. 3, 18–21.

Dick, W., Carey, L. and Carey, J. (1978). *The Systematic Design of Instruction.* Glenview, IL: Foresman and Company.

Docebo. (2014). *E-Learning Market Trends & Forecast 2014–2016 Report.* Retrieved 27 February 2018, from https://www.docebo.com/landing/contactform/elearning-market-trends-and-forecast-2014-2016-docebo-report.pdf

Ferreira, R. R. and Abbad, G. (2013). *Training Needs Assessment: Where We Are and Where We Should Go?* Retrieved 27 February 2018, from http://www.anpad.org.br/periodicos/arq_pdf/a_1369

Gerlach, V. and Ely, D. (1971). *Teaching & Media: A Systematic Approach.* Boston, MA: Pearson.

Guerrero, S. and Barraud-Didier, V. (2004). High Involvement Practices and Performance of French Firms. *The International Journal of Human Resource Management, 15*(16), 1408–1423.

Hansson, T. (2007). The Problem(s) of Change Revisited. *Dialectica, 61*, no. 2, 265–274.

Harless, J. H. (1987). An Analysis of Front End Analysis. *Performance Improvement, 26*(2), 7–9.

IFLA. (2014). *Working Group on Guidelines for Digital Libraries.* Retrieved 27 February 2018, from https://www.ifla.org/digital-libraries/guidelines

———. (2016). *Digitization Strategic Initiatives and Research.* Retrieved 27 February 2018, from https://scholar.google.co.in/scholar?q=%E2%80%A2%09IFLA+(2016).+Digitization+Strategic+Initiatives+and+Research&hl=en&as_sdt=0&as_vis=1&oi=scholart&sa=X&ved=0ahUKEwiol4TyqsXZAhWLwI8KHU-EB6cQgQMIJjAA

Kapp, Karl M. (2017). *The Gamification of Learning and Instruction: Game-Based Methods and Strategies for Training and Education*. San Francisco, CA: Pfeiffer.

Kaufman, R and Lopez, I.G. (2013, February 25). Needs Assessment for Organizational success. *American Society for Training and Development*. Chicago, IL: ASTD Press.

Kim, Y. and Ployhart, R. E. (2014). The Effects of Staffing and Training on Firm Productivity and Profit Growth Before, During and After the Great Recession. *American Psychological Association, 99*(3), 361–389.

Kirkpatrick, D. (1994). *Evaluating Training Programmes: The Four Levels*. San Francisco, CA: Berrett-Koehler.

Mager, R. and Pipe, P. (1970). *Analyzing Performance Problems*. Retrieved 27 February 2018, from https://eric.ed.gov/?id=ED050560

McClelland, S. (1994). A Model for Designing Objective Oriented Training Evaluations. *Industrial and Commercial Training, 26*(1), 3–9.

McGehee, W. and Thayer, P. W. (1961). *Training in Business and Industry*. New York, NY: John Wiley.

Morrison, G. R., Ross, S. M. and Kemp, J. E. (2004). *Designing Effective Instruction*. New Jersey: John Wiley.

Motorola Solutions. (2013). *Motorola Training Solutions*. Retrieved 27 February 208, from https://www.motorolasolutions.com/en_us/services/managed-support.../training.html

OECD. (2016). *International Student Mobility and Foreign Students in Territory Education: How Many Students Study Abroad?-OECD Fact book*. Retrieved 27 February 2018, from www.oecd-ilibrary.org/...2016/international-student-mobility-and-foreign-students-in-

Rothwell, W. J. and Kazanas, H. C. (1994). Management Development: The State of the Art as Perceived by HRD Professionals. *Performance Improvement Quarterly, 7*, no.1, 40–59.

Rummler, G. A. and Brache, A. (1995). *Improving Performance: How to Manage the White Space in the Organization Chart*. San Francisco, CA: Jossey-Bass.

Shepherd, C. (2011). *The Blended Learning Cookbook*. London: Saffron Interactive.

Training Magazine. (2015). *2015 Training Industry Report*. Retrieved 27 February 2018, from https://trainingmag.com/trgmag-article/2o15-training-industry-report

Unilever. (2016). *Unilever Future Leaders Programme*. Retrieved 30 January 2018, from https://www.unilever.com.bd/careers/graduates/uflp

Wiggins, G. and McTighe, J. (2011). *Understanding by Design*. Retrieved 27 February 2018, from https://www.ascd.org/ASCD/pdf/siteASCD/publications/UbD_WhitePaper0312.pdf

Witkin, L. R. and Altschuld, J. W. (1995). *Planning and Conducting Needs Assessment: A Practical Guide*. Thousand Oaks, CA: SAGE Publications.

International Compensation Management

4

LEARNING OBJECTIVES

The objectives of this chapter are to:

❏ discuss contemporary approaches of international compensation management and their implications for business organizations.

❏ illustrate the macro and micro trends of compensation management in a global scenario, along with an analysis.

❏ enable better understanding of the legislative provisions of executive compensation.

❏ describe compensation management in 18 selective countries, enabling a global understanding.

❏ present the salient features of international compensation management including taxation, risk compliances and payroll processes.

Compensation and benefits are undoubtedly the most vital function in IHRM theory and practice. With the growing need for movement of HR across borders, international compensation management has come to occupy centre stage. International compensation management as a practice has been in existence in global corporations for decades, but it is primarily confined to addressing the needs of expatriates and their situations. Further, although international compensation management has been explored and studied from multiple dimensions, financial and tax experts study and analyse compensation management mainly from a taxation and payroll administration perspective rather than as a reward system. The basic purpose of international compensation management is to attract, motivate and retain talent. Hence, it is important to discuss this practice more from an HRM point of view with the financial management angle as an affiliate area.

International Compensation: Macro Trends

According to ILO estimates, monthly average wages adjusted for inflation known as real wages grew globally by 1.9 per cent between 2010 and 2015. Real monthly wages almost doubled in Asia between 2000 and 2011, and increased by 18 per cent in Africa, 15 per cent in Latin America and Caribbean, and 5 per cent in developed economies. However, real wages in many other nations especially in developed economies have seen a decline. Inflation is a key determinant of

Table 4.1	Global Inflation Rate, Productivity Index and Real Wage Growth Rate

Year	Inflation Rate (%)	Labour Productivity Index	Real Wage Growth Rate
2010	3.68	109	2.2
2011	5.05	111	1.0
2012	4.07	112	2.2
2013	3.66	112	2.0
2014	3.23	115	1.8
2015	2.78	116	2.0
2016	2.9	117	1.8

Source: Compilation based on http://www.ilo.org/travail/areasofwork/wages-and-income/WCMS_142568/lang--en/index.htm; http://www.ilo.org/travail/areasofwork/wages-and-income/WCMS_142568/lang--en/index.htm (accessed on 7 March 2018).

movements in international compensation. As can be seen from Table 4.1, the inflation rates are progressively declining year after year. As per IMF, in 2015, inflation rates in more than 85 out of 120 economies were below long-term expectations and about 20 per cent of countries were in deflation. A recent trend also indicates that wages in developing countries are slowly converging towards average wages in developed economies though the gap between them is still much wider. For example, when measured in purchasing power parity, the average wage in developed economies is estimated at approximately USD 3,000 as compared to average wage of USD 1,000 in developing economies. The estimated world average monthly wage is about USD 1,600.

Following are the other macro trends:

- The gap between wages and productivity is growing because during the last five years, wage increase globally is not commensurate with productivity increases resulting in declining labour income share in economies of nations. More and more enterprises seem to favour moving surplus generated to investors rather than to employees. Economic Policy Institute (2015) argues that productivity has increased by a whopping 73.4 per cent worldwide during the period between 1973 and 2015, while pay has grown only by 11.1 per cent (productivity has grown 6.6 × more than pay).
- Various studies have shown that across most countries, the gender gap in compensation for equal work has generally narrowed over a period of time but is not yet fully closed. In 2014, in the EU-28 as a whole, women were paid on average 16.7 per cent less than men. The biggest pay difference among EU nations was found in Czech (22.5 per cent), Germany (22.3 per cent) and the United Kingdom (20.9 per cent). However, the current gap appears to be anywhere between 0 and 45 per cent as per ILO report on global wages.
- During recent decades, wage inequality has increased in many countries around the world. This is a worrying trend since growing inequalities can create adverse social and economic consequences for societies. Fiscal policies and taxation system of nations, however progressive they may be, fail to arrest the growing divide. For example, the ratio of CEO pay to average worker pay has gone up from 24 times in 1965 to 262 times in 2005 in the United States.
- There is a growing trend of increasing wage inequality among enterprises and industries. It appears that compensation levels in emerging enterprises are far higher than in traditional

bricks-and-mortar industries. For example, growing compensation gap in the United States is attributed to growing polarization, with highly skilled workers cluttering in some enterprises while low skilled workers concentrating in other enterprises.

- The compensation gap that exists within an enterprise is also considerable worldwide. This gap is reported to be wider in mega enterprises employing more than 10,000 employees. Various studies in Europe show that at the very top end of the curve, the top 0.1 per cent of employees are paid EUR 211 per hour, while the enterprises in which they work pay EUR 45 an average per hour. Many CEOs effectively determine their own pay and benefits, and corporate governance of many firms fall short of ensuring fair compensation.

- Labour wages have a strong positive correlation with household incomes across the countries. Hence, GDP of countries will get impacted if share of labour wages in the overall economy does not grow.

- Pay equity and transparency have become a major issue globally with all companies, particularly those that are intended to be progressive. Glassdoor's (2016) Global Salary Transparency Survey found that 70 per cent of employees across seven nations, namely, the United States, Canada, the United Kingdom, France, Germany, the Netherlands and Switzerland, believe that transparency is good for employee satisfaction and 72 per cent believe that it is good for business. The global survey also reveals that 59 per cent of men and 51 per cent of women employees believe they have a good understanding of how pay is determined in their companies. However, 69 per cent of employees felt that they need to have better information and understanding of what fair pay is for their position and skill set. Another survey conducted by Towers Watson points out that only 49 per cent of employees globally feel confident of pay equity and transparency. According to 'Transparency in Corporate Reporting' published by Transparency International (https://www.transparency.org/whatwedo/publication/transparency_in_corporate_reporting_assessing_emerging_market_multinat [accessed on 7 March 2018]) covering about 124 of the world's largest traded companies worth USD 14 trillion and spread across 25 countries, pay transparency is yet to be real. Interestingly, Todd Zenger in his *Harvard Business Review* article published in 2016 argues against pay transparency stating pay transparency is a double-edged sword which is capable of doing much more damage than good because it can cause more attrition, productivity decline and conflicts.

Increasing Legislation of Executives' Remuneration Practices Across the Nations

The following codes have stipulated remuneration principles, duties of remuneration committee, remuneration report submission to Annual General Body Meeting (AGM) and individualized disclosure of director's pay in Europe:

- UK Combined Code of Corporate Governance (2006)
- Italy Governance Code (2006)
- Unified Corporate Governance Code, Spain (2006)
- German Corporate Governance Code, 2008 and Appropriateness of Management Board Compensation Act, 2009
- The Dutch Corporate Governance Code, 2008
- Belgian Corporate Governance Code, 2009
- French Code de Commerce, 2010/French Industry Based (MEDEF/AFEP) Pay Recommendations
- Finnish Corporate Governance Code, 2016

International Compensation Management: Strategy and Approaches

Global HR consulting firm Mercer, in its survey covering over 90 firms, has found that the number of organizations implementing a global compensation strategy across nations is growing with over 85 per cent of respondent organizations stating that they have a well-defined international compensation programme in place. The study also finds that a large number of organizations have a programme of fixing and administering international compensation rather than a well-crafted international compensation strategy and approach. However, on scrutiny of these compensation programmes, an inference can be drawn of the approaches organizations have taken and strategy that they have followed. Another survey conducted by Aon Hewitt on international workforce reveals that close to 70 per cent employees are dissatisfied with the implementation of compensation and benefits programmes. HR professionals themselves are found to be performing limited role in international compensation management due to variety of reasons including perception that international compensation is more in the scope of financial and compliance management which HR professionals are not well equipped with. Design of an international compensation strategy is complex because organizations face multiple complex challenges and priorities as listed below:

- **Compliances:** Laws and regulations governing compensation, benefits and incentives are different in different countries, and compensation is one area which is highly legislated at some level in all countries in multiple ways such as immigration laws, taxation laws and wage laws.
- **Practices:** There are similarities and dissimilarities in compensation practices among nations.
- **Compensation strategy** needs to be aligned with organizational business strategy and plans.
- **Global consistency and uniformity** needs to be maintained while being sensitive to local needs and requirements.
- **Diverse standards:** Living standards and inflation rates are different in each of the regions in which the companies operate.
- **Employee expectations:** Expectations from employees can be similar or different depending on the level, function, role and region.
- **Culture:** Compensation practices do arise from local culture so compensation approach needs to consider this aspect. Compensation is a collective subject in some countries and highly individualized in others.
- **Competitiveness:** International compensation costs are considerable for many organizations and their budgets, so the design should be competitive.
- **Alignment with other HR systems:** Compensation model and strategy shall be aligned with other HR systems such as recruitment, job evaluation and performance management.
- **Key for talent:** Compensation is a key strategy to attract, motivate and retain the talent.

Further to these challenges discussed, global organizations while designing and executing an international compensation strategy often face a conflict between two major approaches. The first approach involves the need to align the compensation system with global operations on same model, principles and processes for better optimization, to attain efficiencies of scale, sharing of resources, experience and knowledge of management practices. Integration, uniformity, consistency and standardization at the global level are at the core of this school of management thought. This is chiefly driven by economic considerations and urges to ensure strategic alignment with organizational focus. In consonance with this, an international compensation strategy too shall strive to achieve uniformity, alignment and integration. Here the emphasis is on aligning compensation approach with organizational strategy, structure and systems. This approach can also be understood as being internally focused since aligning with organizational context is the dominant factor while designing compensation approaches and methods. The second approach is more sensitive to local complexities, local market dynamics and local cultural aspects. This is more an external focused approach where a design of compensation system is influenced by forces operating in that country/region which is to a great extent outside the control of an organization. This approach tends to seek more flexibility and differential compensation system in the same organization depending upon the country of operation and local realities. Few global organizations have also tried to blend both these competing models into one since it is hard to be one-sided in the realm of managerial decision-making. However, the blending creates confusion in the minds of implementers of international compensation processes whenever they are faced with situations that require decisions on the ground as part of day-to-day operations. They are not quite clear which of the two approaches to adopt, integration or differentiation. For example, should the compensation package of an executive be in line with global compensation structure or local package? Answer to this question can be derived from the overall approach of the compensation policy of a firm.

Further, a question arises about how a compensation strategy can be designed without factoring local realties especially from a compliance perspective. In this context, the argument advanced is that compliance to regulations is always part of the best practice and merely designing a system to comply is a minimalist approach. Creating differential approach suited to local requirements such as national compensation trends, industry conditions, talent dynamics and competition from local players may aptly address a subsidiary or country operations more effectively but lack of global alignment can cause shrink in opportunities, operational inefficiencies and cultural misalignment with global identity of a firm. However, deciding the approach to strategy, global or national orientation, entirely depends upon the dual objectives of IHRM and international compensation management. Both the approaches have their advantages and disadvantages. There is enough evidence in strategic management research and literature which supports that alignment of a compensation system with overall corporate strategy can yield greater impact on the performance of a company and other studies reveal that close alignment between compensation model and individual, and small group work will result in greater performance of a company since a macro global compensation model may not ensure tighter alignment between individual performance with pay. However, various research studies in the last four decades with empirical evidence have established that the linkage between a firm's performance and executive compensation is weak. Hence, for some, it is more important to bring alignment between performance and compensation rather than deliberating whether there shall be one global system of compensation or region-focused system. Further, the studies have found that compensation has been increasing whenever firms are performing well (sometimes rate of compensation increases are more than a firm's performance level), but there is no commensurate change whenever firm's performance targets are not met or when firm's performance is on decline. For example, *The Wall Street Journal* (2010) reports that many CEOs received substantial salaries and bonuses in 2010 when their companies experienced significant declines in the stock market.

Firms choosing a global orientation to their international compensation strategy can adopt various approaches. Bloom, Milkovich and Mitra (2003) have found firms embracing different models while designing a global compensation system as described here. The key findings of 'Global Compensation Programs and Practices Survey' (through electronically accessible instrument) conducted by WorldatWork (2014; The Total Rewards Association) covering about 461 respondent organizations globally are also presented to capture the practices in vogue.

- **Adapter:** Firms that chose to adopt local conditions to determine compensation strategy are called adapters or localizers. These organizations provide different schemes/benefits/compensation structures which are tailor-made to a particular country of operation. In this approach, country subsidiaries or branches tend to function almost independently from the firm's headquarters. Therefore, the number of compensation systems in such firms can be equivalent to number of countries/locations they operate in. It is challenging to get a global picture of compensation system in this scenario since the system is highly fragmented. However, the benefit is that an adapter can address local needs precisely and can respond to changes in local talent and compensation market sharply and promptly. Even when headquarters circulate a compensation scheme, it can be a guideline rather than a mandatory process, so affiliates can choose to extend implementation of the scheme or not. Control and audit of compensation practices can become a vexed process and establishing equivalence among compensation systems of various business units and subsidiaries becomes a nightmare. Investments can get duplicated in design and roll-out of highly individualized compensation systems. A global firm may lose its natural benefits of being a global firm by adapting to local conditions instead of influencing them with its global knowledge and resources.
- **Exporter:** Firms that chose to pursue a consistent and uniform compensation system across all countries are called exporters. Here the strategy is one-company-one-compensation system. The administration, control and audit of compensation and benefits function tend to be centralized at headquarters. Affiliates/subsidiaries/branches may have a collaborative role in design of compensation systems but not a decisive one. Compensation system in any country of operation is merely a mirror image of same policy and process of global compensation system. The advantages here are efficiencies, a global identity, a common mindset among employees and their easy mobility from one business to another business unit and one country of operation to another country of operation. Disadvantages with exporter approach are trying to force a one-size-fits-all approach despite uniqueness of each line of business or country of operation, insulating an organization from local realities which is a powerful determinant of attracting right talent, distortion of the objectives when a system is moved from headquarters to local operations, conflict between headquarters and local units with local unit managers seeing it as deprivation of their operational freedom and imposition of headquarters' ideas which are influenced by realities that exist in country of headquarters rather than country of subsidiary operations, perceived impossibility of factoring all local compensation trends and practices into a global compensation system and challenges with change management whenever an innovative scheme is to be implemented since it has to be at a global scale.

Global Compensation Structure and Strategy
Key Findings of Survey of Organizations

- Multinational companies in the United States remain fairly evenly split with regard to how they approach their global compensation structure: centralized (53 per cent) and decentralized (47 per cent).
- While 49 per cent of all respondents see more momentum towards greater centralization of their organization's compensation structure in the next two years, 42 per cent do not anticipate any shift—either towards greater or less centralization. Only 9 per cent see more decentralization occurring.
- Respondent organizations who self-reported a globally centralized compensation structure for their company said that the primary objectives for adopting this type of structure were to establish a consistent link between rewards and results, have a consistent positive link vis-à-vis market and maintain internal equity.
- Among those self-reporting a decentralized global compensation structure, the most common unit of compensation organization is country specific, followed by region and a combination of business unit and country specific.
- Nearly half (47 per cent) of those with a decentralized global compensation structure give it a mixed review in terms of effectiveness, but an additional 42 per cent say it is either a mostly or very effective structure.
- While 53 per cent of respondents characterize their company's global compensation structure as centralized, a slightly larger per cent (59 per cent) said that their organization has a global compensation strategy with policies and strategies that are applied uniformly in all operations around the world unless individual country compliance dictates otherwise.
- Majority (56 per cent) of respondents indicated that their organizations use either global grades or global bands or both.
- While 66 per cent of organizations with a centralized compensation structure have an HR information system that covers operations globally, only 41 per cent of organizations that are decentralized have a global HR information system.
- Organizations which report a centralized compensation system are also more likely to have a centralized performance management system (86 per cent of centralized organizations versus 47 per cent of decentralized organizations).

- **Globalizers:** Firms that chose to design and implement a global compensation system are called globalizers. In this model too, there will be one global compensation system across all the countries/locations/business units. The main difference between the models of exporters and globalizers is that in the globalizer model, firms simply neither opt for headquarters' compensation system nor extend the implementation of headquarters-determined compensation system to all the countries/locations/business units but decide on a compensation strategy and approach keeping in view the global factors and realities, ideas and practices of all countries where a firm operates. Here firms strive to stitch together the best practices gathered across all the countries. The advantage with this model is one seamless process and approach wherein employees experience equality regardless of the country or business unit they work in apart from all the other benefits that an exporter model offers. The main challenge with this model is that it is an insurmountable task to blend all the best practices into a single compensation system however much firms may try.

Often, such efforts create chaos and pulling together multiple elements results in a compensation strategy that may lack a clear focus and distinction.

- **Conformers:** When firms become susceptible to pressures of subsidiaries/local operations/ business units and opt to accord priority to compliance with a country's local laws and regulations over implementation of the best practices which are presumably superior in their design to regulations, the firms are called conformers. This model provides opportunities for various subsidiary nations of a global organization based on their overall influence to capture a decisive role in most of the compensation matters. Here the headquarters are concerned about their own inadequacy in their understanding of compensation administration in various countries so they leave these matters to subsidiaries to decide by playing a mere coordinator's role. All advantages that accrue in an adapter model do occur with this model too in addition to subsidiaries experiencing empowerment and taking all the ownership to execute a compensation strategy that would possibly succeed locally. Similarly, all disadvantages that occur with a fragmented compensation system as described in adapter model do exist here with much more propensity since the role of headquarters in this model is seen to be more subdued.

- **Avoiders:** When firms decide to avoid complying with local compensation practices in order to push through a global compensation system that is understood as well aligned to their business strategy, they are called avoiders. The difference between this model and the globalizer model exists in the basic approach. In a globalizer model, a firm strives to blend all the best practices assembled from various countries in which the firm operates, while in this model, a stand-alone compensation system that espouses the business approach of a firm is given priority and a local compensation practice that conflicts with the global compensation system is avoided regardless of its merit. The chief motive of firms for pushing through this model across the countries is driven by cost reductions since a global compensation system can cut down costs and create optimization. The disadvantage with this model is that it can create formidable conflicts and undermine moral standing of country managers and a firm's practices can be viewed suspiciously.

- **Resisters:** This is similar to avoiders but firms here choose to comply while showing resistance. In this model, country managers are not fully convinced with executing the global or headquarters-determined compensation strategy so resistance comes in various forms such as country managers protesting stating that the compensation system proposed by headquarters is not compliant with local practices or local regulations and the same can become a deterrent in attracting right talent and existing workforce morale can be compromised and so on. While some of these arguments are logical, they can be resolved easily if country managers have not exhibited resistant behaviour. In brief, a global compensation system as designed by headquarters will be implemented reluctantly since the influence of subsidiaries is not enough not to comply, but due to this covert resistance, the chances of success with the compensation system are limited.

Recent trends seem to suggest that there is a positive movement towards a centralized model with a uniform global compensation system. This may be partly due to pace of globalization and organizations' thrust to attain competitiveness in their management practices. For example, a study conducted by Towers, Perrin, Forster and Crosby (1979) reported that the number of European firms with the American style of pay for performance schemes has increased multifold. Several Japanese firms knowingly or unknowingly have started incorporating some of the Western compensation elements into their compensation model and at the same time many multinational companies which are fascinated with Japanese management techniques have started leaning towards some of the Japanese compensation concepts which lay more emphasis on collaboration and less on individual achievements.

Another way to understand the international compensation strategy and approach is by using the four types of compensation approaches that firms deploy as discussed here:

1. **Contingency approach:** This approach basically advocates acknowledging local sensitivities, situations and realities while designing a compensation system. It is a situational approach seeking greater flexibility in compensation strategy.
2. **Equity approach:** This is based on principle of pay for performance. The approach involves the practice of linking compensation closely to individual employee performance and achievements rather than focusing on global and regional contexts and factors.
3. **Resource-based approach:** Here firms take a market-sensitive strategy. The belief is that compensation shall be determined by local market conditions such as demand for talent and compensation trends in order to attract and retain right talent. It is seen as strategic to look at HR dynamics surrounding the immediate organizational environment to choose a compensation strategy rather than internal situations.
4. **Agency approach:** Linking host of organizational factors and stakeholders interests/goals with employee compensation strategy and approach to achieve the goals is called agency approach. Some firms take this approach to determine their international compensation strategy in order to establish relationship between investors and employee interests.

International Compensation Practices and Policies

In order to develop an international compensation management practice and policy, it is important to study and understand the compensation practices prevalent in selective countries as discussed next. The compensation structure, payroll, taxation and overall orientation can be different in different nations though some of these are merging into a common stream at some level paving way for emergence of international compensation model to cater to global organizations.

International Double Taxation

In a globalized world and cross-border careers, employees earn income or salary in more than one country. However, employees would get taxed in their country of residence for entire earnings as per income tax rules/slabs applicable in that nation and also become liable to pay income tax in the country where that income accrues. This is called double taxation which is irrational and unjustified. Therefore, to avoid this irrationality in tax system, many nations had entered into bilateral double taxation agreements with each other. For example, India has double tax treaties with over 88 countries. This agreement works in two ways. First, tax is deducted at the source in the country where income is earned and the employee receives a tax credit which he or she can produce in the country of residence to offset the tax payable. Second, the employee, on submitting proof of country of residence, has tax deduction exempted at the country of accrual.

The United States

It appears that organizations in the United States prefer more and more market-based compensation structures rather than traditional and broadband-based structures as they gravitate towards enhancing the competitiveness in their people policies. A survey conducted by WorldatWork in collaboration with Deloitte Consulting in 2012 covering over 900 organizations in the United States has found that 64 per cent of organizations use market-based compensation structures, 23 per cent use traditional structures, 12 per cent use broadbands, 8 per cent use set-up structures, 4 per cent have no formal structure and 5 per cent have a combination of all or can be categorized as others. The definition for these structures is drawn based on the pay ranges each structure would accommodate and range of mid-point progression. Market-based structure typically has range spreads of 30 per cent to 80 per cent and mid-point progression of 10 to 15 per cent. Traditional structure has range spreads of 20 per cent to 40 per cent and mid-point progression of 5 to 10 per cent. Broadbands structure has range spreads of 80 per cent to 200 per cent with no defined mid-point and step structure has range spreads of 20 per cent to 40 per cent and mid-point progression has range spreads of 5 to 10 per cent with defined points within the ranges. The data show that in the United States salaries are driven more by market forces than anything else.

Employee compensation in the United States companies typically consists of: base pay, bonus/variable pay/performance-linked pay, commission, employees' stock option plans, retention bonuses and benefits consisting of holiday pay, retirement plans, health insurance and vacation. Some of these compensation components are described briefly here:

Risk-based Compensation Practices

Few aggressive corporate organizations particularly in banking and financial services industry in the United States do implement executive incentives as a part of compensation package. This can be categorized as risk-based practice because potentially they may motivate executives to attain performance objectives by all means. In order to regulate these practices, the US bank regulators have stipulated the following principles:

- Balanced risk: As per this principle, all risks associated with such aggressive incentives shall be assessed in terms of amount of incentive and its association with material targets of an organization.
- Risk monitoring: All performance-driven incentive schemes covering senior leadership of a company must be subjected to risk audit and assessment, and shall be monitored by risk officers.
- Corporate governance: All independent directors on the board of a company must have an oversight on the incentives of senior leadership and these board members can ideally take steps to involve experts to review the incentive schemes in the light of the best corporate governance practices.

Base salary: This refers to the salary component which is fixed and often closely related to worth of a job in relation to other jobs in an organization. Aon Hewitt's survey on base salaries in the United States shows that the base salary has seen an increase of about 3 per cent in 2013 comparing to a 3 per cent dip in 2009. The base salary revision trends for the period 1993–2015 are shown along with inflation rate in Table 4.2.

Table 4.2	Base Salary Trends	
Year	**Percentage of Base Salary Increase**	**Inflation Rate (%)**
1993	4.3	3.0
1994	4.0	2.6
1995	4.0	2.8
1996	3.9	3.0
1997	4.0	2.3
1998	4.2	1.6
1999	4.2	2.2
2000	4.3	3.4
2001	4.3	2.8
2002	3.6	1.6
2003	3.4	2.3
2004	3.4	2.7
2005	3.6	3.4
2006	3.6	3.2
2007	3.7	2.8
2008	3.7	3.8
2009	1.8	−0.4
2010	2.4	1.6
2011	2.7	3.2
2012	2.8	2.1
2013	3.0	1.5
2014	3.1	1.6
2015	2.8	0.1

Source: Compilation based on https://www.globalcompensation.net/us-salary-survey (accessed on 7 March 2018).

According to a CNBC (2015) report, the average and median US salary stood at USD 44,569 and USD 28,031, respectively, in 2014. Many organizations in the United States deploy job evaluation methods to determine the base salary, while few other organizations simply follow the industry practices.

Bonuses/incentives: Bonuses and incentives are critical components in the compensation structure of executive in the United States. According to Forbes, US companies spend an estimated USD 38 billion on bonuses and incentives per annum; 99 per cent of organizations are found to implement one or other type of bonus or incentive plan for their employees. There are different incentive plans that companies use such as annual incentive plans, discretionary bonus plans, profit-sharing plans, gain-sharing plans, project bonus and retention bonus.

Compensation Strategies: It Is Not Always about Incentives

Mercer, an HR consulting firm, has conducted a worldwide study in 2012 on sales salaries covering 63 markets in order to understand how companies compensate their sales personnel. It is found that globally, only 45 per cent of companies pay sales incentives to their employees. Incentives are most common in Egypt (75 per cent of organizations have sales incentive plans) and least common in Poland (used by only 24 per cent of organizations). Another study conducted on sales compensation in the same year by WorldatWork and Alexander Group reveals that companies tend to change sales compensation plans often such as altering goal/target framework, scope and value proposition, and redesign and realignment. In 2012 alone, about 69 per cent of organizations have changed their sales compensation plan and 46 per cent plan to change in the following year. The study also states that organizations have different approaches to reward sales credits whenever more than one sales executive is involved; some organizations split the reward, while others double the credit. Studies have also found that overall work environment and ecosystem for sales is equally important to that of sales incentive plans per se.

Stock options plans: US organizations also widely use stock option plans to incentivize their employees and consider them as long-term incentives which help both in performance and retention of employees. Securities and Exchange Commission (SEC) (https://qz.com/878025/sec-10-k-filings-show-us-companies-cite-regulations-as-an-obstacle-much-more-than-they-did-20-years-ago/ [accessed on 7 March 2018]) data shows that since 1980, the number of employees holding stock options has increased about ninefold. However, there are different types: some involve investment by employees as they are granted at market price and others are with no investment but linked to performance goals. The types of stock option programmes observed in the United States are: stock option scheme, restricted stock, phantom stock, stock appreciation right, long-term cash plan, performance shares/units and equity overhang.

Social security benefits: Workforce in the United States is largely covered by the government-administered social security measures provided they are citizens/permanent residents. Initial monthly retirement benefits payable to average wage earners with a stable work history is about USD 1,300. Employers must also offer health care insurance coverage to full-time employees and failure to do so make them liable for penalties. The 401 (k) contributions are also largely matched by the employers. The current tax rate for social security is 12.4 per cent and Medicare is 2.9 per cent deriving contributions equally from employee and employer.

Fringe benefits: Vacation, corporate credit cards, executive dining, conveyance, chauffeurs, housing, enhanced health care, club memberships, golf reimbursements, low-cost loans, security, paid parking, wealth management, qualified retirement planning, transfer of property and so on are commonly implemented fringe benefits in the US companies for employees particularly in managerial and executive category. Although fringe benefits are taxable, employers may not treat them as wages, so there is a probability to make an error here of not bringing these payments under taxable income.

Deductions: Deductions on account of federal income tax, social security tax, Medicare tax, city tax, county tax and state income tax are applicable to all employees.

Payroll process and income tax: Administration of payroll is a key operational aspect in compensation management in the United States. Income tax rates are progressive ranging from 3 per cent to 33.2 per cent depending upon the cash income level of employees.

Setting Up Payroll Process in the United States

- Obtain an employer identification number from the Internal Revenue Service (IRS) since it is necessary for reporting about employees to state agencies and taxes to the IRS.
- Obtain local ID number since in few cases it is required to process taxes.
- Define clearly the difference between independent contractor and employee since taxes, social security contributions, Medicare and unemployment taxes are different.
- Help employees to fill Form W-4: federal income tax withholding form for facilitating of withholding applicable taxes.
- Decide frequency of salary pay/pay period in adherence to the local law: bi-weekly or monthly.
- Document standard operating process (SOP) for payroll process.
- Choose an appropriate payroll system either in-house or outsource to a third party.
- Report payroll taxes systematically to concerned IRS on quarterly basis.
- Create a clear document and maintain all records related to payroll of all employees including deductions and withholdings which can be payrolled process-wise.

Canada

According to Statistics Canada, real wages in that country increased by about 14 per cent during the 30 years between 1981 and 2011. The biggest rise came from wage trends during the period between 1998 and 2011, when average wages increased by about 38 per cent, while inflation pushed up the cost of living by about 28 per cent, a 10 per cent net increase. However, if data is considered for the period between 2006 and 2011, real wages have fallen as wages grew by 8 per cent, while inflation had gone up by 9 per cent. In other words, as per Bank of Canada (2015) estimates based on inflation data, someone earning CAD 50,000 in 1992 should be earning about CAD 72,480 by 2015 to have kept up with the real wages. Average salary in Canada now is about CAD 45,000 per annum. The average Canadian salaries by sector based on North American Industry Classification System as in 2016 are: mining, quarrying, oil and gas exploration (CAD 107,065), utilities (CAD 89,955), construction (CAD 62,461), manufacturing (CAD 56,446), retail ($29,398), transportation and warehousing ($52,383), finance and insurance (CAD 65,348), real estate ($48,887), educational services (CAD 53,109), professional and technical services (CAD 69,032) and public administration (CAD 63,840). According to National Household Survey (NHS) data, the second generation immigrants are making more money than average salaries of employees in Canada. For example, average immigrant salary is standing at CAD 50,699 against the national average of CAD 45,128.

Analytical Study on the Evolution of Canadian Wages Major Findings

Statistics Canada had conducted a major study on Canadian Wages in the year 2013 to examine the evolution of compensation trends during the last three decades (1981–2011). The key findings of the study are:

- Gender bias in wages still exists in Canada though the gap between men and women's salaries is diminishing lately. Canada stands at seventh position in highest pay gap between men and women among OECD countries. As of 2013, women were paid 92 per cent equivalent wages that of men for the equal work/job. Between 1981 and 2011, average hourly wages of men increased by 11 per cent and in contrast women's average wages went up by 26 per cent during the same period. The gap has decreased due to increase of productivity of women workforce at a faster pace than that of men and from changes in education, job tenure, occupation and union status providing equal opportunities.

- Average wages of workforce aged 45 to 54 grew roughly 20 percentage points faster than those of their counterparts aged 25 to 34 during the period between 1981 and 1998. In contrast, workforce aged 25 to 34 experienced faster wage growth than their counterparts aged 45 and 54 from 1998 to 2011.
- Though highly educated employees (university graduates) still earn more than high school educated, the gap is progressively decreasing particularly during the period between 2000 and 2011. The wages during the said period increased by 2.7 per cent for university graduates, while it was 7.2 per cent for high school educated employees. The said narrowing gap is attributed to higher demand for less educated workforce in industries such as construction, oil and gas exploration and mining.
- Wage growth seems to have varied across the industries with finance industry offering significantly higher wage growth rates (20.1 per cent) against the average wage increase of 6 per cent. Good wage growth has happened post-1998 during which many industries have experienced double-digit growth in wages.
- Among the occupations, managerial jobs have seen higher wage growth rate (26.9 per cent) outpacing the average wage growth of all other occupations (average increase of 2 to 15 per cent) due to changes in job characteristics of these jobs.

There is a considerable salary inequality between highest and lowest paid in Canada like many other nations and this gap appears to be widening during the current decade. The highest salary average is at approximately CAD 381,300, while the lowest salary average is CAD 27,600 per annum. As per the Conference Board of Canada (2016), the inequality of wages in Canada is pegged at 0.32 on the Gini index, an increase from 0.281 in 1989.

The salary structure consists of base, bonus/performance-related pay and commissions. Talent management and rewards pulse survey conducted by Willis Towers Watson in the year 2016 shows that 20 per cent of organizations in Canada link pay to performance though only one-third of them find that performance-related pay is effective in accruing anticipated benefits. Typical benefits in Canada would include employment insurance (health insurance and life insurance), Canadian pension plan, education and training benefits, housing benefits, benefits to help employee's family with the costs of raising children and compassionate care plus schemes. Fringe benefits are automobile benefits, board and lodging, gifts, awards, low-interest loans, meals, tuition fees, recreational and club reimbursements, transit passes, counselling services, travel allowance, discounts on merchandise, Internet service and subsidized school services.

Income tax/payroll tax in Canada has two components, a federal tax and a provincial tax. Federal income tax rate is a minimum of 15 per cent to a maximum of 33 per cent and provincial tax (Ontario) is a minimum of 5.5 per cent to a maximum of 13.16 per cent depending upon an employee's income. An employer in Canada is legally responsible for deducting Canada pension plan contributions, employment insurance premiums and applicable income tax deductions as mentioned before. In order to run the payroll process in Canada and effect necessary deductions, an employer must obtain a business number (BN) or must update Canada Revenue Agency if BN already exists. Employer also needs to register with Ministry of Finance to remit employer health tax and with Workplace Safety and Insurance Board for depositing premiums. Payroll is generally administered bi-weekly though options for weekly and monthly payroll process are available.

Depending upon the approach of a company, payroll can be run in-house or can be outsourced to third-party payroll agencies.

The United Kingdom

Compensation practices in the United Kingdom are quite varied with organizations experimenting with rich variety of different compensation models ranging from traditional fixed wages for work hours model to shared capitalist model with multiple objectives to excite employees with greater opportunities to earn more, to gain tax benefits, to align compensation with profit maximization and implement profit/loss-sharing methods. The most popular form of compensation has been profit-related bonuses. The United Kingdom government itself has encouraged shared capitalist practices by offering tax advantages to companies. The United Kingdom is a nation where compensation practice is a combination of a rigid practice with regulations and collective bargaining processes playing a dominant role as far as average worker salary is concerned including stipulation of minimum wages and flexible compensation practices targeted at executive category which are mostly driven by market forces and competition.

Real wages in the United Kingdom too seem to be plummeting almost equivalent to the levels in Greece. According to *Financial Times*, employees in the United Kingdom face more than a decade of lost wage growth and will earn no more by 2021 than they did in 2008. Average earnings fell 9 per cent between 2008 and 2014 as wages failed to keep pace with inflation. It is estimated that average real incomes will grow just 0.2 per cent a year between 2015 and 2020 which is slower than the 0.5 per cent annual growth between 2010 and 2014. This is an interesting situation because the United Kingdom has seen good growth of employment which is generally associated with real wage upward movement but in this exceptional situation, the United Kingdom has seen a decline. This, however, is attributed to low productivity and consequential low earnings and a decline of GDP by almost 10 per cent.

Salary Survey of Compensation and Benefits Professionals in the United Kingdom Interesting Facts

A study has been conducted on 543 compensation and benefits administrators as part of a salary survey in the United Kingdom to understand how these professionals react to compensation practices. The interesting facts are:

- The mean salary difference between male and female benefits professionals is about GBP 15,000 mirroring gender pay inequality that exists in all occupations implying that even benefits administrators are not free from discrimination.
- Only 9 per cent of the administrators are satisfied with their compensation, while 28 per cent are dissatisfied and remaining are neither satisfied nor dissatisfied.
- Eleven per cent of benefit administrators are themselves not members of any pension plans although they hold primary responsibility to promote the same.
- Five per cent of benefits administrators are not clear about their own pension schemes.
- Twenty-five per cent of benefits administrators have received stock grants.
- Seventy-two per cent of benefits administrators received annual bonus based on their individual performance.
- Almost 31 per cent of benefit administrators work part-time.

There are a wide range of benefits schemes that corporate organizations implement in the United Kingdom such as pensions, childcare vouchers, retail/leisure vouchers, charitable donations, training fees, mobile phones, interest-free loans, bikes for work, company car schemes, income protection, gym membership, canteen food, bus travel, long service awards, health care, pet insurance, buying/selling holidays, travel insurance, private medical insurance, life assurance, share schemes, share save, self-invested pensions (SIPs) and computer schemes. Most of these benefits are designed to be tax-free or tax-saving instruments. Forbes (2010) study found that 69 per cent of employers offer benefit schemes to their employees on voluntary basis in the United Kingdom. However, the efficacy of many of these schemes is vague. For example, Towers Watson Flexible Benefits Research study shows that only 51 per cent of such benefit schemes are measured to establish their benefits to employees. On the other hand, a Chartered Institute of Personnel and Development (CIPD; 2015) survey reveals that 78 per cent of employees do not appreciate the value of voluntary rewards. Voluntary benefits and pension schemes are at the core of compensation practices in the United Kingdom and are part of government-inspired salary sacrifice arrangements. According to a 2015 survey by Pensions and Lifetime Savings Association (PLSA), 90 per cent of active defined contribution pension scheme members invest in their employer's default pension fund because many of them are not savvy in making investment decisions. All these experiences prove that there should be better communication around benefits and their returns to employees. For example, Mercer's UK total rewards survey results point out that only 29 per cent of employers define a total rewards strategy, whereas 62 per cent of them in practice are implementing total rewards and only about 60 per cent of the 29 per cent believe that their strategy is helpful in attracting and retaining the talent.

An employer intending to set up and manage payroll process and national insurance in the United Kingdom must register with the UK government and set up a Pay as You Earn (PAYE) with Her Majesty's Revenue and Customs (HMRC) as a legal requirement. In addition to making salary payments, a payroll process also has the function of statutory payments, statutory sick pay, statutory maternity pay, ordinary statutory paternity pay and shared parental pay at regular intervals. HMRC provides a calculator for arriving at applicable taxes and contribution to the insurance for each employee which must be adhered to. An employer must make sure that its payroll SOP shall factor all the steps and processes stipulated by HMRC for running payroll in a legally compliant manner.

Germany

Unions, co-determination forums and collective bargaining process are at the core of German employee compensation system. According to an economist report, nearly 90 per cent of employee wages are regulated and determined as a part of collective bargaining wage agreements rather than through a pure managerial action or individual employee–employment contract negotiations. Wages are set by sectoral collective agreements. Compensation system is largely welfare- and socialism-driven and employers have limited flexibility in driving performance-based discriminatory-oriented compensation models in German industries. Therefore, industries which need flexibility to motivate employees through monetary incentives due to competition of the sector had to move part of their manufacturing operations to other parts of the world. *Financial Times*' study reveals that almost 35 per cent of labour-intensive manufacturing units were shifted to locations outside of Germany by 2004.

Compensation System at Deutsche Bank

Deutsche Bank has modified its compensation approach in 2016 to achieve a sustainable balance between employee and shareholder interests. Further, the bank claims that attracting and retaining the most capable employees on a global basis is central to its compensation strategy. The cornerstone of this concept is pay for performance within a sound risk management and governance framework. The new compensation system also seeks to align with internal and external expectations.

Wage increases have not kept pace with productivity which has been on the rise in Germany continuously for the last several years as shown in Table 4.3. Generally, wage trends in Germany have been stagnant for some time. The question of why German wages are not rising faster is one of the biggest riddles of the economy according to a *Financial Times*' report. The average growth rate of real wages as measured by aggregate statistics between 2008 and 2015 is a meagre 0.9 per cent. Studies also point out that general employees and junior executives in Germany are well paid, while senior German management professionals like CXO level are paid far less compared to corporate executives in developed countries like the United States and other European countries.

Firms in Germany have started using performance-related pay models only since the 1990s. However, performance-related pay is also largely regulated by collective bargaining process and it is group oriented rather than individual-based pay. Mostly, performance pay is linked to organizational goals and all employees get similar percentage (quantum) of pay based on actual target achievement on annual basis. Few German organizations also practice some form of profit-related pay and employee share ownership. Taxes in Germany are progressive and depending upon your income, tax can be between a minimum of 14 per cent and a maximum of 45 per cent of gross salary (of course, 0 per cent tax if annual income is less than EUR 8,354). All types of remuneration and benefits received by an employee constitute taxable income. However, certain components are tax exempted: payments from health or accident insurance, maternity grants, kindergarten fees, rent at the place of work and meal allowances, subject to limits.

Table 4.3   Inflation Rate, Productivity Index and Real Wage Correlations: Germany

Yes	Inflation Rate	Productivity Index Points: Increase	Real Wage Increase
2008	2.63	2.3	0.7
2009	0.32	2.1	0.6
2010	1.10	1.9	0.8
2011	2.07	2.7	0.9
2012	2.01	2.0	0.6
2013	1.50	1.8	0.9
2014	0.91	1.9	0.6
2015	0.23	2.2	1.1

Source: Compilation based on https://tradingeconomics.com/germany/wage-growth (accessed on 7 March 2018).

Wage Revision for German Public Sector Employees

After a long gap of many years and amidst threat of strike earlier, German employees are likely to see a good hike in their pay making public sector employment better. The federal and local governments reached a collective bargaining agreement with trade unions on pay rise covering about two million employees. As per the agreement, there will be pay hike of 4.75 per cent which will be implemented in two phases. The first increase of 2.4 per cent will be effective by 2016 and remaining 2.35 per cent by 2017. The hike which is considerable in the recent wage history is likely to influence the other pay agreements in Germany.

Table 4.4   Gender-based Pay Gaps: Germany

Year	Men's Income (in EUR)	Women's Income (in EUR)
2011	2,988	2,381
2012	3,031	2,345
2013	3,078	2,391
2014	3,191	2,643
2015	3,205	2,671

Source: Compilation based on http://ec.europa.eu/eurostat/statistics-explained/index.php/Gender_pay_gap_statistics (accessed on 7 March 2018).

Germany with 21.6 per cent is one of the biggest gender pay gap nations in Europe as shown in Table 4.4. This huge pay gap difference is attributable to gender concentration in certain industries and traditional collective bargaining agreements which have positioned women employees in lower pay grades.

Social security benefit which is very generous is a major compensation benefit applicable to all employees in Germany. There are two types of social security benefits. One is called employee social security consisting of health insurance, compulsory for employees whose wage is less than EUR 53,550 and nursing care insurance. The second one is called employer social security consisting of pension insurance, unemployment insurance, health insurance and long-term care insurance. Payments made in the form of premiums for these benefits account for almost 40 per cent of gross compensation of employees.

Payroll is administered once a month in organizations in Germany. Employers need to obtain all applicable registrations from the tax and social security authorities including an eight-digit number for identification of the company.

France

Compensation and benefit management in France is highly regulated and subject to collective bargaining and negotiations. A very intriguing element with France is that though the rate of unionization is only about 8 per cent, the rate of collective bargaining coverage is almost 98 per cent. Wage agreements can be drawn at sectoral, industry, company, regional and national level. As per the

Ministry of Labour, Government of France, in 2013 alone, signed 962 industry level agreements of various types of which 422 dealt with pay increases. The distinction with collective wage agreements in France is that there are multiple types of bargaining agreements depending upon the need and scope. For example, one type of agreement covers all types of wages, benefits, conditions and guarantees and the second type is targeted to cover special situations and third type addresses the instrument of individual employee negotiations. Though compensation system in France for decades has been collective, the recent trend suggests growing popularity of individualism in compensation management at least in private corporate sector. Also, bonuses, importantly individualized bonuses as a percentage of total pay, are on upward movement since 2004 and constituted an estimated 21 per cent of the total pay in 2014. Real wage in France, like in many nations in Europe, has seen a steady decline when compared to inflation as shown in Table 4.5. According to OECD, the rise of rate of pay inequality in France is higher than in many other wealthy countries (it went up by 1.6 per cent in 2014 alone) though inequality in income among its population has seen a decline, thus creating a paradoxical situation. For example, compensation of CEOs of Cotation Assistée en Continu (CAC) index companies have gone up double digit compared to the 0.7 per cent wage growth of other employees. The study also found that France was a slow mover when it came to decreasing the gender pay gap. Women in France still earn 14 per cent less than men.

The distinctive feature with benefits in France is that its pension system is classified into four types based on employee categories: blue-collar or clerical employees, junior supervisors, supervisors and senior executives. Contributions to this benefit come from employers and industrial bodies and amount of pension is dependent upon salary levels of employees. Employers in France pay 27.5 per cent of total labour costs in social security contributions, almost the highest of anywhere in Europe. The typical monetary benefits would include subsidized travel, Reduction du temps de travail (RTT) days, a kind of overtime payouts, restaurant vouchers, paid days off for weddings, subsidized health care, 13th month bonus, renting of the employee's flat, payment of phone bills and mileage allowance.

Table 4.5 **Inflation Rate, Productivity Index and Real Wage Correlations: France**

Year	Productivity Index Points	Inflation Rate	Average Wage Increase
2006	0.57	1.68	0.7
2007	0.47	1.49	0.5
2008	0.81	2.82	0.4
2009	0.23	0.09	0.4
2010	0.17	1.53	0.3
2011	0.02	2.12	0.4
2012	0.01	1.96	1.0
2013	0	0.86	0.5
2014	0.73	0.51	0.6
2015	0.81	0.04	0.4

Source: Compilation based on https://www.ecb.europa.eu/pub/pdf/scpwps/ecbwp1360.pdf?76adf63a5e82e0922 604cc6c257a1f77 (accessed on 7 March 2018).

The French Tax system is highly progressive with seven slabs depending upon the income/salary level with a minimum of 0 per cent to a maximum of 45 per cent income tax. In France, the income tax return is generally a family return with spouses and children jointly reporting their income. The larger the family size, the lower the income tax. Managing payroll process in France is a complex operation due to numerous individual and collective wage agreements, different working hours and vacation time calculations apart from pension and social security contributions. Employer needs to register the company and seek 14-digit numbers for company identification, deposit of taxes and to run the payroll.

Switzerland

Compensation practices in Switzerland are to a great extent similar to the practices in the United States and the United Kingdom. While compensation practices that are applicable to operating core or works committee level employees are partially regulated through canton/federal rules and collective bargaining agreements, executive compensation has followed a highly discretionary, competitive and individualized structure. Executive compensation packages especially at CXO level are highly debated and controversial given their abnormal growth disturbing the pay parity ideal. As per Towers Watson survey in 2013, the executive compensation has gone up by three times in comparison to normal wage growth. There is no legal minimum wage in Switzerland but in 2013, unions had negotiated to include minimum wage as an element in collective bargaining agreements but actual minimum wage rate is not yet realized due to rejection of the same in a referendum conducted in 2014. The average wage as of 2016 was CHF 6,276 per month. The average wage growth has been at 1.63 per cent during the last two decades till 2016. The annual wage hikes generally hovered around 0.50 per cent in the last five years against the average core inflation growth of about 0.30 during same period resulting in marginal growth of real wages, while productivity has seen a dip of nearly 1.1 per cent at an average. Pay inequality is a major issue in Switzerland drawing attention of both corporate and public leaders. As per Swiss Federal Statistical Office (2016), the gender gap has been growing and as of 2015, women earned 18.9 per cent less than men for equal work. The pay difference between highest paid and average paid is also on the rise. The highest paid employees have earned an average of CHF 11,512 per month against the lowest paid average of CHF 3,886 per month.

Distinct element in Swiss compensation structure of employees is its excessive focus on variable pay probably owing to significant presence of financial industry. Stock option plans, performance-based pay, deferred compensation and cash bonuses are very common to the extent that they are highly debated and the Swiss Financial Market Supervisory Authority had to issue guidelines on remuneration of employees in this regard. Income tax is progressive and levied both at canton level and federal level for compensation income up to CHF 150,000. Unlike other nations, remittance of income tax is the sole responsibility of employees and employers have no legal obligation necessarily to do deduction at source. Tax rates are also different for employees residing in different cantons as the communal tax is different. Income tax for income up to CHF 150,000 can be anywhere from 9.6 per cent to a maximum of 23.5 per cent. The income tax rate applicable for income of CHF 500,000 and above can vary from a minimum of 15 per cent to a maximum of 33 per cent.

Social security contributions are made both by the employee and employer equally at the rate of 5.125 per cent each aggregating to 10.25 per cent towards AHV (first pillar of coverage of old age and survivorship: 8.4 per cent), IV (first pillar of disability: 1.4 per cent) and EO (coverage of salary payment in the case of military service and motherhood: 0.45 per cent). In addition to this, contribution of 1 per cent is made towards unemployment insurance and any additional contribution depends upon the nature of industry and employer for accidents/insurance. Payroll process in Switzerland is simple and a company can run a payroll without even registering with Swiss authorities. However, it is helpful for payroll to be run locally if a company has considerable number of employees employed locally.

The Netherlands

A large number of employees, almost 84 per cent of workforce (6 million out of 7.1 million), in the Netherlands and their wages fall within the purview of collective bargaining process. According to the Ministry of Labour of the Netherlands, 731 wage agreements reached in 2015 across all industries and sectors. Large companies negotiate their own wages, while small and medium ones follow industry level wage agreements. Variable pay which is mostly performance-related pay is gaining momentum in the Netherlands but this is a greater trend in company-centric wage agreements rather than industry or sectoral agreements. Compensation and benefits practices in the Netherlands are quite mixed due to the reason that some industries in the country are highly internationalized pursuing global benchmarks and few industries remained very country-centric furthering national practices. For example, percentage of foreign CEOs at AEX companies doubled in just two years from 24 per cent in 2002 to 48 per cent in 2004 and percentage of foreign CEOs stood at a whopping 59 per cent by 2015. However, even in national practices, the influence of both Anglo-Saxon and Continental Europe trends can be seen. The managerial talent however across all the industries is increasingly globalized in the Netherlands. On the other hand, compensation practices are significantly influenced by the Tabaksblat Code. A major trend observed was reform of equity-based compensation which used to be highly discretionary, subjective, traditional stock option grant plans but has become more performance oriented and more of a deferred compensation tool in the recent past. In the entire compensation structure, equity and long-term incentives have become key elements at least for employees in executive category in the Netherlands as more and more companies move towards competitive business performance.

The Dutch Tabaksblat Code

The Code was adopted by the parliament in 2003 which applies to all listed companies in the Netherlands effective 2004. The Code comprises voluntary guidelines but firms need to explain when their practices diverge from the practices suggested by the Code. According to the Code, a supervisory board member shall not be granted any shares in the company. Variable compensation shall be related to measurable long- and short-term targets. Severance pay shall not exceed one year pay. Options to acquire shares shall only be exercised three years after grant date or at the end of employment. Shares shall be retained for at least five years after the grant date.

Real wages have seen up and down trends during the period between 2003 and 2015. Wage growth has been better due to low level of inflation during the said period except in years 2005,

2006 and 2001 to 2013 when inflation surpassed the wage growth. Though wage inequality comparatively is a lesser problem in the Netherlands, it does seem to be on an upward trend recently. The inequality has increased by about 0.8 per cent during the period 2004 to 2014. Wages have increased an average of 1.30 per cent in 2017 against an average wage increase of 2.23 per cent during the period from 1991 to 2016.

Compensation structure practised by the Dutch companies usually consists of base salary, annual bonus plans, deferred bonus plans, performance pay, stock options, performance shares, restricted shares and the benefits include retirement benefits such as pension plan, health insurance, sickness benefit, social security insurances, company car, personal loans, vacation allowance/holiday pay, housing subsidies, telephone and laptop provision. Social security in the Netherlands can be classified into three types: employee insurance schemes, general insurance schemes and social provisions. Also, each company should have its own pension scheme.

Dutch income tax system which is progressive stipulates a minimum of 2.35 per cent to a maximum of 52 per cent tax depending upon the income, status of partner: working/non-working, type of work and residency of an employee. Payroll tax comprises income tax and social security contributions. Like many other nations, a company needs to obtain registration from the Companies House and also a wage tax number so that all payroll levy and deductions can be remitted referring this number. There is no legal need to run payroll within the country and payroll is generally administered on a bi-weekly basis.

Finland

Finnish wage and compensation practices are dominated by unions and collective bargaining agreements whose main objective is to drive socialistic form of wage structure without losing sight of productivity. Almost for the last five decades, compensation practices were not only subject to collective bargaining process but were also industry/sector wide and highly centralized. However, since 2007, a new trend has started with unions and managements driving firm-wise agreements which provide more flexibility and address an organization's needs more precisely. Currently, the mainstream practice is that 50 per cent of wage is influenced by sectoral agreement and 50 per cent by a company level agreement. Average wage in Finland has been moving up steadily and currently standing at 3,384 EUR per month. Wages were increasing at approximately 1.3 per cent between 2012 and 2016 with 2016 showing the lowest increase at 0.8 per cent. Real wages were growing at about 0.3 per cent during the same time. Inflation, productivity and wage increase trends in Finland are quite steady during the last six years with almost negligible marginal movement. Wage inequality in Finland is not a major challenge. The difference between highest paid and lowest paid is no more than a 5.4 times difference and is almost the lowest pay inequality among EU nations. Senior executive pay is also subject to compliance with Finnish Remuneration Code (Corporate Governance Code, 2015). Pay inequality among genders is also considerably low with current difference for equal work standing at about 7 per cent. There has been a huge drop in gender pay inequality during the last 20 years by almost 45 per cent.

The salary structure of Finland employees is largely similar to standard models consisting of basic pay, allowances/prerequisites, bonus, social security contributions and stock plans. The significant difference is that Finland comes across as much more egalitarian than other EU nations in compensation practices including prerequisites. Stock option/share plans are also common consisting of all employee share plans, phantom option plans, cash plans and performance share plans. Social security contributions in Finland are organized into several brackets: Medicare contribution (1.32 per cent of municipal taxable income by an employee and 0.75 per cent by an employer), group life insurance contribution (by an employer at the rate of 0.067 per cent of an employee's salary), accident insurance premium (1 per cent contribution by employer), unemployment insurance premium (0.5 of the salary paid by the employee and 0.75 per cent by an employer), pension insurance premium (5.55 per cent by an employee and 17.75 per cent of an employee's salary by the employer) and per diem contribution (0.84 per cent of the salary income paid by an employee).

An organization can choose to run payroll locally within the country or remotely and company registration with Finland government and tax identification numbers are required if payroll is to be managed locally. Income tax payable by an employee on salary can be 6.5 per cent at the minimum and 31.75 per cent at the maximum.

Sweden

Though wages in Sweden, like in many European nations, are collective and regulated by wage agreements reached between employers of industry/sector/company and trade unions as a part of collective bargaining process, the trend of individualized compensation and individually negotiated wage agreements is growing rapidly. There are currently about 600 collective agreements covering over three million employees governing wages. More and more employers and unions are seeking company-wide wage agreements in the place of industry-wide agreements for better results though as of now almost 90 per cent of agreements are drawn at a central level: industry or sector wise. There is a clear evidence for greater use of individual wage agreements in respect of supervisory and executive staff and also in IT and telecom industry across all levels of employees. Swedish Financial Supervisory Authority has stipulated certain regulations in relation to executive remuneration and performance-based pay to avoid risk-taking and short-term gains. The guidelines mandate that at least 60 per cent of variable pay payment which can have potential impact on the risk exposure of a company shall be deferred to at least three years.

Sweden ranks highest in its hourly labour costs with EUR 43 per hour of wage among EU nations whose average is EUR 29 per hour as per Germany's Federal Statistical Office (Desstatis). Real wages in Sweden have been appreciating in contrast to many nations since wage increase has been outpacing the rate of inflation. The pay disparity is also vanishing and wages of blue-collar workforce in particular has been increasing faster than white-collar workforce since 2006 as per Confederation of Swedish Enterprises equalizing the pay. Similarly, disparity between the pay of men and women workforce is declining. For example, due to higher wage increase for women workforce (due to higher wage revisions in women-dominated industries) since 2004, the gap has reduced by 1.3 percentage points between 2004 and 2007 alone and currently the gap stands at less than 1 per cent. Though the disparity between industry sectors is also thinning, IT and telecom lead in highest wages.

Social security contributions made by employers on behalf of their employees are an important element in the overall compensation structure. The contributions cover pension, health insurance and other social benefits which account for 31.42 per cent of gross salary. However, percentage of contribution for employees under the age of 26 years is only 25.46 per cent. Employees also need to contribute 7 per cent of their wages to the pension system. The social security system takes care of childcare, parental leave, health care, and accident care and disability assistance. In order to set up the payroll process in Sweden, a company shall register with Swedish Tax Office and with Swedish Companies Registration Office. Taxation involves three components: the municipality (24 per cent), the county council (7 per cent) and the central government taxes. The minimum tax is 0 and maximum is 51 per cent applicable based on salary level of an employee.

Denmark

Compensation practices in Denmark are largely governed by collective bargaining agreement processes and have more of a socialism-based approach but competitive compensation models too exist. There are three types of compensation systems prevalent in the country. The first is practised by Danish-based industries that cater to needs of their own country/market and are primarily limited to Denmark wherein more an egalitarian and collective compensation system is practised. The second type is Danish multinational companies whose primary market is exports wherein a combination of competitive pay like individual bonuses and performance-related pay practices are adopted in some measure along with a socialistic pay. The third kind of organizations is pure multinational companies operating in Denmark whose practices are dominated by their parent country practices and largely leaning on individualized compensation practices. However, the government interference even in collective bargaining-driven wage models is very limited. The latest trend in Denmark is that the collective bargaining process is mostly confined to negotiating a minimum or standard wage applicable to a sector which will be implemented by all companies both in private and public sectors paving way for negotiations/flexibility for company-wise perks and performance-related pay and individualized compensation components. This trend is seen mainly in IT, telecom, and research and development sectors.

As of 2016, the average salary in Denmark is DKK 531,320 (gross) and DKK 325,146 (net). Wages have been increasing at an average of 2.5 per cent in the last 10 years against the average increase of inflation at about 1.8 per cent during the same time. Real wages in Denmark have been rising steadily due to low inflation rates compared to wage increases during early 2000's though there were very nominal hikes but it has been stable since 2010 with a positive bias towards increase of real wages. Historically, wages as a proportion of total output/productivity is high in Denmark. Productivity has increased by about 1.0 per cent against wage increase of 2.5 per cent during the last 10 years.

Denmark is truly an egalitarian workplace with high emphasis on social security system. The social security contributions cover health insurance, child allowance, maternity benefit, holiday pay, disability benefits, sickness benefits, pension schemes and unemployment benefits. Social security contribution shall be made by both the employer and employees. The actual contribution is determined by income and tax rate applicable to an employee. Usually contribution towards social security and occupational insurance will not exceed 8 per cent of gross pay for an employee. Further, employees and employer are liable to contribute to supplementary old-age pension. This contribution is a fixed monthly amount of DKK 284 and is paid one-third by the employee and two-thirds by the employer.

Performance-related pay is picking up momentum in Denmark. Currently, pay up to 20 per cent of gross salary payable to an employee can be towards allowances and performance-based pay. There are also instances where senior management performance pay is stretched to a 50 per cent but it is a rarity. The performance pay is generally allocated based on performance appraisals and dialogue between employee and the manager. The Danish government has also introduced performance pay for its employees since late 1990s. However, performance-based pay is not viewed favourably by many in Denmark as they believe it can lead to gaming the system in order to earn this incentive. Pay inequality does exist; gender pay inequality is at approximately 12 per cent and the gap between highest paid to lowest paid is about nine times.

Income tax rates are high compared to many nations and the rates are progressive in Denmark with minimum tax being at 8 per cent and maximum standing at 56 per cent. Payroll can be administered either locally or remotely. A firm is required to register with Danish government to run payroll locally and shall maintain record of all employees and their details including income tax number.

Hungary

Hungarian compensation practices applicable to works level employees are collective and subject to collective bargaining process at a company level although the system is flexible and there is also a strong trend lately favouring individualized pay packages. Collective bargaining agreements are also highly decentralized with management, rather than unions, playing an influential role unlike in many countries in the EU and such wage agreements are largely confined to average wage hikes. According to the European Commission, about 250,000 of 1.2 million workers in Hungary are not even paid minimum wages of HUF 87,150 per month. Executive compensation is individualized and mostly follows the Anglo-Saxon models of competitive pay with emphasis on variable/performance pay and fringe benefits and stock options. Wages in Hungary are not frozen and they are subject to downward adjustment unlike other EU nations where only upward adjustments are practised and they are frozen for any downward adjustments. Average wage in Hungary as of 2016 was at HUF 28,577 per month, the highest in a decade. Wage hikes at an average have hovered around 18 per cent per annum for a decade and highest pay increases of around 24 per cent are seen since 2014. Employees in Hungary are also experiencing real wage growth of about 5.2 per cent at an average in the recent past with wage hikes superseding inflation which is at an average of 7.3 per cent per annum and productivity increase of 2.7 per cent.

Guaranteed cash compensation (basic pay) is the most major element in compensation structure of employees accounting for almost about 65 per cent of total pay and bonuses occupy the role of second most preferred component. The common prerequisites which are more driven by tax considerations than competitiveness of pay are meal vouchers, vacation voucher and voluntary health fund contribution, back to school support, Internet subscription, local travel and entry to sports events. According to Hay Group survey in 2014 (www.haygroup.com/us/press/details.aspx?id=37635 [accessed on 7 March 2018]), 37 per cent of firms have offered stock option plans or shares to their employees. Social security contributions are made both by employees and employer, and covers benefits such as health, pension and unemployment. Employers shall contribute 22 per cent of gross salary and employees a total of 18.5 per cent of gross salary (towards pension scheme contribution of 10 per cent, health insurance and labour market contribution of 8.5 per cent) as social security contribution.

Payroll is administered once a month in Hungary and companies intending to run their own payroll need to register with Labour Department along with details of incorporation. Social security contributions and income tax deductions need to be made on account of VAT. Income tax applicable to salaried income is flat at 16 per cent and deducted at source.

Poland

Compensation practices in Poland are varied and mixed including competitive compensation practices which are not bound by any agreements as well as collective agreements drawn in an organization which are applicable to either all employees or one section of employees. Wages and compensation matters are not unionized and subjected to the extent that collective bargaining agreements prevail in other nations in EU providing enough flexibility. Interestingly, wage agreements drawn at organization level are also kept confidential from others and government generally does not interfere. Individualized compensation models such as performance-based pay and bonuses are commonly present. At the same time, there are many instances where organizations seem to be implementing collective bonus models. Unions have a say and government interference is limited ensuring minimum guaranteed wage and all other wage practices over that guaranteed wage are flexible, individualized and circumstantial. According to Central Statistical Office of Poland (2017), wages in Poland have been increasing between 2.1 and 4.3 per cent at an average during the last five years (2011–2016). However, real wages have declined by almost 1 per cent during the same period and also productivity by almost 0.8 per cent. The average gross wage in Poland stands at PLN 4,050 per month as of 2016. Though exact data is unavailable, the pay inequality between men and women for the same kind of work is considerable though lower than average of EU as per Poland government estimates and also the pay gap between highest paid and lowest paid is wider than in other EU nations. Often, reason for growing pay inequality is attributed to infusion of foreign capital in Poland and immigration of Poles to other EU nations and its impact of wages of domestic market.

Salary structure is standard consisting of basic pay, variable pay, bonus, allowances, prerequisites and social security contributions. Social security contributions are made both by employer and employee, and it comprises of pension contribution of 19.52 per cent of an employee's salary (employer 9.76 per cent and employee 9.76 per cent), disability contribution of 6 per cent (employer 4.5 per cent and employee 1.5 per cent), accident insurance contribution of 0.67 per cent paid by employer and sickness contribution of 2.45 per cent paid by an employee, employee's guaranteed benefits fund contribution of 0.1 per cent by employer and health insurance contribution of 9 per cent out of which 7.75 per cent is adjusted against the tax payable by an employee.

Employers must be registered with National Court Register for setting up payroll process and are also required to do social security registration for remitting the social security contributions. Employers can choose either bi-weekly or monthly frequency for running the payroll. The income tax rate that is applicable depends upon the salary level consisting of two slabs: 18 per cent for annual income up to PLN 85,528 and 32 per cent over this amount.

The Czech Republic

Compensation and benefits practices in the Czech Republic are largely governed by collective bargaining agreements reached as per the Czech Labour Code and other related regulations. In few cases, there could be specific company level collective agreements providing a difference in pay practice but that too restricted to be within approved standard deviation range. Rate of minimum wage depends upon job type and can range from CZK 11,000 to CZK 22,000 per month in 2017, while the average wage is CZK 26,287 per month. Employees in the country have seen a wage growth of about 3.62 per cent at an average during the period between 2011 and 2016 but real wages have witnessed a marginal dip of about 0.4 per cent though core inflation has been steady at about 2.2 per cent and this is due to steep escalation of housing rentals in Prague and increase in productivity by an average of 4.8 per cent. The gender pay gap in the Czech Republic is the highest of all EU nations at a whopping 22.1 per cent in 2016 and general pay gap between highest paid and lowest paid is about 41.1 per cent. The gender pay gap seems to be chiefly contributed by the really low number of women employees in management cadre.

Salary structure for employees in the Czech Republic typically consists of a standard salary, bonus and fringe benefits and social security contributions. Importance of fringe benefits is a growing among the workforce in the country due to tax benefits and these include meal tickets, 13th month pay, supplementary pension insurance contribution, premium health care, vacation, transport subsidy, mobile phone and free drinks at workplace, company weekend functions and extra holiday and computer for personal use. It is estimated that 34 per cent of average wage bill is per cent on benefits excluding social security contributions and direct performance-related pay. Employees and employers contribute towards social security scheme consisting of benefits such as pension, unemployment and sickness benefit. Employees contribute 6.5 per cent of their gross taxable income and employers contribute an amount equivalent to 25 per cent of the gross taxable income of an employee.

In order to manage payroll, an employer shall register with the Czech Government Labour Office and obtain necessary permission and code numbers for remitting social security contributions, health insurance premiums and income tax of employees. Czech has some of the lowest income tax rate for employees. Currently, the tax rate is 15 per cent but it can be 22 per cent for salary (additional tax of 7 per cent towards solidarity over and above 15 per cent standard tax) that is over CZK 1.2 million per year.

The People's Republic of China

It is complex to summarize or infer the compensation practices in China since practices vary from province to province and different from urban to semi-urban to rural regions. Government limits its role to execution of minimum wage though it oversees the wage practices in private sector. Executive compensation is quite competitive and heavily influenced by multinational companies that have set up manufacturing bases in many parts of China and introduction of stock option/ownership programmes since 2006. Performance-based pay is also gaining importance at least in executive compensation management. Wages in China have been growing at a double-digit rate for almost 12 years with an average hike of almost 11 per cent during 2010–2016 as per National Bureau of Statistics of China (2016). Average wage as of 2016 was CNY 62,031 per annum. Real wages are also on the rise given single-digit inflationary trends and productivity increase at an average of 3.9 per cent. In 2016 alone, real wages have gone up by an average of 7.1 per cent. As per ILO estimates, wages in China have grown three times more than the wage growth in G20 economies. However, the forecasts for 2017 show that this trend is likely to slow down and double-digit wage growths may be a practice of the past paving a beginning for single-digit hikes given the slowdown in the economy and increasing wage bills blunting China's cost advantage. There is also a move on the part of the government to freeze the minimum salary level in order to stabilize wage levels which have grown three times in annualized compound terms since 2004. For example, highly industrialized Guangdong provincial government has announced that it will be freezing minimum salary for two years. Gender pay gap in China is significant and it is on the rise and it is estimated to be a difference of almost 38 per cent with women getting paid lesser for same kind of work. As per IMF estimates, pay gap between highest paid and lowest paid is also wide indicating an average difference of over 200 times and income inequality is pegged at 0.8 on Gini index.

Administering payroll in China would involve close liaison with government agencies because there is a requirement of registrations and a host of deductions and rules that are vastly different for Chinese employees and foreign employees. Payroll is run once a month. There would be payroll deductions such as individual income tax, social security contributions and payroll tax. Remote payroll option does not exist in China. Income tax rates in China are really progressive and can be anywhere from a minimum of 3 per cent to a maximum of 45 per cent of gross salary. Though it varies from province to province, a contribution of 8 per cent shall be deducted from employees' salary towards social security for the benefits covering pension, health insurance and unemployment insurance, and employer shall contribute 20 per cent of salary for the benefits covering pension, health insurance, maternity insurance, work-related injury insurance and unemployment insurance. In addition to the social security benefits, fringe benefits such as transport reimbursement, Chinese New Year bonuses, free counselling, vacations and additional training opportunities, meal vouchers are becoming part of the pay structure. Equity-based compensation practices such as employee stock option plans are also in vogue though largely restricted to senior and middle management levels and they tend to be cashless more often despite strong government intervention in ownership structure of many firms in China.

Singapore

Though National Wages Council (NWC, 2016) plays a role in the formulation of general guidelines on wage matters which are applicable to both public and private sectors, compensation practices in Singapore are quite flexible. In fact, NWC itself played a key role in freezing and stabilizing wages on quite a few occasions in tandem with economic trends and has also given a fillip for introduction of variable pay system. The flexible compensation practices include more decentralized wage negotiation process tailored to requirements of organizations, their profitability and interests of employees and employer. Though workplace wage agreements exist, individual wage agreements/negotiated contracts have become more common reflecting individualized compensation practices and competitive pay structures. Discretionary bonuses, skill-based pay, performance-based pay and other target-driven variable pay and benefits are widely deployed in Singapore organizations. Employee stock option plans which had gained popularity with organizations in the country in late 1990s are still being practised albeit in a selective manner. Salaries have been growing at an average of 4.8 per cent during 2010–2016. Average wages in Singapore as of 2016 were at SGD 4,646 per month. Real wages have been growing due to declining inflationary trends and stable productivity. A government estimate puts the real wage growth in the last seven years at 18 per cent. According to the Ministry of Manpower, women were paid 10 per cent lesser than men for equal kind of work in 2015 and this gap is progressively reducing with more and more women employees getting into managerial and professional jobs. A distinct feature with compensation structure in Singapore is its performance-related pay with coverage of almost 89 per cent of employees as per Hays Asia Salary Study of 2015 (https://www.hays.com.sg/salary-guide/index.htm [accessed on 7 March 2018]).

Salary structure in Singapore generally consists of base pay, bonus, variable pay, overtime, social security contributions and allowances, and equity-based compensation mainly targeted at employees in middle and senior cadre. Pay benefits include attendance allowance, standby duty allowance, anniversary cash awards, cost of living allowance, dirt allowance, commission, education allowance, education/training reimbursement, festive allowance, extra duty allowance, gratuity, mobile phone reimbursements, housing rental expenses, holiday expenses, laundry expenses, meal expenses, national service pay, personal clothing allowance, transport and staff welfare benefit. Companies need to register with Singapore government for running payroll and are also obligated to prepare an annual report in prescribed formats for the purpose of employees' income tax. Income tax has multiple slabs in Singapore starting from a minimum of 2 per cent for income from SGD 20,000 up to SGD 30,000 and to 20 per cent on income of SGD 320,000 plus per annum. Employees who are Singapore nationals and permanent residents need to contribute 20 per cent of their gross salary towards social security and employers need to contribute 16 per cent of gross salary. This is also known as Central Provident Fund (CPF) contributions in Singapore. In addition to this, employees need to contribute to ethnic fund and employers need to pay towards skill development levy. Employers hiring foreign workers are also required to pay foreign workers levy.

Japan

Japanese compensation practices are relatively well coordinated and tied to a firm's performance to a large extent given the nature of relationship-based corporate culture. Compensation system, although aligned with a firm's performance, is quite different from the flexible and competitive Anglo-American compensation system. Therefore, a distinct element with compensation system in Japan is its seniority-based wage system (known as Nenko Wage System) where an older or senior employee sometimes gets paid more wages than a younger or junior employee regardless of their roles. However, given global competitive markets, some Japanese firms have been making efforts to move away from this practice especially due to the fact that the younger people are shying away in accepting lower pay as per this principle. Also, a commonly witnessed practice is that most employees in Japan are paid bonuses twice a year in alignment with profits of a firm in addition to regular base pay and variable pay that is linked more to an individual's target achievement and performance. The bonus accounts for at least one-fourth of an employee's annual salary. Collective bargaining process and negotiations by unions are largely confined to base pay revisions. Shunto wage agreements are a case in point here. Wage hikes in Japan since 1995 are very low and real wages have gone up by merely 0.3 per cent. During the period 2009–2016, 2.1 per cent has been the average pay hike and the inflation has been at the same level standing at about 2.07 per cent during the same time with productivity steadily ahead of real wage growth. The average annual salary in Japan is JPY 4,890,038 as in 2016. The pay gap between men and women is significant with a gap of about 30 per cent as of 2016 as per OECD data, indicating Japan is one of the highest gender pay gap nations. The pay inequality between permanent employees and temporary contracts is also considerable, and currently permanent employees are paid around JPY 5 million against the JPY 2 million paid to temporary employees for the same kind of work. The difference between highest and lowest paid is also widening despite Japan being known for its social equality. The difference is about 0.069 on the Gini index. Employee stock options are also popular in Japan. Broadly, companies offer stocks to employees, both in managerial and non-managerial cadres, by acquiring their own stock in advance and through issuance of new stock.

Pay structure typically comprises base pay, variable pay and bonuses apart from prerequisites. Commonly found benefits include paid vacation, health care, pension, commutation expense, annual medical check-ups, mobile phone, laptops and meal vouchers. Social insurance which is mandatory for all employees and for which equal contribution shall be made both by employees and employer on a monthly basis consisting of: health insurance, social pension, nursing insurance and children upbringing benefit. Contribution towards upbringing of children is made only by the employer. Also, employees are covered under labour insurance covering benefits like unemployment insurance for which contribution is made both by employee and employer, and accident compensation insurance for which contribution is made by employer.

Payroll is administered once a month generally on 25th of every month. Tax on salary income is deducted on a monthly basis and shall be remitted by the employer. There are two types of income tax in Japan, one at a federal level and the being a resident income tax. There are seven income tax slabs applicable depending upon annual income, 5, 10, 20, 23, 33, 40 and 45 per cent. In addition to this, municipal tax and prefectural tax are also deducted from the salaries of employees through payroll process.

The Philippines

Compensation practices in the Philippines are partly regulated by the Labor Code through wage agreements and mandatory/voluntary guidelines and partly negotiated by employees and employers on their own. Gradually, competitive pay structures and practices are growing in the country with more and more multinationals setting up businesses. Minimum wage rates are different for agricultural and non-agricultural workers and the wages also differ by industry and occupations further classified as A, B, C and D. Minimum wage as of 2016 was at a minimum of PHP 295 to a maximum of PHP 353 per day depending upon the nature of occupation. The average wage was standing at PHP 8,280 per month combined for agriculture and non-agriculture sectors and it was PHP 31,127 per month for industrial sector as of 2016. Wages in the Philippines grew at an average of 6 per cent during the period 2012–2016 as per Willis Towers Watson. This rate is lower than the growth rate in other nations such as India, Pakistan and Bangladesh but higher than in Singapore and Hong Kong. As per estimates based on latest surveys and studies, this trend is likely to continue with the Philippines catching up with double-digit wage growth in the immediate future. Real wages in the Philippines are growing since growth of nominal wages is ahead of the core average inflation rate of 2.1 per cent and productivity growth rate of about 4.7 per cent. The pay gap between men and women is comparatively lower at 10 per cent and this is also on a progressive decline as per the Department of Labor and Employment's estimates. Pay among employees in public sector has stayed ahead of employees in private sector by almost 30 per cent as per the data published by the Office for National Statistics. The salary gap between highest paid and lowest paid is continuously widening but it is hard to capture the average percentage or ratios given the data deficit.

Social security contribution covering benefits such as sickness, disability, maternity and retirement pay and contingencies, contribution to national health insurance programme, contribution to home development and mutual fund, 13th month pay, service incentive leave, and meal and rest period are mandatory for all organizations to implement. Social security contribution amount depends upon the monthly salary and contributions shared by employer at the rate of 7.37 per cent of the salary and 3.63 per cent by the employee. Other benefits commonly seen are midyear bonus, rice allowance, meal subsidy, tuition fee subsidy, employee's educational assistance programme, attendance bonus, loyalty token and vacation. In order to run payroll, companies need to register with the Philippines government and also open seek identification numbers for remitting income tax and social security contributions from respective government departments. Income tax rates are progressive starting at a minimum of 5 per cent for salary range up to PHP 10,000 to a maximum of 32 per cent for a gross salary of PHP 500,000 and above.

Australia

Australian compensation practices are partly regulated to ensure minimum wage and wage equality to a rational extent and there is enough flexibility for organizations to experiment and design competitive individualized pay packages. Wage awards or agreements for each industry and sometimes specific to a company are common. Minimum wages are regulated both at federal level and provincial level. Federal minimum wage is about AUD 657 a week, while average wage ranges from AUD 75,936 to AUD 88,327 per annum depending upon the province. As per Fair Work Commission (2015), the real minimum wage rose by almost 11 per cent between 1997 and 2012, and stands at AUD 672 per week in 2017. Despite the efforts of the Australian government, gender pay inequality is at about 18 per cent with men being paid more than women for equal work according to Australian Bureau of Statistics. The ratio between average highest paid and lowest average paid is approximately 38 times as of 2015 indicating that while the gap is considerable, it is not as high as in some developed nations. Though real wages were on the rise since 2005, it is on the decline during 2016 due to general slowdown of economy and productivity.

Social security contributions in Australia are closely tied to tax deductions and current social security rate stands at 11.50 per cent and the benefits are funded through these tax deductions. Only exception is that a deduction of 1.5 per cent of gross salary is made towards Medicare. Income tax rates are progressive with no tax up to AUD 18,200 income, 19c for each dollar of income over AUD 18,200 and 32.5c for each dollar over 37,000, 37c for each dollar over 80,000 and 45c for each dollar of income earned over AUD 180,000 per annum.

Summary

The chapter explores (a) macro trends impacting international compensation strategy and approaches, (b) international compensation structure and systems of selective multinational companies, (c) international compensation practices and policies in 18 selective countries, (d) risk-based compensation practices, (e) minimum wages, (f) payroll process set up in various nations, (g) inflation rates, productivity, real wages and taxation trends, (h) gender-based compensation practices and (i) flexible benefits, incentives, bonuses and base salary trends. Orientation and philosophy of selective nations towards compensation of employees is discussed and deliberated in detail along with emerging trends.

QUESTIONS FOR DISCUSSION

1. How macro factors such as inflation, taxation and economic growth of a nation and micro factors such as profits, revenue growth and productivity of an organization impact wages?
2. What macro trends are impacting an international organization's approach towards compensation and benefits management?
3. Discuss about increasing legislation regulating executive compensation.
4. What are the various approaches and models of international compensation management?
5. Centralization or decentralization? What works well for management of compensation in an international organization?
6. What is double taxation in payroll?
7. Discuss about gender-based pay discrimination.
8. Discuss about real wages and wage growth in European countries.
9. Compare and contrast compensation practices in North America versus Asian countries.
10. Pay for performance: is it real?
11. Analyse state of global compensation administration based on various international surveys.

CASE STUDY

Wagonriders is a Germany-based automaker that has operations and manufacturing bases across the globe. The company has a great history and is a pioneer in developing mid-range passenger cars. Its product range includes hatchback, MUV, SUV, sedan and estate, and supermini type vehicles and recent development is its foray into manufacturing and marketing blueTEC clean diesel engine cars. The company has also entered into collaboration with two other prominent German luxury automobile manufacturers to strengthen marketing of their respective products mutually. Wagonriders is facing a steep challenge from Japanese and American car manufactures in the North American market. The company sales are falling dramatically for the past four years. The volumes have dropped from about 857,000 units of sales in 2013 to 279,672 units in 2016. The car maker's analysis of its poor performance in sales has revealed two primary reasons as key contributors for this fall. These are as follows: (a) American and Japanese manufactures are able to compete due to lower prices and (b) these companies offer better sales compensation and sales incentives to their staff in North America than Wagonriders. As a result, the company has lost some of its star performers in the sales department over a period of time. Compensation and incentive practices of the company are largely socialistic that are not able to motivate employees in North America. The management consulting firm engaged by the automaker has come up with similar findings and recommends redesigning its compensation approach in order to address the sagging morale of its front-end sales staff. The company's approach towards compensation has so far been effective with majority of staff, working in various countries and is time tested. The company is reluctant to expose its employees' compensation to market fluctuations and individual employee performance levels since it is largely team-based work. In fact, in all these years the company has taken pride in the fact that its compensation model insulates employees from volatility and promotes collective work. However, the consulting firm has argued that sales will decline further if the issue of pricing and sales incentives is not addressed on war footing.

Discuss what compensation approach should the company take towards its sales staff in North America. Whether the approach should be same across all countries of operations or different for different countries? Should compensation be market and employee performance sensitive or the approach of insulation works well in the long run?

Bibliography

Aon. (2016). *2016 US Salary Increase Survey*. Retrieved 8 March 2018, from http://www.aon.com/human-capital-consulting/thought-leadership/talent/2016-2017_salary_increase.jsp

———. (2017). *How is Global Uncertainty Impacting Employee Engagement Levels?* Retrieved 8 March 218, from http://www.aon.com/engagement17/

Bank of Canada. (2015). *Indicators of Capacity and Inflation Pressures for Canada*. Retrieved 28 February 2018, from https://www.bankofcanada.ca/rates/indicators/capacity-and-inflation-pressures/

Bloom, M., Milkovich, G. T. and Mitra, A. (2003). International Compensation: Learning from How Managers Respond to Variations in Local Host Contexts. *International Journal of Human Resource Management, 14*, 1350–1367.

Central Statistical Office of Poland. (2017). *Wages in Poland*. Retrieved 30 January 2018, from www.stat.gov.pl

CIPD. (2015). *Reward Management Survey Report*. Retrieved 28 February 2018, from https://www.cipd.co.uk/knowledge/strategy/reward/surveys

CNBC. (2015, October 20). *The Average American Made $44.6 Last Year*. Retrieved 28 February 2018, from https://www.cnbc.com/2015/10/20/the-average-american-made-446k-last-year.html

Deutsche Bank. (2016). *Compensation Practices and Structures—Deutsche Bank Responsibility*. Retrieved 8 March 2018, from https://www.db.com/cr/en/compensation--structures.htm

Economic Policy Institute. (2015). *Causes of Wage Stagnation*. Retrieved 28 February 2018, from http://www.epi.org/publication/causes-of-wage-stagnation/

Eurofound. (2017). *Statutory Minimum Wages in the EU 2017*. Retrieved 8 March 2018, from https://www.eurofound.europa.eu/observatories/eurwork/articles/statutory-minimum-wages-in-the-eu-2017

Fair Work Commission, Government of Australia. (2015). *Awards & Agreements*. Retrieved 30 January 2018, from www.fwc.gov.au

Financial Times. (2016, November 24). British Workers Face Worst Decade for Pay in 70 Years. Retrieved 8 March 2018, from https://www.ft.com/content/d56b46f6-b237-11e6-9c37-5787335499a0

———. (2017, March 10). German Labour Costs Register Biggest Rise Since Financial Crisis. Retrieved 8 March 2018, from https://www.ft.com/content/b0d70dcf-e383-3294-bc26-8d6e1e80ccf4

Forbes. (2010, April 21). *Money is Not the Best Motivator*. Retrieved 28 February 2018, from https://www.forbes.com/2010/04/06/money-motivation-pay-leadership-managing-employees.html#58304fa43e13

———. (2012, September 26). *Can $38 Billion Employee Incentives Boost Corporate Profits?* Retrieved 8 March 2018, from https://www.forbes.com/sites/petercohan/2012/09/26/can-38-billion-employee-incentives-industry-boost-corporate-profits/#21e94ee06321

Glassdoor. (2016). *Are you Being Paid Fairly? Global Salary Transparency Survey*. Retrieved 28 February 2018, from https://www.glassdoor.com/blog/paid-fairly-glassdoor-global-survey-reveals-salary-transparency-perceptions/

International Labour Organization. (2013). *Global Wage Report 2012/13: Wages and Equitable Growth*. Geneva: ILO. Retrieved 8 March 2018, from http://www.ilo.org/global/research/global-reports/global-wage-report/2012/lang--en/index.htm

International Monetary Fund. (2015). *World Economic and Financial Surveys: World Economic Outlook Database*. Retrieved 28 February 2018, from https://www.imf.org/external/pubs/ft/weo/2015/02/weodata/index.aspx

Mercer. (2012). *Designing Sales Commission & Incentives*. Retrieved 28 February 2018, from https://www.mercer.ca/content/dam/mercer/attachments/global/Talent/human-capital-agenda/Anthology%202013/sales-incentive-harmonisation-at-the-indesit-group-europe-2013-mercer.pdf

———. (2014). *Few Total Rewards and Business Strategies Fully Align: Total Rewards Survey Analysis*. Retrieved 8 March 2018, from https://www.mercer.com/newsroom/few-reward-and-business-strategies-align-say-mercer-survey.html

Mercer. (2016). *Global Compensation Strategy Trends Study—2017*. Retrieved 28 February 2018, from https://www.mercer.com/newsroom/global-talent-trends-2016.html

Morgan McKinley. (2016). *Morgan McKinley Salary Guide 2016*. Retrieved 8 March 2018, from https://www.morganmckinley.co.jp/en/salary-survey

National Bureau of Statistics of China. (2016). *National Database*. Retrieved 30 January 2018, from www.stats.gov.cn

National Wages Council. (2016). *National Wages Council Guidelines 2015/2016*. Retrieved 28 February 2018, from http://www.mom.gov.sg/newsroom/press-releases/2016/0531-national-wages-council-guidelines-2016-2017

OECD. (2014). *Rising Inequality: Youth and Poor Fall Further Behind*. Retrieved 8 March 2018, from https://www.oecd.org/social/Focus-Inequality-and-Growth-2014.pdf

———. (2016a). *Closing the Gender Gap: Sweden*. Retrieved 8 March 2018, from https://www.oecd.org/sweden/Closing%20the%20Gender%20Gap%20-%20Sweden%20FINAL.pdf

———. (2016b). *Highlights Japan*. Retrieved 8 March 2018, from https://www.oecd.org/japan/39696303.pdf

Pensions and Lifetime Savings Association. (2015). *Pensions and Lifetime Savings Association Five Year Trend Data from Annual Survey*.

Philippines Statistics Authority. (2016). *Annual Labour and Employment Status*. Retrieved 8 March 2018, from https://psa.gov.ph/content/2016-annual-labor-and-employment-status

Stastisches Bundesamt. (2014). *Labour Costs Comparison Between EU Countries for 2013*. Retrieved 8 March 2018, from https://www.destatis.de/EN/PressServices/Press/pr/2014/GenTable_201405.html

Statistics Canada. (2013). *The Evolution of Canadian Wages over the Last Three Decades*. Retrieved 28 February 2018, from http://www.statcan.gc.ca/pub/11f0019m/2013347/userinfo-usagerinfo-eng.htm

———. (2016). *National Household Survey Data Tables*. Retrieved 8 March 2018, from http://www12.statcan.gc.ca/nhs-enm/2011/dp-pd/dt-td/index-eng.cfm

Swiss Federal Statistical Office. (2016). *Gender Pay Gap Between Women and Men*. Retrieved 28 February 2018, from https://www.degruyter.com/view/j/sjs.2016.42.issue-3/sjs-2016-0020/sjs-2016-0020.xml

The Conference Board of Canada. (2016). *Canadian Income Inequality*. Retrieved 28 February 2018, from http://www.conferenceboard.ca/hcp/provincial/society/income-inequality.aspx

The Labour Inspectorate, Ministry of Social Affairs and Employment-Netherlands (2015). *Wage Rates & Agreements*. Retrieved 8 March 2018, from https://www.vro.nl/files/chain-liability.pdf

The Wall Street Journal. (2010). Performance for Pay? The Relationship Between CEO Incentive Compensation and Future Stock Price Performance. Retrieved 28 February 2018, from https://www.wsj.com/articles/SB10001424052748704281204575003351773983136

Towers, Perrin, Forster and Crosby. (1979). *Incentive Compensation in the Banking Industry*. Stamford, CT: TPF.

Transparency International. (2017). *Corruption Perceptions Index 2016*. Retrieved 8 March 2018, from https://www.transparency.org/news/feature/corruption_perceptions_index_2016

Willis Towers Watson. (2014). *Flexible Benefits to Boost Engagement*. Retrieved 8 March 2018, from https://www.towerswatson.com/en/Insights/Newsletters/Europe/HR-matters/2014/05/flexible-benefits-to-boost-engagement

———. (2016). *North American Employers Give Pay for Performance Programs Low Marks*. Retrieved 28 February 2018, from https://www.willistowerswatson.com/en/press/2016/02/north-american-employers-give-pay-for-performance-programs-low-marks

———. (2017). *Global Perspectives on Pay Equity and Transparency*. Retrieved 8 March 2018, from https://www.towerswatson.com/en/Insights/Newsletters/Global/strategy-at-work/2016/viewpoints-qa-global-perspectives-on-the-growing-importance-of-pay-equity-and-transparency

Worker Participation. (2013). *Collective Bargaining. Developments in Collectively Agreed Pay 2013*. Retrieved 27 February 2018, from https://www.worker-participation.eu/National-Industrial-Relations/Countries/France/Collective-Bargaining

WorldatWork. (2012a). *Global Sales Compensation Trends Survey*. Retrieved 28 February 2018, from https://www.worldatwork.org/docs/research-and-surveys/2012-sales-compensation-trends-survey-report-full-report.pdf

———. (2012b). *Pay Structures—Develop a Framework from Start to Finish: Survey of Salary, Structure, Policies and Practices*. Retrieved 28 February 2018, from https://www.worldatwork.org/docs/research-and-surveys/survey-brief-salary-structure-policies-and-practices.pdf)

———. (2014). *Global Compensation Programs and Practices Survey*. Retrieved 28 February 2018, from https://www.worldatwork.org/docs/research-and-surveys/Survey-Brief-Compensation-Programs-and-Practices-2014.pdf

Zenger, T. (2016, September). The Case Against Pay Transparency. *Harvard Business Review*. Retrieved 28 February 2018, from https://hbr.org/2016/09/the-case-against-pay-transparency

5

Industrial Relations:
Labour Codes, Laws and Regulations
Management—North America

LEARNING OBJECTIVES

The objectives of this chapter are to:
- ☐ enable practitioner understanding of the Labor Code of the United States.
- ☐ enable practitioner understanding of the Canadian Labour Code, along with its interpretation.
- ☐ discuss the essential labour laws and regulations in the United States, along with selective case studies.
- ☐ illustrate the philosophical and ideological differences between the dynamics of labour legislation and IR in the United States and Canada.

I ndustrial relations, labour laws, codes and regulations have a long history in the United States and Canada. Both the countries have laid down the fundamental labour laws on the foundations of no discrimination, equal opportunities, rights and responsibilities of employees and employers, and collective decision-making. Labour laws are primarily driven at federal level in the United States, whereas it is at the provincial level in Canada, though both countries also consider federal and provincial governments equally important in achieving industrial harmony. Current state of labour laws and codes is unable to cope with the changing needs of employment society due to various factors such as fast-changing demographics because of a high immigration-driven workforce, changing technology towards automation, soaring contingent workforce and globalization of economy. In general, enforcement and promulgation of labour laws are weakening as both the countries have started placing more emphasis on economic efficiencies as they are forced to compete on cost factors with other countries and eagerness to attract capital. Further, the recent trend is that governments are more inclined to make labour and employment regulations on their own as executive decision rather than in the form of collective regulations.

There are great similarities between labour codes and legislation between both countries but there are also dissimilarities. The key differences are: (a) employment contract laws and collective legislation is largely driven at provincial level though there is a federal code in Canada, whereas the same are driven at federal level in the United States, (b) at-will employment is widely prevalent in the United States and not a mainstream employment practice in Canada, (c) privacy laws and employee data is highly regulated and stringent in the interest of employees in Canada and the same is mostly in the interest of employers in the United States, (d) non-solicitation and non-compete clauses which are generally seen in employment contracts are highly restricted in their validity in Canada, (e) overtime payment is applicable across all grades and applicable to a wide range of employees in Canada and restricted to category of employees in the United States, (f) reduction of pay or benefits can be construed as constructive dismissal in Canada and it is not as widely accepted interpretation in the United States and (g) whatever employment scenarios not explicitly stated in contracts will go in favour of employees in Canada and it is subject to qualification in the United States. Both countries have seen increasing number of claims in forums administering the labour issues and benefits causing significant bureaucracy and stress on the system. Also, there is general decline of union enrolments and emphasis on building employer–employee relationships with growing individualism across the organized industrial sectors. The following sections are dedicated to describe key aspects of various labour codes, laws and regulations of both these countries.

Labour Laws in the United States

It is imperative to understand and have a solid grasp of the Labor Code and various federal labour laws in the United States in order to manage HR in a compliant and harmonious manner. Comparatively, job/security laws are weaker, working hours are longer and annual leaves are lesser in the United States. Employee at-will is considered as almost a substitute to collective bargaining process in the country; therefore, understanding of the employment contract and laws is must. The US labour legislation can be classified into three clusters: the first cluster focuses on well-being of employees such as Fair Labor Standards Act (FLSA), 1938, Family and Medical Leave Act (FMLA), 1993 and Occupational Safety and Health Act, 1970; the second cluster pertains to anti-discrimination and equal rights legislation such as Equal Pay Act (EPA), 1963; Age Discrimination in Employment Act, 1967; Genetic Information Nondiscrimination Act, 2008 and The Pregnancy Discrimination Act, 1978; and the third cluster focusing on employee–employer relationship such as National Labor Relations Act, 1935 and Labor Management Relations Act, 1947. The following sections capture salient features of these Acts from a practitioner's perspective.

The Fair Labor Standards Act of 1938

The objective of this enactment is to ensure living standards necessary for health, efficiency and general well-being of workers. Every employer shall pay to each of his or her employees not less than a minimum wage of USD 5.85 an hour at the beginning and USD 6.55 an hour after 12 months and till 24 months and USD 7.25 an hour after 24 months. No employer shall discriminate employees based on sex in terms of wages for equal work on jobs, the performance of which requires equal skill, effort and responsibility, and which are performed under similar working conditions. However, pay is made on the basis of a seniority system, a merit system and on quantity or quality of production. Working hours of employees normally shall not exceed 48 hours in a week. If employees are engaged in work for more than 48 hours a week, they shall be paid overtime at the rate of 1.5 times their normal wage rates. No employer shall be deemed to have violated this law by employing any employee for a workweek in excess of the maximum workweek applicable to such employee if such employee is employed pursuant to a bona fide individual contract or pursuant to a collective bargaining agreement. Any person who wilfully violates provisions of this law shall attract a fine of not more than USD 10,000 or imprisonment for not more than six months or both. An employer who violates provisions concerning employees shall be liable to the employee or employees affected in the amount of their unpaid minimum wages or their unpaid overtime compensation and an additional equal amount as liquidated damages. An organization that has more than 200 full-time employees and that offers employees enrolment in one or more health benefits plans shall automatically enrol new full-time employees in one of the plans offered. No employer shall discriminate against an employee with respect to his or her compensation, terms, conditions or other privileges of employment because the employee has received credit under section 36b of the internal revenue code (IRC) or because there is information relating to a violation by an employee in regard to such credit or because the employee has testified or is about to testify in a proceeding concerning such violation.

Secretary of Labor notifies from time to time the list of occupations in which employment of persons less than 18 years of age is prohibited. Except in such notified occupations, persons of a minimum of 16 years of age can be employed by adhering to the due procedures laid down in this legislation. No employer shall employ any oppressive child labour in commerce or in the production of goods. In other words, the Act stipulates 16 years as the minimum age for employment in manufacturing or mining occupations although certain youth between the age of 14 and 16 may, under certain specific conditions, be employed. The minimum age is 18 years for occupations which are notified as hazardous or detrimental to the health and safety of minors in the age group of 14 and 16. The Secretary of Labor is also authorized to issue notification permitting the engagement of persons in 14 and 16 years age group in occupations which will not interfere with their health and well-being such as in agriculture outside school hours, delivery of newspapers, performing in motion pictures and being employed by own parents. Any person who violates the provision related to child labour shall be subject to civil penalty of USD 11,000 for each act of violation.

Family and Medical Leave Act, 1993

The purpose of this Act is to entitle employees to take reasonable leave for medical reasons, for the birth or adoption of a child and for the care of a child or to attend to a spouse or parent who has a serious health condition. An employer covered by FMLA is any person engaged in commerce or in any industry employing 50 or more employees for at least 20 calendar workweeks in the current or preceding calendar year. Separate entities will be deemed to be parts of a single employer for the purposes of this Act.

For the purpose of this legislation, eligible employee means an employee who has been employed for at least 12 months by the employer with respect to whom leave is requested. An eligible employee shall be entitled to a total of 12 workweeks of leave during any 12 months period. The 12 weeks leave entitlement on account of birth or adoption of a child or to attend to a spouse, child or parent ailing from a serious health condition will elapse if not availed at the end of 12 months period. An eligible employee who is the spouse, son, daughter, parent or next of kin of a covered service member shall be entitled to a total of 26 workweeks of leave during a 12 months period to take care of an ailing family member. This leave shall only be available during a single 12 months period. An employee intending to avail the leave shall provide a 30 days' notice in order to avoid any disruption to the operations. In addition, the employer may require an employee to submit documents as evidence of the ill health of the employee or employee's family members. Likewise, the employer can also seek from employee a fitness certificate to return to work. FMLA leave may be taken intermittently or on a reduced leave schedule under certain circumstances. When an employee takes leave on an intermittent or reduced leave schedule, only the amount of leave actually taken may be counted towards the employee's entitlement.

Employer has the responsibility to restore the employee in the same or equivalent position when the employee returns from leave. However, an employer can deny such restoration if the denial is necessary to prevent substantial and grievous injury to the operations of the employer. During any period that an eligible employee takes leave, the employer shall maintain coverage under any group health plan for the duration of such leave at the level and conditions which the employee would have been provided if the employee had continued in employment. The employer may recover the premium that the employer paid for maintaining coverage for the employee under such group health plan if the employee fails to return from leave after the period of leave except in conditions where such inability to return is due to the circumstances beyond the control of the employee. The principal duty of an employer is without endorsing any group health product to permit the insurer to publicize the programme to employees and to collect premiums through payroll deductions and to remit them to insurer. FMLA leave can be taken for treatment of substance abuse. However, treatment for substance abuse does not prevent an employer from taking employment action against an employee. The employer shall not take action against an employee because he or she has exercised his or her right to avail leave for the treatment. Generally, FMLA leave is unpaid leave. However, FMLA permits an eligible employee to choose to substitute accrued paid leave for FMLA leave. If an employee does not choose to substitute accrued paid leave, the employer may require the employee to substitute paid leave for unpaid FMLA. Leave taken pursuant to a disability leave plan would be considered FMLA leave for a serious health condition. Employer shall post and keep posted summary and salient features of this legislation for the benefit of employees in conspicuous places on the premises of the employer where notices to employees are customarily posted. A complaint of violation of FMLA rights can be filed by e-mail or telephone call with the Wage and Hour Division, US DOL. FMLA rules stipulate that employers shall make, keep and preserve records pertaining to their obligations in accordance with record keeping requirements of the Act. Nothing in FMLA supersedes any provision of state or local law that provides greater family or medical rights than those provided by FMLA.

Employee Polygraph Protection Act, 1988

The purpose of this Act is to prohibit private employers from using any lie detector tests either for pre-employment screening or during the course of employment. Every employer shall post and keep posted on its premises a notice explaining the Act. However, an employer can request an employee to be subjected to a polygraph test if there are charges involving economic loss or injury to the employer's business such as theft, embezzlement, misappropriation or an act of industrial espionage or sabotage. The terms economic loss or injury to the employer's business include both direct and indirect economic loss and injury. Economic losses or injuries which are the result of unintentional or lawful conduct would not serve as a basis for the administration of a polygraph test. The employer has the burden of establishing that the specific individual or individuals to be tested are reasonably suspected of involvement in the specific loss or injury. Analysis of a polygraph test chart or refusal to take a polygraph test may not serve as a basis for adverse employment action. Employer who subjects an employee to a polygraph test shall maintain related records for a period of three years. No employer or examiner can disclose results of a polygraph test other than to the subjected employee and authorized governmental agencies and courts.

National Labor Relations Act, 1935, and Labor Management Relations Act, 1947

The purpose of this legislation is to set processes and methods through which employees and unions, and employers and their unions can negotiate collectively and resolve disputes and to clearly define what shall and shall not constitute unfair labour practices apart from promoting rights of labour unions and employees, and full freedom of association. The Acts and Regulations exhort that protection by law of the right of employees to organize and bargain collectively safeguards commerce from injury, impairment or interruption and promotes the flow of commerce by removing certain recognized sources of industrial strife and unrest by encouraging practices fundamental to the friendly adjustment of industrial disputes arising out of differences as to wages, hours or other working conditions and by restoring equality of bargaining power between employers and employees. Amendment of 1947 to the Act has paved the way for constitution of National Labor Relations Board. The board has the powers to make amends and rescind the rules and regulations as may be necessary to carry out provisions of this legislation and ensure the objectives are met.

In pursuance of this Act and as per section 157 of the Regulations, employee has the right to self-organization, to form, join or assist labour organizations to bargain collectively through representatives of his or her own choosing and to engage in other concerted activities for the purpose of collective bargaining or other mutual aid or protection. An employee need not join a labour organization as a member if that person belongs to a religion or holds a belief that objects to being part of a labour organization. Employees' rights under this legislation include bargaining collectively through representatives for wages, hours, terms and conditions of employment and to strike and picket if required. It is illegal for employers to prohibit employees from talking about or soliciting for a union during non-work time, questioning an employee about union activities and supporting a union, or to fire, demote, threaten, transfer, reduce hours or change shift of an employee because he or she belongs to a union.

It shall be deemed an unfair labour practice if an employer restrains, coerces or interferes with employees in their rights to dominate or interfere with formation or administration of any labour organization. Employers shall also not indulge or exhibit any discrimination in hiring or extension of benefits to any person or employee based on membership to a labour organization. No employer can refuse to bargain collectively with the representatives of his or her employees. Likewise, it will be an unfair labour practice for a labour organization to bargain with an employer or restrain or coerce employees in the exercise of their rights and cause or attempt to cause an employer to discriminate against an employee because of that employee's membership to a labour organization. Labour organizations or their representatives shall not force or restrain any employee to join any labour organization. Forcing any employer to recognize or bargain with a particular labour organization when some other organization is certified as the representative of employees or forcing an employer to show prejudicial attitude in favouring or disfavouring employees based on their membership to a labour organization is also considered an unfair labour practice. Forcing an employer to pay any money for which no services are rendered by employees is also an unfair labour practice. However, labour organizations are within their rights to express any views, arguments, opinions or to disseminate information or to publicize whether in oral or written or visual, or graphic form in order to create awareness and education among employees about their rights and legitimate expectations. A preliminary investigation will be made whenever a complaint of unfair labour practice is filed on priority and if the preliminary investigation establishes the charge, the matter will be taken up by the attorney with United States District Court for appropriate injunctive relief pending final adjudication. Further, whenever any person is charged with having engaged in an unfair labour practice, such charge shall be given priority over all other cases.

It is the mutual obligation of employer and the representatives of employees to collectively bargain in relation to wages, hours and benefits, and other terms and conditions of employment and in execution of a contract or modification of the same. Neither employer nor labour organization nor their representatives shall terminate or modify the contract unilaterally. However, an agreement reached between both parties, in the course of implementation, can be modified or amended, or repealed with mutual consent and agreement by following prescribed procedure as laid down in the Code of Federal Regulations. National Labor Relations Board in certain circumstances can supersede labour organizations and employers the moment the Board intervenes to resolve a dispute and assumes the role of representative of employees. The Board is empowered to prevent any person from engaging in any unfair labour practice affecting commerce. Though representatives of a labour organization which is certified as a collective bargaining agent are the ones that negotiate with employer, an individual employee is not barred from negotiating or expressing grievance with the employer for redressal as long as the solution is not inconsistent with any collective bargaining agreement that is in force. Collective bargaining units can be different for different skills, crafts and professions. Employees of a particular group can decide to vote in favour of or against other groups for the purpose of collective bargaining. A labour organization shall serve an advance notice of not less than 10 days if it plans to go on strike or picket, or any such concerted act of refusal to work in health care institution.

The labour policy of the United States promotes and encourages the use of voluntary arbitration to resolve disputes over the interpretation or application of collective bargaining agreements. Arbitration award is required to be made within 60 days from the date the dispute is raised. The Federal Government has created an agency called Federal Mediation and Conciliation Service (FMCS) with the amendment in the form of an Act in 1947. Labour organizations and employers shall strive to resolve the disputes amicably and if the disputes are not settled, they can be taken up with FMCS for speedy resolution. These disputes can be in relation to interpretation or implementation of collective bargaining agreements. FMCS is also assisted by the National Labor-Management Panel comprised of members who have an outstanding background in the fields of management. It is the duty of this panel to advise in the avoidance of industrial controversies and the manner in which mediation shall be administered. FMCS is authorized to create contracts and awards in order to fulfil its objectives as long as such outcomes are arrived at with the participation of labour organizations.

Impact of Wagner Act, 1935 on Taft–Hartley Act, 1947

The Wagner Act is also known as National Labor Relations Act of 1935 and was also referred to as Labor's Bill of Rights. In the backdrop of the great economic depression, the Wagner Act was the first piece of a major legislation in the history of labour laws in the United States, empowering trade unions and granting rights to workers and employees in a formal and firm manner. The Act, for the first time, also made it clear that IR is a domain that falls within the purview of the federal regulator. This was despite steep opposition from Republican senators who had argued that it does more harm than good to the livelihood of employees. The Federal Government becoming an arbitrator in IR disputes, even in the cases where there was no interstate commerce, could be seen as usurping the position with arbitrary powers. The prime objective of this Act was to provide the right to workers to organize themselves collectively by forming unions, the right to negotiate and bargain with employers and the right to strike at work. The Act also provided for trade union shops so that they could enlist workers as members, while it also provided closed shops so that employees could choose not to become members. In accordance with this Act, the National Labor Relations Board was established. However, post the implementation of the Act, it was widely criticized, highlighting that the workers were accorded unreasonable rights and that the trade unions had become so powerful that they became a barrier to business growth. There were apprehensions that communists had seeped into these unions to try subvert the democratic norms of the United States. These developments lead to a review of the Wagner Act, primarily due to two reasons: first, the Second World War had placed extreme demands on the economy to perform well and optimize all indusial operations and assets in the country. Second, the Republicans had gained majority control in the Senate, who felt that the growing power of trade unions was neither good for the economy nor for the polity of the country. Apart from these, the period post the implementation of the Wagner Act experienced many major strikes causing a slowdown of industrial activity in the country. Striking of work often was seen as thwarting the progress of the country. Experts offered suggestions that trade union rights should be curtailed to a rational level, while some accountability for stable operations should be placed on the trade union executive leadership. Further, there were also views that there should be a mechanism for redressal of union demands and grievances before the trade unions could resort to striking, through the introduction of a third-party involvement. Accordingly, the Taft–Hartley Act was passed, curtailing the rights of the trade unions and introducing provisions related to unfair labour practices. In fact, to begin with, there were two bills proposed which were almost similar in nature and content: the first was by Fred Hartley, a right-winger and the other one was by Robert Taft, a conservative representative. Therefore, both these bills were ultimately combined into one and became known as the Taft–Hartley bill. The Act, which was more like amendments to the Wagner Act, mandated (a) trade unions to provide 60 days' notice before they could resort to a strike, (b) empowered the President to constitute an inquiry into the disputes before the unions could cause a strike, (c) refer disputes to the National Labor Relations Board, (d) if required, obtain an injunction, stopping the strike by any unions/employees, led by the Attorney General, (e) a trade union could press for negotiations/collective bargaining and issue a strike notice only in a case where it enjoyed the support and membership of the majority of employees. The Act also placed restrictions on the rights of unions to call for strikes, significantly improving on the original provisions of the Wagner Act and made them more accountable to explain and account for the financial funds.

Till the promulgation of Taft–Hartley Act in 1947, trade unions enjoyed enormous clout and power to the extent that individual employees, who were reluctant to become members of the union, could be threatened with loss of employment. Trade union leaders using various persuasive, as well as pressure tactics, increased the trade union members from 3.5 million in 1935 to 15 million by 1945. However, the membership saw a steep decline post the implementation of the Taft–Hartley Act (union membership fell from 35 per cent to 12 per cent). However, the employers were never in a position to express their views on trade unions. Compared to the Wagner Act, the Taft–Hartley Act was perceived as an attempt at balancing the power structure, even though each of these Acts were brought into force keeping in view the social, economic and political realities of that period. The Taft–Hartley Act was seen and interpreted by Democrats as a piece of legislation brought in order to weaken the potency of trade unions and tilt the power structure in favour of big businesses. Powers of the trade unions were further curtailed by bringing in additional unfair labour practices through a legislation called Labor Management Reporting and Disclosure Act of 1959, which was not part of the Taft–Hartley Act. Though the Wagner Act has been widely criticized, mostly by neo economists, business leaders and Republican leaders, the provisions of the Act helped immensely towards progress, with amendments in the form of Taft–Hartley Act. Therefore, it is logical to state that the Wagner Act was the fundamental basis for bringing in Taft–Hartley Act, even though the latter was seen as an Act brought to weaken the position of the Wagner Act. The Taft–Hartley Act was also seen by many as an instrument of neutrality because it balanced the powers among state, unions and employers. The Act also provided for a much detailed framework to resolve industrial disputes. It also places obligations as well as rights on both players: trade unions and employers. The Taft–Hartley Act also significantly recognized the rights of individual employees to either become members of a trade union or to support or not support a certain agenda, something which did not exist in the Wagner Act. This move was interpreted by some experts as a method of weakening the collectivism and bargaining power of the trade unions, the fact remains that it gives space for individual employees', apart from avoiding the exploitation of employees by the hands of a trade union. Though both these Acts were founded on different ideologies, treating them as opposing tools may not be a rational argument. It is more logical to see the Taft–Hartley Act as an evolved legislation of the Wagner Act. An analysis of implementation of this legislation shows that Taft–Hartley Act had not stopped or ceased the rights of trade unions to call for strikes, but only made for them being more responsible while doing so, while also making the strikes less violent.

Equal Pay Act, 1963

Though the EPA is motivated to protect interests and rights of women employees, its provisions, in fact, address concerns of both sexes. The Act applies to all categories of employees unlike FLSA which does not apply to executives, administrators and professional employees in most of the cases. Under the EPA, wages definition includes all payments made to an employee as remuneration for employment. EPA prohibits discrimination by employers on the basis of sex in the wages paid for equal work on jobs, the performance of which requires equal skill, effort and responsibility, and which are performed under similar working conditions. It is unlawful to classify a job as being meant only for men or women unless sex is a bona fide occupational qualification for the job. When factors such as seniority, education, experience are applied, such application shall be done on a gender-neutral basis. The minor differences in the degree or amount of skill or effort, or responsibility required for the performance of jobs will not render the equal pay standard inapplicable. If a person of one sex succeeds a person of the opposite sex in a job at a higher rate of pay than the predecessor and there is no reason for the higher rate other than difference in gender, a violation as to the predecessor is established and that person is entitled to recover the difference between his or her pay and the higher rate paid to the successor employee. Testing and establishing equality of jobs is based on principles such as jobs requiring equal skill in performance, equal effort in performance, equal responsibility in performance and performance under similar conditions. Additional duties shall not be a defence for the payment of higher wages to one sex where the higher pay is not related to extra work and when the extra work involves negligible time and peripheral importance to the performance and outcomes of a task. Claiming employing a particular sex over the other is expensive and so preferring one sex therefore is considered discriminatory under this legislation. Any collective bargaining agreement that would make differences in pay based on sex is null and void as per provisions of the Act. However, an employer can continue to pay higher wages to an employee over another employee of the opposite sex if such employee was being paid that rate of salary in the previous job but transferred to a lower job due to ill health under the principle of red circle rate. Likewise, an employer may pay higher wages in a situation requiring an employee for a shorter period to perform the work of a job classification other than the employee's regular work and such differential cannot be termed as unequal pay or discriminatory. Any violation under the EPA is amount to violation of Civil Rights Act on 1964. No labour organization or agency shall make any attempts or pursue any agenda or engage in any activity that is aimed at achieving discrimination in pay based on sex for same job.

Age Discrimination in Employment Act, 1967

The Age Discrimination in Employment Act, 1967, prohibits discrimination on the basis of age with respect to individuals who are at least 40 years of age. As per this law, it is unlawful for an employer to discriminate an individual in any aspect of employment because that individual is 40 years old or older. However, the law does not envisage providing extra concessions or preference to older people as stated in any manner. No employment notices shall carry advertisements that say that only young people in their 20s or 30s are preferred or invited to apply. However, help wanted advertisements which express preference for older people of over 60 years, advertising jobs that supplement their pension or that are seeking retirees are not discriminatory. Though, per se, help wanted notices that seek disclosure of age of applicants is not discriminatory, such information seeking can lead to old age individuals being discouraged from applying and so these advertisements will be scrutinized carefully in order to avoid a possibility of discrimination. In other words, a request on the part of an employer for information such as date of birth or age on any employment application form is not in itself a violation of the Act but because the request for such details may tend to deter older applicants, it possibly indicates discrimination against older individuals. So employment applications that seek age and other related details will be closely scrutinized to assure that such request is for a permissible purpose. Employers generally tend to cite that bona fide occupational qualifications is the reason for preferring younger workforce so employment applications seeking such bona fide occupational qualifications for a job shall ensure such requirement is logical and genuine and the same can be subjected to close scrutiny to ensure non-discriminatory practices. Many state and local governments have enacted laws and regulations which limit employment opportunities based on age. Unless these laws and regulations meet the standards for the establishment of a valid bona fide occupational qualification requirement, the same shall be superseded by provisions of this Act. Whenever reasonable factors other than age defence is raised, the employer bears the burden of proving that the job is not age discriminatory and that it is for other valid factors. A differentiation based on the average cost of employing older employees is unlawful. If age is listed as one of the factors to effectively perform the job, a clear defence will need to be drawn around how this factor is linked to effective performance and how it will help with achieving or can achieve the employer's stated business objectives and plans. Seniority systems which segregate, classify or discriminate individuals based on race, colour, religion, sex or national origin are prohibited and unlawful. However, seniority systems drawn for pensionary benefits or similar benefits application cannot be termed as discriminatory. Involuntary retirement schemes shall also be qualified under this law and shall confirm the terms of a retirement pension plan as the same has the potential for discrimination based on age. However, no provisions of this Act make it unlawful for a plan to permit individuals to elect early retirement at a specified age at their own option. The practice of life insurance coverage is to remain constant until the retirement age, after which there can be gradual reduction. No employee hired prior to normal retirement age may be excluded from a defined contribution plan. The Act does not prohibit an organization from retiring employees who attain the age of 70 years and who are serving under an employment contract of unlimited tenure. All apprenticeship programmes are also covered under this legislation, so no discrimination on the basis age shall be made. Equal Employment Opportunity Commission (EEOC) is responsible and empowered to make regulations and to implement and supervise the provisions of this Act. EEOC can make inspections and investigations on its own in order to ensure effective implementation of the legislation. Complaint related to violation of this Act can be made in person or by telephone or by email to any office of the commission. A complaint shall contain details of respondent and description of the charge. Generally stating, the complaint shall be made within 180 days from the date of occurrence of such violation. A complaint made can be amended to clarify or amply the allegations made during the progress of proceedings adding additional facts. Upon receipt of a charge, the commission shall promptly attempt to eliminate any alleged unlawful practice by informal method of conciliation. An agreement reached as a result of commission intervention shall require respondent to eliminate such discriminatory practices and provide relief to the complainant. Every employer shall ensure to take all actions for publicity of the provisions of this Act by displaying the features of the Act in prominent places where it can easily be accessed by employees.

Americans with Disability Act, 1990

The purpose of this Act is to ensure equal employment opportunities to persons with disabilities and to eliminate discrimination against individuals with disabilities. It is unlawful for an organization/employer to discriminate on the basis of disability in regard to recruitment, promotion, award of tenure, demotion, lay-off, termination, rehiring remuneration, job assignments, leaves, benefits training and participation in social and recreational activities. No employer is allowed to use selection practices and tests that tend to screen out persons with disabilities. Physical attributes, vision requirements and other such factors can be used as the criteria only when such attributes are directly related to performance on the job and such exceptional conditions when permitted are diligently scrutinized. It is also unlawful for organizations to conduct medical examination on an applicant or to make inquiries as to whether an applicant is an individual with a disability or to make inquiries about the severity of a disability. However, an employer can make pre-employment inquiries into the ability of an applicant to perform job-related functions. If a medical report is obtained, it shall be maintained confidentially. A medical examination can be conducted only if such a medical test provides a result that is essential for performance of the job and is consistent with business necessity.

Genetic Information Nondiscrimination Act, 2008

This Act promulgates prohibition of use of genetic information in employment decision-making and restricts employers from seeking, requesting and requiring or purchasing genetic information report and regulates maintaining confidentiality of genetic information and provides remedies for individuals whose genetic information is acquired, used or disclosed in violation of its protection. It is unlawful for an employer to discriminate against an individual on the basis of the genetic information of the individual in regard to hiring, discharge, training, compensation, terms, conditions or privileges of employment. However, an organization can offer financial incentives to encourage individuals to provide family medical history voluntarily in order to assess whether an employee is at an increased risk of acquiring a health condition in the future in order to have the employee participate in disease management programmes that promote healthy lifestyles and to meet health goals. Similarly, when employees disclose voluntarily family medical history of diabetes, high blood pressure or heart disease for health management, it will not amount to violation of this legislation. Where an employer in order to comply with requirements under FMLA solicits information on health condition, it cannot be termed as violation. Also, when an employer acquires genetic information about an employee in order to assess biological effects of toxic substance, it is no violation. An entity is not violating when it requires, requests or purchases genetic information or information about the manifestation of a disease, disorder or pathological condition of an individual's family member who is receiving health or genetic services on a voluntary basis. The prohibition on acquisition of genetic information including medical history applies to medical examinations related to employment. An organization must inform health care providers not to collect genetic information, including medical history as part of a medical examination intended to determine the ability to perform a job, and must take additional reasonable measures within its control. Also, information obtained as permitted under this law must be maintained in electronic form and separate from personal files and such information should be treated as confidential. If an employer either asks a health care provider for genetic information or advises an employee to undergo medical tests in order to get genetic information, it amounts to violation of the provisions of this Act.

The Pregnancy Discrimination Act, 1978

The Act stipulates that women affected by pregnancy and related conditions must be treated the same as other applicants and employees on the basis of their ability or inability to work. Women under this law are protected against practices such as termination, refusal of promotion because she is pregnant or had an abortion. No woman employee who is pregnant shall be forced to stop working till she decides or her medical condition suggests that she should be on leave. When a woman returns from maternity or pregnancy-related leave, she shall be offered the same role and work. Unless the woman employee on leave has informed that she does not intend to return to work, her job must be held open for her return on the same basis as jobs are held open for employees on sick or disability leave. A woman employee who is unable to work for pregnancy-related reasons is entitled to disability benefits or sick leave like any other employee who applies leave on medical grounds. An employer shall extend facilities such as modified tasks and alternative assignments to a pregnant employee who is unable to carry out normal duties because of the condition of pregnancy. An employer cannot single out or subject a pregnant employee to tests in order to assess the employee's ability to work except when such tests are independent of pregnancy condition. The seniority policy shall consider and include all medical leave taken due to pregnancy. Also, such leave shall be reckoned for calculation of all time-bound or seniority-bound benefits like vacation leave quantum. A pregnancy-related medical expense should be reimbursed in the same manner as are expenses incurred for other medical conditions. The amount payable for the costs incurred for pregnancy-related conditions can be limited to the same extent as costs for other medical conditions. The Act provides for extension of medical benefits for abortions necessitated by medical condition, whereas in other circumstances it is voluntary for employer to extend such benefits. Pregnancy Discrimination Act does not cover leave on account of childcare purposes because the principles would require that leave for childcare purposes be granted on the same basis as leave which is granted to employees for other non-medical reasons.

Occupational Safety and Health Act, 1970

The purpose of this Act is to ensure safe and healthy working conditions for all working men and women by encouraging employers and employees in their efforts to reduce the number of occupational safety and health hazards at their places of employment. The Act also attempts to stimulate both employers and employees to design initiatives and programmes that provide safe working environment by laying down provisions defining responsibilities and rights of both the employer and employees to achieve safe and healthy working conditions. Under the legislation, Secretary of Labor is given the responsibility to set mandatory safety and health standards through Occupational Safety and Health Review Commission. Occupational safety and health standard means a standard which requires conditions or the adoption or use of one or more practices, means, methods, operations or processes, reasonably necessary or appropriate to provide safe and healthy employment and places of employment. Any person affected by a standard issued may, at any time prior to the 60th day, file a petition in the court challenging such standard. Nothing in this Act shall be construed to supersede or in any manner affect any workmen's compensation law or to enlarge or diminish or affect in any other manner the common law or statutory rights, duties or liabilities of employers and employees with respect to injuries, diseases or death of employees arising out of or in the course of employment. Every employer shall ensure a place of employment and workplace to an employee that is free from hazards and source of likely death and every employee is responsible to adhere to the occupational and safety standards as applicable. As per the Act, authorized authority can inspect and investigate during working hours or at other reasonable times the working places, infrastructure, premises, machinery and question in order to ensure compliance to the standards. Every employer is obligated to make, keep and preserve all records pertaining to the prescribed occupational and safety standards for the perusal of inspection authorities. Secretary of Labor issues instructions related to record keeping which shall be complied with. Any employee or representative of employees who believe that there is a violation to the standards at workplace can complain and solicit inspection. No employee or person shall be discriminated because he or she has made a complaint which is unlawful. Civil penalty of up to USD 7,000 can be levied for each of the violations on the employer. If death is caused due to violation of standards, a fine up to USD 10,000 and imprisonment of up to six months can be imposed. If there is a possibility of accident proneness at a workplace, the same can be treated as accident deemed to have happened and authorities can initiate action accordingly, terming it as serious violation. Occupational Safety and Health

Commission will take necessary initiatives in collaboration with employer to create awareness and education among employees about occupational safety health standards from time to time. The Commission will also conduct periodic and comprehensive assessment of the efficacy of the worker and supervisor training programmes developed and offered with assistance from government grants.

Canada Labour Code

It will be a mammoth effort to capture employment laws which will run into volumes since the employment matters are significantly provincial than federal. Thus it depends upon each province. Nevertheless, Canada Labour Code is cardinal and also functions as principal guiding statute to all laws of provinces. The Code focuses on all facets of employment cycle that include welfare/ security of employees/employment conditions, occupational health, safety and employee– employer relationships as described briefly in the forthcoming content. Canada Labour Code is a composite legislation comprising three parts: Part 1 deals with provisions relating to IR, Part 2 deals with occupational health and safety, and Part 3 focuses on standard hours, wages, vacations and holidays. These parts and the salient features are discussed briefly in the following paragraphs.

Part 1: Industrial Relations

The objective of this part is to define provisions, procedures and methods in order to encourage harmonious relations among employees, employers and labour enforcement agencies and to recognize freedom of association of employees and protection of their rights in consonance with convention 87 of the ILO and promotion of common well-being. Part 1 applies to all industrial undertakings, corporations and businesses.

Employees are free to join trade unions, and employers are free to join their associations to participate in lawful activities. The Code also provides for establishment of Canada Industrial Relations Board comprised of a chairperson and vice chairperson appointed by the government and six members drawn equally from employees and employers. The duties of the Board inter alia include: the certification of trade unions as bargaining units for a defined unit, the hearing or determination of any application, complaint dispute or difference that is made or referred to the Board and to give declaratory opinion on employee matters. The Board is empowered to decide on any matters before it without holding an oral hearing. The Board can make or issue any order or decision, or stipulate any terms and conditions or order any such things in relation to an employee or an organization in order to attain objective of harmony and common well-being. A trade union which is seeking to be certified as the bargaining agent for a business unit of an organization must make an application to the Board who on following proper procedure and on satisfying itself with the entire factors can certify or reject such application. Employers shall not alter wages, allowances, working hours and all such relevant terms and conditions of employment without discussion and consent of certified bargaining agent. The Board may refuse to certify a trade union as collective bargaining agent if it believes that the trade union is dominated or influenced by an employer. Trade union will be certified as bargaining unit for a specific unit based on various groups of employees in an organization such as professional employees, supervisors and other employees. This means there can be one bargaining agent for each group. A trade union in order to qualify for certification should have at least 35 per cent of all employees in that unit as its members and shall not exceed 50 per cent of employees as members of that unit. Every trade union must follow proper procedure in extending the membership to the employees and the Board may refuse to recognize employees as members of the trade union if proper procedure and eligibility criteria are not followed while giving union membership to employees. The Board may also permit two or more employers and two or more employee unions to come together as one collective bargaining agent for clearly identified units as a single unit. Any collective barging agreement drawn by such unit shall be binding on all employers' members of such group and trade unions who had come together for certification as bargaining agent. The employer representative may require each employer of employees in the bargaining unit to remit its share of the costs that the employer representative has incurred or estimated to incur in discharging its responsibilities to arrive at a collective bargaining agreement and to oversee the implementation of terms and conditions of the agreement. Once a trade union is certified as sole bargaining agent, such trade union is authorized only to negotiate to draw agreements with employer which shall be binding on all employees and the employer. If any trade union or employees believe that a trade union which was certified as bargaining agent does not enjoy support of requisite employees, they can approach the Board for revocation of the certification. Whenever a trade union is merged with another union, the new entity will automatically assume the previously certified status of collective bargaining agent. Similarly, whenever there is merger or acquisition, or transfer of undertaking, the new employer shall respect rights and privileges of certified trade union same as that of pre-merger. The new employer is also bound by all previous collective agreements drawn and in force and shall not alter the features and terms of the agreement unilaterally. In other words, a collective agreement that applied to employees employed in an organization/business unit at the time of the change or sale continues to apply and is binding on the employer or the person to whom the business is sold. An employer who succeeds a previous employer shall not only continue to apply the terms and conditions of employment without change as was before but also must pay to the employees their wages without any change that adversely affect employees. A trade union duly certified as bargaining agent of a unit and its employer shall commence the negotiations at least four months before expiry of the current collective agreement. If any collective bargaining agreement provides for revision of certain terms of the agreement on a given date, either party shall commence the discussion for the revision. Whenever a notice for negotiation is given by one party to the other, the discussion shall commence within 21 days of the said notice. Even when there is delay in negotiating new terms of collective agreement, employer cannot alter the pay levels or terms and conditions or any rights and privileges of employees in any disadvantageous manner and instead shall continue to apply the terms in vogue till a new agreement is drawn. The introduction of any new technological changes that are likely to impact livelihood or collective agreement provisions relating to employees shall be discussed and any issues identified shall be resolved before implementation. Employers must provide a detailed description of the nature of the proposed technological change, the names of employees who are likely to be impacted and the rationale for the change. The Board may perform an evaluation of all relevant aspects and direct the employer not to implement the technological changes for a period not exceeding 120 days and can order reinstatement of any employees displaced due to the technological changes with back wages.

All collective bargaining agreements must contain a provision that any differences arising out of interpretation, application and implementation must be settled finally without stoppage of work through arbitration process. To resolve the disputes, an arbitrator or arbitration board comprised of chairperson and members are elected by mutual consent of both the parties or will be appointed by the minister. Powers of an arbitrator or a board would include: the power to interpret provisions of collective bargaining agreement and provide relief, power to make interim order as may be necessary and deemed fit and power to expedite arbitration proceedings to protect rational interest and power to determine whether a particular issue falls within the purview of arbitration or otherwise. Arbitrator or board is required to complete its proceedings within 60 days from the date of such reference and provide relief orders. A collective bargaining agreement shall be valid for a year if no validity period is defined in the agreement. Employers are bound to deduct trade union membership contribution fee from the wages of employees regardless of whether they are members of that trade union or not provided a clause allowing the deduction is included in a collective bargaining agreement. A trade union in pursuance to a collective bargaining agreement can make referral of candidates for employment opportunities and these referrals must be dealt with fairly and without discrimination. Government has created a mechanism called the FMCA under the Department of Employment and Social Development with a mandate to assist the minister in ensuring harmonious IR and assisting the unions and employers in collective bargaining process and in implementation of collective bargaining agreements. Department may appoint conciliation officers and board consisting three members to undertake the responsibility of conciliation services. It is encouraged to include a provision in all collective bargaining agreements that all differences and disputes will be referred to conciliation and must be addressed within 14 days and once referred to conciliation, the right to strike or lockout is taken away till the conciliation proceedings are complete.

Unless a lockout not prohibited has occurred, a trade union is bound to provide 21 days notice to the employer from the date of intending to strike with details such as the nature of dispute and date of strike with a copy to the minister. Unless a strike not prohibited has occurred, an employer must provide a 21 days' advance notice from its intending date of lockout with details of dispute and date of commencing the lockout to trade union with a copy to the minister. During a strike or lockout not prohibited, the employer, employees and trade union must strive to ensure uninterrupted services and supply of goods to the extent necessary to prevent an immediate danger to the safety and health of the public. The Board also on receipt of a copy of notice regarding impending strike or lockout as the case may be should direct both the parties to ensure uninterrupted service or supply of goods in public interest and impose such measures as necessary in order to achieve this objective. At the end of a strike or lockout, an employer must give preference to employees who are members of the collective bargaining unit in reinstatement of service comparing to other employees who are not members. Strikes and lockouts are prohibited during the currency of operation of a valid collective bargaining agreement except in the case where a trade union has given advance notice and it is in adherence to the guidelines provided in the Labour Code. No employer can declare a lockout and no trade union can declare a strike unless both the parties have made attempts to bargain and have failed, a notice is given to the minister who in turn institutes conciliation proceedings which either fail or could not resolve the issue to mutual acceptance of the employer and the trade union and on lapse of 21 days from the day of the minister's communication of no intention to further pursue the conciliation proceedings. No employee is allowed or can participate in a strike unless that employee is a member of the bargaining unit. The minister, after affording an opportunity to a trade union and employees to represent their interests and only on satisfying himself or herself that there is in fact a contravention to the procedure because a trade union has declared or resorted to strike the work, can declare the strike illegal and direct the trade union to revoke or abandon the strike and direct all employees to resume the work immediately. Likewise, on receipt of a complaint from trade union or an employee that an employer has intention to declare or has announced a lockout contrary to the Code, the minister after affording an opportunity of being heard to the employer and on satisfying that there is contravention, the lockout can be declared illegal and employer will be directed to commence the operations immediately. No employer or person acting on behalf of the employer is allowed to interfere with the administration and affairs of a trade union and to contribute to a trade union financially. If it does so, the same will be treated as unfair labour practice. Employers also shall not use coercion, threat, intimidation, promise or undue influence on the union to get through its way. However, an employer can provide the premises for functioning of a trade union office, provide free transport to trade union office-bearers during collective bargaining meetings and provide financial assistance to employee welfare and pension schemes. Employers shall not treat employees who are members or seek to be members of a trade union in employee legitimate entitlements and neither can the employer suspend or transfer or lay off or indulge in any pressure tactics. No trade union can compel an employer to negotiate with it when it is not a certified collective bargaining agent and this will be treated as unfair labour practice and will be dealt with as per provisions of the Labour Code. Trade unions also cannot approach or pursue an employee to become member of the union or espouse a cause during working hours without consent of an employer. The Board can certify a trade union as the bargaining agent despite a lack of evidence of majority support if the Board is of the opinion that but for the unfair labour practice, the trade union had the support of a majority of the employees on the unit. Every employer who declares a lockout contrary to the provisions of the Labour Code will be declared as guilty and can be fined a minimum of USD 1,000 to a maximum of USD 10,000 per day of lockout and a trade union which goes on strike in contravention to provisions of the Labour Code will be declared guilty and can be fined from a minimum of USD 1,000 to a maximum of USD 10,000 per day of strike. Minister can conduct meetings periodically with employers/employers' associations and trade union/trade union associations and experts to discuss about IR scenario and initiatives required to maintain industrial harmony.

Also, minster under the Code can appoint a commission to be designated as an Industrial Inquiry Commission for investigation of the matters important for protection of employee rights and to ensure productivity and effective functioning of business organizations. The Board may grant permission on receipt of a request application from a trade union for granting access to one of its representatives to a premise which is reasonably isolated, and owned and controlled by an employer to approach the employees with a view to protect interests of employees. All employee members of a trade union shall have access to the financial statement of trade union organization.

Part 2: Occupational Health and Safety

The objective of this part is to lay down the provisions that are helpful to prevent accidents and injury to health arising out of and in the course of employment. Every employer is required and bound to ensure that the health and safety of every employee working in the organization is fully protected. Employer also must provide all safety gears, devices and materials to all persons who are given access to the workplace. The Labour Code provides for exhaustive guidelines and standards that shall be maintained by the employer in relation to physical workplace, machinery, hazardous material handling, ergonomics and maintenance of safety records. Employers must also take adequate measures to educate and create awareness among employees about importance of safety and health. Training of employees in supervisory and managerial positions on safety measures and safety management is mandatory and also all members of policy and workplace committees, and health and safety representatives are required to receive the stipulated training. The Code encourages every organization to form a safety policy committee or to entrust the responsibility for safety and health to works committees. Every employer who normally employs directly 300 or more employees shall establish a policy health and safety committee. Where less than 300 and more than 20 employees are normally employed, an employer shall establish a policy committee to look after and dispose all the matters related to work safety. Efforts shall be made to publicize the workplace telephone numbers of representatives of said committee so that employees can access them easily. Employer representatives and officers shall consult the committee members on regular basis in matters related to implementation and monitoring of programmes related to safety. No member of policy and works committee is personally liable for any act, decision or direction given in good faith. While at work, every employee must use all safety gear and clothing given by the employer for the purpose of protection, adhere to the prescribed standards, procedures and protocols set in an organization, cooperate with safety representatives in ensuring safe workplace and report to the employer if anything is likely to cause danger to the safety of workplace. No employee is personally liable for any omission done in good faith as advised by an employer or procedures in vogue. If an employee is killed or seriously injured in a workplace, no person shall, unless authorized to do so by the minister, remove or in any way interfere with or disturb any wreckage, article or thing related to the incident. An employee who believes that a particular process or circumstances has probably led to an accident can make a complaint to his or her supervisor and if the supervisor and employee fail to agree on an approach, they can bring the complaint to safety policy or works committee for resolution. If the complaint is still unresolved, either employee or employer can refer the matter to the minister who can initiate an investigation and based on the report of investigation a decision will be arrived at which shall be binding on all the parties. The minister may initiate health surveillance programme in order to assess the occupational and health issues and also can inspect work premises in the presence of employer and employee representatives and representatives of works and policy committee. The minister is also required to investigate every death of an employee that occurred in the course of employment. If aggrieved with the decision of the minister, an employer or employee, or trade union can make an appeal to appeals officer within 30 days for review of the decision. The appeals officer is bound to provide a decision on review with reasons for his or her decision in writing. A decision taken by an appeals officer is final and can neither be questioned nor subject to review by any court. The Code also provides full protection to an employee who has testified or is about to testify in a safety dispute. Any person or organization not adhering to the Code directions will be declared as guilty and penal actions will be taken which include monetary and imprisonment or both depending upon severity of violation.

Part 3: Standard Hours, Wages, Vacations and Holidays

The purpose of this part, as the title suggests, is to prescribe working hours, general holidays, vacation pay and to stipulate conditions for wages.

The standard hours of work of any employee shall not exceed 8 hours in a 24 hours day and 40 hours in a 7 days week cycle. Hours of work in a week shall be scheduled in such a way that employees are able to get one full day's rest in a week and that day as much as possible must be on a Sunday. However, an employer may ask employees to work excess hours in exigencies if the same is agreed to as a part of collective bargaining agreement subject to a condition that the total working hours including excess hours shall not exceed 48 hours in a week. Also, such modification of working hours must be notified to employees concerned well in advance by the employer. General holiday under the Code means New Year's Day, Good Friday, Victoria Day, Canada Day, Labour Day, Thanksgiving Day, Remembrance Day, Christmas Day and Boxing Day. Every employee is entitled to paid holiday on a general holiday. If an employer substitutes a general holiday with another holiday due to exigencies of work and with prior permission, the employer shall put notice at all conspicuous places for information to all affected employees. Whenever there is change in schedule of work and if employees insist on a secret ballot stating that the change does not have the consent of majority employees, the labour inspector shall conduct a secret ballot. An employee who has not completed 30 days of service in an organization is not eligible for paid general holiday. Employees on continuous operations work are not eligible for paid holiday on a general holiday if they are asked to work on a general holiday but refuse to work. If holiday falls on a day when an employee working day coincides as per work schedule, such employee is entitled to be paid one and half times of normal wages for that day. Whenever the employees work excess hours, they are entitled to wages one-and-a-half times of regular wages. Employers are also obligated to pay employees not less than minimum wage as prescribed by the government from time to time. An employer can employ a person who is less than 17 years of age only in occupations specified by the Code regulations and subject to adherence to the relevant conditions put in place by the Governor in Council. An employer shall ensure equal wages for same or similar work regardless of gender, religion, nationality or race. A labour inspector who suspects that an employer is indulging in discriminatory practice can bring the same to the notice of Canadian Human Rights Commission for investigation and appropriate action. Employees are entitled to 4 per cent of wages or 6 per cent of wages as vacation pay if an employee has completed six consecutive years of work in the same organization. Employees are eligible to be granted a vacation of at least two weeks and three weeks after completing six consecutive years of work in an organization and with vacation pay and additional one week in respect of every year of employment in the same organization. Vacation pay for all purposes will be treated as wages. Intervening general holidays will not be counted as vacation leave and it will be extended by equal day/days of general holidays. Employers shall complete full and final settlement when an employee ceases to be an employee of that employer within 30 days. The continuity of service of an employee is protected on transfer from one employer to another on account of merger and acquisition, and transfer of undertaking scenario. An employer while making payment of wages must provide a statement of wages with details such as: the period for which the payment is made, the rate of wages, details of deductions made and the actual sum being paid to the employee. Employers should not make deduction from the wages of employees except for authorized deductions as required by a federal or provincial Act or regulations, amounts of deduction authorized by the courts and deductions authorized by the employee in writing.

An employee who is pregnant is entitled to a leave of absence during the period from the beginning of pregnancy to the end of the 24th week following the birth. Every employee who completes six months of continuous service in an organization shall be granted maternity leave of up to 17 weeks which may begin not earlier than 11 weeks prior to the estimated date of confinement and end not later than 17 weeks following the actual date of confinement. In order to see grant of maternity leave, an eligible employee shall apply with the support of a medical certificate from a qualified medical practitioner. In case a child is hospitalized soon after the birth, employee is eligible for additional leave to the extent of hospitalization period subject to cumulative leave not to exceed 52 weeks. During the period of pregnancy or nursing, an employee can request an employer for modification of duties/functions if the current duties and responsibilities can potentially pose threat to health and safety of the employee. An employer can agree to modify the job based on the request or can refuse if the employer has reasons to believe that the current role can in no way adversely affect the health of the employee. However, the onus to prove it will be on the employer. An employee will have the right to claim the same role on return from maternity leave or on completion of maternity period. Employee shall apply for such modification of role with at least two weeks' notice. Every employee who has completed six months of continuous service in an organization is entitled to paternity leave of 37 weeks to take care of newly born child or adopted child, and such a leave can be granted only during the first 52 weeks period. If the child is hospitalized soon after the birth, employee is entitled to grant of additional leave to the extent of hospitalization duration subject to the condition that the cumulative leave on account of this shall not exceed 104 weeks. The aggregate of leave that can be taken by a couple ordinarily shall not exceed 37 weeks and 52 weeks in case of hospitalization of the child. Every employee is entitled for grant of compassionate care leave up to eight weeks to take care of a seriously ailing (with a significant risk of death within 26 weeks) family member or a cohabitant with whom the employee has conjugal relationship based on a certificate issued by a qualified medical practitioner. Every employee who is a parent of a child and has completed six months of continuous service in an organization is entitled for grant of leave up to 37 weeks in order to take care of ailing child based on a certificate issued by a specialist doctor. Every employee who has completed six months of continuous service in the employment of same employer is eligible for grant of leave up to 104 weeks in the event of death of own child as a result of a crime. Employee is also eligible for grant of leave up to 52 weeks in the event that his or her own child is missing or has disappeared as a result of a crime. However, an employee is not eligible for the said leave if the same child is charged with the crime. For the purpose of this leave, child means a person who is under the age of 18 years.

In general, an employee is expected to give four weeks' notification for grant of leave unless there is rational reason for inability to provide such advance notice. Employer in exigencies can interrupt granted leave of an employee and ask the employee to report for work. Employee can also interrupt own leave or shorten the grated leave by providing reason and advance notice to the employer. This interruption can be taken in the case of maternity or paternity leave in which case an employer needs to convey acceptance or refusal of an employee's request with reason within a week. No employer can insist that an employee go on maternity leave unless the employee requests for it. However, if an employer has a strong reason to believe that a pregnant employee is unable to perform a critical function of her role due to pregnancy, the employer can ask her to go on leave. The onus to prove this will be on the employer. Employer shall protect the right of an employee who is on maternity leave in the matters of promotion, training and other benefits during the leave. The leave shall not be grounds to refuse any such opportunities and it is obligatory on the part of employer to reinstate an employee who has returned to work post-maternity leave without dilution of the role held immediately before proceeding on the leave. In exceptional conditions where an employer is not able to offer the same role due to valid reasons, the employer shall offer comparable role with same wages and benefits. The pension, disability, health benefits and the seniority of an employee remains unaffected due to leave which is authorized and rated as per the Labour Code. Employee who is required to pay contributions for benefits such as pension and insurance in normal course shall continue to do so during the leave period and the employer also shall continue to pay all matching contributions or stand-alone against an employee as was due in normal course of employment. No employer can dismiss, terminate, demote or take disciplinary action against an employee during her pregnancy and during her maternity leave. Every employee is entitled to be granted bereavement leave of three days in case of death of an immediate family member, and leave of three days with normal wages is applicable to an employee who has completed at least three months of continuous service in an organization.

An employer who intends to terminate 50 or more employees at the same time or within a period of four weeks shall obtain prior permission from the Minister of Employment and Social Development and is also obligated, as part of employment contract or as per the terms of collective bargaining agreement, to provide 16 weeks' advance notice in addition to the normal notice period to employees who are going to be terminated. Employer must give a notice also to Canada Employment Insurance Commission and trade union which represents the employees to be terminated. The minister will direct the employer to appoint a joint planning committee consisting of at least four members of whom two members shall be drawn from employees or trade union representing employees that will be terminated as per the employer's notice. Where there is more than one union representing redundant employees, there shall be one representative from each trade union. The role and responsibility of this joint planning committee is to explore all possibilities to avoid employee terminations and, if unavoidable, to create adjustment programmes to minimize the impact and assist in outplacement of employees and make fast closure of benefits such as wages, notice and severance pay and other benefits payable to employees. If the joint planning committee is unable to reach a consensual decision or a decision that is agreeable to employee representatives, minister can appoint an arbitrator to assist the committee to successfully evolve an adjustment development programme. An employer is required to serve at least two weeks' notice in individual employment terminations or the duration as specified in collective bargaining agreement. However, the said two weeks' notice is not mandatory in respect of employees who have not completed at least three months of continuous service in an organization. Where termination is not of dismissal for cause of an employee who has completed 12 months of continuous service in an organization, employer must give severance pay of two days for every completed year of service. Employers are discouraged from terminating employees who are on sick leave. No employer shall dismiss, suspend, lay off, demote or discipline an employee on the grounds that garnishment proceedings may be or have been taken. Every employer shall subscribe to a plan that provides an employee, who is absent from work due to work-related illness or injury, with wage replacement payable at an equivalent rate to that provided for under the applicable workers' compensation legislation in the employee's province of residence. An employer must provide the same role and responsibility when an employee returns from absence of work due to work-related injury or illness unless the said injury incapacitated an employee to perform core functions of the role he or she held prior. Every employer that provides benefits to its employees under a long-term disability plan must insure the plan with an entity that is licensed to provide insurance under the laws of province. An employee who has completed 12 months of continuous service in an organization and is not a member of a trade union or is not covered under collective bargaining agreement provisions, if terminated or dismissed, can file a complaint with labour inspector. The employee must make the compliant within 90 days from the date of such dismissal and the inspector shall make inquiry and convince both the parties for an alternative action. If inspector is not successful in convincing the parties, he or she shall submit a report to the minister for an appropriate action on the matter. The minster can seek explanation from the employer in writing or can refer the matter for adjudication. The decision arrived at during the proceedings of adjudication is final and binding on all the parties. However, either party who is not convinced with the decision of adjudicator or the minister can approach Federal Court.

Employers must disburse wages and salaries once in 30 days or early periods as stipulated in collective bargaining agreement or as per the practice of the employer. A predictable practice of paying salaries from a periodicity perspective shall be established by the employer. Every employee enjoys the basic right to employment without being subjected to sexual harassment and every employer must ensure and take all measures to provide a sexual harassment-free work environment. Sexual harassment in the Labour Code is defined as any conduct, comment, gesture or contact of a sexual nature that is likely to cause offense or humiliation to any employee or that might, on reasonable grounds, be perceived by that employee as placing a condition of a sexual nature on employment or any opportunity for training, promotion or any such benefit of opportunity. Every employer must issue a policy statement on this subject and ensure this is well communicated within an organization so that all employees are aware of this. The policy statement should not only define what sexual harassment constitutes but also the disciplinary and penal actions applicable. The policy also must include necessary provision of anti-discriminatory practices propounded and observed by Canadian Human Rights Commission and employees' right to approach the Commission for redressal of any discriminatory and sexual harassment complaint.

An employee who is a member of reserve force and has completed six months of continuous service in an organization is eligible to be granted leave of absence to attend reserve force duties as and when required. An employee must ensure that the request for grant of this leave is applied four weeks in advance. Employer must make efforts to reinstate the employee on return from the said leave and if not possible for substantive reasons the reinstatement shall be done in comparable positions with same wages and benefits. No employer shall dismiss, demote or transfer, suspend or lay off because an employee is a member of reserve force and is intending to take leave. Governor in Council will notify the regulations in regard to quantum of leave that can be granted and circumstances in which the leave can be granted or refused by an employer. The leave period shall be counted towards continuous service of employees.

To enforce provisions related to working hours, vacation leave, health and safety, maternity/paternity leave, general holidays, and terms and conditions of employment, the minister may appoint any person as a labour inspector with a mandate to facilitate, supervise, coordinate and monitor. The labour inspector can seek information, documents, payroll stubs and proof of insurance for long-term disability protection, returns and records from the employer in order to satisfy himself or herself with the implementation of this part of Labour Code provisions. The inspector can also enter the premises of work at all reasonable times for inspection and verification. No inspector is required to give a testimony in any civil suit or civil proceedings with regard to information gathered during the discharge of his or her duties. An inspector is also personally not liable for anything done or omitted to be done in good faith. An aggrieved employee who has a reasonable ground to believe that his or her employer has not followed the Code can file a complaint with the inspector for investigation and necessary resolution. However, the employee must make the complaint within six months from the date of occurrence of such violation. Any person who contravenes provisions of this part will be declared guilty and is liable for the USD 50,000 fine if the offence is committed for the first time, USD 100,000 if the offense is committed for the second time and USD 250,000 if the offense is committed for the third time. Proceedings in respect of an offense under this part may be instituted at any time within but not later than three years.

Summary

Employment laws and regulations in North America (those pertinent to corporate organizations especially from the perspective of foreign entrepreneurs and international organizations) were discussed. The chapter was organized into three parts with the first part dedicated to the introduction and guiding principles of labour laws in the United States and Canada, second part focusing on three clusters of labour legislation in the United States and the Labour Code of Canada in the third part, provisions of the employment laws were presented from a practitioner's perspective with emphasis on easy understating and relevance to HRM operations.

QUESTIONS FOR DISCUSSION

1. Construct an employment contract in conformity with the provisions of FLSA, 1938, to be issued to 18 campus undergraduates passing out of one of the US universities and who will be posted in Houston.
2. Is data pertaining to an employee such as academic and experience background details protected in Canada? And elaborate whose responsibility is it to maintain data confidentiality.
3. What is the procedure to seek collective bargaining agent certification under Canada Labour Code?
4. What are the pros and cons of anti-discrimination laws for business growth in the United States?
5. Whether significance of labour laws is on decline in the United States? If yes, why and if no, substantiate?
6. Compare and contrast labour regulations between Canada and the United States in regard to leave, vacation and health.
7. Discuss whether age discrimination laws in North America are progressive or regressive.
8. Describe IR legislative measures in North America and how effective are they to forge harmonious relationships between employees and employers.
9. Write an analysis on exit clauses of employment in the United States.

CASE STUDIES

Case Study 1

Exit Management at Richard Lewis Inc.

Richard Lewis Inc. is into manufacturing of high-speed elevators. The company has manufacturing bases located in states of North Carolina and Florida in the United States and in Calgary, Canada. In these locations, 4,700 employees are working and break-up is: 1,700 employees in Calgary, 2,931 employees in Florida and remaining in North Carolina plant with 21 per cent of gender diversity, 6 per cent of minorities and 0.7 per cent of disabled persons in employment. The company has reported losses for 23 consecutive quarters with almost empty cash balance on its register. Investors have cautioned the board members that neither will they allow raising of any fresh loans from financial institutions nor are they ready to pump in anymore funds unless actions are initiated to cut the flab in cost structure, most importantly excessive number of employees engaged in the plants and also to consider shifting the manufacturing bases to low-cost centres in China actively and immediately. Brand equity of products is high, design and manufacturing facilities meet state-of-the-art standards. Cost structure is very high due to steep wage bill since average compensation of employees is industry best and employees who had become surplus over a period of time due to advancements in work processes and automation have never managed to exit from the rolls of the company. Further, at least 63 per cent of various parts and equipment used in manufacturing elevators are sourced from Taiwan and China leading to escalation of supply chain-related costs since the market share for products is on decline in North America and buoyant in Asia and Europe. Employment contracts are mix of at-will and no explicit mention of exit-related clauses. Employees were hired during the period 1997–2004 with hardly any fresh recruits during the last 10 years. The board has decided to exit at least 2,500 employees in the current financial year and raise loans to meet severance costs as well as to execute the plan of shifting two of its manufacturing plants to low-cost centres outside North America. The company is committed to respecting law of the land and follows proper processes to implement the plan. Discuss a plan on how the exits can be managed without industrial disturbance, non-compliance to employment laws while balancing the severance costs.

Case Study 2

Wage Fairness at Zon Am

The wage fund theory postulates that an increase in wage of a particular section of employees in an organization will cause a proportionate decrease in salaries of another section of employees. The marginal productivity theory suggests that wages of employees of any section gets determined based upon the demand and supply curve rather than any other productivity factor. In this context, how do we attain the objectives of the FLSA which was founded on the basic premise of fairness to all sections of employees at all times?

Example: Zon Am is an online retail company in the United States growing at 23 per cent CAGR annually. The company's HR critically comprises of three groups: the first group includes procurement specialists, who perform a pivotal role in sourcing goods at the right time at the right price and with high quality. Performance of these employees plays a significant role in the company's profitability, apart from continuously expanding the product and portfolio range. The second group is the supply chain specialists whose performance contributes towards customer satisfaction and inventory management. The third group is those of the software engineers who are the backbone of the company search engine which is the interface between the company and customers. Each category has their own skill sets which are complex enough, while the performance challenges are equally formidable. Now, let us discuss how we decide upon the compensation and benefits for each category of these employees. Should there be a sale level and a quantum of remuneration based on the overall fund availability or should it be different for each category based on the demand and supply? While determining this, how do we ensure that the company is compliant with the provisions of FLSA?

If the compensation and benefits of one group are higher than any other group, it may lead to a situation wherein one group might enjoy more benefits at the cost of the other group; as the overall compensation budget of a company would factor remaining on the basis of affordability (implying it is a zero-sum game, which means the dollar will move from one group to another and not by adding an

(Continued)

(Continued)

extra dollar to the existing fund!). If compensation levels and benefits have no distinction, then it may breed a non-performance culture, apart from not being in tune with the demand and supply reality of talent in the market. On the other hand, creating a distinction may contribute to a dilution of fairness since performance complexity and the skill dexterity required are at par for all categories of employees in this case. Discuss how can we can bring a distinction in compensation and benefits without nullifying the spirit of FLSA. Also discuss whether differentiation in the terms and conditions of employment based on the category of employees is unfair under the statute.

In addition, also discuss, in the context of a raging debate on executive compensation, where it was seen that the senior management consumes the major part of the wage budget pie in some cases; is such corporate behaviour contrary to FLSA which was promulgated to empower weaker sections of employees with bargaining power?

Case Study 3

Job Security During FMLA

Jessica John was working with a Chicago-based leisure and travel company as a tourist guide for the last six years as a permanent employee. Her performance had been consistently rated as high and she had received appreciation from her clients on record. She had applied for and been granted maternity leave under FMLA. She was to return on the expiry of the duly sanctioned leave but could not do so due to post-delivery complications. She kept postponing the date to resume work based on her doctor's advice. The company too sanctioned leave from time to time, which lasted for about nine months in addition to the initial period of maternity leave. During Jessica's leave period, the company could not leave the position unfilled, so they went ahead and hired a replacement. Jessica was advised to work with her replacement on joining back on duty. She was reluctant and refused to work along with the replacement employee, stating that it eroded her job responsibilities. She argued that her position was downgraded compared to the pre-leave period, when she was handling the job independently, and that asking her to report to a peer is tantamount to demotion of her position in material terms. Jessica made a compliant under FMLA to the company's internal redressal committee on the issue. The committee, on review of all the circumstances, recommended offering an alternative position to Jessica which she could handle independently. Accordingly, the company issued a communication to Jessica, moving her to a business development position. However, stating the reason that she had neither the skills nor prior experience in performing such a role, Jessica declined the offer and moved the case to the court, filing a petition that the company did not comply with provisions of FMLA in protecting her job during her maternity leave, and that the company indulged in an illegal practice of replacing her. *Discuss:* what could be the outcome of this case under FMLA. As per the law, is Jessica right as the FMLA guarantees protection of the same job during the leave, or is the company right in offering an alternative position?

Case Study 4

Constructive Dismissal and Canadian Labour Code

Peter Samuel is a finance director with a general insurance company based in Toronto. The company is not happy with Peter because of his poor interpersonal handling of colleagues, even though he manages to meet his key performance targets. Hence, the company HR department which is tasked with separating Peter has begun negotiation to buy out his employment contract. In the meantime, two developments have taken place: one, the company announced an employee stock grant programme to all employees who were active on the rolls, and second, Peter applied for the employee stock as per his eligibility. Subsequent to these developments, Peter has gone on leave for three weeks, which he had applied for much before the negotiation for his separation had started. The company, believing that Peter is engaging in delay tactics to prolong his separation from the company in order to gain employee stock options grant, and also to gain undue separation benefits, has gone ahead and put him on suspension on the basis of poor peer interaction. The employee stock option programme stipulates that employees who are on suspension would not be eligible for grant of said options, resulting in Peter becoming ineligible.

Peter has now approached the Ontario Labour Relations Board seeking to strike down his suspension notification on the grounds of constructive dismissal which is against the provisions of Canadian Labour Code. His argument was that the company, in order to avoid grant of stock options and to weaken his negotiating capability in the context of ongoing employment contract buyout discussion, imposed suspension on him as a pressure tactic. Meanwhile, the company has defended its stance citing reasons such as poor peer relations resulting in workplace toxicity and continuous delays being caused by Peter with the anticipation of stock option grants, while also looking to thwart the progress of legal termination of employment contract. Discuss whether suspension of Peter from the services is tantamount to constructive dismissal under the Canadian Labour Code.

Case Study 5

Joining a Competitor Firm

David Rogrecker was employed as a sales director in an IT services firm, ORG Fintech, based in Calgary. Having served for 14 years, David voluntarily quit the service of ORG and joined a competitor firm Global Fintech in Winnipeg, Manitoba. ORG got to know that David had joined a competitor firm and challenged this in court. They asked for a restraining order against any IT services industry clients from approaching David, citing a clause that restricts its employees from pursuing a sales career in the IT industry for a period of 24 months from the date of leaving ORG services. The employment contract that was agreed upon by David and ORG in fact comprised a clause that prohibited him from pursuing a sales career in any competitor firm in IT services industry. David defended his action averring that his employment contract with ORG had stipulated and that he would not solicit any employment, which he had adhered to. He suggested that he merely accepted an opportunity presented by Global Fintech, without him approaching them or without soliciting any employment with them, and therefore had not violated any employment contract clause. His lawyers argued that imposing a condition that David, their client, shall not pursue a sales career in IT industry is tantamount to depriving his livelihood and vitiates the spirit of Canada Labour Code. Discuss whether it is legally valid to build a clause in an employment contract that restrains an employee from pursuing a career in the same industry; whether it is legal to restrain someone to work for a competitor firm and whether it is legal under the Canada Labour Code to exercise an employment non-solicitation clause.

Industrial Relations:
Labour Codes, Laws and Regulations
Management—Europe

6

LEARNING OBJECTIVES

The objectives of this chapter are to:

❏ enable practitioner understanding of the labour codes of Germany, Switzerland, The Netherlands, Poland, France, Hungary and the Czech Republic, along with their interpretation.

❏ enable practitioner understanding of the essential labour laws, regulations and employment conditions of European nations.

❏ illustrate important case laws, providing deeper insights into the implications of various legislative measures for people management.

❏ discuss the IR scenario, collective bargaining process and international workers' unions in HRM in business organizations.

❏ analyse European directives on labour and employment, and their implications on various legislative measures of member nations.

It is a whole world in itself when it comes to labour codes, laws and regulations, and a wide canvas of IR in Europe. Though there is a common thread in the form of EU and its directives pertaining to employment matters, still each country in Europe has its own labour code and labour laws. Labour laws and regulations in European nations can be classified into two clusters: one cluster is comprised of a set of labour laws promulgated to ensure good working conditions, living standards and equality, and are driven by EU guidelines as per the Treaty on the Functioning of the EU, while another cluster is comprised of labour laws and regulations arisen out of its own needs and historical conditions of each nation.

In general, labour laws and regulations in European nations are more generous, socialistic and protective towards employees and less employer-friendly compared to North American labour laws. Though some members of EU such as France, Sweden, Switzerland and Poland are attempting to bring in reforms to transform labour laws that are less cumbersome to businesses, there is still a long way to go to attain balance among all stakeholders' interests. IR legislation like works council related are far exhaustive and in quite a few instances organizations cannot do anything without obtaining approvals from the said councils. While this will ensure social justice, many times the processes are lengthy, tardy and dilutive leading to business under performance.

Therefore, enabling nations to compete internationally, yet ensuring social harmony and justice, is a complex task for these countries. Relationships between employer and employees are very formal and so all working conditions and expectations shall be formal and structural. Nothing can be left open in employment contracts or in employee policies and nothing can be assumed unless it is in a formally articulated format. Regulations concerning maternity, working hours, performance appraisals and training, welfare and security aspects are stringent. This orientation of labour laws is founded in the respective constitutions of these nations, making the countries duty-bound to attain social justice and solidarity. This labour law environment only calls for solid understating of laws and regulations and in no way are they barriers to conduct business or make investments in Europe. There are many international organizations that successfully perform and grow in these nations while adapting their HRM framework in compliance to these laws. With this objective, the following text presents labour codes and laws of selective nations and also EU directives on labour and employment.

European Union Directives on Employment and Labour

The Treaty of Amsterdam, EU, has given a beginning to members of EU to recognize that employment issues are central to economic and monetary development in the region as a part of social policy agenda. This was followed up with The Treaty of Nice and social agenda set in Lisbon that provided direction to member nations on variety of issues involving working conditions, employment contracts and collective bargaining in the form of EU directives which are discussed next. Basically, there are 14 directives issued by the EU covering 12 subjects under the broad theme of working conditions and there are 5 directives issued by the EU covering 8 subjects under the broad theme of employee involvement.

Individual Employment Conditions
(Council Directive of 14 October 1991)

The objective of this directive is to: make employment relationships formal, provide employees with improved protection against possible infringements of their rights, make employees fully aware of main terms and conditions of their employment and promote working conditions. This directive is applicable to all employees of the member nations of EU. An employer under this directive is obligated to:

- notify an employee of the essential aspects of employment contract/relationship.
- ensure that the employment contract mentions the names of parties to the contract (employer and employee), the place of work, title, grade, brief description of work, date of commencement of employment relationship, the expected duration of the contract, leave, notice period, remuneration and working hours and details about collective bargaining agreements in force. Whenever an employee of the EU is required to work in a non-EU nation, the contract of employment shall include in writing additional details such as the duration of employment abroad, the remuneration specifying currency, benefits while working abroad and conditions governing repatriation. This directive will not affect the prerogative of member nations to introduce laws on this subject more favourable to employees.

Fixed-term Work (Council Directive of 28 June 1999)

This directive is applicable to all fixed-term employees. This directive aims to improve the quality of fixed-term work by ensuring the application of the principle of non-discrimination and establishing a framework to prevent abuse from the use of successive fixed-term employment contracts or relationships. The word fixed-term employee refers to a person who has an employment contract entered into with an employer and the end of the contract is determined by objective conditions such as reaching a specific date, completing a specific task or the occurrence of a specific event. No fixed-term employee shall be treated less favourably than permanent employees. Employers are obligated to share all permanent job opportunities within the company with fixed-term employees to provide them with the opportunity to secure permanent employment. Employers must extend all training and development opportunities to these employees to enhance their skills and career opportunities. They must also share data and details of fixed-term employees with trade union representatives and must also specify reasons justifying engagement of fixed-term contracts.

Temporary Agency Workers (Council Directive of 19 November 2008)

This directive is applicable to employees who have a contract of employment with a temporary agency and who are assigned to work temporarily in both private and public undertakings under their supervision and direction. The objective of the directive is to ensure protection and equal treatment of temporary agency employees. Prohibition or restriction of employment on the use of temporary employees shall not be done to the prejudice of protection of such employees. Temporary agency workers shall be informed of any vacant posts in the user undertaking to give them the same opportunity as other employees in that undertaking to find permanent employment. Temporary employee agencies shall not charge employees any fees in exchange for arranging for them to be recruited by the user undertaking. All temporary employees must be given access to the collective facilities such as canteen, childcare and transport services under the same conditions applicable to employees directly employed by an undertaking. Temporary employees must also be extended training and development opportunities. The directive also envisages that member nations shall provide for penalties for violations of provisions laid down in this directive and also put in place judicial procedures to deal with such violations.

Health and Safety of Employees (Council Directive of 25 June 1991)

This directive is applicable to employees governed by fixed duration contracts of employment concluded directly between the employer and the employee and to temporary employees employed in an organization through an employment agency. The objective of this directive is to ensure these employees are provided and cared for through measures intended to secure their safety and health at the workplace. Under this directive, all member nations are required to ensure that all fixed-term and temporary agency employees are provided with the necessary training in order to keep employees at work safe and healthy, and to avert all occupational hazards. Member nations also have the option of prohibiting employment of these categories of employees at certain workplaces or in certain jobs or tasks that cannot guarantee their health and safety. Member nations are also urged to deploy medical surveillance on organizations and industries to identify workplaces which are susceptible to safety, health and hygiene issues and can be sources of occupational hazard, in order to prepare adequate measures to prevent the same.

Protection of Young People at Work (Council Directive of 22 June 1994)

Young person here is defined as any person less than 18 years of age. A child is defined as any young person less than 15 years of age. Adolescent is defined as any young person of at least 15 but less than 18 years of age. The directive contains the following provisions:

- Children and adolescents must be considered specific risk groups, and measures must be taken with regard to their safety and health.
- Employment of children and adolescents should be prohibited and the minimum working age should not be lower than 15 years.
- Every employee should guarantee that young people's working conditions are appropriate to their age.
- Young people should be protected against any specific risks arising from their lack of experience, absence of awareness of existing potential risks or from their immaturity.
- Maximum working time of young people should be strictly limited and night work by young people should be prohibited.
- Training, either practical or theoretical, undergone by young people in the course of their plant work experience should be counted as working time.
- Young people should be given the minimum daily, weekly and annual periods of rest and adequate breaks. Eight hours a day and 40 hours a week should be the maximum inclusive of all training and developmental participation. Young people are entitled for 30 minutes of break for every 4.5 hours of work.
- Member nations should take adequate measures to prohibit child employment and young people should be protected against economic exploitation and against any work likely to harm their health and safety or physical, mental, moral, social development or jeopardize their education.

Working Time (Council Directive of 4 November 2003)

This directive concerns aspects such as minimum periods of daily rest, weekly rest and annual leave, breaks and maximum weekly working time and certain aspects of night shift work and patterns of work. Member nations are urged to take action to ensure that in instances where the working day is longer than six hours, every employee is entitled to a rest break with a defined duration. Every employee is entitled to a minimum daily rest period of 11 hours in a 24 hours period. Also, there shall be measures put in place to ensure that for every 7 days period, every employee is entitled to a minimum uninterrupted rest period of 24 hours plus the daily 11 hours rest (35 hours minimum per week). The average working time for each 7 days period including overtime shall not exceed 48 hours. The minimum period of paid annual leave may not be replaced by an allowance in lieu, except where the employment relationship is terminated. Normal hours of work for night workers shall not exceed an average of 8 hours in any 24 hours period. Night work employees are entitled to a free health assessment before their assignment and during the work at logical intervals. Wherever a night work employee suffers from health problems which are connected with the performance of work, the said person must be transferred to day work.

Employer Insolvency (Council Directive of 22 October 2008)

The directive stipulates that member nations shall take measures to provide for protection of employees in the event of insolvency of their employer and to ensure a minimum degree of protection in particular in order to guarantee payment of any outstanding claims by the employer. This is applicable to employees' claims arising from contracts of employment and existing against employers who are in a state of insolvency. As per Article 7, member nations shall take necessary measures to ensure that non-payment of compulsory contributions due from the employer to the insurance institutions under national statutory security schemes does not adversely affect employees' benefits entitlement. Similarly, there shall be measures aimed at protecting the rights of employees in respect of old age benefits.

Transfer of Undertakings and Safeguarding Interest of Employees (Council Directive of 12 March 2001)

This directive is applicable to all transfers of undertakings that occur as a result of mergers and acquisitions, transfers and moving part of business/operations to another employer. Council members strongly believe that it is necessary to provide for the protection of employees, in the event of change of employer, to ensure that rights of employees are safeguarded. In this pursuit, the following conditions are stipulated:

- The rights and obligations of existing employer shall be transferred to the prospective employer in the event of transfer of undertaking/business operations.
- The existing employer is obligated to notify the prospective employer well in advance of such transfer being affected and about all the rights and obligations which will be transferred to the new employer. However, the existing employer's failure to notify and well inform the new employer about the obligations and rights will not affect the rights of employees in any unfavourable manner.
- The new employer is bound by all the terms and conditions agreed in any collective bargaining agreement on the same terms as applicable to the existing employer until the date of termination or expiry of the collective agreement.
- Even in cases where there is no collective bargaining agreement, the new employer is obligated to protect the terms and conditions of employment and interest of all employees including pensionary benefits and social security measures.
- If the contract of employment or the employment relationship is terminated because the transfer involves a substantial change in working conditions that are detrimental to the

employee, the employer shall be regarded as having been responsible for termination of the contract of employment or the employment relationship.

- Both the employers exercising the responsibility of transfer and the representatives of the employees may agree to alterations, insofar as current law permits, to the employees' terms and conditions of employment designed to safeguard employment opportunities by ensuring the survival of the undertaking, business or part of the business.
- Provisions related to safeguarding of employment terms and conditions may not be applicable in the event that an organization is the subject of bankruptcy or insolvency proceedings. However, member nations shall exercise caution to ensure that employers do not simply feign bankruptcy in order to avoid their obligations to employees.
- Under the directive, both existing and prospective employer shall be required to communicate to the representatives of their respective employees affected by transfer matters such as the date or proposed date of the transfer, the reason for the transfer, the legal, economic and social implications of the transfer for the employees and any measures envisaged in relation to the employees. This information must be provided by the employers before the transfer is carried out. Employers shall hold consultation with employees and their representatives covering measures contemplated in relation to the employees in the context of such a transfer.
- Member nations are advised to promulgate provisions that provide an opportunity for employees to raise issues or disagreements through an arbitration board, if required. Members are also urged to create national legal measures necessary to pursue the judicial process in case employees believe that they are wronged by the employers' failure to comply with the provisions of transfer of undertaking.

Employee Consultation (Council Directive of 11 March 2002)

This directive is applicable to member nations in establishments/undertakings where 20 or more employees are employed. The objective of this directive is to establish a general framework seeking out minimum requirements for the right to information and consultation of employees. The employees and employers are encouraged under this directive to adopt practices for consultation and information sharing between employer representatives and employee representatives covering employee-related areas or issues within the company that can impact well-being of employees. It is felt that there is a need to strengthen and promote mutual trust within an organization in order to improve risk anticipation, make work arrangements more flexible and facilitate employees' access to training, make employees aware of adaptation needs and promote employee involvement in the operation and future of the organization to increase its competitiveness. Timely information and consultation is a prerequisite for the success of the restructuring and adaptation of an organization to the new condition created by globalization of the economy. The directive also presupposes that generally employee involvement is restricted to direct employee benefits seldom extend to economic matters that have an important bearing on well-being of employees and protection of their interests. Therefore, the directive suggests that the scope of employee involvement shall be extended to these economic aspects without prejudices to genuine business interests. The objective of this directive shall be achieved through the creation and implementation of a standard framework consisting of principles, definitions and arrangements for information and consultation among employees and employers suiting rational needs and wishes. Such information sharing and consultation should care for not only rights but also for obligations of both employer and employees. The said consultation and information sharing can lead to collective agreements which can govern a defined matter. In order for employee representatives to carry out their responsibilities in an effective and fair manner in employee consultation and involvement programmes, the state shall ensure adequate protection to these representatives.

Collective Redundancies (Council Directive of 20 July 1998)

Collective redundancies are defined as dismissals affected by an employer for one or more reasons not related to the individual workers concerned where in a period of 30 days, 10 or more employees are dismissed in an establishment employing less than 100 and at least 30 in establishment employing more than 300 and at least 10 per cent of workers are dismissed in establishment employing between 101 and 299. However, this directive is not applicable to collective redundancies that are carried out as part of employment contracts where persons are employed for a defined task/assignment for a defined time period and are dismissed on expiry of such defined period. Employers are advised to hold consultation with employees to discuss and arrive at an agreement whenever collective redundancies are contemplated. These discussions are also expected to focus on finding ways and means to avoid implementation of collective redundancies and on finding mitigation plans if redundancies are unavoidable. Before the collective dismissals are carried out, the employer is obligated to provide the following information to the employees: the reasons for the projected redundancies, the number and categories of employees to be made redundant, the number and categories of employees normally employed, the period over which the projected redundancies are to be effected, the criteria proposed for the selection of the employees to be made redundant and the method for calculating any redundancy payments. Employers are also obligated to provide this information in writing to the competent public authorities at least 30 days before such contemplated redundancy action can take place. Trade union representatives/employee representatives can also approach judicial authorities for remedies and resolve disputes arising out of such redundancies.

European Works Council (Council Directive of 6 May 2009)

The objective of this directive is to improve and encourage information sharing and consultation between employers and employees/employee representatives/trade union representatives, lay down a well-defined process for such information sharing and consultation, define scope of the consultative councils and matters that must be considered within the said council and safeguard interests of employees. The central management of an organization is solely responsible for setting up works council or creating conditions and procedures needed for creation of work councils such as deciding the composition of European Works Council, the number of members and the allocation of seats, taking into account where possible the need for balanced representation of employees with regard to their activities, category, gender and term of office. The information of the European Works Council shall relate in particular to the structure, economic and financial situation, probable development and production, and sales of the organization. The information shall also cover employment trend, organizational investments and changes, new working methods, production processes, mergers, cutbacks, closure of business units/operations and collective redundancies. The said European Works Council, once set up, shall have the right to meet with the central management at least once a year, to be informed and consulted by the members of central management. The operating expenses of the European Works Council shall be borne by the organization. Also, it shall establish a special negotiation body for which members are needed to be elected from employees and management of an organization. The number of employee representatives for such negotiating body should be proportionate to the total number of employees in an organization. The special negotiating body shall have the task of determining, along with the central management, by written agreement, the scope, composition, functions and term of office of the European Works Council or shall make arrangements for implementing a procedure for the information and consultation of employees. The negotiating body can seek advice and expert opinions from specialists and community trade union representatives when the need is felt. All expenses related to conduct of meetings by the said body shall be borne by organizations. Employee representatives who are members of the Works Council and the special negotiating body should be extended training opportunities which they would require to effectively carry out their responsibilities. Employee members should also be extended necessary protection to ensure their safety and should be enabled to participate in all Works Council activities and further the goals without fear of implications to them.

Labour Laws in the United Kingdom

Labour laws and regulations in the United Kingdom have a long history which has gone through many phases such as laws meant to exploit black workers, to intensively protecting the rights of citizen employees, to achieving a balance between employee and employer interests. Guiding principles of labour laws include right to work and form associations, welfare and security of workers, and equality and fairness in labour management relations. Though some labour laws are in conformity and a consequence of EU directives, the United Kingdom has its own distinctive laws. The laws are neither stringent and elaborate, like they are in few European countries from an employer perspective; nor as liberal as in the United States, like at-will employment contracts and fewer laws regulating labour matters. Some provisions of labour laws applicable to employees who are UK citizens are different for non-citizen employees. Key labour laws and regulations that principally fall in the areas such as terms and conditions of employment, equal pay, pensions and labour relations as discussed next.

Transfer of Undertakings (Protection of Employment) Regulations 2006

The objective of Transfer of Undertakings (Protection of Employment [TUPE]) is to protect and safeguard interests of employees when ownership of business in full or part changes to a new employer. TUPE is promulgated by the government of the United Kingdom in accordance with the European Council Directive of 2001. The intent of TUPE is to preserve the continuity of employment, and terms and conditions of employees who are transferred to a new employer when ownership change takes place. The regulations also provide limited opportunity to modify the terms and conditions of employment contracts through a consultative and mutual consent process provided that in aggregate such variations are not prejudicial to the interest of employees. Employees cannot waive their rights under the regulations. Changes to terms and conditions agreed to by the parties that are entirely positive to employees are not prevented. The new terms and conditions of employment agreed to in a permitted variation must not breach other statutory entitlements. The regulations also stipulate specific provisions to protect employees from dismissal before or after the transfer in such context. TUPE regulations are applicable to all organizations, both public and private, regardless of their size. Following are the salient features of TUPE:

- Employer shall inform all employees in writing about the proposed or decided transfer of ownership well in advance.
- The new employer takes over the contracts of employment of all employees who were employed by the transferor immediately before the transfer.
- The new employer takes over any collective agreements made by or on behalf of the transferor employer.
- An employee's period of continuous employment is not broken by a transfer and for the purpose of calculating entitlement.
- The new employer cannot pick and choose which employees to take on.
- Employees cannot be terminated or dismissed because of transfer of ownership. Such dismissals will be automatically unfair for the purpose of unfair dismissal law. The transferred employees who find that there has been or will be substantial change for the worse in their working conditions as a result of the transfer have the right to terminate their contract and claim unfair dismissal before an employment tribunal. However, dismissals on grounds of redundancy are permitted if they are because of economic, technical and organizational reasons subject to adhering to all stipulations and redundancy payments and treatment. Consultation with employees and their representatives is mandatory before any such redundancy process is taken up.
- Transferred employees retain all the rights and obligations existing under their contracts of employment with the previous employer.
- Rights related to redundancy and early retirement benefits that are linked to an occupational pension scheme are likely to transfer under the TUPE regulations to the new employer.
- The transferor employer must provide the new employer with information which will assist them to understand the rights, duties and obligations in relation to those employees who will be transferred. The information should also include employee-related details such as the identity of the employees who will be transferred, their details as contained in the personal records, collective bargaining agreement as applicable to these employees, instances of disciplinary actions, instances of grievances raised by employees and legal actions pending or in implementation and so on.
- The regulation stipulates obligations on both existing and prospective employers that they shall inform and consult employee representatives about the transfer of employees and measures being taken to protect employees' interests.

Employment Rights Act 1996

Employment Rights Act is a consolidated legislation bringing together all enactments that relate to employment rights in the United Kingdom. The legislation which was enacted in 1996 consists of 15 parts and 245 sections. A brief summary of this legislation which is critical to employment and IR in the United Kingdom is presented here.

Part 1: Employment particulars

This part stipulates that every employer shall provide a written employment contract to an employee within two months of the beginning of such an employment relationship. The contract will need to specify the names of employee and employer, the employment start date, remuneration details, hours of work, holidays, the length of exit notice, title of the job, brief job description, place of work, collective agreements which may affect the terms and conditions of employment and the employee pension rights, if applicable. Every employee is entitled to itemized pay statement and must be informed of the disciplinary and code of conduct rules.

Part 2: Protection of wages

Part 2 of the legislation focuses on wage deductions, regulations relating to payment by employees to the employer and calculation of wages. An employer shall not make a deduction from wages of an employee unless such deduction is authorized by a statute or based on the consent of an employee. However, this is not applicable where a deduction of wage is made as a consequence of disciplinary proceedings. An aggrieved employee can file a claim or raise dispute in an industrial tribunal if any deduction is made contrary to the law. Wage is defined as sums payable to an employee on account of guaranteed pay, bonus, commission, holiday pay, statutory sick pay, statutory maternity pay, payment for time off and remuneration under a protective award but does not include any advance payment, pension payment and redundancy payout.

Part 3: Guarantee payments

An employee who is employed to work part of a day is entitled for guaranteed pay as per this legislation even in conditions where there is a diminution in the requirement for the kind of work for which a person is employed. However, this condition is not applicable to employees who are engaged on a complete specific task/assignment. Similarly, this condition does not envisage protecting wages of an employee who has unreasonably refused to work.

Part 4: Protected shop workers and betting workers

This Act recognizes all shop and betting workers as protected. A shop worker or betting worker may at any time give his or her employer written notice (opting out notice) to the effect that he or she objects to Sunday working. Even a person who is employed as a shop worker and his or her contract provide for Sunday working can opt out by giving an opting out notice.

Part 5: Rights not to suffer detriment

This section is intended to specify obligations of the employer and to provide rights to employees to ensure their safety and health while at work. An employee has the right to not be subjected to any detriment by any act or by his or her employer's deliberate failure. An employee has the right to approach industrial tribunal if he or she is subjected to any detriment in contravention of this legislation. An industrial tribunal can award compensation as damages in favour of an employee and against the employer if deviations are established.

Part 6: Right to time-off work

An employee who is a member of a local government authority, a statutory tribunal, a police authority, prison visiting committee, relevant health body, education body or environment protection agency shall be granted reasonable time off to attend meetings or do any other thing approved by the body concerned. An employee who is permitted to take time off is entitled to normal remuneration by his or her employer for the period of absence. An employee who is pregnant and has, on the advice of a registered medical practitioner, made an appointment to receive antenatal care shall also be granted time off. An employee who is a trustee of a pension scheme shall be granted time off to attend the meetings and remuneration shall be paid as normal. Employee representatives/trade union representatives are entitled to take reasonable time off during working hours to perform the duties required in their roles.

Part 7: Suspension from work on medical grounds

An employee while suspended from work by his employer on medical grounds is entitled to be paid remuneration for a period not exceeding 26 weeks. An employee who is suspended from work by the employer on the grounds that she is pregnant or has recently given birth or is breastfeeding shall be given the said leave (maternity leave) with normal remuneration. An employer can offer suitable work that would fit her circumstances instead of offering suspension on maternity leave.

Part 8: Maternity rights

An employee who is absent from work at any time during her maternity leave period is entitled to the benefit of the terms and conditions of employment which would have been applicable to her if she had not been absent. Maternity leave period commences on the first day after the beginning of the sixth week before the expected week of childbirth or when childbirth occurs. An employee who intends to return to work earlier than the end of her maternity leave period shall give her employer notice of not less than seven days from the date on which she intends to return. An employer is not entitled to postpone an employee's return to work to a date after the end of her maternity leave period.

Part 9: Termination of employment

If an employer decides to terminate the employment contract of an employee, the employer is obligated to provide not less than one week's notice if the employee's period of service in the organization is less than two years, not less than one week's notice for every additional year of service if employment is more than two years but less than 12 years and not less than 12 weeks' notice if service is more than 12 years. This law does not prevent notice period waive off if either party wants to waive off its right by accepting a payment in lieu of notice period. However, such notice period clauses are not applicable to employment contracts which are for a defined period. Employee is entitled to normal remuneration during the notice period. An employee is entitled to be provided by his or her employer with a written statement within 14 days of dismissal giving particulars of the reasons for the employee's dismissal. An employee can approach industrial tribunal if employer fails to provide the said written statement.

Part 10: Unfair dismissal

An employee under this part is entitled to not be dismissed by his or her employer unfairly. Dismissal is defined as termination of an employee's contract by an employer. If an employee is not permitted to return to work post maternity leave, that act is also termed as dismissal. In determining whether the dismissal of an employee is fair or unfair, the responsibility lies with the employer to provide reasons for the dismissal and such reasons shall relate clearly to capability, conduct or redundancy-related issues. Capability here means capability assessed by reference to skill, aptitude, health or any other physical or mental quality. If an employee is terminated during her pregnancy or while she is on maternity leave, the dismissal is treated as unfair. An employee dismissal shall be regarded as unfair if the reason for dismissal is that an employee has disregarded the instruction of his or her employer because the employee believes with sufficient reason that carrying out such instruction will pose threat to his or her health and safety. Similarly, if an employee who is a shop worker or betting worker is terminated because the employee refused to work on a Sunday, it is deemed to be unfair dismissal. If any employee is dismissed because such employee is member of a trade union or a pension trust, it shall be treated as unfair dismissal. An employee termination because of redundancy also shall be treated as unfair dismissal if proper redundancy process is not followed by the employer. If the employee believes he or she was unfairly dismissed, he or she can present a complaint to an industrial tribunal. If an order of reinstatement is made by the tribunal, the organization shall treat the complainant in all respects as if he had not been dismissed.

Part 11: Redundancy payments

An employee is entitled to redundancy payment if he or she is terminated for redundancy reasons. However, an employee is not eligible for any payouts for termination on account of lockouts by the employer. Redundancy can take place when an employer has ceased or intends to cease the business or part of the business in which an employee is employed so far. An employee shall be taken to be laid off for a week if he or she is employed under a contract on terms and conditions such that his or her remuneration under the contract depends on his or her being provided by the employer with work of the kind which he or she is employed to do but he or she is not entitled to any remuneration under the contract in respect of the work because the employer does not provide such work for him or her. An employee is not entitled to a redundancy payment by reason of being laid off or kept on for short time. An employee does not have the right to a redundancy payment unless he or she has been continuously employed for a period of not less than two years with the relevant date. Also, an employee who retires at the age specified in the contract of employment or at the age of 65 and above will not be eligible for redundancy payment. An employee is eligible for redundancy payment of one and a half week's pay for a year of employment in which the employee was not below the age of 41 and one week's pay for a year of employment in which he or she was not below the age of 22. An employer who fails to comply with this law will be liable for fines apart from damages payable to the employee in some cases.

Part 12: Insolvency of employers

This part primarily deals with employee's rights in the event of insolvency of employer. Issues such as payment to employees and limit on amount payable and transfer to Secretary of State of rights and remedies are discussed.

Part 13: Particular types of employment

This part deals with crown employment, House of Lords' staff, House of Committee's staff, parliamentary staff, employment outside Great Britain, offshore employment, national security-related provisions and short-term employment.

Part 14: Continuous employment

An employee's period of continuous employment shall be treated as beginning on the employee's 18th birthday if that is later than the day on which the employee starts work. A continuous year means a year of 12 calendar months. For the purpose of continuity of service, breaks are defined as those breaks that have risen due to employee's incapacity to work in consequence of sickness or injury, absence from work on account of temporary cessation of work and absence of work wholly or partly because of pregnancy or childbirth. The continuity of service up to one week spent on a strike or lockout does not amount to break of service. Any change of control of ownership will not cause any break of continuity of service.

Part 15: General and supplementary

This part deals with provisions related to reciprocal arrangements with Northern Ireland and reciprocal arrangements with Isle of Man, repeals and revocations, title, extent and commencement.

Equal Pay Act, 1970

The objective of this Act is to prevent discrimination, as regards terms and conditions of employment between men and women. The Act stipulates that for men and women employed on like work, the terms and conditions of one sex are not in any respect less favourable than those of the other. Further, the Act mandates that a women is to be regarded as employed on like work with men if her work is the same or is of a broadly similar nature and the difference if any is not of practical importance and a woman is to be regarded as employed on work rated as equivalent with that of men if her job is given equal value in terms of the demand made in matters such as skill and decision-making. An employee, who is aggrieved and believes provisions of this law are not followed, can approach an industrial tribunal and also can opt for judicial process. If ordered by the tribunal, an employer is bound to pay remuneration equal with arrears. Where a wage regulation order is made or collective bargaining agreement is made previously, enactment of this legislation containing any provision that discriminates men and women in pay shall be referred by Secretary of State to Industrial Tribunal for declaring what amendments need to be made to these instruments.

The Employment Equality (Religion or Belief) Regulations, 2003

The purpose of this Act is to lay down provisions regulating and preventing discrimination to people at work due to their religious affiliations or preferences to certain beliefs. Discrimination under this regulation is defined as discrimination against another person on the grounds of religion or belief, that is, if A treats B less favourably than he or she treats or would treat other persons or if A applies to B a provision, criterion or practice which he or she applies or would apply equally to persons not of the same religion or belief as B but which puts or would put persons of the same religion or belief as B at a particular disadvantage when compared with other persons. This legislation also explains what constitutes discrimination by way of victimization and harassment on grounds of religion or belief. It is considered harassment if a person engages in unwanted conduct which has the effect of violating another person's dignity or creating an intimidating, hostile, degrading, humiliating or offensive environment for the other person. It is unlawful for an employer in relation to employment to indulge or subject any person to religious or belief harassment. It is also unlawful for an employer to discriminate against people based on religion or belief in offering employment opportunities. However, if it is established with regard to the nature of employment that being of a particular religion or belief is a genuine and determining occupational requirement, the same can be allowed in exceptional circumstances. Similarly, there shall be no discrimination based on religion or belief in vocational training or in assisting a person in employment opportunities or in institutions for higher studies. Employer will be ultimately accountable and liable for any unlawful act committed by a person in an organization that constitutes harassment or victimization as defined in this law. The Act also carries provisions in Chapter 4 providing protection to Sikhs from discrimination in connection with requirements that relate to wearing safety helmets. An employee who finds contravention of the provisions laid down in this law can approach industrial tribunal who in turn can pass an order declaring the rights of the complainant and the respondent and an order requiring respondent to pay the compensation corresponding to damages could be offered by a court in judicial proceedings. An employment tribunal shall not consider a complaint unless the same is filed within three months of occurrence of an unlawful act.

Trade Union and Labour Relations (Consolidation) Act, 1992

Part 1: Trade unions

A trade union is not a body of corporate but is capable of making contracts and is capable of suing and being sued in its own name. To sum up, a trade union has a quasi-corporate status. No trade union or trade union member can be made unlawful by reason that is restraint of trade. This part also deals with procedures related to trade union property, trustees, remedy against trustees for unlawful use of union property, prohibition on use of funds to indemnify unlawful conduct, nominations by members of trade unions, payments out of union funds on death of member, liabilities of trade unions in proceedings in tort, repudiation by unions of certain acts, limit on damages awarded against trade unions, restrictions on enforcement of awards against certain property, trade union administration, duty to keep accounting records, annual returns, accounts and audit, election to trade union positions, requirements to be satisfied with respect to elections, voting and appointment of scrutinizers, right to require employer to stop deductions of union dues, duties of employer who deducts union contributions, use of employer's premises for secret ballot, restriction on application of funds for political objects, passing and effect of political resolution and effect of trade union amalgamations.

Part 2: Employers' associations

This part explains what an employer association means and what it constitutes, the list of employers' associations in Great Britain, quasi-corporate status of employers association, exclusion of common law rules as to restraint of trade, administration of employers association, regulation of employers association properties, restriction on the use of employers association funds for political objects and federated employers associate administration.

Part 3: Rights in relation to union membership and activities

It is unlawful for an employer to refuse employment to any person because someone is or is not member of a trade union or is unwilling to take steps to join or cease to be member of a trade union. A person who is thus unlawfully refused employment has a right of complaint to an industrial tribunal. However, the tribunal can entertain a complaint only if the same is filed within three months from the date of such occurrence. It is considered refusal of employment if an employer refuses or deliberately omits to entertain and process a person's application or enquiry, causes a person to withdraw or cease to pursue his or her application, refuses or deliberately omits to offer employment or makes an offer but prevails upon a person not to accept the offer. Similarly, it is unlawful for an employment agency to refuse a person any of its services because he or she is or is not a member of a trade union or because he or she is unwilling to become a member or cease to be a member of a trade union. No organization can refuse to deal with a supplier or a prospective supplier of goods and services on union membership grounds. A dismissal will be treated as unfair if the same is done on the grounds that someone is a member of a trade union or not a member of a trade union or has taken part or proposed to take part in the activities on an independent trade union. Employer shall permit an employee who is office-bearer of a trade union, time off during working hours for reasonable time for the purpose of carrying out negotiators with the employer, to participate in trade union activities and to study and undergo training related to aspects of IR.

Part 4: Industrial relations

Scope of a collective bargaining agreement can include: terms and conditions of employment; engagement or termination of or suspension of employment provisions; allocation of work between employees or group of employees; matters of discipline; trade union membership; facilities for trade union office-bearers; rights of trade union representatives; wages and benefits. A collective bargaining in order to be enforceable shall be in writing. Employers are obligated to consult trade union representatives if they intend to declare any employee redundant and eventually dismiss the employee. An employer, apart from consulting a trade union, shall also notify the Secretary of State in writing if the employee intends to dismiss as redundant 100 or more employees within 90 days or 10 or more employees within 30 days of such a proposal. Failure to notify the Secretary of State shall amount to offense and the employer will be liable on summary conviction to a fine. Advisory, Conciliation and Arbitration Service (ACAS; government of the United Kingdom) has the responsibility to define and provide codes covering relationship standards between employers and employees, and take all measures to promote improvement of IR and encourage collective bargaining process. ACAS can also offer assistance in dispute resolution through designating some of its officers as conciliation officers and arbitration officers. ACAS may give employers' associations, employees and trade unions such advice as it thinks appropriate on matters such as: organization of employees and employers for collective bargaining purposes, procedure for recognition of trade unions by employers, negotiations of terms and conditions of employment, procedures for avoiding and settling disputes and grievances, communication between employers and employees, facilities for trade union officials, procedures related to termination of employment, disciplinary matters, manpower planning, labour turnover and absenteeism, recruitment, promotion and vocational training of employees and job evaluation and equal pay.

Part 5: Industrial action

It is lawful to participate in peaceful picketing near an establishment of an organization for the purpose of communicating information or persuading or requesting fellow employees to abstain from working. However, unlawful picketing is not permitted. An act done by a person in contemplation or furtherance of a trade dispute is not accountable in tort only on the grounds that it induces another person to break a contract or interferes, or induces another person to interfere with its performance or that it consists in his or her threatening that a contract will be broken or its performance interfered with or that he or she will induce another person to break a contract or interfere with its performance. An act is not protected if the reason is that a particular employer is employing or has employed or might employ someone who is not a member of a trade union or is failing or has failed or might fail to discriminate against such a person. An act done by a trade union to induce a person to take part or continue to take part in industrial action is not protected unless the industrial action has the support of a ballot. Entitlement to vote in the ballot must be accorded equally to all the members of the trade union. A person who wilfully violates contract of service either alone or in combination, endangering human life or causing serious body injury or exposing valuable property and found to be guilty will be liable for summary conviction to imprisonment for a term not exceeding three months or a fine. Also, a person is considered to have committed an offense if he or she compels any employee using violence or intimidation or persistently follows that person from place to place.

Part 6: Administrative provisions (ACAS)

This part elaborates the process involved in setting up of ACAS, its functions, constitution, council formation, terms of appointment of members' council and their remuneration. ACAS shall appoint conciliation officers who will have the custody of all documents submitted for the purpose of Trade Unions Act, Industrial Relations Act and The Trade Union and Labour Relations

(Consolidation) Act. ACAS will also appoint Central Arbitration Committee consisting of chairman and other members as the chairman may direct.

Part 7: Miscellaneous and general

This part deals with applicability of this law and provisions to Crown employment, House of Lords' and House of Commons' staff, health service practitioners, police service, armed forces and exemption on grounds of national security and excluded classes of employment, applicability and title of the legislation.

Terms and Conditions of Employment (The Working Time Regulations, 1998)

The objective of this legislation is to promulgate provisions regulating working hours and employment of children and young persons and measures related to them. These regulations are applicable only to Great Britain. As per this Act, no employee shall be allowed to work more than 48 hours in a week, including overtime. However, an exception can be made to the 48 hours condition provided there is a mutually consented agreement between an employer and the employee that defines the number of working hours. Such an arrangement can be terminated by an employee by giving seven days' notice to the employer. An employee who is engaged in night shift shall not be allowed to work more than eight hours in a 24 hours cycle. Employer shall take all measures to subject an employee to free health assessment before engaging any person onto night shift work and for the employee should continue to be subjected to a free health check-up at regular intervals. No young worker is allowed to be employed during the period between 10 PM and 6 AM. Also, a young worker can only be employed after being subjected to health assessment and capability assessment and on being found fit to work without health hazards. Young worker means a worker who has attained the age of 15 but not the age of 18 and is over compulsory school age. An employee whose medical report reveals that he or she is suffering from health problems which are considered to be connected with night shift shall be given transfer to day work. Where the pattern according to which an employer organizes work is such as to put the health and safety of a worker employed at risk, in particular because the work is monotonous or the work rate is predetermined, the employer shall ensure that the worker is given adequate rest breaks. An employer shall maintain all health records of employees and preserve such records for at least for the last two years from the date on which they were made. An employee is entitled to a minimum of 11 hours rest in a 24 hours cycle and a young worker is entitled to a rest period of not less than 12 hours in a 24 hours cycle. An employer shall ensure that his or her employee gets an uninterrupted rest period of not less than 24 hours in each seven days period. Alternatively, an employer can also provide an uninterrupted 48 hours rest period in a 14 days period. Employees must also be given rest breaks of a reasonable duration for continuous six hours work and the duration of the rest breaks shall be as per the collective bargaining agreements and a young worker shall be given rest break for every 4.5 hours of work. An employee is entitled to four weeks of leave for every year's work. Leave to which a worker is entitled under this regulation may be taken in instalments but it may only be taken in the leave year in respect of which it is due and it may not be replaced by a payment in lieu except where the worker's employment is terminated. An employer may require the worker to take leave to which the worker is entitled or not to take such leave on particular days. If an employee is engaged with due compliance on work during rest period, such employee shall be allowed compensatory off of equivalent period and the health of the employee shall be safeguarded through appropriate measures. An employer who fails to comply with any provisions and or relevant requirement under the regulations shall be guilty of an offense. An employee who is aggrieved that his or her employer has failed in protecting his rights under these regulations and failed to ensure his or her safety and health can approach an industrial tribunal for remedy. An employee has the right not to be subjected to any detriment if he or she has refused to comply with any instructions of his or her employer which are contrary to the regulations laid down in this legislation.

Employment Act, 2002

The objective of this Act is to stipulate conditions and regulations related to paternity and adoption leave and pay, maternity leave and pay, employment disputes, compromise agreements, equal pay, fixed term and flexible working, and employment and training.

Health and Safety at Work Act, 1974

The purpose of this Act is to provide statutory provisions for securing the health, safety and welfare of persons at work and controlling use of explosive or highly flammable or otherwise dangerous substances and preventing use of such substances. It is the responsibility of the employer to ensure the health, safety and welfare at work of all the employees. Part 1 of the Act especially focuses on the general duties of employers in respect of their employees. Employer is obligated to publish a written policy/statement with respect to measures of safety and health at work and arrangements for the time being in force for carrying out such policy. It shall be the duty of every employee at work to take reasonable care for the health and safety of self and other persons who may be affected by his or her acts or omissions at work and comply and cooperate with the employer in implementation of all safety and health measures. No person shall intentionally or recklessly interfere with or misuse anything provided in the interest of health, safety or welfare in pursuance of any of the relevant statutory provisions. Two bodies: Health and Safety Commission and Health and Safety Executive are set up as per this statute in order to assist and encourage persons concerned with matters relevant to safety and health at workplace and provide information and advisory services on the subject. These bodies also are empowered with powers to investigate, inspect and file reports on the safety and health matters. Commission also can create, approve and issue suitable safety and health codes to be observed at workplaces. Failure to observe such codes will amount to committing a civil or criminal offense and proceedings can be levelled against persons responsible for such failure. Safety inspectors can issue prohibition notices if they find that any activity is unsafe and causes harm to health of employees. Commission's inspection authorities can call for information as they deem required from employers in order to satisfy themselves with measures being taken to ensure safety. The Act also stipulates that there shall be formation of the Employment Medical Advisory Service for providing advisory services in relation to health of employed persons. Functions and responsibilities of the said advisory services is dealt with in part 2 of this legislation and part 3 is dedicated to building regulations, special provisions as to material and so on unsuitable for permanent buildings and part 4 is focused on miscellaneous and general provisions.

The Employment Equality (Sexual Orientation) Regulations, 2003

Under the said regulations, it is unlawful for an employer to discriminate against a person based on gender unless being a particular sexual orientation is a genuine and determining occupational requirement. Otherwise, it is unlawful for an employer to discriminate against any person based on sexual orientation for employment opportunity in a regular or contract job. Sexual orientation is defined as sexual orientation towards persons of the same sex, persons of the opposite sex or to both persons of the same sex and of the opposite sex. For the purpose of this regulation, a person is deemed to have been discriminated if this person is treated less favourably when compared to another person on grounds of sexual orientation or if a provision or set of provisions or criterion, or practice is applied not equally for the same sexual orientation. Putting a person at a disadvantage when compared to other persons without a substantial reason or with an inability to logically and morally explain why such discrimination is made and to achieve what aim of good can be termed as a clear discrimination. It is considered sexual harassment under these regulations if a person subjects another person to harassment on grounds of sexual orientation. Violating dignity of other person, creating an intimidating, hostile, degrading, humiliating or offensive environment clearly constitute unwanted conduct attracting provisions of the said regulations deeming the same as harassment and discriminatory. It is also unlawful for an employer to discriminate against a person in the arrangements made for the purpose of determining to whom employment offer shall be made or in the terms and conditions of employment or refusing a job opportunity or deliberately not offering employment. Discriminating against employees in the areas of promotions, transfers, training or any such benefit shall be strictly avoided in pursuance to the regulations. Anything done by a person in the course of his or her employment shall be treated for the purposes of these regulations as done by his or her employer as well as by him or her whether or not it was done with the employer's knowledge or approval. Employers have the responsibility in proceedings to establish in their defence whenever there is a complaint that they took all reasonable steps to prevent the employee from performing that act which constitutes discrimination. Under the regulation, the burden of proof falls on the employer accountable as respondent to prove that he or she did not commit the offense. An employment tribunal shall not consider a complaint unless it is presented to the tribunal within three months from the date of occurrence of such offense and within six months in some cases.

Pensions Act, 2004

The objective of this legislation is to make provisions relating to pensions and financial planning for retirement and provisions relating to entitlement to bereavement payments and related aspects. Pensions Act is implemented and supervised by the Pensions Regulator consisting of a chairperson, chief executive and five other nominated persons. The scope of the Pensions Regulator includes: protecting the benefits under occupational pension schemes, personal pension schemes, reducing the risks and promoting good administration of work-based pension schemes. The Pensions Regulator also provides education and assistance to the employers and employees in relation to work-based pension schemes and can also issue restraining orders, repatriation orders, wind-up of occupational pension scheme orders and freezing orders. An organization which is intending to introduce a pension scheme shall apply to the regulator providing details such as: name of the scheme, the address, the full names and addresses of each of the trustees or managers of the scheme and the categories of benefits of the scheme with contributions and calculations and determinants of calculations. The Regulator may issues codes of practice containing practical guidance in relation to the exercise of functions under the pension's legislation and regarding the standards of conduct and practice expected from those who exercise such functions. Primary duty rests on the trustee and the employer to report to the Regulator if there is a breach or potential breach of the provisions of this law. The Regulator can appoint persons to inspect the premises of an employer for the purpose of investigation whether an employer is complying or has complied with the legislative requirements under this Act. This comprehensive piece of legislation also deals with constitution and functions of The Board of the Pension Protection Fund, information relating to employer's insolvency, pension fund protection and fraud compensation in part 2 and scheme funding in part 3, financial planning for retirement in part 4, occupational and personal pension schemes and safeguarding pension rights in part 5, financial assistance scheme for members of certain pension schemes in part 6, cross-border activities within EU in part 7 and state pension in part 8.

Personal pension scheme here means a pension scheme that is not an occupational pension scheme, and occupational pension scheme means a pension scheme providing benefits to the people with service in employment. An employer can make contribution for his or her employees based in the United Kingdom or based outside of the United Kingdom if the pension scheme is established under irrevocable trusts and that the trustee of the scheme is resident in the United Kingdom. Whenever there is transfer of undertaking to which the TUPE regulations apply, the transferee employer shall secure that the contributions in respect of all TUPE employees are made to the stakeholder pension scheme of which the employee is a member. On the termination of an employee's pensionable service, member of an occupational pension scheme acquires a right to elect an option like a cash transfer sum or a contribution fund. The trustees of an occupational pension scheme must not accept any contribution to the scheme unless the trustees are authorized by the Regulator.

Labour Code and Laws in Germany

German Labour Code is very complex since it originated from multiple sources. The sources include: German Constitution, European directives and treaty law, German Civil Code and German Labour Laws. Supplementing these sources, there are numerous labour law case studies and interpretations given by various courts over a period of time which form the basis for employment actions and labour management. The German Civil Code and important laws are discussed in the following paragraphs.

German Civil Code, 2002, with Amendment Act, 2013

Labour and employment-related matters are dealt with from section 611 to section 630 of German Civil Code. It is important to understand these sections for effective management of HR in Germany and more importantly to ensure their compliance. These sections dwell upon employment contracts, safety and health aspects, wages and termination of service and employment contracts and provisions thereof.

Section 611: Primary duty of employer and employees in an employment contract is to oblige and ensure implementation of the contract by an employee performing the services as promised and the employer granting the remuneration as agreed.

Sections 611a and 611b were repealed.

Section 612: It is deemed that any services rendered are in order to gain remuneration at a rate agreed, and in the absence of any agreement, the remuneration shall be paid as per the tariff rate which can be assumed as minimum wage rate.

Section 612A: No employee shall be subjected to victimization in any manner either through less favouring in employment agreement or through other measures because he or she has exercised the rights in a permissible way.

Sections 613 and 613A: The claim of services is not transferable. However, if a business is passed on to another owner, then rights and duties are transferred to the new owner in relation to the employment relationship. No change to employment relationship or to the employment contract can be effected due to the change of business ownership. Apart from individual employment agreements, all collective agreements need to remain valid. The previous employer is jointly and severally accountable and liable along with the new owner in discharge of provisions of all employment-related contracts, instruments and agreements in letter and spirit. The Code does not permit termination of an employment contract on account of ownership transfer. As and when any merger or acquisition is likely to take place, all employees shall be communicated the date of ownership transfer, reasons for transfer and how the transfer may or may not affect the employment relationship and social, economic and legal consequences of such transfer. Employees will have the right to object to the ownership transfer by lodging a complaint with the previous employer seeking explanation.

Section 614: Employees shall be paid their remuneration on completion of the service period or at the end of individual time periods as agreed upon.

Section 615: Employees shall not be held responsible for no performance if an employer fails to provide the opportunity for rendering service as agreed upon and entitlement for remuneration remain intact. In other words, employer is liable to bear the risk of loss of working hours due to poor management of allocation of work. Likewise, if an employee wilfully refuses the work or refuses to perform on own volition and without reasonable grounds, remuneration need not be paid.

Section 616: If an employee is prevented from performing the services for reasons for which an employee is not responsible in any way or if an employee is incapacitated and thus unable to perform temporarily due to ill health or on account of an injury, the employee is entitled to remuneration either through employer or through accident insurance policy in applicable circumstances.

Section 617: Employer is obliged to provide medical relief and food during the illness apart from usual wages and leave up to six weeks in the event of an employee falling ill and if the illness is attributable to the occupational hazard or employment conditions, then till the date the employee recovers. Employer can rescue from this care if arrangements are made either by way of insurance company or by health care provided by the public institution as far as medical care and food is concerned.

Section 618: Employer is liable to take all steps to maintain work premises, equipment, devices, installations and other work-related machinery in a shape that an employee can perform without safety risk and there shall be all protective measures in place to guard all employees against danger to life and limbs. Damages and other punishments would be made applicable if an employer fails to provide a safe workplace and fails to keep a professional supervision for ensuring protective and safe work environment.

Sections 619 and 619A: The responsibilities of an employer in ensuring safe workplace and responsibilities as enumerated in sections 617 and 618 cannot be diluted or altered to the disadvantage of employees by way of any employment agreements/contracts or collective barging instruments and the same if attempted will be null and void. An employee can file and claim compensation of damages if an employer fails to adhere to his or her duties in ensuring safe workplace or for breach of a duty under the employment contract.

Section 620: The employment relationship can be terminated on expiry of the term as agreed mutually and as codified in the employment contract or by way of mutual voluntary consent.

Section 621: If the relationship is not employment based but service based, the same can be terminated and released on any day based on remuneration pay cycle. If the remuneration is paid on daily basis, then the relationship can be terminated next day and if the pay cycle is weekly based, it shall be terminated towards weekend and if the payday follows monthly cycle, it shall be 15th of a month and if pay cycle is quarterly based, six weeks' notice period is mandatory. In case the periodicity is not defined for remuneration payment, then a two weeks' notice for termination of service relationship is stipulated.

Section 622: The Code mandates that in order to end employment relationships, a minimum notice period of four weeks must be observed. Further, it states that a minimum of one-month notice period shall be compulsorily followed in the event of employment relationship having lasted more than two years, two months if it lasted for five years, three months for eight years of relationship, four months for 10 years, five months for 12 years, six months for 15 years and seven months if the employment relationship has been sustained for 20 years. However, in case of probationers, a maximum notice of two weeks is sufficient. No employment contract or a collective agreement is valid if it consists of any elements that are contrary to this section and only exception can be in the case of employment contracts which are temporary, part-time or for fixed tenure wherein modification of notice period clause is allowed.

Section 623: All terminations of employment contracts or separation agreements shall be in written form and electronic form is excluded for the purpose of validity of the instrument as per the Code.

Section 624: The minimum notice period of six months is stipulated if any service relationship arrangement is stated to be lifetime or if it has lasted for more than five years. No deviation is allowed.

Section 625: A service relationship would be meant to end on expiry of the service period as agreed upon in the contract mutually and in the eventuality of continuing the service relationship beyond the agreed period would result in the service relationship being automatically renewed and becoming valid for indefinite period. A logical grace period is permitted to end the service relationship on the slippage of actual end date as long as the same is within the logical limits and without much delay.

Section 626: A service relationship can also be ended without notice period observance in exceptional circumstances wherein certain facts compelled such a decision such as when continuing the relationship would seriously jeopardize the interests of establishment/institution/organization/persons/operations. The facts and background for the exceptional decision must be robust and compelling, and subsequent upon weighing all the options including interest of all parties involved in the service relationship.

Section 627: The exception to following section 626 as discussed before is permissible when a service relationship is not an employment relationship as defined in section 622 implying that even a two weeks' notice is mandatory for positions which are trust based and expected to be in the higher level and obliged to perform services without being in permanent service relationship with fixed earnings. The positions whose performance and functioning is based on high trust but not necessarily in senior levels can be given a notice period equivalent to a logical period required to find an alternative service relationship.

Section 628: A person rendering the services as a part of service relationship is entitled to part remuneration equivalent to the period of service rendered without being remunerated and damages for loss of opportunity as applicable if a relationship is ended in breach of the relationship contract by the engaging party. However, if the person rendering service in breach of relationship ends the service before expiry of the valid period then he or she is not entitled to part remuneration for the period of service rendered without being remunerated and damages if any contemplated. The engaging party is entitled to reimbursement if person rendering service has been paid in advance equivalent to period of service that is meaningless for the final outcome. The section envisages that the party responsible for dissolution of service relationship shall have primary liability to mop up the loss of the other person due to such act unless that act is necessitated in extraordinary situation.

Section 629: The person rendering service is entitled to a continuing relationship and if terminated, shall be allowed and must be granted by the person who is obliged to provide the service, a reasonable time to seek another service relationship if such a demand is placed.

Section 630: The person who is engaging party in a service relationship is obliged to provide reference letters stating experience, nature of service and conduct on termination of the service relationship and the person rendering the service may demand such a reference letter. This letter must be given in written form and electronic form is excluded unless the party rendering service opts for electronic copy.

Co-determination Legislation in Germany

The history of co-determination in Germany goes back to 1848 when there was demand for establishment for factory committees with rights to participate in decision-making. In the period beginning 1919 when Weimar Constitution Act came into existence and had provided for workers participating in economic development of company with equal rights, till 2006, Germany has seen co-determination as an important labour movement and law. Co-determination means creating forums for workers participation in management of not only employee matters but also business and operations. At a company level, apart from Works Constitution Act, 2001 which will be discussed in detail in the following pages, there are three acts promulgated and implemented in Germany which strengthen the practice of co-determination.

Co-determination Act, 1976

The Act is applicable to all companies employing 2,000 or more persons including joint stock companies, limited liability companies, cost book companies under mining law, trade and industrial co-operatives and companies with limited partners holding share capital. The Act, however, is not applicable to institutions with religious orientation and purpose. There shall be a works council and the composition will depend upon strength of employees working in the company. The council should have six shareholders and six elected employee representatives if an organization employs less than 10,000 employees, eight shareholders and eight elected representatives if persons employed if an organization employs more than 10,000 but less than 20,000 and 10 shareholders and 10 employee representatives if an organization employs more than 20,000 employees. Also, it is mandatory that out of the said employee representatives, a minimum of 1 person each representing daily wagers, regular non-managerial employees and managerial employees must be included in the overall permissible number of employee representatives. The election of employee representatives can happen through direct voting by all employees if the total number of eligible employee voters is less than 8,000 and through votes cast by delegates if numbers of eligible employee voters in an organization is more than 8,000. Trade union representatives to the council must be nominated by trade union executives. The purview of this joint council encompasses all employee issues, financial, production, operation and marketing matters of the business/company and bound by statute of trade secrecy. Labour director will be a member of the joint council with a duty to ensure compliance and facilitate the council to achieve the objectives as set in the Act.

Co-determination Act, 1951

The Act is applicable to coal, iron and steel industry and all companies which fall in this industry whether they are joint stock companies or limited liability companies. The composition and overall strength of the council can range from 11 members to 21 members with equal representation from employees and shareholders depending upon share capital of a company. The employee representatives to this forum will be nominated by the works council and extremal members by trade union executive and neutral members by the labour department. All employee and company-related matters fall within the purview of this forum.

Third Part Act, 2004

This Act is not entirely new and is in fact replacement legislation for former Works Constitution Act, 1952 to a great extent. The Act is applicable to companies with employee strength ranging from a minimum of 500 and a maximum of 2,000. The Act is not applicable to institutions with religious orientation. In few cases, members to this forum representing employees are nominated by the works council and in others they are directly elected by the eligible employee voters. In order to secure a place to contest elections to become member of this forum representing employees, the nomination shall be espoused by at least 10 per cent of the employees that are eligible for voting. Members representing shareholders are nominated by the company board. Total number of members to the forum ranges from 3 to 21 depending upon amount of share capital of the company.

Works Constitution Act, 2001

This Act was promulgated in the year 2001 and was amended in 2013 with an objective to establish work councils to identify and resolve the employment issues along with the employer in order to attain harmonious IR and promote a democratic process in employee management issues through collective agreements.

Part 1

In accordance with part 1 of the legislation, works councils shall be elected in all establishments that normally have five or more permanent employees with voting rights including three who are eligible. The employer and the works council shall work together in a spirit of mutual trust having regard to the applicable collective agreements for the good of the employees and establishment. Members of works council in order to exercise the rights and powers granted under this Act shall have the access to enter into the establishment at all reasonable times subsequent to notifying the same to the employer and without causing disturbance to the normal operations of the establishment. The said works councils can be formed company wide or for each branch or for a combination of companies or establishments keeping in view how to serve the best interests of the employees and establishments. Employees for the purpose of this Act and for inclusion to represent in works councils are defined as 'the members of an organization that are legally empowered to represent the corporation'. This Act is not applicable to executive staff who, under their contract of employment, are entitled on their own responsibility to engage and dismiss employees on behalf of the establishment and endowed with general authority.

Part 2

This part focuses on composition and election of the works council, term of office of the works council, conduct of business of the woks council, works council meetings, constitution of central works council and combined works council.

All employees who are 18 years of age and above and working for more than three months in an establishment will have the legal voting rights. All employees with voting rights who are employed as homeworkers for more than six months in an establishment are eligible to become members of works council. However, six months condition is not applicable in case of an establishment whose duration of existence is less than six months. The membership strength in a works council of an establishment will depend upon the number of employees eligible to vote. There will be one member in a works council if number of employees eligible to vote is less than 20 and three members for a strength of not less than 50 employees entitled to vote and it can go up to 35 members where in any establishment, the number of eligible voters is between 7,001 and 9,000 employees after which, the number of members in a works council can be increased by two members for every additional number of 3,000 employees. Regular election to the works council shall be held once every four years generally any time in the months of March and May every year. However, election can be held at the end of two years if the number of employees in an establishment is increased or decreased by more than 50 per cent since the last election was held. Election also needs to be held if majority of works council members resign or if the works council election is dissolved by court orders. The works council shall be elected by secret ballot. Employees with voting rights and trade unions represented in the establishment are entitled to submit lists of candidates for the works council elections as member candidates. A list of nominees submitted by employees shall be espoused by at least 20 per cent of employees in order to be eligible to contest and similarly a list submitted by trade union shall be signed by two office-bearers. Election to the works council is held in two steps. The first step would involve electing an election board that would conduct elections and announce winners and the second step is the actual conduct of secret ballot, counting and declaration of results. The works council generally appoints an election board 10 weeks ahead of expected validity of the current works council with a three members team out of which one will be identified as chairman of the election board. If a works council fails to appoint an election board in a timely manner, the same will be taken care of by a labour court.

Employees who cannot, in person, participate in an election meeting in which the works council is elected need to be given opportunity to cast their votes remotely in writing. As much as possible, the nomination to the election of works council shall be done in a manner that would provide representation to all parts of an establishment and to all groups of employees. The gender that accounts for a minority of staff shall be at least represented proportionate to their respective strength in an establishment. An election to the works council may be contested by an application made by three or more eligible employees or by a trade union office-bearer before the labour court if any of the laid-down processes of elections are not adhered to or if there has been any infringement that has coloured the election results. Any attempt to unduly influence the election results or intimidation of any employees or election board members is grossly unlawful.

In case of establishment split (divestiture), the works council shall continue in office and take care of respective departments till a new works council is elected. On split, an election must be conducted to elect a new works council for each of the parts of split-up establishment or for combination of establishments (merger) within six months from the date of such split-up. A similar procedure applies in the event that two independent establishments are merged. On account of dereliction of duty by any members of works council, one-fourth of voting eligible employees or a trade union can apply to a labour court to pass an order for removal of such works council member. A labour council continues to function to safeguard interest of employees till an establishment is closed/shut down. A substitute is to be chosen from unelected list of employees who were there to contest for works council membership in case any member leaves the council whatever may be the reason. The works council needs to elect two members from its council members as chairperson and vice chairperson. A works committee shall be constituted comprising members elected from the council itself as per this Act if total numbers of members in any works council is in excess of nine members to deal with the day-to-day business of the works council.

The employer is required to participate in works council meetings to which he or she is specifically invited and employer can be accompanied by a representative of employer's organization. All decisions in the works council shall be made based on majority vote/espousal and at least 50 per cent of the members shall be present to qualify the quorum. Minutes of the proceedings and decisions shall be documented and signed by the members and chairperson. The post of the member of works council is unpaid and honorary. However, members of the works council shall be released from their normal work and duties without loss of pay to the extent necessary to perform their responsibility as a member. During the tenure of membership in the works council and after a year from the date of demit of membership, a member employee shall be paid at lower than other employees at the same level and the same shall apply to promotions and other benefits. Each member of the works council is entitled to three–four weeks leave during the tenure of membership to participate in training and pursue other educational courses that have been approved by the competent central labour authority to acquire knowledge in collective bargaining, negotiations and other labour relations matters. Also, members of the works council who have been released from normal duties enabling them to attend works council responsibilities shall not be deprived of any vocational training participation opportunities being extended to other employees.

Any expenses arising out of the activities of the works council shall be defrayed by the employer and also the employer shall extend necessary facilities such as venue, information and communication facilities and staff to assist in conduct of meetings and logistics, and for day-to-day operations of the works council. Under the law, it is unlawful to collect any donations or contributions from employees towards functioning of the work councils. The works council is expected to call and organize meetings once in every calendar quarter. The works council meetings would also be called for on the request of an employer with specific agenda or as and when one-fourth of employees ask for a meeting to discuss any particular issue. Employer shall make disclosures to the works council by circulating report to the members of the works council on staff questions and social affairs in the company including the status of equality between women and men, and the integration of the foreign employees working in the establishment and other important employee and business matters as far as there is no risk of a disclosure of trade or business secretes.

Part 3

Part 3 of the Act describes the provisions related to the youth and trainee delegation with an aim to protect the interests of young and trainee persons engaged in an establishment. In establishments that normally employ five or more persons under the age of 18 years or persons less than 25 years of age receiving vocational training, there will need to be members elected from this group to the works council to represent this group in meetings in proportion to their strength in an organization through secret ballot and adhering to the similar procedure to that of election to works council members. This election of youth and trainees shall be held once in every two years. The purpose of such inclusion of trainees in works council meetings is that there is a possibility that regular employee members may overlook the interests of this section. The works council invariably makes sure that these elected members of trainees particularly represent their groups especially when discussions related to the trainees and the youth arise. The delegation shall be involved in matters such as vocational training, continued employment of persons employed for training purposes, treatment of trainees and young persons in comparison to the treatment of regular employees, safety regulations and other collective bargaining agreement aspects directly connected to the well-being of young members and trainees. The works council must record all information and make all records available to the delegation in discharge of their duties as a delegation. Where there are several youth delegations such as in a conglomerate, these wings can be combined to take care of interest in a unified manner as long as they do not dilute the specific focus on some local issues.

Part 4

This part is dedicated to principles and sections concerning collaboration by employers and co-determination, execution of joint decisions, work agreements, secrecy, employees' rights to participate and to make decisions and duties of work council and such.

The Act envisages that the employer and the works council shall meet together at least once a month for joint conferences to discuss and reach an agreement on issues of difference. Both employer and works council must refrain from disturbing the industrial peace and causing any industrial action unless such action is warranted to realize their genuine expectations during a collective bargaining agreement process. Whenever a need arises, a conciliation committee must be set up and can be a standing conciliation committee if required to resolve issues between an employer and the works council especially on the matters of vital difference. The said conciliation committee must be constituted comprising assessors appointed in equal number representing the employer and the works council and an independent chairman acceptable to both the parties. The conciliation committee must reach decisions based on majority agreement and shall attempt to resolve issues promptly. However, a conciliation committee can attend to only those issues that are referred by the employer and the works council with mutual acceptance. The costs of the constitution and operation of a conciliation committee shall be borne by the employer. However, members of conciliation committee are not entitled to any remuneration. All agreements reached between an employer and employees must be executed by the employer unless otherwise mentioned in such agreement as an exception and works council shall not interfere with the execution and day-to-day to operations of implementation of such agreements. Even on expiry of the agreement drawn as a part of employer–works council proceedings, it will continue to be valid till such time a fresh agreement replaces the exiting one. All members of the works council, youth delegation and conciliation committee shall not be subjected to any prejudice in participating in any vocational training programmes and other career enhancement programmes because they happen to be members of such forums and shall not be obstructed whichever way from discharging their responsibilities effectively as members to protect employee interests. Members of the works council are required under this law to maintain secrecy of information and must refrain from divulging any business, trade or competitive information or classified data during and even after they cease to be members. In accordance with the Act, the works council's main responsibilities would include: (a) ensuring implementation of labour laws, collective bargaining agreements and safety, and health regulations, (b) safeguarding terms and conditions of employment and benefits of employees, (c) promoting interest and protecting young employees, trainees, disabled persons and elderly employees, (d) ensuring equal treatment of women and men at work including benefits, career opportunities and remuneration for equal value work, (e) promoting integration and assimilation of foreign workers, (f) encouraging work-life balance in the establishment, (g) consolidating and making recommendation of employee aspirations, benefits and plan to the employer and (h) making recommendations for the benefit of establishment furthering interests of an organization.

It is also important to discuss the responsibilities of an employer in the context of works council and in general as envisaged in this legislation and these responsibilities would include: (a) providing comprehensive and authentic information to the works council enabling the members to discharge their duties effectively, (b) giving access to the members to the relevant documents and its premises at all reasonable times, (c) providing expert advice and support as and when required and essential to works council members to gain knowledge on the issues, (d) informing and educating all employees of their tasks and responsibilities, and how their contributions could help the establishment and about health and safety measures and precautions and (e) informing the employees about measures envisaged concerning technical plants, works procedures and operations or jobs and their effects on his or her job and skill update imperative. Employees shall also be informed of how their remuneration is calculated and fixed, and should be given access to self-personal file.

The works council holds the right to codetermination in matters such as: (a) design and implementation of remuneration models, principles, revisions and fixations applicable to employees, and mode and frequency of payment, (b) bonus, perks, productivity incentives and other monetary benefits applicable for specific purposes, (c) methods and processes meant to apply in performance of employees and their measurement, (d) leave, vacations and procedure for sanction and regulation of the same, (e) implementation of suggestion schemes and information to employees seeking suggestions and updating process, (f) hours of work, breaks, weekly offs and overtime, (g) allotment of accommodation if company owned and the guidelines and their governance, (h) principles governing teamwork and formation of teams and allocation of tasks, (i) conduct of employees, (j) general terms and conditions of employment if the same is not prescribed by the legislation and (k) health, safety and occupational hazards.

Employer by this law is bound to inform works council well in advance if there is any plan or contemplation for alternation of works, relocation of offices belonging to the establishment and also any change likely to happen to work procedures, flow of work, manpower planning resulting in staff movements and provide the relevant documents. Employer necessarily needs to discuss with works council before finalizing the guidelines on recruitment, transfers and dismissal-related subjects. If works council insists, an employer must notify all vacancies of certain type of jobs internally before advertised the same seeking applicants from outside the organization. Employer and works council must take active interest in promoting vocational training and employer shall discuss with the works council in setting up vocational training infrastructure, facilities, curriculum and participation of employees in these programmes. Appointment and removal of training officer of the vocational training falls within joint purview of employer and works council.

As discussed before, all staff movement/transfer issues especially collective in nature must be discussed and agreed upon with the works council and no employer can take unilateral decisions in this regard to effect the movements. The works council can refuse staff movements in certain circumstances such as when staff movements are likely to result in dismissal of employees, result in non-compliance of earlier collective bargaining agreements and associated instruments, result in disadvantage to the organization or when the movements are due to prejudice against employees. Works council, if not in agreement with the proposal of the employer for movement of employees based on valid grounds, must inform the employer in writing with the reasons. In such a situation, employer can approach the labour court for a decision. Employer can also affect the transfer on temporary basis if such movements are urgent and important while discussing the matter with works council or while approaching the labour court for final decision. However, the works council can contend the urgency of these movements. These temporary transfers are liable to be cancelled if labour court decides otherwise terming the proposal of transfers as not legitimate and invalid. An employer is liable for imposition of penalties if he or she fails to act on the court order of rescinding the staff movement. Employer must also consult the works council for every dismissal action without fail. Works council may refuse the dismissal proposal or action citing valid reasons and facts. Works council can also request an employer to transfer or dismiss an employee on the grounds of unlawful conduct or for indulging in any racist activities.

In organizations employing 100 or more persons, it is mandatory to establish a finance committee and this committee shall consult the employer in all financial matters and report to the works council. This committee shall comprise a minimum of three and maximum of seven members who would be appointed by the works council from the employees working in the establishment and at least one member out of these must be from the members of the works council. The matters that fall within the purview of this committee are: (a) the economic and financial status of the organization, (b) investments ongoing and proposed, (c) marketing plans, (d) any financially driven special initiatives like rationalization, (e) production techniques, work methods and introduction of new technologies, (f) cutting down operations/production and closure of part of full-scale operations of an organization, (g) any divestiture, mergers, acquisitions and related portfolio changes and (h) any other substantive changes that are likely to affect the interests of employees in the organization. The finance committee is required to meet once a month and employer's representative must also attend these meetings.

Part 5

Part 5 of the Act deals with special regulations applicable to particular types of industries and establishments which include shipping industry and aviation industry. The Act stipulates that a ship's committee needs to be appointed on board every ship that normally has five crew members with voting rights including three who are eligible. The ship's committee works similar to the works council and is competent to deal with the matters of co-determination. The ship's committee and master of the ship can enter into ship's agreements. In addition to this, there shall be a fleet works council elected consisting of crew members. Crew members who serve on the fleet works council shall continue to receive their seamen's pay even if they are employed offshore. The ship's committee must make all decisions and discussion with the master of the ship not in contrary to the collective agreements and decisions of the fleet works council. The fleet works council as per this legislation must be kept fully informed on the shipping movements of the shipping company. The Act also mandates that a body representing the flight personnel of aviation companies needs to be set up by way of collective agreement.

Part 6

Offenses for violation of this legislation are dealt with in part 6 of the Act. Behaviour that causes undue interference with the election of the works council, obstructing the legitimate activities of the works council, prejudicial treatment of works council members, any action with ulterior motive to undermine the role of works council, breach of secrecy as described in the legislation are defined as violation to the spirit and letter of the Act and would attract pecuniary penalties and in some instances imprisonment.

The Minimum Wages Act, 2014, and Amendment Act, 2016

The Act consists of four parts with 24 sections and was promulgated by the Federal Government with an objective to stipulate minimum wage for each hour that is actually worked.

Part 1

Matters such as setting the general minimum wage, mandatory nature of the wage, due date for payment of wages, minimum wage commission, governance and procedures are discussed in part 1 of the Act. In accordance with the legislation, each employee is entitled to payment of wage at the rate not lesser than the minimum prescribed wage amount and all employers are bound to adhere to this. The minimum wage that is to be followed is 8.50 euros for every hour of actual work effective January 2015 and this rate is subject to renewal from time to time. In cases where piecemeal wage method is followed, the same can continue to be practised as long as the minimum wage that is paid even in such circumstances is not less than 8.50 euros per hour of work. Any collective bargaining agreement must factor this rule and no provision of such agreement shall have contradiction. The employer is obligated to pay the minimum wage on the due date as agreed between them as a part of employment contract/agreement or at the latest on the last bank working day of that month. One-off bonus payments like Christmas bonus can be counted towards the minimum wage in the month that was actually paid. The Act also allows, though not explicitly stated, the inclusion of any profit-sharing type wages for the purpose of calculating minimum wage provided such payments are regular and irrevocable. The minimum wage Act is silent on overtime payment. The Act does not exclude periods of on-call duty and, therefore, the hourly minimum wage rate is applicable to on-call duty hours. No expenses allowance or reimbursements can be considered for the purpose of minimum wage payment calculation. Also, any payments made by an employer towards any employee saving scheme contribution shall not be qualified for minimum wage calculation. Where there is a practice of remunerating employees through kind such as by providing lodging and boarding, the expenses even when logically quantified in monetary terms cannot be counted towards qualifying the minimum wage requirement because the Act envisages that all payments for being qualified towards minimum wage shall be in direct monetary terms. Deferred compensation amounts will be eligible to be counted towards minimum wage because they are towards retirement benefits of employees. Employers as per this legislation are required to maintain records and keep all the details of each employee's working hours: start and end of the work day and actual hours worked and location of the work.

The Federal Government as per the Act establishes a standing minimum wage commission with a valid term of five years comprising seven members including chairperson with voting rights and two members chosen from expert community without voting rights. The members of the commission shall act independently, perform their activities on honorary basis and their compensation and reimbursement of travel expenses will be decided on case-to-case basis by the chairperson. The minimum wage commission shall pass the resolution starting January 2017 announcing minimum wage rate based on need for protection, inflation and keeping in view the fairness and competition and at the same time the rate of minimum wage shall not blunt the competitiveness of organizations. The minimum wage commission is also expected to evaluate its decision on minimum wage continuously along with facts and submit a report together with the resolution stipulating minimum wage once every two years to the Federal Government. A resolution can be passed with a simple majority of the voters who are present and minimum quorum should be half of its total membership. Chairperson, unless the voting is divided equally, must refrain from voting in normal circumstances in order to remain a neutral person. While deciding the minimum wage rate, the commission must ensure to hear the versions of employers/ employer organizations, trade unions, associations representing economic and social interest, NGOs and others who are likely to be affected by the minimum wage rate.

Part 2

Part 2 of the Act focuses on enforcement of civil claims and contracting entity's liability. The Act is intended to ensure a subcontractor who engages persons for a principal employer's work shall remain accountable to comply with the minimum wage rate and payments. Wherever the subcontractor fails to comply with the provisions of the Minimum Wages Act, the principal employer/firm will have ultimate accountability to ensure compliance and to make sure that the subcontractor pays the wages or the principal employer pays the wages. This provision was made in order to ensure that employers avoid circumventing the implementation of the legislation by engaging subcontractors.

Part 3

Enforcement of the Act is dealt with in part 3 of the Act. The custom authorities are responsible for monitoring and ensuring compliance of the Minimum Wages Act by employers. The Customs Department is empowered to inspect all employment contracts and other related business documents and employers are obligated to cooperate. The Federal Government in selective cases may liberalize the requirement of these provisions for inspection. Employers with the registered office in Germany or abroad are obligated to pay workers who are employed by them in Germany directly or indirectly the minimum wage rates. There are steep penalties for violation of this legislation based on the type of non-compliance and the fine can go from 50,000 euros up to 500,000 euros.

Part 4

The extent of applicability and scope of the Act are discussed in this part. The Act stipulates that it applies not only to employees and subcontractors but also to interns. Internship which is mandatory under the Education Law in respect of schools, colleges and vocational training regulations and if not for more than three months duration will not fall within the ambit of this legislation. Also, the Act is not applicable for the first six months of employment in case of persons engaged who are categorized as long-term unemployed. Employees who are employed outside of Germany are entitled and covered under this Act only when their employment contracts are made in Germany. Exemption for internships must be processed at the beginning of the internship duration and if the duration of training is likely to be in excess of three months, then minimum wages are applicable. The Act is due for revision in the year 2020.

The General Equal Treatment Act, 2006

The objective of this legislation is to ensure equal opportunities to all citizens of Germany since not everyone has the same chances and opportunities and to prevent and eliminate discrimination. The core purpose is to prevent discrimination on the grounds of race, ethnic origin, gender, religion, disability, age or sexual orientation.

Part 1

This Act was promulgated in the year 2006 and was last amended in 2009. In any of the following areas, discrimination is strictly prohibited in a more pronounced manner:

- Opportunities to pursue education/courses
- Social treatment
- Social security and health care protection
- Access to supply of goods and services which are available in public domain
- Employment opportunities: recruitment and selection
- Career opportunities/hierarchical promotions
- Opportunities to access and participate in vocational training programmes including practical work experience
- Terms and conditions of employment offered to same level of employees with similar educational and experience background
- Remuneration and benefits
- Working conditions
- Company pension schemes and retirement benefits
- Dismissals
- Collective bargaining agreements
- Membership and involvement in an organization of workers/trade unions or professional bodies and organization of employers or any forums in which someone qualified can become a member and certain benefits are accrued.

Discrimination is broadly defined into two types. Direct discrimination occurs when one person is treated less favourably in comparison with other person(s) in comparable situation on any of the discrimination grounds as mentioned before. For example, a woman because of her pregnancy is treated less favourably than another woman for the opportunity to participate in a training programme. Indirect discrimination occurs when a person is put in a disadvantageous situation because a policy or process, or a guideline or a rule is made or a practice is followed that is devoid of objectivity in treating everybody equal. Any type of harassment that violates dignity of a person or any behaviour of intimidation or hostile treatment and creating an offensive environment is tantamount to discrimination for the purpose of this Act. Any behaviour or action, or any instruction that attempts to discriminate against a person on any of the before described grounds will attract punitive action. However, in certain circumstances, unequal treatment is allowed if such treatment is maintained to remove a natural disadvantage a person suffers in relation to others. For example, a disabled person may get special treatment or relaxation of some standards in employment opportunities so that the person can overcome that disadvantage which he or she has got. Similarly, there can be, in some circumstances, an occupational requirement that would presuppose preferential treatment to a particular type of persons or a gender which may not fall within the purview of discrimination. This is called a positive and affirmative discriminatory action.

Part 2

Provisions which are meant for protection of employees against discrimination, permissible limits of discriminatory treatment on the grounds of religion, age, employer obligations and employee rights and prohibition of victimization are discussed in this part of the legislation. As briefly mentioned in part 1 before, discrimination in some specified circumstances would not fall within the definition of discrimination. These are: (a) stipulating a minimum or maximum age limit for some employment opportunities, experience range or seniority of preferring particular type of experience and exposure, (b) seeking persons with a specified training or vocational internship, (c) ensuring a person has left with reasonable period for contribution before this person is given opportunity to participate in a comprehensive training and educational programme, (d) prescribing special conditions for being eligible for vocational training and promotion opportunities, (e) stipulating minimum age requirement and physical standards for certain type of jobs where such specifications are rationale requirements, (f) fixing upper age limit for participation and inclusion in social security scheme, (g) enabling employees to claim pension schemes by qualifying them for termination of employment rather than dismissal and (h) differentiation in benefits, especially social benefits created in accordance with collective bargaining agreement as per Works Constitution Act based on age and length of service and also based on relative economic strength of employees. Employers have the primary responsibility to ensure prohibition of discriminatory practices in an organization for which all efforts shall be made to put in place preventive mechanisms. There must be educational and communication programmes launched within an organization drawing attention of all employees regarding what constitutes discrimination and how to avoid it systematically and also initiate disciplinary measures such as cautioning, warning, relocating, demoting and dismissing where employees violate the prohibition of discrimination rules. Employees have the right to file a complaint and seek action whenever they experience discrimination in connection with their employment in an organization and employer must create a system and administrative apparatus competent enough to deal with these matters swiftly and professionally. In case an employer refuses to act on or any action is absent despite elapse of reasonable time, an employee has the right to refuse to work and still claim wages and benefits till such complaint is addressed in proper manner. Employer is also liable to pay damages in conditions of violation of prohibition of discrimination practices. However, damage clause is not applicable if such discrimination incident happens not due to breach of any duty by an employer. The damage wherever applicable shall be equivalent to the economic loss hypothetically or actually incurred by an employee and where no economic loss is involved, an employer will still need to compensate for the act of discrimination equivalent to three months' pay. There shall be no prejudicial treatment meted out to an employee because he or she has made a complaint under this legislation. Works council also has the responsibility to approach a court if there is a gross violation by any employer in implementing anti-discrimination law resulting in unequal treatment of employees. All parties to a collective bargaining agreement that would include employees, employee representatives, employers and their representatives must be actively held responsible for proper implementation of this legislation and all steps must be taken to avoid any violations. All claims of violation must be lodged within two months from the time of such occurrence to take cognizance and initiate appropriate action. However, in specific conditions, claims are entertained even after expiry of two months period. Whenever a complaint of discrimination is lodged, the onus is not only on the person to adduce the facts in support of such a complaint but also on the party against whom the complaint is made to prove the innocence by presenting relevant facts.

Part 3

Provisions related to protection against discrimination under civil law and permissible differences of treatment and matters related to enforcement are discussed in part 3 of the Act. The Act states that the provisions as enumerated in this legislation cannot be made applicable to obligations related to family law and succession. The Act is also not applicable in case of rental housing where certain social, cultural and economic factors play a role. Certain differences made on the grounds of sex, disability, age, religion and sexual orientation may not be discriminatory and do not amount to unequal treatment if they are based on objective grounds and satisfy the requirement of protection of privacy or personal safety.

Part 4

Defence of rights, burden of proof and support from anti-discrimination voluntary organizations are described in part 4 of the Act. People who are at a disadvantage and subjected to unequal treatment can seek support from anti-discrimination voluntary organizations, and legal advisors from these organizations are allowed to represent them in court hearings. Anti-discrimination voluntary organization is defined as an association that commits itself to defend interests of victims of unequal treatment and aids complainants in their fight to attain justice and helps in restoring equal treatment as intended in this Act. The said anti-discrimination organizations are required to be permitted under the law to be empowered to manage and advise the legal affairs of disadvantaged persons.

Part 5 and Part 6

The establishment of federal anti-discrimination agency entrusted with the responsibility of implementation of this Act is discussed in part 5, and legal sanctity, tasks, authority and relationship with non-governmental organizations in this pursuit are in part 6. All aggrieved persons who have faced discrimination can approach the anti-discrimination agency for redressal of their complaints and agency shall provide independent assistance. All federal authorities and other public institutions are required to collaborate and assist wherever needed enabling federal anti-discrimination agency to discharge its responsibilities effectively. The federal anti-discrimination agency must appoint an advisory council comprising members from social groups, experts and organizations to advise the agency on important matters related to regulation and enforcement of anti-discrimination practices. The members of the council must carry their responsibilities as envisaged in the Act and are expected to perform on voluntary basis. However, they are entitled to claim travel expenses (per diem) and hotel stay expenses.

Part 7

In this part, concluding provisions such as transitional issues and clauses prohibiting the change of any tenets or provisions of this legislation by any instrument are discussed. The Act explicitly prohibits drawing up any agreement or including any provisions in any collective or individual instrument that contradicts or derogates any provisions of this Act in any manner. The issues related to this legislation or regulation will prevail: German Civil Code and specifically provisions related to anti-discrimination and harassment vis-à-vis this Act. It is meant that all issues that have risen before the year 2006 will be dealt with as per the Civil Code and any case that has occurred post 2006 will be dealt with in accordance with this Act.

Protection Against Dismissal Act

The employment matters of dismissal are dealt with primarily in two places in German law: one is through sections from 611 to 630 in German Code and second is through Protection Against Dismissal Act (PADA). There are also innumerable judicial pronouncements and interpretations that have shaped the issue of employee dismissals and termination of employment contracts. An important related legislation in this context is the Part-Time and Fixed Term Employment Act which also deals with dismissals, especially the preconditions for limiting the term of an employment contract and the legal consequences of an invalid term limitation. In accordance with all legislation pertaining to termination and dismissals, the contract of employment can be terminated by either party, employer or employee, by adhering to certain procedures. Both parties have the opportunity to challenge the decision in appropriate forums including court of law if any one party acts unilaterally and more so contrary to the employment or collective agreement and relevant law. A valid termination of employment contract must observe: (a) termination of employment contract by mutual consent in writing mentioning any benefits or severance pay if payable/obligations from both sides, (b) on death of an employee, (c) pursuance to a court order either by way of a suo moto instruction or validating an employer or employee's argument defending their decision of termination of employment contract, (d) expiry of defined period of employment contract validity, (e) resignation tendered by an employee according to the employment contract seeking release from the services and (f) refusal to resume work as a consequence of a court ordering reinstatement because the dismissed employee found new employment. The most important aspect to be noted is that neither German Civil Code nor PADA can have any applicability in cases where the employment has ended due to end of the contract period as mutually agreed on in the employment contract.

In the context of PADA, any dismissal in normal circumstances shall happen only in accordance with provisions on the said Act. It needs to be noted that core objective of this legislation is to preserve the employment relationships in all normal conditions. Any termination of employment has to be the last resort. Employer can terminate an employment contract if it is established that a person has misrepresented the facts and gained the employment without risk of PADA applicability. In cases of lockout of business due to prolonged strike observed by employees, the employer can seek the measure of termination of employment contract based on valid grounds. Any termination of employment infringing upon maternity benefits of an employee is deemed to have violated provisions of this legislation. Employers also carry responsibility to terminate the contracts promptly based on valid reasons and any delay or reluctance on the part of employers in initiating termination in valid cases will give fillip to a view in the minds of employees that such acts will not attract termination and if attempted in future by the employer can be perceived as an act of injustice. In accordance with PADA, termination of employment contract is just and fair if it is due to an employee's misconduct or urgent operational reasons or business imperatives which render continuation of employment impossible. However, the onus of proving that a termination decision is just and fair rests on the employer. Reasons such as misconduct, urgency of business operational requirements and misrepresentation of facts by an employee can attract ordinary dismissal, while severe breach of contract, criminal offenses and so on can attract extraordinary dismissal. Serving prior notice to an employee is not mandatory if it is extraordinary dismissal. All ordinary dismissals can be affected only subsequent to serving at least four weeks' notice and the notice period grows proportionately in the case of employees who have completed employment service in the same organization exceeding two years continuously and employee is more than 25 years of age. This condition is equally applicable to employees when they intend to terminate the contract of employment. Wherever there is a need for mass retrenchment which is as per the law, an employer shall exercise a social selection keeping in view factors such as length of service, age, family obligations and disability, and efforts must be made to protect employment of people who are less likely to get alternative jobs. However, these criteria need to be followed in case of employees whose services are essential to run the organizational operations and these employees can be kept out of the purview while adopting the aforementioned criteria. Two weeks' notice for termination of employment would be adequate as far as employees on probation are concerned unless the individual employment agreement specifies otherwise.

Notwithstanding anything contained in this legislation, in accordance with Works Constitution Act, wherever works council exists, employers mandatorily need to inform the council about all terminations citing the grounds/reasons. The works council may raise objection but this resistance cannot stop the decision of the employer to effect termination. However, council objections may provide substantive ground for an employee to approach the court for stalling the termination effect. As per PADA, severance pay has to be given in order to avoid litigation or to abstain from initiating legal procedure by an employee. Court can also order severance pay in the event of rendering a termination as legally invalid and an employee is reluctant to resume the work due to discomfort with the dispute or if the decision is just intolerable to both the parties. The amount of severance pay is equivalent to 12 months' pay and this can be more depending on an employee's length of employment and age. An employee who is aggrieved with the decision of termination needs to approach competent court of law within three weeks from the date of such termination and in exceptional cases the condition of three weeks would be relaxed.

French Labour Code

The French Labour Code which was comprehensively refreshed in 1973 has since been amended multiple times for further simplification and practicality. Despite these efforts, the Code is still reckoned as one of the most complex and voluminous labour codes in the world. The Labour Code is made in three parts: all labour laws are enumerated in part 1, regulations in part 2 and decrees in part 3. Part 1 of the Code which is relevant here consists of a total of nine books (more like parts), and each book is further composed of chapters and sections. These are discussed briefly in the following content.

Book 1

Book 1 is primarily dedicated to laws pertaining to employment agreements comprising five titles as discussed further.

Title 1

Matters such as contracts of apprenticeship, contracts of employment, collective labour agreements, wages and penalties are discussed in this title in a vivid manner.

In accordance with the Code, an apprenticeship programme whose objective is to provide practical training and impart vocational skill to young workers shall last for a period of two years and in exceptional cases for three years. Apprenticeship training shall be formalized by way of a contract and must be implemented partly within an organization and partly in an apprenticeship training centre. This contract of apprenticeship must explicitly contain obligations of an employer such as imparting vocational training, paying wages for the period of apprenticeship to the trainees. Wage of an apprentice must be equivalent at least to the minimum wage thus applicable for such trade/skill. Rules to be followed for overtime payment must be the same as those applicable to the regular staff. The apprenticeship training centres shall be set up in joint collaboration between the state and professional bodies, industrial organizations and public establishments representing economic interests of their respective fraternity. There shall be model agreements drawn up for this purpose involving all the parties as discussed here and these agreements must address inter alia the total number of hours set aside for training activities for each skill/trade, infrastructure requirements, curriculum, methodology, assessment and governance of these centres. An apprenticeship contract can be terminated by either of the parties with mutual consent. It is not permitted to engage apprentices on training or in work for more than eight hours a day and 40 hours in a week and they shall not be engaged during night shifts. Apprentice is entitled to five days as paid leave to appear for examinations leading to acquisition of diploma certificate in addition to the normal allowed leave period. No person under the age of 16 and over the age of 20 years is qualified to be an apprentice. Employers are not permitted under this law to engage persons for apprenticeship unless those persons have been recognized for departmental vocational training specifically by respective professional bodies in consultation with the works council. Employer needs to undertake all responsibility for enrolling and ensuring that a person undergoes vocational training as an apprentice systematically and attends requisite examination leading to the technical education diploma corresponding to the training specified under the apprenticeship contract. State has the authority to supervise and monitor the technical, instructional and financial management of apprenticeship training centres across the country. The state is also empowered under the Code to impose penalties and cancel the agreements concerning the apprenticeship training centres if it finds that there is negligence and lack of compliance as outlined in the Code in running and managing the centres. The action can include closing down the apprenticeship training centre and levying penalties on the defaulters.

Title 2

A contract of employment which is a critical element in workplace management is discussed in part 2 of book 1 of the Code.

All employment contracts shall be made in writing and if not in writing then such employment arrangements are assumed to be for an unspecified period. An employment contract intended to be executed in France shall be executed in French and if the contract is meant for an alien then it can have a language translation. An employment contract can be for a fixed period or for an unspecified period. Fixed contracts will come to an end on expiry of the stipulated period by serving one month notice before expiry, and length of notice period in unspecified period of service contracts can be as per the mention in that contract or depending upon length of service, a notice period can be for a minimum of one month or as per collective bargaining agreements or relevant laws as applicable. Any notice period contrary to these instruments shall be null and void. Employee is also obligated to observe the notice period condition and failing to do so will attract proportionate damages. No employer can terminate services of an employee without reasons or due process and doing so can lead to reinstatement of that employee. Employees are entitled to severance pay for termination or dismissal of services before expiry of the employment contract. On expiry of employment contract, an employer must provide experience, conduct and reference letter to the employee. Employer is liable to allow an employee leave of 20 days if such employee is a candidate to the national assembly or to the senate. Employers cannot refuse to employ a woman because she is pregnant and a woman is not required to disclose the fact that she is pregnant. Also, a woman employee cannot be terminated during pregnancy. However, she can terminate a contract either before six weeks or after 10 weeks of confinement. An employee is entitled to leave for bringing up a child adopted or born up to the child becoming three years' old. Temporary employment is permitted only in certain conditions such as occasional peak periods of work, urgency of completion of work, temporary absence of regular employee and resumption of work post breakdown of the machinery or establishment. No employer is permitted to indulge in subcontracting the work or outsourcing the work on piecemeal basis in order to avoid regular employment or regular wages and benefits.

Title 3

This part deals with collective bargaining agreements and sets rules governing collective relationships between employers and employees. A collective agreement would cover aspects related to employment conditions, working arrangements and social security measures and such measures will need to meet minimum standards of relevant laws; however, measures favouring employees more than prescribed standards are allowed. Collective agreements can be drawn enforceable in an establishment or at a national, regional level or for industry-wide adoption and are valid for a period of no more than five years. Provisions of collective agreements signed by both the parties will be applicable not only to existing employees and employer but also to future employees and shareholders. The labour minister is authorized to form a joint committee comprised of representatives from employees, employer and professional bodies for drawing up collective agreements. The collective agreements must cover issues such as freedom of opinion, right of association, minimum occupational wage, more pay for hazardous work, equal pay for equal work, procedure for recruiting and dismissing employees, period of notice, welfare facilities, conciliation procedures for resolving disputes, leave with pay, apprenticeship and vocational training, special conditions applicable to women and young persons, severance pay, part-time employment and remuneration, employment of temporary staff, employment of disabled persons, wages, overtime work, shift work, night work, bonuses, allowances and retirement schemes. If a joint council fails to conclude an agreement in reasonable time frame in an establishment/ organization, the minister of labour can extend an agreement of a similar establishment till such time as it draws up its own. Employees and employer must abstain from doing anything that can weaken execution of a collective agreement and such actions can attract legal liabilities.

Title 4

Wage-related aspects are dealt with in this part. The onus is on the employer to ensure equal remuneration for men and women for the same or equivalent work. There shall be a minimum wage and that rate must be fixed keeping in view the purchasing power of employees by linking the minimum wage with consumer price index. The minimum wage must be revised in line with trends of consumer price index. Wages to employees shall be paid at least on a monthly basis.

Merely an employee accepting a pay slip will not deprive that person from raising any claims in future. However, claims shall be raised before expiry of five years period from the date of occurrence of such claim. Insurance scheme shall be financed by the employer and the amount of remuneration paid to an employee would form the basis for rate of contribution to the said insurance. Wherever employees are paid for effort or piecemeal basis, it must be ensured such payment meets the criteria of the minimum wage rate. Employees wage occupies first due payment in case of bankruptcy or liquidation proceedings. Employers are not permitted to cause any deduction to the wages of employees other than the deduction of no more than one-tenth of total wage payment towards offsetting the advance money paid. Attachment of salary payments of employees as ordered by civil courts is permitted and employer shall carry the deductions as advised. Any service charges like tips in a restaurant offered to employees shall not be reckoned for the purpose of wage rate. An employer's insistence on employees to spend part of their wages buying provisions from the store located inside an establishment is legal unless an employment contract contains provisions waiving this off. This provision is applicable to company stores attached to industrial establishments managed by companies whose capital belongs to retired employees.

Title 5
Penalties are described in this part of the Code pertaining to provisions as discussed in book 1. As per the Labour Code, any deviation or non-compliance either wilfully or accidentally will be taken as a cognizable offense and penalties, and in some serious negligence cases, imprisonment can be imposed on the defaulters.

Book 2
Subjects such as regulation of employment, conditions of work, hours of work, rest and leave, public holidays and leave which are applicable to all industrial establishments are presented in this part as discussed next.

Titles 1 to 6
No persons below the age of 18 years can be employed in an industrial establishment other than for the purpose of apprenticeship training. To monitor the working conditions and stipulate standards, a national agency for the improvement of working conditions is constituted which functions under the Ministry of Labour. The agency is made of members representing employees/ trade union organizations, employers/association of employers and members of parliamentary committee dealing with social and economic council.

The hours of work shall not exceed 40 hours a week. Employers in consultation and in consent with works council and after informing labour department can carry these 40 hours of work over four or four and half working days as the nature of work would call for. The said 40 hours of work is to be taken as actual work hours in exclusion of any rest/lunch breaks. Part-time work involving fewer hours can be allowed subsequent to consultation with works council in selective occupations and trades. There shall be clear definition of terms and conditions of employment including seniority and other rights laid down in either collective agreements or other written instruments. The severance and retirement benefits shall be granted to the extent depending upon length of service rendered in an establishment. Refusal to work extra time beyond normal/agreed working hours shall not be construed as fault of the employee nor can such refusal call for any punitive action. If a full-time employee opts to work part-time or if a part-time employee opts for full-time employment, he or she must be given prior claim whenever suitable opportunity arises in an organization. Employees are entitled to overtime for hours beyond 40 hours in a week at the rate of 25 per cent more than standard rate of wages up to 48 hours and this increase shall be 50 per cent more for work beyond 48 hours a week. The number of hours worked in a week shall not exceed 50 hours including overtime and there can be very few exceptions in extraordinary circumstances. No woman can be employed in any establishment during night shift which is defined as work between 10 PM and 5 AM. Also, a woman employee must not be asked to work more than 10 hours a day including overtime. All employees are entitled to weekly rest of 24 hours and this must be given on a Sunday and no person shall be asked to work more than six days a week. Wherever services need to be operated throughout a week, employees must be given Sunday break on rotation while allowing weekly break on other days. An employee is entitled to extra wages for foregoing Sunday off and working on that day at the rate of 13 per cent more than normal wage rate. All establishments need to observe the following days as statutory public holidays in a year: 1 January, Easter Monday; 1 May, Ascension Day; Whit Monday, 14 July; All Saints' Day, 11 November and Christmas Day. Every employee shall be entitled to leave at the rate of two days per month worked totalling 24 days of paid leave in a year. Women employees and apprentices under the age of 21 years are entitled to two extra days of paid leave in addition to the standard 24 days a year. Employees are also eligible to claim equivalent compensation for leave days that have been not been availed at the time exit on account of termination or retirement. No woman employee may be employed for a total of eight weeks before and after her confinement. However, it is not unlawful to employ a woman during the six weeks after the confinement. All employees are entitled as per the Code to special paid leave in certain eventualities: four days of special leave on account of self-marriage, one day for demise of parent, one day for marriage of own child and two days for death of spouse or child. Every establishment mandatorily shall observe health and safety standards stipulated in the Code in areas such as lighting, ventilation, drinking water, rest rooms, removal of dust and fumes, fire safety, sleeping accommodation for staff, food hygiene, occupational hygiene and occupational hazards prevention guidelines, and governance shall be through various in-house councils on safety and occupational health as prescribed in the Code.

It shall be unlawful to allow distribution of any alcoholic beverages other than unadulterated wine in establishment or work premises and no person can enter the premises in a drunken state. An occupational medical service shall be made available to assist employees. Head of establishment or manager, or director is accountable to ensure execution of all provisions as discussed, failing which, they are liable for fine and in some serious negligence cases, imprisonment with a term of two months to two years. A repeated offender may be dealt much more harshly and can be banned from professional work for a period of five years in addition to having a monetary penalty imposed and a period of imprisonment.

Book 3

Issues revolving around placement and employment are discussed in book 3 of the Labour Code as presented next.

Titles 1 to 6

In accordance with this part of the Code, every person seeking employment must register with the National Employment Agency being managed by the government. All employers are required under this law to notify all vacancies to the said employment agency. However, employers are permitted to advertise their vacancies in the press and other mass media by adhering to the guidelines stipulated by the employment agency from time to time. Any employment notification seeking details such as age of the applicant, the existence, origin and other discriminatory factors would be unlawful. It is not binding on the applicants to accept the job offers forwarded by the employment agency. The Code also permits private placement agencies to operate legally but such agencies cannot offer services free of charge. The only exceptions are the agencies run by joint councils and associations of trade unions and employers which are recognized by the state. All private placement agencies offering services for return shall be registered with the state. The placement expenses charged by an office operating in return for payment shall be covered entirely by the employer and no amount shall be received from an employee. No placement agency, operating either free or on a chargeable basis, can be run by persons who also run hotels, merchant or broking business or agents dealing with sale of pawn tickets. All establishments must file returns loaded with the information of persons recruited or terminated with details to the government-run manpower services department at regular periodicity. No employer can terminate employees in a collective manner without discussing with staff and negotiating the process to be followed for the same and the employer is also required to file with competent administrative ministry providing a 30 days' notice for granting approval. If in any establishment two or more employees are dismissed without obtaining approval, the employees would automatically be eligible for reinstatement with full back wages and are qualified to file for damages. Government may come forward to take up partial liability of paying supplementary allowances as a preventive measure to rescue the business in order to avoid dismissals for economic reasons in exceptional conditions when entire industry is in depression due to market conditions. Government shall set up a National Employment Fund with an objective to assist employees to adapt themselves to the changing economic conditions through mobility and by acquiring new skills that are relevant to the industry and ensure continuity of their employment. In order to enable unemployed persons to move from a region where there is underemployment to a region where there are employment opportunities, they must be provided with mobility allowance, transfer bonuses, compensation for transport, removal and reinstallation expenses grant through National Employment Fund. Persons of over 60 years of age who may not be suitable for resettlement may be granted special allowance. Young persons also need to be assisted with mobility allowance to relocate to new locations, and budgetary support for this shall be extended by the government. In addition to these measures, all unemployed persons are eligible for substitute allowance provided the unemployed person fulfils the criteria of age, fitness for work, background of previous employment and is still actively looking for employment for livelihood. Entitlements of an unemployed person to a substitute income will not depend upon whether an employer is contributing to such allowance or not. An employee who continues to be employed in an establishment and suffers loss of wages due to closure of establishment or cease of operations can be provided monetary relief by the state. No unemployed person shall be entitled to benefits as discussed here for more than twice in any period of five years. An employee receiving daily allowance may be required to perform work at least two hours every day. The rate of subsistence allowance shall not be less than 90 per cent of the minimum wage. Young persons who have reached 16 years of age and have also completed vocational training will be given flat rate allowance for a limited period for maintenance.

Employers of all industrial establishments must employ ex armed force personnel, war widows, war orphans and war-disabled persons at a proportion of at least 10 per cent of their total staff. The employment and resettlement of handicapped persons is a critical element in the employment policy and therefore the Code calls for concerted action by the representatives of employers and trade unions to extend all the support for vocational training and retraining of handicapped persons enabling them to be employed in normal production setting. Government will grant necessary financial assistance to industrial establishments to enable them in this pursuit. This financial assistance can be used to redesign and reinstall the machinery and working set-up in a manner that suits the handicapped persons so that they can be employed engaged at the workplace. Handicapped persons shall enjoy a prior claim to employment up to a certain percentage to be specified by orders made by the minister of labour for each region, industry and activity. The specified percentage of handicapped persons to be employed in occupations shall be same for private and public sector establishments. The wage payable to a handicapped employee shall not be less than the wage being paid to a normal person employed in the similar job or shall be as per wages specified in collective agreement for employees. Where an employee is dismissed, the notice period applicable to a handicapped/disabled person shall be double the normal notice period duration. Handicapped persons will be given exclusivity in light jobs over the normal persons and handicapped persons who cannot be placed in normal working environment must be given a sheltered workshop. Persons with three or more dependent children in case of men and two or more dependent children in case of widows must be given priority in employment opportunities.

Clandestine employment is strictly prohibited other than in emergencies such as an impending accident or while managing rescue operations. It is the one where people are employed without maintaining a record or register and doing away with all information related to employed persons. No foreign person can be engaged in employment in France without a valid visa, work permit, connected documents and contract of employment. The work permit shall specifically contain occupation/area of work that the foreigner is engaged on and shall have all other details as prescribed in the regulations. However, foreigners who complete 10 years of work in an occupation will be permitted to continue to work in a gainful engagement in any territory in France. Employers who engage foreign persons need to make contribution to the National Immigration Office and any expenses incurred including travel charges for bringing person into France shall not be chargeable to the foreign employee. The National Immigration Office which is the nodal centre for managing all foreign employees needs to stipulate the percentage of foreign persons who can be employed in any establishment in France in occupations/operations/departments/branches/industry.

Book 4

Provisions related to trade unions, works committees and associations are discussed here.

Titles 1 to 6

In accordance with the Code, the purpose and objective of trade unions is to defend and support economic and commercial interest of the society and protecting rights of employees. Members of trade unions who hold civil rights should not have been convicted for any offense under the election code of the country. A person who has ceased to work can also continue to be member of a trade union provided that he or she is engaged on the work for at least a year. Trade unions for all practical purposes are bodies of corporate and will have rights to sue and be sued. They can acquire property and run subsidy schemes for the benefit of their members, manage retirement funds for their members and run courses to educate them. However, they cannot distribute dividends or disburse payment of profits to their members. Trade unions shall be consulted and negotiated with for resolution of disputes. They are free to forge federations and combine or create joint forums in order to achieve their objectives. A federation will enjoy all the rights of a trade union entity. An employer based on membership of a trade union can involve them in all people management-related matters such as recruitment, allocation of work, work conduct, training, retraining, promotions, remuneration, benefits, social benefits, disciplinary matters and terminations. Employers are authorized to deduct trade union members' contributions from their wages or can choose to contribute on their own instead of causing deductions. Employers are barred from exerting any form of pressure or from applying any undue influence either for or against a trade union and such behaviour will attract damages and liabilities. Trade union members can meet once a month within the premises of an establishment but outside their actual workplace and outside working hours. No trade union delegate can be dismissed from the service without obtaining approval from labour inspector unless such an action is highly necessitated to dismiss immediately. Trade union delegates are elected through secret ballot once a year. Employers are required to give time off to a maximum of 15 hours a month to the delegated to discharge their trade union duties. Employers shall also provide necessary infrastructure such as an office or a place for trade union delegates to function. Employer representative who is generally the head of establishment must meet trade union delegates at least once a month and also in urgent cases as and when required based on the request for meeting made by the union.

Setting up of works committee is mandatory in all establishments where 50 or more persons are employed. The works council shall be consulted on matters of improving the conditions of employment, work and life of all employees working in an establishment, training and development, working hours, welfare facilities, utilization of 1 per cent housing contribution levied on wages and housing condition of foreign employees. The works committee is responsible for managing all welfare facilities set up in the undertaking for the benefit of employees. The employer's annual contribution towards financing of welfare facilities shall not be less than what has been granted as an average per year in the last three years. Works committee also has within its scope a role to recommend reward scheme that would be apt for employees to motivate them to make valuable contribution and suggestions. It must be regularly briefed about the general operations, production programmes, employment situation and plans of an establishment. All plans for reduction of staff or redundancies must be discussed and opinions of works committee will need to be factored or shall be forwarded to the labour inspector. Works council members must also be provided with profit and loss account statement, the annual balance sheet, the auditor's report and all such documents which are available to general shareholders. Works committee members can also seek help of chartered accountant to assist the committee in their understanding and analysis of financial statements for which the fee shall be borne by the establishment. Members of the works council are bound by secrecy in all matters related to marketing plans, production processes and any competitive information. Works committee shall have equal representation from employees, trade unions and employer/representatives of head of establishment. There shall be at least one delegate each representing groups such as commercial staff, production workers, supervisors, engineers, and departments and diversity. All employees who have been continuously employed at least for a year, have been French nationals and have reached the age of 18 years are eligible to vote to elect members of woks council representing employees. No person who has been convicted or imprisoned for disgracing the nation and removed from the office of a trade union shall qualify to contest for elections to the works committee. Where an undertaking has more than one establishment, there can be equal number of establishment committees who would function on the same lines as that of works committee but coordinated by a central works committee to bring in undertaking wide issue resolution. Employees including apprentices are eligible for grant of 12 days' unpaid leave for attending courses, seminars and training programmes on trade unions and related subjects organized by national level institutions recognized for such education. However, an employer can refuse grant of such leave in exceptional circumstances substantiating the same. Organizations and state are expected to take initiative to provide training and education to trade union office-bearers and members of works committee on social and economic issues and to organize these programmes, state may grant financial assistance. Non-compliance of any of the provisions enumerated in book 4 of the Code would attract fines.

Book 5

Establishment of individual dispute boards, duties of the board, conciliation committees, judicial committees and panels for interim proceedings, collective disputes, mediation and, arbitration and enforcement of collective agreements is discussed in this part of the Labour Code as given further.

Titles 1 to 3

In order to resolve disputes which may arise in connection with employment contracts and aspects covered under the Labour Code and which could not be settled through conciliation proceedings, individual dispute boards are established with members equally representing employees, unions and employers. Individual dispute board will have all conciliation and judicial powers in discharge of their duties. An individual dispute board which is set up for each defined jurisdiction/geographic area will be organized into five independent sections: one each for management, industry, commerce and commercial services, agriculture and miscellaneous services. Again each of these sections is organized into two chambers: one chamber for judicial committee and one for conciliation committee and each chamber consisting of four representatives of employer and four representatives of employees. Members of individual dispute boards are elected for a term of six years arranged in such a way that half of the members are replaced once every three years. The president and vice-president of the board will be chosen in rotation once a year: once from employer and once from employees. Representatives of employees are elected through secret ballot with employees participating in voting. All members of individual dispute board are trained on behalf of the government and financed by the government enabling them to discharge their duties effectively. An employer must permit employee members of individual dispute board six weeks' time off to participate in training programme to acquire necessary knowledge and hone skills and also paid time off to discharge their duties as members as and when necessary.

In accordance with the Labour Code, a strike shall not constitute a breach of contract of employment, unless it is due to serious fault of an employee or trade union or group of employees. No employer is permitted to resort to any discriminatory measure or punitive action against an employee or set of employees because they had gone on strike. In other words, right to strike is regarded as the right of employees and trade unions. However, the Code stipulates that advance communication/notice and plan of strike must be served to the employer and no lightning strike paralyzing the entire undertaking is allowed. Contrary to these provisions, if employees cause stoppage of work, an employer can impose disciplinary action as per the standard process. All disputes must be resolved as much as possible through collective negotiations or by referring to individual dispute boards before either party resorts to serious measures such as strike or disciplinary measures. Conciliation proceedings must be instituted immediately whenever collective labour disputes occur, especially in connection with the revision or renewal, or drafting collective agreements. The conciliation agreements reached between the parties to the proceedings shall be set down in the minutes of the meetings and shall be binding on the parties. During the conciliation proceedings, chairman of conciliation committee can appoint a mediator to study greater details of the dispute and make recommendations for redressal. A list of mediators in consultation with representatives of employees and employer will be drawn and a mediator can be chosen from this list by the chair person. The mediator is empowered extensively to collect all the relevant information including financials from the employer and conditions of employees and views of unions. The mediator is expected to submit a report to the minister of labour on completion of all data collection and interpretation and the recommendations shall be published for consumption of all parties within three months from the date of submission. Wherever a collective agreement has provided for deploying arbitration procedure on failure of conciliation proceedings, both the parties can choose to appoint an arbitrator or both parties can come to an agreement to opt for arbitration through a written understating if an existing collective agreement does not provide for the same. The arbitrator shall not make an award on any items other than those mentioned in the record of the failure to conciliate the parties. An arbitration award must be substantiated with supporting evidence and documents, and an award once submitted shall not be subject to appeal save in exceptional conditions. Arbitration awards can be reviewed when appealed by a central court of arbitration. The court is expected to give its verdict within eight days from the date of filing for an appeal. An arbitration award is binding on all the parties. However, if a court quashes an award in full or part, either party can appeal for appointment as second arbitrator and the second award shall be binding without involving another chance for appeal or revision.

Book 6

This part of the Code focuses on implementation of labour laws and regulations including governance, labour inspection and obligation of employers and penalties applicable in case of deviations/non-compliances.

Titles 1 to 3

Labour inspectors are primarily responsible to ensure implementation of various provisions of the Labour Code and labour laws and regulations that are promulgated from time to time. Labour inspectors can take help and support of police officers attached with jurisdictional court in discharge of their duties especially when they need to file cases for breach of law. There shall also be medical inspectors assisting labour inspectors and the primary responsibility of the medical inspectors is to ensure execution of health and safety-related provisions. Labour inspectors have the right to enter into all establishments and are authorized to take samples, seek documents, inspect production floors and speak with employees and inspect all the registers that are required to be maintained under the law. On inspection, if the labour inspectors suspect contraventions to the law, they shall first collect prima facie evidence. A report must be prepared in two copies if prima facie evidence exists and one copy shall be filed with public prosecutor and another with Ministry of Labour. A labour inspector is obligated under oath to not reveal any production secrets or processes observed during the inspection or through perusal of all documents and production process documents/manuals/plans. Any breach of oath by an inspector of labour is punishable under the penal code. A labour inspector in conjunction with medical supervisor must keep constant watch on all establishments to ensure employee health and workplace conditions. When an employer, either existing or new, intends to employ persons, he or she must provide a declaration to that effect providing details of people to be employed in an establishment. There shall also be a declaration to be filed with Ministry of Labour. This process shall also be followed when an employer intends to employ persons of less than 18 years of age or whenever there is a change of ownership of transfer of establishment or when there is an intention to employ persons who worked earlier with the same establishment but ceased to work for the last six months.

Book 7

This part is dedicated to special provisions related to certain specific industries such as energy, mining, queries, building industry, public works, transport, communication, manufacturing industries and employment conditions including wages, health and safety provisions, settlement of disputes of employees working in these industries. The part also specifies provisions related to certain occupations and professionals such as journalists, seafarers, performers and mannequins.

Title 1

No employee is permitted to work in any underground mine for more than 38 hours and 40 minutes a week. Any time spent by an employee in the underground of a mine is tantamount to actual work in the mine for the purpose of calculation of working hours. It is unlawful to employ women in underground mines and to employ persons who have not reached the age of 18 years. Consent for exceptions needs to be obtained from occupational safety committee and general mining council. There shall be a specialized medical practitioner of mines available all the time at the workplace to safeguard and take care of employees' health and safety. There shall be medical services available all the time for which expenses shall be borne by the employer. Sufficient number of delegates shall be appointed for each mine depending upon number of persons employed whose job is to inspect the mine on regular basis to establish the safety and occupational health measures. Delegates are expected to report to the Ministry of Labour if any contraventions to working hours, employment of women and weekly rests are noticed. A delegate needs to visit all shafts, galleries and work sites twice a month to ensure safety and must visit immediately if any accident takes place and report must be filed. The said delegates are chosen through secret ballot elections participated in by all employees working in a mine and the elections are held once in three years. After being elected as delegate, he or she must undergo vocational instruction and training course organized by the department of mines for which paid leave shall be granted by the employer.

Title 2

Provisions related to employees working in manufacturing industries are discussed here. All persons working in industrial establishments as employees and homeworkers who supply raw material or parts of goods or who produce spare parts meant for final goods of an establishment from a place other than premises of these establishments are covered under these provisions. All homeworkers are also defined as employees for the purpose of this section of the Labour Code. It shall not be lawful for an employer to pay wages to homeworkers less than regular employees for the same kind of work or outcomes. Employer shall maintain register with details of all homeworkers. A collective agreement shall be drawn between homeworkers and principal employer detailing the outcome of the work expected or goods to be produced with time and quality stipulations and proportionate wages and benefits. This collective agreement stating wages can be subject to review from time to time based on the request of homeworkers or the employer. All disputes related to matters covered under the collective bargaining process or wages or work measurement shall be raised and settled within five years. Homeworkers can have their own trade unions to represent them and protect their interests and file disputes.

Title 3

Compensation for workers engaged in construction and building industry especially in bad weather conditions and provisions related to connected matters are discussed in this part. All the persons employed in direct construction activities such as in public works, construction of building and civil engineering work and construction of timber frames or in areas such as plumbing and roofing are covered under this section. Bad weather means atmospheric conditions and flooding actually making the performance of the work dangerous or impossible in regard to the workers' safety and health. All employees working in bad weather conditions are entitled to special allowance in addition to the regular wages and these workers must be paid their wages for the duration where actual work could not be carried out due to adverse weather conditions even though workers are at the site or could not be reached due to impossible conditions. However, employees who are off during that period or on leave will not be entitled to these wages or special allowance. The special allowance will not be counted towards calculation of social charges/deductions. The decision to stop the work due to bad weather conditions will be taken either by the contractor or by the principal employer. Wages paid due to such a condition shall be borne by the principal employer and National Equalization Fund for paid leave in the building industry and public works.

Title 4

Employment contracts and provisions related to seafarers are discussed in this part. The Code envisages that there shall be special rules drafted and made applicable to seafarers on board and crews in the merchant navy involving employment matters such as minimum wage growth rate, collective agreements and dispute resolution, and safety and health on board merchant vessels respecting human life at sea and accommodation on the board ship. Minster responsible for the merchant navy in collaboration with Minister of Labour shall draft and oversee the execution of these special provisions for the benefit of the said employees.

Title 5

This part of the Code discusses provisions applicable to commercial travellers, representatives and agents who work in establishments that exist to organize travel arrangements and do not own or run commercial operations on their own as a separate business entity. All commercial travellers, agents and representatives who work in these establishments irrespective of whether there are employment contracts between these agents and establishments or not are deemed as employees as per this section of the Labour Code. It is encouraged to have employment contracts formalizing the relationship between agents and agencies. The contract can stipulate a condition that an agent by virtue of the employment contract shall not work for any other agency or for any specific product or brand for commercial purpose or otherwise. The contract validity can be for a specific time frame in-built with a probation period of no more than three months' duration and termination of the contract must provide for one month advance notice. These employees are eligible for wages and incentives based on their contribution of orders and monetary value of the same. An employee will continue to be eligible to receive commission/incentive for the orders brought even after this employee has left the organization on account of termination of an employment contract by the employer. The commission earned by commercial travellers and representatives shall be settled at no more than three monthly intervals.

Title 6

This part of the Code describes the provisions in relation to professional journalists, performers and mannequins. Journalists, correspondents and editors fall within the purview of professional journalists for the purpose of this Code. When any media drafts the services of a journalist, it is deemed that there is an employment contract arrived at between both the parties irrespective of whether there is a written agreement or not. No employment contract shall be terminated without providing an advance notice of one month if service of a journalist with an employer is three years or less and it shall be a minimum of two months' notice if service rendered is more than three years or equivalent remuneration is to be paid in lieu of the notice period. There shall also be severance pay equivalent to one month's salary for every year of service rendered to a maximum of 15 months and where there is a dispute of calculation of severance remuneration, the same shall be decided by the arbitration board. Journalists are also entitled to one month paid leave if total service length of a journalist with an employer is at least one year and it shall be five weeks' paid leave per year for journalists who have completed 10 years of service. Journalist who is paid on piecemeal basis shall be entitled to the work commissioned by the media employer regardless of whether the same has been published or not. Agreement between a journalist and an employer will be the referring instrument to decide whether a journalist's work can be published in more than one media or not. All journalists shall be issued professional identity cards in accordance with guidelines of the government.

The definition of performer in this context would include opera singers, actors, dancers, variety artists, musicians, popular singers, extras, conductors, orchestrators and executors. There shall be a contract of employment with each individual performer or jointly with a group of performers based on the nature of artistic work. Each of the performers shall be paid wages for physical appearance or in-person performance and any payment made on account of sale of copies of recorded version shall not count as part of wages. Agencies and individuals are legally permitted to charge and recover fees for placement of performers with an employer's entertainment house/office. Local government agents such as the municipal administrator will be responsible for inspecting and ensuring that the performing houses and agencies would conduct business as per the law and regulations and that the legitimate interests of performers are protected as envisioned in the Code.

Mannequin for the purpose of the Labour Code is defined as any person of either sex who is responsible for either presenting models or new fashions, particularly in the fields of clothing or costume jewellery, in person to the public or for posing of any kind of presentation, even if such activities are only carried out occasionally. When a mannequin is engaged using any type of contract for remuneration, that contract will automatically become contract of employment in the context of the Labour Code. If any commission or royalty is paid for sale or resale of a performance of the mannequin where personal presence is not required and a recorded version will suffice, the commission or royalty paid will not count as part of remuneration.

Books 8 and 9

Special provisions relating to overseas departments are discussed in book 8 and continuing vocational training as part of long-term education are discussed in book 9 of the Labour Code. The provisions relating to overseas departments include agreements relating to employment, regulation of employment, hours of work, occupational medical services, placement and employment, and labour disputes which are specific and shall be drawn for each department with the approval of the Ministry of Labour and Ministry of Foreign Affairs. As mentioned in foregoing content, there shall be lifelong vocational training which shall be the duty at national level in France. The vocational training shall consist of both initial training enabling people to join the workforce and also retraining that helps people to keep updating their skills in tandem with changing work trends. The continuous vocational training is an effort of large-scale collaboration among the local and national governments, private sector establishments, trade unions, industry bodies and vocational training institutes. The trainings that shall be launched span around:

programmes based on long-term education or continuous training in order to acquire and improve the knowledge base, training programmes designed and executed to impart advanced skills enabling people to progress in their careers and move up to take on higher responsibilities, refresher and retraining programmes targeted at persons who are facing redundancy to acquire relevant skills to get re-employed, pre-training schemes providing preparation for working life and basic training curricula to train unskilled persons to acquire basic skills so as to be employed gainfully in industrial/service/agriculture establishments and also training focused on sports and physical training. The state shall play a vital role in continuous vocational training. Hence, an inter-ministerial forum is created under the supervision of the prime minister to oversee the implementation of this programme. The state shall contribute towards the cost of remunerating vocational trainees and also provide financial assistance to all those institutes participating in and imparting continuous vocational training. As per provisions of this part of the Labour Code, all employers employing 10 or more employees in their establishments shall contribute to the development of continuous vocational training by contributing financially and taking part in shaping training courses and imparting them. All employers employing 50 or more persons in their establishment are legally bound to provide the evidence and submit reports informing the government of their participation in and contribution to the continuous vocational training initiative. Employers are also obligated to discuss this matter with their respective works councils. The state shall play an active role in recognizing the courses and issuing certificates. All persons participating in continuing vocational training courses would be automatically enrolled into social security schemes.

Labour Code and Laws in Switzerland

Swiss Code of Obligations (SCO) is the basic and cardinal law that defines and regulates the labour and employment matters in Switzerland. Articles 319 to 362 of the Code (Title Ten) focus on labour and employment matters as discussed in the forthcoming content. The other important labour and employment laws in Switzerland would include:

1. The Federal Act on Information and Consultation of Workers (Workers' Participation Act, 1993)
2. The Federal Act on Equal Treatment of Women and Men (2011)
3. The Federal Act on Data Protection
4. The Federal Act on Personnel Recruitment and Hiring Out of Employees
5. The Federal Regulation Against Excessive Compensation in Public Companies
6. The Federal Merger Act

Section 1 (Articles 319 to 343)

This section deals with individual employment contracts.

Where there is an arrangement between an employee and employer to work for defined hours or undertake to work in the service of an employer for a limited or unlimited period, it is deemed that there is an individual employment contract. An employee is expected to carry out the tasks in person unless the contract of employment provides otherwise. Employer can issue directives and specific instructions regarding the work to be carried out by the employee. The Code stipulates that an employee must carry out his or her assigned responsibilities/tasks diligently and shall not be employed anywhere else for gain especially when such work is meant for competition of the present employer. The employee shall not divulge or share any confidential information or documents, or trade secrets obtained while in service during the employment relationship and afterwards till such time as to not jeopardize the business interest of the employer.

Although an employee is expected to work for the number of hours as agreed to in the employment contract or collective bargaining agreement or as per the standard employment condition, he or she might be expected to work extra hours to the extent that he or she is able and consciously expected to do so. The employers shall compensate the employee for the overtime work in consultation with the employee by paying normal salary plus one quarter of the normal salary or providing time off equivalent to the duration of overtime. Employer is obligated to pay salary and share of profits if an employee is entitled as per the employment contract on the basis of the financial results for the financial year as calculated in accordance with the statutory provision. Employees must also be paid commissions where applicable as per the employment contract and on closure of transactions and it is lawful for the employer to reduce the commission if the transaction enters into effect partially or fails to conclude. Employees are entitled to prorate bonus payouts proportionately if their services are terminated in the middle of or before completion of the year. Salaries to employees shall be paid at the end of the month unless the employment or collective bargaining agreement states otherwise provisioning shorter payout cycles. Employees must be provided with a written statement of salary details. Deductions to be made or payments to be made for the benefit of employer even in accordance with an individual agreement stand void. If an employee is in hardship and requests an advance against salary due for work already performed, the employer must advance such sum as may equitably be expected of him. Though an individual employment contract may provide for higher deduction from the salary, generally employers are expected not to cause deductions of more than 10 per cent of the salary payable or the cumulative deduction shall not exceed more than a week's salary. If the performance or time to deliver goods or services is lost due to the employer's fault, no salary deduction can be made nor is employee obliged to make recovery of the loss of time or performance. However, employers are authorized to make deduction on account of employee contribution to employee benefits schemes, health insurance, personal accident insurance, life insurance and so on and deposit the contributions with respective funds. Employees are also entitled to amount of salary for being unable to attend to work due to reasons not personally due to them such as falling ill, injuries out of an accident, legal obligations or to attend to public duties. Employer must ensure to provide adequate work to engage an employee of piecemeal work fully and employer also has the flexibility to convert piece-based work into time-based work if circumstances would require or unable to provide piece work. In these conditions, a piece-based work employee is entitled to salary at the rate of average salary earned previously. Employees in addition to the salary and benefits are eligible to receive reimbursements for expenses incurred during the performance of a job including transport for commuting based on the expense statement submitted. In order to safeguard health, safety and right working environment, employers must take all measures so required including providing medical care and assistance. Employers also must ensure that employees are not sexually harassed and that any victim of sexual harassment suffers no further adverse consequences.

Employer must observe provisions of Data Protection Act in handling the employee data and must deal or collect employee data to the extent required for job suitability-related decisions.

Employees are entitled to one day off per week which is generally on Sunday and at least four weeks' holiday and five weeks in the case of employees under the age of 20 per annum with all pay and amount equivalent to that an employee might lose in the form of benefits. Employees under the age of 30 are also eligible for grant of one week unpaid leave per year to participate in leadership development or extracurricular activities. Female employees are entitled to maternity leave of 14 weeks at least.

Employees are entitled to receive a reference letter indicating the nature and duration of the employment relationship, quality of work and conduct from the employer at any time. Employer is obligated to communicate to an employee in writing, within one month of joining, the details such as the names of the contracting parties, the date of commencement of employment with the employer, the employee's job description containing duties and responsibilities, salary and other benefits as applicable, working hours, weekly off and any changes to these terms shall be communicated to the employee 30 days in advance. All fixed-term employment contracts come to an end on expiry of the term and either party is eligible to receive six months' advance notice if the employment relationship has lasted for 10 or more years. Employment relationship of unlimited term can also be terminated by issuing due notice with reasons for the termination of relationship. The duration of notice period may vary in consonance with individual or collective bargaining agreements or as per standard employment contracts. An organization which is intending collective redundancies must consult employee organizations and offer details such as reason for mass redundancy, number of employees and their details, who will be impacted by the redundancy, the date of redundancy commencement and provide an opportunity to the employee representatives to offer an alternative plan to avoid collective redundancies. An organization's action of terminations falls within the ambit of mass redundancy when it contemplates terminating at least 10 employees within a 30 days span in a business normally employing more than 20 and less than 100 employees or at least 10 per cent of the employees in a business normally employing 100 or more but less than 300 employees or at least 30 employees in a business normally employing at least 300 employees. Employer as per the Code is required to issue a notification to the cantonal employment office with a copy to employee organizations about the planned mass redundancy plan with requisite details subsequent to end of consultations with employees. Cantonal office can mull over the solutions to the problems likely to arise due to this situation. It is also important to consider whether the collective redundancy might potentially jeopardize the business.

Inventions and designs produced by the employee alone or in collaboration with others in the course of the work shall belong to the employer. However, when an invention or design is produced, an employer must inform that employee about the intention to acquire it and fix a fair remuneration for the same keeping in view economic value of the invention/design and the extent of contribution of an employee or employees. An employee is liable to pay damages if he or she infringes upon the competition. Whenever there is a transfer of ownership from previous to future employer, the rights and obligations of employment relationship will be passed on to the future employer (acquirer) and any fallout between both the employers are liable for claims. An employee's employment relationship would come to an end with due notice period if the employee refuses to be transferred to the new employer due to transfer of ownership. The Code stipulates that an employer who is planning to transfer the ownership shall communicate to the employees/employee organizations the reason for transfer of ownership and its legal, economic and social consequences for the employees and consultation shall be done with them in advance. Where an employment relationship with an employee of at least 50 years of age comes to an end after 20 years or more of service, the employer must pay the employee a severance allowance. The said allowance is payable to spouse or registered partner or children if an employee dies while in service.

Section 2 (Articles 344 to 355)

This section deals with special individual employment contracts. Basically there are three types of special employment contracts that the Code has described. These are: apprenticeship contracts, commercial traveller's contract and homeworkers contract. These are briefly discussed next.

Apprenticeship Contract

The Code stipulates that employer must extend opportunities for apprenticeship training and observe certain rules and methods while implementing this provision. For an apprenticeship contract to be legally valid, it must be in writing and the contract must specify the nature and duration of the vocational training, probation period which shall not be less than one month or more than three months, supply of work tools, vocational activities and description, allocation of work, apprenticeship stipend to meet boarding and lodging expenses, contribution towards insurance, holidays and supervision of apprenticeship training. Apprentices are entitled to receive a certificate from the employer stating nature and duration of vocational training on successful completion of the said training and the certificate may also contain details of skills, achievements and conduct of the apprentice if a special request is made to include these details. The apprentices on their part are expected to perform sincerely during vocational training to achieve the objectives of such programme. An employer can terminate a vocational training contract during the probation period by issuing a notice of seven days for reasons such as the apprentice is intellectually or physically unable to meet the minimum aptitude standards, ill health, issues involving moral turpitude, lack of availability of a professional trainer or a specialist to train the apprentice or the conditions to effectively impart apprenticeship training not existing.

The Commercial Traveller's Contract

A commercial traveller undertakes to broker or conclude all transactions on behalf of an employer of a commercial business in exchange of payment of salary. An employment relationship of a commercial traveller with an employer is formalized through a written contract containing details such as duration and termination of the contract, authority of commercial traveller in discharge of duties/performance, pay and benefits, and other working terms. A commercial traveller must abide by the rules of pricing and commercial terms while executing the business transaction and regularly report all business activities and pass on orders and bring to the notice of the employer any key information related to the client. No employer can make an agreement whereby a commercial traveller becomes liable for a client payment not made or any other type of client performance or obligation that resulted in no payment partially or fully by the client and no recovery can be made from the commercial traveller in all these eventualities. A commercial traveller's role is limited to broking a transaction unless agreed differently. An employer is obligated to recognize and pay the customary commission for all the deals that have taken place in an area or zone that has been allocated to a commercial traveller as his or her scope regardless of whether the deals have been closed by the traveller or by the employer on his or her own. Salary of a traveller shall not be stopped because he or she could not travel for which he or she is not at fault. A commercial traveller with the consent and knowledge of respective employers can work for multiple employers instead of exclusively working for a single employer. In this scenario, if it arises legitimately, liabilities will be shared by the employers equally or proportionately. The commercial traveller must return to the employer all documents, artefacts, samples, price lists, intellectual property, client data and any other property or tools given to him or her at the time of leaving the employment relationship.

The Homeworkers Employment Contract

Homeworker is one who has undertaken work on his or her own or along with his or her family members at their own home or in the premises of the employer to carry out work as per the standards laid down in return for the salary. The Code recognizes this arrangement as an employment contract between an employee and employer, and extends certain provisions that shall be observed by both the parties. The employer must inform the homeworker of the terms and conditions, and description of duties and responsibilities along with resources being provided. The homeworker must commence and carry out the work as defined and accepted, and deliver the results. Wherever homeworker is at fault in delivering substandard or defective work/output, the same shall be rectified at the homeworker's own cost and effort. An employer is expected to notify any defects promptly, failing which, it will be assumed that the work carried out is as per agreed norms and no future claims will be entertained. Employer is obliged to pay salary only when work is executed as agreed and where a homeworker is engaged on continuous basis, the employer shall disburse the salary twice a month and the employer is also obliged to pay salary if a homeworker could not carry out the work on any day not due to his or her fault.

Section 3 (Articles 356 to 362)

The provisions concerning collective employment contract and the standard employment contract are discussed in this section of the Code as presented next.

A collective employment contract as per the Code is defined as a contract reached, concluded and signed off by employee representatives and employer governing nature of employment, termination, duties and obligations of both the parties, dispute resolution method and mechanism, pay, benefits, working conditions, productivity issues, conduct and process of monitoring the execution of the collective agreement. There shall be no obligation that a contract can impose on either party to necessarily join an association or union nor can a contract attempt to exclude a particular profession or occupation being held by an employee to receive a vocational training. All collective employment contracts including the manner in which they can be amended or terminated shall be recorded in writing. Any agreement reached between employee and employer contradicting the compulsory provisions of a collective agreement is void unless such contract provides more favourable benefits to the employee. Both the contracting parties hold primary responsibility to ensure compliance to the provisions of collective agreement and must see that harmonious IR prevail and refrain from any hostile action on matters regulated by the collective employment contract. The Code clearly mentions that the mandatory laws of confederation and cantons take precedence over the collective employment contract wherever there is a conflict, and the collective agreement supersedes these laws if it favours the employee more.

Standard employment contract is one that is drawn up by cantons to provide a basic tenet of employment contract in order to protect interests of employees. Federation takes up the responsibility of issuing a standard employment contract if it is applicable and extended to more than one canton. Essentially, the standard employment contract functions as a model employment contract or a basic employment contract which shall form the basis for minimum terms that shall be maintained in any individual employment contract in areas such as working hours, weekly off, leisure time, minimum wages and employment conditions. The federation or canton which is responsible for issuing these employment notifications shall constitute a tripartite committee consisting of members from employees, employers and representatives from the state to mull over and formulate the contract. The members of tripartite committee are authorized to collect all business documents that may be helpful in discharge of their duties and are bound by trade secret policy. The standard employment contract is mainly applicable to employees in domestic jobs, agriculture and female employees and minors.

Dutch Labour Laws

Though there is no single consolidated labour code governing labour and employment matters in the Netherlands, the Dutch Civil Code, especially Titles 7.10 and 7.11 focusing on employment agreements and collective agreements, occupies the centre place. These titles along with relevant articles are discussed further. The other labour laws that are applicable and relevant in the Netherlands are:

1. The Work and Security Act, 2015
2. The Working Conditions Act
3. The Act on Minimum Wages and Minimum Holidays Allowance
4. The Working Hours Act
5. The Equal Treatment Act
6. The Dutch Works Councils Act

Title 7.10 of the Dutch Civil Code (Articles 610 to 692)

Provisions of this title will be applicable to employment agreement reached between an employee and employer especially when there is a conflict or when any term or condition of employment is inferior when compared to what is stipulated in this Code. However, this title is not applicable to employees working in service of the state. Irrespective of whether there is a formal agreement or not, if a person performs a work for 20 hours a month and continuously for three months, it is presumed that there is an employment agreement. In this context, the Code envisages that both employee and employer must behave as befits a reasonable and fair employee and employer. A minor who has reached the age of 16 years can enter into an employment agreement. An employer shall make changes to the existing employment contract only when authorized in writing and such change is subjected to the test of fairness and reasonableness. An employer is obligated to pay wages at agreed intervals (not shorter than a week and not longer than a month) only in the form of money, shares, stocks, options, debt claims, coupons, holiday cheques, services and services performed by the employer, housing and boarding. Wage rates as given in collective agreement are applicable if it is not given in individual employment agreement. Employer will remain liable for the wages if paid in any kind or method other than that prescribed in this title. Employees are entitled to receive an electronic copy of the pay slip. Employee is not eligible to receive wages for the duration in which he or she has not performed as per the contract and in conditions where that non-performance is at the volition of the employee. Where the employee is unable to perform the contracted work due to sickness, pregnancy or the delivery of a child, the employee remains entitled to 70 per cent of the wages for a period of 104 weeks. Employee is not eligible for the said benefit if the sickness is caused by self intentionally or deliberately or if he or she has delayed the recovery from a sickness or concealed the information relating to an illness during the recruitment stage. Employer will be within the right to seek an independent medical expert's opinion on this matter. Any provision in the employment agreement authoring the employer to make unauthorized deductions to the salary is null and void. Employer can affect offsetting the wages in certain conditions as defined in the Code. These are deductions from the wages as authorized and committed by an employee, premium payment to the pension fund, contribution to the insurance, deposits to the saving funds, any legal claims as allowed by the courts and deduction in order to comply with any contractual obligation.

In accordance with the Dutch Code, for every year in which the employee has been entitled to wages over the full contracted working hours, he or she builds up holiday entitlements of at least four times the working hours contracted per week. However, the full contracted working hours clause is not applicable to a pregnant employee who will continue to be eligible for holiday accumulation although she has not worked for the full contracted hours and exception of contracted work is applicable in cases where employees are on sick leave or adoption leave. The employer must observe minimum holiday condition and give opportunity to employees to avail the holiday entitlement. Employee can also plan holiday period which shall last for at least two weeks at a time and must inform the employer about the plan well in advance. Employees are entitled to wages during holiday period and shall not waive off the right of holiday in exchange of compensation. The payment or compensation in lieu of holiday entitlement is allowed only at the time of ending the employment contract. Employees are also entitled to political leave without wages to attend the meetings of the First Chamber of the States-General (Parliament). Courts can decide the quantum of leave to be granted on account of this cause if an employer and employee is unsuccessful in determining the quantum of leave that can be granted.

No employer can practise discrimination and must treat all women and men equal in all employment matters including offer of employment, terms and conditions of employment, training, promotion opportunities and termination of employment. It is permitted to derogate this clause in practising discrimination for positioning women in advantageous position in order to remove the disadvantage that existed and also permitted to give preference to one gender over the other when required in certain functions which necessitate this. Discrimination could include the work harassment or sexual harassment. No employer shall treat an employee adversely because that employee has brought the issue of discrimination on to the surface and because he or she made a complaint. Employers are also precluded from discriminating against employees based on whether their employment type is full time or part-time or temporary, or contractual unless such treatment is rationally justified in certain issues. There can be a probation period mutually agreed on between an employee and employer in writing lasting a minimum of one to a maximum of two months depending upon the duration of employment contract validity. Employer can enter an agreement with an employee about the non-compete clause restricting the employee's right to work in a certain way. However, this shall not cause undue disadvantage to an employee and in the event that it does, the court can set aside such an agreement. An employment contract which shall be in writing and made at the cost of the employer shall contain details such as the name and domicile of both the parties, the place/places where the work is to be performed, position and nature of work to be performed by the employee, the date of commencement of engagement, duration of employment, entitlement of holiday, duration of termination notice to be observed by both the parties, working hours per day/week, details and membership to pension scheme, wages and benefits, and related matters. Employees are also entitled to receive a testimonial at the time of employment termination comprising details such as the start and end date of employment, nature of work performed by an employee, the way the employment contract is ended and damages if any. An employee working for fixed term or temporary period will have the right to know if a vacancy for indefinite period arises. As much as possible, an employer must provide alternative work if an employee is unable to perform the work for which he or she is engaged as per the contract due to sickness. The employee is obligated to follow instructions and perform the alternative work provided by the employer. The employer must arrange and maintain spaces, rooms, machines and tools in which the work is performed and take all safety measures that are reasonably necessary to ensure safe working conditions. The employee has to perform the work personally and in performing the work a replacement can be brought in only with the consent of an employer.

Employer's rights and obligations towards all employment contracts engaging employees shall remain valid in the event of transition of an enterprise to a new employer. For the first year, both the old and new employer shall be responsible to protect all terms and conditions of employment contracts both individual and collective jointly and severally. Post a year of transition, the new employer shall be solely responsible. The employer is also obligated to inform all employees on the date of transition if works council does not exist and of the reasons for transition and about the legal, economic and social consequences of such transition to employees and business. Termination of an employment contract by either party shall be in writing adhering to the notice period clause. Employer is not legally permitted to cause termination of an employment contract of an employee who is unable to perform due to sickness unless the sickness has lasted more than two years or unless the Social Security Agency has permitted the termination. Employer also cannot terminate a female employee who is on maternity leave or an employee who has refused to work on Sunday or an employee who is a member of a works council. Employer must observe the notice period of minimum one month to maximum four months depending on length of service of an employee while initiating termination where it is permitted. An employee can initiate notice of termination by giving one month notice. Either party initiating termination of employment must provide reason for the action. However, either party is empowered to terminate an employment contract with immediate effect based on urgency. The urgency reasons may include an employer not paying agreed wages or not respecting the obligations, an employer battering or insulting the employee, an employee grossly neglecting the duties and responsibilities, an employer placing unreasonable demand such as asking the employee to work for another employer without reasonable offer and an employee being unable to perform the work due to continued illness. However, if it is established that the urgency clause is not properly applied, the party who has taken the decision is liable for damages. The court apart from imposing damages may order reinstatement of the employee with full back wages.

The Code also provides for a secondment agreement which is defined as an employment agreement under which the employer within the framework of his or her business or professional practice places the employee at the disposal of a third party in order to perform work under the supervision and direction of that third party by virtue of an agreement for the provision of service between the third party and the employer. A secondment agreement comes to an end as and when employer decides. However, a contractual obligation shall no longer be valid and shall have no effect on the employee in performing the work of the employer if the employee has completed more than 26 weeks of work. Both the employer and third party are jointly and severally responsible to pay wages as per the applicable minimum wage and minimum holiday allowance.

Labour Laws in Finland

Labour laws and regulations of Finland are primarily influenced by Nordic model of employee relations. Therefore, employee association and employer forums, collective bargaining agreements and consultations are widely prevalent. Key labour and employment laws applicable in Finland are discussed further.

Employment Contracts Act, 2000

The basic objective of this Act is to provide a framework to draw up employment contracts, stipulate minimum terms of employment, provide protection of employment and define rights and obligations of employers and employees in employment relationship and procedure for termination of employment. Under this Act, an employment contract is presumed to be for an indefinite period unless it specifically mentions a definite end date (a fixed-term employment contract). Employment contract is not subject to formal requirements: it can be oral, written or electronic. Each fixed-term contract has to be drawn up for a justified reason. Consecutive fixed contracts are highly restricted. An employment contract can introduce probationary period lasting no more than six months. Apart from regular employment, the Act permits part-time, contract and temporary employment. Termination of employment by the employer is restricted except in cases where there in serious violation of the duties by an employee and incapacity to work. Collective terminations are allowed after following due process on account of economic recession or production-related reasons. Employees who have had their employment terminated for reasons that are not their fault are eligible for severance pay to the extent of 1,500 euros. In case of wrongful termination, an employee is entitled to 24 months' wages. An employee also can initiate termination of employment contract by providing the reason. Either party must serve a notice of 30 days for termination of employment contract. The Act also provides for maternity leave of 105 days and paternity leave of up to 12 weeks and childcare leave based on the need. Employees are also eligible for sick leave and disability leave. An employer must ensure safety and health in the workplace in order to protect employees from accidents and health hazards. Employees who could not come to work due to illness are eligible to receive pay during first nine days from the employer and subsequently are entitled to draw sickness allowance as per the Sickness Insurance Act. Minimum requirements of an employment contract are: pay and benefits, payday and period, start and end date of employment, lay-off procedures, notice period, duties and responsibilities, non-solicitation, working hours, holidays and applicable provisions of collective agreements.

Working Hours Act, 1996

The Act stipulates the maximum working hours of 40 hours per week and 8 hours a day. The weekly limit may, however, be exceeded by means of a schedule and laid down by the employer in advance providing for working hours not exceeding 40 hours a week on average over a period of 52 weeks. Overtime is allowed up to 138 hours within a period of four months and up to 250 hours in a year.

Holidays Act, 1973

Employees earn their holidays as per the Act. An employee earns two and a half days of holidays for every month of work totalling to 30 days in a year. Employees are eligible to claim holidays at one stretch during the period of May through September. In addition to these holidays, employees are also eligible for public holidays such as Independence Day, New Year's Day, Good Friday and May Day.

Young Workers' Act, 1993

The Act permits entering into an employment contract with a young person who has attained the age of 15 years and does not fall in the category of compulsory school attendance condition. An employer who is employing young persons must take special measures such as training, education and medical examination and restrictive practices must be followed in engaging them in overtime and night shift work, while working hours would be the same as those of an adult worker. No more than 80 hours of overtime work per annum is permitted. The minimum daily rest period shall be 12 consecutive hours and 38 hours in a week.

Equality Act, 1987

The Equality Act prohibits discrimination on the grounds of sex, age, origin, language, religion, family ties, conviction, opinion, trade union activity, political activity, health and disability as laid down in the Constitution of Finland. The prohibition of discrimination must be observed in all walks of labour management including hiring, training, promotion and transfers. The Act imposes on the employers to promote equality at workplace and adjust working conditions to make them suitable to both the sexes as well as initiate preventive measures to avert sexual harassment. Employers must also appoint equality ombudsman to oversee the implementation of equality administration in an organization. An employer may deviate from the requirement of equal treatment only for a justified reason having taken into consideration the duties and nature of work of a role/job.

Collective Agreements Act, 1946

The objective of this Act is to promote industrial peace by defining procedures to be followed for joint negotiations, drawing up collective agreements, dispute resolution mechanism and obligations of all parties to a collective agreement and applicability, and scope of collective agreements. All collective agreements come with an obligation to maintain peace by all parties during the implementation of the said agreement. The Labour Court can order the payment of a compensatory fine for breach of the peace obligation. The Act also stipulates the procedure for election of shop steward and chief steward by members of the trade union who play an important role in collective bargaining process. Both parties are obligated to ensure implementation of a collective agreement in letter and spirit. The Labour Court is a single special court established to deal with disputes connected with collective agreements. The Court is made up of members from employers and employees, and neutral bodies/agencies/experts. The scope of the Court encompasses all disputes concerning interpretation and execution of collective agreements. However, a labour court may entertain a dispute only when the dispute settlement has failed at the level of grievance settlement procedure.

Labour Laws in Sweden

Swedish labour laws are modern and both employee and employer-friendly. The labour legislation framework is inspired by civil law making process in which people themselves make laws on need basis to protect societal interests. Similarly, most labour laws are made and implemented with active participation by trade unions and associations of employers. Joint forums are formed as per the collective bargaining process to address any issue and bring in mandatory legislation. Sweden is also at the forefront in adapting some of the key labour management initiatives as prescribed by both ILO and EU. Sweden has reached a state of maturity in farming its labour law and transforming it as and when need arises. Some of the key laws that focus on employment protection, wages, terms and conditions of employment and labour dispute resolution process are discussed in the following paragraphs.

The Labour Disputes (Judicial Procedure) Act, 1974

The Act deals with all disputes relating to interpretation and implementation of collective bargaining agreements other than those related to bankruptcy and cases concerning criminal injuries and damages related to such issues.

Chapter 1: Scope of the Act and instances wherein this legislation is not applicable and role of arbitrator are discussed in this chapter. A dispute before being subjected to judicial review and resolution can be referred for arbitration provided there is a joint agreement expressing consent by the employer and employee representatives.

Chapter 2: The jurisdictional issues between district courts and the Labour Court and appropriate competent authority within the judicial system to decide disputes related to collective bargaining agreements are dealt with in this chapter. In general, the Labour Court is the competent court to take up all collective barging disputes and adjudicate upon. A labour court also can set aside the decision of the district court if it finds the same is not appropriate in terms of jurisdiction and competency authority purview. The Labour Court can also act as court of review of the decisions taken by the district court in disputes relating to industrial action. However, in such circumstances no decision against district judge can be initiated. Decisions of the Labour Court if appealed can be taken up by the Supreme Court.

Chapter 3: Composition of the Labour Court and governance-related matters are discussed here. A labour court shall consist of four chairpersons and four vice chairpersons and seventeen other members and all of them must be Swedish citizens. One of the four chairpersons will be chosen as president. Three members, one chairperson and one vice chairperson shall be appointed from the group who have no affiliation either with employer or employees and are completely neutral persons but possess knowledge of labour and employment matters. The other members must be chosen from Swedish Employers' confederation, Swedish Association of Local Authorities and Regions, Swedish Agency for Government Employers, Swedish Trade Union Confederation, Confederation of Professional Employees and Swedish Confederation of Professional Associations. The Labour Court fulfils a quorum when a chairperson and no less than four other members are present.

Chapter 4: Procedure of a court proceeding and general provisions are described in this chapter. Any persons representing employer or employee organizations can file a dispute in the Labour Court and their respective associations and federations can join the cause. Any persons wishing to institute proceedings before the Labour Court shall make an application in writing to the Court for issuing summons against the other party. The Labour Court shall determine the case as early and bring about a resolution.

Employment (Co-determination in the Workplace) Act, 1976

The Act consisting of 69 sections is a comprehensive framework regulating and facilitating relationships between employees and employer. It recognizes the right of association as a lawful right of all employers and employees, and the right of association shall not be infringed upon. The Act also acknowledges the right of employees to negotiate with the employer on any matters relating to the relationship between the employer and any member of the organization who has been employed by that employer. Employers before taking any decision on matters falling within collective bargaining or before bringing any changes must negotiate with employees' organization. An employer must negotiate with affected group if an issue does not fall within the purview of collective bargaining scope. An employer cannot terminate services of an employee who falls within the purview of collective bargaining without negotiating with employee unions/organization including during the event of redundancy due to insufficient work or transfer of undertaking. An employer shall first discuss with local employees' organization on employment matters and reach the central employees' organization for negotiation only when it has failed at local level. Employer must grant permission and paid time off to employees who are authorized by employee organizations to negotiate and participate in joint meetings. Employee organizations and their office-bearers are entitled to receive all information from the employer relating to how business is doing, production, operations and finance-related information and how HR policies are shaping up. If either party, employee or employer organization, quotes certain documents to support their view, they will be required to furnish these documents if the other party solicits the same. A collective bargaining agreement that is concluded in writing as per this Act shall be binding on all members of the organization. There shall be no other agreements or arrangements between any employee and the employer that would conflict the collective bargaining agreement in operation. The terms and conditions of an employment contract and provisions of collective bargaining agreement applicable to an employee shall remain valid at least for a period of one year when services of that employee are transferred to the new employer as per the Employment Protection

Act, 1982. Where there is merger or acquisition, the provisions of collective bargaining as applicable to the old employer will be extended to the new employer mutatis mutandis. Validity of a collective bargaining agreement comes to an end on expiry of the period as agreed and embodied in that agreement and on issuance of notice by either party on reaching the end date. An employer shall not resort to unilateral decision on any issue relating to collective bargaining agreement where there is difference of opinion over the way it is implemented or in interpretation of a clause. Whenever an employer wants some other person to perform an assignment or portion of work on his or her behalf without engaging that person as an employee, employer must bring this issue to the notice of employees' organization for them to take a view. An employer can go ahead and implement decisions, without prior negotiations with employee organizations, if these decisions are urgent and the employer needs to move on them without any delay in the interest of business and organization. However, post implementation of the decision, the employer shall immediately inform employee organization about the decision and the need for its urgent implementation. Employer and employees who are bound by a collective bargaining agreement may not initiate or participate in stoppage of work or resort to strike or blockade or boycott, or any other industrial action which is against the labour stability obligation as agreed to by both the parties during or after the collective bargaining agreement process. Similarly, an employer shall not resort to any lockout or stoppage of remuneration or file a lawsuit or any pressure tactics during this phase. Indulging in any of these actions is deemed to be unlawful. Employee organizations or employer shall serve seven days' notice to the other party when planning industrial action. The Act also provides for establishing a National Mediation Office to advise and help employees and employers to approach collective negotiation in a constructive manner and facilitate dispute resolution as and when needed. Either party breaching the provisions of collective bargaining agreement is liable to pay damages of compensation.

Wage Guarantee Act, 1992

The Act comprising 36 sections was promulgated with an objective to guarantee the wage payment to employees in the event of bankruptcy and reconstruction of a business in its entirety. If an employer fails to make wage payments and pension release, state will take the responsibility to be liable to fulfil the loss suffered by employees. However, in order for the State to take up this responsibility for payment of due wages, insolvency proceedings must have been instituted against the employer. No employee can claim loss of wages if the bankruptcy has occurred in the past prior to the current one but will be eligible subject to fulfilling the insolvency conditions for the current bankruptcy. A person entitled to maintenance is entitled to a guarantee amount for maintenance allowance secured by attachment of pay. The Swedish Social Insurance Agency is not entitled to guarantee amounts for maintenance support that have been paid under the Social Insurance Code. Employees are entitled to the guaranteed payment even in cases where resignations from the services are tendered and if the employees are released one month after the bankruptcy declaration. Employee wage payment and pension releases occupy priority over the other claims/debts/due payments in a bankruptcy and business reconstruction scenario. The guaranteed payment clause is applicable in aggregate to a maximum of eight months' employment period. An employee who receives income from other employment shall notify the same to the bankruptcy administrator. It is the responsibility of a bankruptcy administrator to collect relevant information, data and all proofs and prepare a list of claimants and process the same for payment while informing this decision prior to the County Administrative Board. The bankruptcy administrator can lodge claims which in his or her opinion are indisputable. An employee working in an organization which has been put into bankruptcy in another Nordic or EU country can still file a claim but the same shall be dealt with as per Swedish law and conditions. The County Administrative Board shall be responsible for all payments of unpaid wages as per this legislation and before the said payments are made to employees, the Board must impose taxes and deductions as normally applicable. An employee who is aggrieved with the decision of bankruptcy administrator may file a case within three weeks from such decision in the district or the Labour Court. An employee is legally liable to return the guaranteed amount received if the decision taken earlier is revoked based on new facts.

Employment Protection Act, 1982

This Act is applicable to all organizations in private and public sector and to all employees except apprentices and those in managerial positions. The objective of the Act which consists of 43 sections is to provide a framework for formation and termination of employment contract of fixed or indefinite period of employment and conditions of re-employment. Employment contracts are generally for indefinite period in Sweden. However, fixed employment contracts can be entered into in exceptional conditions where the assignment shall end on a definite time frame due to nature of work such as when the employment is for substituting someone temporarily or when the employment is seasonal or if the employee is likely to attain the age of 67 which is retirement age in Sweden. An employee under this legislation is entitled to remain in employment up to the end of the month when he or she attains the age of 67 and is also entitled to re-employment if opportunity exists but he or she cannot be given a preferential turn. If an employee has been employed for a period of five years for fixed period employment, for in aggregate more than two years, the employment is automatically transformed into indefinite period of employment. There shall be mandatory notice period to be observed by both employees and employer for termination of an indefinite period contract of employment and the period of notice can be as indicated in the employment contract. However, notice period shall be for a minimum of one month and can go up to six months based on the length of service of an employee. Notice of termination by an employer must be in writing, handed over in person and shall be based on facts. Employee and employee organizations are entitled to consult and negotiate with the employer regarding termination of employment. When a process of termination or notice period is disputed, the same shall be referred to adjudication of the dispute and in this condition, release of the employee cannot be caused till the adjudication is over. Where an employee is unavailable to personally receive the notice, the same can be mailed but effective date starts only after 10 days from the date of dispatch. Fixed employment contracts come to an end on expiry of the validity of the said contract. The law permits having probationary period for a maximum term of six months and then expiring automatically. The employer can either appoint in regular terms or terminate the employment relationship of a probationer. Every employee is entitled to receive written information from the employer within one month from the date of employment containing names of employee and employer, date of commencement of employment, job description of employee with duties, responsibilities, designation/title, probationary terms, if applicable, period of employment whether fixed or indefinite, pay and benefits, leave, working hours, weekly off and safety matters and collective bargaining agreement in operation. Employee who has been terminated and put on notice period is entitled to normal salary and benefits till the last working day. However, an employee whose services are called off and is employed with another employer during his or her notice period, income accrued from such engagement can be deducted by the foregoing employer. Employee must also be granted leave as and when requested for to search for alternative employment, visit employment agencies and attend interviews/recruitment process. Employer can summarily dismiss an employee for grossly neglecting the work or obligations to an employer and employee is entitled to seek details and facts leading to the dismissal. Employer based on shortage of work can lay off employees by following the due process. Employees whose employment has been terminated on account of shortage of work are entitled to re-employment whenever opportunities arise. An employee must have served at least for one year in the last three years in order to be eligible for right to priority in re-employment. If an employee rejects the re-employment opportunity extended to him or her, the right for priority in re-employment will be forfeited. Right of re-employment is limited to the unit where that employee was employed earlier though an employer may be managing multiple units. An employer who violates any provisions of this Act shall be liable for damages for loss suffered by the employee as well as pay and other employment benefits to which the employee may be entitled. An employee who fails to comply with the provisions of the Act shall be liable for damages as sought by an employer equivalent to the loss suffered due to the employee's behaviour. If an employer fails to comply with a court order rendering a termination invalid, the employment relationship of a fixed employment contract is dissolved and employer is liable to pay an amount equivalent to a minimum of 16 months' pay to a maximum of 32 months' pay based on length of service of an employee in that business unit. This amount is excluding any damages the Court may impose based on gravity of violation. An employee who is aggrieved and not in agreement with the employment termination or summary dismissal may approach the Court within two weeks from the date of termination and in exceptional cases within 30 days failing which the claim will not be admitted and will elapse.

Working Hours Act, 1982

The objective of the Act is to stipulate working hours of all employees. As per Section 5 of the Act, regular working time may not exceed 40 hours per week. Where exigencies demand including on-call duty, the working time shall not exceed 48 hours per week. Any working time beyond 40 hours per week is considered overtime. Overtime work is permitted to a maximum of eight hours, that is, 48 hours including overtime a week. Employer shall maintain a record of all working time and overtime of all employees in a systematic manner as prescribed by Swedish Work Environment Authority. Employee representatives, trade union office-bearers and individual employees are entitled to inspect this record. All employees are eligible to receive two weeks' advance notice whenever a change in working time is contemplated by an employer. Employees are entitled to a minimum uninterrupted rest period of 36 hours per seven days period. As much as possible, rest period shall be scheduled during the weekend. No employee shall be expected to work more than five hours continuously without a reasonable break. The duration of the break must be satisfactory and shall be commensurate with working conditions and nature of work performed by employees. There shall also be meal breaks which can be clubbed with normal break of work and in addition to this, work must be organized in a way that allows work pauses. Swedish Work Environment Authority is vested with the responsibility of overseeing implementation of this legislation in all establishments and to perform supervisory role.

Annual Leave Act, 1977

The objective of this Act is to provide for annual leave benefits including leave, holidays and pay in lieu of annual leave. Employees are entitled to 25 days of annual leave per annum and this leave can be availed without reckoning Saturday and Sunday, and public holidays such as Christmas and New Year's eve as leave days. During the annual leave, employees are entitled to holiday allowance. Any collective bargaining agreement reached in contravention to this quantum of leave and associated conditions as stipulated in this Act will be null and void. Employees whose employment lasts for less than three months will not be eligible for any leave but are entitled to a holiday allowance. Employees who change jobs during the year will be entitled to leave with the new employer to the extent that the employee has not already availed such leave with the previous employer. Employee and employer can reach an understanding about the dates during which the employee would avail the annual leave. If no agreement is arrived at, annual leave dates shall be scheduled during the period of June–August for four weeks. Annual leave unless an employee expressly agrees shall not be coincided with lay-off or termination notice period.

There are two distinct elements in this Act. These are: (a) calculation of days of annual leave with pay and (b) calculation of holiday pay. Calculation of days of annual leave method is: the days when the employee has been completely absent from the work without pay shall be deducted from the days that the employee has worked during the year. Absence on account of annual leave, lay-off, Saturday and Sunday, and in general all days that afford an entitlement to holiday pay shall be counted towards the period of employment. The difference is divided by the number of days in the qualifying year. The factor is multiplied by 25. Calculation of holiday pay as stipulated in the Act is: it is the percentage rule comprising 12 per cent of the employee's pay that has become due in qualifying year and payable weekly or monthly as normally an employee is eligible to receive the pay. An employee who has not availed the annual leave and entitled to 20 days or more annual leave can carry these leaves forward to subsequent leave year. Days of annual leave with pay that have not been carried over and which could not be scheduled during the annual leave year are compensated by holiday pay. Employees are entitled to compensation in lieu of annual leave that has not been availed at the time of leaving services of the company due to resignation or termination of employment contract by the employer. An employer who breaches any provisions of this Act is liable for damages excluding any compensation that might have been due to an employee. The amount of damage to be imposed will be fair and proportionate to the loss an employee incurred due to the violation of a provision by the employer.

Parental Leave Act, 1995

The objective of the Act is to entitle employees to grant of parental leave for own or adopted child. There are six types of parental leave in accordance with the Act as discussed here: (a) female employees are eligible for maternity leave of seven weeks prior to the estimated date of delivery and seven weeks after the birth of the child, (b) full-time parental leave with or without full parental benefit till the child reaches the age of 18 months, (c) part-time parental leave in which an employee can be granted reduction of normal working hours, (d) part-time leave in which an employee can be granted reduction of working hours by a quarter of normal working hours till the child reaches age of eight years, (e) grant of leave for temporary period to take care of the child and (f) grant of full-time leave during which an employee is entitled to child-raising allowance.

An employee who intends to avail any of these leaves must provide two months' notice to the employer prior to the commencement of leave. Likewise, when an employee is intending to return to work, he or she must give notice to the employer. An employee on parental leave shall not be treated unfavourably in decisions pertaining to promotions, vocational training, remuneration changes and work distribution or given notice of termination, summary dismissal or pay-off.

Prohibition of Discrimination of Employees Working Part Time and Employees with Fixed-term Employment Act, 2002

The objective of this Act is to provide protection to part-time or fixed-term employees, rationally owed to them, against any bias or discrimination in their pay and other terms and conditions of employment. The Act explicitly prohibits discrimination that may occur in two ways: the first one is called direct discrimination and is demonstrated through people policies and processes such as pay, vocational training opportunities, working conditions and other terms and conditions of employment which are unreasonably unfavourable to part-time or fixed-term employees than to regular employees. The second type of discrimination is indirect wherein all policies and processes appear to be neutral but the manner in which they are implemented or the way that these employees are treated are adversarial. The Act prohibits both these forms of discrimination by an employer and employee representatives. Discrimination under this Act attracts serious damages.

Labour Laws in Denmark

Denmark is a highly unionized and yet very disciplined labour market and is governed by a set of labour and employment laws covering entire life cycle of employment. Basically, there are seven important Acts that mostly complete the employment legislation landscape and these Acts are discussed further briefly.

The Employers' and Salaried Employees' (Legal Relationship) (Consolidation) Act, 2005

The Act consisting of 22 sections is intended to provide a framework for the relationship between employers and salaried employees. Salaried employee here means (a) a person who is employed to work more than eight hours a week to supervise the work of other persons, (b) a clerk or assistant employed in office and (c) a technical person. The Act is also applicable to employees on fixed-term contracts. Employers shall not terminate employees without providing prior notice of one month if the employment has lasted for six months and three months' notice if the employment has lasted longer than six months; the notice period can go up to six months based on the length of service. No severance allowance will be payable, if the employee on termination of the employment relationship receives an old age pension from the employer. An employer can terminate services of an employee for negligent service and the employer is also entitled to claim damages for the loss suffered and can claim up to half month's salary for a month of unauthorized absence of the employee from work. However, it shall not be considered unauthorized absence if the employee is absent due to illness. Also, an employee keeping away from work in order to attend national duty/service shall not be deemed as being on unauthorized absence. A salaried employee is not entitled to receive any salary during the first period of national service but the employer in the event of any subsequent periods of national service is required to pay the salary. A female salaried employee is eligible for grant of 4 weeks of leave before the confinement and 14 weeks after the confinement during which period the employer shall pay half of the salary to the employee. An employee is eligible to receive full salary during the maternity leave if she is dismissed during or before the said leave period. Group of salaried employees are entitled to negotiate with the employer about their pay and benefits regardless of number of employees in the group. Either party is entitled to solicit services of a mediator/conciliator who can be appointed by industrial court if they are not successful in reaching an agreement through mutual negotiations. A salaried employee can perform services outside his or her employment provided the same will not cause inconvenience to the employer's business. An employee who has been terminated from the services but on notice period can appear in recruitment activities conducted by other agencies/organizations during the working hours without causing major disturbance to the work. A salaried employee can demand a reference certificate from the employer in writing indicating duration of service, type of work performed, salary and reason for termination of employment contract. An employee who has left the services of an employer will be eligible to receive 50 per cent of the normal salary he or she had drawn if he or she is bound by the anti-compete clause and shall not be employed in other organizations nor contact the customers. If the employee obtains other work which will not infringe upon competition, salary earned from that work can be set off from the partial salary payable by the employer. It shall be illegal for employers to advertise that a candidate who is not liable to perform the national service/duty/military service is preferred in the employment.

The Danish Holiday Act, 2004

In accordance with the said legislation, employees are entitled to holiday with pay and allowances. Neither an employee nor an employer is permitted to make deviation from the provisions of this Act and make any waivers. An employee shall be entitled to 2.08 days of paid holiday for each month of employment during a calendar year (25 days per year) and it shall be proportionately calculated if the length of employment is shorter than a year. Intermittent weekends and other public holidays are not counted towards holiday period of an employee. At least 15 days of the holiday shall be given as a consecutive period. The employee must plan and inform the employer about holiday dates as early as possible. The wage during the holiday shall be the ordinary wage and benefits/allowances normally payable and also employee shall receive a holiday supplement of 1 per cent of the wage. Holiday allowance is payable at the start of holiday by an employee. Employees who fall sick are also eligible for the grant of paid holiday to a maximum of four months provided an employee has worked at least a year in an enterprise. If an employee is prevented from taking holiday before the end of the holiday year, the holiday allowance, wages and wage supplement during holiday shall be paid to the employee. Under this statute, the director of the National Directorate of Labour may seek information from an organization with details such as number of employees employed, period of employment, the periods during which a person has taken holiday, the date of termination of employment and wages paid to employees. There shall be an independent institution called Labour Market Holiday Fund under the Ministry of Employment to support benefits implementation of this Act. Any violations of provisions of this Act will attract fines and penalties.

Danish Sickness Benefit Act, 2009

Sickness benefits are paid to the employee for the first 14 days of the employee's absence and are paid by the local authority (municipal administration) subsequent to the 14th day. The employee receives 90 per cent of the salary subject to maximum of DKK 3,016 per week during the sickness. The Act stipulates that an employer must conduct an interview with the employee within four weeks from the first day of reporting sickness and determine when the employee will be able to return to the work. An employee, who is unable to return to work after elapse of eight weeks from the first day of sickness, can request the employer to offer him or her a retention plan. There shall be a fitness certificate to be filled in by employee and employer on the first part and by a qualified physician on the second part in order to certify that the employee can resume work.

Danish Act on Transfer of Undertakings and Protection of Employees, 2002

The objective of the Act is to protect rights of employees in the event of transfer of ownership of an enterprise. The Act stipulates that the terms and conditions of employment, both individual agreements and collective agreements, shall be protected and enterprises failing to protect the terms will result in deemed dismissal of service of employees. Employers are required to consult with employees/employee representatives during planning of transfer of ownership and failing to do so will attract fines. Employer must make clear communication about ramification of undertaking transfer to employees. Employees are generally expected to accept the change of ownership as long as this change does not cause any detriment to their terms and conditions of employment. Even in the case of bankruptcy-led transfer of undertaking, employee rights shall be protected. According to Danish law, it is the fundamental right of an employee to choose the employer. Therefore, an employee who is not ready to accept the new employer is free to terminate the employment contract.

Consolidation Act on Equal Treatment of Men and Women, 2006

According to the Act, there shall be no discrimination on ground of sex in employment opportunities, career matters and related aspects. The Act basically focuses on three principal elements: prohibition of direct discrimination practices, prohibition of indirect discrimination practices and prohibition of sexual harassment. Direct discrimination means absence of equal treatment between two persons of different gender in identical situations and indirect discrimination means applying different policies or processes or implemented them differently for different genders. Harassment shall be understood as taking place when any form of unwanted verbal, non-verbal or physical conduct is exhibited in relation to a person's sex. All employers shall observe the principle of equal treatment of men and women in connection with recruitment, compensation, benefits, transfers and promotions, working conditions and vocational training. Time spent on maternity leave shall be included for the purpose of calculating seniority and a female employee returning from maternity leave is entitled to return to the work/job she was performing prior to the leave. Exception can be made only where the nature of an occupation or work profile seems to fit well for a particular gender. Serious penalties and fines are applicable for deviations and violations.

Collective Redundancies Act, 1994

The objective of the Act is to lay down the framework for termination of employees collectively due to economic necessities of a business. An employer must comply with provisions of this Act when he or she chooses to terminate employment of many people within a period of 30 days. Many employees for the purpose of redundancy in this Act is defined as: terminating 10 employees in an organization which employs more than 20 and less than 100, terminating 10 per cent of employees in an organization that employs at least 100 but less than 300 employees and terminating at least 30 employees in an organization that employs 300 or more persons in an organization. The Act envisages that an employer who is contemplating collective redundancy must consult employees/employee representatives and inform them of the circumstances that have led to the collective redundancy situation. Employer and employee representatives must determine the process of selection of employees for redundancy. The employees so identified must be communicated and provided with applicable notice period and the employer must also inform the relevant Regional Employment Council.

Employment Contracts Act, 2010

The objective of this Act is to mandate a formal employment contract with minimum requirements where employees work at least eight hours a week on an average and likely last for 30 days. This is similar Salaried Employees' (Legal Relationship) (Consolidation) Act as discussed before and many provisions are the same. The Act stipulates that working hours in a week shall not exceed 48 hours and the employee shall be provided with daily rest of 11 hours for every 24 hours period. In addition to holidays earned, employees are entitled to 11 public holidays in a year. Temporary workers are entitled to the same rights and benefits as that of permanent employees.

Hungary's Labour Code

Hungary's Labour Code consisting of five parts has put in place the fundamental regulations for decent work based on fundamental rules of free enterprise and the freedom of employment while factoring the economic and social interests of employers and employees equally. The Labour Code is applicable to employers, employees, employee interest groups, works councils and trade unions in Hungary.

The Code encourages employers and employees to enter into an employment relation formally through an employment contract embodying the terms and conditions that are logical, equitable and fair to both the parties. The basis of employment contract shall be mutual trust and cooperation and they shall not engage in any conduct that amount to breach of rights and legitimate interests of either party. In other words, wrongful exercise of rights that can injure the legitimate interests is prohibited. The employment contracts can be terminated with mutual consent or unilaterally by adhering to the agreed process. In the event of such employment contract termination, both parties must settle all accounts within the agreed time frame. Employment contracts can be amended from the existing status as long as the amendments are mutually agreeable and do not cause disadvantage to employees. Any amendment or modification that is contrary to this principle either directly or indirectly is null and void. Employees should exercise responsibility and good conduct during their employment relationship and take care to not jeopardize the rational economic interests, reputation and image of an organization. Employees are expected to maintain confidentiality of business secretes and shall not disclose any data, events, incidents or share any documents, reports and returns with any unauthorized person who has the potential to cause detrimental consequences to the employer. However, personal rights of all employees are highly protected and they will not be permitted to waive off their rights. An agreement may not be enforceable if either party has wrongly presented any data, facts or circumstances during the course of negotiation and while drafting of agreement or contract. Such agreements if passed through can be contested for rescission, when a party notices the truth.

Employer has the right to subject a person to an aptitude test as part of the selection process and shall not disclose information relating to a candidate for job or of an existing employee except as provided in the regulations of the Code. Employers are not allowed to monitor behaviour of employees beyond the work and the monitoring is to be restricted to the extent of employment relationship. Protecting the human dignity is essential here. Any surveillance techniques if used in an organization to monitor employees shall be well informed and be within the knowledge of employees. The Code stipulates principle of equal treatment pertaining to employment relationships and remuneration. Employees regardless of gender, religion, race and creed shall be treated equally for performing same or similar work. There shall be no discrimination in wages, working conditions, training, promotions, transfers and rewards as long as the work is same or similar in quality, quantity and experience, skills required are same and responsibilities are comparable. Any agreement that infringes upon any employment regulation or that is entered in to by way of circumvention of any employment regulation shall be null and void. If any errors crept into an agreement or an agreement that is entered using coercion by either parties shall be subject to amendment. If either party needs or seeks amendment or alternation to the agreement thus entered into shall opt to file within 30 days of entering into agreement. There shall be a formal employment contract for commencing the employment relationship. The contract must address inter alia issues such as working hours, wages, benefits, role and responsibilities of the job, leave and procedure for grant of leave, notice period for termination of employment contract, location of work, term of validity of employment contract, features of collective bargaining agreement in force and their applicability to the new employee and employee rights and obligations. An employment contract can be modified on need basis with mutual consent. The duration of probationary period shall not exceed three months unless the collective bargaining agreement provide for a longer duration. Even in such a case, this period allowed shall be no longer than six months. An employer is obligated to provide seven days' advance communication to the employee if such employee is identified for being deputed overseas for work. This communication must cover aspects such as the place and country of deputation, duration of deputation, wages and currency, and conditions governing the deputation term. The responsibility for the implementation of occupational safety and occupational health requirements lies with the employers. The employee's fitness for the job for which he or she is being considered shall be examined free of charge before taking up work and on a regular basis during the tenure of the employment relationship. Employees have the right to refuse to do a particular work or task if they have reasonable grounds to believe that carrying out such task or engaging in such work can create health hazard. Employees are obligated to observe all the rules and regulations, not indulge in additional employment or work for pecuniary gains while employed in an organization, foster teamwork and perform to the expectations and be trustworthy by exhibiting expertise and skill at work. Employees can be exempted from work if they are medically temporarily not fit to do the work, when undergoing medical tests/examinations or when attending court proceedings as a witness if summoned by the courts. Employees are entitled to four hours' paid leave to donate blood, one hour twice daily in case of breastfeeding mothers till baby reaches the age of six months and thereafter an hour daily till baby becomes nine months old. Employees are eligible for two days' paid leave in case of death of a close relative. Employees are required to be given exemption when they attend elementary school classes and vocational training programmes as stipulated in collective barging agreements.

The Labour Code also prescribes that in case of transfer of undertaking or transfer of ownership where transfer of employees is automatically involved, the existing employer shall make sure that prospective employer is fully briefed about the employment agreements, obligations and employee eligibilities, entitlements and ensure that terms and conditions of employment shall be protected. If the existing employer has failed to inform or prospective employer has failed to know about it, it will have no bearing whatsoever on the obligation of the new employer about the liabilities. Employees shall be informed at least 15 days before the date of such transfer details about protection of their working conditions, and terms and conditions of employment. Employers have the right to depute employees to the other employer for work as a part of assignment. However, an employee cannot be transferred to another location without the consent of the employee. Likewise, an employee cannot be transferred to another location without the employee's consent from the time that her pregnancy diagnosed till the child reaches three years of age or 16 years in the case of a single parent or if the employee is nursing a close relative who is seriously ill. An employment contract can be terminated with mutual consent. Either party terminating the contract must provide notice pronouncing clearly grounds for termination of the contract. However, no employer is permitted to terminate the employment contract of an employee during pregnancy, maternity leave, a leave of absence taken without pay for caring for a child, any period of actual reserve military service or while the employee is on treatment for human reproduction procedure. An employer is obligated under the Code to substantiate the employment contract termination. However, an employer can call for termination based on performance reasons and behavioural factors. Employers also can terminate employment contracts in the eventuality of liquidation or bankruptcy proceedings levelled against the company. Employers are not required to justify terminating pensioners and fixed duration employment contracts on expiry of their validity period. Generally, the notice period for termination is 30 days and this 30 days' notice period shall be extended by five days after three years of service, 15 days after five years of service, 20 days after 10 years, 30 days after 15 years, 40 days after 18 years of service and 60 days after 20 or more years of service in an organization.

The Labour Code stipulates a well-defined process to deal with collective redundancy. A collective redundancy process is applicable to an organization when an employer wants to terminate at least 10 employees within a period of six months when employing more than 20 employees but fewer than 100 employees or 10 per cent of employees when employing 100 or more but fewer than 300 and termination of 30 employees within a period of six months when employing 300 or more employees in the company. The employer is obligated to carry out consultations with the works councils if the employer is intending to carry out collective redundancy. Works council must be given in writing the entire description of proposed collective redundancies, number of employees to be affected and the criteria, timelines for implementation, reasons and justification by the employer. Works council representatives must hold consultations and discussion with the employer representatives mainly focusing on the possible ways and means to avoid the collective redundancies and the principles and process to govern redundancies and approach to mitigate the difficulties to employees. Once the agreement is concluded between both parties, the collective redundancies shall be affected within 30 days from the date of signing the agreement. Employees who lose their jobs due to agreed collective redundancy plan will be entitled to severance pay at the rate of one month pay in addition to the notice pay if their service with the company is less than three years, two months for service up to five years, three months for the service up to 10 years, four months for service up to 15 years, five months for service up to 20 years and six months for service up to 25 years of employment. However, an employee who is in receipt of pension will not be entitled to any severance pay and employees who are dismissed on grounds of behaviour and ill health will not be eligible for severance pay when they are terminated but not as a part of collective redundancy. The reasons shall be spelt very clearly that though their termination has coincided with collective redundancy, they are not part of the said process. Employer has no obligation to provide advance notice or any notice period for terminating employees who are on probationary period. Employer shall settle all dues including leave wages upon the termination of employment contract promptly providing all accounting details to the employee preferably on the employee's last day of work. Employer is obligated to provide a written assessment of the work and performance of the employee if the employee has worked in the company for a year or more on his or her last day of work enabling the employee to use it as reference cum experience certificate for future endeavours. An employer not only needs to reinstate the employee but also pay full back wages and damages if an employee is proven to be terminated from the service wrongly and contrary to the provisions of the Labour Code. However, the employee, if having terminated fixed employment relationship unlawfully, shall be liable to pay compensation in the sum of absentee pay due for the time remaining from the fixed period up to a maximum of three months' absentee pay.

The working hours for employees in a company as per the Code shall not exceed eight hours in a 24 hours cycle. In case where the collective bargaining agreement permits the working hours to be stretched to a maximum of 12 hours, employers and employees can enter into an agreement to reduce working hours making it part-time or making the working hours flexible. Working hours in a week shall not exceed 48 hours or 72 hours in the case of standby jobs. Time spent relating to on-call duty shall be reckoned for the purpose of normal working hours. As per the Code, public holidays in a year that shall be observed by all organizations are: 1 January, 15 March, Easter Monday, 1 May, 20 August, 23 October, 1 November, and 25 and 26 December. However, organizations in public interest services and by nature of their business will be permitted to work during the said public holidays. Employees shall be given at least 11 hours of uninterrupted rest period after the conclusion of daily work and before the beginning of the next day's work. Employees who have completed at least a year of service in an organization are entitled to vacation time of 20 working days in a calendar year. In addition to this vacation time, employees are entitled to extra vacation time that is calculated based on their age. One working day of extra vacation time for employees over the age of 25 years, two working days over the age of 28, three working days of vacation over the age of 31, four working days for service up to 15 years, five working days over the age of 35, six working days over the age of 37, seven working days over the age of 39, eight working days over the age of 41, nine working days over the age of 43 and 10 working days over the age of 45. Further, in addition to these days, an employee with one child will be entitled to two working days, an employee with two children will be eligible to four working days and an employee with more than two children will be eligible for seven working days. On termination of employment contract, an employee is entitled to vacation leave proportionate to the working period spent in that year. Unless a collective bargaining agreement stipulates otherwise, vacation leave shall be availed to contain at least 14 consecutive days at a time. An employee is also entitled to sick leave of 15 working days in a calendar year whenever the employee is incapacitated to perform the work due to ill health or lack of fitness. Women employees are entitled to 24 weeks of maternity leave. Maternity leave shall also be granted to a woman employee who has been given custody of a child for the purpose of adoption. In the absence of any collective bargaining agreement covering this issue, maternity leave shall be allocated so as to commence four weeks prior to the expected time of birth. Employees are entitled to unpaid leave at the times requested for by them for the purpose of taking care of the child till the child reaches the age of three. In order to avail aforementioned leaves, an employee must apply for sanction of leave normally 15 days in advance. Employers shall maintain records of attendance, leave and overtime. The rate and volume of overtime shall be as agreed upon in the collective bargaining agreement. The amount of overtime, however, shall be limited to a maximum of 300 hours in a given year. Employers are legally bound to pay wages at the minimum not less than minimum wages prescribed as mandatory by the government from time to time. Employers cannot extend performance-based pay or make incorporate it into the salary of an employee unless such employee's employment contract provides for it. If wages are paid on the basis of performance, the performance parameters/factors must be determined at the time of goal-setting by the employee and the manager keeping in view the past performance and calculations covering the potential to perform to meet the goals at a particular level. In the event of any dispute arising out of decision of performance-related pay, employer will have the onus to prove the decision and its rationality. Employees are eligible to receive a minimum pay at mandated levels or 50 per cent of salary eligible in cases where the entire pay is performance based. Employees in addition to their base wages are also eligible for wage supplements. Employees who are asked to work on Sundays will be eligible to 50 per cent of supplement pay equivalent to base wages in addition to the regular salary and employees who are asked to work on national holidays will be eligible for 100 per cent of base pay as supplement wage and employees working in night shifts are eligible for 30 per cent to 50 per cent of supplement wages depending upon the time of the shift. In accordance with collective barging agreement provisions and in pursuance to employment regulations, employees shall be paid 50 per cent of supplement wages for working overtime. Where overtime work is ordered on the scheduled weekly rest day, an employee is entitled to 100 per cent supplement wage in addition to normal salary and this supplement wage can be 50 per cent if employer is willing to provide time off equivalent to overtime duration. Employees are entitled to 20 per cent supplement wage for standby duty and 50 per cent supplement wage for on-call duty. In situations where on-call and standby duty is common, employer can create a salary method comprising base salary and supplement salary payable monthly along with payroll. Shift premium and night shift supplement wage shall be taken into consideration when determining the amount of absentee pay if the employee, for at least 30 per cent of the scheduled working time, is working in shifts. All wages shall be paid in Forint currency and paying through vouchers or other substitute means and instruments is not allowed. Wages shall be paid to employees on or before the 10th of every month taking into account the current one month performance/work and employees shall be given a pay slip explaining the calculation of payout. Employees shall be paid salary on the preceding day if payday happens to be a holiday. In cases where employee salary is exclusively drawn on piece/hourly based rate and is performance driven, such employees shall be paid 50 per cent of salary as advance till such time as the performance output and consequent salary payable is determined. Employers are liable to pay salary along with proportionate interest on the pay if payouts are delayed and the salary to be paid is equivalent to delayed duration. Deductions other than those authorized by the government official notification are not permitted. Deductions which are beneficial to the employer are completely forbidden unless these deductions fall within the purview of authorized list. No employee is permitted to waive off his or her legal right to authorize employer to make deductions which are not permitted. However, employer is allowed to recover or set off if excess salary is paid to any employee erroneously but this can be done after 60 days.

Employers are liable for damages if the employer causes any breach in implementation of any provisions of the Labour Code or/and provisions embodied in any other employment regulations in force. The burden of proof and onus to prove will lie with the employer in the context of any charges of breach of implementation. Employees have no entitlement to relief for actions/behaviours of negligence and suitable action can be initiated against them. However, no liability shall apply with respect to any damage that is considered unforeseeable or that resulted from the employee's wrongful conduct or that was incurred due to the employee's failure to perform his or her obligations to mitigate the damage. In other words, an employee shall be discharged of liability if such employee is able to provide facts that the failure was due to reasons which are not under the control of the employee. Liability that will be determined will be proportionate to the culpability of an employee for the failure. In circumstances where there is no definite proof to prove or otherwise, employee is allowable for partial culpability. In some cases when employers can insist and collective agreement provides for, an employee will be required to provide bank guarantee for joining and performing certain roles where cash handling or inventory handling is involved. Collective agreements are not applicable to executive employees. An executive employee is one who is defined as an employee who is employer's director or deputy director or employees working under them directly supervising work of other employees. Executive employees are expected to work under flexible working conditions and they are liable for damages caused by their negligence. Executive employees are discouraged from entering into any employment relationships in addition to the one with the existing company and they are also forbidden to acquire shares in a business association which is engaged in the same or similar activities or that maintains regular economic ties with their employer. An executive shall not conduct business transactions which are falling within the ambit of the current organization's trade either in his or her own name or in the name of his or her family and is required to report if any of his or her relatives are engaging in a business that is in the same area/field of business of his or her current employer.

The Labour Code also stipulates certain regulations relating to temporary work, functioning of temporary agency organizations and working conditions of temporary employees and organizations that are intended to utilize temporary employees. Temporary work agency is defined as an employer who places employees with whom the agency has employment relationship and through a formal employment contract in another organization for temporary work to be supervised by the temporarily hired organization. Duration of temporary assignment of an employee in a borrowed organization shall not exceed five years. A temporary work agency ought to have been registered with Hungarian government. Engaging in employment and assignment of temporary workers without being registered is illegal. An organization that is planning to use services of temporary agency must enter into a formal agreement specifying conditions of engagement. The organization hiring services of a temporary agency must inform works council about the arrangement and no organization is allowed to sublet the services of temporary employees it hired from a temporary agency. Any agreement of contract reached between an organization and temporary agency will be invalid if it envisages that employees need to pay any fee to temporary agency for the services rendered and if it includes a provision in the contract banning provision of employment by an organization to a person whose contract with temporary agency is ended. Organizations are obliged to provide notification to all temporary employees about vacancies in the company from time to time maintaining frequency of at least once in six months. Temporary work agency must incur all the expenses related to travel and medical examination expenses of a person who is being offered a job. Organization availing temporary agency services must inform the government about details such as working hours, work location, assignment details, goals and non-wage benefits that will be extended to a temporary employee. Basic working conditions of temporary employees in relation to protection of pregnant women and nursing mothers and protection of young workers shall be on par with legal stipulations, and treatment accorded to these employees must be equal to that of regular employees in respect of dignity and protection. Employer rights in this context include expecting temporary agency to adhere to all labour and employment, and tax-related regulations while conducting its business and clamping damages on the agency and its employees if there is loss to the organization wilfully and out of negligence in any manner.

The Labour Code also specifies provision relating to non-compete clause. An employee who has left an organization shall not engage for up to two years in any conduct that can jeopardize the interest of his or her previous employer in any manner. In order for employee to honour this condition, an employer must take measures to protect interest of employees by providing adequate compensation for livelihood for this two years period. The amount of compensation in such situations will depend upon the impediment such a restriction can create on the employee and in any case the compensation offered should not be less than one-third of the salary being drawn by the employee. The Code also prescribes the regulations in order to protect interests and ensure rights of employees, employers and employee associations and works councils with an aim to attain harmonious relations, and peace and equity. Trade unions, works councils and the employer must identify their representatives for negotiations and discussions to sort out issues and enter into collective bargaining agreements. Employees can be represented by the shop steward, works council, central works council or the corporate level works council. Representatives of works councils shall be elected by employees, and employer will nominate representatives on its behalf. The ratio of representation on works councils from employees and employer shall be equal. The elected works council will be operational for a period of five years. Such identified representatives and their details must be shared amongst themselves. Employers are encouraged to share all information with employee representatives in order to achieve clear understanding of business and economics. Expenses incurred for conduct of elections to elect representatives for works council shall be borne by the employer. However, employers are not required to share information or data that can potentially cause harm to the business interests of an organization. The Code exhorts that all parties must respect each other's pace and rights. The size of works council will depend upon the employee strength in an organization. There shall be three-member works council if total number of employees working in an organization is less than 100, five members if the strength is less than 300, seven members for less than 500 employees organization, nine if this number is less than 1,000, eleven for less than 2,000 and thirteen member works council if total number of employees working in an organization exceeds 2,000. Employees nominated as works council members shall have the legal capacity and shall have been employed by the employer in the said organization for a period of at least six months. Members of the works council are elected by secret ballot and each member nomination must be espoused by 10 per cent of employees or 50 employees who are eligible to vote. A central works council can be elected by a group of works councils where multiple works councils exist in an organization. In the event of merger of organizations, a new works council shall be elected within three months. All works council meetings must be held in person as much as possible. Works councils must be unbiased. They are free to support or obstruct a strike call. However, if a works council supports a strike, its mandate in other issues including cause of strike shall be distanced from its functioning. Employer and works council together can set up a conciliation committee to resolve the disputes, and decision of such committee shall be binding on all the parties provided employer and works council and trade unions agree to this condition while constituting the committee.

The Labour Code, the Republic of Poland (Kodeks Pracy)

The Labour Code of Poland consisting of 15 sections was first introduced in 1974 laying down the regulations related to labour relations, employment contracts, wages and benefits, equal employment opportunities, working hours and conditions, leaves, health and safety provisions and collective labour agreements. The key purpose of the Labour Code is to define rights and duties of employees and employers in Poland. The following paragraphs present the Labour Code briefly.

Section 1: General Provisions

This section proclaims that no person or party is allowed to exercise any right that would defeat the social objectives of mutual existence. The Labour Code is applicable to all employees and employers in Poland, though there can be special provisions only relevant to few sections of employees based on their nature of work. The state promulgates the minimum wages payable from time to time and all persons have the full freedom to choose their work. Employment discrimination based on age, race, gender, religion, nationality and trade union membership is completely prohibited under the Code. Employees are provided with rights concerning remuneration, rest periods, health and safe working conditions, welfare and cultural needs, and training and development opportunities and trade union membership. Employers are obliged to provide conditions that would encourage employees to exercise such rights freely and without fear. Employees also have the right to claim equal remuneration for same work. The state labour inspectorate is the competent authority to ensure enforcement of the Labour Code and supervise its implementation in organizations.

Section 2: Employment Relationship

This section defines the employment relationship. An employer may solicit information including name, surname and parent's name, date of birth, education and employment history in order to provide an employment opportunity. An employment contract can be entered into for a definite or indefinite period of time based on the need. An employment contract must specify details of parties to the contract (employee and employer), nature of work, remuneration, place of work, working hours and such employment contract shall be in writing. An employment contract can be terminated:

- By mutual agreement of the employee and the employer
- On expiry of the employment contract period
- By either party serving the notice period of resignation as per the employment contract
- On liquidation or bankruptcy of a firm

An employer must consult trade union organization before terminating an employment contract and shall take opinion into account. An employee aggrieved with the termination can appeal in the Labour Court. Employer can terminate an employment contract of an employee if such an employee is found to have violated the basic duties or committed a crime for which the sentence is passed or lost a valid license to perform a job. If the employee-initiated termination of employment contract is not justified, an employer can claim compensation for the same. An employer can also establish work practices such as telecommuting and the same can be regulated as per the Labour Code provisions provided in Section 2. An employment contract on the basis of cooperative employment conditions will be governed by the legislation of cooperatives.

Under this section, the Code also provides for transfer of services of an employee to another undertaking as a result of merger/demerger/acquisition/takeover without causing adversely impacting the employment status and conditions of an employee.

Section 3: Salary and Benefits

Collective bargaining agreements usually govern the remuneration and benefits of employees but in the rare event that a collective bargaining agreement does not exist, the employer shall determine the rules regarding the same and publish. All such collective bargaining agreements are drawn in discussion and agreement with trade unions. Remuneration typically consists of basic remuneration, additional remuneration not to exceed 20 per cent on account of qualifications, specific performance category, and seniority and other work-related benefits. Remuneration levels and benefits shall be arrived at keeping in view work profiles and specific work performance-related requirements and in consultation with trade unions. Also, employers can prescribe work standards drawn in a collective manner to measure effectiveness of employees' performance. All employees have the right to know the basis on which remuneration is calculated and arrived at. Employees are eligible to receive remuneration for up to 33 days in a calendar year when affected by a contagious illness and also for the duration of recovery when met with a work-related accident. Employee's dependent family members are entitled to receive bereavement payments in case of employee's death and the bereavement payment amount depends on the length of service of an employee.

Section 4: Duties of Employer and Employee

Under the Labour Code, employers shall:

- educate employees about their duties and rights.
- create working conditions which are conducive and stress free for good performance.

- implement discrimination-free work practices.
- ensure safe and healthy working conditions.
- disburse remuneration timely, correctly and equitably.
- provide vocation development opportunities through training and development.
- implement objective performance assessment practices.
- keep all employee-related records.
- act against workplace bullying.
- issue work certificate in case of employment relationship expiry/termination. The employee is entitled for work certificate within seven days.

Duties of an employee include:

- complying with organizational rules set as per the Labour Code and collective bargaining agreements.
- complying with working hours and norms.
- observing all safety and health norms.
- complying with rules relating to confidentiality.
- showing diligence to company assets and tools.
- observing all non-compete rules as signed up.

Employees are also entitled to training leave of a minimum of six days and a maximum of 21 days to appear for external examinations and certification programmes. Employer may grant special benefits encouraging employees to acquire additional qualifications and skills. Employers can design and implement schemes that reward employees who show exemplary performance in their work. Employers can also initiate punitive action if employees fail to adhere to safety norms or to comply with established processes or if employees exhibit a pattern of unauthorized absenteeism.

Section 5: Employee Liabilities

An employee is financially liable if he or she is found to have caused damage to the employer's property, tools and machinery wilfully. Such liability can be equal to the proportion of the damage cost subject to the maximum of three months' salary. However, burden of proving an employee's fault lies with the employer.

Section 6: Working Hours

Working hours must not exceed 8 hours in a 24 hours cycle and 40 hours in a 5 days working week. Any public holiday falling within a 5 days workweek will fall within the definition of working day, and although it is a holiday, it will be calculated as a work day for remuneration purpose. Weekly working hours inclusive of overtime must not exceed 48 hours. However, such a regulation is not applicable to supervisory and managerial job holders. Employees are entitled to uninterrupted weekly rest of 35 hours. There can be breaks for a maximum of 60 minutes for lunch or to attend to personal matters in exclusive of the 8 hours work schedule. Basis request of employees and if agreed to by the employer, an employee can opt for a short week by working 12 hours a day. Based on organization and work need, employer can also introduce shift system of work. Overtime shall not exceed 150 hours in a calendar year. Employees are entitled to 100 per cent bonus over and above normal remuneration for overtime work carried out during night shift, Sundays and public holidays and at the rate of 50 per cent on other days. Employee can also ask for time off equivalent to 1.5 times overtime in case they prefer this over payouts. Night shift is defined as work carried out during 9 PM to 7 AM and employees who work in night shifts are entitled to 20 per cent more pay over their normal remuneration.

Section 7: Leave Provisions

Employees who complete one year of service or more and less than 10 years are entitled to 20 days of leave in a calendar year. If the employee has been working in the firm for more than 10 years, he or she is entitled to 26 days of leave. For the purpose of calculation of length of service for leave eligibility, the years spent in acquiring educational qualification from basic vocational courses onwards will be taken into account. An employee is eligible to avail the leaves as and when required by following necessary protocol. At the time of employment termination, all unused leave will be converted into cash payout to the employee. Employees are eligible for remuneration including average variable pay during the leave period.

Section 8: Employee Entitlement for Parenthood Benefits

Women shall not be employed to perform certain types of work that are not conducive to their health and such work profiles are notified by the government. No woman employee can be terminated during pregnancy or while on maternity leave. Also, no woman employee who is pregnant or with a child up to the age of 4 years can be employed in night shift or expected to do overtime work. A female employee is entitled to maternity leave of 20 weeks for giving birth to one child, 31 weeks in the case of twins and 33 weeks in the case of giving birth to three children, 35 weeks for four children and 37 weeks for five children. The same number of leaves can be granted to an employee who has adopted children. Also, an employee is entitled to an additional 8 weeks of maternity leave in certain circumstances which can be granted. A male employee is eligible for 2 weeks of paternity leave to raise a child. A female employee who is nursing a child has the right to two half-hour breaks which shall be counted as working hours.

Section 9: Employment of Young People

A young person under the Poland Labour Code is defined as someone who has completed 16 years of age but is not yet 18. Young persons who are not yet 16 cannot be employed. Employment of a young person is permitted only when such a person has completed at least basic secondary school. However, a young person can be admitted for apprenticeship for the purpose of vocational training. Young persons can be employed only in such jobs that would not endanger their health and on being medically cleared to carry such a job. Employers shall maintain a separate register with details of such young persons employed. Working hours of a young person shall not exceed 8 hours in a 24 hours cycle. Also, young persons shall not be asked to do overtime work and can be employed in night shifts only in exceptional circumstances. A young person who is employed is eligible for 12 days leave for every 6 months of work. Government will notify which jobs a young person can be employed in.

Section 10: Health and Safety

The employer shall take all measures to ensure safe and healthy working conditions for employees. Employer, under the Labour Code, is obligated to organize work free from unsafe and unhealthy conditions, adhere to principles of health and safety, provide training to employees on safety, monitor and act against all occupational hazards, ensure facility of first aid, put in place all preventive measures and implement all governmental orders related to work safety and health. Employees have the right to refuse to work or perform a task if they see any work-related danger. Such an act of refusal shall not cause any disadvantage to the employee or result in any negative consequences. No machinery, equipment, raw materials and so on can be used without understanding their implications to work safety by an employer.

Employers shall maintain a record of all accidents and as and when any accident occurs, the same shall be notified to the government authorities with explanation of what action is being taken up to avoid reoccurrence of such accidents. If an employee is diagnosed with an occupational disease, the employer shall notify the same to the local sanitary inspector and take steps to eliminate such risks and organize all medical assistance to the affected employee. Employer shall hold training programmes on safety and health for the benefit of employees at regular intervals. Employees should confirm that they are familiar with safety norms before they undertake any duties. Organizations employing 100 or more employees must ensure that a safety service desk managed by an employee is in place specifically for this assignment. Organizations who employ 250 or more employees must appoint a health and safety work commission to advise on safety matters. The commission shall regularly verify, inspect and validate safety measures and organize safety and health sessions for employees.

Section 11: Collective Labour Bargaining Agreements

Collective agreements are concluded and drawn through negotiations between employers and trade unions. Such agreements are binding on both parties. Employers are obligated to present the economic situation of the company to trade unions for fair negotiations, and unions are bound by secrecy to not disclose such data. Both parties can seek help of experts during negotiations and all collective agreements shall be in writing for a definite or indefinite period. A collective agreement can be drawn covering areas such as employment contracts, remuneration, benefits, performance appraisals, training and development, leave and holidays, health and safety, work performance norms and responsibilities of employers and employees in mutual coexistence. Collective agreements can be cancelled/terminated with mutual consent or upon expiry of the validity period. Similarly, amendments to collective agreement can be effected with mutual consent. All collective agreements shall be registered with relevant government authorities. The registering authority can refuse to register a collective agreement if the same is not drawn as per the employment regulations and the Labour Code. Both employers and trade union representatives have the obligation to communicate to all employees about the contents and implications of the collective agreement. Obligations of collective agreement will be moved to the new employer in a merger or acquisition scenario. If both employer and trade union representatives decide to suspend the implementation of a collective agreement due to financial situation of an organization, the same is allowed.

Section 12: Redress of Disputes

An employee, who is dissatisfied or aggrieved with non-implementation of employment contract or settlement of any claims, can approach conciliation commission for resolving the dispute. If conciliation efforts fail to yield results, the employee can approach the court. The conciliation commission is appointed jointly through nominations by an employer and trade unions. Employer shall provide all infrastructure and logistical support to such commission's functioning. Said commission shall endeavour to settle the disputes within 14 days from the date of dispute application by an employee. No settlement that contravenes the law and the Labour Code is valid. If the commission fails to conclude proceedings with a settlement within 14 days, the same shall be referred to the Labour Court. The settlement reached in conciliation commission or in the Labour Court shall be implemented by the employer without fail. If employer fails to adhere to the settlement, the same shall be enforceable as per the Code of civil proceedings. In case an employee feels that a settlement violates his or her rights or is against his or her basic interest, the settlement can be challenged in the court.

Section 13: Penalties

An employer is liable to be penalized at a minimum of 1,000 zlotys to a maximum of 30,000 zlotys if the employer fails to maintain personal files and documents of employment matters, is in violation of the Labour Code's provisions, terminates an employment contract unilaterally without notice and without just and fair reason, fails to issue a formalized employment contract in writing, fails to issue a reference certificate, fails to observe safety and health norms, fails to disburse remuneration on time or fails to implement court decree.

Section 14: Limitation of Claims

Claims arising out of an employment relationship are barred by a limitation of three years from the date on which the claim becomes enforceable. This time limit cannot be reduced or extended. However, an employee or employer can pursue the claim even after expiry of the said three years provided the other party agrees to the same.

Section 15: Miscellaneous Provisions

The Ministry of Labour and Social Policy will issue notifications, both binding and advisory, from time to time, on employment matters to be observed by employers, employees, trade unions and to be enforced by the labour inspectorate, conciliation commissions and the labour courts. Wherever labour and employment matters are not covered by the Labour Code and labour law, the same shall be regulated by the civil code.

The Czech Labour Code

The Czech Labour Code is a sort of composite law that stipulates conditions regulating labour contracts, collective bargaining process and agreements, labour dispute resolution, working conditions and social security provisions and so on. The Labour Code comprises 14 parts and 396 sections dealing with various aspects of employment matters as discussed next.

Part 1: General Provisions

Part 1 comprises of five chapters dealing with scope of the Labour Code, definitions of employee, employer, fundamental principles of labour relations, equal treatment, prohibition of discrimination and consequences on breach of these provisions. The chapter mandates that employment of persons up to the age of 15 years or older until conclusion of their compulsory school attendance is prohibited. This Labour Code is applicable to all public and private institutions. Definition of employee, employer and management staff is provided in Chapter 2. Fundamental principles of labour relations are dealt with in Chapter 3 which primarily stipulates that the employer must ensure equal treatment for all employees and comply with the principles of equal pay for equal work, must educate each and every employee about labour relations and contents of labour contract. Employers shall also take all measures to create labour relations in compliance with the Labour Code. Trade union organizations are entitled to take part in labour relations and in collective bargaining process. As per Chapter 4, employers shall ensure equal treatment of all employees with regard to working conditions, vocational training, career advancement and remuneration for the same work; any form of discrimination is strictly prohibited. However, where differential treatment is necessitated due to nature of work and related work conditions, the same can be allowed without prejudice. Chapter 5 prohibits any act by any employee giving up the legal rights. Trade unions are authorized to conclude collective bargaining agreements on behalf of employees regulating wages, working conditions and other benefits as well as duties of employees. Collective agreements are binding on both employees and the employer.

Part 2: Employment Relationship

This part encompassing four chapters stipulates provisions related to formation of an employment relationship, employment contract, alterations of an employment relationship and termination of an employment relationship. Employer can define the skills and competencies required for a job in order to hire persons and can make possessing such skills a prerequisite to quality to be interviewed/selected for the job. Employer can set up necessary selection process, seek data of candidate-related job skills and brief the candidate of the terms and conditions of employment contract and subject the candidate to undergo an entry level medical check-up before the conclusion of employment contract. Employment contract reached between an employee and employer shall form the core basis for employment relationship. An employment contract under the Labour Code must include nomenclature of the job, job description, place of work and the employment contract shall be in the written form. The Code also allows for a person to be put on trial for a period not exceeding three consecutive months before a definite employment contract is arrived at. The trail period shall be agreed to in writing failing which such an arrangement will be considered void. An employment offer/contract made is valid for seven days. An employment contract typically shall carry:

- the employee's full name,
- nature of duties and role,
- place of work,
- working hours and schedule,
- remuneration details,
- method of salary payment,
- details of collective bargaining agreements with particulars such as working conditions and
- employer name.

Employer has the fundamental responsibility to sufficiently explain to the employees about their rights and duties arising from the employment relationship. Employee must also make efforts to acquaint self with various statutory provisions and rules concerning occupational safety and health, and aspects of collective barging agreements and regulations. Employer shall, within agreed time frame, notify the trade union about new employment relationships. Employment contracts can be arrived at for a defined fixed period or be open-ended. An employment contract can be altered with mutual consent of employee and employer at any time during the operation of an existing employment contract. An employee can be transferred to perform alternative work from that of stated work in employment contract in situations that warrant the change, such as health-related reasons as proven by medical documents, enabling a woman employee for breastfeeding, transfer in the interest of an employee and due to government/judiciary orders and if the employee is unable to perform the job assigned in a consistent manner. An employee can also be transferred to another place based on business requirements and with the employee's consent.

An employment relationship can be terminated through:

- **Mutual consent/agreement:** An employment relationship can be terminated by mutual consent drawing an agreement in writing. If the agreement is not in writing, the same shall be void.
- **Notice of termination:** An employee can offer resignation with or without stating reason by giving a notice of at least two months. An employer can terminate an employment relationship; an act referred to as 'dismissal' and shall categorically state a reason for such dismissal failing which it shall be void. Employer can cause termination of an employment contract only in specific conditions such as: if the employer's firm is closed, relocated, restructured or if the employee does not meet the prescribed statutory conditions to perform the job or if a person is unfit to carry out the job for health reasons or if the employee is found to have seriously breached statutory provisions relating to performance of the job. However, no employee shall be terminated during protection period. Protection period definition is inclusive of an employee who is called for military exercise, or to perform a public office, during pregnancy of a female employee and an employee who is found unfit for night shift work medically. However, an employee can be terminated immediately if the employee is sentenced for a criminal offense/if an employee has breached the duty relating to work performance. Employer is also obligated to notify the trade union within a defined time period of all such terminations and in some cases the employer shall discuss with and obtain the consent of the trade union before such

terminations are effected. All fixed-term employment contracts shall be terminated on expiry, failing which, especially in circumstances where the employee continues the work even after expiry of the fixed term, the same shall be construed as employment contract entered into a phase of an indefinite period.

- **Collective dismissals:** Collective dismissal is defined as a situation in which terminations numbering 10 employees or 10 per cent of the total HR of an organization takes place within a period of 30 days and with reasons as specified in the Labour Code. An employer shall inform the trade union in writing before any collective dismissal is effected providing details such as reasons for collective dismissal, the number of employees being impacted, the period within which these dismissals will happen, criteria proposed and redundancy payment. An employer shall hold consultation with trade union leaders to reach an agreement with regard to measures to be taken to avert collective dismissal. Also, employers must inform the competency labour office of all the particulars related to the collective dismissal.
- **Severance pay:** Depending on the reason given for termination and subsequent agreement, an employee is entitled to receive a severance pay of a minimum of three months to 12 months of his or her average monthly earning. This severance pay shall become payable the very next day of termination of employment.

Part 3: Agreement on Work Performed Outside an Employment Relationship

This part provides scope and opportunity for employers to employ any person outside the conventional and formal employment relationship and for a duration not exceeding 150 hours of work in a calendar year. Such a work activity outside an employment relationship if reached shall be formalized through a written agreement which can be terminated with 15 days' notice.

Part 4: Working Hours and Rest Periods

This part consisting of nine chapters is provided to stipulate regulations related to length of working hours, part-time work, schedule of working hours including flexibility, standby, safety provisions and rest periods and rest days, overtime work and night work.

The length of normal weekly working hours shall not exceed 40 hours per week and in case of employees who work in shifts or construction or mining industry shall not exceed 37.5 hours per week. These working hours are scheduled over five days a week and the working hours shall not exceed 9 hours of work per day in normal course. Employers can also choose flexible working hours involving when to start and end the work in a day. There can be multiple flexible working schedules (flexitime) and an employee can choose a particular schedule. An employee is entitled to have a work break for food and rest lasting not less than 30 minutes. These breaks will not be counted as part of working hours. Where employees are required to work in shifts, the employees shall not be asked to resume the work before 12 hours from the last work schedule have lapsed. The employer shall schedule working hours in such a way that the employee has one continuous rest period of 35 hours per week in a consecutive seven days' stretch.

Overtime can be availed only in exceptional circumstances. However, overtime work shall not exceed 8 hours of work in a week and 150 hours within one calendar year. No night shift work shall exceed 8 hours in a 24 hours' cycle and employees who work night shifts must be provided with the facility of medical examination at regular intervals to check occupational health hazards. Also, an employee shall be medically examined and can be given night shift work only when found to be fit. Employer, under the Labour Code, is obligated to keep and maintain records related to working hours, overtime work, night work and any standby work hours if applicable. Employers are also required to consult trade unions in deciding matters related to work hours, overtime, night work, safety, health and so on.

Part 5: Occupational Safety and Health Protection

This part prescribes standards to be maintained for protecting and ensuring safety and health of employees and for managing occupational health hazards and averting the risk. The costs of ensuring occupational safety and health shall be borne by the employer. The duties of employer include:

- proactively seeking out risky factors, identifying causes and sources of risk,
- putting measures in place to test employers on a regular basis in order to protect them, if risks cannot be averted,
- planning of risk prevention measures,
- taking all measures to not allow employees to carry out prohibited type of work,
- ensuring first-aid facility,
- providing employees with all safety gear and facilities and
- keeping a record of all injuries/health hazards/deaths.

Employees are entitled and have the right to a safe workplace and to participate in the creation of a hazard-free work environment. Also, employees shall make efforts and take care of their own safety and health, and participate in safety training offered. Employee shall not consume alcohol and shall inform superiors if they find anything at the workplace that can cause safety issues. Trade unions and their representatives must be encouraged to participate and offer comments related to safe workplace.

Part 6: Remuneration for Work and Standby, Income from Labour Relationship and Deductions

All employees are entitled to receive wages and such wages shall be equal for similar work regardless of gender. No employer can pay less than minimum wage regardless of nature of work and the wage levels can be fixed based on complexity of work, job profile and skills involved. Employees are also entitled to overtime work at the rate of 25 per cent more than normal wages and 20 per cent more for night shift work. There are 16 salary grades and 12 salary steps in each salary grade. Every employee shall be placed into and paid according to the salary grade and step, failing which the specifications of the Labour Code will need to be followed. These salary grades are drawn based on different types of work and the skills involved. These salary grades and steps are promulgated by the government through a decree. Government prescribes provisions governing how employees can be placed in these salary grades, how salary funds can be utilized and how retirement funds can be managed. All managerial employees are eligible for a premium salary over and above the salary grade of 5 per cent at minimum and 60 per cent at maximum. There are four management grades or stages defined for this purpose. Further, based on performance, an employee can be accorded a personal premium salary up to 100 per cent over and above the prescribed grade as performance bonus. All the salary data shall be accessible by the government. An employee's salary is subject to deductions such as personal income tax, social security insurance, general health insurance contribution, trade union membership contribution and salary advance as authorized by an employee.

Part 7: Reimbursement of Expenses to Employees in Connection with Their Work Performance

All employees are entitled to reimbursement of travel fare, accommodation, incidental and meal expenses for journeys undertaken in connection with business/work and employees shall also be reimbursed for visiting a family member if such a journey is in excess of seven days. This part of the Labour Code exhaustively describes the provisions related to how much per diem is permitted in domestic and foreign travel and limits for accommodation and incidental expenses. This part also focuses on eligibilities and obligations of employers in case of transfer of workplace and reimbursements related to such a situation.

Part 8: Obstacles to Work

This part prescribes the provisions related to maternity/paternity contexts. It also deals with provisions for when an employee is temporarily unfit to perform the job and describes how such cases shall be handled. A woman employee is entitled to 28 weeks of maternity leave and in case of twins or more children, she will be entitled to 37 weeks of leave. A female employee is expected to commence the maternity leave six weeks before the expected childbirth. An employer is obligated to excuse absence of an employee when such an employee is called for military duty. Employees are also eligible for salary during participation in training programmes. Employees are entitled to receive salary at the rate of 80 per cent when work is stopped due to technical snags or problems of supply of raw material.

Part 9: Leave with Pay

Every employee is eligible for annual leave of four weeks in a calendar year at the minimum. Employers are expected to formulate leave policy in accordance with the Code elaborating the process of applying leave and are expected to sanction and manage overall administration of the leave system. Employers need to consult trade unions in case of collective leave sanctions.

Part 10: Care of Employees

This part focuses on working conditions, vocational development and special working conditions. The provisions lay restrictions associated with pregnant employees who may not be allowed to work in areas where working conditions are not conducive. Female employees are also entitled to additional breaks during breastfeeding stage. This part of the Labour Code also prescribes that all employees shall be provided training and educational opportunities to upgrade their skills and regulations related to employing adolescents.

Part 11: Compensation for Damage

Employer shall exercise all cautions and take all steps to secure safe and hazard-free environment for employees and ensure there are no possibilities for causing damage to the organizational assets. An employee is obligated to ensure work does not cause any damage to the property and if an employee finds that certain working conditions cannot ensure safety, the same shall be communicated to the employer. If any damage occurs due to negligence and poor performance of an employee causing loss to the employer, liability can be levelled against the employee appropriately. An employee is liable for loss of tools and personal protective equipment. There can be agreement between employee and employer about the type of liabilities. The damage can be calculated at the rate of cost of such loss of equipment or 4.5 times an employee's average monthly wages. Employers are liable to pay losses if damages of assets have happened as a result of inadequate or unsafe work arrangements by the employer. Where an employee has to put in extra efforts to avert the danger due to lack of proper measures, an employer is liable to pay damage to an employee.

Part 12: Information and Consultation Procedure

All employees have the right to information and consultation related to all labour relationship matters individually and collectively. Trade union representatives are also obligated to carry out their responsibilities in an equitable manner not causing any discrimination or injury to the rights of any employee. They shall also communicate to employees in a logical manner about the outcome of their activities and efforts. Where there is no trade union, employer may create a sort of work council providing sufficient opportunity to represent employees and may participate in all matters related to labour contracts and working conditions. Trade union organizations shall be consulted on all matters related to employment such as wages, benefits, social security, safety and health, training, appraisals and also issues concerning economic situation of the organization and any organizational restructuring. This part also exhaustively deals with European Works Council, constitution, nominations, and elections and representation.

Part 13: Miscellaneous Provisions

An employer can set workload norms based on consultation with trade unions and after taking into account capabilities of employees and by complying with statutory norms. Employees are bound to perform as per their capabilities, must avail fruitfully all working hours and shall discharge their duties in a diligent and productive manner. An employee can engage in gainful activity outside the employed organization only with the prior consent of employer. Managerial employees are obligated to create proper working conditions for employees, to guide and mentor them and ensure they are properly rewarded. Employees are also bound by non-competition agreements and related clauses. Employer shall maintain personal files of employees and, on the termination of employment, shall issue a verification certificate with details such as period of employment, details of work done, qualifications and wages. Where an employee requests for reference, an employer is bound to provide the same within 15 days of such request. Employee who is not in agreement with his or her reference certificate provided by the employer can approach competency court for redressal.

Trade union organizations shall ensure that the Labour Code is compiled by them and the employer, and any deviation shall be brought to the notice of competent government for initiating necessary corrective action. The Code also recognizes that any document delivered using the Internet or Intranet, or any other electronic means is deemed to have been served. Wherever there is transfer of ownership or merger, or demerger, the rights and liabilities will be transferred to the new employer without adversely impacting employee rights and benefits.

Part 14: Transitory Provisions

This part deals with certain provisions related to employer's liability for damage, scope of liability, compensation for loss of earnings during incapacity for work, compensation for lesser employability, compensation on an employee's death and compensation in case of medical treatment and funeral, and compensation for the survivor's maintenance and so on.

Summary

Labour codes, principal laws and regulations of European nations: Germany, France, the Netherlands, the Czech Republic, Poland, Hungary, Sweden, Switzerland, Denmark and Finland and also labour laws of the United Kingdom were discussed in this chapter along with salient provisions. EU directives on employment and labour were also illustrated together with their explanation. European labour laws can be classified into three categories: the first category is a set of laws and regulations made to promote bi-patriate forums like works councils in order to ensure collectivism, sustainability and harmony. The second set of laws are related working conditions and living standards focusing on protection of employment, wages, benefits, working hours, overtime, occupational and general health, social security, employment standards and safety, and third set of laws are related to anti-discrimination, privacy of data and diversity promotion. Laws and regulations were presented in a manner that practitioners and students can grasp with ease and in a practical context.

QUESTIONS FOR DISCUSSION

1. Discuss the role of European directives on employment and labour in shaping labour legislation in member nations.
2. Compare and contrast the labour codes of the Czech Republic, Poland and France.
3. What are the differences between labour laws of the United States and Germany?
4. Discuss key features of TUPE legislation in the United Kingdom.
5. Write on pros and cons of co-determination legislation in Germany from both employer's and employees' points of view.

6. Discuss role of works councils in determining working conditions of employees in European nations. What is the role of trade unions versus works councils?
7. Discuss data protection legislation and how it helps in employee data management.
8. Write on guiding principles of European labour laws.
9. What are key differences in health and safety legislation among EU nations?

CASE STUDIES

Case Study 1

Mazvode Sale and EU Directives

Mazvode is a telecom company with operations across Europe which is being sold to Banana as asset sale. Mazvode employs nearly 18,000 employees across 12 nations. The sale agreement stipulates that all employees shall be absorbed by the new entity and where required can negotiate new employment contracts involving representatives of works council. Though the works council has given its consent for the sale, it said the same is conditional subject to mutual agreement on transfer of employee services to the prospective employer (acquirer). The right to refusal shall be provided to employees to accept or not to accept the new employment contracts without any prejudice or liabilities and in case employees are not ready for employment with the acquirer whatever may be the reason, separation agreements shall be drawn in consonance with labour laws. The new employment contracts need to adhere to the provisions of TUPE legislation of respective countries such as Germany, France, the United Kingdom, Sweden and Switzerland, and as per directives of EU on the matter. Discuss what kind of employment contracts need to be created in order to be complaint with respective directives and regulations of EU on TUPE. In case employees refuse to accept the employment contracts, what shall be the nature of severance contract that can be offered?

Case Study 2

Resignation During Transfer of Undertaking

Kate Harrison was working as an accountant in London-based Mercantile Bank of the United Kingdom for the last seven years. She had been a permanent employee and her performance was rated as 'met expectations'. Mercantile Bank had been taken over by another UK Bank called Bank of Wales, along with all assets and liabilities, including all employees on an 'as is where is basis'. However, Bank of Wales on review of all positions and employees in both the banks contemplated to offer alternative positions to some of its employees in order to avert the situation of redundancy due to duplication of roles and work. Kate declined to accept an alternative role offered to her, which was from the accountancy to the audit department. She declined this citing no prior experience in the audit function will eventually pull her performance levels down due, which she did not want to happen. Subsequently the bank offered her to move in the same role to a different location about 80 km from her current location of work. Kate rejected this offer citing personal reasons for her inability to move. The bank has politely informed her that she could continue to work at her current location but she might not have full-fledged work for some time as her current responsibilities were merged with existing accountants of Bank of Wales. Kate, expressing unhappiness at the unfolding of these events, resigned from service. Later, she went on to approach the court seeking an order to convert her resignation from service as constructive dismissal by the employer under the TUPE. Her argument was that she was entirely dependent upon this employment for her livelihood and she would have never resigned but for the circumstances created by the Bank, materially changing the profile of her job, while the offers of alternative opportunities were lame rather than a sincere attempt. The Bank defended its position stating that it never wanted Kate to leave the services of the Bank and in fact wanted her to continue in her existing role, although it would not continue to carry the same responsibilities as handled by her in the past. It also added that perhaps the Bank could have restored her responsibilities in due course as integration efforts between both the banks were still in progress. Discuss whether Kate's resignation from the Bank can be construed as constructive dismissal under the provisions of the TUPE; or is it merely her voluntary resignation in the light of the law, especially when bank has not affected her transfer physically.

Case Study 3

Employment Reference in the Eyes of Law, UK

Alison Frederick was employed with Sun Telecommunications as a service technician. In accordance with the employment contract that was signed between Alison and Sun, the previous employer is obligated to provide employment reference to the prospective employer on request of an existing or former employee. Alison had resigned from the job and was released from the services subsequently. A year after leaving the job in Sun, Alison had sought a reference letter to be addressed to her prospective employer which Sun Telecommunications provided diligently and promptly. However, there was an allegation of misconduct against Alison while working at Sun on which there was an inquiry in progress at the time of her leaving the services. However, Sun had closed the proceedings of disciplinary inquiry into the allegation since Alison had left the job. Now the crux of the issue was that Sun, while rendering the reference letter, mentioned that there was an allegation of misconduct against Alison while she was in the service at the Sun. Due to this, the prospective employer had withdrawn the proposal of offering the role to Alison. Aggrieved Alison approached the court charging Sun Telecommunications of breach of duty and care, and wrong action to deprive her of the opportunity. Her claim was that the charge of misconduct was never proved, and at best, it was an unfounded complaint against her by some jealous colleagues. She also brought to notice that Sun, while referring to the alleged misconduct in the employment reference letter, had not adequately explained that the charge was never proved, and as a result, the employment reference letter was factually incorrect and misleading. Sun Telecommunications defended its action stating that in the first place, it is legally not under any obligation to provide a reference letter but did so with good faith. Sun also mentioned that it can never conceal vital information like a complaint of misconduct made against the employee while working with them, as they considered themselves a transparent organization. Discuss whether the court should dismiss the case or fine Sun Telecommunications of wrongdoing.

Case Study 4

Termination of an Aged Employee Under The Equal Treatment Act, Germany

David Kruzner was employed with New Machine Transporters (NMT), an automobile manufacturing company based in Frankfurt for the larger part of his career and was let go during the company restructuring process as his job was declared redundant. Kruzner approached the labour court petitioning that his termination by NMT was illegal under The Equal Treatment Act since some other employees working in similar roles were retained while he was asked to leave, which is a gross discriminatory action. The petition also read that he was discriminated because he was 53 years' old and other retained employees were younger than him. NMT defended its action stating there was no discrimination and that it was not illegal as The Equal Treatment Act did not envisage, nor prohibit, the

(Continued)

(Continued)

employer to separate employees on the grounds of redundancy, as long it adhered to the laid-down legal process, which the company followed sincerely. NMT also argued that David was working for a subsidiary of NMT which had less than 10 employees on its rolls so The Equal Treatment Act is not applicable to the case at all. Discuss whether NMT breached the terms of employment contract. Are the Equal Treatment Act provisions applicable in this case? Also discuss whether or not there was any discrimination.

Case Study 5

Jurisdiction of French Labour Court

LHD had a commercial agreement with MNL Pharmacy to manage delivery of its products across France for the last eight years. A team of 93 employees from LHD had been managing courier and delivery operations exclusively for MNL's operations. LHD and MNL could not reach a constructive understanding when the contract came up for renewal. LHD cited that increasing costs had sought for upward revision of prices, while MNL was expecting a discount to the existing price point due to its own financial challenges, in addition to the competitive conditions prevailing in the supply chain industry. After a series of discussions, the negotiations fell through and MNL went ahead and entered a contract with Airlinks for handling its courier and delivery operations. LHD approached MNL to make a provision in-built in its new contract with Airlinks for absorbing all the 93 employees who were working in MNL operations on existing terms and conditions of employment. MNL refused to make it a mandatory provision and suggested LHD contact Airlinks to take the 93 employees as MNL believed that if it insists on such a condition, Airlinks might seek higher fees/prices in the contract. Airlinks refused to take the employees of MNL stating that the company was already saddled with surplus employees and taking additional employees would create redundancy as well as surplus man-power for their company. LHD, aggrieved with the situation, approached the Labour Court seeking a directive for MNL and Airlinks to absorb all 93 employees along with the transfer of work. MNL in its argument presented to the court that: (a) since this was a commercial arrangement, it was a commercial dispute in which the Labour Court had no jurisdiction to hear the case and (b) the very purpose of outsourcing the delivery and courier work to a third party was to have business flexibility and therefore LHD insisting on guaranteeing the employment of its people is not maintainable under the French Labour Code. Airlinks had defended its action of refusal averring that the company maintained distinct culture and skill development approach which is at its core competence and absorbing employees from another company would cause dilution of this approach. Airlinks also mentioned that its business will be in jeopardy if it keeps taking over employees from other companies as and when competitors lose their business due to commercial and performance issues. Petitioner company, LHD, countered the argument on the basis that the principal ramification of non-renewal of contract was the loss of livelihood of 93 employees who have been sincerely engaged on MNL operations for the past eight years, adding that non-renewal of contract is nothing but transfer of work to another company and therefore transferring services of employees is a logical consequence. Discuss: Does the French Labour Court have jurisdiction in this dispute? Was Airlinks bound to absorb 93 employees? Should MNL have negotiated with Airlinks to have a provision in the contract for absorbing the employees?

Case Study 6

Dismissal of an Expatriate Employee in the Netherlands

Kevin Keening was working with an elevator manufacturing company headquartered in Richmond, Virginia, for the past 13 years in Kansas City, United States. Kevin was transferred to the Netherlands for a period of 3 years to work on the launch of new range of elevator accessories. Based on a compliant of inappropriate behaviour amounting to sexual harassment from a male colleague, Kevin's services were summarily dismissed by the management of the company. Kevin was made eligible for an unemployment benefit from the Netherlands government as per the existing provisions. However, aggrieved with the company decision, Kevin filed a petition with the Cantonal Court alleging workplace harassment, discrimination and an unfair decision by the company to dismiss him from the services. He claimed that in no way could he have caused any sexual harassment to a male colleague since he is not a homosexual. His petition went on to explain how such a dismissal is illegal as per the Dutch Labour Code. The company had defended its positon arguing that Kevin being an expatriate cannot be governed by the Dutch Labour Code, but by the laws of the United States, where the company was headquartered. The United States was also where Kevin was originally employed and where the initial employment contract was drawn. Kevin's stance was that he was issued a deputation cum transfer notification by the company office based at Rotterdam and was brought under the company rules applicable in the Netherlands for all purposes, and hence, the Dutch Labour Code was applicable to him. In addition, his deputation contract never mentioned that any dispute that may arise would be resolved as per the US law. The original employment contract of Kevin that was issued in the United States also had no mention about the scope and jurisdiction of the dispute redressal by legal authorities. Discuss whether the Dutch Labour Code is applicable in such cases of expatriates. Whether a Cantonal Court has jurisdiction to deliberate on this case? Whether a sexual harassment complaint made by a peer of the same gender is legally valid and can be taken into cognizance under the Code?

Case Study 7

Wage Guarantee Under Employer Insolvency, Sweden

Donco, a furniture manufacturing company based in Stockholm, declared insolvency due to insurmountable losses and lack of funds to run operations. The company was in huge debt, without any money left even for basic maintenance of assets, while all its assets were mortgaged. It had employed about 160 people whose employment contract specified a mandatory three months' notice for termination of their services. As a result, the company, with great difficulty, arranged for funds to pay three months' notice salary to all its employees, while terminating their services based on shutting down of the company and insolvency proceeding. It declared that there was no choice but to close down since no opportunity whatsoever existed to revive the company. The Employees Union demanded that employees be paid an insolvency notice salary since the decision of the management to close down the company was abrupt, causing loss of livelihood to employees and as they needed more time to find alternative employment. The Unions' view is that as per Sweden's Wage Guarantee Act, employees are not only eligible for the mandatory notice period in the event of termination of their services but also eligible for an additional notice period in case of company insolvency. The company raised its hand stating it had no money to pay further nor was it legally liable to pay the amount as claimed by the Union. Donco also mentioned to the court that in spite of employer insolvency, it paid notice salary to all the employees as a responsible and progressive employer, despite financial dire straits and that insolvency-related salary payment was not applicable in the present case. Discuss: As per the provisions of Wage Guarantee Act, whether or not the employer who terminated services of employees is liable to pay additional salary as claimed, in addition to the notice period salary as stipulated in the employment contracts.

Case Study 8

Sick Leave Under the Danish Sock Benefits Act

Martin Claus was a graphic designer working with a Danish ship building company as a permanent employee. Martin had applied for three weeks of leave on the grounds of back pain and sought

(Continued)

extension of the same four consecutive times, each lasting for 9 to 26 days, leading to a cumulative absence amounting to 71 days. The company accordingly had sanctioned paid leave and assured all the assistance to Martin to do well at work. About three months after the incident, Martin sought six weeks of leave on the grounds of recurring back pain once again. The company neither sanctioned nor refused the leave, but did not release the salary for the period, seeking a fitness-to-work certificate from the employee. The company's HR department had advised the employee to attend the sickness leave review and counselling that Martin did not comply with and never attended the counselling session. As a result, the company refused to grant him leave. Martin, after submitting the fitness-to-work certificate, resumed work and claimed salary for the past six weeks. The company refused to pay on the grounds that Martin did not attend the leave counselling session which was a prerequisite under the Danish Sick Benefits Act. Martin approached the labour tribunal claiming the benefit and citing the reason that he could not attend the counselling session as he was unable to come to work. He mentioned that if the company was so keen on this, it should have deputed a HR employee to his residence. In addition, inability to attend the counselling session cannot be a legally viable reason to refuse paying the salary to an employee who suffered sickness.

Discuss: Under the Danish Sickness Benefits Act, whether the said employee is eligible for salary during the sick period.

7

Industrial Relations:
Labour Codes, Laws and Regulations
Management—Asia and Australia

The objective of this chapter is to enable practitioner understanding of the essential labour and employment laws, along with their interpretations in the following countries:
- ❐ People's Republic of China
- ❐ Japan
- ❐ Singapore
- ❐ Australia
- ❐ The Philippines

S alient features of labour law and regulations of five nations, People's Republic of China, Japan, Singapore, the Philippines and Australia, are discussed in this chapter. Labour legislation in these countries has been evolving rapidly comparing to any other countries due to a variety of factors such as: influence of colonial rule in the beginning of industrialization, people movement for independence of their societies and social reform, urge for economic development and growing desire to compete internationally and attract capital from foreign investors. Labour laws which had begun with protectionism were slowly moved to egalitarianism and to the current state of flexible and competitive market-driven regulations. Even a nation like China which has a communist government and committed to 'three irons' (iron rice bowl, cradle to grave tenured employment; iron wage; and iron chair, state-controlled labour management) has systematically moved to employer-friendly and competitive labour market policies. Labour legislations in these nations are although comparable but each of them has its distinct evolution and identity. Australian labour law is primarily guided by the premise of reasonableness and fairness. With the promulgation of Workplace Relations Act, 1996, the Howard government has ensured the necessary balance among labour unions, employers and the government. Since then, the labour environment has moved to become more business-centric, and individual employment contracts have started substituting collective employment contracts. The forthcoming contents discuss key Australian labour laws and regulations vividly. The labour laws of Japan are chiefly influenced by the guiding principles as laid down in its constitution: (a) right and obligation to work, (b) a ban on child labour and (c) freedom of workers' association. As a consequence, three important areas in Japanese labour law are: the Labour Standards Law, the Trade Union Law and the Labour Relations

Adjustment Law. Evolution of labour laws in the Philippines was impacted by political and social changes at each stage: being a Spanish colony and later as British colony and the current modernization of labour market. Similarly labour laws in Singapore that has a flavour of being a British colony have moved to more competition-friendly tripartite framework.

Labour Laws in China

China's labour reform took a watershed development in the year 2008 when a slew of measures were announced in the form of labour legislations. The legislations were introduced with the intent to strike a balance between economic development, labour competitiveness and protection of labour laws. These legislations essentially include the following:

- Labour Law of the People's Republic of China, 1995
- Labour Contract Law of the People's Republic of China, 2008
- Regulation on the Implementation of the Employment Contract Law of the People's Republic of China, 2008
- Law of the People's Republic of China on Labour Dispute Mediation and Arbitration, 2008
- Employment Promotion Law of the People's Republic of China, 2008

Salient features of aforementioned laws are discussed here.

Labour Law of the PRC, 1995

This law came into force in January 1995 with an objective to protect the legitimate rights and interests of employees as well as to give a fillip to the economic development in China. The law consists of 13 chapters and each chapter consists of a number of Articles as briefly discussed here.

Chapter 1: General Provisions

Chapter 1 of the said law consists of nine Articles mainly dealing with applicability, scope, responsibility of the employers, state, rights of unions, state councils and the labour department. Basically, this law applies to all organizations and institutions: state or non-state, where there exists a labour and employer relationship regardless of the size and profile of organizations. The law also stipulates that labours have the right to be employed on an equal basis, obtain remuneration and receive training and welfare measures. Under this law, the employer has the responsibility to establish perfect rules and regulations in accordance with various laws acknowledging labour rights and obligations. The state on its part shall take measures to promote employment, formulate labour standards and coordinate labour relationships with an objective to enhance living standards of employees. Employees' right to organize collectively and form unions is discussed in this law encouraging labour to take part in democratic management. The labour management department under the state councils shall take charge of the management of labour of the whole country, whereas local government shall take charge of the management of labour in areas under its jurisdiction.

Chapter 2: Promotion of Employment

Chapter 2 consists of six Articles focused on generation of employment, prohibition of employment of juveniles, non-discrimination and equal rights of women employees. National and local governments are primarily charged with the responsibility of promoting industries with a view to generate employment, develop various kinds of job agencies and employment service centres. This chapter also dwells on employment of people with disabilities, minorities and demobilized soldiers. Organizations can employ people under the age of 16 provided this is done through special arts and sports guaranteeing their right for continuity of education.

Chapter 3: Labour Contracts and Collective Contracts

This chapter which is the king pin of this law consists of 20 Articles dealing with a wide range of issues. The law stipulates that labour contracts shall be executed between labour and employer to establish rights, interests and obligations of both the parties. Such contracts shall be drawn through a consultative process keeping in view the cardinal principles such as equality and voluntariness. All labour contracts are legally binding and both parties shall observe and fulfil their obligations without deviation and failure. Any contract which is drawn contrary to the principle laid down in this law shall be void and shall not be binding. Further, Article 19 envisages that labour contracts shall be drawn in written form and shall contain clauses such as: time limit of the contract, content of work, labour protection and labour conditions, employee remuneration, discipline, conduct and conditions for the termination of contract and liabilities for violations of the contract. Under the law, it is mandatory that all labour contracts be drawn only through consultation. Time limit is the essence of labour contracts in China. Time can be fixed or flexible, or organizations can also opt for probationary period before any contract is termed as final. However, no provision under this law mandates making commercial secrets of the employer open and employees are bound by secrecy. There is a provision for revoking labour contracts upon mutual agreement of the parties. Article 27 stipulates that the employer, when seeking to cut down the number of employees either due to consolidation or bankruptcy, shall engage in a discussion with trade unions and seek their opinion and report to the labour department. Employees who are retrenched shall have the first right to be hired back as employees whenever hiring resumes. No employee shall be terminated during pregnancy or after having acquired or partially acquired a disability due to occupational injuries.

When contracts are in dispute, labour unions can raise them with arbitration authorities or file lawsuits. If any organization has not yet formed a trade union, it can assign the collective agreements to employee representatives as authorized by the employees. It shall be ensured that all labour contracts shall be filed with respective labour departments and the said filed labour contracts will take effect on expiry of a period of 15 days if no objections are received.

Chapter 4: Working Hours, Rests and Leaves

Nine Articles of this chapter are dedicated to working hours system, prolonged working hours, weekly off, holidays and annual leaves. In accordance with Article 36 of the said law, an employee shall be assigned work no more than 44 hours a week on an average and 8 hours a day. Employees are entitled for at least a day off for every week's work. In consultation with trade unions, an employer can prolong working hours by 3 hours per day not exceeding 36 hours a month.

Employees are legally entitled to receive wages at the rate of 150 per cent of their normal wages for prolonged working hours. If an employee is asked to work on the weekly off day, wages at the rate of 200 per cent of normal wages shall be paid. As prescribed by the state council, all employees who complete one year of continuous service are eligible to receive a defined number of annual leaves. Every year, all employees are entitled for paid holiday during New Year's Day, Spring Festival, International Labour Day and National Day excluding provincial specific holiday as stipulated by relevant regulations.

Chapter 5: Wages

Articles 46 to 51 deal with wages, wage revision, guaranteed minimum wages and periodicity of wage payment and wage deductions. It is mandatory for employers to follow the principle of equal pay for equal work. Pay revision can happen on the basis of the business and economic growth, and the state has control over the payrolls. Employers can fix the wage levels based on economic efficiency and jobs. All employers are bound by minimum wage levels as prescribed by provincial governments from time to time. Wages shall be paid on a monthly basis and shall not be delayed without any reason.

Chapter 6: Labour Safety and Sanitation

This chapter focuses on stipulating working conditions from a safety and sanitation perspective. The state fixes the norms for safety and sanitation standards and these norms shall be strictly adhered to by the employers. The objective of this chapter is to prescribe proactive and preventive conditions to avoid accidents and occupational hazards as well as to ensure hygiene. This chapter also empowers the state to lay additional rules related to health check of employees and also training for certain employees who are engaged in special operations. Employees are also obligated to strictly follow rules on safe operations. The state is made responsible to study, collect data, analyse and devise actions periodically at a macro level to ensure safe work operations.

Chapter 7: Special Protection for Female Staff and Workers and Juvenile Workers

Articles 58 to 65 are devoted to provide protection to women employees and children employed below the age of 16. It is forbidden to employ women during their menstrual period in mines in low temperatures. It is also forbidden to prolong their working hours or to ask them to work in night shifts. The same conditions also apply during breastfeeding period when babies are less than a year old. Women are also entitled to maternity leave of 90 days. The law also stipulates that no underage workers shall be employed in under wells and mines or in any harmful work and that employers shall carry out regular physical examination of underage workers who are in their employment.

Chapter 8: Vocational Training

Articles 66, 67, 68 and 69 encompass issues related to development of professional skills, enhancement of work abilities, institutionalization of social groups and occupational classification by states. The law mandates that employees who are to be engaged in technical work be offered training before they are employed in such positions. Every employer shall establish a system for vocational training, provide funds for vocational training as per state regulations and organize vocational training covering employees in a systematic manner. The state is also obligated to identify and notify classification of occupations and set up professional skill standards and vocation certification programmes. Every organization shall carry out testing and appraisal of professional skills of employees as authorized by the government.

Chapter 9: Social Insurance and Welfare

This chapter is promulgated to ensure social insurance and welfare of employees. Every organization and employer shall ensure to set up a social insurance fund and a system to take care of employees when they retire, suffer diseases/injuries, become disabled, unemployed or during post-maternity period. Articles 70 to 76 exhaustively prescribe the procedures and method of setting up of a social insurance fund and the ways such a fund can be utilized. Organizations charged with the task of administering social insurance funds shall collect, keep and use the said funds in accordance with the law and take the responsibility for guaranteeing and investing these funds for better returns. Level of social insurance to be offered vary from time to time based on the social and economic development.

Chapter 10: Labour Disputes

This chapter deals with the process to be adopted in redressal of labour disputes in a fair manner that safeguards the legitimate rights and interests of both employer and employees. The procedures prescribed under the law range from conciliation, arbitration to adjudication by filing lawsuits. The law also encourages settling the disputes through voluntary consultation. Article 80 stipulates that a labour mediation committee can be set up inside an organization comprising of representatives from the trade union and employer with a condition that the chairperson shall be drawn from the trade union. When disputes cannot be resolved to the satisfaction of both the parties at the mediation committee level, the same can be referred to arbitration committee. Arbitration committee comprises of representatives from labour administrative department in addition to representatives from trade union and employer. The chairperson for arbitration committee comes from labour administrative department. A dispute referred in writing by either party shall generally be settled within 60 days. Employer as well as trade union has the right to approach People Court by filing lawsuit within 15 days. If there is no lawsuit, the settlement accorded at arbitration level shall be implemented on expiry of 15 days period.

Chapter 11: Supervision and Inspection

This chapter elaborates on administration and execution of this law with the help of Articles 85–88. The labour administrative department is made responsible for implementation of the law and local governments for the supervision of execution and accomplishment of objectives of the law. Labour administrative department is empowered to supervise and inspect organizations in order to satisfy itself with observance of the law. Supervisors and inspectors of the labour administrative department are made responsible to impartially enforce the law and have the right to verify the documents and data if necessary.

Chapter 12: Legal Responsibilities

This chapter of the law explains penalties incurred in case of violations; these penalties could include criminal charges. Articles 89 to 105 provide an exhaustive summary of what constitutes a violation, proportionate penalty to be incurred and the process involved in imposition of such penalties. For example, the labour administrative department will issue warnings and carry an audit of damages caused to the labour if regulations and processes administered in an organization are contrary to this law. Penalties for violations can be monetary such as paying wage remuneration to the labour, fines, taking into custody and pressing criminal charges. Likewise, there are penalties imposed or criminal charges levelled against trade union representatives or employees if they are found to be violating any articles of this law. Any trade union representative or employee if found to be abusing the powers given under the law or neglecting his or her duties will be disciplined by the labour administrative department suitably. If employees or trade union representatives are found to be causing economic loss to the organization deliberately, they will be charged. Similarly, officials of the labour administrative department shall also carry their responsibilities impartially and diligently, failing which, they will be charged.

Chapter 13: Supplementary Provisions

Article 106 states that governments at provincial, regional and municipal level are obligated to define the rules for implementation of this law and submit the same to the state council for registration. Once registered, these rules shall be implemented in letter and spirit. The last Article of the law, Article 107, proclaims that this law shall take effect on 1 January 1995.

The Labour Contract Law, 2008

The Labour Contract Law came into existence effective 1 January 2008. The core objective of this law is to improve the labour contractual system and articulate clearly the rights and responsibilities of employer and trade union representatives in ensuring reach and implementation of labour contracts. The principal features of this law are outlined here.

Chapter 1: General Provisions

This chapter focuses on purpose, process, nature and scope of labour contracts, and rights and obligations of trade union representatives and employers in putting in place mutually consented to labour contracts in conformity with the law and regulations. Employers have the responsibility to engage trade union representatives in order to formulate rules concerning remuneration, working time, break, vacation, safety and sanitation, insurance and welfare, training of employees and discipline. Employers shall convene a meeting with trade union representatives and put forward a draft proposal covering all these issues and finalize the proposal in consultation with them. Labour administrative departments are expected to form a three party mechanism comprising of trade union representatives, employer and officials of administrative labour department. The responsibility of this committee is to establish a sound mechanism for harmonious relationships between employer and employees, and to provide a healthy environment for establishing dispute-free labour contracts. The labour unions have the responsibility to form a collective mechanism and guide employees to fulfil their obligations under labour contracts.

Chapter 2: Formation of Labour Contracts

This is the most critical and pivotal chapter in this law. It stipulates that no person shall be hired without a written contract, and such a contract shall clearly capture the employer's name, domicile, name of person in-charge, the employee's name, domicile, identity card number, time limit for the labour contract, job description, work location, work hours, break time, leaves, remuneration, welfare, benefits, social security, work conditions, probation, training, confidentiality and protection against and prevention of occupational harm, if any. Employer has the responsibility to clearly inform and educate an employee about these clauses in the labour contract. Every employer shall maintain a roster for inspection by administrative labour department. No employer can expect or stipulate conditions that seek to provide guarantee or collect money or property from an employee. Labour contracts can be for a fixed period or for a period required in order to complete a task or assignment. In case, there is no mention of a fixed contract period, it shall be interpreted that such a contract is for an indefinite period provided an employee has worked for not less than a year. This chapter also stipulates certain conditions related to probation period—probation shall not exceed more than six months if the employment is for over three years and remuneration shall not be less than 80 per cent of actual remuneration. Employer can seek a service agreement for a defined period from employees wherever employer invests money in training the employees. If an employee violates the stipulation regarding the service time period, the employee shall pay the employer a penalty for breach of contract. However, the penalty shall not exceed the training fees/cost incurred by the employer. Only senior managers and senior technicians can be subjected to non-competition clauses since they can have access to company secrets.

Chapter 3: Fulfilment and Change of Labour Contracts

All labour contracts will remain valid in the context of all mergers and acquisitions or transfer of ownerships or split of business operations. They can be modified as and when required provided there is mutual agreement between employer and trade union representatives/employees. Labour contract forms the fundamental basis for the relationship between an employer and employee. Therefore, each party shall ensure execution and strict implementation of all the provisions of agreed labour contracts drawn in consonance with the law.

Chapter 4: Dissolution and Termination of Labour Contracts

Employment contract can be dissolved with the mutual agreement of an employee and employer by providing 30 days' notice or 3 days in case of probationers. An employee can unilaterally terminate the contract if an employer fails to fulfil the stated obligations such as paying remuneration or ensuring safe working conditions or social security benefits. Likewise, an employer can terminate a contract if an employee is found to be violating rules and procedures or could not prove recruitment credentials submitted while being hired or causes damage to the employer's property or simultaneously maintains other employer relationships and withholds this information from the employer, thus adversely affecting the business interests of the employer.

Employer can also terminate the contract by notifying in writing giving 30 days' notice or 30 days' wages if an employee is sick or injured for non-work related reasons or if an employee is found to be incompetent in the position even after having undergone the requisite training for the job.

Conditions for laying off 20 or more employees or 10 per cent of the total workforce include informing trade unions and the labour department 30 days in advance. A detailed explanation of circumstances leading to such lay-offs will need to be provided after seeking views from trade union representatives. Employer is also required to, under the law, inform labour reduction plan to the labour department. Lay-offs are only permitted in the event of bankruptcy, or when encountered with serious difficulties in production and business operations, or change in technology and prevailing economic situation. The law also prescribes the process to be adhered to for identifying the labour for reduction under lay-off plan.

No employee shall be terminated even as part of lay-off plan if he or she:

- is engaged in operations exposing him or her to occupational hazards and has not undergone an occupational health check-up clearing him or her of any occupational disease.
- has lost capacity to work partially or fully due to occupational hazard/disease.
- has contracted an illness or sustained a non-work related injury for which treatment is still in progress.
- is in confinement or is pregnant or in nursing period.
- has been working continuously for 15 years and is left with only 5 years for retirement.

Any employer found to be violating these provisions can be ordered to rectify and can be subject to undergo penalties. Employers are also required to pay economic compensation based on the number of years an employee worked, at the rate of 30 days' wages for every completed year of service. Employers are also obligated to preserve all the documents and labour contracts in situations such as this for a period of at least two years.

Chapter 5: Special Provisions

This chapter presents conditions applicable in case of collective contracts. In the place of individual contracts, employees can get together to negotiate with the employer on various matters including remuneration, working hours, vacation, work safety, hygiene and benefits. The collective contracts which are concluded by unions and employer shall be submitted to labour administrative department for their validation. Once a labour collective agreement is approved, the same is binding on the employees and employer. Both the parties are entitled to press for arbitration of litigation in case of breach of contract implementation. Section 2 of this chapter deals with worker dispatch service. This is like a subcontracting or staffing agency. As per the law, the employment contract shall be between the worker dispatch service organization and the employee and the duration of the contract shall be for not less than two years, and remuneration and benefits shall be not less than minimum wages prescribed by the people's government from time to time. There shall be an agreement between a dispatch service provider and entity accepting the workers from such agency. The entity engaging the employees from dispatch service providers shall perform certain obligations which include providing proper working conditions, training, overtime remuneration where applicable and normal wage adjustments and further these employees shall be paid wages equivalent to wages paid for the entity's own employees for the same jobs. Entity is also allowed in turn to dispatch these employees to the other employer. Dispatch services shall be used only for temporary, auxiliary and substitute positions.

Section 3 of Chapter 5 is dedicated to part-time employment provisions. Part-time employment is mainly calculated on an hourly basis and weekly hours shall not exceed 24 hours and day hours shall not exceed 4 hours. A part-time employee can enter labour contract with more than one employer. Wages of part-time employee shall not be lower than minimum wages prescribed by the government.

Chapter 6: Supervision and Inspection

The labour administrative department of local government is responsible for implementation and supervision of this law within their jurisdiction and state council is responsible for the entire country. The local government is also responsible to formulate appropriate rules to enforce this law. Employee or trade union or employer, or employer representative is entitled to seek arbitration or adjudication if there is a breach of or failure of implementation of this law. Labour administrative department can reward and recognize meritorious people who report violations.

Chapter 7: Legal Liabilities

This chapter deals with penalties for violations of the law by employers, employees and trade unions. Penalties could include warning letters, an order to rectify the mistakes, paying double the normal wage level or monetary fines up to 5,000 yuan. Officials of the labour administrative department are also subject to penalties and disciplinary action if they neglect their responsibilities in enforcing the law. All the parties are subject to criminal charges if they indulge in any criminal act or violence, or sabotage.

Chapter 8: Supplementary Provisions

The chapter prescribes that all employment practices being followed before promulgation of this law shall be structured in adherence to this law. For example, an employer is obligated to put in place a written labour contract in place immediately for any existing employment relationships however old it may be according to this law. Similarly, working hours, overtime, remuneration and so on shall be brought in line with provisions of this law immediately.

Regulation on the Implementation of the Employment Contract Law of the PRC

The primary objective of this law is to promote implementation of the Employment Contract Law and enhance harmonious employment relationships.

Labour administrative department, trade unions, employers and employees shall make all efforts to implement the Employment Contract Law in letter and spirit. All firms including legal firms, accounting firms, foundations and partnership firms fall within the purview of the Labour Contract Law. This law came into force effective September 2008. This law also explains the importance of drawing employment contracts, time limits, aspects to be covered underemployment contract, employee transfers from one undertaking to another undertaking, duration of employment contracts, procedure for termination of employment contacts, probation and training. An employment contact can be terminated or concluded in the following circumstances:

- The employee and the employer agree.
- The employer fails to pay remuneration on schedule.
- The employer fails to provide safe and hygienic working conditions.
- The employee gives 30 days' notice of intention to quit.
- Employer denies right of employees.
- Employer fails to provide social insurance.
- Rules and procedures adopted in employment contract or employee relationships are contrary to the law.
- The employer compels the employee to work restricting personal freedom illegally.
- The employee fails to meet the employment conditions during the probation.
- The employee violates the rules and procedures set up by the employer.
- The employee seriously neglects the duties so assigned.
- The employee simultaneously entered into employment with another employer.
- The employee is under investigation for criminal liabilities.
- The employee is found to be incompetent for the position.
- The employee is sick or is injured for non-work related reason and is unable to carry out the duties.
- The company/firm is restructured according to the Enterprise Bankruptcy Law.
- The employer changes products, or technological or business operations change.
- Change of economic situations.
- An employee reaches mandatory retirement age.

Employment contract of employees who are engaged on a specific task/assignment can also be concluded on completion of said task/assignment. Every employer is bound to follow the laid-down procedure for conclusion of employment contracts, preserve all such documents and present them to the labour department whenever verification is being carried out. Employers are also obligated to pay remuneration or economic compensation in certain cases when employment relationships are concluded as per the law. Employer is liable to pay a fine of up to 20,000 yuan but not less than 2,000 yuan on failing to set up roster of employees. Disputes that have risen between an employee and employer related to labour contracts and are unresolved can be referred to mediation and arbitration administered by labour administrative department and the decision of the department shall be binding on the parties.

Law of the PRC on Labour Dispute Mediation and Arbitration

Twin objectives of this law are: to settle in a timely manner the labour disputes and promote harmonious and stable relations. This law is applicable to the labour disputes arising from the confirmation of a labour relationship, conclusion, performance, modification or termination of a labour contract and removal/termination/resignation/retirement of an employee. This law is also applicable to disputes concerning work hours, vacations, social insurance, benefits, training, remuneration or injuries arising out of work.

The law prescribes that wherever and whenever there is a dispute, the parties—employer and employee—shall make all efforts to settle the dispute based on facts and by adhering to the principles of fairness and timeliness. If any party disagrees or fails to reach a mutual agreement on settlement, the same can be referred to mediation by either of parties. Either party in writing appeals to a mediation committee citing facts and salient features of dispute and disagreement. Mediation committee comprises employee as well as employer representatives with trade union representative as the chairman. Where an agreement is reached through mediation, both parties shall be made to sign a mediation agreement paper which shall be binding on them.

If the mediation is also not successful in bringing in a mutually agreed settlement, the same can be referred to arbitration within 15 days from failure of such a settlement. During the arbitration process, employer or employee will have primary responsibility to present the evidence based on who is controlling the dispute matter. Labour administrative department of people's government shall form a tripartite labour mechanism to redress the dispute. Generally, an arbitrator who is appointed by the people's government is a serving judge or a lawyer with minimum of three years practising experience. Parties: employee/trade union and employer will have the opportunity to be represented by an attorney in the arbitration process. The arbitration process shall be conducted openly unless the dispute involves a national secret, trade secret or personal privacy. A dispute subjected to arbitration shall be included within a year. If the dispute is serious and complex, the same can be arbitrated by an arbitration tribunal comprising of three arbitrators including a chief arbitrator. Both the parties have the right to cross examine during the proceedings and all tribunals shall maintain written records of hearings. An application of arbitration can be dropped if parties reach a mutually acceptable agreement. The arbitration awarded shall be final and binding on all the parties and takes effect immediately. However, both employee and employer have the option to approach people's court within 15 days from the date of receiving the arbitration award. No fees shall be charged for the labour dispute arbitration.

Employment Promotion Law of the PRC

The objective of this law is to promote employment, eliminate employment discrimination, institutionalize equal employment opportunities and ensure vocational training. The law consists of nine chapters focusing on achieving the said objectives. People's governments are expected to have goals to increase employment for the development of economy. In order to achieve this, local and provincial governments shall create conducive employment conditions by regulating the talent market and strengthening the vocational education and training.

The state council is charged with the responsibility of establishing coordination mechanism for employment promotion work throughout the country and study significant problems in employment work with a view to address them in timely and effective manner. The labour unions, federations, youth leagues and other social organizations are expected to participate in generating employment in the country. The state encourages labour-intensive businesses, and creates and implements fiscal policies thereby giving impetus to employment generation and economic development on a sustainable basis. Every employer has the absolute right to pursue the employment practices and hiring in a fair manner and this law will help in that pursuit. Under this law, state is also obligated to establish a sound employment insurance system so as to ensure the basic living of unemployed persons and promote their employment. Also, enterprises pursuing plans to provide employment support to unemployed persons and disabled persons will be eligible to receive tax concessions. Local governments are also responsible to move people from low employment areas (moving out areas) to employment areas (moving in areas) to improve employment opportunities for rural people. People's government at all levels is also responsible to create an environment for fair employment, eliminate employment discrimination and formulate policies and take measures to support and aid the people who are finding it difficult to get a job and at the same time shall support and encourage enterprises by creating right economic environment to set up business operations. Governments at various levels are also obligated to create a uniform plan to set up vocational colleges and schools, skill development training institutes, pre-employment training sources and encourage workers to participate in these initiatives. State shall also adopt vocational qualification license system for workers engaged in special jobs such as those related to public safety and personal health. Government at all levels shall have the targets and accountability to generate training and employment opportunities through policy and operational support. Employers, both existing and prospective, will be encouraged with right aids and support to create employment and all intermediate agencies that do not follow the law and create false employment practices will be dealt with punitive actions.

Labour Laws in Singapore

History of labour legislation and laws in Singapore started during colonial regime of the British. The laws were aimed at averting and regulating industrial strife more than providing protection and ensuring welfare of employees. Subsequently, Japanese who took Singapore under its protection and supervision did not focus on creating a sustainable legal framework. However, on its freedom and self-governance, Singapore started modernizing not only its economy but also employment and labour-related aspects. During the period of 1970s and 1980s, Singapore government has brought in a series of labour laws and regulations through tripartite model/forums. These are discussed in the following chapter. The guiding principle of Singapore labour legislation is to promote economic development while attaining employee welfare and security as the legislation would reveal.

Retirement and Re-employment Act, 1993

The purpose of this Act is to make provisions regulating retirement age and process for re-employment and matters connected with it. Re-employment as per this statute is defined as employment of an employee by the same employer on or after the date the employee attains retirement age. The retirement age of an employee shall be not less than 62 years. No employer shall dismiss on the grounds of age any employee who is below 62 years of age. An employer or person responsible will be sentenced with imprisonment up to six months and or penalized with fine up to SGD 5,000. An employer can gradually reduce the salary of an employee who attains the age of 60 years and in case it is disagreeable to an employee, both employer and employee can agree for retirement. Employers are also allowed to reduce the salary of other employees based on factors such as employee's productivity and performance, and wages can be different for different jobs and occupations and different based on academic qualifications. However, salary reduction on account of age factor shall not exceed 10 per cent of the total salary. In order to re-employ retired employees up to age of 67 years, an employee needs to be assessed by his or her employer and should be medically fit to continue to work, and performance must be satisfactory. In the case of re-employment, employer and employee must enter into new employment contract defining the job scope, duties and responsibilities, and performance goals apart from other terms and conditions. The re-employment contract terms can be different from the previous employment. Any such contract should have at least minimum service duration of one year. If an employer reasonably satisfies that an employee does not qualify for re-employment based on an objective criterion and job factors, the employer must provide an adequate notice to the employee before termination. Similarly, an employee who does not want to be re-employed by his or her existing employer must serve a notice to the employer communicating the intention of non-continuance on re-employment. An employer who is not able to re-employ an employee who is retiring due to lack of vacancies may offer to retire the employee and offer financial assistance based on tripartite guidelines as a single lump sum payment or as mutually agreed. An employee who is terminated before attaining the age of retirement can file a complaint with the minister claiming reinstatement. Minister can direct the commissioner to carry out the necessary inquiry. Based on the commissioner's report, the minister can order reinstatement with full back wages and also fix wages afresh or minister may order to pay such compensation as reasonable. While determining the said compensation, minister may consider factors such as: the loss incurred by an employee due to such termination of services, availability of alternative job opportunities to the employee, efforts taken by an employer to mitigate the employee loss, and age and length of service rendered by an employee in that organization. If an employer fails to comply with directions and orders of the minister, a fine of up to $10,000 and imprisonment up to 12 months or both can be imposed. Employees and employers who are in dispute in regard to re-employment or termination of an employee before the age of retirement or specified age can seek conciliation services to resolve such dispute by writing to the commissioner. An employee or employer who is dissatisfied with the decision of the commissioner can approach high court within 14 days from issuance of the order. The commissioner is empowered to inspect work premises without notice and inquire any person related to a complaint or can inquire into terms and conditions of employment generally offered by an employer, orally examine a person who may be familiar with facts and incidents of a compliant, seek presentation of documents, relevant records and report from an employer, direct an employer to produce any employee along with terms and conditions of employment offered to that employee and take photographs and shoot videos. Any person who hinders the inquiry by the commissioner or an investigating offer is liable for punishment of up to 5,000 dollars and or imprisonment up to six months. The ministry by an order can exempt persons or organizations as deemed fit and also such exemptions can be stopped or new conditions for exemption can be applied. Any collective bargaining agreement drawn between employees and employer that lack agreement with provisions of this Act are null and void. The minister can issue tripartite guidelines on the issue of re-employment of eligible employees and regulations connected to this subject which need to be adhered to by organizations.

Skills Development Levy Act, 1979

The purpose of this Act is to set up a skill development fund by imposing a levy on employers with a view to build vocational skills that are valuable and useful to organizations and economic growth. The skill development levy payable by an employer is at the rate of 0.25 per cent of the remuneration of an employee. In some cases, minister considering relevant factors can determine the skill development levy payable by an organization. However, the level charged cannot exceed 4,500 dollars per employee in a month. The minister can also order exemption of an organization or a group of organizations from the purview of skill development levy in public interest. The skill development fund is financed through collection of skill development levy from organizations, all penalties and fines recovered on account of violation of this Act, all interests and dividends accrued of the investments made with proceeds of the fund and all donations received for skill development and funds granted by the government. The funds granted by the government will be an amount equivalent to the levy received through collections. The fund will be spent to promote, develop and upgrade skills and expertise of already working people and people who will be joining the workforce and for retraining of employees that have been laid off or retrenched. Specifically the funds will be utilized to build training and development facilities, to offer loans to employers to procure training equipment, simulators and apparatus, and to grant subsidies for training employees and to develop course curriculum and courseware. Government under this statute has established an agency called Singapore Workforce Development Agency in conjunction with another legislation called Singapore Workforce Development Agency Act of 2003. This agency will handle all the matters related to implementation of this Act. Any employer who claims fund grants based on false statements or wrong reports or any person who gives baseless and untruthful complaints will be charged and liable to penalties of up to 3,000 dollars and imprisonment of up to three years. The agency is authorized to make investments with the usage of funds and shall publish an annual report of receipts, fund size, investments, returns, grants, spend and fund availability. Accounts related to this fund are subject to audits, and failure to furnish information as sought by an auditor will attract penal impositions by the administrators of the agency. The audited report will be placed before the Parliament. The agency is responsible for defining and applying the guidelines regarding the manner of imposing the levy, collection, and investments and grants.

Central Provident Fund Act, 1955

The purpose of this Act is to make provisions for provident fund (PF) to protect employees' financial future, to set up a Central Provident Fund Board and to define regulations related to contributions, withdrawals, administration of the fund and grants by the government. There is a Central Provident Fund Board set up with representation of two persons each from government, employers and employees. The Board also has appointed officers, inspectors and employees to enforce the provisions of this Act. As per the legislation, a CPF has been set up into which all contributions are paid. The Board is the trustee of this fund. The Board will decide investments of the fund in areas such as fixed deposits in the banks, purchase of property and construction of buildings and investments in accordance with standard investment power of statutory bodies. The Board also will declare interest rate for contributions from time to time and such interest shall not be less than 2.5 per cent per annum and it can be in excess of 2.5 per cent with the approval of Ministry of Finance. The first schedule of the Act specifies the rate of contribution for different wage groups and this contribution shall be paid by employers at intervals not exceeding six months. However, employers need to recover contribution from employees out of their monthly wages payable. If an employer upon deducting the contribution from employees' wages fails to deposit the amount with the fund within the prescribed six months' time limit, the employer is punishable with penalty of 10,000 dollars or seven years of imprisonment or both. An employee apart from contributing to fund at standard rate can also voluntarily contribute at higher level provided such employee is a citizen or permanent resident of Singapore. No employer is permitted to recover or offset any money or attach any damages against the PF available to the credit of an employee. Withdrawal of an amount from the fund by an employee can be permitted by the Board if member has attained the age of 55 years, if the member not being citizen of Singapore is intending to leave the country permanently and has no intention to return, is physically or mentally incapacitated from continuing in employment or is suffering from terminal illness or disease. The Board in some cases allows the withdrawal by employees less than 55 years of age if they are unemployed for a period of more than six months. Members are also permitted to withdraw the balance for purposes such as payment towards purchase or acquisition of an immovable property or to repay the loans drawn for purchase of immovable property. Withdrawal is also permitted for payment of tuition fees at approved educational institutions for pursuing self-education or for children's education. The Board approves the educational institutions that fall within this category periodically. Nominee of an employee will be eligible to receive balance proceeds in case of death of an employee. Part 3A of the Act clearly explains the division of fund-related assets in matrimonial proceedings. Part 3B aims to set up a lifelong income scheme established and maintained by the Board. Employees at the time of becoming members of the fund can apply for joining in lifelong income scheme and based on the eligibility the Board can approve the same. Members of this fund need to make contributions at the rate and amount decided by the minister. The purpose of this scheme is to provide a monthly income for remainder of life, once retired, to an employee through the annuity plan. The Act also provides for Home Protection Insurance Scheme. The purpose of this scheme is to establish and maintain a home protection insurance to provide that on the death or incapacity of a member of the scheme at any time during the period in which the member is insured, his or her liability to repay his or her housing loan to a housing authority or an approved mortgage secured by a mortgage on the immovable property to that authority or approved mortgagee shall be discharged by the Board. This scheme is automatically applicable to member employees of PF who have withdrawn money from their balance to finance to purchase or acquire an immovable property/house. Double insurance of an immovable property is prohibited; so if an employee has insured against mortgage of his or her property through other schemes and models, he or she can be exempted from coverage of this scheme. An employee needs to be medically fit and a certificate in this regard shall be obtained in a prescribed format in order to be eligible to become member under this scheme. On becoming a member, contribution at a rate as decided by the Board is recoverable from employee's salary. The Board also has established a Dependents' Protection Insurance Scheme as provided in this legislation as part 5 of the Act with an objective to provide economic security to dependents of an employee on his or her death and provide economic security to employee himself or herself in case of incapacity. However, this scheme is not applicable to a person who is not a citizen of Singapore, at an age of 60 or more and if opted to be out of coverage of this scheme in writing and approved by the minister for such exemption. Part 6 of the Act provides for establishment of Medishield Scheme with an objective to protect and provide for reimbursement or to pay the full or part of the costs incurred by an insured person for the medical treatment or services received by him or her in an approved hospital at any time during the period of insurance. The Act also envisaged a scheme for members to provide for supplement income called Workfare Income Supplement Scheme. The scheme has a provision to provide loans/credits and cash payment to a member of employees subject to certain terms and conditions. The Act has incorporated stringent penalties and sentences for violation of its provisions and submission of wrong certificates and statements.

Employment (Part-Time Employees) Regulations, 1996

The purpose of these regulations is to protect interests and rights of employees engaged in part-time work and also to provide a rational process for maintenance of part-time employees. There shall be a contract of employment for part-time employees covering aspects such as hourly basic rate of pay, working hours in a day and in a week, number of working days in a week and hourly gross pay inclusive of all allowances clearly specifying each item. An employee is eligible to be paid his or her normal daily wages when he or she works on a rest day at his or her own request and double the normal rate of wages when he or she works on a rest day on his or her employer's request. Part-time employees are also eligible to receive overtime wages at the rate of 1.5 times the normal hourly wage rate. Part-time employees are also eligible for paid holidays. The annual entitlement to paid holidays of a part-time employee shall be in proportion to the entitlement of a similar full-time employee. The employer is required to pay a part-time employee an hourly gross wage rate applicable to such employee during the annual leave. Part-time employees also have an option to swap their wage eligibility for holidays and leave with an allowance if employer also agrees. Part-time employees are also entitled to sick leave and childcare leave, and women employees are entitled to maternity benefit leave and quantum of such leave shall be as per the notification issued by the minister.

Employment Act, 1968

The purpose of this Act is to stipulate basic procedure and conditions for employment contract. Any employment contract reached and made between an employee and employer that is less favourable to an employee when compared to standards given in this Act will be considered null and void. An employment contract can be terminated by either party, employer or employee, by giving advance notice as per employment contract. The length of the said notice maintainable shall be same for employer and employee. The Act prescribes a minimum of one day notice if an employee has been working for the employer for less than 26 weeks, one week's notice for more than 26 weeks and less than 2 years of work, 2 weeks' notice for more than 2 years and less than 5 years and 4 weeks' notice if a person has been employed for more than 5 years. However, with mutual consent, such advance notice can be waived off. No employment contract can be entered into with a person who is less than 18 years of age. A valid employment contract is deemed to have been terminated if an employer fails to pay wages as stipulated or if an employee is on unauthorized absenteeism from work for more than two days. Misconduct by an employee will attract dismissal from the service and in lenient cases a downgrade in the position. An aggrieved employee who is awarded punishment can file a complaint with minster or commissioner within 30 days of dismissal for review of the same. Minister or commissioner on review of all the records and facts of the case can either reinstate the employee or validate the decision of the employer. If an employer fails to comply with the instructions of the minister, such employer will be liable for penalty up to SGD 10,000 or 12 months imprisonment or both. In case notice is not given as required, whichever party is breaching the contract shall pay an amount as stipulated in the Act that is generally equivalent to the notice period salary. Change of employer or transfer of undertakings, mergers and acquisitions will not alter the terms and conditions of employment contract unilaterally or to the disadvantage of employees. Any employer who enters a contract of employment with any employee contrary to provisions of this Act will be held in violation and guilty of an offense. Salary period applicable to all employees shall not be less than once a month and such monthly salary shall be disbursed on or before expiry of the seventh day of completion of a month. Overtime payment shall be made within 14 days of completion of salary period. A dismissed employee shall be paid with final settlement of any dues payable within three days from the last working day. All salary payments are subject to income tax clearance and no employer can make any salary deductions which are not authorized under this Act. The authorized deductions include: on account of absence from work, damage or loss of goods or loss of money directly attributable to an employee due to negligence, deduction on account of lunch, housing, recovery of advances and adjustment of overpaid salary, income tax deduction as applicable. Another category of deductions is those on account of PF and insurance schemes as applicable and requested by an employee, and any contribution to cooperative societies and other deductions as requested by an employee and allowed under the statute. No employer shall make any deductions by way of discount, interest or any similar charge on account of any advance of salary made to any employee. The Act also specifies certain conditions for employees drawing a monthly salary not exceeding SGD 4,500. These conditions are: employees shall be given a weekly off on Sunday or any other day as decided by an employer with or without pay. Employees engaged in shift work can be given 30 hours off continuously at any time. No employee can be forced to work on a rest day. If an employee requests to work on a rest day, he or she can be allowed and paid salary at normal rate and if an employer wants an employee to work on a rest day then employer shall pay wages at twice the normal wage rate. Working hours shall not exceed 8 hours in a day and 44 hours in a week and there can be no more than 6 consecutive working hours without a rest break. An employee must be given 45 minutes of such a rest break which is inclusive of working hours. However, an employer can ask employees to work overtime or work on a rest day in case of an accident or essential services to the community or urgent work to be completed in a definite period. Interruption of work which is not allowed due to technology or machinery limitation and work that is essential for the Singapore economy and considered essential economic activity by notification of the minister can be allowed to work on a rest day. No employee shall be allowed to work overtime for more than 72 hours in a month. Employers also can have wage models which are based on task or project. An employee, in addition to holidays, weekly off and sick leave, is also entitled to annual paid leave at the rate of seven days per annum if an he or she has worked for the employer for not less than three months and one day additional to this seven days period for every completed year of service up to a maximum of 14 days per annum if he or she has more than three months service with the employer. All paid leave and unpaid leave approved by an employer will be counted towards uninterrupted service of an employee. An employee will forfeit his or her entitlement of leave if he or she goes on leave without approval and spends 20 per cent of total working a days on leave even it is approved with or without pay. Employees who complete three years of service are eligible for retrenchment benefits if terminated on redundancy grounds and for retirement benefits other than PF on completing five years of service with an employer. Employers and employees can make negotiations and draw collective wage agreements covering wages including performance or productivity-based variable pay which shall be payable on attaining the targets. Employers can also introduce annual wage supplement which is a single annual payment to employees adding to an employee's total wages. The minister would also make wage recommendations and adjustments periodically and publish in the official gazette. An employer and trade unions can take this as basis for their wage negotiations. Principal employer when engaging contractors and subcontractors through any agency or directly will be responsible for employment matters and liabilities jointly and severally. Every contractor and subcontractor needs to apply for registration and obtain permission from the commissioner. Engaging as contractor or subcontractor without necessary registration and permissions will be considered an offense. An employee who is employed to work for a duration not exceeding 35 hours a week is regarded as a part-time employee. Child is defined as someone who has not completed 15th year of age and a young person is one who has completed 15th year of age but not completed 16th year of age for the purpose of this legislation. No child shall be employed in any industrial or non-industrial undertaking except in cases where such undertaking is run by own family and even in this context such employment shall be based on medical fitness certificate issued by a medical officer. No young person shall be employed in any industrial undertaking as declared in official gazette. The minister can also prescribe conditions for employment of young persons and wages applicable to such employment. Any person or employers contravening these conditions are liable for penal action.

Every female employee is entitled to absence from work during the period of four weeks immediately before her confinement and eight weeks immediately after the confinement. If any female employee works during the benefit period before her confinement, such employee will be entitled to extra wages at the rate of double the wage, wage at normal eligibility and additional one more time wage equivalent to normal wage. A female employee who is intending to avail this leave shall apply for leave at least one week in advance and in case an employee fails to give the said advance information of one week, the employee will be paid at the rate of only half of her eligible wages. Female employees are also encouraged to notify the employer as soon as possible and practical to inform about their confinement. No employer can terminate services of a female employee who is on maternity benefit period duly approved and such act if occurs will be treated as unlawful. It is null and void even when a female employee voluntarily opts out of the purview of the benefit or relinquishes any benefits guaranteed under this legislation. An employer who fails to comply with provisions of maternity benefit is liable for imprisonment of six months or fine of up to SGD 5,000 or both. Employees are also entitled to childcare leave in addition to sick leave, annual leave, holidays, weekly offs at a minimum of two days to maximum of 14 days. Employers are required to pay gross pay during grant of this leave. Not granting childcare leave without cause by employer is tantamount to offense and will attract penal clauses. Employees are eligible for holidays as per the Holidays Act. If a holiday intervenes when an employee is on leave, the same shall be continued to be considered as a day on leave. An employee who absents himself or herself from the work on the working day immediately preceding or succeeding a holiday without prior consent of the employer will not be entitled to paid holiday. Employees are also entitled to be paid sick leave at gross salary level if certified by a medical practitioner at the rate of 14 days for non-hospitalization and up to 60 days for hospitalization provided that an employee has been working for the employer at least for the last six months. Employees who are in receipt of compensation for temporary incapacity will not be eligible for paid sick leave for the same period.

All employers without exception shall maintain and keep a register exhibiting the name, address, basic rate of pay and allowance, amount earned and deductions made from the earnings of employees. Such register shall be maintained and kept at the place of work where these employees are engaged for ready inspection. The commissioner under the Act can also solicit reports and returns periodically to satisfy himself or herself with implementation of the Act. An employer who refuses to provide the information as solicited by the commissioner without substantive reason or who furnishes unauthenticated and wrong information will be termed as guilty and necessary action for conviction up to six months or fine up to SGD 5,000 or both will be imposed.

Labour Laws in Japan

Japanese labour law is derived from the Japanese constitutional framework which emphasizes the right to work, employee's security, freedom of association and prohibition of child labour and discriminatory practices in employment. In pursuance to these provisions, the successive Japanese governments have brought in a number of labour legislative measures such as Employment Insurance Act, Employment Security Act, Labour Contract Act, Equal Employment Opportunity and Treatment Act which are presented in the following along with other connecting laws.

Employment Insurance Act, 1974

The Act consisting of 86 Articles is promulgated with an objective to assure standard of living for the unemployed, redress the unemployment problem and promote stability and welfare of workers. The employment insurance is administered by the government. Benefits for unemployment as per this Act include: (a) job applicant benefits covering basic allowance, skill acquisition allowance, lodging allowance, and injury and disease allowance, (b) employment promotion benefits covering employment promotion allowance, moving expenses and wide area job-seeking expenses, (c) educational training benefit covering payment for the educational training and (d) continuous employment benefit covering basic continuous employment benefit for elderly, basic childcare and re-engagement benefits and family leave care benefits. People who are in receipt of job applicant benefits shall make all efforts to develop vocational and professional skills and find employment in right earnest. If any person by deceit receives unemployment benefit, the same shall be recovered at double the amount thus paid as a benefit. In order to be eligible for basic allowance under unemployment benefit allowance, a person should have been insured at least for a period of six months during the preceding one year period from the date of employment separation. The recognition of unemployment is given by the Public Employment Security Office to which a qualified recipient has applied for employment, once every four weeks calculated from the day the person is reported to have been separated. The basic allowance will not be paid unless a qualified recipient has been unemployed for a period of seven days at least from the date of his or her application for employment to the Public Employment Security Office. The number of days for which basic allowance is paid will depend upon the basic period of calculation and age of the insurer. The basic allowance for an extended duration than eligible period can be paid if the recipient undergoes public vocational training as directed by the chief of the Public Employment Security Office. However, the extended period for the benefit payment will be restricted to the period equivalent to the duration of such vocational training. Also, a person can be paid basic allowance for an extended period under wide area employment placement activities if government finds it difficult to place an applicant in the area of his or her residence due to fewer employment opportunities there and if decided to pursue employment opportunities in a wider area. The basic allowance is paid once every four weeks. The Public Employment Security Office can refuse to pay basic allowance for a month if a person refuses to accept employment opportunity as per wide area employment placement or if a person refuses to undergo public vocational training offered except in cases where the wage offered by such employment opportunity is substantially low or where place of job opportunity is too far making it difficult for the applicant to move. In the case where a qualified recipient becomes unable to work due to sickness or injury after reporting in person and applying for employment in the Public Employment Security Office following separation from employment, an injury and disease allowance is payable.

Employment promotion allowance is payable to persons as identified by the chief of the Public Employment Security Office. The allowance at a calculated applicable rate is payable during unemployment period for a specified period. There will be two categories of persons who can be eligible for this allowance. They are qualified recipients and specially qualified recipients. The amount of allowance payable to them will also differ based on their category. Persons who are already in receipt of job applicant allowance are not eligible to receive employment promotion allowance. Persons who accept employment opportunity facilitated by the Public Employment Security Office and if that causes dislocation of home address, that person will be eligible for moving expenses. The amount of allowance will be notified by an ordinance of the Ministry of Health, Labour and Welfare. Insured persons, excluding continuously insured elderly persons and specially insured persons in short-term employment, are eligible for educational training benefits to be paid for undergoing and completing specially designed training courses. The amount of training allowance is as specified by the Ministry. The educational training benefit is not payable to those who attempt to receive the same through deceit or other wrongful conduct. The basic continuous employment benefits for the elderly are payable for the months in which wages are paid to an insured person. Months subject to payment means the months within the period from the month containing the day on which the insured persons reached 60 years of age until the month containing the day on which the person reaches 65 years of age. The re-employment benefits for the elderly are payable for the months subject to payment after re-employment where a qualified recipient has become an insured person due to taking suitable employment after reaching the age of 60 years. If a person is in receipt of or is eligible to receive employment promotion allowance, then the person will not be paid re-employment benefit. The basic childcare benefit is payable to an insured person who has taken leave as per the ordinance of the Ministry of Health, Labour and Welfare. The amount of the basic childcare leave benefit for a single payment unit period shall be an amount equivalent to 30 per cent of the amount obtained by multiplying the amount equivalent to daily amount of wages. The re-engagement benefit for persons taking childcare leave shall be paid when an insured person qualified to receive payment of the basic childcare leave benefit has been employed by the business operator who employed him or her as an insured person during the period of the leave pertaining to said basic childcare leave benefits. The family care leave benefit is payable when a person has taken leave in accordance with instructions of the Ministry of Health, Labour and Welfare to take care of a family member. A family member here refers to insured person's spouse, a person in a relationship with insured person where a marriage relationship is de facto, parents or children. The amount of the basic family care leave benefit for a single payment unit period shall be an amount equivalent to 40 per cent of the amount obtained by multiplying the amount equivalent to the daily amount of wages. Government also takes necessary action to stabilize employment of persons in order to prevent unemployment and redress the employment problems by providing necessary assistance and aid to organizations which are compelled to curtail business activities due to economic changes and recession. Organizations are not allowed to lay off employees and are required to support continuous employment practices and to employ workers through replication.

Act for Securing the Proper Operation of Worker Dispatching Undertakings and Improved Working Conditions for Dispatched Workers, 1985

The objective of this legislation which is an affiliate law of Employment Security Act, 1974, is to ensure proper working conditions for dispatched workers, and also to ensure employment opportunities in order to stabilize employment situation. Dispatched worker means a person employed by an employer who becomes the object of worker dispatching. Worker dispatching means causing a worker employed by one person so as to be engaged in work for another person while maintaining that person's employment relationship with the former. No person can engage in worker dispatch business and no company can dispatch workers without a valid license from the Ministry of Health, Labour and Welfare. However, services such as construction work, port transport services and work listed as per Security Services Act, 1972, are excluded from the purview of worker dispatch practice. The Ministry, after satisfying itself with the ability of an individual or a company for properly managing the employment of dispatched workers, will grant the license. The business operator of worker dispatching shall maintain the records of number of dispatched workers, the number of persons who have received the worker dispatching services and the amount of fees for the worker dispatching. Also, the operator shall take all measures necessary for the proper management of personal information of workers thus employed. An operator and a dispatching worker shall never disclose to another person or a company any secret learned in the course of employment. The parties to worker dispatch are required to create a contract with terms related to the contents of work, the name and location of business where the dispatched workers are to be engaged, nature of supervision, working hours and working days of dispatch engagement, matters relating to work safety and health, termination of the contract and manner in which the complains will be dealt with. Under the law, a business operator must endeavour to promote the welfare of dispatched workers who are intended to be employed or are already employed, by taking initiatives to secure employment opportunities, and education and training opportunities and improve their working conditions. Further, no person or a company can terminate a worker dispatch contract based on dispatched worker's nationality, sex and social activities or due to the dispatched worker's affiliation to a labour union. A dispatching business operator cannot enter into a contract with a dispatched worker depriving him or her of the opportunity to be employed by the client after his or her employment contract termination with such dispatching operator. Similarly, a dispatching business operator cannot arrive into a contract with a client prohibiting employment of a worker who had been dispatched to the client if that client wants to employ the worker on termination of employment contract between the dispatched worker and his or her employer.

Dispatching practice is permitted to the extent that the same does not damage the stability of employment. Unless the work is highly specialized or is for a specified period, dispatch work is not encouraged. A client must create, maintain and preserve proper management record regarding dispatch work with details such as the name of the dispatching business operator, the days on which the dispatch work was performed, the hours of starting and ending work and the time of rest breaks, the nature of work in which the dispatched worker was engaged and complaints, if any. A dispatching business operator or a person managing dispatching who violates any provisions of this law is punishable with one year imprisonment and fine up to 3,000,000 yen.

Employment Security Act, 1947

The purpose of this Act is to ensure opportunities to the people to gain employment meeting their skill sets and also to create a balanced supply and demand situation for labour market through regulation and facilitation of placement services. The Act also encourages freedom of job selection without causing conflict to public interest and provides for equal treatment on job opportunities independent of religion, race, creed, sex, social status, family origin, previous profession and membership of labour union. The government is responsible to provide free employment placement to job seekers helping them gain job opportunities compatible with their abilities as well as to meet performance standards of jobs. The government also has obligation under Employment Insurance Act to provide vocational guidance and placement services to the insured persons which it can meet with the help of provisions laid down in the present legislation. The Act also envisages good cooperation and collaboration among all the agencies like the Public Employment Security Office, placement business services and labour supply business providers. The Public Employment Security Office shall maintain relevant personal and professional information related to job seekers. This office also takes up the responsibility to post and publicize all job opportunities along with relevant details such as wages, hours of work, prospective employer, location and skills required. Public Employment Security offices offer their services to all persons free of charge providing them assistance in relation to employment placement, vocational guidance, employment insurance businesses and other related services to ensure job opportunities to registered job seekers. The Public Employment Security Office must make all efforts to obtain job opportunities for job seekers without disturbing their domicile or relocating them. It can seek information from all organizations and trade unions in order to collate job opportunities existing at any point of time and these organizations are legally obligated to provide such data in the prescribed manner. It is not allowed to introduce job seekers to organizations where there is a labour dispute or strike, or lockout in progress in order to maintain its neutrality to such labour disputes. The Public Employment Security Office is also responsible for providing vocational guidance and assistance with placement opportunities for physically and mentally disabled and for offering any special guidance that may be required. It also endeavours to build relationships with schools and colleges, and their placement offices in order to identify job opportunities suiting the skills and interests of the students. If a business operator working in the area of job placements is also in port and construction business, he or she shall ensure that no job placement services shall be offered as a service to the port or construction part of business.

Industrial Accident Compensation Insurance Act, 1947

The objective of this legislation is threefold. First, to ensure safety and health of workers and their families by way of regulation of working conditions; second, to facilitate and provide insurance benefits as a fair protection against injury, disease, disability or death arisen in the course of employment and third, to promote social rehabilitation of workers who have suffered an injury or disease from an employment-related cause. There are two types of insurance benefits available to employees under this statute: (a) insurance benefits in respect of injury, disease, disability or death of workers resulting from an employment-related cause that is referred to as 'employment injury', (b) insurance benefits in respect of injury, disease, disability or death of workers resulting from commuting that is called 'commuting injury'. Commuting is defined as round trip between the worker's residence and workplace. If there is a deviation from the route of journey without a logical reason, the benefit may not be applicable, (c) follow-up medical examination benefits. Further, these benefits are organized into medical compensation benefits, temporary absence from work compensation benefits, disability compensation benefits, compensation benefits for surviving family, funeral expenses, injury and disease compensation pension and nursing care compensation benefits.

The insurance benefit is payable at a basic daily benefit rate as prescribed to a worker who suffered an employment or commuting injury and in case of death to the family of deceased worker. Medical compensation benefits shall be granted to cover medical examination charges, purchase of medicines or therapeutic materials, medical treatment procedures, operations and admission to hospitals. Temporary absence from work compensation benefit is payable from the fourth day on which a worker is not drawing wages due to his or her inability to work and earn wages. However, no temporary absence from work compensation benefit is payable where a worker is detained in a penal institution. Also, this compensation will not be paid to a person who receives an injury and disease compensation pension. The disability compensation benefit is payable in accordance with disability grades set by the Ministry of Health, Labour and Welfare from time to time and this amount is payable as a lump sum. The surviving family in the order of spouse, children, parents, grandchildren and grandparents will be eligible to receive lump sum compensation if due. The amount of funeral expenses and nursing care compensation amount will be as per the amounts specified by the Ministry of Health, Labour and Welfare. Medical treatment benefit is payable to an employee based on such employee's claim for an injury or disease suffered due to commuting. Nursing care benefit is payable to an employee who is entitled to receive a disability pension when that employee requires constant or occasional nursing care. The government may undertake the following services towards social rehabilitation of workers who are covered by this insurance: establish and operate services for medical treatment, assist victim families in obtaining education by extending loans, create services for prevention of employment injuries and secure working conditions which are safe and healthy. Premium Collections Act would prescribe the amount of premiums to be collected for meeting the medical expenses under this Act. The basic daily benefit amount payable as benefit under this Act is as prescribed in Article 12 of the Labour Standards Act. When a person who is entitled to insurance benefits dies, the same is payable to the family of the deceased. An employee is entitled only to one benefit at a time. For example, a worker is receiving benefit for temporary absence of work due to injury and if the same person becomes eligible for disability benefit, the temporary absence benefit will be withdrawn. The right to receive insurance benefits shall not be affected by the retirement of the worker. The national treasury subsidizes part of the expenses incurred as a part of this legislation within budgetary limits. Any person aggrieved with a decision related to insurance benefits prescribed as a part of this Act can file a complaint with Labour Insurance Appeal Committee.

Labour Contract Act, 2007

The principal charter of this Act is to promote harmonious relationship of employee and employers, and to provide guidelines and standards for voluntary negotiations and contracts, and to ensure protection of workers. The Act envisages treatment of employer and employee on equal basis, espouse faith, respect their respective rights and obligations, and give due recognition to prevailing conditions of both sides. Employer holds the ultimate responsibility to create awareness about contents of a labour contract among employees. All labour contracts must be in writing as much as possible. Labour contract scope covers items such as wages, safety, working conditions, working hours, disciplinary matters and employment, and transfer of employees. This Act is not applicable to an organization where an employer employs only their relatives. A labour contract can be for a fixed period or for a continuous period as decided as part of a labour contract. A labour contract that is reached between employer and employees will form the basis for all working conditions and neither party can change them unilaterally. However, with mutual agreement, an existing labour contract can be amended or rescinded. An employer can make modifications to a labour contract, provided such changes are well communicated to employees in advance and such changes do not cause any disadvantage to the employees. Employer shall take all measures to protect rights of employees in all situations and must not cause dilution of their rights and likewise employees shall respect objectives of business organization and further the business interests respecting rights of employer.

Labour Tribunal Act, 2004

The objective of this legislation is to create a legal redress system for resolution of labour disputes through conciliation and also to set up labour tribunals which can offer expert support in bringing around prompt, effective and appropriate dispute settlement. A district court automatically assumes the jurisdiction authority for labour dispute arising in the district and consideration of a fact of location of a business organization operation. However, a court can transfer the case to another court if it believes such transfer is suitable on various grounds enumerated in the Act. The aggrieved party, either an employer or employee or employee representatives, can file a petition describing the nature of labour dispute which can be admitted in the tribunal for proceedings. The proceedings are conducted through a labour tribunal consisting of a labour tribunal judge drawn from the district court and two labour tribunal members who are experts in labour relations and related matters. Labour tribunal is expected to conclude the proceedings and deliver the judgement in a maximum of three sittings. The tribunal, in cognizance of evidence and rights of parties involved and consideration of nature of dispute, must make attempts to encourage for conciliation failing in which it will offer its labour tribunal decision that will be binding on both the parties. Both the parties have equal opportunity to file review petition of the tribunal decision within two weeks in a court. Parties also have the option to withdraw the dispute from labour tribunal before a decision is made. If parties fail to comply with tribunal orders, a fine up to 100,000 yen can be imposed.

Labour Union Act, 1949

The purpose of this Act is to encourage employees to form a collective action group by way of trade unions and associations so that they can be in a better position to negotiate with the employer in collective matters concerning wages, working hours and conditions, and to protect their rights and interests. The term and scope of labour union does not include membership of officers and persons in supervisory positions. Trade unions whose primary purpose is political or social movement do not fall within trade union ambit under this legislation. A trade union is required to submit evidence to the effect that it qualifies to be recognized as trade union as per definition of this Act basis which the Labour Relations Commission can permit the union to participate in collective bargaining process. Officer-bearers of a union shall be elected through secret ballot and general body meeting shall be held at least once in a year and all the financial contributions and funds are subject to audit by a qualified accounting professional. No union can start a strike in any business organizations without support of majority union office-bearers. The Act also has defined unfair labour practices. No employer shall treat any employee in a prejudicial or unfair manner because such employee belongs to a trade union. Employer also shall not refuse to negotiate with representatives of a trade union nor can control or interfere with formation and management of a trade union. Also, employers should not show favouritism by sponsoring financially a trade union or their activities. However, it will preclude an employer from contributing to a public welfare fund and providing space for trade union office activities. Employers are also not allowed to claim any damages on accounts of losses suffered due to legal strike or justifiable disputes. The Labour Relations Commission is the competent authority to conduct an inquiry and initiate investigation into unfair labour practices if reported or noticed on its own. All collective agreements must be drawn in writing and implemented for the period as defined in such agreements. If any such agreement does not specifically provide for duration validity of a collective agreement, the same can be terminated by either party by giving advance notice of 90 days in writing. Collective agreements drawn in conflict to lower working conditions standards as prescribed in other statutes shall be void. A collective bargaining agreement that is applicable to three-fourths of the workmen in an organization will automatically be applicable to the rest of the workmen who might not be party to such agreement or joined the organization later.

Act on Childcare Leave, Caregiver Leave, and Other Measures for the Welfare of Workers Caring for Children or Other Family Members, 1991

This welfare legislation is promulgated with an objective to ensure childcare, nursing care for elders, time off to attend to sick family members while continuing in employment. The Act also provides provisions for smooth return to work by workers after attending to such duties at home. The Act in general encourages and promotes caring for family members in need in order to promote a more humane society. A worker must be granted leave for taking care of a child who is less than a year old and such worker in order to be eligible for leave must have been working for that employer for at least one year at the time of applying for such leave. The leave can be granted for a period till the child reaches one year of age. An employer cannot refuse childcare leave to an eligible worker and also an employer shall not treat disadvantageously or terminate services of a worker who is on childcare leave or at the time of applying for childcare leave. The duration of childcare leave eligibility can also differ and depends on consumption of maternity leave. A worker whose family member is in need of care can apply for caregiver leave provided the worker has completed at least one year of service in that organization. Caregiver leave is granted for taking care of a particular family member only once and the duration of the leave depends upon the nature of each case. A worker who is taking care of a child before the commencement of elementary school may obtain leave to look after said child as specified by ordinance of the Ministry of Health, Labour and Welfare as necessary for taking care of or preventing the illness of the said child. Employers also shall not allow employees who are taking care of children with age less than three years to work more than the scheduled hours of work. Also, employers shall not engage or permit workers who have elementary school going children to work in night shifts. Employers are expected to make special efforts to re-employ the persons who had resigned and left employment in order to attend to children or the elderly. Government is also required to make initiatives to offer free counselling, vocational training and placement services to such persons who have left employment to take care of ailing family members or to take care of children. The state also should take measures as per this statute to increase awareness among employees, employers and general public regarding importance of work-life balance and eliminate practices that hinder balanced family life and career pursuits. Government also must set up family support centres across the country to help employees and employers. An aggrieved employee who is denied any of the facilities and benefits that the Act offers can file a complaint with his or her employer or press for labour conciliation. The Act also prescribes penal provisions for violations.

Act on Improvement, etc. of Employment Management for Part-time Workers, 1993

The purpose of this Act is to create and implement regulations to protect interests of part-time workers, their working conditions and welfare, and also to promote their careers towards regular employment. A part-time worker under the Act is defined as a person who is engaged on the work for duration in a day less than normal working day and less than that of duration of the work accorded to a normal regular employee in an establishment. As per this Act, an employer is obligated to ensure fair and balanced working conditions, training and welfare of part-time workers and to take measures for moving them into regular employment based on opportunities. Employers are expected to make attempts to provide necessary support, guidance and opportunities to part-time workers for moving them up in their work and career. Government is also expected to support employers and business organizations in their efforts to provide better treatment to part-time workers. The Ministry of Health, Labour and Welfare must consult labour council, trade unions and employee representatives and part-time workers in order to formulate guidelines from time to time to enhance working conditions and opportunities for part-time workers. Part-time work is prohibited in instances where the work being carried out by part-time workers is same or similar to that of regular employees and this will be treated as discriminatory tactics by employers in order to gain undue business cost advantages. Further, wherever there is similarity in job profile and responsibilities and job does not provide for full time, then wages should be equal to regular employees for the duration of work. Training and education support normally provided to regular employees preparing them to ably perform the jobs shall be extended to part-time employees for the same jobs as lack of training results in their part-time status being unchanged perennially. All part-time workers or prospective part-time workers have the right to be well informed about their wages, working conditions and working hours and other employment-related matters at the time of applying for such part-time job opportunities. As per the regulations issued by the Ministry of Health, Labour and Welfare in regard to this Act, all organizations must make efforts to appoint an employment manager for taking care of welfare and prospects of part-time workers. Government in accordance with this legislation launches various vocational and skill training programmes targeted at persons wanting to become part-time workers voluntarily.

Equal Employment Opportunity and Treatment Act, 1972

This legislation was promulgated and enforced with an objective to achieve equal employment opportunities, equal treatment and special welfare protection and benefits to women employees during pregnancy and childbearing period. As per this Act, employers are prohibited from practising discriminatory treatment in managing women employees during maternity leave. A competent authority under this Act makes all endeavours to prevent causes that result in discrimination of employment of women and their career growth. No discrimination is permitted in matters concerning recruitment, training, benefits, wages, promotions, retirement age, renewal of employment contract and termination of employment on the basis of sex. The process and criteria adopted to implement employment shall not be biased in favour or against either sex. Employers shall not impose conditions or limitations on marriage, pregnancy or childbirth, or use these reasons for early retirement of women employees. Termination of employment services of women during pregnancy or during the first year after childbirth is not maintainable and must be avoided. Employers also shall ensure that women employees receive necessary professional medical guidance in matters relating to their health and well-being on the jobs and extend time off to women employees to participate in receiving such advice. Based on such health guidance and advice, employers need to alter working hours and working conditions to make them conducive for women employees to work in. The Ministry of Health, Labour and Welfare can seek reports on implementation of provisions of this Act from time to time from employers and the Ministry, through the labour council, is also responsible to make such studies and research in order to identify necessary areas of advice that would be helpful for effective functioning of workforce independent of gender. The Act also stipulated fine and punishment for violation of the provisions.

Industrial Safety and Health Act, 1972

Protecting health and safety of workers, promoting detailed safety standards at workplace, defining roles and responsibilities of employer, employees and government agencies in ensuring safe work environment and putting in place measures to prevent work hazards are some of the key objectives of this Act. Employers shall take all measures to ensure safe working environment; designers and manufacturers are expected to factor safety as key element of their products; construction industry is obligated to initiate special safety measures and employees shall strive to participate not only in matters related to preventing industrial accidents but also wilfully comply with safety measures. The Ministry of Health, Labour and Welfare as per this Act is responsible for consulting labour council in order to formulate standards and plans to ensure their implementation in organizations to achieve accident and hazard-free work environment. Every employer is required to employ and identify a responsible executive as safety manager whose responsibility is to implement safety measures in the organization. The said manger shall also be made responsible for matters related to education and training of workers on safety and health, organizing medical examination of workers at regular intervals to promote health and well-being at workplace, investigate and identify causes for accidents and injuries, and suggest remedial measures. In addition to a safety manager, every employer shall also employ a health officer who possesses license issued by the Director of Prefectural Labour Bureau and shall have qualifications prescribed by the Ministry. In some cases depending upon the classification of industry, employers are also required to appoint industrial physicians from among medical professionals/doctors and such persons shall be made responsible for health care of workers. Safety and health standards are applicable to categories of employees including contract workers and persons engaged by a contractor to execute specific part of a work in a principal employer establishment. Contractors who employ sizable number of workers shall also appoint a safety and health care officer and notify details of such officer to the principal employer. As per standards prescribed by the Ministry, an employer to whom it is applicable shall also constitute a safety committee at each workplace to advice on safety matters. Employers also as per guidelines of the Ministry must set up health committees to oversee the health care measures and their effectiveness at workplace. Causes of health impairment due to radiation, high temperatures, gases, dust, nature of raw materials, noises, waves and other abnormalities must be identified and special measures need to be put in place to avoid or eradicate health hazards for workers. Employers shall also identify probable causes of industrial accidents and injuries due to machinery, instruments, equipment, electricity apparatus and so on and initiate adequate measures to avert them. Efforts must also be made and necessary measures taken to ensure adequate lighting, ventilation, illumination, heating, rest, evacuation and sanitation at workplace. Employers also should put in place an emergency handling system and if any particular operation is believed to imminently cause accident, the same shall be shut down immediately regardless of its importance for overall business operations. Principal employer has the ultimate responsibility and obligations under this statute even for contract employees and so principal employer shall guide and monitor safety and health measures being implemented by contractors to protect their well-being. Employers are required to carry out periodic safety inspections and audits on their own internally of all work premises and maintain records of such inspections. They shall not permit employees who have contracted communicable diseases at the workplace in order to prevent the spread of such diseases and the employer shall take measures for assisting treatment of such employees. List of such communicable diseases are notified by the Ministry of Health, Labour and Welfare. Employer is required to make continuous communication and spread awareness among employees about safety and health guidelines, notifications and standards.

Labour Standards Act, 1947

The purpose of this Act is to stipulate standards for working conditions, terms of employment, regulation of wages and treatment of employees. Standards prescribed in this legislation are kept at a minimum to make the legislation applicable to all industry sizes universally. Therefore, employers are encouraged to practice standards which can be superior and motivate employees. The Act mandates that employers and workers must abide by collective agreements, employment rules and contracts, and that they must carry out their responsibilities with sincerity and discipline. Such rules and contracts must be arrived at with mutual consultation and consent of employees and employer. No employer is allowed to practise discrimination on account of gender, nationality, creed, social status in relation to work assignments, wages, working conditions and general treatment of employees. Employers shall not indulge in forceful tactics to pursue any person to accept the work or a job and must not restrict physical or mental freedom of workers. Employees as per this Act have a right to claim time off for exercising vote and to attend other public duties. The Ministry of Health, Labour and Welfare sends periodic notifications about the minimum wages that shall be paid for different occupations and this is binding on all employers. Labour contracts that do not meet the standards of this statute will be void and not enforceable. Employment contract can be for a fixed period or for an indefinite period as an employee and employer agrees based on profile of necessity of work. There should be a well-defined notice period for termination of employment by both sides and in case any employment contract is silent in this respect, both parties must follow the decision of the Ministry in this regard. Employment contracts also must clearly mention wages, working hours and other relevant working conditions in the manner prescribed by the Ministry as per this Act. Employers shall not make conditions in employment contract such as predetermined damages payable by employees for certain acts of conduct or sum of money payable in case of breach of contract or what and how much money a worker needs to be saving from the wages. However, it does not prevent an employer who wants to encourage employees to contribute to saving schemes provided the same is guided by clear rules and are formulated with the consent of the Ministry and accepted by authorized financial institutions. Employers should not terminate or dismiss any employee during a period of absence on account of medical leave due to injuries/accidents arisen in the course of employment. No woman employee can be terminated during maternity leave. In case of termination in other contexts, employee should be given at least 30 days' advance notice. This 30 days' notice can be reduced or waived off by paying equivalent wages and notice period is also not applicable to employees on probation or to employees who are daily wage earners or on fixed-term projects. Employees on retirement/separation are entitled to receive an experience certificate with details such as role, wages, experience profile and date of retirement/separation. No personal information regarding an employee can be disclosed to any third party without express consent of such employee. Wages need to be paid at least once a month on a definite date. Employees are eligible to claim salary prior to such pay date for days eligible to meet expenses in the event of childbirth, illness and natural calamities. When an employer is unable to provide work, an employee is still eligible to receive 60 per cent of normal wages. Employers need to guarantee minimum wages proportionate to number of working hours even for employees who work on piecework payment method. Maximum number of working hours permitted in a week is 40 hours excluding rest period and maximum number of working hours permitted in a day is 8 hours excluding rest period. However, an employer can reach an agreement with an employee or employee representatives to work extra hours (overtime) on a day or a week or a month subject to the employer paying premium wages or compensatory time off for the extra hours. Employer shall provide at least 45 minutes of rest periods when the working hours exceed 6 hours and at least an hour when working hours exceed 8 hours. Employees are entitled to one day off for every six days of continuous work. The premium wages for extra hours (overtime) shall be at the rate of a minimum of 25 per cent and maximum of 50 per cent of normal wages. Employees who work in night shifts which are defined as work between 10 PM and 5 AM are also eligible for premium wages at the rate of 25 per cent more than the normal wages. Employers shall grant annual paid leave of 10 working days, either consecutively or in a split manner, to employees who have been working in an organization continuously for at least six months and for at least 80 per cent of the total working days. The 10 days eligibility could increase depending upon the employee's tenure in the organization. Leave for a specified period as requested by an employee can be granted or declined on account of business reasons and can be postponed to a later date. Employers are prohibited from employing children under the age of 15 years. However, children above 13 years can be employed in light labour work with prior permission of government agencies. There shall be a separate register maintained in each organization with details of employment of persons between 15 and 18 years. Employer needs to obtain a certificate from the concerned school stating that such employment will not adversely affect the studies of these children who are employed. Wages earned by the minors shall not be paid to parental authorities or guardian and such wages shall go to minors directly. Employers shall desist from exploiting apprentices, trainees, students and such persons who, in order to acquire skills, attend work in organizations.

No person below the age of 18 years is allowed to work in night shifts which are defined as work between 10 PM and 5 AM. Also, persons below the age of 18 years shall not be employed to work on dangerous machinery or to perform work underground as this can potentially cause injuries and health hazards. Women who are on maternity leave or up to one year from childbirth are also not allowed to perform work underground, handle heavy material or work in place where harmful gases are spread as this is hazardous to pregnancy and childbirth. An employer cannot refuse sanction of leave if a woman employee who is expecting a child in six weeks requests for the same. Also, a woman employee who has given birth shall not be allowed to work for six weeks after the delivery. Employers also must make efforts to offer lighter work to pregnant women. Women employees are entitled to two breaks of 30 minutes during working hours exclusive of normal rest breaks till the child becomes one year old. Employers cannot refuse to sanction leave during menstrual period if a woman employee requests for such leave. All expenses incurred on account of medical treatment of an injury or health problem which an employee acquires in the course of employment shall be met by the employers. Employees are also eligible to receive 60 per cent of their normal wages if they are unable to work during medical treatment and recovery period due to such injuries and health problems. If an employee suffers an injury or illness in the course of employment and if he or she remains physically disabled after recovery, the employer is required to pay disability compensation at the rate and amount set in the legislation. However, the employer is not obligated to pay such disability compensation if it is proved that injury is caused by accident due to gross negligence of an employee. This fact needs to be validated by government agency also. In the case of death of an employee due to an accident in the course of employment, the family of deceased is entitled to receive compensation equivalent to 1,000 days' wages at the rate of normal wage last drawn. Aggrieved employees have the right to approach government agencies for arbitration within two years from the date of occurrence of any dispute related to their eligibilities and rights guaranteed under this legislation. Employer who employs 10 or more employees is required to draw basic employment rules clarifying working hours, rest period, leave, weekly off, holidays, shift work timings, method of calculating wages, date of payment of wages, retirement age, retirement allowances, job description, special wages such as overtime wages, premium wages, minimum wage, food allowance, vocational training, safety and health measures, stipulations concerning medical treatment of injuries and ill health arisen in the course of employment. Employers who intend to create dormitory facilities for use of employees must observe all the rules relevant to dormitory establishment and maintenance. Government approval is mandatory for operation of dormitory and so employers are required to submit dormitory plans. The dormitory will need to be constructed ensuring proper ventilation, lighting, illumination, heating, damp proofing, cleanliness, evacuation, adequate accommodation per person, sleeping facilities such as bed and blankets, and so on. In case of violation or non-adherence to prescribed standards, government can order shutdown or seek modification of dormitories attached to business organizations. Labour inspectors are empowered and authorized to carry out inspections of workplaces, office buildings, dormitories and other workplaces periodically to ensure proper standards are maintained. Labour inspectors are delegated with judicial powers to deal with violations. Employers are obligated to publicize and create awareness among employees about salient features and provisions of this Act. Every employer must maintain and keep a roster of employees at each workplace with employees' names, date of birth, personal history and employment status and other relevant details as stipulated in this Act. There shall be a wage register covering all employees at a workplace with details of wage rates, wage calculations, amount of wages, frequency of wage payouts, wage calculation method and wage components. Records such as wage ledger, employee records, safety and health records and other employee records shall be preserved for at least three years. Violation of this Act and its provisions could attract punishment by imprisonment up to one year or a monetary fine of up to 500,000 yen.

Minimum Wages Act, 1959

The objective of this Act is to ensure a minimum guaranteed wage to low-paid workers and contribute to enhancement of quality of living and secure livelihood. The minimum wages are set for hour as unit of wage. Government notifies minimum wages for a variety of occupations and jobs periodically keeping in view inflation rate and quality of living. Every employer mandatorily needs to ensure that wages are not below the rates of minimum wages and in case more than one rate of minimum wage is applicable to any employee due to nature of work, the highest minimum wage prescribed shall be applicable to such employee. Any collective agreement or employment contract drawn indicating wage less than the minimum wage prescribed as per this Act shall be void and disallowed automatically. Every region will have their minimum wages notified and sometimes rate of such minimum wage prescribed can vary but such variance is negligible. Regional minimum wages are set keeping in view inflation, living expenses, dignified living and affordability of organizations. Councils of minimum wages are set up at regional and national levels to deliberate on minimum wages and levels periodically by the Ministry of Health, Labour and Welfare. The said councils are formed with representation from employees, employers and representatives of public interest and experts on the subject. Notice of 30 days is given before minimum wages are revised and new rates become applicable. The government must extend all the support required to ensure systematic and efficient implementation of minimum wages. All the documents, reports returns and records maintained by employers in relation to workers being paid minimum wages shall be made accessible to labour inspectors for inspection periodically. If required, identity of such workers who are in receipt of minimum wages must be presented in person to the inspectors. Any aggrieved worker who believes that his or her rights are not honoured or provisions of this Act are violated can file a complaint with the director of Prefectural Bureau or to the director of Labour Standards Office for taking appropriate measures. An employer shall not take any adverse action against an employee by reason of such employee having filed a complaint. All violations will attract punishments which can be imprisonment up to six months and financial penalty up to 500,000 yen.

Labour Code of the Philippines

The state of the Philippines with an objective to promote employment and protect equal opportunities and conditions of employment has promulgated a decree known as 'Labor Code of the Philippines' in the year 1974. Pursuant to this, the department of labour which is charged with administration of the said Code has formulated and implemented rules and regulations to realize the foretasted objectives.

The Labor Code inter alia deals with agrarian reforms. The chapter describes the process of mandated transfer of the land from owners to tenant farmers by fixing a nominal price. The Code has also stipulated a condition that such tenant owners shall compulsorily become members of the recognized farmer cooperative societies.

Chapter 1 of the Code (Book One) focuses on recruitment and placement practices. A bureau called Employment Services has been set up under the supervision of the Department of Labor and Employment to (a) establish and develop employment programmes, (b) offer vocational guidance, (c) establish and maintain a registration and licensing system to regulate private sector participation in the recruitment and (d) maintain a central registry of skills. Unless license is given, no private agency or person other than public employment office shall engage in recruitment and placement. An overseas Employment Development Board was also created as per the Code to undertake a systematic overseas employment of Filipinos. No entity or employer can hire a Filipino worker directly for overseas assignment/employment other than through the Board. It is mandatory for Filipino workers employed overseas to mandatorily remit portion of income in foreign exchange to their families and dependents residing in the Philippines.

Chapter 2 of the Code (Book One) provides for regulation of recruitment and placement agencies. All private entities and agencies shall comply with relevant provisions of this chapter to participate in recruitment activities either locally or for overseas. Travel agencies and sales agencies are prohibited from engaging in the business of recruitment and placement. Recruitment entities and companies owned at least to the extent of 75 per cent by the Philippines citizens are only permitted to participate in recruitment and placement business. The fees that can be charged by these agencies for employment of workers shall be as per the prescribed rates of the Department of Labor and Employment. Overcharging or keeping custody of educational certificates of candidates or inducing any worker who is already employed to quit to pursue another opportunity and fail to file returns as per guidelines are deemed to be offenses under the Code. Violations committed will attract steep penalties and would also lead to cancellation of licenses to agencies by the Department of Labor and Employment. Any person other than a Philippine national seeking employment in the country shall obtain an employment permit from the Department of Labor and Employment. An employer employing non-resident foreign nationals shall submit a list of such nationals to the secretary of the Department of Labor and Employment.

Book Two of the Philippines Labor Code deals with Human Resource Development Program. The objective of this part is to (a) develop HR, (b) establish training institutions and (c) formulate such plans and programmes to ensure efficient allocation, development and utilization of the manpower. In order to achieve these objectives, the Department of Labor and Employment has formed a National Manpower and Youth Council. The Council is responsible to formulate a long-term national manpower plan and to set up national skill centres and industry boards to contribute to skill development efforts.

Book Three of the Labor Code deals with regulations related to working conditions and rest periods. The normal hours of work of any employee shall not exceed eight hours a day. Hours worked shall include rest period such as meal period which shall be for a minimum of 60 minutes. Also, every employee that works during night shall be paid a night shift allowance equivalent to 10 per cent of regular wage. Night shift is defined as any work rendered from 10 PM to 6 AM. Any work beyond eight hours a day is considered as overtime work for which wages equivalent to 25 per cent of regular wage rate shall be paid for every hour in addition to the normal remuneration. Employees are entitled to a paid day of rest for six days of continuous work in a week. Also, every employee who has rendered at least one year of service shall be entitled to a yearly service incentive of five days with pay. Wages shall be paid twice a month and in any case at least once every 16 days. The Department of Labor and Employment publishes minimum wages for both agriculture and non-agriculture employees and this shall be strictly observed. In case of contract employment where contractors fail to pay dues of employees, principal employer will have the liability. Employees will enjoy the first preference as regards to their wages and other monetary claims in the eventuality of bankruptcy or liquidation of the entity. No employer shall resort to any deductions other than those authorized by the Department of Labor and Employment. This condition applies even in cases where damage of tools and property is reported and such acts are attributed to an employee. The Labor Code has also provided for formation of a National Wages and Productivity Commission whose principal responsibility is to act as national consultative and advisory body to the government in matters related to wages, incomes and productivity. This body is also responsible for stipulating minimum wages and review plans of the regional tripartite wages and productivity boards to determine whether the same are consistent with national development plans.

No woman is permitted to work during night working hours defined as from 10 PM to 6 AM. However, this clause is not applicable to managerial cadre of women employees and also to jobs performed by women that cannot be done by male employees and also in some emergencies where the work is necessary to prevent substantial loss or damage to perishable goods. Organizations shall observe mandatory working facilities as notified by the Department of Labor and Employment at all workplaces such as nursery, separate toilets where women are employed. Every employer shall grant to any pregnant woman employee, who has rendered an aggregate service of at least 6 months in the last 12 months, maternity leave of at least 2 weeks prior to the expected date of delivery and another 4 weeks after normal delivery or abortion with full pay. The maternity leave is applicable only to the first four deliveries. The Department of Labor and Employment is also vested with responsibility to encourage family planning and to incentivize the same through appropriate schemes. Discrimination of women in any employment, employment opportunities, and terms and conditions of employment is strictly prohibited. The acts of discrimination can include payment of lesser compensation, favouring male employees in respect of promotions, training opportunities and assignments.

As per Chapter 2 of Book Three of the Labor Code, no child below 15 years of age shall be employed and any person between 15 and 18 years of age may be employed as per the working hours and conditions stipulated by the Department of Labor and Employment. Chapters 3 and 4 of Book Three deal with provisions related to employment of house helpers which include minimum wage, boarding, lodging, medical attendance, termination and treatment.

Book Four of the Labor Code is dedicated to health, safety and social welfare benefits. As per this, every employer shall ensure first-aid medicines and equipment, and further facilities as the nature of employment may require. Employer is also obligated to train and make ready sufficient number of employees in first-aid administration. In addition to this, where it is prescribed, employers shall also make available employees trained in occupational safety and industrial health matters. The service of a full-time nurse is must wherein more than 50 employees are at work, and a nurse, dentist and part-time physician and an emergency clinic is compulsory wherein 200 or more number of persons are employed in an establishment. This requirement of number of persons employed can be lower if the nature of work is hazardous. The Code also provides for establishment of a Tax-exempt Employees' Compensation Programme whereby employees and their dependents in the event of work-connected disability or death may promptly secure adequate income benefit and medical-related benefits. Coverage of all Filipino employees in the country and abroad in defined cases under the State Insurance Fund is compulsory. Every employer under the said scheme shall deposit an amount equivalent to 1 per cent of the salary credit of each employee. Contributions on this account shall be entirely borne by the employer. The Philippine government takes the responsibility of the solvency of the State Insurance Fund and in case of any deficit, the same shall be covered by supplemental appropriations from the government allocations. Under the scheme, employees are eligible for a variety of benefits and assistance programmes which include medical, partial and permanent disability and death benefits. Employers are also encouraged to provide adult education facility to the employees working in such establishment who lack primary education as a welfare measure for which the Department of Labor and Employment also renders necessary assistance.

Book Five of the Code provides for policy on labour relations. The objective of this part is to promote the free trade unionism, collective bargaining process and to ensure industrial peace and harmony through timely dispute redressal mechanisms. The Department of Labor and Employment has established a National Labor Relations Commission comprised of five members chosen from trade unions, employers organizations and government. The Labor Commission will have jurisdiction through appropriate mechanisms in issues involving unfair labour practice cases, termination of disputes, interpretation and implementation of collective bargaining agreements, claims for actual, moral, exemplary and other forms of damages arising from the employer employee relationships. The Commission also provides for arbitration process and for arbitrators to conciliate and resolve the disputes. Inspectors and other representatives as authorized and appointed by the said Commission can inspect, study and investigate any establishment during all reasonable working hours by serving notice. Decisions, awards and orders of the labour arbitrator are final and executory. However, employees and employers will have the opportunity to appeal against such decisions within 10 days to the Commission on defined grounds such as there is prima facie evidence that the decision of arbitrator is marred by corruption or abuse of the discretionary powers of the arbitrator or that there are serious errors in the findings or facts collected and relied upon. The Bureau of Labor Relations and the Labor Relations Division are vested with original and exclusive authority to act on their own initiative or upon the request of either party: employer or employees. Any compromise agreement agreed upon and signed by employer and employee representatives in the presence of the Bureau of Labor Relations is binding upon all the parties without deviation. The Bureau also has powers to require any person to appear or produce any papers/documents in matters related to disputes. In order to be eligible for legal recognition and connected rights and privileges, an association or union shall be registered by following the relevant procedures under the Code. However, no federation or national union shall be registered to engage in any organization activity in more than one industry. Local chapters will have the same rights and privileges of a federation. A registration of a union or federation can be cancelled on certain grounds such as misrepresentation or false statements or fraud in the minutes or ratification of the resolutions/constitution of such union, failure to submit returns and final reports and failure to comply with relevant requirements and entering into collective bargaining agreement on issues maintaining standards below the prescribed levels of relevant laws. A registered and legitimate labour union will have rights such as being able to act as representative in collective bargaining process and to undertake all activities designed to benefit the organization and its members. All persons employed in organizations have rights to self-organize and form unions of their own. Book Five also describes unfair labour practices vide Chapter 2. Unfair labour practices constitute acts such as: to interfere with, restrain or coerce employees in the exercise of their right to self-organize, to dominate employees as a condition of employment to join in a union, to discriminate in regard to wages, hours of work, to violate a collective bargaining agreement and to dismiss or discriminate against an employee.

Unions and employers are expected to observe collective bargaining process as stipulated in the Labor Code while approaching such agreements. As per this process, any party that desires to negotiate an agreement shall serve the other party with a written notice which must be responded to by the party upon whom notice was served within 10 working days. In case of lack of response, or disagreement, the Board can intervene and enter conciliation proceedings. During the conciliation proceedings, either part is barred from creating any disturbance or from exhibiting any behaviour that impedes progress of settlement. Any collective bargaining that the parties may enter into shall be valid for the term of five years. The parties to a collective bargaining agreement shall include therein provisions that will ensure the mutual observance of its terms and conditions. They shall establish machinery for the adjustment and resolution of grievances arising from the interpretation or implementation of their collective bargaining agreement and of those arising from the interpretation or enforcement of company personnel policies. All grievances submitted to the grievance machinery which are not settled within seven days from the date of submission shall automatically be referred to voluntary arbitration prescribed in the collective bargaining agreement. The voluntary arbitrator will have the power to hold hearings, receive evidence and take whatever action is necessary to resolve the issues of dispute, and cost of the arbitrator and arbitration expenses shall be proportionately borne by both the parties. The award of arbitrator shall contain facts of the case and the final recommendation shall be executable within 10 days from the submission of such report.

In accordance with the Labor Code, workers will have the right to strike and employers to lockout in pursuit of their interests and consistent with national interest. However, no employer or union is allowed to call for strike or lockout on grounds on intra or inter union rivalry. Only in the case of genuine breakoff of negotiations or deadlock situations is either party allowed to serve a notice of 30 months with an intention to strike the work or lockout. Such notices shall be sent to the Department of Labor and Employment without fail. The notice must be drafted and served in accordance with relevant procedure laid down in the Code. During this notice period, it is incumbent upon the Department of Labor and Employment to make necessary attempts to conciliate and resolve the deadlock or differences in an amicable and objective manner. If the dispute is still unsettled after this mediation, unions have the right to strike and employers can go for proclamation of lockout. However, both the parties need to wait for expiry of mandatory cooling-off period upon serving the notice as mentioned before. A decision to declare strike shall always be espoused and approved by the majority of total membership of union. No union shall declare a strike and no employer can announce lockout without having exhausted the collective bargaining process and without serving the prior notice. Any employee who has lost wages due to illegal lockout is entitled to full back wages and reinstatement.

The Department of Labor and Employment is duly authorized and empowered to inquire into the financial activities of legitimate labour organizations and to examine the books of accounts and other records to determine compliance or non-compliance with the law and to prosecute any violations of the law. All unions are authorized to collect reasonable membership fees, union dues, assessments, and fines and contributions for welfare fund, strike fund and cooperative undertakings. In organizations where no legitimate union exists, a labour management committee may be formed voluntarily by workers and employer for the purpose of promoting industrial peace.

Book Six of the Labor Code deals with provisions and procedures related to the termination of employment. An employee is deemed to be a regular employee if the employment contract does not contradict that and if such employee is carrying out work which is integral part of the principal functioning of that organization. No oral contract arrangement contradicting the regular status of an employee is valid as long as such person is employed for regular work. Further, any employee who has continuously worked for a year without break in the past one year will fall under the definition of a regular employee. In case of regular employment, no employer can terminate the services of an employee except for a just cause or when authorized by the terms of employment contract agreed to in writing and not contrary to the spirit of the Labor Code. However, an employer can terminate an employee for causes that would include: serious misconduct or wilful disobedience by the employee of the lawful orders of his or her employer, gross and habitual neglect by the employee of his or her duties, fraud or wilful breach by the employee of the trust reposed in him or her by his or her employer, commission of a crime or offense by the employee against the person of his or her employer.

Employers can also cause termination of employee services on account of installation of labour-saving devices, redundancy or due to retrenchment to stop losses in order to save the organization by serving one month notice to all such effected employees and to the Department of Labor and Employment and shall also pay one month's salary for every completed year of service by such employees. An employer can also terminate services of an employee on the grounds of continuous ill health and of suffering from any disease and whose continued employment is prejudicial to his or her health. Severance pay clause is applicable here too wherein employer shall pay one month's equivalent salary for every year of service rendered by an employee. An employee who is intending to leave an employer shall serve a mandatory notice of 30 days failing which an employer can file damages. However, serving of 30 days' notice can be waived off if such severance of employment initiated by an employee is due to a serious insult caused to him or her by the employer, inhuman or unbearable treatment accorded or due to commission of a crime or offense by the employer. The retirement age of an employee shall be as specified in the collective bargaining agreement and in the absence of such clear definition of retirement age, the age for retirement can be deemed to be on attaining a minimum of 60 years of age and maximum of 65 years of age. On retirement, if an employee has worked for a minimum of five years in an establishment, he or she will be entitled to at least half month's salary or equivalent amount for every completed year of service.

Book Seven of the Labor Code dwells on penalties and liabilities. Any violation of the provisions enumerated in the said Labor Code is declared to be unlawful and considered an offense. The same is punishable with a fine of not less than 1,000 pesos and not more than 10,000 pesos or imprisonment of not less than three months and no more than three years or both at the discretion of the courts. In addition to the penalty, any foreigner found guilty will be deported upon completion of the sentence. All disputes and claims arising out of implementation of the Labor Code or interpretation of collective bargaining agreement shall be settled within three years failing which the same shall be summarily barred. Any unfair claim related to labour practice shall be filed within one year from the date the acts complained of were committed failing which the same will not be entertained.

Labour Laws in Australia

Labour and employment laws in Australia are promulgated at national, state and territory levels. These are discussed at macro level in the following paragraphs and some selective national legislation is also discussed in a detailed fashion.

National Level Legislation

The employment laws which are applicable to Australia nationwide mainly revolve around four acts. The first one is Workplace Relations Act, 1996 and associated acts and bills amending it. Most of the provisions of this legislation have been updated and replaced with the Fair Work Act (FWA), 2009. The objectives of this Act are: establishing and maintaining a simplified national system of workplace relations, enabling employees and employers to opt for the most appropriate form of agreement regulating various employment matters and dispute redressal processes, and balancing the right to take industrial action. The second one is FWA, 2009. This is the most comprehensive legislation intended to lay a framework to enable fairness and representation at work, right to freedom of association, ensure guaranteed safety net of fair terms and conditions of employment, set out rights and responsibilities of employees, employers and organizations in relation to the employment and importantly, it is a model to foster harmonious IR at workplace. The third one is the Anti-Discrimination Act of 1977. The objective of this Act is to prohibit discrimination in all normal circumstances on the grounds of race, gender, sex, transgender grounds, homosexuality, marital or domestic status, disability and age. The Act also promotes equal opportunity in public employment. The fourth piece of legislation is the Independent Contractors Act, 2006. Though this Act has exception in some states and territories, it is still an important legislation governing most of the industrial organizations in Australia nationwide. The objective of this Act is to provide a framework for entering into mutually negotiated and fair service contract between a person and institution that is legitimate and valid, and also to avoid misuse of independent contractor source for bypassing the employment of regular employees or indulge in paying lower remuneration for same kind of work to be performed in regular employment establishment.

Queensland Legislation

The notable legislation that is promulgated and applicable here is Industrial Relations Act, 1999. This Act envisages regulating IR and ensuring harmonious relationships between employees and organizations within the purview of state and local government sector. Another important piece of legislation in Queensland applicable to employees is Work Health and Safety Act of 2011. The main objective of this Act is to provide a nationally uniform and consistent framework to secure the health and safety of employees. The Act also stipulates that there shall be fair and effective workplace representation, consultation and cooperation to execute provisions of this Act.

New South Wales

There are four important Acts promulgated by New South Wales, some on its own and some by way of adoption of national legislation. These are: (a) Industrial Relations Act, 1996 whose objective is to provide regulations to ensure harmonious IR between state government sector and its employees, (b) Work Health and Safety Act of 2011 which was made applicable replacing the Occupational Health and Safety Act, 1983 to ensure health standards and safety measures of employees consistent with national and territories, (c) Workers Compensation Act which was brought into existence in 1987 and amended in 2012 with an aim to provide for the compensation and rehabilitation of workers in respect of work-related injuries and (d) Long Service Leave Act, an old legislation which was notified in 1958 but still operational and is intended to define entitlement of leave and its administration for working in organization for longer duration.

Victoria

Victoria has largely followed the federal labour law because it operates within federal jurisdiction mainly, though it has some legislations of its own. Victoria's specific laws focusing on employees include Sex Discrimination Act and the Racial Discrimination Act apart from Occupational Health and Safety Act of 2004.

South Australia

Entire labour legislation that was promulgated by the Federal Government is extended to South Australia with an exception that it has adopted its own version of IR legislation in the form of FWA, 1994 that is applicable to the employees of state government. The objective of this Act is to facilitate good working relationships between employees and the government, and the Act has also been extended to all employees and employers in South Australian jurisdiction.

Western Australia

Western Australia's specific labour and employment laws include Industrial Relations Act, 1979, Long Service Leave Act, 1958, Minimum Conditions of Employment Act, 1993, Public and Bank Holidays Act, 1972 and Workplace Agreements Act, 1993. Some of these Acts have paved way for national legislation in these respective areas and while there is a greater similarity of the legislation that is implemented countrywide, Western Australia retained these Acts due to distinction in few provisions although these distinctions are very peripheral and incidental.

Tasmania

There is one specific Act called the Industrial Relations Act, 1984 applicable within Tasmania whose scope and extent is limited to employees and government representatives of Tasmania state government.

Northern Territory

FWA, 2009, is only the piece of legislation that is very specific though it is very similar to federal FWA.

Australian Capital Territory

Two specific Acts applicable to Capital Territory are: Discrimination Act of 1991 whose objective is to ensure equal access to goods, services, facilities and accommodation to all the citizens and residents, and to eliminate any kind of discrimination in education opportunities and work- and career-related matters. The second Act is the Public Sector Management Act of 1994 whose objective is to regulate the administration of the public sector in the Australian Capital Territory.

Workplace Relations Act, 1996

Workplace Relations Act is no longer applicable and has been replaced by FWA, 2009. However, it is important to understand this repealed piece of legislation and background as the basic tenets of this Act remain captured in the said FWA. In few states and territories, this remains relevant in some measure.

Workplace Relations Act, 1996, contains 23 parts detailing establishment of the Australian Industrial Relations Commission (AIRC) to a wide variety of terms and conditions of employment as discussed further. Key objectives of this legislation are to promote flexible and fair labour market, facilitate peaceful and harmonious workplace relations, ensure minimum wages and employment conditions for those regulated by this Act, provide a platform of guidance for collective resolutions between employees and employer, ensure safety net entitlements, ensure freedom of association and to assist employees in work-life balance and to promote diversity.

Part 1 of the Act deals with title, objectives, commencement, definitions of terms including employee, employer and employment.

Part 2 mainly focuses on establishment and functioning of Australian Fair Pay Commission (AFPC). The Commission's responsibility encompasses conducting wage reviews, setting and adjusting wage levels for junior employees and employees with disabilities or employees to whom training arrangement applies. AFPC publishes wage setting decisions from time to time.

Part 3 is dedicated to establishment of AIRC. The Commission's composition, powers, appointment, termination, wages and the way the Commission is expected to perform its duties are vividly described in this part of the Act. AIRC is vested with the powers under this legislation that include to take evidence on oath or affirmation; vary or revoke order, direction or decision of the Commission; dismiss a matter or part of the matter; determine the proceedings in the absence of a person who has been summoned and sit at any place and conduct the proceedings, adjourn the proceedings, make interim decisions and make a final decision in respect of the matter to which the proceedings relate. The Commission can also authorize a person to take the evidence on its behalf.

Part 4 of the Act deals with setting up of Australian Industrial Registry and defining its scope. The functions of the Australian Industrial Registry are to provide advice and assistance to organizations in relation to their rights and obligations under this Act and to provide administrative support to the commission.

Part 5 focuses on the functions and powers related to matters of Employment Advocate. The functions of the Employment Advocate are to promote the making of workplace agreements, to provide assistance, education, information and advice to employees, to promote better work and management practices, to provide aggregated information and data to government administrators and to analyse the workplace agreements. Employment Advocate is a person appointed or employed by the Commonwealth or the State or more precisely in writing by the governor general for a period of five years on full-time basis and the Employment Advocate person is accountable to the minister. The Employment Advocate must not engage in any paid employment outside the duties of the office. The governor general can terminate employment of Employment Advocate at any time during the employment period on grounds of incapacity, misbehaviour, incompetence or inefficiency. The Employment Advocate must give written notice to the minister of all interests, pecuniary or otherwise, that could conflict with proper performance.

Part 6 of the Act deals with appointment and jurisdiction and powers of workplace inspectors. The minister may also appoint workplace inspectors to carry on the execution of this legislation as necessary with powers to determine and administer the workplace agreements, awards and the Australian Fair Pay and Conditions Standard (AFPCS). Inspectors can also enter premises of business establishment and inspect any work, material, machinery and appliance or interview any person seeking information, to require a person for custody and to inspect and make copies or take extracts of documents.

Part 7 of the Act deals with the key topic of operation of the AFPCS and also focuses on setting up of key minimum entitlements of employment. The AFPCS prevails over a workplace agreement or a contract of employment that operates in relation to an employee. As per the relevant provisions of this part, an employee who is not a piece rate wage employee must be paid a basic periodic rate of pay for each of the employee's guaranteed hours. If the employee is being paid on piece rate basis, then such employee shall be paid basic piece rates of pay for the work that is at least equal to the guaranteed basic pay rate equal to the guaranteed hours.

If an employee is employed to work a specified number of hours per week, the guaranteed hours for the employee for each week are to be worked out in this manner: Start with that specified number of hours and add additional hours on completion. If no specific mention is made in the employment contract of the number of hours an employee needs to work in a week, this can be assumed to be 38 hours per week. The casual employee must be paid, in addition to his or her actual basic periodic rate of pay, a casual loading that is at least equal to the guaranteed casual loading percentage of that actual basic periodic rate of pay. The default casual loading is 20 per cent. Any adjustment of the default casual loading percentage must be such that the adjusted rate is still expressed as a percentage. If a workplace agreement that covers the employment of the employee contains frequency of payment provisions that apply in relation to the employee's employment, the employer must comply with those provisions in relation to the employee. If no such agreement exists or if there is no such specific mention, then an employer must pay the employee on the basis of fortnightly payments in arrears. It is the responsibility of AFPC to ensure that the resulting guaranteed basic periodic rate of pay for the employee is not less than the commencement guaranteed basic periodic rate of pay for the employee. However, AFPC cannot exercise powers to the detriment of an employee's interest. In other words, AFPC cannot exercise its powers in a way that it considers will not result in an employee of average capacity, being entitled to less basic pay per week than he or she would have been entitled to because of AFPC intervention or exercise of powers.

The standard Fair Minimum Wage (FMW) is AUD 12.75 per hour. However, AFPC can adjust this rate periodically. AFPC can determine FMW to employees in junior employment category, employees with disability and employees to whom training arrangements apply. Australian Pay and Classification Scales (APCSs) is a set of provisions relating to pay and loadings for particular employees. APCSs contain rate provisions determining basic periodic rates of pay for employees whose employment is covered by the APCS and also rate provisions which determine basic piece rate of pay for employees. APCSs also need to provide a detailed description if the rate provisions are different for different employees. APCS will also specify casual loading provisions determining casual loadings for employees whose employment is covered by the APCS and for whom there are no basic piece rates of pay. An employee must not be required by an employer to work more than 38 hours a week. However, reasonable additional work hours can be added if there is an agreement between employees and an employer. Few factors can be considered for determining whether requirement of an employer seeking additional hours of work beyond 38 hours work per week is reasonable or not. These factors are: operational requirements of the workplace, health conditions of an employee, the employee's personal circumstances and safety. Any employer intending to require an employee to work additional hours must provide an advance notice in writing to the relevant employees and such employees intending to refuse the request must do so in writing by furnishing reasons.

Employees under this statute are entitled to be paid annual leave, for each completed four weeks period of continuous service with an employer, of one-thirteenth of the number of nominal hours worked by the employee for the employer during that four weeks period. For example, an employee whose nominal hours worked for a 12 months period where 38 hours per week would be entitled to 152 hours of annual leave which would be 4 weeks. The Act also allows an employer to pay salary equivalent to number of leaves provided if an employee is willing to cash out and forego the leave entitlement. However, no employer can exert undue pressure or force any employee to forego and surrender the leave for monetary benefit and this shall be purely voluntary and based on mutual agreement. Annual leave accrues on prorate basis. Each month, an employer must credit the leave as accrued by an employee. Employees are entitled to avail leave by seeking authorization of their employers and there shall be no maximum limit for an employee to avail the leave and for employer to authorize. The amount of leave is restricted to the amount available to the credit of an employee. An employer must not unreasonably refuse sanction of leave applied by an employee or revoke already granted leave. Employers can also encourage and require an employee to avail the leave thus available to the credit of an employee. In addition to the paid leave as discussed before, employees are also entitled to unpaid carer's leave of two days per occasion when an employee's family member needs support on account of health or household requirement. For leave on more than one occasion, it will be at the discretion of the employer and based on genuine grounds. However, an employer must entertain all genuine requests in this regard. An employee in order to avail unpaid leave must follow due process of informing employer well in advance in writing and seek approval. In exceptional circumstances which are beyond control of an employee, such advance notice is not a must condition. Employees are also eligible for sick leave for the duration that the employee is unfit to perform the job. In order to avail sick leave, an employee must also produce documentary evidence like medical certificate issued by a medical practitioner and in some cases employee can also provide self-declaration. In addition to carer's leave, employees are also entitled to guaranteed compassionate leave which is paid enabling an employee to attend to a sick family member or to support in household duties for a maximum of two days. The two days can be broken into single days also. Employees are eligible for parental leave/maternity leave for birth or adoption. An employee is eligible for maternity leave in case of pregnancy, birth of the child, the end of pregnancy otherwise than by the birth of a living child and death of the child. Paternity leave can be taken by the employee's spouse because of the birth of the child.

A single, unbroken period of unpaid leave up to one week can be granted to a male employee within the week starting after his spouse begins to give birth or after his spouse has given a birth to the child to become primary child caregiver. An employee is also allowed to avail any other leave combined with paternity leave. However, the maximum leave that can be granted on account of paternity leave will be 52 weeks. Paternity leave must end within 12 months after the date of birth of the child. The maximum total amount of maternity leave including special maternity leave and ordinary maternity leave to which an employee is entitled in relation to the birth of a child is 52 weeks. To be entitled to grant of maternity leave, an employee shall submit the necessary documentation issued by a medical practitioner. The application for leave preferably must be given to the employer no later than four weeks before the first day of the intended continuous period of leave. An employee can start availing maternity leave at any time within six weeks before the expected date of birth of the child. A continuous period of maternity leave must include a period of at least six weeks starting from the date of birth of the child. In case an employee intends to continue to work even during the six weeks just before the expected date of birth of the child, then such an employee must submit a certificate from a medical practitioner authorizing fitness to participate in the work. An employer can require an employee to proceed on maternity leave if the employee is unable to produce the aforementioned medical certificate of authorization. An employee will continue to be entitled to ordinary maternity leave in the event of end of pregnancy other than birth of the child and also in the case of death of child. An employer can cancel any untaken maternity leave by serving notice to the employee in conditions where employee is not the child's primary caregiver and having regard to the fact that the employee will not become child's primary caregiver in the immediate near future. Accordingly, the employee's entitlement to any untaken maternity leave in relation to the birth ends with effect from the day stated in the notice. An employee is also allowed to extend the ordinary maternity leave by way of an agreement with the employer, and employee must give four weeks' notice to the employer indicating the date of resuming duty. Employee is also given the right to terminate the employment at any time during the period of maternity leave. An employee who has given four weeks' notice to the employer for returning to work is entitled to the same position the employee held before proceeding on leave, and in case that position has been filled, it is the responsibility of the employer to provide a replacement position that is nearest in status and remuneration to the former position.

An employee is allowed two days of unpaid leave as pre-adoption leave to attend any interviews to gain approval for adoption of a child. Alternatively, employee can also avail any other leave available to his or her credit for same duration as paid leave on account of pre-adoption. An employee is eligible for short-term and long-term adoption leave depending upon circumstances. A short-term leave is meant for actual adoption and long-term leave is for providing care to the adopted child. The duration of leave that can be given for short-term adoption leave is a maximum of three weeks and for long-term adoption leave is a maximum of 52 weeks. In order to be eligible for grant of this leave, an employee must have completed at least 12 months' continuous service with the employer. The process for obtaining the said leave would involve advance intimation by the employee expressing intention to avail this leave on receiving the placement notice by the employee for adoption from the concerned agency. An employee holds the right of termination of employment at any time during the period of adoption leave. Further, at the end of adoption leave, an employee's return to work and protection of position or alternative position is guaranteed under the Act. Period of maternity or parental leave does not break an employee's continuity of service.

Part 8 of the Act deals with workplace agreements which is a critical piece of legislation in setting cardinal principles for entering into agreements between employees and employer, and interpreting and resolving the differences and disputes related to execution of various types of agreements. There are different types of agreements:

- An employer and employee can enter into an agreement for employment which is known as Australian Workplace Agreement (AWA). This is essentially used to regulate the relationship of employment forming basis for employment contract.

- An employer may make an agreement in writing with persons employed collectively, defining and clarifying terms and conditions of employment. These agreements are known as Employee Collective Agreements (ECAs).
- An employer and employee unions/organizations representing employee interests can enter into agreements related to various employment conditions which include rights and obligations. These agreements are known as Union Collective Agreements (UCAs).
- An employer may make an agreement in writing with one or more organizations of employees relating to a new business that the employer proposes to establish. This is known as Union Greenfield Agreement (UGA).
- There can also be an agreement called the Multiple Business Agreement (MBA) wherein more than one employer and more than one employee organization involving more than one business can enter into an agreement covering that part of industry business.

An employee or employer can appoint a person as their respective bargaining agent in relation to the issue being discussed for the purpose of entering into an agreement. These appointments shall be made in writing. When appointed by respective parties, no employer or employee can refuse to negotiate with such a bargaining agent. The employer must provide a reasonable time and opportunity to the employee's bargaining agent to interact, confer, seek clarifications and negotiate, and finalize the agreement. An employer who is intended to enter into an agreement with employees must provide draft of such agreement in writing at least seven days before the date of intending discussions. If the content of an agreement is changed post negotiation in whichever manner, the same shall be treated as a separate agenda for negotiation and shall not be incorporated in the ongoing agreement in whatever fashion. An agreement stands approved provided employer and employees sign and date such agreement under the presence of witnesses. For the purpose of collective agreements, the agreement is approved if a majority of persons vote to approve the agreement. All the signed agreements must be lodged with Employment Advocate within 14 days from the date of approval. An employer is deemed to have contravened the spirit and letter of this statute and particularly relevant provisions if any agreement is lodged with the Employment Advocate without due approval or without adhering to due process as mentioned here. Employment Advocate on receipt of duly approved copy must notify all the parties and issue a receipt to begin the execution of contents of the agreement. An agreement ceases to be in operation if it passed the agreed expiry date or is replaced with another agreement superseding the existing one. Once any agreement ceases to be in operation, it can only be activated again for operation by being signed, approved and lodged with Employment Advocate. There can be only one agreement on a clearly given subject and there shall be no multiple agreements either conflicting or repeating the same. Once an agreement is in operation, the same shall be binding on all the relevant parties. Generally any agreement is valid till the date of expiry or on completion of fifth anniversary, whichever is earlier. An agreement also needs to include procedure for settling the disputes that may arise out of and in the course of implementation of provisions of the agreement. Wherever any agreement does not include the dispute resolution procedure, the model dispute resolution procedure would automatically apply. Any agreement covering terms and conditions of employment entered into contravening laws of the state are void. No employer shall lodge an agreement with Employment Advocate that is contravening the state law in any manner. Employment Advocate on receipt of any agreement must study and advise the employer in writing especially when there is a conflict with the existing law so that the employer can withdraw the same. Alternatively, Employment Advocate can also consider making a variation to the agreement in confidence with both the parties. However, Employment Advocate shall not make these variations without giving an opportunity to both parties to being heard so they can give their views and rationale in writing. It is the responsibility of an employer to publish and circulate the information related to workplace agreements among existing and prospective employees and to illustrate how it can affect their employment conditions.

An employer, who is intending to terminate an agreement, must take reasonable steps to ensure that all eligible employees are given a statement of information. However, no termination can take place unless employees or employee organizations approve such termination in writing with reasons. Employers must also ensure that employees get adequate time to dwell upon and discuss the proposal of termination and completely understand the consequences of approving such termination. In case of collective bargaining agreements, such decision of termination can be made and approved by the majority vote only. No person is allowed to use duress or threaten, or engage in any industrial action in order to coerce a person to agree to make, lodge, approve or terminate a collective agreement. Likewise, making any misleading statements or producing wrong facts with an ulterior motive to gain an approval is a gross contravention to this law. Employer shall not discriminate between employees in any manner because some of these employees are members of or not members of any unions and should not show any bias in engaging one union over the other in negligence to the laid-down process for collective barging negotiations. Any employee or employer or union not convinced with any agreement can challenge the same in the court of law invoking civil legal remedy.

Part 9 of Workplace Relations Act of 1996 focuses on industrial action which means any action such as: (a) the performance of work by an employee in a manner different from that in which it is normally performed or any difference in actions by an employee that results in delayed performance, (b) a ban, limitation or restriction on the performance of work by an employee, (c) refusal of an employee to perform any work which is logically part of an employee's job expectation and (d) lockout of the establishment by an employer, thus rendering employees out of employment. The Commission can bar any party from resorting to or participating in any industrial action in exceptional circumstances such as when an industrial action endangering life, the personal safety or health, or the welfare of the population or when it adversely affects the employer or the employees and when such action can cause significant damage to the Australian economy or an important part of it. In order to resort to any protected industrial action, either party attempting the industrial action must serve three days' advance written notice with explanation for such intended action. The notice must also state the nature of such intended action. If such advance notice is not served, then any industrial action cannot be termed as protected industrial action meaning it may be devoid of legal protection. During the bargaining period, an organization of employees that is a negotiating party or an employee who is a negotiating party and the employer or employer representatives in pursuit of their claims can organize or engage in industrial action against each other in adhering to the due process. This is called protected action. Engaging in industrial action in relation to a proposed collective bargaining agreement is not protected action if it is to support or advance claims to include prohibited content in the agreement or the industrial action is not protected if it is engaged in while the bargaining period is suspended. Any person who is not a protected person cannot engage in industrial action and in the event that they engage in such action, it will be deemed to be an unprotected industrial action. A protected person for industrial action means: an organization of employees that is a negotiating party to the proposed collective agreement or an employer who is a negotiating party to the proposed collective agreement. However, either party cannot indulge in industrial action without exhausting all peaceful and functional remedies to reach a collective bargaining agreement in normal course. No law in force in a state or territory can interfere with any protected industrial action unless such action is likely to involve personal injury, wilful destruction or damage to the property and unlawful use of property.

Part 9 also describes the process which allows employees directly concerned to choose, by means of a fair and democratic secret ballot, whether to authorize industrial action supporting or advancing claims by organizations of employees or by employees directly. Unless majority of employees chose an industrial action through a protected action ballot, the same will be termed as unprotected industrial action. Employees' organization or member of a union can apply to the Commission following due process for authorizing a protected secret ballot. The said application must include: the issues to be put for employees to choose in the ballot along with the nature of proposed industrial action, details of employees who can participate in the ballot and rules regulating the ballot process as authorized by the Commission. It is an offense to make or communicate any declaration or statement that is misleading, misrepresenting and contrary to the facts while organizing or participating in a protected ballot process. The Commission will have the responsibility to authorize and apply regulations for conduct of the ballot expeditiously and no later than 10 days from the date of lodging such an application. It can also order the employer of the relevant employees or the applicant to submit a list of employees who may be eligible to participate in the ballot and to submit all other relevant information necessary for a transparent and objective process. The Commission may appoint an authorized ballot agent to conduct the ballot and declare the results. An industrial action proposed in the ballot will qualify as protected action if 50 per cent or more eligible voters favour/approve such an action in the ballot conducted by an authorized ballot agent. An important condition is that at least 50 per cent of the eligible voters out of total eligible voters list must participate in the ballot. Employer and employees who are bound by a collective agreement shall engage in any industrial action as long as the agreement is in operation and has not passed the date of expiry.

Part 10 of the Act centres on the subject of awards with an aim to ensure that minimum safety net entitlements are protected and also that the awards are simplified and transparent. An award covers terms such as: hours of work, rest breaks, notice periods, incentive-based payments and bonuses, annual leave loadings, monetary allowances, redundancy pay, dispute settling procedures, type and nature of employment and conditions for outworkers. However, certain conditions are not allowable award matters. These are: rights of an organization of employers or employees, conversion from casual employment to another type of employment, prohibitions on an employer employing employees in a particular type of employment, restriction on the range or duration of training arrangements, restriction on the engagement of independent contractors and restrictions on the engagement of labour hire workers. However, an award may include machinery provisions including but not limited to commencement, definitions, titles and arrangement, and a model anti-discrimination clause. The Commission may rationalize, review and simplify, and revoke an award on defined grounds in order to protect the rightful interests. Employees or employer can approach the Commission on valid grounds for the said actions by providing facts and a rationale for such a request. Till an award is in operation, employees, employees' organization and employers are bound by the terms of the award.

Part 11 of the Act focuses on transmission of business rules, that is, to provide for the transfer of employer obligations under certain instruments when the whole or part of a person's business is transmitted to another person. All agreements which are operational at the time of transmission of a business from old employer to new employer will remain operational, and status quo shall be maintained and no change whatsoever can be incorporated. The new employer will occupy the position of the old employer for all purposes related to such agreements and are bound by the agreements. The new employer, however, is bound by the collective agreement only in relation to the employment in the business being transferred or employees being transferred as a part of such business transmission. Old employer's rights and obligations that arose before time of transmission are not affected and the old employer will remain accountable for all issues originated before the effective date of business transmission. The new employer can apply to the Commission for revoke of the existing collective agreement if necessary on valid grounds such as the terms and conditions of employment that the new employer intends to offer are superior to the standards the current collective agreement provides for. No collective agreement needs to be moved to the new employer's ambit if not even a single employee is being transferred due to transmission of a business unit. Similarly, the transmitted award ceases to be in operation in relation to a transferring employee's employment with the new employer if the new employer makes an AWA with the transferring employee after the transmission. The new employer also becomes liable for a transferring employee's entitlements in relation to all the benefits including parental leave, continuity of service and so on.

Part 12 deals with minimum entitlements of employees. An employer must not require an employee to work for more than five hours continuously without an unpaid interval of at least 30 minutes for a meal. All employees are entitled to public holidays as paid days. These are: 1 January (New Year's Day), 26 January (Australia Day), Good Friday, Easter Monday, 25 April (Anzac Day), 25 December (Christmas Day) and 26 December (Boxing Day) and any other day declared by state or territory government by way of legislation. However, an employer in reasonable circumstances and depending upon nature of service/operation can require an employee to work even during the public holiday. There shall be equal remuneration for work of equal value and shall comply with all anti-discrimination conventions. Employees are entitled to conciliation regarding the matters relating to their termination or proposed termination as per the established processes. They are also entitled to arbitration process if the conciliation process is unsuccessful and they can approach the Commission if arbitration too is unsuccessful in resolving the issue and if there are fair grounds to challenge the arbitration process. An application made in this regard, if found frivolous, vexatious or lacking in substances, can be rejected. An employer shall not cause termination of an employee on the grounds of: temporary absence from the work because of illness or injury, participation in trade union activities, filing a complaint against an employer, race, colour, sex, age, physical or mental disability, refusing to negotiate an agreement or absence from the work during maternity/parental leave. All terminations shall carry mandatory notice period and serving of a written notice as per the collective agreement or notice shall be provided as stipulated in this Act (at least one week if service period of an employee is not more than one year, two weeks if service period is more than one year but less than three years and at least four weeks if the total service period is more than five years).

Part 13 is dedicated to dispute resolution process with an objective to encourage employers and employees who are parties to a dispute to resolve it at the workplace level and to introduce greater flexibility for the resolution of disputes by allowing the parties to determine the best forum in which to resolve them. The model dispute resolution process is automatically applicable in case the workplace agreements/collective agreements do not provide any dispute resolution process. The model dispute resolution processes cover all the disputes related to: entitlements under the AFPCS, disputes about the terms of a workplace agreement, disputes about the application of workplace determination, disputes about the application of awards and disputes related to meal breaks and public holidays and parental leave. As much as possible, either party must make genuine attempts to resolve the disputes amicably without pressing for conciliation or arbitration proceedings. An employee who has a dispute must make attempts to reach the supervisor or review manager to settle the matter. An employee who is party to a dispute must continue to work as normal while the dispute is being resolved unless such dispute is causing imminent risk. In case an employee is not satisfied with the resolution offered by the supervisor, he or she can opt for alternative dispute resolution process in which a neutral person is appointed to study the dispute and offer the solution. The neutral person can invoke an appropriate method such as conferencing, mediation, assisted negotiation, neutral evaluation, case appraisal, conciliation or arbitration to resolve the dispute in an objective manner. The neutral resource persons can be made available by the Commission on submission of application of dispute by an employee and in some cases a refusal may be accorded if the case is devoid of merits. The alternative dispute resolution process is conducted in private. Alternative dispute resolution proceedings come to an end once an amicable solution is found or if either party refuses the solution proposed, thus leaving the ground to the Commission to end the matter in fittest of things.

Part 14 of the Workplace Relations Act, 1996 deals with compliance, penalties and general provisions relating to civil remedies. An employee can apply for penalty or other remedy under this division in relation to a breach of an applicable provision of AWA, AFPCS, a term of an award, a term of collective agreement, a term of an order of the Commission and any section of the legislation. An eligible court may impose a penalty if evidence of contravention exists. Similarly employers apply for grant of damages in relation to a breach of an applicable provision.

Matters related to the Right of Entry are described in part 15 of the statute and this part has the following objectives:

1. To provide a framework that balances (a) the right of organizations to represent their members in the workplace, hold discussions with potential members and investigate suspected breaches of employment law and instruments, (b) the right of employers to conduct their businesses without undue interference or harassment.
2. To ensure that employers and employees, and their organizations understand their rights and obligations in true spirit.
3. To ensure that permits are issued to eligible members to enter premises and inspect records. The industrial registrar is the appropriate authority to issue the permit in favour of a person or an organization on consideration of all facts and genuineness and eligibility.

At the time of issuing permit, a registrar may impose conditions that limit the circumstances in which permit has effect. A permit that was issued automatically expires at the end of the third anniversary of the date of issue or when the official in whose favour the permit is issued ceases to be a member of that organization, whichever occurs early. A permit holder who suspects on reasonable grounds that a breach has occurred or is occurring can enter premises during the working hours. However, permit holder is bound to provide a 24 hours' advance notice to the employer communicating the intention and purpose of entry and inspection of the premises and records. But if such an advance notice can cause dilution or might result in the destruction, concealment or alteration of relevant evidence, then permit holder can gain an exception approval from the Registrar and in such circumstances the condition of advance notice is waived off. Permit holder is also allowed to hold discussion with relevant employees to garner the information.

The objectives of Part 16 of the legislation include: (a) ensuring that employers, employees and independent contractors are free to become or not become members of industrial associations, (b) ensuring that employers, employees and independent contractors are nor discriminated against because they are members or not members of any industrial association, (c) ensuring effective relief to employers, employees and independent contractors and enabling them to exercise their rights to freedom of association and (d) providing effective remedies to penalize and deter persons who engage in conduct which prevents or inhibits employers, employees or independent contractors from exercising their rights to freedom of association. No person must be coerced in any manner to become or not become a member of any industrial organization and each person has absolute freedom of association. No employer can threaten to terminate or terminate, or take any punitive action or exhibit any bias against any employee or independent contractor because such employee has become or not become member of any industrial organization. Similarly an employee or independent contractor must not cease work or refuse to continue to be engaged in work because the employer is or is not a member of any industrial association. No employee or a person employed in any organization shall be discriminated against because applicability or non-applicability of any legal instrument such as AFPCS.

Offenses in relation to the Commission are dealt with in part 17 of the Act which basically stresses that a person shall not (a) insult or disturb a member of the Commission in the exercise of powers or in course of performance of functions and responsibilities, (b) interrupt the proceedings of the Commission, (c) use insulting language towards a member and (d) write or speak words meant to influence a member of the Commission improperly. No person shall be threatened or intimidated because of providing information or evidence to the Commission in its inquiry or study, or review of any proceedings. A person who is not summoned to appear before the Commission shall not disobey the orders or refuse to be sworn or refuse to answer or refuse to produce a document that is being sought. Conflicting with any of these provisions amounts to offense, and appropriate action including penalty and imprisonment can be imposed based on the nature and gravity of an offence.

Part 18 deals with bearing financial costs associated with proceedings and efforts made to resolve the disputes. As per the statute, costs shall be borne by the party who is to be blamed for dispute arousal or party responsible for action of contravention. In case the complaint is frivolous or if the party instituted the proceedings vexatiously or filed without proper cause, then the party responsible for filing it shall be ordered to pay all the costs. The costs shall include all legal and professional costs, and disbursements and expenses of witnesses.

Part 19 of the statute details various miscellaneous provisions such as conduct of officers, directors and employees or agents for the purposes of this Act, court powers, interim injunctions, trade secrets, enforcement of penalties, acquisition of property and related regulations. Jurisdiction of the federal court, the procedure of interpretation of awards, appellate jurisdiction, representation of parties before the court or federal magistrate court and particular rights of intervention of minister are dealt with in part 20 of the Act, while matters referred by Victoria, that is, extension or additional inclusion of provisions as a result of the referral of certain matters to the Parliament of the Commonwealth are detailed in part 21. Special provisions concerning contract outworkers in Victoria in the textile, clothing and footwear industry are discussed in part 22, and matters pertaining to school-based apprentices and trainees are discussed in part 23 and in the final piece of the legislation.

Fair Work Act, 2009

FWA of 2009 has replaced the aforementioned legislation of Workplace Relations Act, 1996 in all respects.

FWA is an elaborate legislation consisting of six chapters enacted with an aim to:

- provide workplace relations framework that is fair to employees, flexible to businesses and promote productivity and economic growth,
- ensure guaranteed safety net of fair, relevant and enforceable minimum terms and conditions, national minimum wages,
- assist employees to balance their work and family responsibilities by providing flexible work arrangements,
- prevent discrimination and encourage freedom of association and to protect against unfair treatment,
- provide accessible and effective grievance redressal mechanism,
- achieve productivity and fairness through institutionalization of enterprise level collective bargaining process and rules to regulate industrial action,
- provide for terms and conditions of employment and
- set out rights and responsibilities of employees, employers and organizations in relation to the employment.

Chapter 1

Chapter 1 of the Act centres on introductions and definitions, and meaning of employee, employer, base rate pay, full rate of pay, industrial action, ordinary hours of work, piece worker, continuous service, transfer of employment and so on, and this chapter also clearly describes the extent of application of the Act and interaction with state and territory laws.

Chapter 2

Chapter 2 deals with principal provisions of this legislation as discussed further.

While providing employment contract of terms and conditions, an employer must ensure that such employment contract shall not contravene provisions of Employment Standards. Similarly, a modern award or an enterprise agreement shall not exclude the National Employment Standards. A modern award is not applicable to an employee at a time when an enterprise agreement applies to that employee. Only one enterprise agreement can be made applicable to an employee at any given point of time. The National Employment Standards are minimum standards that apply to the employment of national system employees. They also provide guidance on what to include what is not desirable in awards and enterprise agreements. As per the National Employment Standards:

- An employer must not request or require an employee to work more than 38 hours in a week unless the additional hours of work are reasonable. The employee may refuse to work unreasonable additional hours. Factors such as health and safety of employees, employee's personal and family circumstances, need of the workplace, entitlement for overtime payment play an important role in determining whether the ask for additional hours of work is reasonable or unreasonable.

- An employer must give a pay slip to each of its employees and shall also keep these slips for seven years as employee records as per the regulation of this chapter.
- An employee who is a parent or has the responsibility for the care of a child of under school age can request the employer for a change in working arrangements such as hours of work, pattern of work and change in location of work. The employer is expected to decide to grant or refuse such a request within 21 days from the date of such written request from the employee. Decision of refusal must be on valid grounds.
- An employee who has completed 12 months of continuous service is entitled to parental leave and related entitlements. The leave that can be granted under this category is for birth of a child or for miscarriage or for adoption. For this purpose, an employee is entitled to 12 months of unpaid parental leave and such leave shall be availed in a single continuous period. An employee is also eligible to take any paid leave available during the period of the said unpaid leave. A pregnant employee in normal circumstances will be asked to take leave six weeks before the expected date of birth. However, this condition of having to take six weeks' leave prior to childbirth can be relaxed based on medical certificate which states that such advance leave is not warranted. Employee is also eligible to request the employer for grant of additional 12 months' unpaid leave on expiry of the first 12 months. The employer can refuse such a request on valid grounds. No extension beyond 24 months is allowed.
- A female employee is entitled to unpaid special maternity leave on account of pregnancy-related illness or if she has been pregnant and the pregnancy ends within 28 weeks of the expected date of birth. A female employee in this context is also entitled to seeking transfer to a safe job if the current can potentially create challenges to her health. An employee is also entitled to return to the same job or an available job if the same position no longer exists on completion of parental leave.
- Employees are entitled to four to five weeks of paid annual leave depending upon nature of award, and such leave accrues progressively during a year of service according to the employee's ordinary hours of work and accumulates from year to year. The employer must not unreasonably refuse to agree to a request by the employee to take paid annual leave. Employees are entitled to salary in lieu of untaken leaves. However, employers can ask an employee to avail the leave instead of any monetary payouts. In addition to this leave, an employee is also entitled to 10 days of paid personal leave for each completed year of service. This leave can be availed during employee's illness or any unexpected emergency. Also, an employee is entitled to two days of compassionate leave for each occasion to attend to family member's illness or death. Employees are also eligible to seek grant of leave on account of community service participation such as jury service, voluntary emergency management activity and natural disaster.
- Employees are entitled to be absent during public holiday and they are eligible to be paid normal salary during such public holidays.
- No employee shall be terminated from the services of an enterprise without being given written advance notice ranging from one week to four weeks and above based on the length of service of an employee. Employees on termination of their employment are entitled to redundancy pay of minimum of four weeks to a maximum of 12 weeks and above based on their length of service in the employment. However, employees are not entitled to any such pay when their services are transferred to another employer without interruption and with protection of existing terms and conditions of employment.

The Act envisages that modern awards may set minimum terms and condition for national system employees in particular industries and occupations. Modern awards can also have terms that are ancillary to the National Employment Standards. The modern awards must ensure the following in order to extend minimum safety net of terms and conditions:

- Living standards and needs of low-paid workers are addressed.
- Encouragement of collective bargaining.
- Promotion of social inclusion through increased workforce participation.
- Promotion of flexible modern work practices and the efficient and productive performance of work.
- Implementation of equal remuneration for work of equal or comparable value
- Simplification and avoidance of overlaps of awards.
- Minimum wages along with skill-based classification and career structures, incentive-based payments, piece rates and bonuses.
- Clarity on type of employment such as full-time employment, casual employment, regular part-time employment, shift work and flexible working arrangements.
- Overtime work conditions including payments for work during holidays.
- Annualized wage arrangements and allowances, leave and superannuation. An employee's base and full rates of pay are significant in determining the employee's entitlements under the National Employment Standards.
- Procedure for consultation, representation and dispute settlement.
- Outworker terms.
- Redundancy process and redundancy wages.
- Terms for providing for or specifying the determination of the ordinary hours of work for each classification of employees.
- A modern award must not include an objectionable term and it should not include terms that discriminate against an employee on account of race, colour, sex, age, physical or mental disability, marital status, religion, political opinion or social origin.
- Modern awards shall provide provision for review of the award contents once in four years.

An enterprise agreement is made at the enterprise level and provides terms and conditions for the national system employees. It shall include the following matters:

- Relationship between employer and the employees
- Base pay and wages, benefits and allowances
- Hours of work
- Public holidays
- Flexible working arrangements
- Dispute redressal mechanism
- Redundancy provisions
- Industrial action-related workplace determination

An enterprise level agreement is reached subsequent to collective bargaining process and necessary approvals.

The part of the legislation also stipulates conditions and process to be followed in arriving at minimum wages of national system employees who are eligible for the same based on socio-economic factors. While setting minimum wages, it must be ensured that national minimum wages for various skills and trades are taken into consideration as notified from time to time. An employer must not contravene a term of national minimum wage order. Factors such as performance and competitiveness of an organization including productivity, inflation, social inclusion, living standards, needs of low paid and principle of equal remuneration for work of equal value shall be considered.

This chapter also stipulates provisions related to transfer of business and associated transfer of enterprise agreements, awards and other collective bargaining instruments. The objective of provisions here is to protect employee's terms and conditions of employment under enterprise agreements, awards and other mutually agreed upon provisions between employees and outgoing employer and interest of employers in running the business. Requirements of transfer of services of an employer to the new employer include a three months' notice to the employee and a clear connection being established between employee and the new employer.

Chapter 3 of the Act deals with rights and responsibilities of employees, employers and organizations. Rights basically involve protection of freedom of association and involvement in lawful industrial activities and anti-discrimination clause providing relief for persons who have been discriminated against or victimized. Any action involving termination of services of an employee or causing injury or intimidation or the refusal to employ a prospective employee or discriminating against or altering the position of existing employee unfavourably is called an adverse action and this chapter lays down the conditions to deal with such actions. Similarly, the chapter also stipulates conditions for employees who refuse to follow the legitimate instructions of the employer in carrying out work or deliberately causing hurdles to productivity on no valid grounds. The chapter also describes and sets guidelines for protected action ballots with an objective to establish a fair, simple and democratic process to allow a bargaining representative to determine whether employees wish to engage in particular protected industrial action for a proposed enterprise agreement. All industrial action-related matters and their regulations are also covered in the current chapter including payments relating to periods of industrial action and rights of entry. An employer may stand down an employee during a period in which the employee cannot usefully be employed because of industrial action or breakdown of machinery or equipment for which an employer is not responsible or any other stoppage of work for which employer in any manner cannot be held accountable. During this period, an employee is not entitled to any salary payments.

Chapter 4 is about civil remedies, compliance and enforcement-related issues. An employee or employer who experiences contravention of this law or any instrument of collective or individual agreement can seek civil remedy and seek enforcement of an entitlement or restoration of a condition that ought to have existed. The courts are also empowered to impose pecuniary penalties as appropriate. A court may apply the rules of evidence and procedure for civil matters while hearing proceedings relating to a contravention. An employer is required to pay any pecuniary penalty thus imposed or any amount that is payable to an employee to the Commonwealth. A court may not order a person to serve a sentence of imprisonment if the person fails to pay a pecuniary penalty imposed under this Act and court may attach property or assets if any.

Chapter 5 deals with administration and governance of this Act, including the establishment of fair work in Australia. The underlying principle is that administration and enforcement must be simple, transparent, quick, fair and just, and shall take all actions to achieve harmonious and cooperative workplace relations while reckoning equity, good conscience and merits of the matter. The Act also mandates establishment of a fair work ombudsman to monitor compliance with this Act and establishment of fair work instruments or, if required, to investigate and inquire into practices that are contrary to this legislation.

Chapter 6 and final part of this Act is about miscellaneous provisions and equal remuneration applications and disposal of unlawful termination of applications, complaints and general protection applications that do not relate to dismissal and issues relating to the powers of FWA and other persons to deal with a dispute of an award, agreement or contract of employment.

Anti-Discrimination Act, 1977

The Act consists of 10 parts stipulating provisions and regulations related to prohibition of racial discrimination, sexual harassment, sex discrimination, discrimination based on marital or domestic status or on the grounds of disability, homosexuality, age discrimination, transgender as discussed next part wise.

Part 1 of the Act describes the commencement, definitions and reference of certain employers.

Part 2 is focused on provisions relating to racial discrimination. It is unlawful for an employer to discriminate against a person on the grounds of race in issues such as: (a) determining who should be offered employment, (b) in the terms on which the employer offers employment, (c) denial of employee access or limiting the employee access to training or promotion opportunities and (d) dismissing or subjecting an employee to any other detriment. It is also unlawful to discriminate against any person for joining or failing to accept the application for membership in an industrial organization based on race. It is also unlawful for a person to incite hatred or ridicule a person or group of persons based on the race of a person.

Part 2A of the Act prohibits sexual harassment. A person sexually harasses another person if the person makes an unwelcome sexual advance or an unwelcome request for sexual favours to the other person or the person engages in other unwelcome conduct of a sexual nature in relation to the other person in circumstances in which a reasonable person having regard to all the circumstances would have anticipated that the other person would be offended, humiliated or intimated.

Part 3 deals with issues related to sex discrimination. A person discriminates against another person on the grounds of sex if he or she treats the aggrieved person less favourably than, in the same circumstances, or in circumstances which are not materially different, he or she would a person of the opposite sex or if he or she requires the aggrieved person to comply with a requirement or condition with which a substantially higher proportion of persons of the opposite sex are able to comply and with which the aggrieved person is not able to comply. It is unlawful for an employer to discriminate against or in favour of people in employment offers or opportunities in training, career and benefits, and so on based on sex preferences. However, this legislation does not render unlawful discrimination against a person on the grounds of sex where being a person of a particular sex is a genuine occupational qualification for the job.

Provisions related to discrimination on transgender grounds are enumerated in part 3A of the legislation. A transgender person here is someone who, whether recognized as transgender or not, identifies as member of the opposite sex by living or seeking to live as a member of the opposite sex. No transgender employee shall be treated differently from other employees and shall not be shown a discriminatory treatment in whatever manner in all official dealings. An employer shall not require a transgender to amend self to suit the conditions convenient for the majority of employees. No person is allowed to behave in a manner that ridicules or spreads hatred towards a transgender person. In other words, transgender vilification is strictly prohibited and is unlawful in any circumstance. It is not unlawful to show discrimination in any sporting activity for members of the sex with whom the transgender person identifies.

Part 4 is dedicated to provisions and regulations related to discrimination on the grounds of marital or domestic status. It is unlawful for an employer to treat any employee differently on the grounds of marital or domestic status than, in the same circumstances, he or she would an employee of a different marital or domestic status. However, nothing in this part renders unlawful discrimination on the grounds of marital or domestic status in the terms and conditions appertaining to a superannuation or PF where the terms and conditions are based on actuarial data which is reasonable to rely on.

Part 4A is about discrimination on the grounds of disability. Consistent with anti-discrimination approach, no employer shall discriminate against a person with disability in employment opportunities, career, and training and benefits in whichever manner. However, it is not unlawful for an employer to discriminate against a person with disability in certain circumstances where a person's disability will come in the way of his or her carrying out the inherent requirements of a particular employment or a job/position that would require a person without disability and an employer will put to unjustifiable hardship if the said clause is imposed without consideration independent to the reality. Also, nothing in this section renders unlawful discrimination against a person on the grounds of disability if the disability concerned is an infectious disease and the discrimination is reasonably necessary to protect public health. Part 4B stipulates provisions related to discrimination on the grounds of a person's responsibilities as a carer. A carer is described as one who has the responsibility to take care of a child or a family member who is sick or injured and such employee may require some flexible arrangement at work in order to fulfil his or her responsibility as a carer. An employer by law needs to provide some relief as defined in the legislation and because of that, such employee shall not be put to any disadvantage in treatment or opportunities failing which will be considered as discrimination by an employer.

Part 4C of the Act vividly describes what constitutes discrimination on the grounds of homosexuality and clauses to prohibit such behaviour in organizations. A person's homosexuality for the purpose of this legislation includes a reference to the person being thought to be a homosexual person whether he or she is in fact a homosexual person or not. It is unlawful to discriminate against a homosexual person in all spheres of employment matters including contract employment, membership to industrial organizations and in allotment of accommodation/ club membership and any form of vilification is strictly prohibited and categorized as an offense.

Part 5 deals with unlawful acts such as victimization of an aggrieved person. No person shall be victimized or harassed, or intimated because he or she has brought proceedings against a discriminator, given evidence or information against a discriminator. However, a person, who is found to have indulged in making a false complaint or who has made baseless allegations leading to proceedings without a reasonable case or credible event, will be penalized. A person shall not publish or cause to be published an advertisement that indicated an intention to commit an act that is unlawful under this Act.

Part 6 of the Act focuses on the general exceptions to this Act. Any action or behaviour of a person cannot be treated as unlawful if a person has acted or behaved in that way to comply with any other legislation passed or existing before this Act or in consonance with an order of the tribunal or order of any court.

Parts 7 and 8 of the Act describe the Anti-Discrimination Board, its constitution, appointment of members and their removal and governance; part 9 describes the functions of the president, the tribunal and the Board and part 9A focuses on equal opportunity in public employment matters. Part 9B is about intergovernmental arrangements and part 10 deals with miscellaneous provisions.

Independent Contractors Act, 2006

This Act came into existence in the year 2006 and its primary objectives are:

- to protect the freedom of independent contractors to enter into services contracts,
- to recognize independent contracting as a legitimate form of work arrangement that is primarily commercial and
- to prevent interference with the terms of genuine independent contracting arrangements.

A service contract under this Act is defined as a contract entered into for rendering services to which an independent contractor is a party and that has the requisite constitutional connection. The said independent contract can be made only in a territory of Australia and at least one party must be a body incorporated in Australia in order to be valid under this legislation. The following are identified as unfairness grounds as far as an independent contractor contract is concerned:

- The contract is unfair.
- The contract is harsh or unconscionable.
- The contract is unjust.
- The contract is against the public interest.
- The contract is designed to avoid the provisions of Workplace Relations Act, 1996.
- The contract is designed to avoid any other law promulgated by a state or territory.
- The contract is designed to avoid an award, agreement or any other instrument made under collective bargaining process.
- The contract is made providing remuneration which is less than the rate of remuneration for an employee performing similar work.

An application can be made to a court urging the court to review a services contract on aforementioned grounds or on the grounds that such contract is harsh or unfair or both. Nobody can commence any other proceedings related to a contract when the same is under the review of a court. The court while reviewing an application in this context may have regard to (a) the relative strengths of the bargaining positions of the parties to the contract, (b) whether any undue influence or pressure was exerted on or any unfair tactics were used against a party to the contract, (c) whether the contract provides total remuneration, that is, or is likely to be, less than that of an employee performing similar work and (d) any other matters that the court thinks is relevant. The court is empowered to pass an order setting aside the whole or a part of the contract or an order varying the contract. The court can also make an interim order if the conditions necessitate the same.

There are state or territory laws regulating and governing matters related to independent contractor engagement and contracts. A reform opt-in agreement can be entered into by writing and after being signed by the parties to the effect that state or territory contractor laws are to no longer apply to a specified service contract or simply that the parties no longer want the state or territory contractor laws to apply to any of the service contracts of a specified class or classes. However, a person must not take any action or threaten to take any action or refrain or threaten to refrain from taking any action with intent to coerce another person to enter into or to not enter into a reform opt-in agreement.

Summary

The foregoing chapter discusses key legislative measures and their transformation over a period of time in selective countries in Asia such as PRC, Japan, Singapore, the Philippines and also legislative measures in Australia. Though legislative evolution and kinds of laws that exist have similarities and dissimilarities in these nations, the common thread running across is that their transformation from a protective form of state labour policy to egalitarian to more competitive and market-friendly form. Some of the legislative measures appear to have been aimed to ease the conditions to the extent that fuel the efforts to compete with developed economies much more aggressively. As more and more organizations are internationalizing in and out of these nations, it is paramount to track the labour legislation and their relevance to IHRM practice. With this objective, the chapter was devoted to key labour laws and regulations.

QUESTIONS FOR DISCUSSION

1. Discuss the importance of 2008 labour law transformation in China. How does this transformation intend to give a fillip to economic development?
2. What kind of foreign company employment contract is legally tenable in China under the Employment Contract Law of the PRC?
3. What is the purpose of Skills Development Levy Act, 1979 of Singapore and how does it contribute to skill building initiatives?
4. Discuss the terms and conditions of employment as applicable to dispatch employees in Japan.
5. What are the salient features of Labour Standards Law in Japan?
6. Write a critique on the Philippines Labor Code.
7. What are the key legislative measures at national level in Australia?
8. Discuss the role of Workplace Relations Act, 1996 in transforming labour management relations in Australia.

CASE STUDIES

Case Study 1

Collective Bargaining Agents

Ceaz is an engineering company which has operations across Asia and Australia. It has 12,500 employees working in these continents on regular rolls and another 74,300 employees as contingent workforce. Trade unions in Australia have raised dispute with labour administration authorities that terms and conditions of employees that include wages, leave, working hours and welfare measures should be reviewed and revised as the current policies are employee adversarial and discriminatory as they are different for regular employees and contingent workforce though they carry similar work. About 3,800 regular employees and 16,200 contingent employees are engaged in Australia. Trade union leaders have also started connecting with employees in other countries such as China, Singapore, Japan and the Philippines, and Ceaz fears that these disputes may spread into other countries. The company has realized that it needs to address these issues on priority not only to resolve the current crisis but also in order to be compliant with respective IR legislations since it has neglected forming collective bargaining forums. It has decided to initiate the process for forming joint councils and bargaining agent where is it is applicable by approaching the respective government authorities/labour department. Discuss how to approach the issue, form joint forums/collective bargaining fronts as per IR acts of these nations as described in this chapter.

Case Study 2

Dispute Regarding Absence of an Open-ended Employment Contract Under China's Labour Contract Law

Changchang was working with All China Mobile Telephony for the last 12 years as a technical associate based in Shanghai. He had worked in three stints each time, lasting about four years each. Since each of her employment contract was for a fixed period of four years, she was meant to gain a fresh employment contract each time at the end of previous employment contracts validity. When the latest contract had come to an end, she sought a fresh employment contract for which the company had responded positively. They issued it again for a fixed term of four years on the same terms and conditions of employment. However, this time round, the company went ahead and terminated her services before the completion of four-year term, as part of downsizing the company operations. Aggrieved with the company's decision of her termination from employment, Changchang approached the Labour Dispute Arbitration Committee on the grounds of breach of employment contract and breach of China's Labour Contract Law of 2008 provisions. In her petition, she appealed to the arbitration committee that in the first place, she should have been issued an open-ended employment contract in the place of fixed employment contract, since she had completed more than 10 years of service with the company. In addition, she suggested that she should not have been terminated from the services before completion of the fixed term as agreed upon by both the parties, that too without a justified cause and without providing a proper opportunity and notice for her to search alternative job opportunity. She sought reinstatement of her services with back wages and penal charges. The company defended its position arguing that her first three contracts were issued prior to 2008, implying that there was no such law mandating that an employee was entitled for an open-ended employment contract on completion of 10 years of service. Second, downsizing of operations was a reason justified

(Continued)

(Continued)

enough to terminate employees from the services. Hence, their action did not breach any law or provisions of employment contract. Discuss: Whether or not the company complied with provisions of the Labour Contract Law, 2008? Whether the Act covers the duration of employment contract entered before 2008? Whether downsizing of operations is a reasonable and legally valid situation to be called as justified cause for termination?

Case Study 3

Majestic Infosys Case of Skill Development Levy, Singapore

Majestic Infosys, Singapore, is a subsidiary of Majestic Infosys, UK, employing over 120 software engineers in Singapore. Among 120 employees, 18 were foreign workers deputed from the United Kingdom and were employees of the parent company. The company had been paying foreign workers levy as per the law diligently. All 18 employees had been drawing a salary of over 8,000 Singapore Dollars per month. The Labour Department of Singapore on audit found that the company had not been paying the levy under Skills Development Levy Act for these 18 foreign employees ever since they were posted in Singapore. Disputing the audit objection, alleging non-compliance, Majestic Infosys approached the labour court to set aside the audit report of the labour department. The court, on going through the case, directed the company to obtain permission from the public prosecutor, without whose consent the court could not take cognizance of the case. Accordingly, the company approached the public prosecutor for sanction of the case to approach the court for the dispute redressal. The public prosecutor, while refusing to permit the case to be admitted in the court, suggested that the audit report as well as the decision of the labour department was right and upheld the position. According to the public prosecutor, the company is not only required to pay foreign workers levy but is also liable to pay skill development levy based on the remuneration level of these 18 employees. Discuss whether the decision of the public prosecutor was right in the eyes of skill development levy law or that the assumption of Majestic Infosys that there was no need to make separate payments for skill development when foreign workers levy was paid?

Case Study 4

Working Conditions Dispute Under Labour Standards Act, 1947, Japan

Haruto was working as an image-processing assistant with Tubishi Medicals as a permanent employee for the last 41 years. His performance was always regarded as good and he had received appreciation several times for his work. On attaining the age of 65 years, he was retired from the services of the company as per his employment contract and HR policy of Tubishi. However, keeping in view the good performance, skill and experience of Haruto, the company engaged him as a fixed-term employee for a period of three years on new terms and conditions of employment. The new fixed-term contract offered him a salary equivalent to 70 per cent of his old salary in the same job. Haruto, expecting lenient working hours and standards, agreed to the new contract offering him a lesser salary and started working. However, he experienced no such leniency and in turn was expected to give improved performance and longer working hours. Unhappy with the situation, Haruto challenged the decision of the company offering him lesser salary for the same job in the court. Tubishi Medicals had defended its position, stating that it is a regular practice in Japan to offer lesser salary for a fixed-term employment compared to open-ended regular employment contract, and so it had not violated any working conditions provisions as laid down under the Labour Standards Act. Additionally, nothing was concealed from Haruto since his employment terms and conditions, especially his new salary, were well communicated and he had voluntarily accepted the same. Hence, his argument of assuming lenient working hours in the new employment contract was unfounded. Discuss what could be the outcome of this dispute in accordance with Labour Standards Act, 1947 of Japan?

Case Study 5

Can Negative Social Media Comment Amount to Bullying Under Fair Work Act, 2009, of Australia?

John Mathews was working as project manager with Msoft, an IT services company in Sydney. John had approached the Fair Work Commission complaining about workplace bullying on the basis of social media comments posted against him by his colleagues. John had complained against four of his colleagues with whom he had a tiff sometime back, saying that they are trolling his Facebook account and making unfriendly comments, which amount to cyber bullying constituting misconduct, under the anti-bullying provisions of FWA, 2009. The other employees had defended saying there was nothing unfriendly about their comments. First, they had accepted John's friendly request to join them on Facebook and did not engage on their own. Second, they did not make any unfriendly comments, but merely stated that they did not like the pictures posted by John on his account. Third, this entire issue had occurred outside the workplace and had no connection whatsoever with work and so the Fair Work Commission should not take cognizance of the complaint. Finally, comments on social media, regardless of their nature, cannot be called as bullying behaviour under anti-bullying provisions of the said Act. However, John stoutly denied their stance on the basis that the tiff he had with the colleagues was purely work related, and that tiff led to them making hostile gestures collectively on Facebook, and as a result, the complaint falls within the purview of Fair Work Commission. John also submitted a medical certificate demonstrating the mental torture and anxiety such comments had caused, debilitating his health. Discuss: Whether social media comments, if unfriendly, can be termed as bullying under the FWA? Whether the aforementioned incident of posting 'dislike' comments to the pictures is work related or purely personal in nature? Who in this case is on the right side of law? John or his friends?

International Performance Management

LEARNING OBJECTIVES

The objectives of this chapter are to:
- ❏ discuss contemporary approaches of IPM and their implications for business organizations.
- ❏ describe the fundamental constructs of IPM.
- ❏ illustrate innovative performance management practices in global corporations.
- ❏ analyse and enable understanding of how performance management practices need to be reinvented in a global context.
- ❏ present the influences and constraints of IPM design.

The theory of IPM is lagging behind its practice as practitioners are quickly realizing that IPM is the kingpin of IHRM that can significantly help organizations achieve their corporate goals, while academicians continue to grapple with performance appraisal systems and frameworks. IPM works as a powerful independent variable in global organizations to attain multiple objectives of an institution that include: (a) making organizations highly competitive by leveraging HR capabilities and potential, (b) transforming organizations through institutionalizing a performance-oriented culture wherein employees see a direct and positive correlation with what they do and how it enables organizations to achieve financial and non-financial goals, (c) translating organizational goals into action plans, tasks and programmes, and aligning them to respective role holders, (d) getting organizational structures and business systems to function efficiently and effectively, (e) helping employees to realize their career and skill acquisition aspirations and (f) integrating operations, systems, culture and management style across the organization's geographical presence.

A recent Watson Wyatt survey points out that 30 per cent of employees feel that the performance management system of their companies does not help improve their performance, while a little more than 40 per cent of respondents said the goal-setting process is a mere formality lacking logic, rigour and alignment. CIPD survey of HR professionals in 2015 revealed that 55 per cent of these professionals did not consider performance appraisals effective. Another study conducted by Deloitte Consulting covering hundreds of HR managers across the industries in North America found that 58 per cent of them did not believe that the performance management systems deployed in their respective companies are robust enough to provide any positive results. Yet another large survey conducted by Worldatwork and Sibson Consulting in 2010 found that 58 per cent of organizations rated their performance management systems as a Grade C or below. Companies such as Kelly Services, Microsoft, Google, Adobe, Deloitte, PWC, Accenture and KPMG have publicly announced a change of their performance appraisal system while doing away with conventional performance reviews and bell curve practices. A Deloitte survey of several hundred organizations in 2014 had found that 70 per cent of organizations either changed or were likely to change their performance management in the immediate future. Though there is a school of argument within the performance management theory that the implication of performance management practices to organizational performance is unclear, the recent review by De Waal and Kourtit (2013) clearly establishes the strong positive linkage between performance management systems and financial performance such as increased revenue and profits, decreased costs and non-financial benefits such as improved communication, closer collaboration, better knowledge sharing, better strategic alignment, improved employee satisfaction and commitment, improved innovation, enhanced customer delight and higher operational efficiency. In a survey conducted by Development Dimension International (DDI) in 1998 covering CEOs of 88 organizations across the world, it was revealed that the respondents strongly believed that the performance management system implemented in their organization strongly drives the business and cultural strategies. Yet another study conducted by William Schiemann & Associates in the year 1996 with a sample size of 122 organizations with a revenue size of USD 27 million to USD 50 billion points out that organizations which have measurement-based performance management systems outperformed organizations which lacked such a systematic performance management practice. Mercer, based on the results of a study comprising of 1,200 employee respondents, avers that productivity of employees can be enhanced by almost 50 per cent with the application of an objective performance management system. Hewitt, based on the analysis of Boston Consulting Group's database that tracks the financial performance of 437 publicly listed US companies, found that performance management systems can have a significant impact on financial performance and productivity of the said organizations. Further, the study concluded by stating: companies that have performance management practice reported better revenues, good profits, strong market and stock performance as well as better productivity per employee when compared to competitors which lacked the practice of performance management. Strengthening this argument, Watson Wyatt, in a study covering 37 selective global companies, has established a positive implication of performance management systems to overall organizational performance.

PwC's Seven Innovative Practices in Performance Management

PwC, the experts in global consulting, based on a survey of several international organizations and a comprehensive study of contemporary practices and their results, have developed the following seven performance management innovative practices:

1. Abandon the traditional annual performance cycles and opt for continuous appraisals and feedback that can enable employees to gain performance improvement in real time.
2. Release the focus and pressure on evaluation and rating appraisals as this is a backward-looking approach and instead focus on a forward-looking approach by practising continuous conversations based on development and improvement of performance.
3. Simplify the process by utilizing tools and technology and get rid of complex and bureaucratic processes and physical documentation/forms.

4. Remove individual employee ratings and forced choice distribution methods which are judgemental and move towards development and career building.
5. Alter the link between pay and performance appraisal and bring in reward linkage.
6. Gain insights from rich performance management data in real time and take corrective steps as a continuous improvement process.
7. Integrate various people challenges driving business performance and bring talent management, engagement, retention, communication and workforce agility together.

Source: https://www.pwc.in/assets/pdfs/publications/2016/performance-management-in-india-a-change-beckons. pdf (accessed on 8 March 2018).

However, the black box continues to be which mechanism in performance management system creates what kind of impact, while which mechanism causes more or less impact is also unclear. According to Callahan (2007), performance management is inherently compromised because it is used for diverse and often conflicting purposes. Way back in 1995, Keith Grint, based on a comprehensive review of performance management practices, stated that 'rarely in the history of business can a system have promised so much and delivered so little'. Echoing the sentiment, Sylvia Vorhauser Smith (2012) avers that there is no practice like performance management that is so broken but still is universally reviled by both managers and employees. In recent years, the topic of performance management practice has become central for discussions in corporate organizations with many of these organizations re-evaluating their performance management practices. For example, a survey conducted by Mercer Consulting seeking response from its entire clientele worldwide reveals that almost half of these organizations are intending to change their existing practice of performance management. A standard performance management system is important for global organizations since it can be an effective tool to obtain same standards of performance across countries, regions and units. Bloom, Dorgan, Dowdy and Reenen (2006) based on their extensive study argue that good performance management systems deployed in multinational companies have contributed to obtaining the replication of same standards of performance across different regions, markets and cultures. Further, standardization of performance management can help achieve a uniformed institutionalization process, while localization can create divergence, evolving into a divide over a period of time, failing the global character of an institution. When an institution is committed to producing equal standards and same quality of products and services across the countries, weaning away from standardization of performance management weakens this commitment of equal standards. However, the advocates of localization argue that companies attempt to impose their culture and beliefs of parent country over the host country and employees tend to be hostile about it. The fundamentals on which the basis of a performance management system is designed should keep in mind that performance behaviours of employees in one country may not be applicable in some other countries. Further, there are local realities which need to be factored for a performance management system to actually work on the ground. When culture is different in different countries, imposing a single system may create conflicts. The fact is that truth lies somewhere in between standardization and localization. This argument is not unique to performance management but is applicable to all facets of management of an international organization. Hence, global organizations shall strive to identify the drivers of both these schools and conciliate them without distorting the basic character of a performance management system. Ultimately, the core objective of performance management is same across countries and workforce—to help employees upgrade their capabilities and improve their performance. The process of implementation can be blended with local realities for effective execution.

Performance Management System: Good Practice

The Federation of International Employers (2017) stipulates the following good practices for effective usage of performance management system in member organizations:

1. Ensure that the performance management system is designed and deployed based on consensus obtained from all the key stakeholders: management, trade union representatives and members of works council and performance management practitioners (neutral players).
2. Remove details such as individual's gender, age and date of birth from all documents and data gathering forms to avoid prejudices and discrimination.
3. Train all managers, supervisors and employees in goal-setting, goal appraisals and performance counselling and coaching.
4. Ensure regular feedback given to employees highlighting positives and negatives instead of springing a surprise towards end of the year.
5. Motivate employees to voluntarily participate in performance appraisal process and begin the process with self-assessment.
6. Ensure that performance appraisal discussions are positive and progressive, and create a framework for performance appraisal discussion that lays emphasis on employee comfort and confidence.
7. Managers shall be attentive to listen to employees more than them speaking and advising.
8. Take great care to select performance criteria in an appropriate way, primarily based on those factors that the individuals were informed about at the outset, at their last performance appraisal, formal memos or through their job description.
9. Create a system of openness and transparency in performance weightage and appraisal criteria and remove subjectivity as much as possible.
10. Avoid perceptions based on recent events or weighing too much on recent incidents, events, failures and achievements.
11. Do not allow managers to misuse the system to suppress employees, take vengeance, vent out their own frustrations, shift the blame or make employees a scapegoat.
12. Do not allow use of performance management merely as an instrument of reward/punishment and do not establish a rigid relationship between performance appraisal and reward/punishment.
13. Create a performance management measurement that clearly distinguishes the hard data from soft data and interpret soft data with care and objectivity.
14. Review not only on the basis of performance on the goals but also on potential in terms of competencies, skills and attitude, and their relevance to the career graph of an employee.
15. Do not allow disproportionate focus on positives and negatives unless a situation extraordinarily warrants it. There shall be equilibrium. The appraiser should prepare questions with sensitivity and use right set of language and logic. There is a need to balance criticism and appreciation.
16. Ensure that employees' performance assessment is handled constructively and any gaps are addressed through training and skill upgradation.
17. Explore alternative working methods for underperforming employees including teleworking, mentoring and virtual work teams.

18. Lay down clear guidelines to govern consistent inadequate performance level including analysing reasons and providing necessary support to help in improving performance and avoid situations of employee exit or unfair dismissal as far as possible.
19. Do not confuse the normal appraisal process with disciplinary or dismissal procedures. If formal action is required due to performance problems, the employee should be given clear notice of an initial consultation meeting. Only where the employee's conduct has been seriously in error or they refuse to cooperate in necessary changes, should immediate dismissal be considered.
20. Document the appraisal discussion objectively, describing hits and misses, focusing on potential and developmental dimensions.
21. Set clear goals for the next appraisal cycle in discussion with the appraisee and, if required, pushing the manager's agenda must be done carefully and rationally and should be substantiated with reasons.
22. Provide a good performance appeal system wherein an aggrieved employee can seek review and remedy in a confident manner.

Source: https://www.fedee.com/human-resources/performance-appraisal/ (accessed on 8 March 2018).

Performance Management: Approaches

Performance management approaches emanated primarily from a variety of micro and macro factors. The micro factors are (a) overall organizational strategy and culture, (b) leadership style/top management approach, (c) ownership of organization, (d) nature of industry/sector domain and (e) profile of the workforce and trade unionism. The macro factors include (a) sociocultural background of the immediate society where the organization primarily operates, (b) market competition and economic factors and (c) historical background of people management practices surrounding the operations of a company. Even though the practice of performance management in an international organization is influenced by operations in various countries and while there is also a need to bring the performance standards on a uniformed basis, the said factors do play a role. No approach of performance management can be termed as superior to the other as each one of them has its pros and cons. It is the micro and macro factors as described before that would determine the suitability and probability of success of an approach more than the approach itself. There are instances where organizations went ahead implementing a particular approach because the top leadership believed in its advantages. This approach was sometimes not successful because of the absence of a complimentary ecosystem. Therefore, each approach needs to be weighted in the context of an organization's environment and suitability. The approaches can be broadly summarized as illustrated in the following.

Objective-based approach of performance management: This is a competitive and professional approach wherein organizations adopt a uniformed and systematic process involving goal-setting for employees at the beginning of the performance assessment period, interim visit of goals and mid-term review of goal performance, year-end performance evaluation against the goals, performance feedback, potential assessment focusing on competencies and linking performance assessment findings with compensation, development and career planning of employees. The process in an objective-based approach tends to strive for transparency, measurement criteria and at times involves multi-rater approaches to avoid subjectivity. This is also an individual employee-driven approach, though the performance management system is informal and is applicable to all grades of employees. This is an impersonal system where the focus is on comparing performance in relation to goals and benchmarks. Though this drives objectivity and clarity of assessment criteria, the objective system is fraught with criticism. The main commentary supporting this is that even though the system aspires to be objective, managers are often indulging in manipulation of the system to allow their perceptions to dominate the assessment. Managers may appraise performance the way they see things rather than the way they actually occurred. In brief, the objectivity of the system can get corrupt and may become very subjective. The second major remark has been that not all performance goals are hard data driven and measurable; in fact, the highest level of performance is also contextual and qualitative. This qualitative performance behaviour cannot be captured by hard data driven objective-based performance management system.

Criterion-based approach of performance management: An increased focus on the person being compared to the role is referred to as a criterion-based approach. Here, competencies of a person play a dominant role in performance assessment because the approach advocates that higher proficiency in competencies required to perform a job effectively automatically leads to higher performance. The goal-focused performance assessment may be able to provide data on immediate performance condition but the approach does not lead to ensure sustainable performance in the future and on-performance consistency, whereas the criterion approach is a reliable predictor of performance, both short term and long term. Goals are set annually and reviewed periodically; however, they are not task-related goals but competency-related goals. Employees are given targets to achieve in terms of number of competencies and proficiencies that they are expected to acquire and hone during the appraisal period. A number of organizations based in European countries and also in Asian countries like Japan follow this approach for performance management of employees. This approach is also referred to as development-oriented performance management system.

Emerging Global Performance Management Trends

A global survey on performance management systems was conducted by Mercer Consulting in the year 2013 in order to understand and assess the trends covering 1,056 organizations, representing multiple industry segments operating in 53 countries. The key findings are:

- Organizations which have a practice of setting individual performance goals comprise 95 per cent, and 94 per cent of them conduct a formal year-end performance appraisal assessments and discussion.
- Performance rating scales exist in 89 per cent of respondent organizations, a five-point rating scale is deployed in 57 per cent of organizations and 33 per cent provide for people management rating as a key competency for managers; 30 per cent of global organizations report that they have forced choice distribution of performance rating system.
- Organizations which are implementing self-assessment as a key step in appraisal cycle comprise 82 per cent.
- Competencies are assessed in 86 per cent of organizations.
- Organizations which are linking individual performance with compensation of an employee comprise 89 per cent.
- Organizations which view that the performance management system being applied in their respective organizations would need rework comprise 51 per cent.

- Organizations which are currently using multi-rater performance appraisal system comprise 33 per cent and 22 per cent use a 360-degree feedback system.
- Organizations which believe that performance management contributes to drive higher performance comprise 43 per cent, while 21 per cent feel it is good to provide performance feedback and 15 per cent view that performance management helps employees to focus on right things and to move in right direction.
- A mere 3 per cent of respondent organizations feel that performance management system in their respective organizations provides exceptional business value.
- Organizations which claim implementing a pay for performance principle comprise 90 per cent, but only 40 per cent of them actually track and measure the alignment between performance ratings and compensation decisions.
- Organizations which believe that their organizations need to encourage a candid performance discussion between appraisee and appraiser, and create a system around it comprise 31 per cent.
- Organizations which see a strong need to link the performance appraisal findings with employee developmental planning comprise 20 per cent.
- Respondent organizations believe their managers are moderately skilled in managing various facets of performance management system: 65 per cent of the managers are moderately skilled, holding formal performance evaluation discussion with employees, 62 per cent are moderately skilled in setting simple, measurable, achievable, realistic, time bound (SMART) goals, 60 per cent are moderately skilled in ensuring performance evaluations are fair and equitable, a majority 48 per cent are marginally skilled in linking individual performance to actionable development planning, only 5 per cent are highly skilled in having a candid conversation with direct reports about their performance and only 3 per cent are highly skilled in providing career development coaching to employees.
- Only 35 per cent managers regularly talk about performance management as a core business process.

Source: https://www.mercer.com/content/dam/mercer/attachments/global/Talent/Assess-BrochurePerfMgmt.pdf (accessed on 8 March 2018).

Marxist-based approach of performance management: There are organizations in European countries such as in Poland, Czech, Sweden, Finland and Denmark, and Asian countries, such as China, who advocate a socialistic form of performance management. This approach is developed on a belief that performance in an organization is always collective so breaking it into individual-based performance management is unrealistic and intended to create discretion with the management. The conservative form of Marxist orientation also believes that implementing individual employee-oriented performance management is preceded by breaking the tasks into miniscule tasks, depriving creativity and agility, and it is done with the sole intention of making an organization less dependent on cerebral skill of people. Hence, believers of this approach strongly argue that performance management practices shall be based on teamwork and collective form, and goals must be set describing a target assignment or a programme that a group of employees are responsible to achieve it. This group will either win/achieve together or fail collectively, and any singling out of an employee or few employees is irrational and lopsided. Furthermore, this school of performance management avers that often it is unnatural to classify a particular task as superior to the other task since hierarchy of tasks does not exist in reality. Merely bowing to demand and supply forces to judge the value of a task is opportunistic. Therefore, Marxist-based performance management recommends a socialistic form of performance management. Further, the Marxist purists argue that performance management system practised in several organizations is intended to serve the purpose of its masters and is designed to benefit them and exploit employees.

Capitalistic-based approach of performance management: Proponents of this approach advocate for individual employee-based performance management and lay emphasis on distinguishing good performance from poor performance at an individual level. The proponents also believe that goals must be set to achieve tasks and that it is an effective way to simplify complex work. Defining work at a group level in broad fashion would generate two consequences: First, it will breed inefficiencies in the form of social loafing, and second, the work definition will be so broad that every employee will try to make his or her own sense of it, leading to a less concerted and coordinated performance. Rewards and punishments are closely tied with findings of the performance evaluation of an employee. This approach, at best, provides an opportunity to an employee to build the skills and competencies required to perform a job effectively, but will not be empathetic to poor performance, regardless of the reason. This is a competitive and very judgemental approach suited to organizations that face market competition. Organizations that employ a capitalistic-based performance management approach have also made attempts to improve the system by creating systems to avert bias and to avoid the adverse impact of the practice on morale of employees. Critics of this approach argue that it is highly discriminatory, ruthless and inhuman system that destroys teamwork and tires employees without achieving any extraordinary benefits.

Measurement-based performance management: This approach is an extension of capitalistic-based performance management as discussed earlier. In order to overcome the limitations of the capitalistic approach, performance management experts and market-driven corporate organizations have adapted some measurement techniques. Techniques such as Balanced Scorecard and Productivity Measurement and Evaluation System (ProMES) are used in setting and evaluating employees' performance. This is basically a results-based approach of performance management system by design. The approach is aimed at creating transparency, objectivity, removing ambiguity and avoiding all the bias. This approach, while suitable for task performance, will not be able to address the contextual performance, behaviours and attitudes. Organizations are social systems and the way they are structured is way too complex. There are a lot of limitations while trying to measure these complex human interactions and dynamics of social systems and the biggest criticism against measurement-based practices is that they lead to contraction of understating and ultimately negatively impact overall performance of employees. Furthermore, employees will not be able to see the big picture even though the goals might have been drawn from the ultimate organizational objectives because the measurement-based approach promotes narrow focus and micro thinking by design and application.

Deloitte's Performance Management System: A Reinvention

Deloitte realized that even though its performance management system was considered fair, it was not able to address the changing organizational needs and focus. Managers were seen spending thousands of hours in determining the performance ratings and balancing them, rather than using the performance management system to improve the actual performance. Deloitte's internal study had revealed that managers were spending close to 2 million hours of productive time a year in rating performance of employees and assessing of skills and knowledge of employees which continued to be very subjective. In order to overcome this situation, Deloitte reinvented its performance management system in 2015 consisting three key objectives:

1. **Recognizing performance:** The first objective is like many other performance management systems. It should be capable of recognizing and rewarding right performance at task/programme/assignment/activity/engagement levels. This approach helps in identifying the successful projects from not so successful projects. This is a pooled view of the organization with facts and figures so room for bias is highly limited.

2. **Recognizing persons:** Once performance is recognized, the process of identifying person/persons responsible for that performance will begin. Instead of asking managers how a person has performed, the question that will be asked at the time of completion of a project will be: What is your future plan for your reportee? What you are intending to do with that person on completion of the project? Also, opinion is obtained from the immediate manager to understand the future plans, instead of trying to understand who had contributed for the success of a project. This way, managers tend to be honest in sharing their feelings and intentions, instead of just performance ratings. This is the second objective of the new performance management system. This data is obtained throughout the year as and when projects are completed, instead of a one-time exercise in a year. The data of a year is consolidated for each employee. Additional data on employees if they contributed to projects for which they were formally not assigned is also collected and accounted for.

3. The third objective of the newly invented performance management system revolves around **fuelling the performance**. All employees are provided with a self-assessment tool to check themselves on weekly basis. The tool itself, or if required with the assistance of immediate manager, springs areas and skills on which an employee can focus on in order to further enhance performance as well as capabilities. This automatically leads to a continuous improvement process.

Source: https://www2.deloitte.com/insights/us/en/focus/human-capital-trends/2017/redesigning-performance-management.html (accessed on 8 March 2018).

Hybrid approach of performance management: There are organizations particularly that have global operations and follow a mixed set of performance management practices. In some countries of operation, there is a market-driven and competitive performance management system, while a socialistic system in other countries and sometimes a mix of all in the same country because of historical reasons like acquisition of companies without integrating them or allowing freedom to each of their business units to follow their own system of performance management. While all these instances of mixed system are due to lack of conscious effort and focus, the hybrid system of performance management system that few organizations drive are deliberate and planned. Few global organizations prefer a hybrid system to accommodate different approaches that suit a particular type of business or geography given the nature of conglomeration of businesses and portfolios.

Quality-based performance management: The quality approach leads performance management to follow the path of continuous improvement and also as a proactive approach to work on averting errors and overcoming weaknesses. Customer satisfaction is at the core of the system here. Performance of all employees is guided and coached through these principles. This system believes that continuous improvement is the key for customer satisfaction and as long as customers are happy with the products and services, the business will grow. Hence, employees' performance shall be centred on continuous improvement and nothing else. In consonance with this philosophy, a quality-driven performance management system advocates for self-assessment on a voluntary basis. Managers help employees discover their strengths and limitations, and also make customer feedback a vital input into the employee development plan. Teamwork and supporting each other is an important factor too. Most performance management systems are quantity driven and focus only on volumes, without bothering about good and bad volumes, resulting in a loss of long-term focus. In contrast, a quality-driven approach insists on sustainability and innovation. Feedback and development of employees, consistent with findings of strengths and limitations, is more important here than using performance assessment for temporary rewards and punitive actions. Therefore, the perception and acceptance of the system among employees is very high. This approach is highly practised in many Japanese organizations.

Three Foundational Constructs of Performance Management Practice

There are three constructs that explain the function and value of performance management in the eyes of employees and are illustrated below:

Construct 1: Equity. An employee compares their own hard work (inputs and outputs) and rewards received with the hard work (inputs and outputs) and resultant rewards of the peer group and adjudge whether a performance management system is fair and equitable or not. Employee motivation to work harder and produce more output goes up when there is a perception of equity, while performance plummets if the perception is that there is no equity in performance management. Therefore, it is critical that a performance management system is balanced and ensures both internal and external equity.

Construct 2: Assessment of gaps. Employees are eager to know their performance levels and very receptive to genuine feedback. They would like to have a precise assessment that would enable them to understand the gap between their aspiration level of performance and actual level and therefore identify the exact gaps. This performance management system shall be capable of providing very authentic feedback and can work as a great motivator for employees to improve their performance on a continuous basis and also generate confidence in the performance management system. On the other hand, performance management system can lose its relevance if employee confidence in the feedback process is poor.

Construct 3: Social comparison. Human beings always prefer to gauge their performance in comparison with others. Employees seek information on how they are performing in comparison to their peer groups so that they know whether they need to improve or continue to perform at the current level. This also leads to competition amongst employees. A performance management system must provide this information in an authentic manner. Organizations have tried to address this need through a bell curve or forced choice distribution models. However, there has been large-scale resentment against forced choice distribution models in the recent past due to lack of fairness in the administration of the same. Nevertheless, the basic urge is that employees seek to know where they stand vis-a-vis with others.

Comparative-based performance management: As the title suggests, this approach essentially differentiates and slots each individual employee performance level in comparison to others. Various performance rating scales such as ranking, point system, forced choice distribution, grading and paired comparison are used to evaluate an employee's performance. The system generally evaluates each individual employee performance on a stand-alone basis in reference to the goals set at the beginning of the performance appraisal cycle, based on which a certain number of points are given. These points are used to compare the points awarded to other employees and then compared in order to slot where the employee stands. Further, this system also forces the appraiser to slot an employee in a category as per pre-defined criteria. Though understanding of this system can be simple and appears very logical as a concept, it can create inconsistencies and subjectivity. Different raters use rating scales in different ways and the comparison principle tends to upset employees who see that their work and performance are not up to the expected standards. However, the system works well for employees who are very competitive and eager to know where they stand in comparison to others in terms of performance levels. Of course, they expect rewards also to flow according to this assessment, creating further bitterness among majority of the employees.

Competency-based performance management: New Age organizations particularly have experimented with competency-based performance management. This approach consists of both attributes and behaviours. There are various tools such as graphic rating scales, mixed standard scales, behaviourally anchored rating scales and behavioural observation scales which are employed to measure the behaviours, attributes and also functional/domain competencies of employees as a reliable measure of performance. While this can fuel the developmental orientation to performance management, it may fall short of defining and assessing the immediate performance on the job, which is critical for the overall organizational performance. This approach works well for research and development organizations more than organizations which are in a competitive market and need to produce rapid results through operations.

International Performance Management: The Influencers of a Global Process

The critical questions in the context of IHRM are: (a) What approach of performance management is the most ideal for international organizations? (b) How do country-specific regulations, culture, leadership and set-up of an organization impact each of the performance management processes? (c) What shall be the role of a parent organization and host country subsidiary in design and implementation of the performance management system? And (d) what shall be the core objectives of an IPM system. Both empirical evidence and experiences of organizations are very limited to test any hypotheses on these questions. Answers to these questions are not easy and simple; however, a debate can at least help in providing a directional view and can lead to build a globally aligned model. Let us examine each of these questions.

Role of culture and regulations in a global performance management system: Culture definitely impacts the way goals are set, evaluated and feedback is offered. Theory and practice of conventional performance management might not have offered any key insights into the role of culture, but according to latest empirical work and experiences that were reported on culture, point out that culture impacts success of the performance management process at each stage. For example, goals are merely handed over to reportees in high-power distance countries, while not only their goals but organizational performance goals are influenced by reportees in low-power distance countries. The goal-setting process involves an elaborate explanation of tasks, milestones, linkage of goals with their role and relationship of individual performance goals with overall organizational priorities, measurement criteria of performance, rating methods, alignment of rewards in some cultures, while in others, handing over/communicating a broad statement of tasks/activities expected to be carried out, is seen as adequate. It is also evident that in few cultures, the role description itself is considered as a performance goal sheet. The evaluation tends to be objective and focuses on goals set at the beginning of the year, devoid of any commentary on the person, while in some countries, the discussion revolves more around the person and incidentally about the goals. Here, the belief is that a manager is appraising a person in an overall frame and not merely on tasks performed as a part of the job. Therefore, when feedback is offered, it is taken in different ways: in Western culture, it is perceived as assessment of employee performance on a given task, while in oriental culture, it is seen as a judgement on the person. Hence, implication of cultural aspects must be carefully evaluated at each stage of design and execution of a performance management system. An extraordinary rate of failure of performance management practices can be attributed to misalignment of culture in quite a few cases.

Building an overall ecosystem for high performance culture has gained prominence in recent times. This phenomenon is generally known as high performance work systems. The core purpose of high performance work systems is to create a work environment that boosts employee engagement, involvement, productivity, customer service and innovation, catapulting an organization into a high performing one. Though the said system comprises of many practices and components as shown in Box 8.1, culture is key and cardinal to it. More and more international organizations are opting to build high performance work systems in order to enhance performance, as well as forge a common work culture across the units located in various countries. In order to realize a high performance work system, an international organization must identify the performance management practices, fill the gaps and bring all these practices under one umbrella of functional scope, with an aim to extract the benefits and also to drive a global practice in a consistent manner across the countries of operations.

Box 8.1 | **High Performance Work Practices**

Though the term 'High Performance Work Practices' (HPWP) has become very popular but what does it precisely mean, what does it constitute of and importantly, what practices are part of this and what is its impact on the organizational performance. These are several valid questions still being debated. CIPD, UK, on an extensive study of said practices has come up with a definition as well as components of HPWP as illustrated below:

Components: According to CIPD, HPWP primarily is made up of and based on few key components such as (a) vision: a vision based on customer delight and tailoring products and services to meet the needs and expectations of each customer, (b) leadership: inspiring the top management team which is capable of creating momentum and excitement among the employees and driving them towards the accomplishment of the company vision, (c) culture and processes: an ecosystem comprising of people development processes and culture that is aligned to the company vision and objectives, (d) empowerment: decentralization, distribution of decision-making, self-management and confidence in capabilities of employees to deliver what is needed to meet customer expectations all the time and (e) governance: a fair system that recognizes right performance, commitment and treats everybody fairly, irrespective of them working or left, and with a fair reward system.

Practices: The practices of HPWP are (a) realistic job previews: all prospective employees and candidates for a job are provided with clear job descriptions and specifications, (b) deployment of psychometric tests for selection: behaviours and motivational orientation are scientifically measured and accorded equal importance to that of functional and hard skills in selection of candidates, (c) an effective induction: on joining, employees are well inducted into the organization to make them an integral part, quickly expelling any kind of alienation, (d) lateral training: emphasis on continuous learning and providing ample opportunities for experienced employees to undergo training and to upgrade their skills, (e) continuous appraisal: appraising an employee's performance is regular and continuous, and is neither a one-time event nor a mere formality, but a constructive measurement, (f) feedback: regular and developmental feedback based on the information collected from multiple sources intended to help employees with a realistic and unbiased view of strengths and areas of development, (g) compensation: pay based on individual employee performance and potential while also based on equitable and merit-based criteria, (h) incentives and bonuses: yearly and half-yearly incentives and bonuses linked to company profits and achievements, thereby aligning an individual goals and performance with that of company objectives and performance, (i) role clarity and flexibility: each employee is given role clarity and also provided with flexibility to amend the job description that would facilitate better performance, job enrichment and effectiveness of a role, (j) multi-skilling: employees are encouraged to hone more than one skill as work is becoming more and more inter-disciplinary and are provided with both on- and off-the-job opportunities to seek exposure to a multi-skill environment, (k) use of work improvement teams: forming and nurturing work teams that are not only capable of meeting current work demands but also work towards continuous improvement of work methods and processes, (l) engagement of problem-solving teams: often high performance comes from engaging special problem-solving teams comprising of complementary skills, instead of believing that the top management is there to solve all the problems, which is unrealistic, (m) smooth flow of business communication: all employees are communicated about the business plans of the organization in order to enable them to gain a big picture understating and also to make them an integral part of the organizational functioning and progress, (n) sharing of information on the company performance: employees are updated from time to time on the performance of organization on the targets which are set and shared with all employees which help to build trust and also make them feel as a part of an organization, (o) no forced exits: since the focus is on continuous performance appraisal, feedback and developing of employees, it automatically helps employees to catch up with performance standards, thereby avoiding the necessity of compulsory redundancies, (p) avoidance of voluntary redundancies: the development focus and overall ecosystem focusing on fairness presents a situation wherein an organization avoids voluntary redundancies as well as attrition, (q) single status treatment: organization applies all the rules, regulations and processes treating every employee equally rather than following hierarchy and exceptions, wherein some employees are treated less equal comparing to others and (r) harmonized holiday and benefits entitlement: consistent with the principle of single status, all employees are given equal holiday entitlement and all direct work-related benefits are extended to all employees without differentiation or exceptions to cultivate equality and respect.

Employment regulations and trade unions have a role to play too and significantly influence the practice of performance management, albeit many employers and managers tend to believe that this is one area which is completely at the discretion and prerogative of the organization. Various IR laws have stipulated regulations concerning equity, equality and fairness of performance management systems. The role of trade unions, especially when a performance management system is tied up with rewards and compensation, is very high. In fact, many unions see performance managements systems as a ploy by the employers to break the collectivist and pluralistic orientation of employees. For example, a survey conducted by G. E. Robert in 1994 (www.emeraldinsight.com/doi/abs/10.1108/ER-08-2015-0167 [accessed on 8 March 2018]), to understand the barriers to implementation of performance management, found that 59 institutions had cited trade unions as the major barriers for practising performance management practices. Another comprehensive survey conducted by Nurse in 2005 covering about 120 organizations revealed that a performance management system was not present in majority of the unionized organizations. For example, in 2011, the Telecom Trade Unions in the United Kingdom passed a resolution committing the most comprehensive fightback against the ethos and culture of performance management unanimously. The Federation of Unions demanded that company such as British Telecom must cease its cavalier and brutal application of performance management policies, failing which the union threatened to launch ballot for industrial action. Trade unions of the financial sector in the United Kingdom have vetoed and protested against the use of bell curve in performance appraisal systems. The role of trade unions and regulations becomes more complex for international organizations which are pursuing a path of standardization. In this context, the argument of localization of performance management practices gains momentum again. It is therefore important for international organizations to consider the role of regulations and trade unions as positive rather than a barrier. It is beneficial to enlist the support of trade unions who can give a fillip for successful design and execution. In order to achieve this, organizational leadership must create a forum of trade union representatives drawn from all countries of operations of an organization. This forum can debate and generate options for helping employees to improve their performance and avenues for enhancing their capabilities which can be called as a performance management system. The distrust among trade union leaders in regard to performance management has arisen not only due to ideological differences but also because organizational leaderships have tried to approach performance management as a managerial tool to control and maximize the output, instead of considering this tool as a developmental source and a model of optimization for mutual benefit. This behaviour leads to a perception that performance management is meant for managerial personnel, and even if it is extended to the staff, the aim will be to exploit them. Hence, organizations need to make substantive efforts to expel this perception and transform performance management as an issue of mutual interest. Trade union leaders or works council representatives must be involved right from the beginning of conceptualization and design of the performance management system. Organizations must devise a performance management system that focuses on softer aspects such as development, counselling, coaching, mentoring and feedback in the first phase, and focus on harder aspects such as discipline, rewards, compensation, promotions and succession planning in the second phase. Leaderships of few organizations have done disservice to the cause of performance management by projecting an image that this system is meant for hard decisions essentially, and only incidentally focuses on softer aspects, resulting in stiff resistance from trade unions and employees. Leaderships of organizations also need to overcome the belief that trade unions tend to resist performance management, no matter what the pitch and benefits may be for employees, as this is a misplaced notion on their part. Unions resist because of apprehensions and because of refusal by the management to involve them at right stages of performance management. There are experiences with a few organizations within the EU which show that when trade unions were consulted, and their participation was sought willingly in countries such as the Netherlands, Sweden, France and Denmark, it paid huge dividends in terms of rolling out successful performance management systems.

It is also imperative for international organizations to identify provisions related to participation of trade unions and works council members in performance management apart from fairness-related aspects. None of the provisions stipulates organizations to follow a particular performance management approach, except that whatever an organization follows must be objective, transparent and equitable. A review of IR legislation of major countries reveals that there is no constraint other than that the purpose, process, application and coverage must be discussed and consent of works council members is expected to be obtained before the roll-out of a performance management system. The outcome actions of performance assessment relating to the staff must also be discussed proactively with unions/works council. This can also work as a check and balance system for an organization instead of leaving the entire administration to few managers without any third-party observation. However, there is a persistent fear that the involvement of state through labour legislation and regulations, and unions/works councils through their urge for negotiations will deprive managements of organizations the necessary flexibility, speed and agility to administer the process which needs to be real time in a competitive world. Even though there is some truth that whenever a process is subjected to democratization, it is susceptible to a slowdown in change management cycles, it is not unique to performance management. On other hand, this will help in speedy implementation since all stakeholders are on board with the system voluntarily.

Top leadership style is an important influencer of an overall approach and mode of performance management implementation in any organization. A study of performance management of organizations proves that a democratic leadership prefers a consensual and collaborative approach, a market-driven leadership would opt for competitive performance management system, an autocratic leadership tends to go with a centralized and control-oriented system, while a paternalistic leadership style influences to embrace development-oriented performance management system. There are also instances wherein there is a clash between leadership style and the approach of a performance management system due to historical reasons like the current performance management system was introduced by the previous leader, while the new leader's style does not agree with the system in vogue, or that the performance management system was designed keeping in view the elapsed organizational strategy. In such circumstances, the implementation of performance management takes a beating and loses its focus. Therefore, the need to bring close alignment between styles of top leadership and the approach of performance management assumes greater significance. Performance management is a great source for leadership to engage with employees at all levels, present a big picture in terms of organizational objectives and show how each employee contributes to this big picture through the cascading effect. The leadership must spend substantive time and commit resources to involve employees at every stage of performance management including while determining the approach. However, the leadership must refrain to use the performance management system for control purpose to begin with as discussed before and should rather proceed with highlighting how the system is designed to support the employees' cause, especially employee skill and career development. In a nutshell, the leadership style must be seamlessly integrated and aligned with the approach of performance management. This will remain a perplex situation for international organizations since it needs to be decided whether the alignment process is relevant at the level of global or local leadership. The answer is that it shall be uniformed since ideally there should not be any difference between global and local leadership styles and preferences so that the alignment can be achieved at the same level for a global performance management system to succeed. It does not mean that the minor deviations to address local realities cannot be accommodated. While providing rational space for adjustments representing local sentiment, the alignment on the big picture should not be overlooked.

The high impact leadership behaviours to build a great performance culture in an international organization revolve around five critical elements: (a) co-create vision, mission and define organizational objectives: a leader must inspire employees at various levels to participate in building the company vision and defining objectives/milestones in translating the vision, (b) co-create operational plans: merely creating a vision statement or articulating objectives is not adequate unless this progresses into concrete action plans depicting the role of employees with their roles and responsibilities, (c) creating change leaders: a leader can create a lasting impact only by inducting the right people and developing the right set of next level leaders who are capable of change and transformation, (d) building collaboration and trust: unless there is trust and confidence apart from collaboration, achieving goals of performance management will be a mere dream; and achieving them is the core job of a leader and (e) developing and rewarding the talent to lead to high performance levels: a good performance system can make even an average person demonstrate high performance, while a bad system can make even an outstandingly capable person perform poorly. An effective leader creates a system that helps in developing and rewarding employees leading them to high performance levels.

Role of parent and subsidiary companies in performance management: The way roles are to be played by headquarters of an international organization and its subsidiaries have a significant influence on performance management. This is a classic situation like the centralization versus decentralization discussion. There are other experts who view that there are three ways this can be addressed: (a) exporting a performance management model to subsidiary operations which is designed and rolled out by parent company headquarters, (b) adapting a parent country performance management model with modifications to suit to each subsidiary country and (c) collaborative effort and a flexible model where the parent country and subsidiary countries implement a yin and yang kind of model to drive performance management. Defining and clarifying roles of parent and subsidiary companies is very crucial for international organizations for several administrative and functional reasons. This is an area of contention for many organizations since headquarter-based HR department thinks that performance management is a global function and also a source of integrating people practices globally, whereas the subsidiary company tends to believe that performance management is primarily about performance of employees managing country operations on which the headquarter HR department may not have full appreciation and understanding. These disagreements, unless resolved and guidelines are clearly laid down defining the roles, can lead to confusion and would result in counterproductive effects on the performance management practice. Experts of performance management, on studying international organizations across countries, have argued that the headquarter/parent country can play a lead role in the design of a global performance management system based on inputs received from various subsidiaries, while subsidiaries can be made primarily responsible for implementation of the system in collaboration with the parent country's HR department. However, this is easier said than done. It was often found that organizations stipulate this guideline at a macro level and leave it to the countries to operate. Mere high-level guidelines will not be adequate to address many issues that come up during both design and implementation phases. Therefore, there should be detailed governance on this important function along with a dispute redressal mechanism. Experiences point out that subsidiaries feel that their inputs are not given due weightage in the final design of performance management system, while parent country managers think that they need to reconcile and accommodate views of everybody, so that in the process, some compromises are made to achieve the end closure. Hence, international organizations should develop a framework for analysing inputs received from subsidiaries and also applying negotiable scope and non-negotiable scope with a rationale. All inputs received need to be reasoned out and non-qualified ones should be published to subsidiaries with reasons. Similarly, the essence of a global performance management system needs to be well communicated to the subsidiaries along with how too many local factors can cause dilution of the performance management system. It is a sincere continuous dialogue between two groups that can actually enhance the effectiveness of the system.

The governance framework can contain the following steps which can help international organizations in their endeavour to roll out a global performance management system.

Step 1: Identifying primary roles. Defining who will play the primary and complimentary role in various phases of performance management is the first step in the right direction. Typically, a performance management programme in international organizations may go through three phases: (a) design phase, (b) implementation phase and (c) review and renewal phase. Empirical evidence suggests that the parent country set-up must opt for the lead role during the design phase with subsidiaries complimenting the effort as discussed before. During the implementation phase, subsidiaries must perform a dominant role with the support of the parent country department, while both parent and subsidiaries must play a collaborative role during the review and renewal phase. If required, depending upon the complexity, size and spread of operations, the phases can be further broken into sub-phases, clarifying roles in each of these parts. Various studies have shown that performance management has failed to take off in international organizations due to unresolved differences between parent and subsidiary country operations teams, each developing serious suspicion and lack of respect for each other's views and ideas. Hence, clarifying roles has a significant place in the overall performance management programme.

Step 2: Goal-setting. Reviews of vast literature on the goal-setting process along with corporate experience establish that goal-setting is useful since it provides direction, focus, clarity, visibility into the future, energy and discovery of strengths. Subsidiaries are expected to ensure that all employees carry well-defined goals which are properly documented. Goals must be set in a manner that the performance management design has envisaged and mandated without exceptions. In order to ensure a logical cascading and build relevance to global as well as country objectives, the goals must reflect three clusters of goals: (a) overall company objective, (b) overall country objective and (c) role objectives. Though discretionary performance is vital to innovative behaviour and effectiveness, it is also equally important to standardize the goals at each level. Therefore, a parent company can take up the initiative of building a key performance area (KPA) dictionary at a company level, while subsidiaries should do the same for country and role-level dictionaries. These dictionaries can assist managers and employees to undertake the goal-setting process in a meaningful manner. In large international organizations, employees tend to approach goal-setting as a ritual rather than an opportunity, which would make their work exciting and fruitful. Therefore, while dictionaries can be directionally helpful as a guide, managers and HR specialists should create engagement tools that can capture personal attention. One way of handling this could be creating performance groups/teams, dedicating a day for performance goal activity and motivating them to work on setting up their goals for the year. Unless subsidiaries take an active role in goal-setting, the performance management system will be confined to just a showcase. Cultures that are not planning friendly tend to abhor goal-setting as a theoretical exercise since they believe that actual performance demands and expectations are susceptible to change all the time. This behaviour will cause tardiness in goal-setting. As part of an IPM practice, organizations must build and popularize case studies highlighting the positive benefits of goal-setting for employees. It is often witnessed in many international organizations that a goal-setting activity may take place, but the quality of the exercise and standards of goals set are disputable. Ensuring standards in the goal-setting process is the real test for organizations and the success of performance management lies in this process. While KPA dictionaries can obtain minimum acceptable standards in the quality of goals, they will be short of attaining the right fit of performance goals with the capabilities and potential of individual employees. A PwC survey covering a wide range of international organizations found that while the surveyed organizations said they use SMART goals, the actual data revealed that only one-third of goals qualify the framework of SMART. Managers and employees should be trained in the goal-setting process and there must be group of well-trained specialists drawn from all units and functions of a subsidiary who can assist in the goal-setting process. Though there are many ways that goals can be set, the widely recommended framework is referred to as SMART. Further, each employee should be able to see a clear linkage between individual goals with the goals of the operations. In no circumstances should these appear as stand-alone or unconnected. Studies conducted on the goal-setting process during the last few years repeatedly point out that this is often viewed as ineffective by the employees and they see that the way goals are set does not lead to high performance. However, another set of studies show that when a goal-setting process is systematic, it has contributed towards higher productivity. The goal-setting process is also to be viewed as not just a one-time event but as an ongoing process providing opportunities intermittently to evaluate and to align with a changing direction and focus of an organization, as and when required. This flexibility can lead to the goal-setting process to be more realistic and effective in addressing the employee needs in real time. Usually it is seen that the parent company's HR department staff is enthusiastic to intervene with the goal-setting process in subsidiary countries in order to satisfy themselves, but many times this can create a sense of suspicion and can also be seen as supervising the subsidiary management, leading to an eventual loss of trust. The parent country headquarters can explore possibilities of approaching this in a collaborative manner by participating in the process based on the invitation of subsidiaries, rather than on their volition. Subsidiaries also should not be shy to enlist support of the headquarters when needed, instead of claiming unchecked autonomy.

Goal-setting is essentially a participative process between an employee and a manager and it should not be seen as a prescriptive medication by the managers. However, a study in Europe covering 17 different multinational organizations operating in over 21 countries showed that this process is treated by managers as their prerogative and an instruction led method is deployed dominantly, nullifying the participative spirit. In conditions like these, the reactions of the employees tend to be negative. International organizations must include goal-setting as a participative and high employee engagement task in their process guidelines. Goals must not focus only on tasks and initiatives that an employee performs but also include developmental efforts to enhance the skills and capabilities of employees. When goal-setting involves not only work tasks but also developmental targets, employees would see this as a process which will enhance their careers, rather than a mechanism for monitoring their work. Finally, a study done by experts at regular intervals on goal-setting process and quality of goals can provide valid insights which can be used to refine the process as well as prove to be a good governance mechanism. CIPD (the professional body of HR professionals in the United Kingdom) prescribes the following critical factors in goal-setting:

- **Clear and challenging goals for simple jobs:** Set clear, outcome-based and challenging goals for jobs in which tasks are straight forward and predictable.
- **Behaviour and learning-centric goals for complex jobs:** Set outcome-based goals for jobs that are not specific but focus more on behaviours and learning outcomes.
- **Mutual participation:** Goal-setting is a collaborative process, and managers and employees should be involved in the process and mutually determine the approach towards performance.
- **Recruit people with a learning zeal:** Recruit employees based on learning enthusiasm and capability rather than performance angles, since the motivation to learn will lead to great performance in a sustainable manner.

- **Encourage employees to seek execution goals:** A goals setting process must encourage and lead employees to opt for goals that are action centric and implementation focused, describing how, where and when they will act and develop strategies to deal with potential setbacks.
- **Provide pertinent goal-setting data:** Employees must be provided with all data and information that is relevant for them to set challenging yet realistic goals, commensurate with their capabilities and the nature of the job they perform in organization. This will enable them to develop a mindset of engaging in goal-setting in a constructive manner.

Step 3. Goal appraisal: This is the most critical step in the entire process as most of the effectiveness of performance management comes from and depends upon how this step is designed, and most importantly, how it is executed. Often it is seen that disenchantment of employees with performance management occurs due to mishandling of the goal assessment process. Employees in all nations and companies expect fairness and procedural justice in the assessment of their performance. Managers and performance management administrators should make efforts to eliminate all kind of biases and errors that commonly occur and cause damage to the entire system. Though processes are found to be relatively robust in international organizations and capable of ensuring procedural fairness, the system still provides for a high degree of arbitrariness and discretion to managers. Discretion is essential in the assessment process, but this should be handled very professionally, ethically and fairly. However, there are more incidents of failure on the part of assessors than successes with assessment processes. Bias is found to be a very complex phenomenon in performance assessment cycles. Common biases are known as: halo effect, horns effect, contrast effect, leniency error, central tendency error, recency error, first impression error (primacy effect) and similar-to-me error. Biased behaviour is both psychological and sociological. Many organizations assume that all managers are well equipped to handle performance assessments and neglect the rater's training. The fact is that a majority of managers are not skilled at handling performance appraisal assessments. They are liable to make mistakes and wittingly or unwittingly, they allow biases to creep in. Managers tend to give an impression that they are evaluating and judging the person rather than the person's goals, vitiating the entire exercise. Few of the common assessment errors can be resolved through balancing the performance assessment processes, some through training managers and sensitizing them and some through audits. Training of raters (managers) can be broadly classified into five types:

1. **Behavioural observation development training:** This training helps managers observe employees' performance, collect information properly, categorize and analyse it, drawing inferences on the goal performance. Training includes imparting skills such as detection, perception and recognition of patterns and important incidents and events related to performance, integrating them to find out the performance behaviour. This training can also sensitize managers on common rating errors like the halo effect.
2. **Performance dimension training:** This is also known as multidimensional or frame of reference performance appraisal training. The purpose of this training is to equip managers to notice and acknowledge that the actual performance of employees on a goal is the result of them possessing and applying multidimensional disciplinary skills rather than applying a single dimension of discipline of skill. Research indicates that managers usually observe the single dimension of performance (for example, executing a task timely, while not noticing whether the task is executed with requisite quality) and extrapolate it to other

dimensions or simply neglect taking into account the performance of an employee on other dimensions.

3. **Rater error training:** Here managers are sensitized and made knowledgeable about common errors that managers make while assessing goals that may not be deliberate, but sill creep in like the halo effect/central tendency. There are also deliberate errors which are relationship based. The managers are trained to avoid them and be conscious of these maladies.

4. **Accuracy training:** Managers under this cluster are trained to observe the factors, traits and conditions that facilitate performance, rather than the performance dimension itself. This is more of a competency-based approach. Competency proficiency of an employee is also a reliable indicator of not only their current performance but also, to a great extent, the potential of the person on those goals. This helps immensely in building development plans for employees. Even though confining to the direct dimensions of performance of goals is adequate in goal assessment and rating, it can give a fillip to build a robust performance assessment system if it includes observing the competency dimension of performance.

5. **System training:** Managers are trained on the company process, policy and tools of goal assessment. Each company, over a period of time, develops its own system of assessment and overall ecosystem which a manager must be fully aware of. This is more like an orientation programme for managers so that they are at ease in administering the goal assessment process. Orientation programmes can also throw an opportunity to managers to question and debate the validity of the process that in turn can help in continuous improvement.

Sixty-two Per Cent of the Performance Evaluations Are Idiosyncratic and Based on Perception

According to a research, covering a sample size of 4,492 employees, conducted by Michael Mount, Steven Scullen and Maynard Goff (2000) on how performance ratings actually measure the performance of employees: 62 per cent of the performance ratings were attributable to individual perceptions and peculiarities of managers, while a mere 21 per cent of the ratings reflected actual performance.

Still, there will be scope for errors which can be addressed by creating an appellate system. Creating checks and balances is definitely a step towards obtaining sanctity of assessment integrity but organizations must strive to build a culture of fairness in performance management. This is more relevant to international organizations because process maturity can ensure the governance, but culture is the key to secure the spirit of performance management. International organizations, especially the technology- and knowledge-driven companies, have adopted a process of year-long journals to overcome the assessment biases. Employees are expected to record their progress on daily basis in collaboration with their managers and peer group. This journal becomes the basis for the annual appraisal discussion and ratings. The goal assessment process must be made an exercise, meant not only for gauging and rating the performance level but also as an instrument to better understand the work processes, strengths and areas of development. The exercise must be democratic, transparent and highly participative. Performance appraisal systems in international organizations typically follow the sequence of self-assessment, followed by managers' assessment, and this sequence is found to create a gap between the two assessments. The gap widens further when managers do the assessment remotely, which is highly common in international set-up. The process of sequential assessment has advantages but potentially creates communication problems too. Organizations can explore the possibility of mutual assessment in person to avert the criticism of performance appraisal process being very non-personal and mechanical in international organizations.

Goal Assessment Meeting—Guidelines

The following process can help in a goal assessment meeting between manager and an employee:

- Set up goal assessment meeting on a mutually convenient date and venue at least with a 10 days' advance notice to the employee.
- Duration of the meeting must be at least 60 minutes.
- Exchange all the documents such as the goal-setting process, goals set at the beginning of the appraisal cycle, self-assessment and any data/information that would be relevant and will be used during the discussion.
- Commence the meeting by creating a sense of ease for the employee and by creating a sincere and positive atmosphere for an open dialogue.
- Review the goals, their description, measurement criteria and any conditions associated with goal accomplishment together.
- Review the associated situations like market conditions and any changes which occurred after the goals were set, and carry a general educational dialogue beyond goals in order to grasp the entire situation.
- Motivate the employee to speak about their achievements towards their goals, one after another; supported by relevant data and information that drives the point.
- Express appreciation for the goals that are met and discuss how achievement of these goals has contributed towards enhancement of skills and led to new insights gathered by the employee.
- Express empathy for goals not achieved and help analyse the reasons, along with how things could have been approached and done differently, facilitating the achievement
- Help identify strengths and how they can be further developed and leveraged.
- Help identify limitations and areas of development and collaborate to develop a plan of action to overcome the limitations.
- Listen to the employee's inputs and observations intently and understand how the organization could have supported them during the appraisal period.
- Propose to the employee specific and overall performance ratings, with the support of information and data; provide reasoning and rationale, and answer all the questions an employee may ask.
- Conclude the rating in collaboration with the employee and firm up with a summary.
- If a serious difference arises between an employee and manager regarding the rating, take a break for a day from the discussion and reconvene next day to revisit the discussion where the manager should firm up the rating.
- Provide an opportunity for appeal if the employee still disagrees with the managers rating.
- Appellate authority can admit a grievance only if there is a prima facie evidence and resolve the matter based on merits.
- Based on the current year's performance and employee developmental plan, employee and manager may mutually identify the performance goals for the coming year.

The goal assessment process must be leveraged to motivate employees and reward them for the right behaviour more than striving for accuracy of the process, since absolute accuracy is hard to attain. Managers have their own anxiety while performing goal assessment for several reasons. Primarily, managers should be motivated to think and work towards goal assessment of employees in a positive manner. If managers are not motivated enough, it does not matter how perfect the performance management system design may be, it tends to fail to deliver the objectives. A motivated manager observes the performance of employees keenly, stores all the relevant information, guides employees in performing their work and takes up the goal assessment exercise as a culmination of all these activities, rather than considering it as an event like judgement day. Managers see goal-setting as an opportunity to reward employees and create an impression on the employees but are also afraid of negative consequences such as upsetting relationships with subordinate employees, possible demoralization of employees and reluctance to receive criticism on their rating behaviour. If managers are not motivated, they tend to neglect critical information and data on the performance behaviour of employees, while merely considering superficial behaviours and shying away from supporting employees in order to enhance their performance. In order to make goal assessment a constructive and positive activity, organizations must make the assessment less of a rating exercise and instead consider it as taking stock of the situation for further progress. Managers must make goal assessment highly individualized, refrain from comparing with other employees and conduct all discussions in confidence and with protection of privacy.

Employees have equal responsibility to that of managers when it comes to goal assessment. They should develop a realistic view of their performance and be honest in carrying out self-assessment. Employees generally view the goal assessment as basis for earning rewards and recognition and are motivated to present a positive picture, regardless of the reality, which might be resulting in self-deprivation of development opportunities. It is difficult for many employees to be hard on themselves to assess their work in a non-personal manner. Normal pitfalls in judging one's own case occur here too and the organizations must make substantive efforts to create awareness and train employees on objective self-assessment. This task is more complex for international organizations since cultural aspects influence the way employees self-assess themselves. In high-power distance cultures, employees are susceptible to believe that they shall rate themselves high, because in any case, managers will bring down the rating. As a result, the employees feel right and tactical to inflate their performance. In low-power distance cultures, employees tend to assess their performance moderately and often take it as a chance to assess themselves based on the data and information. Hence, training employees on self-assessment and creating a guideline of standards to be maintained by employees while doing self-assessment can help to some extent. Ultimately, it is the precedent and the way the sincerity of goal assessment weightage is maintained and governed in an organization that would contribute to setting rightful expectations among employees and managers alike.

Feedback and communication of goal assessment results: In international organizations, due to their size of operational units and multi-country presence, a large number of employees working in these units seem to contribute towards an impersonal way of communicating the performance assessment results to employees, which is often through a digitalized e-mail form. A PwC survey reveals that around 70 per cent of the surveyed organizations see their line managers not prioritizing performance management conversations and feedback. The feedback phase is a great opportunity for managers to communicate not only the performance of employees but also to share with them their strengths and career options. However, many organizations do not succeed in leveraging this phase due to a variety of reasons including apathy and callousness. Employees understand that their work is not cared for due to ineffective communication of the goal assessment outcomes. There are instances a plenty in international organizations wherein employees got to know their performance assessment results through a communication from the HR department rather than hearing from their managers. Such communications merely confine to letting employees know their arithmetic rating but never focus on the logic behind it, leading to the defeat of the entire performance management system. Hence, international organizations must take steps to personalize the feedback and communication process. Technology cannot substitute certain type of human interventions like feedback. Managers must share feedback highlighting the achievements of employees and their strengths that have contributed towards such accomplishment more enthusiastically. Developmental areas in reference to the goal performance should also be shared along with the reasons for such observation. Employees generally receive feedback that is more focused on development and less so on showing them in a poor light. It does not mean that managers will always have positive observations to share, but even negative performance must be explained in a supportive and confidence building format. A feedback session shall never function to create a demoralizing effect. Feedback and communication of goal assessment results must be conducted in a supporting and respectful environment and shall never appear as a mechanism of a manager's control, pulling the rank and imposing authoritatively. Some research studies have shown repeated evidence that positive feedback is more effective and motivates employees to pursue the goals with more vigour, while negative feedback undermines the confidence of employees and discourages them from pursuing the goals. However, self-regulation studies argue that negative feedback holds more influence and motivates employees to correct their actions and get their direction right. Nevertheless, the most important element is that employees should have full confidence in the feedback process in order to act on it. The kind of message the organization is intending to drive also determines the type of feedback. For example, when organizations believe in generating positive feelings amongst employees, they are more likely to follow a social path of providing positive feedback so that the same can enhance commitment. When organizations want to leave a feeling of incompleteness in the minds of employees, signalling that their goal achievement efforts are inadequate, they would prefer negative/critical feedback. Effectiveness of both these types of feedback also depends upon the overall social and culture fabric of an organization. An attempt to provide superficial feedback or giving a positive feedback for the sake of positive feedback, independent to the performance, can cause more harm than benefit as it can degenerate the entire performance management system. Feedback is found to cause impact in three ways when it is constructive, honest and objective.

1. **Reinforcement:** Feedback, particularly when it is constructive and received positively by an employee, helps in reinforcing the performance behaviour. Feedback helps an employee to identify right behaviours and helps gain clarity so he or she is more likely to keep up that behaviour with permanency.
2. **Correction:** Feedback can contribute to identify the right way of doing things from the current way of doing things, leading to correction of work behaviour. Feedback is an opportunity to gain insights into the most effective way of carrying out tasks, post which a manager, on analysis of an employee's method of performing, can help in improvising.
3. **Relationship:** Feedback when handled properly would lead to building a great relationship and partnership between a manager and an employee. Moments during feedback can be very intensive, intimate, candid and transformational, if a manager and an employee collaborate and are trained in feedback sessions.

Model Feedback Process

Though the feedback format is quite contextual, according to Pendelton, Schifield and Havelock (1984), an expert on learning feedback, a practical model is as illustrated below:

- Check whether an employee is ready and keen for feedback
- Let the employee speak and present his or her work and all associated matters
- Let the employee speak on what was done well
- Manager should speak on what was done well according to his or her observation/information
- Let the employee speak on what could be improved
- Manager should speak on how it could be improved
- An action plan for improvement is made collaboratively by the manager and employee

Research and practice show that it is not uncommon to come across managers and employees who do not see positive outcomes with the feedback process. Their negative view is influenced by the manner it is implemented in, where managers are not equipped to provide objective feedback and employees are not ready to receive feedback which is not necessarily all positive. To overcome these negative consequences, organizations must ensure that feedback is non-judgemental and open to discussion rather than something which is cast in stone. Once feedback is offered, an employee must be given adequate opportunity to question, seek supporting information and seek suggestions how to resolve the same. The objective of feedback must be development oriented and never to be a mere critical commentary. Feedback should also be a continuous process rather than a one-time event that surprises an employee. Best practices in communication and feedback highlight that feedback must be specific, non-accusative, constructive, incident specific, precise, timely, focused on behaviour and never on personal characteristics, non-opinionated and in addition to which a follow up is made. Employees must also approach the session with an open and positive mindset rather than with any suspicion. Employees must carefully listen to the feedback, seek additional clarification wherever required to better understand the spirit of the statement made, reflect on the feedback, not associate the power dynamics that might be existing in the normal course during the feedback session, not make excuses, not be silent during the discussion, thank the person giving the feedback and discuss with the manager the next steps so that the feedback can be leveraged to develop the work and performance further.

Summary

Performance management is going through a metamorphosis in corporate organizations as the existing practice is broken and unable to address the growing needs of both employees and employers. Though executives and researchers are unanimous about the potential of this practice to contribute for organizational success, the efficacy of the system has remained in quandary for several reasons. The situation is further complex for international organizations, given the varied expectations of parent and subsidiary operations. In this backdrop, the foregoing chapter is dedicated to discuss critical elements of IPM that include: (a) approaches of IPM, (b) influencers and barriers of IPM practice, (c) benchmarking performance management practices and (d) changing trends of international performance system with a focus on innovative methods to build high performance management work systems.

QUESTIONS FOR DISCUSSION

1. Discuss why trade unions oppose performance management system. What should be done to make trade unions an integral part of performance management system design and application in international organizations?
2. Why multinational organizations such as Deloitte, Accenture and PwC have concluded that their performance management system should be redesigned?
3. Why do some researchers and practitioners aver that there is no managerial system other than performance management system which has promised so much and delivered so little?
4. What are the emerging trends of performance management practice in international organizations and how different is it from the earlier practice?
5. What are the influencers and barriers to effective implementation of performance management system?
6. Why is there so much resistance to forced choice distribution or bell curve application in performance management? Is it a way to dilute performance maximization or to attain harmony?
7. What conflicts are likely to arise between parent and subsidiary units in realization of performance management system?
8. Different cultures prefer different approaches to goal-setting, appraisal and feedback! Is it true or false?
9. Compare and contrast capitalistic versus socialistic models of performance management.
10. Is there an ideal performance management system (PMS) model that would suit international organizations?

CASE STUDY

Kanakasi is a Japanese general insurance company which has spread its operations across the continents with almost 65 per cent (89,000) of its employees working outside Japan. Performance management policy of the company is more developmental, learning and feedback driven in Japan, while the same is highly measured and competitive in North America, goal driven in Europe and a mix of all approaches in other nations of companies units. There is widespread dissatisfaction with performance management practice across as found out in employee satisfaction survey, since performance management has scored minimal. Further study revealed that younger employees in Japan have sought a competitive and incentive-based performance management, while employees in North America have felt that the system should focus more on development rather than being task driven since most of customer engagement performance comes from contextual performance. There are other employees who have argued to do away with performance appraisal system altogether as in their belief it was demotivating than helping any cause. Some amount of dissatisfaction with performance management is common; the problem here seems to be much more acute. Managers too often complain about rating scales and efficacy of the system. The company is forced to review its performance management system globally and take corrective action. Key purpose of performance management system in the company is to motivate high performance, identify capabilities and nurture them for succession planning more than associating monetary and non-monetary incentives though it is expected as an ancillary outcome. Client management and integrity in underwriting are the key attributes the company looks for in employee performance and there should be a system that recognizes and promotes these behaviours. Discuss what model and approach works better in this situation.

Bibliography

Behn, R. E. (2002). The Psychological Barriers to Performance Management. *Public Performance & Management Review, 26*(1), 5–25.

Bloom, N., Kretschmer, T., and van Reenen, J. (2006). "Work–Life Balance, Management Practices and Productivity," Center for Economic Performance Special Paper No. 16.

Buckingham, M. and Goodall, A. (2015). Reinventing Performance Management. *Harvard Business Review*, April Issue, 40–50.

Callahan, K. (2007). *Elements of Effective Governance, Measurement, Accountability and Participation*. Public Administration and Public Policy. CRC Press.

CIPD. (2015). *Resourcing and Talent Planning Survey of HR Professionals*. Retrieved 28 February 2018, from https://www.cipd.co.uk/Images/resourcing-talent-planning_2015_tcm18-11303.pdf

———. (2016). *What is High Performance Working?* Retrieved 28 February 2018, from https://www.cipd.co.uk/knowledge/strategy/sustainable-performance/factsheet

De Waal, A. and Kourtit, K. (2013). Performance Measurement and Management in Practice: Advantages, Disadvantages and Reasons for Use. *International Journal of Productivity and Performance Management, 62*(5), 446–473.

Deloitte Consulting. (2014a, June 10). *It's Official: Forced Ranking is Dead.*

———. (2014b). *Performance Management is Broken: A survey of PMS.*

——— (2015). *Performance Management Redesign*. Retrieved 28 February 2018, from https://www2.deloitte.com/global/en/pages/human-capital/articles/performance-management-redesign-human-capital-trends-2015.html

Development Dimension International. (1998). *Performance Management Practices Survey Report*. Retrieved 28 February 2018, from https://www.ddiworld.com/ddi/.../theglobalizationofhrpractices_fullreport_ddi.pdf

Grint, K. (1995). *Management: A Sociological Introduction*. Indianapolis: Wiley.

Hewitt Associates. (1994). *The Impact of Performance Management on Organizational Success*. Lincolnshire, IL: Hewitt Associates LLC.

Mercer Consulting. (2013). *Global Performance Management Survey*. Retrieved 28 February 2018, from https://www.mercer.com/content/dam/mercer/attachments/global/Talent/Assess-BrochurePerfMgmt.pdf

———. (2015). *Mercer Performance Management Snapshot Survey*. Retrieved 28 February 2018, from https://www.mercer.com.au/newsroom/mercer-Survey-Employees-seeking-next-generation-of-performance-management.html

Mount, M., Scullen, S. E. and Goff, M. (2000). Understanding the Latent Structure of Job Performance Ratings. *Journal of Applied Psychology, 85*(6), 956–970.

Pendelton, D., Schifield, T. and Havelock, P. (1984). *The Consultation: An Approach to Learning and Teaching*. New Delhi: Oxford University Press.

PwC. (2015). *The Changing Performance Management Paradigm: Evolution or Revolution? Is There a Future for Performance Management?* Retrieved 28 February 2018, from https://www.pwc.nl/nl/assets/documents/pwc-performance-survey-2015.pdf

Scottish Trade Union Congress. (2014). *Performance Management and the New Workplace Tyranny*. Retrieved 28 February 2018, from http://uel.web.ucu.org.uk/2015/03/27/performance-management-and-the-new-workplace-tyranny-report-for-scottish-tuc/

Smith, S. V. (2012). *Talent Management in High Growth Markets*. Retrieved 28 February 2018, from https://www.pageuppeople.com/en-ph/news_item/pageup-people-executive-to-discuss-talent-management-in-high-growth-markets-and-neuroscience-of-change-at-hro-today-forum-apac/

The Federation of International Employers. (2017). *Performance Appraisal: A European Perspective*. Retrieved 28 February 2018, from https://www.fedee.com/human-resources/performance-appraisal/

Watson Wyatt Worldwide. (2014). *Pulse Survey on Performance Management—Results*. Retrieved 28 February 2018, from https://www.towerswatson.com/en/Insights/IC-Types/Survey-Research-Results/2014/03/Pulse-Survey-on-Performance-Management

William Schiemann & Associates. (1996). *The National Survey of CEOs on Measurement Based Management Practices.*

WorldatWork. (2010). *The State of Performance Management: A Survey Brief by WorldatWork and Sibson Consulting*. Retrieved 28 February 2018, from https://www.worldatwork.org/docs/research-and-surveys/state-of-performance-management-2007.pdf

9

International Culture Management

LEARNING OBJECTIVES

The objectives of this chapter are to:
- ☐ discuss contemporary approaches of international culture management and their implications for business organizations.
- ☐ describe various models of culture management.
- ☐ analyse the profile of culture in global corporations by drawing practical inferences.
- ☐ present the barriers in building a culture and the actions to leverage multiculturalism.
- ☐ present a multicultural organizational development model.

Culture is at the cornerstone of international HR theory and practice. In fact, the very idea of IHRM as a concept has started with observing, studying, analysing, interpreting and understanding culture and its consequences for organizations that are operating globally. With more and more organizations becoming global, as a result, the workforce is also becoming increasingly global. Even employees whose work confines them to their native nations have also become global in their approach, behavioural orientation and attitude due to the Internet explosion. Though it is a business imperative for global organizations to focus on international and national cultures, it is no less a need for all other domestic organizations. Internationally, culture which used to change in an evolutionary manner with each generation has started undergoing transformation in a revolutionary manner within the span of the same generation with the spurt in cross-border mobility, Internet-propelled social media, television, movies and of course international products and services. As a result, today cross-cultural paradigm has replaced monoculture as the mainstay culture. Nevertheless, various studies have found that national cultures continue to influence the culture of institutions that are set up in a country and spread to other countries. This confluence of national culture with other nations' cultures imported through multinational organizations has created the strong cross-cultural dimension which we refer to here as international culture.

Culture has become as important as business strategy for corporate organizations worldwide. Culture can keep a firm operating in multiple countries as a single entity in its form and content of operation. A study conducted by faculty at Columbia Business School and Duke's Fuqua

Business School surveying more than 1,400 North American CEOs and CFOs over 13 months ending in 2015 had the following findings:

- More than 90 per cent said that culture was important.
- Those who believe that improving corporate culture can improve value of the company comprise 92 per cent.
- More than 50 per cent agree that corporate culture influences productivity, creativity, profitability and growth rates.
- Only 15 per cent believe their firm's corporate culture was where it needed to be.
- Those who believe corporate culture is an important consideration in M&A deals comprise 46 per cent.

International Culture Management: Basics, Concepts and Models

History of corporates worldwide amply demonstrates that while capital, strategy, processes, products, structure, technology and leadership are important, it is culture that ultimately determines the success of an organization and more importantly its sustainability. There are enough case studies and data proving that organizations fail to succeed in the absence of a robust and mature culture. More than 62 research and survey-based studies were conducted during the last three decades covering more than 6,000 small, medium and large firms and an overwhelming number of these studies have found that there was a positive relationship between culture and organizational performance. For example, Kotter and Heskett (1992), in a study of corporate culture impact on long-term financial performance covering over 200 firms over a period of 11 years, found that there was a significant gap between firms with performance culture and firms without it as per Table 9.1.

Issac Dixon (2005), based on a study of culture management in mergers and acquisitions, states that culture has emerged as one of the dominant barriers to effective integrations, and culture incompatibility was found to be the cause of 30 per cent of failed integrations. A study of S&P 500 companies reveals that 85 per cent websites of these companies have a dedicated section on corporate culture describing importance of innovation, integrity and respect in their companies'

Table 9.1   **Culture and Organizational Performance**

	Average Increase for 12 Firms with Performance Enhancing Culture (%)	Average Increase for 20 Firms Without Performance Enhancing Culture (%)
Revenue growth	682	166
Employment growth	282	36
Stock price growth	901	74
Net income growth	756	1

Source: Kotter and Haskett (1994).

culture. A study covering 95 franchise automobile dealerships over six years ending in 2015 has found that culture comes first in consistently predicting ratings of customer satisfaction and vehicle sales. Further, the positive effect of culture on vehicle sales is fully mediated by customer satisfaction ratings. Yet another study conducted by Tata Strategic Management Group (2015) covering 96 organizations of various sizes across the sectors based in India found the following:

1. Companies with strong business strategy–culture alignment reported 2.4 times more profitability than companies with no such alignment. The aligned organizations are likely to report a profit margin of 11.5 per cent against 4.8 per cent by firms where the sync between strategy and culture is weak.
2. The respondent organizations which have agreed that an organizational culture that is aligned with business strategy has a significant contribution to business growth comprise 100 per cent.
3. About 33 per cent of organizations have admitted that the culture existing in their organizations was not one that was nurtured by them as business leaders but evolved on its own.

An empirical study conducted by Hirota, Kubo and Miyajima using Japanese firms' data from 1987 to 2000 has found that the strength of corporate culture significantly affects corporate performance. Another study conducted on over 4,000 employees in the United States by Petty, Beadles, Chapman, Lowery and Connell (1995) found a strong positive correlation between a firm's performance and organizational culture. However, there are researchers who believe that while culture may have positive implications for organizational performance, arguing that culture is a reliable predictor of an organization's financial performance is somewhat far-fetched given the complications in credible measurement of cultural aspects since many of these aspects are intangible.

Multiculturalism does not necessarily create only positive impact; it can also cause a few negative effects. It can cause cultural clashes within an organization leading to dysfunctional group dynamics and consequently a loss of productivity. Homogenous groups or monocultures can enjoy effective communication and seamless teamwork whereas multicultural groups will continue to face communication issues and sometimes resultant distrust despite extensive training. Diverse cultural groups in an organization potentially move towards polarization in the name of protecting their interests leading to fragmentation instead of unity. Some studies have shown that homogenous culture groups have performed far superior to heterogeneous groups on the same tasks.

Organizational Culture and Innovation

Many studies also point out that innovativeness and rate of innovation in an organization is dependent upon the kind of organizational culture that gets nurtured. For example, Boston Consulting Group in its study of Most Innovative Companies in 2014 has found that all organizations that have a successful innovation track record have certain distinct organizational culture elements:

- **Leadership style:** Top management committed to radical projects created different key performance indicator (KPI) system for radical projects, introduced incentives linked to radical innovations and encouraged culture of experimentation. Leadership fully backs and shows commitment to radical innovation projects by designing a KPI system which is non-financial and non-specific but process-centric. Leadership exhibits high tolerance for failures and breeds functional risk-taking behaviour leading to concentration of innovation-specific efforts.

- **Organizational processes:** The way processes are defined in highly innovative organizations encourages iterations and adjustments, provides enough room and time for experimentation and sometimes trial and error attempts, methods that rationally qualify difference between high and low innovativeness, protects radical projects from strict cost control and budgetary constraints, transparent system of project approvals and their targets and project approval being not dependent upon strict ROI projection. It is found that more than 80 per cent of breakthrough innovators allow projects to start with no projection of future returns.

- **Organizational structure and systems:** Innovative organizations were found to have created different governance structure and systems that motivate radical innovation. Structures encourage collaboration and duly recognize interdependency of efforts, and decision-making is consensual and authority is expert driven rather than hierarchical or concentrated. Experimentation and idea generation is at the core of monitoring or review system.

The culture by definition includes language, customs, attitudes, values, religion and norms of a group/community/institution. Basically, there are two major theories analysing culture in organizations. One theory argues that culture is formed on its own through various interactions with environment over a period of time. This is also known as interpretive view of culture. The other theory advocates an approach that culture is formed out of organizational structures, systems and tasks so one can decide the type of culture an organization should have. In that sense, culture is not formed on its own but through a deliberate action. This is known as structural view of culture. It is important to understand concepts and models of culture before we make an attempt to understand the whys and hows of international culture management.

Basics of Culture

Culture consists of certain basic elements, and observing these can help to understand the type and nature of culture:

- **Stories:** members of an organization/institution/community always create and share certain type of stories/anecdotes/analogies about events of past or about leaders or incidents. Studying them will provide underlying motive and intention and behaviours that are being sought.

- **Rituals and routines:** The way things are done in an organization. For example, how the meetings are conducted, minutes drawn, how they begin and end and how proceedings are conducted, events celebrated, sequence, how people are addressed and how certain rules are formulated.

- **Symbols and artefacts:** Logos, designs, signposts, colours, dress code, office layout, furniture, meeting rooms and the likes can help in understanding the type of culture an organization or community is trying to drive.

- **Controls:** This refers to what kind of limitations or controls are applied to lead an organization or community in order to understand the checks on power structures prevalent in an organization/community.
- **Organizational structures:** Hierarchies and flow of work and the way these are organized can reveal how power is structured in an organization and how delegation of power flows. This would also provide an understanding of whether power is centralized or decentralized and how broadly decision-making authority is distributed in an organization.
- **Vision, mission and values:** Many organizations articulate clearly their vision, mission and values and some practice it without explicitly publicizing. This helps in understanding the nature of an organization's goal, purpose, milestones and direction.

All the discussed elements in combination create a paradigm of culture that is believed to help organizations either to achieve or to fail in achieving their purpose.

How culture shapes up, how it drives performance and what processes add up to create it are puzzles for many even in leadership though all of them unanimously agree that culture is the key for organizational success. It is not easy to create a high performance culture and this can happen over a period of time through a series of efforts and creation of supporting organizational systems. Lindsay McGregor and Neel Doshi (2015), organizational culture experts and *New York Times* bestselling book authors, on surveying over 50 companies and over 20,000 employees, have found answers to these questions as discussed here:

- **Why we work determines how well we work:** A comprehensive study in the 1980s found that reasons for people to work are: (a) play, (b) purpose and (c) potential which enhance performance and other factors such as (a) emotional pressure, (b) economic pressure and (c) inertia hurt performance. So, to create a high performance culture, it is important to understand why people want to work. Organizations can look at attracting talent who possess play, purpose and potential traits and discouraging hiring of talent who want to join due to emotional and economic pressures or merely to get out of their inertia.
- **How culture drives performance is another question often asked!** Studies on various service organizations have amply demonstrated that a highly motivated workforce makes all the difference to their sales and customer satisfaction. For example, all hotels of a particular grade have similar infrastructure and location advantage but some of them are more successful than others because service levels differ. A highly motivated workforce is a result of three cultural factors as discussed earlier and these are play, purpose and potential. Studies on commercial airlines sales found that a customer-oriented culture has made a difference of 30 per cent in revenues for their organizations.
- **How is culture formed and what processes can create that?** Culture is shaped up by variety of processes that would include role design, leadership style, organizational identity, career ladders, community, workforce planning, compensation, governance processes, organizational structure and method of performance review. All these put together create an ecosystem that we call organizational culture. Some of these factors may have more influence and some may have lesser influence but all of them are critical to nurture a culture in an organization.

Concepts of Culture

There are two broad schools of culture that are heavily debated and researched on. One is known as an 'ideational system' and the other as 'sociocultural system'. These are briefly discussed further.

Ideational System

This school of thought advocates that culture is psychological and resides in the mind of culture bearers and describes culture as a system of ideas. Ideational system considers culture to be more of a cognitive map rather than an interactive social system. There are four sub-schools of thought supporting this view:

- **Cognitive school of culture:** This school treats culture as a set of functional cognitions organized into a system of knowledge. This knowledge is at the core and is important for members of a group to behave and function in a particular fashion that is acceptable to group members. This group behaviour tends to create organizational norms and organizational climate. The norms and climate are nothing but cognitive maps of a group of people.
- **Structuralist school of culture:** This school avers that culture is universal and exists in a structural form. The belief is that forms of problem-solving and idea generation are the same across the world. Therefore, culture is universal as per this theory. Behaviours, norms, attitudes that an organization promotes tend to spread universally in that organization regardless of location of a country. This school believes that culture exists in a structural form consisting of mental ideas and images.
- **Multi-equivalence structure school of culture:** This school points out that culture is made up of individual ideas, cognitions and norms of many members and is the output of the interrelation and interplay of this result in culture rather than a single idea or image of cognition. Basically, the theory establishes that culture is product of not one person or one idea but interplay of multiple actions, ideas and reactions. Hence, organizations are not necessarily rational systems but aggregate cognitive preferences.
- **Symbolic school of culture:** This school of thought is relevant both from an action perspective and institutional perspective. As per this theory, culture is a product of symbols that are created over a period of time which in turn generate certain types of behaviours, norms and forms in a particular group or in a particular activity. The symbolic culture also underlines that this is the reason why sometimes behaviours, emotions and adherence to norms are not necessarily synchronized with organizational structures, goals and objectives.

Sociocultural System

This theory advocates that culture is the product of social systems manifested as behaviour among the members of an institution. Culture in this context tends to be understood as functional, rational and synchronized with larger interests. This system of thought consists of the further-mentioned schools of culture:

- **Functional school of culture:** This school of thought believes that culture consisting of norms, forms, behaviours, structures and processes exists to satisfy human needs through work and participation in an organized effort. People are considered actors and organizations considered platforms of theatre. Culture that can facilitate fulfilling this need survives and others vanish. The underlying philosophy of this theory is that culture has a functional purpose of facilitation and that purpose must serve fulfilment of human needs.

- **Structural-functionalist school of culture:** This school of thought spreads an idea that organizations are social systems and as such culture cannot reside away from the kind of social system an organization is. Organizations are systems with purpose, goals and needs and always in functional interaction with their environment. Culture is a functional instrument that is in tune with the social system of an organization augmenting its journey.

- **Ecological-adaptationist school of culture:** Organizations which are influenced by their environment adapt themselves as social systems and develop a culture that is in harmony with such environment. The basic theory points out that a conducive culture is built over a period of time out of continuous interactions with the environment and culture that is not in tune with the environment and that cannot adapt itself to that ecology will become extinct. This means that organizations which fail to adapt to the environment will fail and organizations which adapt will succeed.

- **Historical-diffusionist school of culture:** The central argument of this school of thought is that culture, an integral part of social system, is formed over a period of time due to historical reasons and by diffusing the same across a society/institution/group. Many times, it would be challenging to understand the genesis of a social system and order unless historical factors that have contributed to that system are traced. Hence, this school believes that historical events lead to creation of culture and this culture gets diffused over a period of time through individuals/groups/institutions to become mainstream behaviour and customs.

There are other theories proposing culture to be an intersection of society (social, political, economic and judicial systems), history (historical events that trigger societal change) and contingencies (technology and organizations). Interaction of these elements causes generations of culture that binds people and societies.

Social Contract (Rules of Rain Forest and Plantation)

According to Victor W. Hwang (2014), creator of an ecosystem that boosts innovators, culture in business is primarily the conflict between two opposing social contracts. One social contract is based on values of exploitation/efficiency/predictability/production and is known metaphorically as Plantation and the other is based on values of exploration, variance and uncertainty/innovation and titled Rainforest. Both social contracts are valid but come from opposite schools of thought. There are certain rules governing each of these social contracts. Rules of the Rainforest are to break rules and dream, open doors and listen, to trust and be trusted, seek fairness and not advantage, experiment and iterate together, err, fail, persist and pay it forward. Rules of the Plantation are to excel at your job, be loyal to your team, work with those you can depend on, seek a competitive edge, do the right the first time, strive for perfection and return favours.

Harrison's Four Cultural Ideologies

Harrison in 1972, based on empirical data, had come up with four ideologies that can describe and help to understand culture in societies, organizations and groups more objectively. These four culture ideologies exist in organizations/groups/societies complementing and supporting each other, objectives of such organizations and nature of such culture. These are discussed here:

- **Power orientation:** Groups or organizations strive to acquire control over others, are highly competitive, jealous and want to win all the time. Power is centralized and leaders seek absolutely control and authority. Some societies have high-power orientation and some have less. Leaders and members of these organizations place premium on asserting their superiority and make all efforts to conquer others. Leaders in these organizations seek compliant behaviour from followers and loyalty is accorded more importance than performance. Family-controlled enterprises or market-driven organizations mostly fall in this category of culture of power seeking.
- **Role orientation:** Culture of power orientation is person based while culture of role orientation as the title suggests is role based. Here, culture promotes rationality, objectivity, rules, regulations, processes, hierarchy and legitimacy. These are formal societies and everybody functions as per the constitution, and interactions among all people reinforce the orderliness. Large organizations tend to be role oriented and therefore culture that pervades will be role oriented so members interact with each other through their roles rather than as individuals.
- **Task orientation:** This is knowledge-driven culture. Here, people function with an objective to achieve superordinate goal. People tend to be achievement oriented. Hierarchies and formal positions and formal powers hold less importance than a person's performance which contributes to achievement of ultimate goal. Appropriate knowledge and competence is a prerequisite for members here. Structures, roles, process and authority are formed based on how close a performance is to the superordinate goal. Any structures, roles or behaviours that come in the way of achieving this goal will be rejected. Religious institutions and voluntary organizations mostly fall in this category.
- **Person orientation:** Culture here involves complementing each other's efforts and addressing each other's needs. Members' interests are supreme and whoever can serve the cause of all members can assume authority proportionate to making things happen in that direction. People are not seen as cogs in a machine but valued as human beings. Collaboration, trust, mutual respect and common interests are at the core of this culture. All start-ups and entrepreneurial ventures and research/academic organizations are oriented towards task orientation culture.

Martin's Three Culture Perspectives

Martin (1992), based on extensive research and studies on culture, had developed a three cultural perspective framework to understand culture in a more concise manner and classified all culture theories as discussed further:

- **Integration:** Culture is understood as an outcome of integrative, coherent and consistent actions by a group or by members of an institution. It is seen as an integrative force that binds people together to ensure everything is seen by everybody through the same lenses. Any deviation or ambiguity to this common frame is understood as a limitation, and remedial actions are taken to resolve the same. Culture in integration perspective is defined as a set of manifested actions which are in synchrony and consistent with each other and this harmony carves out the characteristic of a group. Theories here are based on inductive logic and consensual behaviour is at the core.

- **Differentiation:** This is opposite to integration theories of culture. Differentiation theories believe that culture is formed due to inconsistencies and deviations leading to formation of subcultures which hold the key for the working of a group. For example, senior management announces a policy but behaves in a manner that is inconsistent with that policy resulting in the formation of a behaviour of disbelief in announced policies. Culture can be more accurately understood through manifested actions of inconsistencies and differences than through integrative framework. Theories here are based on deductive logic, and differences more than consensus lead to formation of culture. However, consensus occurs at a level below in major groups and organizations based on agreement on deviations.

- **Fragmentation:** The foundation of fragmentation theory is that ambiguity is at the core of culture. Culture is formed not because of consistent or inconsistent manifested behaviours by members of a group or institution but rather because of ambiguities that exist due to lack of such behaviours which thus contribute to the creation of adequate space for members to interpret, assume and add to this space through their interactions. Fragmentation theories argue that culture is often the consequence of one or a few major events that cause fragmentation and trigger the formation of culture and not the result of a more deliberate, managerial approach. According to these theories, culture formation is a result of deviant events.

Models of Culture

Researchers' thrust to create a framework that can provide an understanding of culture differences among societies and to attain predictability of culture has led to the formation of different models as discussed further.

Hofstede's Four Cultural Dimensions

Based on his detailed study of IBM's culture around the world, Hofstede Geert, a Dutch Researcher and Psychologist, came up with a seminal model to understand key cultural characteristics of 70 nations, popularly known as Hofstede's four cultural dimensions. These dimensions are as follows:

1. **Power distance index:** Tolerance of people to the centralization of power or unequal distribution of power in organizations is referred to as power distance index. High-power distance implies greater tolerance to unequal power distribution and steep hierarchies and with discretionary power being vested in few people at the top in organizations. Low-power distance refers to low tolerance to centralization of power and discretionary powers and preference of egalitarian work structures. Autocratic leadership structures are generally present in organizations with high-power distance and consensual decision-making practices are seen in low-power distance organizations.

2. **Uncertainty avoidance index:** This dimension refers to the risk-taking quotient. Culture which promotes behaviours of seeking certainty emphasizes adherence to rules, regulations, customs, processes and structures. Belief here is that deviation from standard operating procedure in vogue and taking chances can result in uncertainty, while sticking to them can provide certainty in the form of stability. Uncertainty avoidance behaviour seeks to establish compliance, while no avoidance behaviour prefers flexibility and chance taking in decision-making and even allows for deviations.

3. **Individualism versus collectivism:** Some societies are collective and others individualistic in their behaviour. Collectivist behaviour accords importance to group issues and promotes interdependency while individualistic behaviour attaches no such importance and rather does not feel comfortable with sharing issues with others. Also, individualism characterizes addressing ones needs on self-basis while collectivists seek group espousal.

4. **Masculinity versus femininity:** Masculine refers to assertiveness, materialism, success, and directness and confrontational behaviour. Feminine refers to relationship seeking, emotional quotient, and modesty, caring and discomfort dealing with conflicts.

While Hofstede's work has received acclaim for having collected and put together data from 70 nations as well as criticism for extrapolating a single company's data to draw inferences for entire nations, this has remained a powerful framework to understand culture in the international context.

Trompenaar's Seven Cultural Dimensions

Fons Trompenaar is another Dutch researcher who, while building on Hofstede's work, has come up with another framework called seven dimensions of culture based on a study conducted covering 50 nations. This framework is more focused on implications for managerial behaviour. These dimensions are:

1. **Universalism–Particularism:** This refers to compliances versus exceptions. Universalism refers to complying with rules and regulations in all situations regardless of variations that may occur. Particularism denotes according exceptions to standard rules according to situations or relaxing rules due to extraneous pressures or conditions.

2. **Individualism–Collectivism:** This is an extension of Hofstede's work. The element that has been explored further here is an individual's readiness to submit self-interest in favour of group interests. Individualism refers to resistance to surrendering self-interest and collectivism implies willingness to surrender to group's interest.

3. **Neutral–Emotional:** Some experts emphasize on data, analysis, reports and others rely on intuition and a gut feeling to arrive at decisions. Neutral decision-making refers to objectivity and material evidence and rationality. Emotion refers to subjectivity, feelings and perceptual fairness.

4. **Specific–Diffuse:** This refers to dyadic relationships. In some countries, people accept hierarchical relationships (boss-subordinate) only at the workplace and in others these relationships are accepted not only at the workplace but also in social contexts and relationships.

5. **Achievement–Ascription:** In some societies, people are respected due to their age, caste, religion, social status, formal position and authority, and in some societies people are respected only based on their merit and achievements and not on affiliated factors.

6. **Sequential–Synchronic:** In some cultures, activities and events are seen as sequential and in others they are seen as synchronic. This means that people in synchronic cultures cope with multiple things at the same time and tend to do or attempt many activities simultaneously and not one particular activity at a time. So they take punctuality and sensitivity to time lightly compared to sequential cultures wherein people would attempt one activity at a time and take punctuality seriously.

7. **Harmony–Subjugation:** This dimension refers to how people in different cultural settings respond to the environment and nature. People in some nations live in harmony with the environment while others subjugate it and think of it as being meant for them and not that they are meant for the environment and so their approach towards natural resources and their interaction with the environment tend to be very different.

Trompenaar's work of seven cultural dimensions has also been appreciated particularly for its relevance to business organizations. There is also criticism that in the search for building a typological framework, the study neglects the importance of cultural changes that are occurring in all nations that make it complex to classify them, people and organizations.

Trompenaar also proposed a culture model consisting of four cultures: (a) The family culture which is a power-base-oriented culture, (b) The Eiffel Tower culture which is a task-oriented culture, (c) The guided missile culture which is a role-based culture and, (d) The incubator culture which is development-based culture.

Globe's Nine Cultural Dimensions

This is a study that was launched in the year 1992 and is still continuing involving over 150 researchers worldwide collecting data on cultural values, management and leadership attributes from over 62 countries covering samples representing multiple industries. The GLOBE project based on existing data has come up with a nine-dimensional cultural framework to map countries on the culture. These nine dimensions are as follows:

1. **Assertiveness:** This refers to orientation of people in exhibiting assertiveness. People in some nations have more propensity than in other nations to make their present felt and come across strongly and vocally approving or disapproving something. They are direct and do not concern themselves with how their assertiveness will be perceived. People in some nations would be hesitant to assert themselves openly even when they agree or disagree with something.

2. **Future orientation:** Culture in some nations promotes meticulous planning, saving for future and delaying gratification while the culture in others promotes living in the present and reacting to current situations and showing less intensity for future planning.

3. **Gender differentiation:** This dimension denotes the role stereotype. People prefer role differentiation between men and women in some nations and such differentiation is very low in other nations where no such preference or perception exists of what roles a woman and man have to perform.

4. **Uncertainty avoidance:** This culture dimension was dealt with in both Hofstede and Trompenaar studies as discussed earlier. Order, structure, norms, processes and formality are preferred and seen as mechanisms that provide psychological certainty by people in few

countries. People in other nations do not perceive order and structure as agents of predictability and look at them as rather cumbersome.

5. **Power distance:** As discussed earlier, some nations accept hierarchies and unequal distribution of power and authority and some do not accept, thus causing differences in power distance in societies. This plays an important role in understanding organizational structures and leadership of decision-making.

6. **Institutional collectivism:** This refers to caring for the collective social interest. Societies across the world differ in this aspect with people widely sharing the sentiments, causes and traditions belonging to an institution on one side of the continuum and merely confining to oneself on the other side of the continuum.

7. **In-group collectivism:** This is small group collectivism. In some nations, people view and treat their family members, relatives and friends differently from others and with more pride, while in some other nations, people exhibit no such differentiated treatment.

8. **Performance orientation:** Some societies in the world have high achievement motivation and orientation than other societies.

9. **Humane orientation:** This refers to fairness and generosity. Some nations are high and some are low on this dimension causing cultural differences.

These nine cultural dimensions have been further developed to improve the understanding of their implications for HRM and leadership. The study promotes reckoning these cultural differences while designing HR policies and practices in organizations.

Edgar Schein's Model of Culture

Schein (1992[1988]), a professor at MIT, developed way back in 1988 a widely acclaimed framework known as three levels of organizational culture as discussed here. According to this model, culture is not adopted in a single day but rather formed in due course of time. The three levels in the framework are as follows:

1. **Artefacts:** This refers to the characteristics of an organization that are material and visible and that all employees can feel and live with. Examples include vision, mission statements of companies, dress code and office layout, hours of work, general orientation towards work, physical work settings and behaviour of employees. All these are artefacts conveying the type of culture that exists in an organization.

2. **Values:** This level focuses on psychological aspects such as what and how employees think and feel, and their attitudes, perceptions, orientation towards work, colleagues and customers. Values are deeper than artefacts and develop over a period of time through many experiences, changes and organizational developments. They are at the core of culture and determine the type of culture that is brewing in an organization.

3. **Assumed values:** This is a hidden part of culture. This happens not through any systematic effort or an expressed intent but through latent behaviour. Various employees, when they come in contact with organizations over the course of their career, make certain assumptions and interpretations of what an organization is about and what it stands for. This is reflected in their interactions. Intentionally or unintentionally they pursue that direction of behaviour, thus contributing to a cultural norm. These norms contribute to certain type of behaviours in organizations.

Deal and Kennedy's Culture Model

Terrace Deal and Allan Kennedy are the authors who first coined the term 'corporate culture' back in 1982, garnering huge attention and debate. Based on the framework of high–low risk and fast–slow feedback continuum, the authors have developed a culture model consisting of four types of organizational culture as discussed in the following:

Tough guy culture: This is a macho culture where people need to be tough, hardworking, activity-oriented and action-packed. Stakes are high. Soft-hearted people cannot survive here. This is typical of corporate organizations in investment banking, entertainment industry, advertising and other such industries according to the authors. All sales, real estate, retail and financial markets employees fall in this category. People here are competitive, strive to become stars and work to win. This is the most gruelling of all corporate cultures. Speed, agility and high energy matter while endurance and persistence are hardly present in this culture.

Work hard/Play hard culture: This culture is activity based and people just need to work hard, persist and endure. It is collaborative since people believe that situations are not easy to win solo and so people forge networks. So teamwork is important here. Feedback comes fast so one can initiate remedial actions. It is a world of small activities with low risk.

Bet your company culture: Here, people put company's interests at stake instead of their own, similar to work hard/play hard model of culture. Decision-making tends to be top-down based on inputs sought or available. Leaders take high-risk decisions like major investments, putting company future at risk but feedback comes slow so many cannot see the risk potential immediately. Slow feedback does not mean that there is no stress here, but stress is gradual and persistent. Industries such as infrastructure, mines, energy, capital goods and heavy construction fall in this category and of course some of them show inhibition to risk.

Process culture: This is typical of government organizations. People working in such cultures are often not clear about their end objectives and about why they do certain things. Their efficiency and performance depend upon the ability to implement a process. How good their work is how good they appear to be adhering to this process. Feedback is either slow or never comes through. People in such cultures are mechanical in their approach and insist on compliance without being aware of the pros and cons.

Schneider's Culture Model

Schneider, Brief and Guzzo (1996) while building on Harrison, Deal and Kennedy's works, had proposed a more universally applicable corporate culture model consisting of four dimensions as discussed in the following:

- **Cultivation culture:** Culture that pervades in some organizations is like faith. Everybody believes in that and works towards the goals. Working towards the supposed goal of that faith is very important for its members and gives them utmost satisfaction. Religious organizations, symphony, orchestra, art creation and media fall in this category. People in this culture believe that they are working towards something very valuable and noble. The mere thought of working for the greater cause of society gives energy and leads to a culture of cultivation. The title of cultivation culture is given because this culture is a consequence of careful cultivation by its members.

- **Collaboration culture:** In this culture, self-interest has no place. People come together to complement each other's strengths and work towards a common goal like a family. No status, hierarchy, rank and authority is accepted and only positive relationships among members guide their actions. Voluntary organizations, hospitals, creative institutions, family-owned and family-employed organizations and start-ups work with this culture.
- **Control culture:** This culture exists in rational and objective organizations where material facts, empirical data, evidence, quantifiable analysis and exemplary structures are important. Order, predictability, stability and chain of command are the key characteristics. Emotions, empathy and considerations have no place in this culture and soft approaches are not encouraged. Formal instructions, processes and systems are put in place to regulate actions of its members. Decision-making is impersonal and external facts guide the actions.
- **Competence culture:** This is a culture where knowledge and achievement matters. This school of culture emanated from David McClelland's Achievement Motivation Theory which avers that some societies and people compete against a standard of excellence. People in competence culture seek to do more and more and want to stand apart from others. They compete to create the best. Being superior, high-quality orientation, superseding the existing standards to set new order are paramount for members in this culture. People are hard-working and no monitoring is required as their standards are built inside of their personalities. To them, organizations are mere platforms where they work, test and excel in to achieve something extraordinary through their competence. Competition is used here to compete against their own standards and for their own sake. Formalities and emotional considerations are not as important as orientation of achievement.

Cameron and Quinn's Model of Culture

The competing values framework is also known as OCAI (Organizational Culture Assessment Instrument) in organizational culture theory and is regarded to be the most sophisticated model of culture that is relevant to business organizations. Cameron and Quinn (1999), based on their research of business organizations, have placed organizational culture into four quadrants with competing assumptions. These are as follows:

- **Hierarchy culture:** Control, command and stability are at the core of this culture. Tasks and functions are integrated and coordinated with well-defined decision-making matrix. Standardization and accountability are valued. Organizational structure is formal, authority is respected and rules and processes are central to organizational functioning. Leaders are perceived as effective controllers and coordinators and actions are generally predictable. Maintaining status quo and protecting stability are the chief characteristics. This model of culture often exists in large manufacturing organizations and in government departments/functions. Internal environment and dynamics are more emphasized than external realities.
- **Market culture:** Unlike hierarchy culture, here external realities and environment play a dominant role. Customers, competitors, market changes and business networks are reckoned while arriving at decisions. Efficiencies, profit maximization, winning competition, productivity enhancement are the typical goals. This culture seeks result-oriented behaviour and leaders are hard-driving and demanding. Focus on markets, success, winning competition and aggression is the glue that keeps teams together.

- **Clan culture:** This refers to a climate akin to a family where relationships and team orientation are paramount. Participation, empowerment, regard for people, employee development, commitment, loyalty and common sharing are the key characteristics of the clan culture. Customers are treated like partners and all employees work hard to the best of their abilities to deliver value. Leaders motivate employees through loyalty, mentorship, commitment and relationships. Leadership is paternalistic. Clan culture espouses behaviour of consensus, democracy and concern for people accommodating all. Employees here always try to do their best. Relationships rather than monetary incentives, commitment rather than demands, respect in the place of aggression are evident in clan culture oriented workplaces.
- **Adhocracy:** As the title suggests, culture in adhocracy type organizations is temporary, dynamic and changing forever. Flexibility, adaptability, uncertainty, creativity, ambiguity and interpretations are the key characteristics. Here, roles, responsibilities, processes, structures and authority centres are also susceptible to change. Customers are the only ones who are relatively stable. The zeal to experiment, innovate and create something extraordinary is what holds people in such organizations together. Research organizations, new technology companies and creative places prefer this type of culture. Standardization and control structures have no place here. Leaders guide employees through their knowledge and competence rather than with formal powers and accountabilities.

Charles Handy's Model of Culture

According to culture expert Charles Handy (1993), there are four types of organizational culture:

- **Power culture:** Power tends to be concentrated in the hands of few people who take all the decisions. Decision-making is faster and the line of command is simple, straight and clear. There is no bureaucracy and few rules and processes exist. Employees are evaluated and identified based on what they achieve rather than how. Decisions are usually made to serve immediate interests and make progress even at the cost of long-term priorities. Power is considered aspirational in this culture and exists as a core instrument to enable the progress of an organization. Power culture is a strong culture in its form and fabric and can get toxic.
- **Role culture:** Power culture emphasizes importance of a few people, whereas role culture highlights influence of roles in an organization. Role culture tends to be bureaucratic with tall organizational structures, quite a few rules and regulations and a long chain of command. Process of detailed delegation powers and which role can decide what matters exists. There is limited scope for expert power. Decisions are impersonal and are made as a matter of fact and often as per well-defined rules and structures.
- **Task power:** This refers to expert power. Here, people are focused on achieving goals and performing tasks with their specialized skills. Leadership uses knowledge, information and interpretation capabilities to lead the teams. Extent of power and authority one holds over others is largely dependent upon their competence and falls within intersections because tasks are generally not solo but team oriented. Power is decentralized to teams who hold ownership for tasks like a team conducting surgery in a hospital. Everyone in the team conducting surgery is important as they take decisions in their respective areas.

- **Person culture:** As the title suggests, this is completely person based. There can be multiple people performing the same kind of role, but one person or few persons emerge as the most powerful mostly due to expert power or network power. Such persons tend to wield enormous influence in organizations and many people follow them voluntarily. Leaders here tend to be charismatic and can inspire the followership through sheer personality and style.

Denison's Model of Culture

According to this model, there are four key elements in understanding culture as discussed in the following. Two of these elements, involvement and adaptability, are centred on change and flexibility while the other two, mission and consistency, hinge upon stability and direction principles.

- **Involvement:** This element refers to the degree of involvement of employees at all levels in an organization and the collaboration spirit that exists. Involvement can happen when three conditions exist in harmony as per this model. These are capability development, empowerment and teamwork. If there is only empowerment and no capability development, this can potentially lead to people who are not adequately capable of making decisions. If there is only capability development and no empowerment, an organization may have people who are capable but are not allowed to take decisions resulting in wastage of human capabilities and skills. If there is only teamwork and no empowerment and capability development, people are not geared up to the task and they limit themselves to routine activities and tend to become like a club. Unless all the three conditions coexist, the real employee involvement in organizations is a mere dream. The said three conditions in harmony can be witnessed in organizations with high involvement culture.
- **Consistency:** This culture refers to internal coherence and internal integration. Problem-solving, efficiency and effectiveness at every level in an organization are the key characteristics of consistency culture. Consistency culture oriented organizations tend to be well integrated and coordinated. People in this type of culture possess implicit faith that internal control systems, internalized values, structures, rules, regulations and processes are important for effective functioning. The urge for stability, control and coordination is at the core of leadership. Employees are capable of reaching consensus/agreements even when there are disagreements. Consistency culture promotes looking inwards, internal integration, imbibing internal value system and a common mindset among employees which sometimes can pose a bigger challenge when dealing with external environment and marker challenges.
- **Adaptability:** Adaptable organizations and people who work there are well equipped to adapt themselves with changing environment and dynamics. Adaptability culture encourages an outward-looking and market-facing approach. Hence, organizations are susceptible to change in tune with changing demands of clients, markets and technologies. Adaptable organizations prefer systems and processes that cater to gathering information and changing market dynamics and seamlessly translating them into the inside of an organization in the form of systems, processes, structure, overall decision-making and behaviour of its employees. Adaptable culture drives risk-taking behaviour and imbibes motivation to seek transformation

and influence environmental changes. However, sometimes an adaptable organization waits for changes to happen in the environment and adapts itself rather than driving on its own and in that sense ability of an organization to proactively plan the change is minimal.

- **Mission:** Mission culture exists in organizations which are highly conscious. These organizations and people working there clearly know the destination (vision), purpose (intent/goals), strategic direction (milestones) and efforts (tasks) required to reach the destination and also what contribution they need to make for the success of the organization. Organizational systems, processes, structures and overall culture can also undergo change when vision changes. However, often mission culture also leads to excessive focus on execution sidelining long-range planning and sometimes tends to fail to translate vision into actions due to focus of leadership on execution rather than on design and strategy. Mission culture also relies on integration as a core value.

Theory Z

In 1993, William Ouchi had developed a culture theory which became popular as Theory Z. According to him, it is not few individuals or behaviours that cause organizational culture but the way many things in an organization put together and managed as a whole and in its entirety cause the culture. Theory Z culture is a high commitment and high performance oriented culture which happens as a result of long-term-oriented policies like consensual decision-making, individual responsibility, slow evaluation and promotion, long-term employment, trust, equitable reward system, motivation through self-interest, moderately specialized career paths and informal control systems with explicit measures of performance.

Profile of Organizational Culture in International Organizations

As discussed earlier in the introductory part, although organizational culture requirements seem to be similar in domestic as well as international organizations in the new era of technology-driven business and changing social and cultural dynamics due to millennials, yet culture profile and needs are different for international setting. It is a subtle challenge unlike in the past because national differences in culture were stark but these boundaries are blurred and today in almost every nation there is a mix of national and international culture fabric leading to cross-cultural ethos.

Organizational Culture in America's Best-run Companies

Thomas Peters and Robert Waterman (1982) in their search for excellence in America's best-run companies found organizational culture tied to the success of their companies and they said such high-performance culture existed due to the following elements:

- **Bias towards action:** Execution ability and motivation to act, experiment, explore and decide.
- **Close to the customer:** Customer is at the centre of innovation and for introduction of new products, services and pricing.
- **Autonomy and entrepreneurship:** Overall climate in organization tends to be dynamic, empowered and encourages innovation, risk-taking and constantly tries new ways of doing things.

- **Productivity through people:** High involvement of employees, distributed decision-making and confidence in employees are evident.
- **Hands-on, value-driven effort:** Organization promotes values not only by talking but walking by its leadership, and values are built as the core of organizational functioning, so results are important but they shall be achieved through the values.
- **Sticking to the knitting:** Leadership and people in high performing organizations have a culture of sticking to their core capabilities and main business. They will be reluctant to venture into any business activity that is unrelated to its core business.
- **Simple form, lean staff:** Organizational structures are simple, leaner, linear and there is no matrix and dual channels and there are less procedures and formalities.
- **Simultaneous loose–tight properties:** Organization exhibits control and facilitation behaviours depending upon the situation and issue. Values are tightly controlled and decision-making is flexible. Individual employees can take initiative and can fail but shall adhere to the value system of the company.

Differences in national cultures: Theories as illustrated earlier prove that organizational culture does get impacted by the national culture because organizations become microcosms of that society. Leadership styles, decision-making process, job expectations and other organizational processes to be adapted in an organization shall be in tune with the preferences of local culture. Organizational processes and management systems that lack harmony with local cultural beliefs are fraught with the challenge of resistance and producing counterproductive results for the company. Every nation has its language, religion, customs, traditions and ways of perception which can impact culture of an organization operating in that nation. Table 9.2 lists researchers/ authors and their works that support this view.

Table 9.2   Culture of Employees and Nations

Author/Researcher	Study Findings
Buchanan and Hucznski (2004)	Behaviour of employees is shaped by the organizational culture which is influenced by respective national cultures.
Jung et al. (1989)	Employees of a multinational company's subsidiary will be influenced by the national culture of their country in terms of the country's values, beliefs and customs.
Joiner (2001)	Inconsistency in the organization's culture and national culture held by the leaders has an adverse impact on the performance.
Parboteeah, Bronson and Cullen (2005)	National culture influences absenteeism and people in certain countries believe that absence is more acceptable than people in other countries.
Steinwachs (1999)	Communication effectiveness between a sender and receiver is highly influenced by national culture in which language is an important part.
House, Hanges, Javidan, Dorfman and Gupta (1982)	National culture shapes the style of leadership and the way leaders function.
Schein (1992 [1988])	Organizational culture which is influenced by national culture shapes the leadership.

Source: Author's own compilation.

David Livermore, a leading researcher of leadership and culture, had spent 15 years researching cultural intelligence studying over 55,000 professionals across 98 countries and found several challenges with the global teams due to cultural differences. National cultures are of different types. Some of them are monoculture nations, some are multicultural, few are pluralistic and others are diversified culture societies. Each of these cultures can have distinct influence on people and as a result on organizational cultures. Therefore, international organizations need to be flexible enough to accommodate national cultures to design certain organizational processes, systems and organizational structure and more importantly the way these can be implemented in a country. However, while doing so, organizations shall not lose their identity culture fabric. Organizations need to drive a balance between these two and blend them.

International Culture Management
3 M

3 M has operations spread across the length and breadth of Russia for the last 15 years. While operating in Russia, 3 M did not overlook the importance of blending local positive culture elements like working cooperatively with its teamwork practices. Also, Russian managers are found to be good in dealing with turbulent situations so 3 M has hired only local managers to run its operations withdrawing all expatriates. 3 M is known to make donations to schools and local voluntary organizations keeping in view the long running Russian tradition of charitable contributions to community development that brought a great deal of positive brand image for the company within the country. More interestingly, 3 M in recognition of dysfunctional cultural elements that exist in the country such as bribery and contributing to protection money among corporates has taken an opposite standby not only discouraging these practices but also by popularizing the importance of ethical behaviour among its associates through training creation of ethical leaders in the organization. 3 M experience is considered the best practice in cross-cultural operations where while adapting local positive cultures, interventions are made to overcome the local negative cultures.

According to Erin Meyer, there are stark cultural differences among the nations that can create a huge impact on global business organizations. She had studied a number of countries and their cultures by applying the following eight scales:

1. **Communicating:** People in the United States, the Netherlands, Australia, Germany and Canada are straight talkers and no implicit understanding is involved, whereas people in Japan, India, China, Indonesia and East Asia are implicit communicators who prefer to say anything in a suggestive manner and not directly, thus needing to be interpreted in context to get to the point.
2. **Evaluating:** Russians, Germans, French and Dutch are at ease in giving direct negative feedback while Japanese, Thai, Chinese and Indians prefer to give negative feedback in very indirect manner.
3. **Persuading:** Americans pursue with intuition and outward logic and Indians and Chinese with emotions and French and Italians with evidence and analysis of data.
4. **Leading:** Steep hierarchy is preferred to make leadership impactful in countries such as India, China, Japan, Korea and other East Asian countries and egalitarian approach is preferred in some other countries to the extent that there is hardly any between CEO and the junior most associate.

5. **Deciding:** Sweden, Japan and the Netherlands are consensual decision-making nations while India, China, Russia and African countries are very top-down and countries like the United States, UK are in the middle of these two approaches and France, Italy and Brazil are more top-down, although they make it appear that consensus is preferred.

6. **Trusting:** The United States, Denmark, Germany, the Netherlands, Finland, UK and Australia are task based in their trust probably because these countries have strong legal remedial systems; countries like India, China, Japan, Turkey, Mexico and Russia are relationship-centric nations and countries such as Poland, France, Italy and Spain fall in the middle of these two extremes.

7. **Disagreeing:** People of some nations are at ease with confrontations and express their disagreements and it is not the same with people of other nations who shy away from expressing their dissent openly and directly. Countries such as Israel, Germany, Russia, France, Spain, Italy, Australia and the Netherlands view confrontation as being agreeable and not negatively impacting relationships. People in countries such as Japan, Thailand, Indonesia, China, India, Mexico and Brazil have a tendency to avoid confrontation as the same is feared to negatively impact relationships. The US and UK fall in the middle of this scale where they decide to confront or not, depending on the situation.

8. **Scheduling:** People in countries such as Switzerland, Germany, Sweden, Finland, US, UK, Denmark, Japan and the Netherlands are very punctual and particular about time and they see time as linear. People in India, China, Turkey, Middle East and Brazil view time as flexible and approach it in a fluid manner. France, Russia, Italy and Spain fall in the middle.

There is also a school of thought that argues that the cultural differences that exist within a country are much more formidable than the differences that exist between countries. For example, Kirkman, Lowe and Gibson (2016), based on their research work of meta-analysis of 558 existing studies covering 32 countries over a period of 35 years, found that the biggest cultural gaps are within countries and not between them. They have studied four interrelated values to understand how they exist in the same country. These values are:

- Individuals versus groups
- Hierarchy and status in organizations
- Certainty at work
- Material wealth, assertiveness and competition versus social welfare and harmonious relationships

The research reveals that a country is actually a poor container of culture and a difference of over 80 per cent was noticed on the four aforementioned values within the same country versus a 20 per cent difference in values between countries. Therefore, mentions like Japanese culture or American culture or Indian culture can be misleading as there is significant room for error. Reason for this is that the socio-economic conditions of people in the same country are vastly different and so when they come on board in organizations, they carry different cultural backgrounds. For example, people who live in urbanized areas and rural areas in the same country tend to be very different in their behaviours and attitudes. Therefore, stereotyping by country is likely to lead to a whole host of mistakes.

Pamela Hinds (2000) based on an intensive case study of three large organizations and their teams across the United States, India, China, Japan, Mexico and Germany found that often implementation or adoption of the best practices do not translate into reality due to cultural differences.

Different Cultures See Deadlines Differently

According to Bhaskar Pant (2016, https://www.hbrascend.in/topics/different-cultures-see-deadlines-differently), different cultures perceive time differently. Western cultures tend to view time as linear with a definitive beginning and end. Time is viewed as a fixed and exhaustible resource and so Westerners plan their activities, business operations, milestones and targets along the timelines so as to accomplish them within the time schedule. Consumption of time without results or failure to adhere to a schedule is considered to reflect inefficiency and incompetence. Time is a material resource like money and capital. Some of the oriental cultures, if not all, view time as an endless and cyclical resource. So doing something in harmony and peace and nurturing relationships is more important than merely meeting deadlines because time is abundant and does not carry a material value.

Cross-cultural management: Whitney Johnson, an equity analyst at Merrill Lynch, says that building rapport across cultures is a good way to manage cross-cultural issues. To build rapport one shall learn the language, genuinely enter the other person's world, avoid jargon and employ body language, share a meal and genuinely have an orientation to relish the diversity. All leaders across the globe struggle with managing cross-cultural teamwork, cross-cultural communication, cross-cultural training and cross-cultural performance management because what fits well with one culture seems to be at odds with other cultures. The challenge resides in the design of processes and systems many times and at other times in the method of application. This challenge is further compounded with very moving cultural orientation of people in tandem with social and economic changes.

Three Causes of Cross-cultural Communication Breakdown

Ginka Toegel and Jean-Louis Barsoux, faculty at IMD, Lausanne, based on 25 years of their research of global work groups, have found the following three situations that cause breakdown of cross-cultural communication:

1. **Eliciting ideas:** Some societies are more egalitarian and democratic while some are hierarchical, impacting the manner in which people contribute ideas. For example, employees in the United States voice their opinions, suggestions, ideas and comments freely, while employees in countries such as Japan wait for their seniors to take lead and are sometimes hesitant to so much as voice an opinion. Some societies encourage instant speaking, while others insist on the 'think before you speak' principle. This causes a barrier when dealing with cross-cultural global teams.
2. **Surfacing disagreements:** People in some countries are comfortable with good fights and functional confrontations. In fact, it is seen as a sign of trust and collaboration. In other societies, people try to avoid voicing disagreements to a person's face as they believe voicing them may cause loss of trust and confidence. Therefore, it is difficult to know whether there was real consensus or if there were disagreements. This causes a breakdown in cross-cultural work groups unless addressed because constructive criticism is an important element in global teamwork.
3. **Giving feedback:** In individualistic societies like North America, people see feedback as an opportunity for self or team development and look at it as a reliable source to plug the gaps. In Asian societies, managers are hesitant to offer direct feedback, especially critical feedback, because often people tend to attribute such feedback to personal and group dynamics rather than viewing it as a genuine source for development. Hence, often even team feedback in these societies is offered in

an informal way and in a one-on-one setting leading to even critical feedback looking like soft commentary. When this difference is neglected while giving feedback to a cross-cultural global team, it tends to generate different impact.

Hence, when cross-cultural global teams are to be formed and managed, leaders and organizations must factor the differences and address them before they are brought into action.

These challenges can be addressed by creating a balance and cultural awareness among the teams and by enabling diversified structures that support functioning of cross-cultural teams. According to Tsedal Neeley (2013), professor of HBS, three factors are critical for creating high-performance global teams. These are as follows:

- **Mutual learning:** Global teams when exposed to learning together as a team will discover culture similarities and differences themselves that enrich their learning. Teams usually explore common grounds and relatedness and also notice dissimilarities; organizations must take advantages of positives to address challenges. Also, teams must be encouraged to ask questions, to show curiosity and absorb the differences. When something starts with learning rather than work in a mutual setting, the same can pave a way to build functional teams at global level that are culturally aligned.
- **Mutual understanding:** While a mutual learning process helps in knowing the cultural similarities and dissimilarities, a mutual understanding process enables appreciation of each other's cultures and each other's point of view. This process eliminates communication gaps among global team members and presents an opportunity for the emergence of a unified team. This phase is represented by members not being judgemental and understanding ambiguities as events of learning opportunities.
- **Mutual teaching:** Once a global team moves up the value chain successfully from mutual learning to mutual understanding, automatically the teams have a tendency to identify the mentors, coaches and problem solvers and interpreters among the team members. This is phase of collaboration with team members supporting and teaching each other and progressing towards a shared goal. Trust and appreciation for each other's existence and work are the key traits that mutual teaching generates in global teams.

Five Actions to Leverage Multiculturalism

Abundant empirical evidence exists from business organizations across the globe establishing that multiculturalism helps to enhance innovation and build the best practices and grow much more rapidly. However, organizations need to be conspicuous and take several proactive actions to realize these benefits. Yves Doz (2011), Professor of Strategic Management at INSEAD, on study of several multinational corporations and based on Hae-Jung Hong's research, advises of five actions to leverage multiculturalism that exists in international organizations to create superior services and products through its diversified cultural workforce. These are as follows:

1. Identify creative associations and enable to draw analogies between international and local cultures to develop cross-cultural practices which can be sensitive to local cultures and yet create an international identity for the company.

2. Understand complex contextual dynamics behind the local management practices. This tends to be tacit but shared among the members. It is important for international organizations to understand the interpretation of these which can be helpful in execution of their operations.
3. Proactively anticipate cross-cultural conflicts and address them before they erupt into major barriers. This is critical to effectiveness of global teams.
4. Integrate team members drawn from different cultures systematically and deploy developmental mechanisms. Organizations must create an identity for team members and facilitate the teams to develop their norms for effective performance.
5. Mediate relationships among staff members of headquarters and subsidiary companies and between global teams and local teams because often there would be clashes between monocultures with multiculture-centric teams and staff. Allowing these clashes to be resolved by themselves can be ineffective.

Cross-cultural conflicts: Experiences of global organizations with cross-cultural conflicts are not uncommon. These conflicts continue to cost immense efforts and money if they are failed to be managed systematically. Cross-cultural conflicts occur due to a host of causes. The first being when attempts are made to understand the culture of a group through stereotyped notions. As discussed earlier, macro understanding of national cultures and applying them to a group of employees of that country often leads to erroneous inferences. Believing in the self-view of another's culture, when interpreted through the lens of one's own culture, can be misleading. This often leads to incorrect conclusions and contributes to cultural conflicts among teams working in global companies. The manner in which symbols, artefacts, customs and body language are interpreted and understood can be quite different in different cultures, so a systematic understanding of another's culture in the way it was structured is essential to avoid conflicts. Deep beliefs that each society promotes can also lead to conflicts at workplace particularly in international organizations. Research studies have amply demonstrated that people in countries such as the United States, Australia and Germany show high concern for self-interest goals and tend to be assertive while people in nations such as Japan value others' interests and goals equally and equate being assertive with being self-centric. When employees from these countries come together to work on a project, there is likelihood of cultural conflicts that can adversely impact progress. Differences in leadership styles are yet another source for cultural conflicts in organizations. Tomas Chamorro and Michael Sanger (https://hbr.org/2016/05/what-leadership-looks-like-in-different-cultures [accessed 8 March 2018]) in their study of 'what leadership looks like in different cultures' aver that there are six types of leadership styles which are built on cultural beliefs of respective nations. These are as follows:

- **The synchronized leader:** Leaders in Mainland China, Japan, Korea, Thailand and Latin America are seen as synchronized leaders who focus on processes and work with teams and are often catapulted into leadership roles from rank and file cadres. These leaders work in tune with the staff and are more focused on avoiding risks than on acquiring reward.
- **The opportunistic leader:** Leaders in Germany, Norway, Denmark, the UK, India, Singapore, Hong Kong and Malaysia are self-initiating and demonstrate flexibility to adapt themselves to situations and can handle ambiguities well. They are more risk-taking and ambitious.
- **The straight shooting leader:** In some nations, people prefer leaders who are capable of confronting issues in a straightforward manner. Leaders in these cultures tend to be task

masters and are interpersonally less sensitive. For example, people in Holland like straightforwardness and dislike excessive communication or indirect ways of doing things.

- **The diplomatic leader:** Countries such as New Zealand, Sweden, Canada and much of Latin America were found to prefer leaders who are very tactful in getting ahead. Hence, leaders in these countries are likely to be very careful and keep all conversations pleasant and amicable. Leaders adjust their messages and the way they work with staff echoing the sentiments and beliefs of the staff and gauge the staff on a continuous basis.
- **The kick up/kick down leader:** These leaders exhibit two traits simultaneously, going into details and paying careful attention while also commanding staff with fiery directives without compromise. This leadership style is most preferred in countries such as Turkey, India, UAE, Greece, South Korea and Kenya. These leaders tend to be dutiful and diligent with those above them, while being intense and dominating with their staff.
- **The passive–aggressive leader:** Countries such as Indonesia and Malaysia seek leaders who are cynical, sceptical, critical and resentful. They may try to push the agenda sometimes without entirely understanding its rationality and forcefully attempt to execute the agenda. This style may not work and leads to execution failures in other nations but in these countries it does not appear to be an impediment at all.

The leadership differences as illustrated earlier can cause cultural conflicts. A particular leadership style may work well in some nations but will create disharmony in other nations. According to Professor Quinn Mills (2005) at Harvard Business School, cultural differences among leaders in North America and Asia are considerable. For example, adaptability among leaders is less common in Asia than in the United States. Robert House (1999), director of the Global Leadership and Organizational Behavior Effectiveness Research Programme at the Wharton Business School, says what works in business organizations based in the United States may not work in business environments in other parts of the world, and organizations face a growing need to understand the subtleties and nuances of leadership as it is exercised in different cultures. Before trying to build multinational teams, one must take note of cultural differences among leadership and follower attitudes embedded in culture. Richard Lewis (1999) lays down differences in leadership styles and concomitant cultural attitudes as illustrated in Table 9.3.

Karen Loon, partner with PWC in Singapore and a diversity leader, says that Asian female leaders, unlike female leaders in Europe and North America, value inclusiveness, community and contribution over individuality. The word ambition may not resonate well with non-individualized cultures. As discussed earlier, when leadership styles are applied without factoring local cultural preferences and ethos, it can lead to potential cultural conflicts. Hence, international organizations that usually deploy cross-cultural teams must take proactive actions to foster understanding among the team members about the cultural variations that may creep in and how to tackle them.

Managing International Culture

The consequences of multiculturalism to organizations and communities and their impact on behaviours are complex and powerful. Organizations of contemporary era have no choice but to realize multiculturalism for their own survival. There are three real business reasons why organizations are pushed towards this goal. First, more and more societies/nations are pushing a legal agenda making it mandatory that no organization or individual can any longer pursue

Table 9.3   Nations and Their Leadership Culture

Country	Leadership Culture	Cultural Attitudes
Germany	Hierarchy & consensus	German managers are authoritative with the staff within the framework defined and also motivate staff with solidarity. German employees also seek clear definition of processes, standards and would be keen to know where they stand in their work. Employees are hardworking and work long hours, obey instructions and also insist on fair play and consensual approach to problem-solving.
France	Autocratic	The French prefer an autocratic and top-down management style. However, this is not apparent at first glance. Chief executives of French companies, unlike their German counterparts, take all decisions and perform a supervisory role breaching chain of command. The staff exhibit high tolerance. Dynamics of journey becomes more important than ultimate results and failures are not viewed too negatively.
Japan	Confucian hierarchy	Top leadership wields influence as much as shop floor employees as a team. Japanese leadership does not interfere with day-to-day operations. However, they take policy decisions when required and also ratify all important ideas that originate from the shop floor. It is a clannish culture like family.
Spain	Human force	Spanish leaders are autocratic but with a human face. They are intuitive, seek admiration from their staff and will make sacrifices for them. Their style is to inspire the followers and be able to persuade them towards goals. Decision-making is centralized and opposition is not encouraged.
Sweden	Democratic	The Swedes seek democratic leadership. Leaders are easily accessible and decision-making is consensual with keen participation by staff. Leader is considered as first among the equals and no more than that.
USA	Structured individualism	The US has a materialistic approach. Managers are expected to get things done, find ways to achieve goals and promote teamwork. In order to achieve goals, people believe leaders should be given authority and they must make decisions to create rewards for everybody. Money is a key reward for leaders and followers.

Source: Author's own compilation based on Richard's (1999) work.

monoculture, and deviations are dealt with punitive actions. This is because of growing multiculturalism in the workforce. For example, the proportion of white race employees to all other races in the American workforce was 47 per cent in 1990, and 20 years later by 2010, this proportion was down to a mere 14 per cent. Second, a business organization can no longer create a market for itself when it is still monoculture-centric because more and more customers and distributors see the organization's culture brand being an important factor for growth and monoculture reflecting single community dominance is seen as a sign of imperialism. Third, organizations that do not practise justice, fairness and equality tend to become extinct in the long run as demonstrated through numerous examples in history. To be successful, international organizations have to manage international culture to the advantage of both employees and the organization. Working with multicultural global teams is a business necessity and indispensable for international organizations. In any case, as the discussed contents reveal, multiculturalism contributes to better innovation, generation of novel ideas and creation of better products and services. Discussion also points out that strong culture would contribute to improved organizational performance. Experiences of multinational companies increasingly demonstrate that multicultural organizations can attract and retain the best talent because their culture is one of inclusiveness and they can enter into broader markets because they have broader exposure than monoculture organizations and can better adjust to changes in the environment. Hence, organizations must make efforts to manage international cultures effectively by applying right approaches as discussed in the following:

Acknowledgement: Recognizing the challenges that exist with multicultural teams (cross-cultural communication issues, cross-cultural conflicts and cross-cultural team dynamics) is the first step in the right direction. It needs to be noted that multiculturalism is a double-edged sword as it can accrue valuable benefits to organizations and at the same time pose serious challenges in the form of culture clashes. Often, organizations tend to not recognize or acknowledge that there are challenges. This happens due to various reasons. Sometimes, it is sheer lack of experience that prompts them to think there can be no issues and so global teams are formed or employees from one country to other countries are deputed without an orientation or training. When teams fail to function effectively, organizations may realize that it is due to lack of proactive understanding of multicultural workforce concerns but that realization comes in a little too late, after the damage has already occurred. In few cases, organizations are just insensitive to the needs and challenges of multicultural teams and put themselves in jeopardy as a result. Hence, proactively acknowledging the challenges without loss of time can lead to timely and practical solutions. Working with global teams and multicultural groups is common for international organizations so a prudent approach would be to set up a professional multicultural training system that can train employees to deal with cultures other than their own and to help them understand that their country's cultural ethos can be understood by other country nationals. These trainings can include awareness training on the benefits of multiculturalism and also enable employees to understand the cross-cultural issues from a positive perspective and skill training to equip global team members to work with multicultural teams effectively. The second approach is for international organizations to build multicultural managers who can spearhead international cultures both in their roles as managers as well as in the capacity of multicultural brand managers. It is like building in-house expertise on multiculturalism. These multicultural managers can help in creating a shared vision and shared mindset and multicultural consciousness among employees and enable organizations to adapt to diversity with associated business gains. As a key responsibility, these managers will be required to promote multiculturalism. Erin Meyer (2014), professor at INSEAD and author of the book *The Culture Map: Breaking Through the Invisible Boundaries of Global Business*, points out based on her comprehensive study on 'why successful leaders acknowledge cultural differences' that acknowledging and understanding cultural differences is more important than ever. Leaders need to understand a wider and richer array of work styles than ever before and to be able to determine which aspects of an interaction are simply a result of personality and which are a result of differences in cultural perspective.

Systems/Processes: In order to build high-performing international organizations, systems and processes shall be designed that encourage and facilitate multiculturalism. Processes must be built on the foundation of inclusiveness and must have all prejudices sans lineage to a particular culture eliminated to avoid the domination of parent country culture over the culture of subsidiaries. When international organizations accommodate subsidiary cultures in some measure, they sometimes make the mistake of making it appear as if great flexibility has been exhibited by the dominant culture groups while it is to actually be treated as a basic right and obligation. It is important for all organizations operating in a country to respect local cultural ethos and blend them with organizational practices as much as an organization must protect its integrity and character. It is pertinent to mention that an international organization can always opt to resist dysfunctional elements of local norms if they are contrary to the principles of universal ethics. Of course, no culture of any nation which is sustainable can have a dysfunctional value. A system of incentivizing multicultural practices and attitudes must be put in place and organizations that aspire to grow as true international entities must make multicultural training and induction compulsory at all levels. These organizations will need to demonstrate in letter and spirit a global character instead of serving the country of their origin. Design/Production and market/demand must be international, and concentrating on one at the cost of the other in any nation could lead to an assumption of superiority. Core of management systems and practices must be universal while execution of these practices can be intertwined with flavours of local cultures for better consumption. Systems and processes can perform as great levellers of multiculturalism. Merely wishing for and making sporadic attempts to infuse multiculturalism through one or two interventions without fundamentally altering the approach by deploying necessary systems and processes is mere lip service. Hence, creation of multicultural managers must precede creation of multicultural systems and processes.

Multicultural Organization Development Model

Bailey Jackson and Rita Hardiman, at the University of Michigan in 1981, have developed a multicultural organization development model valuing and capitalizing on cultural differences consisting of three levels and six stages which can help in the transformation of a monocultural organization into a multicultural organization. These levels and stages are described here. There are two stages in each level.

Level 1: The monoculture organization: This level of an organization reflects an image that it is only focused on furthering interests of a particular group and does not believe in multiculturalism but rather in the dominance and special privileges of a particular group, and equality can be only within that special group.

Stage 1: The exclusionary organization: This is an exclusionary state. Organizations make all efforts not only to protect interests of a selective group but also push back other groups and oppress them. These organizations create entry barriers that favour the selective group and restrict other groups from gaining entry or from hiring. It is a self-centric organization.

Stage 2: The club: This type of organization promotes a privileged group whose members protect each other's interests through networking and by finding means to relate themselves to each other. This group pushes agendas and policies that favour them and put the rest at a disadvantage. On the face of it, it may not appear like an exclusionary organization as it tries to project a neutral image. But in reality, a particular social group or executive group has more privilege than other groups.

Level 2: The non-discriminating organization: This is a neutral state. An organization neither discourages nor encourages multiculturalism deliberately. These organizations have a tendency to incidentally recruit people representing all cultures and not by plan. There may not be any system or process support to build multicultural employees and the employees are expected to resolve any issues that arise by themselves.

Stage 3: The compliance organization: At this stage, an organization does not encourage monocultures and wishes for multiculturalism but without disturbing the status quo of policies, processes, structure and systems in the organization. This stage allows looking more favourably towards multiculturalism but without actually initiating substantive actions or complying with the dynamics that arise.

Stage 4: The affirmative action organization: Actions are taken to eliminate any discrimination and efforts are made to create a culture of inclusiveness. Unlike in the compliance stage, here organizations are positioned to take proactive actions to promote multiculturalism and to remove entry barriers and prejudicial processes.

Level 3: The multicultural organization: These organizations are clear that they intend to be multicultural organizations. Therefore, by plan they hire people representing a variety of cultures and create systems and processes that support and spread multiculturalism. They emphasize diverse cultural representation, equitable distribution of power and influence and support multicultural perspectives and the elimination of oppression.

Stage 5: Redefining organization: This is a transition phase. Organizations initiate series of actions to redefine company policies, processes, structure, system and also vision and mission if required to foster multiculturalism with a belief that diversity creates value. Organizations support the social cause of non-discrimination and equal opportunities. Equal distribution of power is seen as an essential element of management.

Stage 6: Multicultural organization: Organizations at this stage clearly reflect multiculturalism in various dimensions and have diversity at the centre. Members of this organization are equally influential and contributions can be seen from all. Multiculturalism becomes the core strength and there is high sensitivity exhibited to all cultures.

It is also important for organizations to carry out a kind of status assessment of their management systems, organizational processes and structures in the context of multiculturalism to map the readiness and gaps. Based on the study findings, an organization can develop a transition plan if required. Studies have shown that many organizations carry systems, processes and structure that are more tuned to mono or neutral cultures than with multicultural operations. According to a few experts, organizations can take the organization development (OD) approach for transition as a more comprehensive strategy. There are others who argue that traditional OD approaches have not worked well to create real multicultural organizations because transition is much more complex than mere systemic change management. Nevertheless, an attempt to redefine systems and processes is definitely a substantive step in attaining a real multicultural organization. Organizations are tardy in making structural changes such as movement of key roles and leadership positions and filling them up with people representing all cultures. Even multinational organizations which have been in existence for several years have been concentrating their leadership roles in selective countries or in the country of origin, although some of them are consciously trying to distribute these roles more equitably. There shall be a strategic programme to implement structure-related multiculturalism which can actually create a sustainable impact through a global leadership programme. Competencies required, especially relationship skills for leaders in multicultural organizations, are quite demanding and it will not be an exaggeration to state that there are few leaders with that calibre because organizations till lately were not systematically focused on building these skills. Therefore, leadership needs to be provided with opportunities to build cultural intelligence quotient as discussed in Box 9.1.

Box 9.1 Four Factor Cultural Quotient Model

Culture expert trio: Linn Van Dyne, Soon Ang and David Livermore (2003) have developed a culture intelligence model that is apt for international organizations to nurture multiculturalism. Cultural intelligence refers to a person's ability to effectively manage different cultures. The model consists of four factors. These are as follows.

Motivational CQ: Curiosity, interest and passion to adapt to cross-cultural environment can be measured through motivational culture quotient. Some people enjoy and seek to engage with multiple cultures, both as an intrinsic interest and to enrich their learning. High MCQ leaders also exhibit confidence in dealing with cross-cultural situations.

Cognitive CQ: This dimension of CQ refers to a leader's knowledge of culture and its constituents and the competence to interpret situations and apply actions at the workplace. This is also known as interpersonal culture competency. High cognitive CQ leaders possess the ability to see through culture systems and their assumptions and correlate them. They are quick in grasping cultural norms and adapting them in their own behaviour and teaching others.

Metacognitive CQ: Planning, strategizing and successfully executing them in a multicultural environment involves deep understanding of the roots of different cultures, the meaning and possible implications for organization and operations. High metacognitive CQ leaders not only understand the culture deeply but can also interpret and deploy it for successful operations. They build a skill of culture predictability which means they can anticipate rightly a particular culture manifestation for different behaviours and approaches. Deep knowledge about cultures and the ability to deploy and blend them with organizational processes and decisions is referred to as metacognitive CQ.

Behavioural CQ: While metacognitive CQ is more about planning and strategizing, behavioural CQ is more about the execution of that planning to accrue multiple benefits. Here, cross-cultures or alien cultures are not a barrier but a strategic advantage to accomplish something extraordinary. Leaders with this CQ can switch between cultures seamlessly and have mastered the art of language (verbal) and symbols (non-verbal) and intelligently use them for superior implementation and for fastening teamwork and collaboration in the company.

Norms: The third step in managing organizations for infusion of multiculturalism is creating norms. Once an organization has gone through the phase of acknowledging the challenges that cross-cultural efforts present either proactively or reactively and systems and processes are created to tackle them as discussed earlier, organizations must move to enforce do's and don'ts referred to here as 'norms'. Though culture is very context sensitive, it will be immensely helpful to lay down the norms for strengthening the multiculturalism in organizations. Experiences prove that balancing majority culture with minority culture is not an easy transformation. Systems and processes can provide the necessary structure but fall short of realizing multiculturalism in spirit unless the desired behaviour is obtained from all employees and leadership. That is possible through applying norms. Organizations over a period of time develop variety of rituals, customs and traditions without evaluating them from the perspective of multiculturalism and they tend to exist as natural things. Many empirical studies point out that the behavioural patterns observed by parent country staff or groups of employees who are the majority are applied across an organization without being scrutinized for whether they are multicultural or monocultural and nor are their implications understood. Hence, organizations shall evaluate the behavioural orientation of their leaders and various customs and traditions afresh in order to integrate minority traditions or alter majority traditions that apply globally. For example, a recent incidence of an e-commerce company putting doormats with a Hindu god printed on top for sale has received wide criticism and backlash from Hindus in India and elsewhere. This has happened because of the American way of doing things where printing national flag on anything is permissible and seen as a celebration while this is a highly restricted practice in India. This is an easily demonstrable example (where norms of one country are applied to another country without realizing the implications) while many rituals, traditions and customs are complex and invisible and a person can only feel them.

Culture experts at American Management Association, after spending nearly 15 years promoting multiculturalism in Fortune 500 companies, believe that creating systems and processes is essential but redefining norms will reinforce the efforts of building multicultural organizations and advocate the implementation of the following:

- Co-create a company statement of multiculturalism with participation of all key employees.
- Articulate a culture goal consistent with company's multiculturalism statement and regularly publish culture demographics internally on a regular basis to communicate how the company is progressing on multiculturalism.
- Make leadership accountable to reach multiculturalism targets and appraise their performance on this parameter at regular intervals.
- Develop culture mentors and brand ambassadors.
- Create an incentive system to encourage people to embrace multiculturalism voluntarily.
- Leverage internal job postings and transfers and job rotations to promote diversity.
- Audit all company processes and schemes in order to eliminate culture prejudices.
- Encourage people to identify themselves with their cultural identity and discourage them from changing their names to match the so-called mainstay culture of a company. Promote cultural associations/groups to capitalize on positive aspects of that culture and also to mitigate barriers.
- Circulate events of success and assignments and tasks on which cross-cultural teams are engaged.
- Create multiculturally driven idea generation and suggestions.

A recent study conducted covering over 12 companies on their multiculturalism initiatives reveals that their attempts are shallow and not deep enough to create a sustainable culture that can yield benefits of diversity. Another example included an organization that changed its hiring policies and processes to promote equal opportunities for all cultural groups and yet its interviewers continued to look for people who appeared to exhibit behaviour that was prevalent in the dominant culture group in the organization. In other words, a system or a process or a rule can ensure diversity and multiculturalism to some extent but not fully because at certain times decisions are subtle and contextual. Therefore, true multiculturalism can only be achieved when people have completely bought into a state of commitment which is possible by relooking at norms of culture. Many cultures are represented by stereotypes and symbols, so organizations need to evaluate them as well. Organizations should also exercise caution to avoid cultural clashes because everything that an organization has need not be necessarily culture prejudicial. Creation of organizational multicultural norms must be supplemented with simple do's and don'ts and all employees can be made aware of these for adherence.

Extinction: Organizations which successfully go through the first three phases of managing multiculturalism transformation are expected to generate data on practices, processes, systems and structures and also identify employees who are not multiculture-friendly and rather end up being stumbling blocks. For example, there are many stereotypes an organization can find in itself.

The suggested approach is to look at them for reorientation at the first instance as much as possible. Once reasonable attempts are made and if they still do not yield desired results, organizations must adopt an approach of extinction. This means bidding farewell to some practices, rituals and traditions which might have lasted for years in a company and changing employees from positions of prominence to less impactful roles if they still show resistance to the new culture. Building multiculturalism is a long journey as it cannot be accomplished in a short span of time. Hence, organizations must be willing to disband and drop systems and people in the course of this journey as continuous renewal is at the heart of diversity. For example, data from several organizations show that though organizations appear to have embraced multiculturalism, the leadership continues to be occupied by homogenous culture groups. Unless these kinds of issues are addressed, the efforts will not yield real results. Unlearning is very important in this process. Cross-cultural movement also has the potential to generate insecurities and cynicism among members of majority culture groups, particularly those that have benefited all along. It is insurmountable to reform some who are not only reluctant but also form groups of resistance to create clashes within an organization. In such situations, it will not be business prudent to show tolerance and so organizations should take the approach of extinction for overall good. Extinction phase is the most challenging phase in managing multiculturalism in organizations as it can cause emotional stress with some groups staging final attempts to thwart the efforts of organizations; an example is when Indians on the face of Americanization had staged a 'Ghost Dance' symbolizing their last endeavour to preserve their culture and identity.

Summary

Though culture is a much broader organizational topic and interdisciplinary, it occupies a strategic place in IHRM. Hence, attempt has been made to capture tenets of international culture in the last chapter of the book. The basic objective of the chapter was to understand international culture models and their role in organizational performance and associated practices. The chapter is presented in five parts: Part I deals with basic concepts and models of international culture management. Profile of culture in international organizations is deliberated in Part II, while multiculturalism and cultural attitudes of selective nations is dealt in Part III and models of managing international culture and multicultural organization development model are illustrated in Parts IV and V, respectively.

QUESTIONS FOR DISCUSSION

1. Multiculturalism does not necessarily create positive impact and can also cause negative impact on organizational performance. Discuss pros and cons of multiculturalism in the organizational performance context?
2. Distinguish elements of an ideational system versus sociocultural system?
3. Does national culture impact organizational culture?
4. Organizational processes and systems that are in conflict with organizational culture fail to deliver results! Is this true or false? Substantiate with examples.

5. What are some of the stark differences between cultures of nations? Take a case of Germany versus Canada and explain.
6. Intra-country cultural differences are much more challenging than inter-country culture! Do you agree or disagree?
7. What causes cultural communication breakdown in international organizations?
8. Is culture formation a consequence of organizational actions?
9. Deliberate how leadership styles impact culture and how culture impacts leadership style.
10. Write a critique on cultural intelligence quotient.
11. How do existing models and theories of culture fail to explain the behaviour of millennials?

CASE STUDY

Chief HR officers of several multinational companies operating in India are often surprised that all employees are aware of salaries of their colleagues precisely, no matter how well all of them are informed of the need to maintain confidentiality of their respective salaries. They have found that this is very peculiar to Indian operations and have never come across this in North America and other European nations. When chief HR officers of some companies realized this challenge, they rolled out increasingly stringent rules and educational communication to sensitize employees of the sanctity of confidentiality of individual employee salary, since it was noticed that a significant reason for employee attrition and dissatisfaction was due to constant comparison of their remuneration levels. Despite all the managerial actions, the problem remained rampant. On further study of this organizational problem, some organizations have understood that this is more to do with culture of collectivism that encourages employees in India to make their salary details public and they also have a strong belief that their salary is a personal matter and not necessarily an organizational matter. Analyse what cultural factors are contributing to this behaviour? Why are employees in North America and Europe able to maintain confidentiality and respect the organizational process on this matter and not employees in India?

Bibliography

Bassi, Laurie, Paul Harrison, Jens Ludwig, and Daniel McMurrer. 2001. "Human Capital Investments and Firm Performance." (www.bassiinvestments.com/downloads/ResearchPaper_June2001_.pdf)

Boston Consulting Group. (2014). *The Most Innovative Companies 2014: Breaking Through is Hard to Do*. Retrieved 8 March 2018, from https://www.bcg.com/publications/collections/most-innovative-companies.aspx

Buchanan, D. A. and Huczynski, A. (2004). *Organizational Behavior: An Introductory Text*. Englewood Cliff, NJ: Prentice-Hall.

Cameron, K. S. and Quinn, R. E. (1999). *Diagnosing and Changing Organizational Culture: Based on the Competing Values Framework*. Boston, MA: Addison-Wesley Publishing Company.

Columbia Business School. (2015). *CEOs and CFOs Share How Corporate Culture Matters*. A Study by Columbia and Duke's Fuqua Business Schools. Retrieved 8 march 2018, from https://www8.gsb.columbia.edu/newsroom/newsn/3874/ceos-and-cfos-share-how-corporate-culture-matters

Deal, T. and Kennedy, A. (1982). *Corporate Cultures: The Rites and Rituals of Corporate Life*. Boston, MA: Addison-Wesley Publishing Company.

Denison, D. R. (1996). What is the Difference Between Organizational Culture and Organizational Climate? *Academy of Management Review, 21*, no. 3, 619–654.

Dixon, I. (2005, March). Culture Management and Mergers and Acquisitions. *Society for Human Resource Management Case Study, 12*, no. 2, 11–17.

Doz, Y. L. and Prahlad, C. K. (1999). *The Multinational Mission: Balancing Local Demands and Global Vision*. New York: Simon & Schuster.

Doz, Y. (2011). Qualitative Research for International Business. *Journal of International Business Studies, 42*, no. 5, 582–590.

Dyne, L. V., Ang, S. and Livermore, D. (2003). Cultural Intelligence: A Pathway for Leading in a Rapidly Globalizing World, in K. M. Hannum, B. McFeeters and L. Booysen (eds.), *Leadership Across Differences: Cases and Perspectives* (pp. 113–129). San Francisco, CA: Pfeiffer.

Gilmozzi, M. (2017, April 5). What Comes First: The Chicken or the Egg? Great Work Cultures. *The Huffington Post*. Retrieved 8 March 2018, from https://www.linkedin.com/pulse/hp-blog-great-work-cultures-what-comes-first-chicken-egg-gilmozzi

Guiso, L., Sapienza, P. and Zingales, L. (2013, September). The Values of Corporate Culture. *Journal of Financial Economics, 117*, no. 1, 60–76.

Handy, C. (1993). *Understanding Organizations*. London: Penguin Books.

Harrison, R. (1972). Understanding Your Organization's Character. *Harvard Business Review*, May–June, 119–129.

Hinds, P. (2000). Choosing Work Group Members: Balancing Similarity, Competence and Familiarity. *Organizational Behavior and Human Decision Processes, 81*, no. 2, 226–251.

Hofstede, G. (1980). *Culture's Consequences: International Differences in Work-related Values*. New Delhi: SAGE Publications.

House, R. J. (1999). *Transformative Organizations: A Global Perspective*. Thousand Oaks, CA: SAGE Publications.

House, R. J., Hanges, P. J., Javidan, M., Dorfman, P. W. and Gupta, V. (1982). *Culture, Leadership and Organizations: The Global Study of 62 Societies*. Thousand Oaks, CA: SAGE Publications.

Hwang, V. W. (2014). *Sign the Social Contract*. The Rainforest. Retrieved 31 January 2018, from www.therainforestbook.com

Jackson, B. and Hardiman, R. (1981). Coaching Leaders Through Culture Change. *Consulting Psychology Journal: Practice and Research, 48*(2), 104–114.

Joiner, T. A. (2001). The Influence of National Culture and Organizational Culture Alignment on Job Stress and Performance. *Journal of Managerial Psychology, 16*(3–4), 229–242.

Jung, T., Scott, T., Davies, H., Bower, P., Whalley, D., Mcnally, R. and Mannison, R. (1989). Instruments for Exploring Organizational Culture: A Review of the Literature. *Public Administration Review, 69*(6), 1087–1096.

Kirkman, B. L., Lowe, K. B. and Gibson, C. B. (2016). A Retrospective on Culture's Consequences: The 35 Year Journey. *Journal of International Business Studies, 48*, no. 1, 12–29.

Kotter, J. P. and Heskett, J. L. (1992). *Corporate Culture and Performance*. New York, NY: Free Press.

Lewis, R. (1999). *Cross Cultural Communication: A Visual Approach*. London: Transcreen Publications.

Livermore, D. (2009). *Leading with Cultural Intelligence: The New Secret to Success*. New York: AMACOM.

Martin, J. (1992). *Cultures in Organizations: Three Perspectives*. New York: Oxford University Press.

McGregor, L. and Doshi, N. (2015). How Company Culture Shapes Employee Motivation. *Harvard Business Review*. Retrieved 8 March 2018, from https://hbr.org/2015/11/how-company-culture-shapes-employee-motivation

Meyer, E. (2014). *The Culture Map: Breaking Through the Invisible Boundaries of Global Business*. Fontainebleau: PublicAffairs.

Neeley, T. B. (2013, March–April). Language Matters: Status Loss and Achieved Status Distinction in Global Organizations. *Organization Science, 24*, no. 2, 476–497.

Nurse, L. (2005, July). Performance Appraisal, Employee Development and Organizational Justice: Exploring the Linkages. *The International Journal of Human Resource Management, 16*(7), 1176 – 1194. Retrieved July 31, 2007 from Taylor & Francis Journals Database, http://www.informaworld.com

Ouchi, W. G. (1981). *Theory Z*. New Delhi: Addison-Wesley.

Parboteeah, P. K., Bronson, J. W. and Cullen, J. B. (2005). Does National Culture Affect Willingness to Justify Ethically Suspect Behaviors? *International Journal of Cross Cultural Management, 5*(2), 27–41.

Peters, T. J. and Waterman, R. H. (1982). *In Search of Excellence*. New York, NY: Harper & Row Publications.

Petty, M. M., Beadles, N. A., Chapman, Deborah F., Lowery, Christopher L. and Connell, D. W. (1995). "Relationships Between Organizational Culture and Organizational Performance." *Psychological Reports, 76* (1 April), 483–492.

Quinn, M. D. (2005). Asian and American Leadership Styles: How Are They Unique? *Harvard Business Review*. Retrieved 8 March 2018, from https://hbswk.hbs.edu/item/asian-and-american-leadership-styles-how-are-they-unique

Schein, E. H. (1992[1988]). *Organizational Culture and Leadership*. John Wiley & Sons.

Schneider, B., Brief, A. P. and Guzzo, R. A. (1996). Creating a Climate and Culture for Sustainable Organizational Change. *Organizational Dynamics, 24*(4), 7–19.

Steinwachs, K. (1999). Information and Culture—The Impact of National Culture on Information Processes. *Journal of Information Science, 25*(3), 193–204.

Tata Strategic Management Group. (2015, 22 July). *Organization Culture Aligned with Business Strategy Impacts Profitability.* Retrieved 8 March 2018, from http://www.tata.com/company/releasesinside/Organisational-culture-aligned-with-business-strategy-impacts-profitability-says-Tata-Strategic-Management-Group-report

Toegal, G. and Barsoux, J. L. (2012). How to Become a Better Leader. *MIT Sloan Management Review, 53*, no. 3, 51–60.

Trompenaars, F. and Hampden-Turner, C. (1997). *Riding the Waves of Culture: Understanding Cultural Diversity in Business.* London: Nicholas Brealey Publishing.

Author Index

Subject Index

Lightning Source UK Ltd.
Milton Keynes UK
UKHW051920200320
360684UK00004B/119